The rough guide to
NEW YORK

=The=
rough
guides

Other available Rough Guides include:
**PARIS, FRANCE, BRITTANY & NORMANDY, AMSTERDAM,
SPAIN, PORTUGAL, GREECE, CRETE, YUGOSLAVIA, EASTERN
EUROPE, SCANDINAVIA, MEXICO, PERU, MOROCCO,
TUNISIA, KENYA, CHINA and HALF THE EARTH:
WOMEN'S EXPERIENCES OF TRAVEL
(co-published with Pandora Press)**

Series Editor
MARK ELLINGHAM

The rough guide to
NEW YORK

Written and researched by
MARTIN DUNFORD AND JACK HOLLAND

With additional accounts by

Phyllis Cohen, John Froscher,
Donald Hutera, Bobbie Kingsley, Allan
Robertson, Sara Schulman
and Mary Watson

HARRAP
COLUMBUS
Rough
Guide

Thanks for help, information and encouragement to: Louise Jones and particularly Deborah Hardy of I Love New York, Peggy Thrush, Danell Jones, Bridget Bouch, Mark Kröne, Louisa Ricketts, Doreen Hamilton, John Fisher, Steve at Wordsmith's, Doug Simmons and the many others who helped to produce this book. And special thanks to Mark Ellingham.

Many thanks, too, to all those who wrote in with comments, corrections and additions: Mike and Marilyn Miller, Laura Drazin Boyes, Eveline Thevenard, David McClelland, Penny Geary, R.G. Bowden, David Smith, Jane Lawrence, Hugh Duffy and A.E.M. van Oijen. Please keep writing!

First published in 1987 by
Routledge & Kegan Paul Ltd
Revised and reprinted 1988 by
Harrap-Columbus Ltd.
19–23 Ludgate Hill, London EC4M 7PD
Published in the USA by
Routledge & Kegan Paul Inc.
in association with Methuen Inc.
29 West 35th Street, New York NY 10001

Computer typeset by Wordsmith's, London N1, and the authors
Printed by Cox & Wyman Ltd, Reading, Berks

Library of Congress Cataloging in Publication Data

Dunford, Martin.
  The rough guide to New York
  (The Rough guides)
  Includes index
1. New York (N.Y.)–Description–1981–
Guide-books. I. Holland, Jack, 1959–
II. Title. III. Series
F128.18DC86 1986 917.47'10443 86–26186
British Library CIP data also available

ISBN 0-7471-0141-8

CONTENTS

Part one BASICS
1

New York City, New York State / Costs, climate and when to go / Getting there (and travel onwards) / Red tape and visas / Health and insurance / Information, maps and tours / Money and banks / Communications: telephones and the post / Media / Police and trouble / Sleeping / Food and drink / Glossary of food terms / Women's New York: problems and contacts / Gay and lesbian New York / Parades and festivals / Sport / Staying on / Other things

Part two NEW YORK CITY
43

Points of arrival / Orientation / Transport / Finding a place to stay

1 Lower Manhattan 57
2 Midtown Manhattan 96
3 Upper Manhattan 125
4 The Outer Boroughs 153
5 Museums 176
6 Shops and galleries 209
7 Drinking and Eating 234
8 Nightlife: Rock, Jazz and Clubbing 260
9 The Performing Arts and Film 268

Part three NEW YORK STATE
279

New York State: an introduction / practicalities

10 Long Island 284
11 The Hudson Valley and the Catskills 298
12 Saratoga, the Adirondacks and Thousand Islands 312
13 The Finger Lakes and Central Leatherstocking 323
14 Rochester, Niagara and Chautauqua-Allegheny 333

Part four CONTEXTS
343

The Historical framework 345
Architectural chronology 353
20C American art: a brief survey 356
Two views of New York City: Quentin Crisp and David Widgery 359
Books 363
New York on film 367
Glossary of New York terms and people 372
New York slang: a glossary 376

Index 378

A hundred times I have thought, New York is a catastrophe, and fifty times: It is a beautiful catastrophe.

Le Corbusier

Part one
BASICS

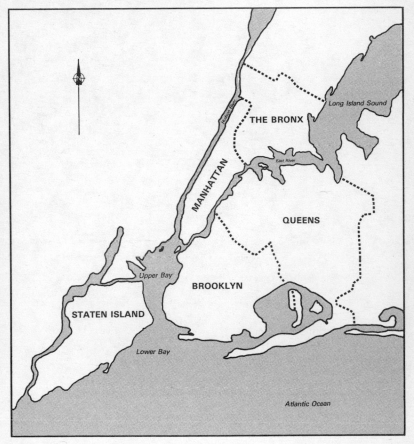

NEW YORK CITY, NEW YORK STATE

New York City is the most beguiling place there is. You may not think so at first – for the city is admittedly mad, the epitome in many ways of all that is wrong (and really drastically wrong) in modern America. But spend even a week here and it happens – the pace, the adrenalin takes hold and the shock gives way to myth. Walking through the city streets *is* an experience, the buildings like icons to the modern age, to the excitement and violence of change and above all to the power of money. And despite all the hype, the movie-image sentimentalism, Manhattan (the central island and the city's real core) has massive romance: whether it's the flickering lights of the midtown skyscrapers as you speed across the Queensboro bridge, the 4am half-life in Greenwich Village, or just wasting the morning on the Staten Island ferry. You really would have to be made of stone not to be moved by it all.

None of which is to suggest that New York is a conventional or a conventionally pleasing city. Take a walk in **Manhattan** beside Central Park, past the city's richest apartments (and they are *rich*) along the Upper East Side, and keep walking. Within a dozen or so blocks you find yourself in the burnt-out degradation of the lower reaches of Harlem. The shock could hardly be more extreme. The city is constantly like that: nowhere in the Western world are there so many (and so explicable) human derelicts alongside so much glaring wealth. For out in the Lower East Side or the legendary South Bronx the city is in crisis, with some of the world's most classic and vivid cases of urban blight, neglect and non-investment.

Whether you seek it or not, you will be made aware of this – and in a perverse way it's these tangible and potent contrasts that give New York much of its excitement. But the city, too, has more straightforward pleasures. There are the different **ethnic neighbourhoods** of Lower Manhattan, from Chinatown to the Jewish Lower East Side or (ever diminishing) Little Italy, or among the arts and gay concentrations of SoHo and TriBeCa, Greenwich and East Village. There is the **architecture** (the whole city reads like an illustrated history of modern design) of corporate midtown Manhattan and the more residential Upper East and West Side districts. And there is the **art**, arguably unrivalled and affording infinite weeks of wandering in the Metropolitan and Modern Art Museums and countless smaller collections.

All of which is just the background. For to enjoy and experience New York the greatest draw of all, whether you're resident or visitor, is in the action. You can **eat** anything, cooked in any style; **drink** in any kind of company; sit through any amount of (or simply continuous) **movies**. The established arts – **dance**, **theatre**, **music** – are superbly catered for, and though the contemporary **music scene** is nowhere as vital or original as in London, New York's **clubs** are varied and exciting – if rarely inexpensive. And if you're into shops or **consuming**, choice is vastly, almost numbingly unique in this heartland of the great capitalist dream.

Specific introductions to each of these subjects, and to the areas of the city (including the four often forgotten Outer Boroughs of Brooklyn, Queens, The Bronx and Staten Island), precede their particular chapters. A **survival guide to the basics** of staying in, and getting to, New York follows this section.

The *Basics* section – and indeed the book as a whole – has been written primarily with the idea of visitors to New York City in mind, though much of the practical information applies equally to **New York State**. The city, though few people (New Yorkers least of all) place great store by the fact, is actually just a small section of the state – not even the capital. If you've only a week or two, then perhaps it's best to follow this disregard. But time beyond this and there are definite reasons (and pulls) for escaping the city and venturing upstate, even if it's just to escape the city's intensity for a while. A short break on **Long Island** is perhaps the most tempting option: the traditional summer resort for New York's better-heeled society and for its artistically inclined, and with beaches that can hardly be bettered. For more natural spectacle there is the wooded beauty of the **Hudson Valley** and the broad, sluggish majesty of the river itself, or further afield the **Niagara Falls** – the most popular statewide target. Less explored, in the north of the state rise the **Adirondack mountains**, with at their heart North America's largest national park, a countryside as remote as anything in the Rockies. A **full introduction** to New York State, detailing both the excitements and practicalities, precedes Part Three of the guide on p.281.

COSTS, CLIMATE AND WHEN TO GO

Without doubt your biggest single problem in New York is going to be **money** – or rather how to hold on to what you have. The pound-dollar exchange rate has crawled up from an all-time low in 1985 to around $1.80 to the £1, but the cost of almost everything here is greater than in Britain and most other parts of Europe.

Accommodation will be your biggest day-to-day item, with rock-bottom rooms in Manhattan starting at $30 a night; even a basic YMCA single goes for around $25. Unless you're staying with friends there's no way to cut corners on this, so if you don't want to be sent home be sure to budget accordingly *before* you leave – something the immigration officials will check on when you arrive.

The bottom line for staying alive – *after this* – is around $15 a day, a figure which will of course skyrocket the more you dine out and party. But the unending variety of places to eat means it is possible to do it well and cheaply. There are bargain **restaurants** (our listings start on p.240) where you'll be well fed for under $5, while the all-American breakfast will set you up for the day for around $1.50, and ubiquitous delis and pizza places provide the cheapest snacks from around $1. Be warned though that at the end of a sit-down meal the expected **tip** can come as a nasty surprise, and **drinking** in Manhattan's better-heeled bars can be horrifically dear. **Transport** too soon mounts up with flat fares of $1 for any Manhattan bus or subway journey.

Climate-wise, New York – city and state – ranges from the stickily hot and humid in midsummer to well below freezing in January. As far as the city goes, winter and high summer (most people claim the city is unbearable in July and August) are much the worst time you could come. Spring is gentler, if unpredictable and usually wet; autumn is perhaps the best season; come at either time and you'll find it not only easier to get things done but the people more welcoming. For **clothing**, bring your warmest coats, woollies and thermal underwear in January (and wellies, stout hats and ear-muffs to combat the blizzards), and a good selection of T-shirts, shorts and the like if you come in July. Also, dress in layers: buildings tend to be absurdly over-heated during the winter months and air-conditioned to the point of iciness in summer.

Average Temperatures

	JAN	FEB	MAR	APR	MAY	JUN	JUL	AUG	SEP	OCT	NOV	DEC
MAX(°F)	39	40	48	61	71	81	85	83	77	67	54	41
(°C)	4	5	8	16	21	27	29	28	25	19	12	5
MIN(°F)	26	27	34	44	53	63	68	66	60	51	41	30
(°C)	-3	-3	1	6	11	17	18	19	16	10	5	-1

For a full and up-to-the minute rundown on daily weather conditions in NYC 'phone 976 1212'

GETTING THERE

From London
Competition is intense on the **London-New York** flight route, and the choice of airlines, tickets and fares is constantly changing. For the best current offers, it pays to shop around: either checking the travel ads in the Sunday papers, *Time Out* or the giveaway *LAM*, or by consulting one of the agents detailed below. Treat our comments as a general guide

only – and one that's likely to have had at least subtle alterations.

Flights tend to **leave London** in the morning or afternoon and arrive in New York in the afternoon or early evening; flying time is 7-8 hours. Coming back, most flights depart in the evening to arrive in London early next morning; flying time is 6-7 hours. Weekend flights are generally more expensive.

Fares vary enormously, according to season, availability and inter-airline competition, which can be intense. **Standby deals** are few and far between, and don't give great savings, and you're usually better off with a regular *Apex* ticket. The conditions on these are pretty standard whoever you fly with – seats must be booked 21 days or more in advance, and you must stay for a minimum of seven nights – as are prices. Low season midweek rates start at around £330 return right now, rising to as high as around £470 travelling on a weekend (ie Friday, Saturday, Sunday) during high season. *Virgin Atlantic* are normally slightly cheaper, and they offer a broader choice of fares, ranging from late savers, which you must book no more than seven days before departure, to ordinary *Apex* tickets. Also, their inflight entertainment is far and away the most genuinely diverting.

Whenever you're travelling, it's always worth phoning the airlines direct to check on current deals they may be offering – or contact the agents we've listed below, who often – especially for students and those under 26 – have the same seats at cheapter rates.

Airline Addresses in Britain include:
Air India   17 New Bond St, London W1 (01 493 4050)
Air Canada   140 Regent St, London W1 (01 439 7941)
British Airways   421 Oxford St, London W1 (01 897 4000)
British Caledonian   215 Piccadilly, London W1 (01 668 4222)
El Al   185 Regent St, London W1 (01 439 2564)
Kuwait Airlines   52 Piccadilly, London W1 (01 409 3191)
North West Airlines   49 Albermarle St, London W1 (01 629 5353)
Pan-Am   193 Piccadilly, London W1 (01 409 0688)

TWA   200 Piccadilly London W1 (01 636 4090)
Virgin Atlantic   Sussex House, High St, Crawley, West Sussex RH10 1BZ (0293 38222)

To by-pass the airlines – and to get a good overview of the various offers – go straight to an **agent** who specialises in low-cost flights. One of the most helpful and reliable are *STA Travel*, who have offices in London at 74 Old Brompton Road, SW7 3LH (01 581 1022) and 117 Euston Road, NW1 2SX (01 388 2261), and in Bristol at 25 Queens Road, BS8 1QE (0272 294399); and Cambridge at 38 Sidney St, CB2 3HX (0223 66966); whatever's going on they should be able to offer the cheapest current deals. Or there are **specialist American flight agents** like *North Atlantic Travel Club* (22 Sackville St, London W1; 01 734 8100). *American Airplan* (Marlborough House, Churchfield Rd, Walton-on-Thames, Surrey KT12 2TJ; 0932 246166) or *Jetsave* (Sussex House, London Rd, East Grinstead, W. Sussex RH19 1LD; 0342 27711) – all of whose brochures you should find in most high street travel agents. Through these companies you can book tickets with most of the major American carriers, and at certain times of the year cash in on some superbly cheap charter fares.

A further possible cost-cutting alternative is to travel as a **courier**. This involves delivering documents transatlantic and though your luggage allowance is severely curtailed (usually down to hand luggage) can prove a highly tempting deal. *Jetservices* (01 759 4991; NYC 718 917 7900) are fairly typical, offering a return flight for around £100: departures daily apart from Friday and Sunday year-round, with a choice of 1-week, 2-week or 9-day stays. *TNT Skypak* (01 861 2345 for an application form), *IML* (01 890 8888) and *Inflight* (0932 857455) also offer courier trips. The situation varies, so phone these – and other listings in the Yellow Pages.

If you're interested in **upstate New York**, bear in mind that places like **Boston**, or even **Montreal** and **Toronto**, can be just as viable as points of arrival, especially if you're heading to the Adirondacks or Niagara Frontier. *STA Travel*, *North American Travel Club* and *American Airplan* offer cut-rate fares to all three destinations. Major carriers are *British Airways* and *TWA*, both of whom fly daily from London to Boston, and *North West Airlines*, who fly there once a week. *Air Canada* and *BA* also fly to Montreal and Toronto roughly once a day.

From elsewhere in Britain
Choices are few. You can fly from **Manchester** with *British Airways* twice a week for the same rates as from London. Or, if you're in **Scotland**, *North West Airlines* fly Prestwick to New York (JFK) once a week, again for much the same prices as the other airlines. Bear in mind that with certain airlines – not least *Virgin* – you can get a return **rail ticket** to London from anywhere in England, Scotland or Wales for just £19 if you buy it in conjunction with your ticket to New York; which may well work out cheaper.

From Eire
USIT, 7 Anglesea St, Dublin 2 (01 778117) offer flights with *Aer Lingus* or *North West Airlines* daily, with two departures each day in summer. The **youth fare** for those under 26 is cheapest at £(Eire)140 single, £280 return; if you're older but a student their **student fare** is £179 single, £359 return. There are no booking restrictions on either ticket. Those unfortunate enough to fit into neither the above categories can content themselves with a North West Orient **PEX fare** at £439 return.

From Europe
Nouvelles Frontières operate weekly charters from Paris and Brussels and offer discount bookings with Air India, either of which can represent a saving on scheduled fares. Their offices can be found at 66 Boulevard Saint-Michel, Paris (4634 5530); 21 Rue de la Violette (Grand Place), Brussels (02511 8013); and 19 W 44th St, New York (212 764 6494). There's also a London office at 1-2 Hanover St, W1 (01 629 7772).

From Australia and New Zealand
Quantas, *Continental*, *United* and *Air New Zealand* fly the **Sydney**-LA/**Melbourne**-LA route. APEX fare in the high season is around Aus $1000 single with a New York add-on fare of US $160. Bar Quantas the same airlines fly from **Auckland** New Zealand to LA: APEX singles around NZ $2300 in the high season;

domestic supplements to New York as above.

Inclusive holidays
Package deals – flights plus hotel accommodation in New York City – can often be a good way of working things if you're only planning a short stay. The best current deal – by far – is the one run by *Miracle Bus* (408 The Strand, London WC2; 01 379 3322) who throw in three nights' accommodation in a tourist class hotel for a little over the cost of the flight. *Virgin Holidays* and *TWA* also run inclusive deals with very good rates for accommodation if you spend a week or more in New York. If you plan to explore upstate, **fly-drive** programmes may also be worth looking into; both *British Airways* and *Pan-Am* offer cars (at around £80 a week) in conjunction with their flights.

To do things in true style you could alternatively take one of *Kuoni*'s hugely expensive short breaks, whereby you sail out on the **QE2** and come back by **Concorde** (or the other way round if you prefer) for an all-in price of around £1300 per person in high season. The sea journey takes about five days, and in New York you stay between 3 and 5 nights at the Waldorf Astoria.

TRAVEL ONWARDS

As far as international travel goes, the most obvious place to head for after New York is **CANADA**, two of whose provinces, Quebec and Ontario, border New York State in the north. There are regular flights to Toronto, Montreal and other gateway cities from New York, and a *Greyhound* **bus** can have you in Montreal in around 8 hours, or in Toronto, via Buffalo and Niagara, in about 11 hours. There are also daily **trains**, run by both *Amtrak* and *VIA* (the Canadian rail system) connecting Montreal with Albany and New York City in about 9 hours. There are more exciting places than **Toronto**, but it's an easy introduction to the country, and an inevitable one if you're intent on seeing Niagara Falls. Most people find **Montreal** more appealing, its firm European atmosphere in blatant contrast to Toronto's sober northern aspect. Historically, Montreal was Canada's 'City of Sin', and there's no city in Canada with a more vigorous street and nightlife. **Quebec**, too, is something of an oddity in North America: very old (with city walls and a 17C cathedral) and with an even more militantly separatist attitude to central government than Montreal. A 3 hour bus journey from Montreal, it's well worth the detour. Practically speaking, there's no *Rough Guide* to Canada as yet, neither is one planned, so here are a few basics...

Getting Around Flights are more expensive than in the States and so are best kept for coast-to-coast travel (watch the newspapers for 'seat sales' – often as much as 50% cheaper); trains are better (best in Ontario and Quebec) and if you're travelling any distance 8, 15, 22 or 30 day passes are available from railway stations; buses, run most widely by *Greyhound*, once again provide the cheapest way of getting around, especially if you invest in an *Ameripass* (see below) which is valid in most parts of the country.

Accommodation As with America, a choice between youth hostels and motels if money's tight. Motels go for upwards of Can$20. Hotels tend to be at least as expensive as America, usually more so.

Information Once in New York, from the Consulate General at 1251 6th Ave (757 4917). In Britain, each province has its own office – Ontario's is at 13 Charles II St, London SW1 (01 930 6404) and Quebec's 59 Pall Mall, London SW1 (01 930 8314) – or for general information on the country there's Canada House, Trafalgar Square, London SW1 (01 629 9492).

Tours *Go-Ways* have the widest selection of trans-Canada trips, from hikes up to the wilds of the Yukon to canoe expeditions through the Algonquin Park. Contact them at 27 Ebury Bridge Road, London SW1 (01 730 6216).

Most people, however, push on to explore the rest of **AMERICA**, which, once out of New York City, can work out surprisingly inexpensive. Again, in the absence of a *Rough Guide* to the country, some notes...

Getting Around It's possible to save on transport costs in a variety of ways, many of which are best organised before you leave Britain. First option is to buy an **Airpass** in conjunction with your transatlantic ticket. Most American carriers offer these, allowing the choice between unlimited travel on the network of one airline for periods of between 30 and 60 days, at a cost of $300-500; or in low season a special deal which gives coupons valid for four flights anywhere on the network for a total cost of under £100. Choose your airline carefully: *North West Orient* and, to a lesser extent, *Delta* and *Republic* give best value since their network of routes is so wide; *Eastern* are obviously strong on the east coast; *Continental* in the south; and *United* on the west coast. If on the other hand you only want to make a couple of journeys you may be better off simply buying **discounted internal tickets** from a travel agent in Britain. *STA Travel* offer these, and also do 'Open Jaw' tickets which enable you to fly into one US (or Canadian) city and back home from another: a facility well worth utilising if you intend doing a lot of moving around once in the States. Slightly cheaper, and a good way of seeing America from the ground, is to purchase a **Bus Pass** from *Greyhound*, 14-16 Cockspur St, London SW1 (01 839 5591). Their *Ameripass* costs from £65 for the minimum 7 days, rising to £140 for 30 days, extensions £15 a day. Greyhound can also organise advance accommodation; see their brochure for details. *Amtrak*, the country's national **railways**, are worth the bother if you're a train fanatic. A national rail pass, valid for 2 weeks, costs about $375 – for a month $525; or there are two-weekly regional tickets available for upwards of $125. Further details from Amtrak.

Coast-to-Coast By far the most popular path to take after New York is to travel across the continent to California – a journey mythologised in the literature of the Beats and still one of the most dramatic in the world. You can of course take the bus, either by utilising a pass and taking in some of the country on the way or by just buying a ticket and getting it over in one go. A one-way Greyhound ticket from New York to San Francisco currently costs around $160 (returns double less 5%) and the trip takes about 3 days. Or there are companies like *Green Tortoise*, who run converted buses regularly at cheaper rates; phone 800 227 4766 for details. But the most notorious – and cheapest – way of getting to California is to use a **Drive-away**, whereby you deliver a car for someone who's basically too lazy to do it themselves. Among many companies specialising in this are *Auto Driveaway Co*, 313 5th Ave, NYC (696 1414); *Auto Caravan*, 110 W 40th St, NYC (354 7777); and *Driveaway Service*, 1457 Broadway (221 6930), but there are plenty more in the Yellow Pages (look under 'Automobile Transporters and Driveaway Companies'). Requirements are that you're over 21, hold a valid driving licence and have anything between $100 and $200 handy as a deposit. This is reclaimable on arrival and other than that there's nothing to pay bar petrol. But bear in mind that while it's accepted that you may want to see a little of the country on the way, there are generally fairly tight restrictions on your delivery deadline and if you're late without good reason you lose the deposit.

Inclusive Tours If it's your first time in the States you may prefer to see the rest of the country on an escorted tour of some sort. This is again something best fixed up before you leave. Of the many operators you could choose, **Contiki**, Wells House, 15 Elmfield Road, Bromley, Kent (01 290 6422) and **TrekAmerica**, 62 Kenway Road, London SW5 (01 373 5085) offer probably the best and most reliable range of tours, Contiki's staying in hotels and motels and TrekAmerica travelling by – and sleeping in – converted minibus. Prices start at around £300 for a 3 week trip, plus flights and not including a food allowance.

Finally a note on **books**. The most practical guide you can take on both countries is *Travellers Survival Kit: USA and Canada* (Vacation Work £5.95) by Susan Griffiths and Simon Calder, which as the name suggests covers both countries; or there's *Let's Go America* (St Martin's Press, £8.95) which is equally practically-based but includes more detail on the States at the expense of Canada. There's no better travelogue on the US than William Least Heat Moon's *Blue Highways* (Picador £3.95): an evocatively written account of his journey through America's backwaters in the early 1980s.

RED TAPE AND VISAS

Visas

With the exception of Canadians, foreign citizens entering the US must have a **non-immigrant visitor's visa** before arrival. To apply for a visa, fill in an application form (available from most travel agents) and send it with your passport to the visa section of the nearest US embassy or consulate. British citizens should note that the temporary Visitor's Passport is not valid – only full 10-year passports.

US embassies and consulates abroad include:

ENGLAND US Embassy, 5 Upper Grosvenor St, London W1A 2JB (01 499 7010).

SCOTLAND US Consulate General, 3 Regent Terrace, Edinburgh EH7 5BW (031-556 8315).

NORTHERN IRELAND US Consulate General, Queens House, Queen St, Belfast BT1 6EQ (0232 228239).

EIRE 42 Elgin St, Ballsbridge, Dublin. (01 688 777)

NETHERLANDS Lange Voorhout 102, The Hague (70 62 4911)

SWEDEN Strandvagen 101, Stockholm (8 630 520

NORWAY Drammensveien 18, Oslo (2 566 880)

DENMARK Dag Hammarskjöld Alle 24, 2110 Copenhagen (1 423 144)

AUSTRALIA Moonhah Place, Canberra (62 733 711)
NEW ZEALAND 29 Fitzherbert Terrace, Thorndon, Wellington (4 722 068)

On the application form you're required to state that you're not a communist or fascist, drug dealer or convicted criminal. Less romantically, you're also asked for evidence that you need to return home once the trip is over. For the latter, commitments of work, study or family are usually sufficient, and though an official-looking statement from either of the first two will aid matters your word is usually all that's required.

The visa you get may last as long as your trip, the whole of that year, or most often indefinitely; and it may let you in to the country just once or as many times as you need. So if you intend to make several visits to the States in coming years, or cross borders to Canada or Mexico, say so — it'll save making future visa requests.

Immigration

Obtaining a visa is only the first hurdle; the next is passing through **immigration control** in the US. On the plane you'll be handed an **immigration form** to complete with the details of where you are staying (if you don't know write 'touring') and the date you intend to **leave** the country. This will be attached to your passport on arrival.

What immigration are really interested in is your **ability to support yourself** financially for the length of the trip, so don't be surprised if they ask to see traveller's cheques, cash, credit cards and return airline tickets to prove that you can. Their rule of thumb is about $150 for each week you intend to stay, and those unable to match that face being turned around for the next plane home. Those **staying with friends** should have a letter showing an address and phone number suspicious officials can ring. If you're really financially stumped (but confident you can resolve this once in New York) one way around the problem is to borrow as much money as you need (or take it out on a credit card), buy the requisite amount of traveller's cheques to show immigration and then return the money via an international money order from any bank. Sneaky, but it works. It would be stupid (that's putting it mildly) to use this technique if you have no viable contacts in the US.

It's sad but true to say that you stand the best chance of a problem-free entry if, as well as complying with the above necessities, you happen to be English-speaking, white, well-dressed, sober and polite to the officials. Remember too that the reason for all this red tape is that the land of plenty is terrified of the idea of foreigners coming to look for work — so even if this is your intention, on no account say so.

Customs

Customs officers will relieve you of the declaration completed on the plane and ask if you have any fresh foods (say goodbye to them if you have) and whether you have visited a farm in the last month (in which case you can say goodbye to your shoes as well). The **duty free allowance** if you're over 17 is 200 cigarettes and 50 cigars — though not Cuban cigars — and 1 litre of spirits or wine.

As well as foods and anything agricultural, it's also **prohibited** to bring in chocolate liqueurs, obscene publications and, oddly enough, lottery tickets. Those caught carrying **drugs** into the country will not only face prosecution but also an entry for all time in the files that immigration officers check the name of each arrival against; this will severely prejudice your chances of going anywhere for years to come.

Extensions — and leaving

The date stamped in your passport is the latest you're legally entitled to stay. Leaving a few days after this won't matter, especially if you're heading back home, but a week or more can result in protracted — and generally unpleasant — interrogation from officials; it's been known for immigration to question overstayers just long enough to miss their flights.

So if you do want to stay on, the best option is to get a **visa extension** before your time is up. This can be done by going to the **US Immigration and Naturalization Service**, 26 Federal Plaza, NYC (206 6500), and applying for an **Issuance or Extension of Permit to Re-Enter the USA.** They will automatically assume that you are working illegally so it's up to you to dissuade them and furnish convincing proof that you can support yourself financially. Taking along an upstanding US citizen to vouch for you is a good idea. You'll also need to think up a good reason to explain why you didn't allow the extra time initially: well-worn but effective excuses include saying your money lasted longer than you planned or that your parents/husband/wife have decided to come over for a while. Should you need a further extension, apply for it at a different office, and keep your fingers crossed.

HEALTH AND INSURANCE

Coming from Europe you don't require any inoculations to enter the States. What you do need is **insurance**, as medical bills for the simplest accident can be astronomical − and there's no way they can be escaped.

It's essential to get insurance *before you leave*: policies can be bought at travel agents or, more cheaply, through an insurance broker. Among British policies, *ISIS* are probably cheapest − not, as many think, open only to students, and with rates starting at about £18 for a week. Their forms are available at almost any youth/student travel offices or direct from 97-107 Southampton Row, London WC1 (01 436 4451) and many other regional offices. On all policies check the small print to ensure the cover includes a sensible amount for medical. expenses − at least $100,000.

If you need to see a **doctor**, lists can be found in the Yellow Pages under 'Clinics' or 'Physicians and Surgeons'. The British Consulate (845 3rd Avenue; 752 5747) also has selected names. A basic consultancy fee is $50-75 before you start talking, and medicines (US 'medications') don't come cheap either; keep receipts for all you spend and claim off your insurance when you return.

Minor ailments can be remedied at a **drugstore**. These sell a fabulous array of lotions and potions designed to allay the fears of the most neurotic New Yorkers, but bear in mind that many pills available over the counter in Britain are prescription only here (for example, most codeine-based pain killers) and brand names can be confusing. If in doubt, ask at a **pharmacy** − you'll find one on almost any corner (for addresses see p.211).

Should you be in an **accident** don't worry about dying on the sidewalk − medical services will pick you up and charge later. For an accident that doesn't require emergency treatment try the *Bellevue Hospital* at 1st Avenue and East 29th Street (561 4141). And for emergency **dental treatment**, the number to ring is 679 3966.

Most insurance policies also cover your money and personal possessions against **theft**. If you have anything stolen report it to the nearest police station (for the address of this phone 374 5000) and don't forget to make a note of their precinct number. What they will issue you with is a reference number to pass on to your insurance company − not the full statement that insurance people usually require. Don't worry about this, your company won't be surprised.

INFORMATION, MAPS AND TOURS

Maps and guides
Before you leave it's worth contacting the **United States Travel and Tourist Administration**, who, while more or less useless in every other respect, hold a good stock of free maps, booklets and glossy bumpf on each region of America, especially New York.
USTTA offices abroad include:
BRITAIN 22 Sackville St, London W1X 2EA (01 439 7433).
NORTHERN IRELAND & EIRE US Consulate Queen's House, 14 Queen St, Belfast BT1 6EQ (0232 228 239)
NETHERLANDS Museumplein 19, Amsterdam (020 790 321)
SWEDEN American Embassy 101 Strandvagen Stockholm (8 630 520)
NORWAY Drammensveien 18, Oslo (2 244 8550)
DENMARK Dag Hammarskjolds Alle 2, 2100 Copenhagen (1 142 3144)
AUSTRALIA 4 Cliff St, Milsons Point, NSW 2061 Sydney (612 957 3144)

For specific New York information and literature, particularly free guides and booklets, contact **I Love New York** (the New York State Department of Commerce Tourist Division). They have a London office at 25 Bedford Square, WC1 (01 323 0648); write or telephone – no personal callers. In New York itself there are *I Love New York* offices at 230 Park Avenue, New York City, NY 10169 (309 0568) and 1 Commerce Plaza, Albany, NY 12245 (518 474 4116) – both of which you can again only write to or telephone. Among the I Love New York info worth picking up is a comprehensive state-wide **map**, a glossy **Travel Guide** to each region of the state, an **Outdoors** brochure giving detailed listings of campsites and where and how to do your hiking and sailing, plus a booklet on **New York City** listing useful addresses and details of all-in packages.

Perhaps more useful – and obtainable over-the-counter once you're in New York – is the information from the **New York Convention and Visitors Bureau** at 2 Columbus Circle (397 8222), and Times Square at 42nd St, between Broadway and 7th Ave. Their offices are open Monday-Friday 9am-6pm, Saturday-Sunday 10am-6pm, and are good for getting hold of up-to-date **leaflets** on what's going on arts-wise and otherwise, bus and subway maps, and information on hotels and accommodation – though they can't actually book anything for you. Their high-gloss **Big Apple Guide** is good too, if rather upmarket, but it'll cost you $10, and for the kind of information it gives – on restaurants, hotels, sights – you'd probably be better off keeping a sharp eye out for the many kinds of free magazines and guidettes you can pick up all over the city like *Where*, *Broadway*, *Key* and *The Guide*. These appear in hotel foyers and the like and include complete (if superficial) rundowns on what's on in the arts, eating out and shops, and a host of ads that might just point you in the right direction.

We reckon our maps of the city should be fine for most purposes; **commercial maps**, like the *Rand McNally* plan of the city and all five boroughs ($3.95), fill in the gaps. Others include the tiny shiny-finished *Streetwise* maps, neatly laid out and not expensive at around $2 from most good bookshops; or, less afford-ably, the *Van Dam* fold-out maps, pricey at $6.95 but very user-friendly. If you're after a map of one of the individual Outer Boroughs try those produced by *Geographia* at $2.95, again on sale in book-shops – or, for Brooklyn, the free plan doled out by the borough's information booth on Cadman Plaza West. Good **map shops**, if you have trouble picking up any of these, include the *Rand McNally Store* and *Complete Traveler*, p.225 for addresses.

As far as **New York State maps** go, the *I Love New York* productions are more than adequate. However for something a little more detailed, *Rand McNally* do maps of specific regions. For hiking and climbing get hold of one of the charts produced by the US Department of the Interior Geological Survey; these go down to scales of 1 inch to 1 mile and cost around $4.00. You usually have to order these – in London from *Stanfords*, 12-14 Long Acre, WC2 (01 236 1321), in New York from *Rand McNally*.

Tours

Apart from equipping yourself with a decent map it's a good idea to orientate yourself by taking a look at the city from the air, either from one of the tallest buildings (say, the Empire State or RCA), or by catching a ride on a **helicopter**. This is expensive but if you've got the money it is an experience you won't easily forget. Best people to fly with are *Island Helicopter* at the far eastern end of East 34th Street, who offer three flights, ranging from $25 for around 15 minutes in the air and views mainly of midtown Manhattan, to a $45 trip that takes you the length of the island from Central Park to the Statue of Liberty, and on which you stay for a good half an hour. You can't book a place, but the helicopters take off throughout the day and evening (until 9pm) seven days a week, so just go down to the heliport and stand in line; bear in mind that in high season you may well have quite a wait. For further details, phone 683 4575.

Cheaper, if not nearly as breathtaking, the **Circle Line Ferry** leaves Pier 83 at the far west end of 42nd Street twice a day in low season, roughly every hour in midsummer; its three-hour voyage around the whole of Manhattan costs $12. This is probably the most popular way of seeing the island first off, taking in everything from the classic soaring views of Lower Manhattan to the bleaker stretches of Harlem and the industrially blighted Bronx. If you pick a fine day there are few better ways of spending an afternoon; but if the weather's bad, things can turn out pretty miserably, and you may find yourself taking shelter in the far from luxurious downstairs bar. Those broke and happy to make do with the wondrous downtown skyline can cut costs completely by simply jumping on the regular **Staten Island ferry**, whose 45-minute journey to the city's remotest borough still costs 25 cents and lays on an equally staggering panorama; or even by just walking halfway across the Brooklyn Bridge and turning around.

Bus tours of the city's streets are extremely – though unjustly – popular. The two standard companies are *Shortline* and *Grayline* (half-day tours around $16, bookable through any travel agent) but on either you'll find yourself swept around so quickly you scarcely get to see anything.

Walking tours, which allow you to get to know a specific part of Manhattan or the Outer Boroughs, are another matter. Usually led by experts, the range is considerable – some are general city strolls, others (like those of the Brooklyn Historical Society) devoted to one particular area. Detailed below are some of the most interesting: note that they don't all operate year-round, the more esoteric only setting up for a couple of outings at specific times of year. If you're interested, phone.

The 92nd Street Y, 1395 Lexington Ave (427 6000). None better, offering a mixed bag of walking tours ranging from straight explorations of specific New York neighbourhoods (like Park Slope Brooklyn or Harlem) to art tours, walking tours of political New York or a pre-dawn visit to the city's wholesale meat and fish markets. Average costs are $8-12 per person, and the commentary is erudite and informative. Look out, too, for the Y's day excursions by bus to accessible parts of upstate New York, and their specialised location talks led by well-known writers and artists. All in all, an excellent and useful organisation, whose brochure is well worth getting hold of.

Muncipal Arts Society, 457 Madison Ave (935 3960). As the name implies, principally tours with an architectural or cultural slant, but no less enjoyable to the layperson for all that. Regular trips around Harlem, the Upper West Side and other neighbourhoods, as well as 'hard hat' jaunts around construction sites for the *really* committed and free Wednesday lunchtime tours of Grand Central Station. Between $5 and $8.

Museum of the City of New York, 5th Ave at 103rd St (534 1872). Sunday walking tours, six months of the year, again around New York neighbourhoods, downtown, midtown and in Brooklyn. Prices a flat $6.

Art Tours of Manhattan, 63 E 82nd St (772 7888). Much the best people to go with if you're interested in first-hand accounts of the city's art scene, establishment and fringe. East Village tours, SoHo and the galleries of Madison Avenue, as well as 'hospitality' visits to an artist's studio, all guided by qualified – and entertaining – art historians.

For **Central Park** the *Urban Rangers* (397 3091) run a varied and free selection of educational walks throughout the year, as does the *Department of Parks and Recreation* at the Dairy (see p.130; 397 3091. Tuesday-Sunday 11am-4pm).

The Penny Sightseeing Company, 1565 Park Ave (410 0080). A back-run four company that specialises in tours of Harlem, claiming to give an 'honest view of Harlem as it is'. Coach-based trips run on Tuesdays and Saturdays at 11am and cost $15; reservations are needed two days in advance. They also offer Harlem Gospel Tours that take in the rousing spiritual singing of a Baptist service: Thursdays at 10am, Sundays at 10.30am, reservations two days in advance, $17. Though harder work, the *Municipal Arts Society's* Harlem tours are much better.

Brooklyn Historical Society, 128 Pierrepoint St, Brooklyn (718 624 0890). Walking tours of Brooklyn neighbourhoods like Brooklyn Heights itself, Park Slope, Greenpoint and plenty more. Costs around $5.

Prospect Park Environmental Center, Picnic House, Prospect Park, Brooklyn (718 788 8500). Don't be put off by the name: these people run much the same range of tours as the Historical Society (above), though concentrating on Prospect Park and around. Costs around $3 per person.

Queens Historical Society, 143-35 37th Ave, Flushing, Queens (718 939 0647). No walking tours as such, but if you write to them enclosing a SAE they'll send a free do-it-yourself walking tour of 'historic' Flushing. Can you resist?

Bronx County Historical Society, 3309 Bainbridge Ave, Bronx (881 8900). Yes, there really is enough in the Bronx to warrant a series of neighbourhood tours, from strolls through suburban Riverdale to furtive hikes across the desolate wastes of the South Bronx. Excellent

value at about $4 per person.

Staten Island Historical Society, 441 Clarke Ave, Staten Island (718 351 9414). Determined not to be left without its own historical society and a set of walking tours, these people run treks around various Staten Island enclaves – an excellent opportunity to see the best of the city's otherwise forgotten borough. From around $2.

MONEY AND BANKS

US currency comes in dollar bills worth $1, $5, $10, $20, $50, $100 plus larger denominations that you're not likely to see. Confusingly, each is the same size and colour, making it necessary to double check before handing notes over. For the record (and for fans of US politicians), a **$1** bill has a portrait of Washington; **$5** Lincoln; **$10** Hamilton; **$20** Jackson; **$50** Grant; **$100** Franklin. The dollar is made up of 100 cents in coins of **1 cent** (1c, known as a penny), **5 cent** (a nickel), **10 cent** (a dime) and **25 cent** (a quarter). New York City – its telephones, cigarette machines, etc. – runs on quarters so always carry at least a dollar's worth. Also, you'll very occasionally find **JFK half-dollars** (50c) and **Susan B. Anthony dollar** coins in your change.

Traveller's cheques and credit cards
Best way to take the bulk of your money is in **traveller's cheques** (*travelers checks* in the US). In Britain you can buy them over the counter at any bank (at a cost of 1% of the amount ordered) and a fast-increasing number of building societies (who generally waive the charge provided you keep a certain amount in your account). The most universally recognised cheques are *American Express traveller's cheques*, available in Britain from the TSB, Lloyds and The Royal Bank of Scotland, and *Visa traveller's cheques*, from the Co-Op, Yorkshire and Barclays Banks. *Thomas Cook's traveller's cheques* (sold at all their major agents) come a clear third. Always buy **dollar cheques** rather than sterling, since most banks, especially upstate, will look askance at anything that doesn't firmly insist on calling itself a dollar.

The advantage of the better-known cheques is that they can be used as

cash in very many shops, restaurants and garages (don't be put off by a "No Checks" sign in the window as this refers to personal cheques). You'll get your change in dollars, and for this reason remember to order a good number of $10 and $20 cheques: few places like to hand over all their spare change in return for a cheque. Additionally, almost all 24-hour Korean greengrocer/delis will cash small cheques – a lifesaver if you run out of cash at 4am.

America is also of course the land of **plastic money**, so if you have a **Visa**, **Access** (here known as **MasterCard**), **Diners** or **American Express** card you really shouldn't leave home without it. All are accepted in just about every shop, most restaurants and for many services, and as well as their buying power, hotels and car hire firms will ask for a card to establish your credit-worthiness and as security: cash, believe it or not, is sometimes treated with suspicion. Very occasionally the fact that your MasterCard has *Access* plastered all over it will cause confusion – which a phone call to MasterCard will soon clear up.

With Access or Visa it is also possible to **withdraw cash** at a bank (watch for the relevant stickers); don't however try to use the **cash machines**, which will gobble up your card leaving you creditless and possibly cashless for the rest of your trip. **American Express** and **Diners charge cards** cannot generally be used to withdraw cash; but an American Express card entitles you to get cash or buy traveller's cheques at any American Express office or, in conjunction with your PIN (personal identification number), you can use the traveller's cheque dispensers found at airports. Diners Club members can cash cheques at any branch of *CitiBank*.

Banks

Banking hours are usually 9am-3/3.30pm, with certain banks staying open later on Fridays. Major banks such as *CitiBank* and *Chemical Bank* will exchange traveller's cheques and currency at a standard rate: other change facilities such as those at airports may offer disadvantageous rates and/or commission charges which it's wise to find out first. Out of banking hours are *Chequepoint*, 551 Madison Ave at 55th St (7.30am–10.30pm 7 days a week) and *Deak-Perera*, 41 E 42nd St at Madison (Monday-Friday 9am-5.30pm, Saturday 9am-5pm). Both will change traveller's cheques and exchange currency.

Emergencies

All else has failed. You're broke and 3,500 miles from home. Before you jump off the Brooklyn Bridge, weigh up the alternatives.

● Arrange for someone to transfer cash from any branch of **Thomas Cook's** in Britain to Thomas Cook's office in Manhattan (address above).

This takes 24-48 hours and costs around $20.

● **Transfer money** from your bank account. Find a bank that has connections with your own (whether it handles credit cards associated with British banks is a good guide) and phone or telegram your bank to telex the money to the specified New York bank. This will take 48 hours at least and cost $10-$30. Alternatively, your bank can wire the money to Thomas Cook's HQ in Peterborough, England, where it will be transferred to Cook's office in New York.

● If there's time, get someone to buy an **international money order** and send it through the post. The commission is low but you'll have to rely on international airmail service (allow at least seven days from London).

● Should you have literally no cash nor access to any, the alternatives include **selling blood** (p.37), **working illegally** (p.36) or throwing yourself at the mercy of the **British Consulate** (845 3rd Avenue, 752 5747) who might (very begrudgingly) repatriate you but will never, repeat never, lend money.

COMMUNICATIONS: TELEPHONES AND THE POST

Phone calls

The American **telephone system** is reliable, though annoyingly privatised ("Thank you for using AT & T" operators mechanically state, as if you had the choice) and expensive, especially when dialling long distance.

The **dialling tone** is a low, continuous rasp or a single low drone; the **ringing tone** a long nasal squark with short gaps; the **engaged (busy) tone** a series of rapid blips; **number unobtainable** is a single high-pitched squeak.

Nine times out of ten you won't dial but jab since push button phones have largely superseded the dial variety. And for non-private calls, you will quite frequently be typing in letters as well as numbers: New York Airport Transport information, for instance, has the 'number', 1 800 AIR RIDE. Which is good for memory if at first confusing to dial: follow the letters on the buttons or dial and make sure not to mistake letter O (on the number 6) with the zero button for the operator.

Normally, **telephone numbers** are in the form of (123) 456 7890. The first three digits are the **area code** and are needed only when dialling a different area. In New York City, the 212 code covers just Manhattan and the Bronx: phoning within this area simply dial the seven-figure number. Outside the area – long distance or to the Outer Boroughs of Queens, Brooklyn, etc. – dial **1** first, then the **area code** and **number**.

Area codes around Manhattan include:
Brooklyn, Queens,
Staten Island(1) **718**
Long Island(1) **516**
New Jersey(north:1) **201**
　　　　　　(south)(1)**609**
To phone into Manhattan from these areas or anywhere else(1) **212**

Where we've given phone numbers for areas outside Manhattan, you'll find codes are included. To check codes elsewhere consult the phone book or dial the operator (see below).

One of the more impressive features of New York life is that the **payphones**, no matter how graffitied or otherwise unpromising, almost always work. Their rates, however, are well above those for private phones – which makes anything other than a local call a costly business.

The basic payphone **charge** for **local calls** (ie calls within the same area code) is 25c, followed by top-ups of 10c. To phone long distance, dial the number and a recorded message will cut into demand enough for the first three minutes.

Making **international calls**, much the same applies. It isn't possible to dial direct, and the operator (0) will detail the initial call cost, which you'll have to load up in quarters after the person you're phoning has answered. When the first three minutes are up the operator may interrupt, but it's more likely you'll simply hear a bleep: after you've hung up the operator will phone back and test your honesty by asking for the extra money. The **cheap rate** for operator-connected calls via a payphone to Europe is between 6pm and 7am, though the price for the initial three minutes is fixed. The minimum cost of a call to Britain is currently $5.50.

To make a **reverse charge** call, dial 1 800 44 55 667 and you'll be connected (toll free) with the British operator. If phoning from a **hotel**, check the cost first as rates are often hiked up. Calling from a **private phone** will mean considerable savings.

When stating a number *don't* use the word 'double' but state the number in full; and remember that telling the operator you can't 'get through' will cause great confusion as 'through' means finished or completed – the correct phrase is to say you 'aren't connected' or 'can't get a connection'.

Any number with **800** in place of the area code is '**toll free**' which means it costs nothing to dial. Many national firms, government agencies, enquiry numbers, hotel and car hire reservations have a central toll free number. To find it look in the Yellow Pages or dial **1 800 555 1212** for toll free directory enquiries.

Unbelievably useful (if hardly the sort of things you'll want to lug around) are the Manhattan **White** and **Yellow Page phone books** – the first an alphabetical list of private numbers and businesses (with the **Blue Pages** containing government agencies at the end) and the other detailing every consumer-orientated business and service in the city, listing delicatessens, grocers, liquor stores, pharmacies, physicians and surgeons by location, and restaurants by location *and* cuisine. It's also handy for finding bike and car hire firms – and just about anything legal that can be paid for. Look for it in most bars, hotel lobbies and the larger post offices.

Service numbers
Emergencies   **911** for police, ambulance and fire
Operator   **0**
Directory Enquiries
411 (Manhattan)
1 555 1212 (local)
1 + (area code) + 555 1212 (numbers in other area codes)

For other useful telephone numbers – to find out the time, weather, etc. – see p.41.

Letters and poste restante
In terms of efficiency the New York (and American) **postal service** comes a very poor second to its phone system. Even within Manhattan mail can take a few days to arrive and a letter to LA might take a week – and that's airmail. Services to Europe take anything between five and ten days, and sending mail abroad surface consigns it to oblivion or at best a couple of months' disappearance.

To Europe, **postcards** go cheapest, aerograms are slightly more expensive while **letters** proper are costlier still once you've passed the half-ounce minimum. You can buy **stamps** in shops, supermarkets and (usually non-functioning) vending machines, but the best place is, unsurprisingly, a post office. These are open 9am-5pm Monday-Friday, 9am-12pm Saturday, and there are a lot around. In Manhattan, the main **General Post Office** at 8th Avenue between W 31st-33rd Sts is open Monday-Saturday round the clock for important services. Letters posted from the General or Lexington Avenue Post offices seem to arrive soonest, whereas the blue bin-like **mail boxes** on street corners tend to take a while.

If you want to send – or receive – something **poste restante**, best have it addressed to the General Post Office 421 8th Avenue, NY 10001. Americans use the phrase 'c/o General Delivery' – though simply writing 'Poste Restante' is unlikely to confuse anyone. To collect letters you'll need two forms of ID (passport, credit card and driving licence form the holy trinity of identification). Mail will be kept for 30 days before being returned to sender – so make sure there's a return address somewhere on the envelope. Receiving mail at someone else's address, be sure your correspondents puts c/o on the envelope, since without that you risk your mail being returned to sender by an over-zealous postperson.

US mail regulations concerning **parcels** are decidedly recherché: post offices are highly specific in the type of container that must be used and won't allow it to be sealed with sticky tape. Buy one of their boxes and read the instructions in the info at the front of the Yellow Pages before you start – turn up with a parcel that breaks the rules and you'll be curtly sent away. Parcels are delivered surface unless you specify airmail and either service costs more the further the destination and the larger and heavier the parcel. To send anything abroad you need a Customs Declaration Form, again available at the post office.

Sending **mail within the States**, always specify the **Zip Code**, the last line of an address which details the specific area. Without the code, letters can end up terminally lost, and certainly delayed. If you're unsure of a Manhattan Zip use the guide in the front pages of the phone book or phone 971 7411; elsewhere ask for the relevant Zip directory at the post office. Lastly, to send a **telegram** (US *cable*) you'll want not a post office but a *Western Union office*. There are long lists of these in all Yellow Pages. If you've got a credit card you can simply phone up (962 7111) and dictate. Prices for international telegrams are marginally cheaper than the shortest possible phone call. For domestic telegrams ask for a **mailgram**, which will be delivered to any address the following morning.

MEDIA

Newspapers and magazines

Gone are the days when New York could support twenty different **daily newspapers**. There are now just three published in the city – the broadsheet *New York Times* (30c) and tabloids *Daily News* and *New York Post* (both 35c) – along with one insurgent from Long Island, *Newsday* (40c). The **New York Times** is an American institution: judged liberal by US standards it's a fairly élitist rag, with a dull old-fashioned layout and typeface enlivened by comprehensive world news and features that have earned it a reputation of the country's number one newspaper. Each weekday there's a special section: Sundays the *Book Review Magazine*; Monday *SportsMonday*; Tuesday *Science Times*; Wednesday *Living* (full of handy yuppie-aligned articles like 'How to Grow Orchids in a Window Box'); Thursdays *Home*; Fridays *Weekend* (good for events). The Sunday edition of the *Times* ($1.25), a thumping bundle of newsprint most of which is advertisement, comes out on Saturday evening in an edition known as the *Bulldog*, which should keep you busy well into the following week.

The two tabloids concentrate on local news, usually screamed out in banner headlines. The **Daily News** is far and away the better of the two, with a fresh, energetic style that comes as a surprise if you're used to British equivalents. Most readable features: the gossip pages, Doonesbury cartoons and the acerbic Jimmy Breslin. Most famous of many racy headlines: succinct summary of the President's attitude to New York during the crisis of the mid-1970's: 'FORD TO CITY – DROP DEAD'. The Sunday edition of the *News* ($1) is if anything more readible than the *Times*, its *City Lights* section giving an excellent overview of the week's concerts, gigs and events. The **New York Post** was once a decent organ, indeed considered better than the *News* and more liberal editorially than the *Times* – to which it was in some ways an adjunct, sharing its readership and offering a local slant to news coverage. But things have changed radically since Rupert Murdoch's News

International Group bought the paper in the 1970s, lurid sensationalism replacing investigative reports and editorials sinking into knee-jerk conservatisms of the most crass kind. All that remains of former glories are the sports pages, considered old unbeatable by those in the know.

Newsday (35c) has worried both tabloids by its increasingly high profile among New York commuters. However it is not an NYC paper – the readership are mainly middle-income suburbanites – and seems unlikely to encroach greatly on the Manhattanite market.

The US doesn't have a tradition of national newspapers – yet. **USA Today** (50c), a new colour daily (and the model for the British *Today*) has been attempting to alter this, printing by satellite on both East and West Coast. You'll see it around in New York – though less often read.

British and European newspapers are widely available. For the British press, the most comprehensive outlet is *The Magazine Store*, 30 Lincoln Plaza (across the road from the main Plaza) where you can also pick up most periodicals. The widest selection of European (and also regional US) papers is available at *Hotalings*, 142 W 42nd (840 1868), or try the kiosks on 42nd St between 5th and 6th Avenues.

Murdoch's News International Empire also cast a shadow over New York's most celebrated **weekly paper**, the *Village Voice* (Thursday, $1). Originating in the Village, this made its name as a youthful, intelligent, vaguely left journal with hard-hitting investigative reporting and interviews – the nearest the city ever got to 'alternative' journalism. Murdoch seemed scared to alter the successful mix of liberal politics and insightful writing, and these days the *Voice* is still a good read and can be a useful pointer to what's on around town. Buy it as matter of course, and if you're further interested in New York journalism supplement with the **East Village Eye** (Thursday, $1.50). Similar in format, the *Eye* is more daring in its exposés and barbs – and it can be impressively unrelenting in its campaigning stance.

A brief glance at the **glossies**. The **New Yorker** (weekly, $1.50) is a stodgy collection of fiction, poetry and reviews, an upmarket mix of *Time Out*, *Punch* and the *Spectator*. Its *Goings On about Town*

pages, however, live up to their description of a 'Conscientious Calendar of Weekly Events' – excellent for theatres, films and galleries. Others include **New York Magazine** (weekly, $1.95) a yuppie-orientated, Murdoch-owned rag that's worth reading for its listings; **Details** (monthly, $2) filled with modish fashion and gossip of nocturnal doings of the intown incrowd; and Andy Warhol's **Interview** (monthly, $2) as the name suggests, given over to talk with a major figure, plus lots and lots of fashion. For wacky news, views and the odd listing, look out too for **The Paper** (monthly, $1.50).

Television

American TV is bad and there's too much of it. The two dozen (plus) stations do come up with a gem once in a while, but to catch it you'll have to sit through an awful lot of crap – not to mention the frequent and clumsy commercial breaks. At some time in the city though you're almost bound to allow curiosity to get the better of you. So, a brief guide to the dial, and the two varieties – broadcast and cable TV.

Broadcast TV offers a choice of eight channels in NYC:

2 WCBS (CBS)
4 WNBC (NBC)
5 WNYW (Independent)
7 WABC (ABC)
11 WPIX (Independent)
13 WNET (PBS)
25 WNYE (PBS)
31 WNYC (PBS)

Notable Broadcast TV programmes include the **Macneil, Lehrer Newshour** (Channel 13; nightly at 7.30pm), the most informed news report; **60 Minutes** (Channel 2; 7pm Sundays), rare investigative reporting; **Saturday Night Live** (Channel 4; 11.30pm) has comedy on Saturday nights (live); **The Cosby Show** (Channel 4; Thursdays at 8pm), currently the country's most popular domestic comedy; and the crass but hilarious **Lifestyles of the Rich and Famous** (Channel 11; sporadic series), which, like the **Crazy Eddie** adverts, have the effect of making you want to bang your head against the wall. If you're hunting for **the news** – and you're not in line for Macneil, Lehrer – you'll find bulletins on channels **2**, **4** and **7** at 7am, 5pm, 6pm, 7pm, and 11pm.

Channels 13, 25 and 31 are **PBS**

(Public Broadcasting Service), and on a different planet as far as quality is concerned, showing drama, documentaries and educational programmes alongside the best that British TV has to export. Watch out for *Masterpiece Theater*, introduced with avuncular condescension by Alastair Cooke.

Cable TV is available in many hotels and some YMCAs/YHAs: channels received depend on how much the subscriber pays. Among the most common are **CNN** (Cable News Network) offering round-the-clock news; **HBO** (Home Box Office), repeated schedules of recently released and popular movies; **LIF** (Lifetime), basically a health channel including the enormously popular Dr Ruth on *Good Sex* (weekdays, 10pm); **MTV** (Music Television) rock/pop/new wave *et al* videos, concerts and interviews – thoroughly addictive; and **SHO** (Showtime), much like HBO. At the far end of the dial are slightly bizarre Spanish stations, frightening hot gospel from Jerry Falwell and other 'religious' nutters, and porno channels. Best way to fathom out what's on and when is to buy *TV Guide* (60c), or check the day's newspapers listings – the *Times* has the most comprehensive.

Radio
The **FM** dial is crammed with local stations of highly varying quality and content. If you possess a walkman radio bring it, as skipping through the channels is a pleasure. Stations are constantly chopping and changing formats, opening up and closing down. For the most complete listings again see the *New York Times*. As an introduction, among the city's most enduring radio stations are:
WPLJ (95.5) Pop/rock/etc. One of many stations that focus (with numbing repetition) on the top thirty hits.
WRKS (98.7) Calls itself KISS 98FM. Aggressively poppy and urban.
WQXR (96.3) Commercial classical station so staid it makes Britain's Radio 3 look bold and innovative.
WNYC (93.9) Adventurous classical music and the best morning news programme – from 6am-8.30am.
WNCN (104.3) Reliable end of the dial classical station.
WKCR (98.9) Excellent jazz.
WBAI (99.5) Non-profit-making independent station with an intelligent variety of features.

AM stations aren't nearly so interesting with but a few good talk shows amid a sea of belting rock and lobotomised 'easy listening'. **WOR 710** is worth dipping into for its interviews. **WINS 1010** and **WCBS 830** are all news; **WNYL 830** all talk.

Finally, if all this American noise is getting on top of you it's possible to tune into the **BBC World Service** on the 49 metre short wave band, or just the World Service news, broadcast on public stations like WPBX on Long Island.

POLICE AND TROUBLE

The **City Police** (aka 'New York's Finest') are for the most part approachable, helpful and overworked. This means that asking directions gets a friendly response, reporting a theft a weary 'Whaddya want me to do about it?'. Each locality has a station, numbered at a **precinct**; to find out which is the nearest phone 374 5000. In **emergencies** phone **911** or use one of the outdoor posts that have a direct line to the emergency services. Out of the city you may have to tangle with the **State Police**, who operate the Highway Patrol – and quite ruthlessly.

Irrespective of how dangerous New York really is, it *feels* dangerous. Perhaps more than any other city in the world a sense of nervy self-preservation is rife here: people make studied efforts to avoid eye contact and any unusual behaviour clears a space immediately: the atmosphere of impending violence is sometimes sniffable.

The reality is somewhat different. There *is* a great deal of crime in New York, some of it violent. But 7 million people live in the city and as far as per capita crime rates go Boston is more dangerous, as are Phoenix, Dallas, Denver, Seattle and half a dozen other towns. New York's tension doesn't automatically mean violence: as with any big city, anywhere, the main thing is to walk with confidence and to be aware of the few places and/or times that you really should avoid. Though crime can and does happen day and night it's unlikely you'll be robbed outside the Rockefeller Center at midday; Times Square at midnight is a different matter. Throughout the text we've outlined places where you should be careful and those few best avoided altogether, but really it's a case of using your common sense; it doesn't take long to figure out that you're somewhere unsavoury.

It is of course the murders that make the headlines: reassure yourself with the fact that 90% of victims are known to their killers, which is to say most are personal disputes rather than random killings. More real a problem – and one that is obsessive conversation among New Yorkers – is **street crime**, especially **mugging**. It's impossible to give hard and fast rules on what to do should you meet up with a mugger: whether to run or scream or fight depends on you and the situation. I'd hand over the money every time and so would most New Yorkers – indeed keeping a spare $20 or so as 'mugger's money' lest your attacker turn nasty at finding empty pockets is common practice.

Of course the best tactic is to **avoid being mugged** and there are a few simple points of mental preparation

worth taking: **don't** flash money, jewellery or your Oyster Rolex around; **don't** peer at your map (or this book) at every street corner thereby announcing that you're a lost stranger; even if you are terrified or drunk (or both) **don't** appear so; **never** walk down a dark side street, especially one you can't see the end of; and in the early hours stick to the roadside edge of the pavement so if approached it's easier to run into the road and attract the attention that muggers hate.

If **the worst** happens and your assailant is toting a gun or (more likely) a knife, play it calmly: remember that he (for this is generally a male pursuit) is probably almost as scared as you and just as jumpy; keep still, don't make any sudden movements – and do what he says. When he's run off hail a cab and ask to be taken to the nearest police station: taxis rarely charge for this; if they do the police will pay. Don't stand around on the street in a shocked condition – this is inviting more trouble. At the stations you'll get sympathy and little else; file the theft and take the reference (see p.10) to claim your insurance back home.

SLEEPING

Accommodation in New York City is a major cost. The only way to cut it radically is to utilise every contact you have – however tenuous – in the city and the Tri-State area. Spend some of your time on a floor or two and suddenly the city, cost-wise at least, isn't all that different from any other.

Otherwise the bottom-line choice is between a room in a **YMCA/YWCA** (a *Y*, as they're known), the **Youth Hostel** (YHA), or, an increasingly popular alternative, **bed and breakfast** in a New Yorker's spare room. Ys charge around $38 a double (though one location, Sloane House, is greatly reduced for those with YHA cards – available, price £6, from 14 Southampton St, London WC2; tel 01 240 3158); bed and breakfast, arranged through one of three official agencies, is usually about $40-50 a double. **Hotels**, which do not normally include breakfast in their rates, also start at around $40 a double, though at this end of the scale they are rarely too enticing. If you want a place you'll

actually enjoy going back to then count on $50 and up – and even so be very selective in where you choose. **Detailed hotel listings** – with our recommendations for all these categories and B&B agencies – begin on p.53.

For **upstate New York**, much the same applies. There are only a scattering of **YMCAs and youth hostels** (though these do have cheap dormitory accommodation for members) and **hotels** run at similar prices to those in NYC. There are, however, cheap and handy standbys in **motels**, which range from seedy truck-stops to somewhat cleaner and quite welcoming places; prices hover around $30 for a double though rarely dip below $20. The *Howard Johnson* and *Holiday Inn* hotel indexes give prices of their upstate hotels/motels (including the reductions made by squeezing several people into a room). They can be worth picking up before you set out – from one of their hotels in New York or in Britain/Europe. Two further upstate possibilities, a little more expensive and out of the way but far more characterful, are **bed and breakfasts**, or, for around the same price, **country inns** – basically European-style guest houses. For further details on both see the **Introduction to New York State** on p.282; specific recommendations are detailed in the relevant town or area sections of the guide.

With almost any hotel room it's possible **to cut costs** slightly if you can fill a double with three or even four people. This is normal practice in the States and managements rarely mind providing an extra bed or two. If you're staying long enough, you may also be able to pay at a special weekly rate, maybe getting one night in seven for free. Some hotels, particularly those that see tourists as a major part of their revenue, also lay on special weekend discounts if you stay two nights or more.

One good thing: almost all US hotels, even the very grottiest, have **TVs** in rooms as a matter of course – so if you've spent all your money on a bed for the night you can always curl up in front of Johnny Carson...

FOOD AND DRINK

There isn't anything you can't eat in New York. The city has more restaurants per head than anywhere else in the States, and New Yorkers not only eat out all the time but take their food incredibly seriously, devoting long hours of discussion to the study of different cuisines, new dishes and new restaurants – which can find themselves received with all the fervour of a second coming. In short, it's food (after money – and the two often go together) which rules, and as you stroll through the heavenly odours that emanate from the city's delis, bagel shops, Chinese restaurants and popcorn palaces, it's hard not to work up an appetite.

Breakfast
Not just in New York but across the USA this is the best value and most filling meal of the day. Most hotels serve breakfast, but it works out much less expensive to go out to a **coffee shop**, most of which do special deals up until 11am, allowing you to eat and drink until you're full for no more than a couple of dollars. If you're on any kind of budget, getting to the coffee shop before 11am is of utmost importance – later in the day sit-down food costs will be considerably higher.

Figuring high on **breakfast menus** are sausages (small, skinless and spicier than British ones) and bacon (streaky, cut very thin and fried to a crisp), along with eggs, waffles and pancakes, the latter thick and heavy, and served with a smothering of honey or maple syrup. Be prepared to be interrogated as to how you want your eggs and be ready to snap back with an answer – breakfast may be taken seriously in the States but it is never taken slowly. Basically, 'sunny side up' means fried unturned, 'over' means flipped over and done on both sides, and 'over easy' turned for a few seconds only. Americans also forget all distinctions between sweet and savoury at breakfast time, and it's quite common to see people consuming piles of syrup-covered pancakes and fried eggs and bacon not only off the same plate but often in the same mouthful.

Lunch and snacks
The Great American Breakfast never spoils the Great American Lunch. Almost all **restaurants** open at lunchtime and it's then that you get the better deals, either because there's a set menu or because prices are simply cheaper.

In New York City, the best lunchtime deals of all are to be had in **Chinatown**. There you can get a massive plate of meat with noodles or rice for well under $3, or, if you're feeling a little more adventurous, feast at a *Dim Sum* restaurant for $4-5. Dim Sum (literally 'your heart's delight') consists of small dishes that you choose from a moving trolley and pay for at the end according to the empty dishes in front of you. For the inexperienced (and Dim Sum is not recommended to vegetarians) there's an element of chance, since Chinatown waiters tend not to speak English and the dishes themselves are often unrecognisable until the first bite. But duckwebs aside, it's mostly pretty accessible fare (see the lists that follow for some of the standards).

Another option for lunch – and one that's not just limited to Manhattan – is to get a **sandwich 'to go'** (ie takeaway) from a **deli**. Once again, be prepared for a quick-fire question and answer session with the assistant, who will not only ask which kind of bread you want – white, wholewheat, rye or french (in which case ask for a 'hero' or a 'sub') – but also whether you want 'mayo' (mayonnaise), lettuce or anything else. American sandwiches are custom-built so don't be constrained by menus, only by your imagination, and bear in mind the size of the thing you're creating: the American sandwich has absolutely nothing in common with the thin limp object you buy in Britain, which is probably why you can expect to pay at least $3 for one.

For **quick snacks**, many delis also do ready-cooked **hot meals**, there are also **vendors** (most concentrated on lower/midtown Manhattan) who sell hot dogs, pretzels and knishes, or for a round dollar you can get a slice of **pizza** (*Ray's* is the most ubiquitous and reliable NYC chain). If you want to sit down or just eat something a touch more wholesome, **coffee shops**, invariably run by Greeks, are open all day and most evenings and serve a variety of straight American dishes at affordable rates. And there are of course regular and familiar **burger chains** like (in descending order of quality) *Wendy's*, *Burger King* and *McDonald's*, as well as a host of other fast-food franchises that haven't yet made it across the Atlantic.

Coffee is drunk widely in the States and is usually fresh and good, served black or 'regular' (with cream or milk). (Confusingly, in other parts of the country 'regular' coffee is black coffee). You can get coffee 'to go' in most delis, and in restaurants coffee is often served 'ad lib', ie you can keep asking for refills at no extra charge. As an alternative for the health-conscious, *Sanka* is caffeine-free coffee. **Tea** is becoming more popular, and will normally be served straight or with lemon; if you want milk request it, and specify whether you want it hot or cold.

Soft drinks (sodas) come in caffeine-free versions as well. On the subject of soft drinks, watch out for **root beer**, a rather nasty concoction not unlike drinking bubble gum, and rainbow varieties of **coke**. These are drunk in three sizes: small (large), regular (bigger), and large (practically a bucket).

Bar food and bargains

Just about every American **bar** serves food of one kind or another. Even in the lowliest there's a good chance they'll cook you at least a burger or a plate of potato skins, and many places offer a full menu, particularly in the slightly more upmarket Irish hangouts. Though bars open late (see *Drinking* below) their kitchens are usually closed by 12pm.

In the **ritzier bars** – basically in Manhattan – there are almost invariably hot **hors d'oeuvres**, laid out between 5 and 7pm Monday-Friday. For the price of a single drink (it won't be cheap) you can stuff yourself silly on pasta, seafood, chilli or whatever. Remember, though, that the more you look like an office-person (it's for them, after all, that the hors d'oeuvres are put out) the easier you'll blend in with the free-loading crowds. Some places even demand you wear a tie.

Another NYC bargain (especially for serious drinking) is **brunch**, usually served at weekends between noon and 4pm. For an all-in price you get a meal (lox and cream cheese on a bagel, steak and eggs or eggs benedict are favourites) plus as many complementary bloody marys, mimosas or glasses of champagne as you can drink.

Bars which serve serious food are detailed along with restaurant **listings** on pp.240-255; hors d'oeuvres places on p.244; brunch venues on p.245. For convenience in locating a nearby place on a walk around the city, they are also cross-referenced by area in the Manhattan and Outer Boroughs chapters.

Restaurants

Specific NYC **restaurant recommendations** – and a rundown of the different areas – appear in the *Drinking and Eating* chapter (p.234), and you'll again find lists for cross-reference at the end of each section in the Manhattan and Outer Boroughs chapters. Similarly, recommendations for upstate restaurants and other eateries are detailed under their town or area. What follows is simply an introduction to the food and to peculiarly New York/American procedures of eating and paying for it.

American cooking tends to be of consistently good quality and served in huge portions. Salads are eaten with every meal, not as a main course but as a starter, and ordering one entails fielding more rapid questions as to the kind of dressing you want. *Italian* (more like European 'French'), *French* (nothing like European 'French'), *thousand island* and *blue cheese* are the usual alternatives. Some restaurants have a salad bar, from which you can help yourself to as much as you can eat while waiting for the main course. Main dishes include steaks and burgers (which are near ubiquitous) and, especially upstate, a good choice of fish and seafood. Vegetables will almost certainly include french fries and baked potato, the latter commonly topped with sour cream and chives. Ordering a burger may be more complicated than you're used to: they're treated like regular steaks and you'll be asked how you want them cooked – rare, medium or well-done.

In New York City, at least, so-called American food inevitably fades into the background when you're confronted with the startling variety of different **ethnic cuisines**. Among them, none has had so dominant an effect as **Jewish** food, to the extent that many Jewish specialities – bagels, pastrami, lox and cream cheese – are now considered archetypal New York. Others retain more specific identities. **Chinese** food, available not just in Chinatown but all over Manhattan, is most frequently (and familiarly) Cantonese though, many restaurants also serve the spicier Szechuan and Hunan dishes. Chinese prices (see *lunch and snacks*, above) are usually the city's lowest. **Japanese** food – generally expensive – is Manhattan's current craze, in particular *sushi* (raw fish) – served as much for the aesthetic arrangement as for the taste, which you'll either love or hate. Other Asian cuisines include **Indian** (becoming more plentiful though nothing like as ubiquitous – or as good – as their British counterparts) and a broad sprinkling of **Thai**, **Korean** and **Indonesian** restaurants, all of which tend to be pricey.

Closer to home, **Irish** food dominates the city's bars with corned beef (more like salt beef than the tinned British bully) and cabbage, shepherd's pie and Irish stew. **Italian** cooking is also, not surprisingly, widespread (though rarely especially cheap); so is **Spanish**, whose huge seafood dishes can make an eco-

nomical night out for those in a group. **French** restaurants are predictably expensive, particularly so of late with the cultish popularity of *nouvelle cuisine*.

More realistically, a whole range of **Eastern European** restaurants – Russian, Ukrainian, Polish and Hungarian – serve well-priced filling fare. **Greek** food is easy to find in most parts of the city (especially, of course, the Greeks' own quarters) and is usually edible and affordable. **Mexican** restaurants are another good-value option, since the food is honest peasant stodge by nature, you get plenty of it and there are no little extras to push up the bill.

Other sundry places include **Cuban-Chinese** and **Kosher-Chinese** hybrids, and any number of **vegetarian** and **wholefood** eateries to cater for any taste or fad. The key is to keep your eyes peeled and not be afraid to be adventurous. Eating is *the* great joy of being in New York, and it would be a shame to waste it on the familiar.

Whatever you eat, **service** will everywhere be excellent, since not only is the notion of customer service deeply engrained into the American psyche, but the system of **tipping**, whereby you double the figure on the bill for tax to work out the minimum tip, can make the staff almost irritatingly attentive. There's no way round this: if you either refuse or forget to tip there's little point in going back to that restaurant again. As far as actual **payment** is concerned, many, though by no means all, restaurants take credit/charge cards (if you use one you will find a space left for you to write in the appropriate tip); traveller's cheques are also accepted at many places (see p.13).

Drinking

Ordinary American **bars** can be enjoyably like the ones you've seen on TV – a few cigar-smoking drunks propping up the counter, with a wise-cracking, philosophising barman. But the average down-market New York neighbourhood bar is still pretty much **male-only** territory and can be intimidating if you try and pretend otherwise. Larger bars are usually more mixed and more inviting. Bars generally **open** from mid-morning (around 10am) to the early hours – 4am at the latest, when they have to close by law.

As far as actual **drinking** is con

cerned, you will probably soon be looking for ways to save money. A round of drinks – even a single drink – in a New York bar can be a sizeable investment. Take note of decor. In a name bar or especially in what New Yorkers call a singles joint you'll be paying $2.00 upwards for an ordinary glass of beer; walk next door to a more basic place, and you'll be down to $1, or even less. Detailed **listings** and recommendations again appear in the *Drinking and Eating* chapter, starting on p.234, and by area cross-reference in the Manhattan and Outer Boroughs chapters.

Specific **savings on drinking** can often be made in the larger bars by ordering quart or half-gallon pitchers of beer, which represent a considerable discount on the price per glass. Look out, too, for 'Happy Hour' bargains (usually 60 minutes stretched somewhere between 5 and 7pm) and two-for-the-price-of-ones. And avoid bars or clubs that offer 'free drinks for ladies' – they tend to be cattle markets or worse.

When you've made your choice of bar the next problem is deciding **what to drink**.

Despite its successful incursion into the British market over recent years, American **beer** enjoys something of a reputation in Europe – for being fizzy, tasteless, and with virtually no alcoholic content at all. While that may be slightly over-stated, even the average American bartender wouldn't make much of a spirited defence of the brew. Americans don't take beer very seriously: it's not a drink to get drunk on, more to quench your thirst, and it's normally served so chilled that the taste barely matters anyway. If you do care, then imported beers like Canadian *Molsen*, Mexican *Dos Equis* and the familiar European varieties are widely available, if also more expensive. And if price is a problem, then bear in mind you can walk in and buy beer at around 60c a can in any supermarket.

Don't be afraid to try Californian **wine**, since not only can it be very good, it's also extremely inexpensive at around $2-$3 for a bottle in a liquor store, $5 upwards for a flagon: *Christian Brul* and *Paul Masson* are the names to look out for. New York State also produces wine, though of a lesser quality – see p.326 for details on the main wineries. French

and Italian wines come more expensive, but they're still by no means costly. In all cases, though, wine does demand a well-filled wallet when in a restaurant or bar: expect 100 per cent mark-up on the bottle.

As for the **hard stuff**, there are a number of points of potential confusion. First bear in mind that whether you ask for a drink 'on the rocks' or not, you'll most likely get it poured into a glass full to the brim with ice; if you don't want it like this ask for it 'straight up'. Don't forget either that if you ask for whisky you'll get the American kind, *bourbon*, of which the most common brands are *Old Grandad* and *Jim Beam* (*Jack Daniels* isn't technically bourbon since it's not made in Tennessee); if you want Scotch or Irish whisky ask for them by nationality or brand name. Neither should you ask for *Martini* if you want the herby drink drunk by beautiful people: to Americans a martini is a mixture of gin and vermouth – vermouth (pronounced 'vermooth') to an American being what we call Martini.

Cocktails are popular all over the States, especially during happy hours and weekend brunch (see above). Varieties are innumerable, sometimes specific to a single bar. But among standards are:

Bacardi	white rum, lime and grenadine – not the brand name drink
Black Russian	vodka with coffee liqueur
Daiquiri	white rum and lime
Highball	any spirit plus a soda, water or ginger ale
Manhattan	vermouth and whisky
Margarita	tequila, triple sec and lime (or strawberry) juice
Mimosa	champagne and orange juice
Mint Julep	bourbon, mint and sugar
Pina Colada	rum, coconut milk and pineapple
Screwdriver	vodka and orange
Tequila Sunrise	tequila, orange juice and grenadine
Tom Collins	gin, lemon juice, soda and sugar
Whisky Sour	bourbon, lemon juice and sugar

With any other names you come across, experiment – that's half the fun.

Buying your own alcohol, you need

to find a liquor store — you won't get anything apart from beer in a supermarket. Which is just one of New York State's somewhat complex **licensing laws**. Other regulations worth keeping in mind are that you have to be over 21 to consume alcohol in a bar or restaurant (and you'll be asked to provide evidence if there's any dispute); that it's against the law to drink alcohol on the street (which is why you see so many people furtively swigging from brown paper bags); and that you can't buy off-licence booze, other than beer, anywhere on a Sunday.

Glossary of Food Terms

American

A la mode	With ice cream
Au jus	Meat served with a gravy made from its own juices
BLT	Bacon, lettuce and tomato toasted sandwich
Broiled	Grilled
Brownie	A fudgy, filling chocolate cake
Brunch	Originally a meal between breakfast and lunch: now a midday meal taken at weekends
Caesar's salad	Cos lettuce in egg dressing with anchovy paste, olives and lemon, served with garlic croûtons and parmesan cheese
Check	Bill
Chips	Potato crisps
Clam chowder	A thick soup made with clams and other seafood. Very tasty and with bread almost a meal in itself. A popular East Coast dish
Club sandwich	Large, overstuffed sandwich
Doggy bag	Bag provided by restaurant for taking home leftovers
Egg cream	Neither eggs nor cream but a drink containing milk, chocolate or vanilla syrup and seltzer
Egg-plant	Aubergine
English muffin	Toasted crumpet
Fillet	The same, but pronounced 'fillay', as if French
Frank	Frankfurter (hot dog)
(French) fries	Chips
Half-and-half	A mixture of milk and cream
Hash browns	Mashed potato shaped into cubes and fried in fat
Hero	Sandwiches made with french bread
Home fries	Fried potatoes
Jello	Jelly
Jelly	Jam
Maitre d'	Head waiter
Muffin	Leavened cake made with bran and/or blueberry
Pecan pie	Pastry cake filled with pecan nuts and custard
Popsicle	Ice lolly
Potato chips	Crisps
Pretzels	Savory circles of glazed pastry sold on street corners
Scrod	Young Atlantic cod
Seltzer	Fizzy/soda water
Sherbet	Sorbet
Shrimp	Prawns
Soda	Generic term for any soft drink
Soft-shell crab	A kind of crab whose shell is soft and edible. Eating an entire crab shell and all may seem a bit hard to get used to, but persevere — it's rightly considered a delicacy on the East Coast
Squash	Marrow
Teriyaki	Sweet and sour sauce
Waffles	Egg batter cooked in an iron and served with maple syrup, honey or butter

| Waldorf salad | Celery, chopped apple and walnuts served on lettuce leaves with a mayonnaisse dressing |
| Zucchini | Courgettes |

Glossary of Ethnic Food Terms

Chinese

Cantonese	Szechuan/Hunan	
Chow	Ch'ao	Stir-fried
Doufu	Tofu	Bean curd
Fun, fon	Fan	Rice
Gai, gee	Chi	Chicken
Har, ha	Hsia Jen	Shrimp (prawns)
Hew	Shao	Roasted
Jyuyuk	Jou	Pork
Ow	Cha	Deep-fried
Ngow yuk	Niu Jou	Beef
Opp	Ya	Duck
Yu	Yu	Fish

Dim Sum (Cantonese)
Bao, bau	Bun
Cha Shew Bao	Steamed bun filled with sweet cubes of roast pork
Chow fun	Fried rice noodles
Chow mai fu	Rice vermicelli
Har Kow	Shrimp dumplings
Jook	Congee, or rice gruel
Kow, gow	Dumplings
Lo Mein	Mixed noodles
Mai fun	Thin noodles
Tang mein	Soup noodles
Wontons	Thin-skinned dumpling filled with fish or meat

Greek
Baklava	Very sweet, flaky pastry made with nuts and honey
Dolmades	Vine leaves stuffed with rice and meat
Feta	Crumbly white cheese made with goat's milk
Gyro	Minced lamb
Horta	Greens, often dandelion leaves
Kasseri	Rubbery cheese made with sheep's milk
Kokeretsi	Grilled lamb innards
Moussaka	Baked aubergine pie, topped with a cheese sauce
Pastitsio	Lamb pie topped with macaroni
Souvlaki	Shish kebab
Spanakopita	Spinach pie
Stifado	Lamb stew
Taramasalata	Paste made of cod's roe, olive oil and lemon juice
Tiropita	Cheese pie
Tzatziki	Yogurt with garlic and cucumber

Italian
Cacciatore	'Hunter's style' – cooked with tomatoes, mushrooms, herbs and wine
Calzone	Pizza turned over so the topping is inside
Alla Carbonara	Sauce made with bacon and egg
Al fredo	Tossed with cream, butter and cheese
Al forno	Cooked in the oven

Posillipo	Tomato sauce with garlic, Neapolitan style
Puttanesca	Literally 'whore style', cooked with tomato, garlic, olives, capers and anchovies
Alla Veneziana	Cooked with onions and white wine
Zabaglione	Dessert of whipped egg yolks, sugar and marasala

Pasta

Cannelloni	Large pasta tubes, stuffed with minced meat and tomato and baked
Cappelletti	'Little hats', stuffed with chicken, cheese and egg
Cappelli d'angeli	'Angel's hair', very fine pasta strands
Fettucini	Flat ribbons of pasta
Fusilli	Pasta spirals
Gnocchi	Pasta and potato dumplings
Linguine	Flat pasta noodles, like Tagliatelle
Manicotti	Squares stuffed with cheese; ravioli are the same only with meat
Tortellini	Rings of pasta stuffed with either spiced meat or cheese
Vermicelli	Very thin spaghetti
Ziti	Small tubes of pasta, popular in New York, often baked with tomato sauce

Japanese

Gyoza	Meat and vegetable dumplings
Karagei	Fried chicken
Kushikatsu	Pork cutlet, with mushrooms and green peppers
Larmen	Noodles in spicy broth
Negimayaki	Sliced beef with scallions
Okonomi	Literally 'as you like it', this is usually used with regard to sush when choosing the variety of topping
Sake	Japanese rice wine, drunk warm, and very strong
Sashimi	Thinly sliced raw fish eaten with soy sauce or *wasabi*
Sushi	Raw fish again, but wrapped up with rice in seaweed. Slightly more appetizing for tentative first-time sushi eaters
Tempura	Seafood and vegetables deep-fried in batter
Teriyaki	Sweet and sour sauce
Tonkatsu	Deep-fried pork with rice
Wasabi	Hot green horseradish sauce

Sushi/sashimi

Anago	Sea eel
Ebi	Shrimp
Ikura	Salmon roe
Kappa(maki)	Cucumber with rice and seaweed
Maguro	Tuna
Nigiri	Rice topped with fish
Tai	Red snapper
Tamago(yaki)	Omelette
Tekka(maki)	Tuna with rice rolled in seaweed (nori)
Toro	Extra meaty part of the tuna
Chirashi	Mixed fish on rice

Jewish

The Jewish faith allows two types of restaurant: those in which meat can be eaten and those where dairy products can be consumed. The two types of cooking can't be mixed. This section includes some Russian and Ukrainian dishes, which, though occasionally spelled differently on menus, are often much the same.

Bagel	Hard bread roll, in the shape of a ring, often toasted
Blintz	Crêpe filled with cheese or fruit and eaten with sour cream
Borscht	Beetroot soup
Challah	Egg-bread, eaten traditionally as part of the Friday evening Sabbath meal

Falafel	(Middle Eastern). Deep fried spiced chick pea balls
Glatt kosher	Type of cuisine and restaurant catering to the diet of ultra-orthodox Jews
Kasha	Cracked buckwheat cooked until tender and served with soup or as a side dish
Knaidel	Meat dumpling. Also known as *matzo balls*
Knish	Pastry filled with cheese, meat, potato, fruit or anything else that comes to hand on sale from street vendors – though the creation they'll sell you bears little relation to the real thing.
Kreplach	Noodle-dough shells filled with *kasha*, meat, potato etc
Kugel	Potato or noodle pudding
Lox	Smoked salmon
Matzo	Flat unleavened bread eaten all year round but particularly at Passover
Pareve	The term for 'neutral', ie something which can be eaten with meat or dairy food
Pirogen	Baked envelopes of dough filled with potato, meat, cheese, or fruit
Schmaltz	Chicken fat
Tzimmes	Literally 'a mixture'. Casserole of meat, vegetables and fruit

Mexican

Burritos	Tortillas stuffed with re-fried beans or beef, and grated cheese
Chiles Rellenos	Stuffed chilis
Enchiladas	Soft tortillas filled with meat and chilli or cheese and baked
Frijoles	Re-fried beans, ie mashed fried beans
Margarita	*The* cocktail to drink in a Mexican or Tex-Mex restaurant, made with tequila, triple sec, lime juice and limes, and blended with ice to make a slush. Served with or without salt
Nachos	Tortilla chips served as a snack before a meal
Tacos	Hard, crispy tortillas, often folded and stuffed with various fillings
Tortillas	Maize dough pancakes used as shells for fillings
Tostados	Crisp tortillas, fried and smothered with meat and vegetables

WOMEN'S NY: PROBLEMS AND CONTACTS

In New York – as with any large, cosmopolitan city – you're likely to experience some level of sexual harassment. And you've probably heard enough about how manic and threatening the streets can appear. What you may find surprising is the sheer crassness of attitude displayed by many American men, and, in a city where women outnumber men by a considerable ratio, the passivity with which some women accept this. On the positive side, the women's movement of the 1960s and 70s has had a much more dynamic effect in New York (indeed throughout East and West Coast America) than in Europe. Women are much more visible in business, politics and the professions. The attitudes around can equally well be *more* progressive and sophisticated...even if it's the negative that first and most powerfully catches attention.

Feeling safe
It must be safe to travel around New York; American women do it all the time. So runs the thinking, but New York does throw up unique and definite problems for women – and especially for women travelling alone and just getting to know this city. If you feel and look like a visitor, not quite knowing which direction to ride the subway, for instance, it's little comfort to know that New York women routinely use it on their own and late in the evening. What follows are a few points to bear in mind when beginning your explorations of the city: if they duplicate, in part, the comments on *Trouble* (see p.18), no apologies.

The truth is you're more likely to feel unsafe than *be* unsafe. Something that can lead to problems in itself, for part of the technique in surviving (and enjoying) New York is to look as if you know what you're doing and where you're going. Maintain the facade and you should find a lot of the aggravation fades away. But also keep in mind that for Americans subtle hints aren't the order of the day: if someone's bugging you let them know your feelings loudly and firmly. Some women carry whistles, gas and sprays, which, while pretty useless in the event of real trouble, can lend confidence and ward off creeps.

Harassment in the city is certainly worse for women than men — and it can be a lot scarier. But it's not always that different, at least in intent. You're far, far less likely to be raped than you are **mugged**. For a few ground rules on lessening chances of mugging, see p.19, but above all be wary about any display of wealth in the wrong place — if you wear jewellery (or a flash-looking watch) think about where you're walking before setting out for the day. If you are being **followed**, step off the sidewalk and into the streets as attackers hate the open. Never let yourself be pushed into a building or alley and never turn off down an unlit, empty-looking street. If you're unsure about the area where you're staying, don't hold back asking other women's advice. They'll tell you when they walk and when they take a bus so as to avoid walking more than a block; which bars and parks they feel free to walk in with confidence; and what times they don't go anywhere outside a cab. Listen to this advice and merge it into your own experience. But don't avoid parts of the city just through hearsay — you might miss out on what's most of interest — and learn to *expect* Manhattanites to sound alarmist...it's part of the culture.

If you don't have much money, **accommodation** is important: it can be very unnerving to end up in a hotel with a bottom of the heap clientele. Make sure that you have a hotel lobby that's well-lit, the door locks on your room are secure and the night porters seem reliable. If you feel uneasy, move. A good choice, for safety and supportive contacts, is the women-only *Martha Washington*. This is detailed, along with the range of hotel accommodation, on p.55. If you're looking for a long-stay room you might also try *Allerton House*, detailed with the apartment information on p.37.

Crisis/support addresses

There are competent and solid support systems for women in **crisis**, or in need of **medical** or **emotional** support. At any of the following you can be assured of finding skilled, compassionate staff.

New York Women Against Rape (477 0819 — or 777 4000 hotline). Crisis counselling, advocacy and support groups for victims of rape or sexual abuse.

The Women's Counseling Project, c/o Barnard College Women's Centre (see below) (280 3063). Referral service that can connect you with a range of medical agencies including abortion and birth control, psychological health and alternative treatment services.

The Saint Mark's Women's Health Collective, 9 2nd Ave (228 7482). One of the foundations of the New York women's community, offering traditional and alternative medicine at sliding scale prices.

Identity House, 544 6th Ave (243 8181). Coming-out groups and individual counselling.

Other feminist contacts

Womanbooks, 201 W 92nd St at Amsterdam Ave (873 4121). New York's main feminist bookstore — and an obvious first point of contact. Aside from books, you'll be able to pick up *Womanews*, the city's monthly feminist newspaper, a good read and reasonably comprehensive for feminist/lesbian events, readings, dances and gatherings. Womanbooks' own noticeboards, too, are a useful resource.

Barnard College Women's Center, Barnard College, 117th St, Broadway (280 2067). Clearing-house for information on women's organisations, studies, conferences, events, etc. They also maintain an extensive library collection of books, articles and periodicals.

Women's International Resource Exchange (WIRE), 2700 Broadway (666 4622).

National Organisation for Women, 9th Floor, 15 W 18th St (807 0721). The largest feminist organisation in the US — active in abortion and lesbian rights and ERA agitation.

More Fire! Productions Apt 16, 63rd E 7th St (533 7667); **WOW** (Women's One World Theatre), 59 E 4th St (460 8067). Feminist theatre groups. If you're interested, WOW welcome visits (and foreign contacts).

Ceres, 91 Franklin St (226 4725). Women's gallery.
Qui Travel, 165 West 74th St (496 5110). Women's/gay travel agent.

See also the lesbian listings in Gay and Lesbian New York *below and the women's/lesbian bars and clubs detailed on p.240.*

GAY AND LESBIAN NEW YORK

Gay refugees from all over America and the world come to New York, and it's estimated that around 20% of New Yorkers (or at least Manhattanites) are **lesbian** or **gay**. The recent passage of the Gay Rights Bill has contributed to the high visibility of gay men and women in the community: NY's State Governor and Mayor, its City Council President and Controller, and the Manhattan Borough President all employ full-time liaison officers to gay and lesbian groups. So too, in the midst of the current horrifying AIDS epidemic, does the Health Department: a major problem, obviously, though one to which the community is extremely responsive.

   Greenwich Village is the traditional and established gay neighbourhood and it's here that you'll find most of the action – bars and nightclubs, bookshops, businesses, theatre, arts and contact/support groups. The **East Village** too has a growing scene, especially for lesbians. Other promising locales include the **East 20s and 30s**, **Chelsea** and (for gay men) **Fire Island**.

   You'll find all **bars and nightclubs** detailed in Chapters 7 and 8: what follows are the more **community/resource** kind of listings. If you need to supplement these (and obviously space forbids a comprehensive New York gay guide) get hold of the *Gayellow Pages* ($3.95), available from either of the bookshops below. For up to the minute info, check also *The Native*, New York's superb weekly newspaper for gay men, or *Womanews*, a monthly lesbian/feminist newssheet. Both, along with the more national *Christopher Street*, are available from many newsstands or from one of the bookshops below.

LESBIAN *AND* GAY RESOURCES

Center
Lesbian and Gay Community Services Center, 208 W 13th St. (620 7310) Occupying a run-down high school this has only been in existence since 1985 but already provides meeting space for over eighty organizations ranging from Gay Alcoholics Anonymous to Gay Advertising Executives. In addition to the numerous groups (which have activities – from sports to political lobbying – going all the time), the Center itself sponsors regular dances and other social events. Call the above number to see what's happening.

Bookshops
The Oscar Wilde Memorial Bookshop, 15 Christopher St (255 8097). The first gay bookshop in America. Unbeatable.
A Different Light 548 Hudson St (989 4850). Excellent selections of gay and lesbian publications. Opens late throughout the week, and often hosts booksigning parties and readings.

Health and well-being
Community Health Project, 208 W 13th St (691 8282) Low-priced gay clinic which can either treat you or refer you.
Identity House, 544 6th Ave (243 8181). Psychological assistance and counselling.
Lambda Legal Defence and Education Fund (944 9488). Legal referrals.
SAGE: Senior Action in a Gay Environment (741 22247). Advice and numerous activities for gays over 50.

Religion
There are numerous gay religious organisations in New York:
Beth Simchat Torah (929 9498). The gay synagogue.
Dignity (868 3050). Catholic.
Integrity (620 0057). Episcopal.
Metropolitan Community Church (242 1212). Protestant.

Theatre and television
There's always a fair amount of gay theatre (and some TV) going on in New York: check the listings in *The Native* and *The Village Voice*.
Stonewall Rep (675 1014). Mixed gay theatre company.

Gay Cable Network. Broadcasts for 90 minutes every Thursday from 10.30pm to midnight on Manhattan Cable Channel J — which you should be able to pick up on a hotel TV.

EXCLUSIVELY FOR WOMEN

Info/help
Lesbian Switchboard (741 2610 Monday-Friday, 6pm-10pm). Because no lesbian organisations receive any centralised funding, the community relies on the committment of small groups of volunteers. One such is the Switchboard — *the* place to phone for information on events, happenings and contacts in the NY community.

Archives
Lesbian Herstory Archives (874 7232 for an appointment). Celebrated and unmissable.

Radio
Lesbian Radio Show WBAI 99.5FM Tuesday 8.30pm. Issues and news for lesbians.

Accommodation
Womyn's Bed & Breakfast (794 8645). Phone for details of women-only rooms in central Manhattan.

See also Women's New York *(p.27)*.

EXCLUSIVELY FOR MEN

Info/help
Gay Switchboard (777 1800 Daily, noon to midnight). Help and what's on info.

Radio programme
Gay Rap WBAI 99.5FM Wednesdays 9pm-10pm. Weekly program for and about the gay male community.

Accommodation
If you're looking for somewhere to rest your head that is specifically sympathetic to gays (or well located for the Village), here are a few more suggestions:
CPI (929 1023). Agency providing clean rooms on the edge of Greenwich Village. Rates start at $25, but reserve well in advance.
Incentra House, 32 8th Ave (206 1020). Doubles $50 up.
Longacre House, 317 W 45th St (246 8580). In the theatre district. Singles start at $30.

See also Fire Island *(p.287)*.

PARADES AND FESTIVALS

New York takes its **parades** seriously: Fifth Avenue is usually the venue and almost every large ethnic group in the city holds an annual get-together — often political or religious in origin, though now just as much an excuse for music, food and dance. Chances are your stay will coincide with at least one: the following list is roughly chronological — for more details and exact dates of parades, phone 397 8222. As you might expect, New York's **festivals** are concentrated in the spring and summer, tending to tie in with ethnic holidays and religious observances. We've included those that take place in Manhattan: for further details, exact dates and lists of events in other boroughs, phone 755 4100.

Parades
The big celebration — and undoubtedly NYC's most famous — is the **St Patrick's Day Parade** on the weekend nearest March 17th. Celebrating an impromptu march through the streets by Irish militiamen on St Patrick's Day 1762, it has become a draw for every Irish band and organisation in the US and Ireland, which in recent years has meant increasing political overtones with Noraid and Sinn Fein out in full force. Much of the city lines the route up 5th Avenue from 44th to 86th Streets, and general dementia runs especially high in Irish bars: should you find yourself in one, steer clear of politics. Best vantage point is St Patrick's Cathedral, where the Bishop of New York greets the marching pipes and bands.

The **Greek Independence Day Parade** (March 25th) isn't as long or as boozy, more a patriotic nod to the old country from floats of pseudo-classically dressed Hellenes. When Independence Day falls in the Orthodox Lent, the parade is shifted to April or May. It kicks off from 5th Avenue to 49th Street. Also in April is the **Easter Parade** (5th Avenue between 49th and 59th Streets), an opportunity for New Yorkers to dress up in outrageous Easter bonnets.

Martin Luther King Jr. Memorial Day (May 17th) marks a procession along 5th Avenue from 44th to 86th Street to celebrate his work for equal rights for blacks. Of several Puerto Rican celebrations in the city, largest is the **Puerto Rican Day Parade** (first Sunday of June), three hours of bands and baton twirling from 44th to 86th Streets on 5th Avenue, then across to 3rd. July 4th sees nationwide celebration of **American Independence Day** and in New York **Macy's firework display**, visible all over lower Manhattan but best seen from Riverside Park between West 80th and West 105th Streets from around 9.30pm on: more local shindigs can be found just about everywhere else.

The **Gay Pride March** on June 28th commemorates the Stonewall riots of 1969 (see p.85); a well-attended celebration of gay rights running south from Columbus Circle. The **Steuben Day Parade** is the biggest German-American event, taking place on the third weekend of September. Baron von Steuben was a Prussian general who fought with Washington at the battle of Valley Forge, which is as good an excuse as any for a costumed parade in his honour from 61st to 86th Street and 5th Avenue. The **Columbus Day Parade** on or around October 12th is, after St Patrick's Day, the city's largest binge, commemorating the day America was put on the map. **Halloween** is celebrated on 31st October in a chase through Greenwich Village culminating at Washington Square, and on the last Thursday in November **Macy's Thanksgiving Parade** runs from 79th Street down Central Park West to Columbus Circle, afterwards down Broadway to Herald Square: lots of bands, celebrities and giant balloons.

Fifth Avenue gets seasonal trimming at **Christmas**, especially in the last two Sundays before Christmas week: the Rockefeller Center lights up its Christmas tree in the first week of December and decorates Channel Gardens, so beginning the festivities. On the two Sundays before Christmas 5th Avenue is closed to traffic, with entertainment on the streets. **New Year's Eve** is traditionally marked by a mass gathering on Times Square where the last seconds of the year signal drunken but good-natured revelry amid the snow.

Festivals

First off is **Chinese New Year**, a noisy, colourful occasion celebrated around Mott Street in Chinatown on the first full moon after January 21st. Dragons dance in the street, firecrackers chase away evil spirits and chances of getting a meal anywhere in Chinatown are slim; phone 267 5780 for further details.

In May the **Ukrainian Festival** fills a weekend on East 7th between 2nd and 3rd Avenues: marvellous Ukranian costume, folk music and dance plus authentic foods. At the Ukranian Museum (12th Ave and 2nd Street) there's a special exhibition of *pysanky* – traditional hand-painted eggs; 228 0110 for festival details. Highspot of May is the **Ninth Avenue Festival** which closes the Avenue between 34th and 57th for the weekend, giving you the chance to snack your way along the strip of delis and restaurants that come out on to the street with their wares.

Smaller, though more interesting, are the **Fiestas de Loiza Aldea** on the second weekend of July, a miniature version of the great Fiestas de Santiago Apostol (Festival of St James the Apostle) in the town of Loiza Aldea, Puerto Rico. Following mass at the Church of San Pueblo at Lexington and 117th, separate processions of women, men and children each carry a statue of the apostle to the footbridge at 102nd St and East River Drive to Ward's Island. Look out for the *Vejigante*, the animal-headed creature covered with horns who symbolises the devil, and *Caballero*, a 16C Spanish nobleman. After the procession there's a festival of Latin music, dance and salsa on Ward's Island, with plenty of Puerto Rican food – try the *pasteles* (spicy meat pies wrapped in a plantain), washed down with *coquito*, a drink made from eggs, coconut cream and rum. Also, check out the **Fiesta Folklorica**, an all-singing, all-dancing spectacle that fills Central Park on the last Sunday in August.

The city's two Italian festivals are well publicised: the **Festival of St Anthony**, held in early June, is a two-week celebration on Sullivan Street from Spring to West Houston, culminating in a procession of Italian bands led by a lifesize statue of the saint carried on the shoulders of four men. More popular, and with great street stalls, is the **Festival San Gennaro**, patron saint of Naples, held along Mulberry Street in Little Italy for ten days during the week of September 19th. Highspot is a procession of the saint's statue through the streets, donations of dollar bills pinned to his cloak.

From early July to late August the **Summer Festival** has outdoor concerts and plays in Central Park, the Rockefeller Center and the South Street Seaport, many of which are free: phone 755 4100 for a daily round-up. Also running from mid-July to August is Lincoln Center's **Mostly Mozart** festival, which starts with a free outdoor performance and continues in a series of cut-price concerts in Avery Fisher Hall: phone 874 2424 for more details. One of the most popular summer events is the series of **concerts** given by the New York Philharmonic in

Central Park and other parks throughout the boroughs, all for free: 755 4100 for a schedule of times and places.

Central Park Mall (72nd St entrance) sees the **Indian Festival** in June or July: Indian music and dance, sari stalls and lots of Indian snacks. Biggest of the Jewish festivals is the **Lower East Side Jewish Spring Festival** (second Sunday in June) on East Broadway between Rutgers and Montgomery Streets, featuring *glatt kosher* foods, Yiddish and Hebrew folk singing and guided tours of Jewish Lower East Side. Another religious-based occasion – and one of the prettiest – is the **Japanese Oban Festival**, which takes place at Riverside Park Mall at West 103rd Street in the early evening of the Saturday nearest July 15th. Slow, simple dancing in the lantern-hung park make this well worth catching.

Dates

January   *Chinese New Year*, Chinatown

March   17th: *St Patrick's Day Parade*, 5th Ave
            25th: *Greek Independence Day Parade*, 5th Ave

April   *Easter Day Parade*, 5th Ave

May   *Ninth Avenue Food Festival*
            Ukrainian Festival, East 7th St
            17th: *Martin Luther King Jr. Memorial Day Parade*, 5th Ave

June   *Puerto Rican Day Parade*, 5th Ave
            Festival of St Anthony, Sullivan St
            Indian Festival, Central Park
            Lower East Side Jewish Spring Festival, East Broadway
            28th: *Gay Pride March*, from Columbus Ave

July   4th: *Independence Day Celebrations*
            New York Summer Festival of Theater and Music
            Mostly Mozart Music Festival at Lincoln Center
            Japanese Oban Festival, Riverside Park
            Fiestas de Loiza Aidea, Lexington Ave

August   *Fiesta Folklorica*, Central Park

September   *Steuben Day Parade*, 5th Ave
            Festival of San Gennaro, Little Italy

October   4th: *Pulaski Day Parade*, 5th Ave
            12th: *Columbus Day Parade*, 5th Ave
            31st: *Halloween*, Greenwich Village

November *Macy's Thanksgiving Day Parade*, Broadway

December *Rockefeller Center Christmas Tree Celebrations*
31st: *New Year's Eve*, Times Square

SPORT

Sport in America is big business, which is to say that for all **spectator sports** financial considerations come first. The Brooklyn Dodgers, New York's official baseball team, upped and left (for LA) as long ago as 1957, and every other professional team intermittently threatens to do the same. Yet New Yorkers are themselves highly sports-conscious and all three NY papers (the *Times* on Tuesdays, the *News* and *Post* daily) devote a great many pages to the subject. Sit in any bar long enough and someone will demand your opinion of their favourite team as the match comes on TV — which might, as at the *McCann* chain, be a special kingsize screen that's the best alternative to actually being there. If you do want to be there, of course, there's **American football**, **baseball**, **basketball** and much else: just check the papers and your venue/ticket details below. And be warned that major events frequently sell out — and that ticket prices are consistently high

Participation sport isn't that cheap either — unless you're prepared to **swim** (either at the local pools or the borough beaches) or, the city's main obsession, **jog**. Other participatory sports, and all **fitness** fads, are firmly in the private sector which ensures that you pay for the privilege. For anyone interested, they do however fill sizeable sections of the city's Yellow Pages.

WATCHING

Baseball
Baseball is America's national game — one that looks like rounders but is immeasurably more skilled and subtle. The season runs from April to October and the city teams are the **Yankees** (alumni include Joe DiMaggio and Babe Ruth), who play floodlit games at the Yankee Stadium in the Bronx, and the **NY Mets** who share Shea Stadium with the Jets — and who were 1986 champions.

Tickets for both venues are around $10, though you can get (unshaded) *bleacher seats* for about half that.

American Football
If you haven't seen an American football game before you arrive in New York you won't have long to wait. All big matches feature on TV and they're a major slot in most neighbourhood bars. For the uninitiated, the spectacle of all-American razamatazz is probably novelty enough, though the game does get more interesting if you can pick up at least some of **the rules**...

Basically, American Football is like rugby. The aim is to reach the end zone with the ball and score a **touchdown** (though players don't actually have to place the ball on the ground). The action is organised into a series of **plays** and each time the player with the ball is tackled to the ground or the ball goes off the pitch, that play is concluded. Only one forward pass per play is allowed — a climax with the players allowed to stop, block or push over their opponents even if they're not in possession of the ball.

The other main unit of the game is a **down**, an attempt to move the ball forward two lines (10 yards) of the pitch. A team gets four attempts to achieve a down — then another four if they succeed. If they fail, possession of the ball goes to the opposing team. In the rambling mysteries of the commentary 'second and 4' means the game is on the second down and four more yards are needed. If it seems unlikely that the offensive team will get the yards required (eg at 'fourth and 9') a **kicker** will attempt to secure a **field goal** by beating the ball between the posts; if the ball is far from the opposition's goal a **punter** comes on to drop kick the ball as far down the field as possible. The opposing team will then take possession and try to run back up the field before being stopped by tackles.

The game lasts for one hour of play, divided into four **quarters** with a break after the second quarter. However the clock only runs when the game is in progress, which means that it can run for three hours or more...more than enough time to master the complexities if you're prepared to ask, sit back and listen.

The **season** stretches from August to June. New York's teams are the **NY Jets** who play at Shea Stadium and the **NY Giants** whose home is the Giants Stadium at the Meadowlands Sports Complex in New Jersey. Cheapest tickets are $8, though these can be tough to get.

Basketball
The basketball season begins in October and runs until June. Strictly the only home team is the **NY Knickerbockers** (Knicks) who play at Madison Square Garden Centre. The **Nets** from New Jersey, however, are considered honorary NYC and play at the Meadowlands Complex, NJ. Tickets around $10-15.

Tennis
The UD **American Open Championships** are held in Queens each September at the National Tennis Centre, Flushing Meadows (718 592 8000). Ticket prices for the big matches are astronomical.

Venues and tickets
Tickets for most events can be booked ahead with a credit card and collected at the gate, though it's cheaper (and of course riskier for popular events) to pick up tickets on the night. For anything at Meadowland book by phoning *Chargit* on 201 935 3900; for Yankee Stadium, either *Chargit* on 944 9300 or *Teletron* on 947 5850. If all else fails try **Mackey's** at 234 W 44th Street (840 2800), a ticket agency for all sporting events.

The four big football/baseball/basketball **venues** are:
Madison Square Garden Center, W 33rd Street and 7th Avenue (564 4400); subway 1,2,3 to 34th Street Penn Stadium.
Meadowlands Sports Complex, Off routes 3, 17, and Turnpike exit 16, East Rutherford New Jersey (201 935 8500). Regular buses from Port Authority Bus Terminal on 42nd Street and 8th Avenue.
Shea Stadium, 126th Street at Roosevelt Avenue Queens (507 TIXX; 672 3000) for basketball fixtures, (421 6600) for football. Subway Number 7, direct to Willets Point/Shea Stadium Station. Dress warmly in Autumn and winter as Shea is a windy icebox.
Yankee Stadium, 161st Street and River Avenue, the Bronx (293 6000); subway CC, D or 4 direct to 161st Station.

Huddle in with the crowds when you leave − it's not a nice neighbourhood.

BETTING

Horse racing, as Europeans know it, takes place at the **Aqueduct Race Track**, ('The Big A') Rockaway, Queens between January and May and June and July. It is possible to get there on a special A train from 42nd Street with a ticket that includes grandstand admission. More details on 718 330 1234 or from Grand Central. **Belmont Park** on Long Island can also be reached on similar all-inclusive tickets from Penn Station and the Long Island Railroad. Details on 516 739 4200; open May-June, August-October.

Somewhat more American in spirit, and also highly popular, is **trotter or harness racing** where horses pull small buggies. Venues: **Roosevelt Raceway**, Westbury, Long Island (516 222 2000) (various dates throughout the year, all-in subway/bus tickets from Penn Station) and **Yonkers Race Track**, Yonkers, NY (March-April, June-July, September, October and December) Get them from Port Authority Bus Terminal − more details in the papers. The **Meadowlands Stadium** has races from January-August starting at 8pm in an enclosed stadium.

To **place a bet** anywhere other than the race track itself you'll need to find an **OTB (Off Track Betting)** office. There's one at Grand Central, where you'll find a pamphlet explaining the laws and complications of the American betting system. Opening hours are Monday-Friday 9am-5pm, Saturday 9am-3pm.

PARTICIPATING

Jogging
Jogging is still very much number one fitness pursuit: the number of yearly coronaries in **Central Park**, the most popular venue, probably runs well into double figures. A favourite **circuit** in the Park is the Receiving Reservoir − just make sure you jog in the right direction, which is anti-clockwise. The East River Promenade and almost any other stretch of open space long enough to get up speed are also well jogged.

If, rather than bust your own guts you'd prefer to see thousands of others do so, the **New York Marathon** takes place on the third or fourth Sunday of October: two million people turn out each year to watch the 16,000 runners complete the 26 mile course that starts in Staten Island to cross the Verrazano Narrows Bridge and pass through all the other boroughs before ending up at the Tavern on the Green in Central Park. To take part you need to apply for an entry form from *Road Runners Club*, P.O.Box 881, FDR Station, New York, NY 10150, or phone their headquarters on 860 4455.

Skating and tobogganing

In winter, the freezing weather makes for good **skating** and **tobogganing**. Slickest place to skate is without doubt the Rockefeller Center rink (757 5730), but you may have to queue. Far better to head out to the Kate Wollman Rink in Prospect Park, Brooklyn (718 965 6561), or to try the rink in Central Park when it's completed. For tobogganing head up to the slopes of van Cortlandt Park in the Bronx – phone 543 4595 to see if the snow's thick enough.

Swimming pools

There are municipally-owned swimming pools across the city:
East 23rd Street Pool E 23rd St and Asser Levy Place (397 3184) 60ft x 30ft.
Gymnasium & Pool Clarkson St and 7th Ave (397 3147) 70ft x 20ft.
Gymnasium & Pool 342 E 54th St (397 3148) 54ft x 50ft.
Gymnasium & Pool W 59th St and West End Ave (397 3170) 60ft x 34ft.
Gymnasium & Pool 35 W 134th St (397 3193) 75ft x 35ft.
 Other **privately-run pools** are mainly membership affairs and very expensive.

Beaches

Few visitors come to New York for the **beaches**, and those New Yorkers with money tend to turn their noses up at at the city strands, preferring to move further afield to Long Island, just a couple of hours away and much better (see p.284). But the city's beaches, though often crowded, *are* a cool summer escape from Manhattan and most are also just a subway token away... The best, in the three boroughs of Brooklyn, Queens and the Bronx, are:

BROOKLYN
Coney Island Beach (At the end of half a dozen subway lines: fastest is the D train to Stillwell Avenue). After Rockaway, (see below) NYC's most popular bathing spot, jam-packed on summer weekends. The Atlantic here is only moderately dirty and there's a good, reliable onshore breeze. 885 1828 for info.
Brighton Beach (D train to Brighton Beach). Technically the same stretch as Coney, but less crowded and given colour by the local Russian community (pick up on ethnic snacks from the boardwalk vendors).
Manhattan Beach (D train to Sheepshead Bay Road, walk to Ocean Avenue and cross the bridge). Small beach much used by locals. 718 965 6589.

QUEENS
Rockaway Beach (A or CC trains to any stop along the beach). Forget California. This seven-mile strip is where New Yorkers – up to ¾ million daily in summer – come to get the best surf around. Best beaches are at 9th St, 23rd St, and 80-118th Sts. 718 634 7065
Jacob Riis Park (IRT 2 train to Flatbush Avenue, then Q35 bus; also B9 and B46 buses on summer weekends). Good sandy stretches, the western ones used almost exclusively by a gay male crowd. 718 474 4600.

THE BRONX
Orchard Beach (IRT 6 local to Pelham Bay Park, then Bx 12 bus). Lovingly known as 'Horseshit Beach' – and in any case less easy to get to than the rest. 855 1828.
Staten Island
Great Kills Park (Bus 103 from Staten Island Ferry Terminal). Quiet and used by locals.
Wolfe's Pond Park (Bus 103 to Main St Tottenville, at Hylan and Cornelia). Packs in the crowds from New Jersey.

STAYING ON

Nobody ever says it's easy to **live and work** in New York City, New Yorkers especially – most of whom, when you broach the subject of prolonged residence, will talk obsessively about their jobs and salaries (assuming they have them), and where they live, or will live, or won't be living any more. Which should give you some idea of the nature of the competition for a good apartment address – definable to the street by most natives, in terms of money, social status and mobility.

As a **foreigner**, you naturally start at a disadvantage, at least as far as contacts go. An English accent will help but don't count too heavily on it. The British Consulate claims that each year an alarming number of Britons wind up in New York City in need of shelter, sustenance and sympathy. Both work and rooms, however, *are* there, if you've got the energy, imagination or plain foolhardiness to pursue them. Below are the basic ground-rules and those matters of bureaucracy which, even if you choose to ignore them, you should certainly be aware of.

Legal (and illegal) work

For **extended, legal stays** in the US it helps if you have either relatives (parents, or children over 21) who can sponsor you. Or alternatively a firm offer of work from a US company or, less promisingly, an individual. Armed with a letter specifying this you can apply for a **special working visa**, available from any American embassy or consulate abroad (see p.8) *before* you set off for the States.

There are a whole range of these visas, depending on your skills, projected length of stay, etc. – but with a couple of exceptions they're extremely hard to get. The easiest tend to be for academic posts or other jobs (in the computer field, for instance) which the US feels it particularly needs to fill. Or for **students** (and occasionally non-students) there are a limited number of *Exchange Visitor Programmes* (EVPs), for which participants are given a *J-1 visa* that entitles them to accept paid summer employment and to apply for a **social security number** (an identification for tax purposes which virtually no

American citizen is without). Most J-1 visas are issued for positions in American summer camps through schemes like *BUNAC* (info on this from 232 Vauxhall Bridge Rd, London SW1; 01 630 0344).

Should all this seem too far-fetched, you could, like thousands of others each year, forget regulations completely and hunt out **work on your own**. To do this you'll have to pound the streets, check the noticeboards (p.40) and the media, and, most likely, invent your own social security number to satisfy your prospective boss. If you're already in New York and decide you want to stay and work this will most likely be your only choice: employment visas can't realistically be obtained in the city. Be advised though that for anyone with only a standard tourist visa, *any* kind of work is **totally illegal**. If you're caught, you could be liable for deportation.

Of more immediate concern, for **temporary workers**, is the business of finding out exactly what people do in New York – and how you can fit in. For ideas (and positions) check the Employment Want ads in the *New York Times* and *Village Voice* and in the plethora of smaller, freebie neighbourhood tabloids available throughout the city.

Possibilities obviously depend on your own personal skills and inventiveness, but among the more general or obvious you might look at some of the following suggestions:

- **Restaurant work**. With over 25,000 restaurants in the city, this is a real standard: wait tables, or be hired as a delivery person, dishwasher, salad-preparer or short-order cook. Experience helps, as does dropping by in person since most restaurants won't deal with you over the phone. And don't forget about **tending bar** in one (or more) of the city's thousands of watering holes: as in the restaurant biz, tips can be excellent.
- **Child-care, house-cleaning, dog-walking**. New Yorkers frequently advertise these tasks on notices posted in supermarkets and corner drugstores, healthfood shops, bus shelters, and on university and college bulletin boards.
- **Telemarketing/Market research**.

Often not too choosey about whom they employ – and sometimes impressed (especially the market research people) with very English English.

• **Agency work**. *Travelers Aid* (207 W 43rd St; 944 0013) puts out a handy list of temp agencies seeking skilled and unskilled labour. These usually require you to apply in advance and to arrive early (like 6am) but, if you're hired, some pay that same night. Most prefer to engage workers who have proper ID and proof of residence, but with over 21 agencies on one floor at 25 W 14th St alone, it's an avenue worth pursuing.

• **Painting and decorating**. Hard work but good rates. Some agencies offer this kind of work – or you can hunt privately through friends and friends of friends.

• **Foreign language lessons**. If you've a language or two try advertising it on a noticeboard or in the *Voice*, etc. Rates can be good.

• **Artist's model**. Pass your name and a contact number around to the various independent studios or artist hang-outs in SoHo, TriBeCa or the East Village. Or try to reach the model booking directors at the art schools themselves.

• **Nightclub bouncer**. For those with physique – and a liking for the hours.

• **Blood donation**. A final, if slightly desperate, option for quick emergency cash. Check Yellow Pages for agencies or hospitals.

Whatever you do (or try to do), proceed with caution. Be selective, if you can. And don't enter into any sweatshop or slave labour type set-up if you're at all suspicious.

Finding an apartment or long stay room
If work can be hard to find, wait till you start **apartment hunting**. Costs are outrageous. A one-room **Manhattan** flat with bathroom and kitchenette in a reasonably safe neighbourhood can rent for as much as $1000 a month, and even in traditionally undesirable parts of the city – the Lower East Side being the most recent and extreme example – gentrification (and property rentals) are proceeding apace. More and more, unless you have established New York friends (or intend to make some fast), the options are being restricted to commuting in from the Outer Boroughs, or even further afield, from Jersey City, say, or Hoboken. It's a fact that the further you get from Manhattan, the lower the rent...

The best **source** for actually hearing about an apartment, or apartment room is, as anywhere, word of mouth. On the media front keep an eye on the ads in the *Voice*, the *New York Times*, *New York Magazine* and other publications: and if you're reading this before setting out for New York consider advertising yourself, particularly if you've a flat in London to exchange. Try the **commercial and campus notice boards**, too, where you might secure a **temporary flat-sit** or a **sub-let** while the regular tenant is away.

Some of the city's many universities and colleges also provide **holiday vacancies**, especially in the summertime. For instance *Barnard College* (Columbia University, 3009 Broadway, NY 10027; 280 8021) offers a variety of dormitory facilities to students, interns and associates from the end of May through mid-August for under $500 a month: write well in advance as they're 'selective' about who gets a room. During a similar period *New York University* has several hundred shared dorm rooms going for a fixed daily rate supplemented by meal plans.

Less satisfactory, perhaps, but a common fallback option are **long-stay hotels**. Two of these cater specifically for **single women on long stays**: *Allerton House*, 130 E 57th St, NY 10022 (753 8841) and the *Martha Washington Hotel*, 30 E 30th St, NY 10016 (689 1900). Others, open to both women and men, include: the *West Side Y*, 5 W 63rd St, NY 10023 (787 4400); the *International Student Hospice*, 154 E 33rd St, NY 10016 (228 7470/4689); the *Chelsea Center* 511 W 20th St, NY 10011 (243 4922); and the *International Student Center*, 38 W 88th St, NY 10024 (787 7706). At most of these costs range from nightly rates of under $15 to weekly charges that vary depending on the facilities available; though bear in mind that most of the cheaper hotels offer reduced weekly rates. Contact the respective reservations managers.

Another, less likely source is **Travelers Aid**. Although they mostly deal with crime victims and (US) travellers stranded without funds, they may refer you to low budget (or even free) temporary accommodation. The **New York Convention and Visitors Bureau** (2 Columbus Circle; 397 8222; or Times

Square & 42nd St) can also be worth a call. They dole out a leaflet listing all reduced hotel rates.

Just possibly, you might also find it to your advantage to resort to one of the city's several **roommate finding agencies**. Oldest and most reliable of these is *Roommate Finders* (489 6862), a non-discriminatory but discriminating company. If you use one of the other agencies – and the *Voice* carries all their names, numbers and descriptions – make sure you read the contract before any money changes hands or papers are signed.

Lastly, for the really organised, other viable accommodation alternatives include **homesteading**, **co-op** and **mutual housing associations**. These revolve around low-rent group occupation and renovation of often abandoned, city-owned buildings. It's the group element – and the commitment that entails – that mark this system as different from squatting. Each individual tenant

contributes the particular skills at their disposal, as well as monthly dues that collectively support normal operating, maintenance and repair costs. Various agencies designed to assist and protect co-op groups and tenant associations have sprung up, providing legal assistance, rehabilitation and repair loan pools, architectural services, tool lending and so on: all very urban grass roots, community-orientated stuff. As for getting involved: in the words of one young British homesteader it's a matter of 'being in the street and seeing what's happening'. Sound advice in any case, but for more direct information call the *Department of Housing Preservation and Development* (75 Maiden Lane, NY 10038; 806 8171) and ask about the *TIL (Tenant Interim Lease) Programme*, or phone the *Urban Homestead Assistance Board* (1047 Amsterdam Ave, NY 10025; 749 0602) and enquire about *Self-Help Work Consumer Cooperative*. And good luck.

OTHER THINGS

AIRLINE OFFICES *Aer Lingus*, 122 E 42nd St (557 1110); *Air India*, 345 Park Ave (407 1416); *British Airways*, 530 5th Ave (687 1600); *British Caledonian*, 415 Madison Ave (935 9550); *El Al*, 850 3rd Ave (940 0708); *Kuwait Airlines*, 430 Park Ave (308 5707); *North West Orient*, 537 5th Ave (736 1220); *Pan-Am*, 600 5th Ave (687 2600); *TWA*, 1 E 59th St and all over the city (290 2121); *Virgin Atlantic*, 96 Morton St (242 1330).

Between them the *airlines offices* at 100 E 42nd St and 1 E 59th St have information and tickets for almost all American domestic airlines.

AIRPORT TAX $3, but invariably included in the price of your ticket.

BABYSITTING The *Babysitters Guild*, 60 E 42nd St, open until 9pm, 7 nights a week (682 0227); The *Babysitters Association*, 610 Cathedral Parkway (865 9348).

BRING... Films, toiletries, cosmetics, razorblades – all of which work out more expensive in the States. And don't forget your credit card(s) – you'll be considered barely human without it.

CAR PROBLEMS See p.282.

COCKROACHES To other Americans New York is known as 'Roach City', and no wonder. The creatures infest every apartment or hotel, however luxurious, and it's no good imagining that a $300-a-night suite will ensure you're free of the things. It won't. Latest invention to deal with the problem is a spray said to render all roaches sterile.

CONSULATES *Australia*, 636 5rd Ave (245 4000); *Canada*, 1251 6th Ave (586 2400); *Denmark*, 825 3rd Ave (223 4545); *Eire*, 515 Madison Ave (319 2555); *Netherlands*, 1 Rockefeller Plaza (249 1429); *New Zealand*, 630 5th Ave (586 0060); *Sweden*, 825 3rd Ave (751 5900); *United Kingdom*, 845 3rd Ave (752 5747).

CONTRACEPTION Condoms are available in all pharmacies. If you're on the pill it's obviously best to bring a supply with you; should you run out, or need advice on other aspects of contraception, abortion or related matters, contact the *Margaret Sanger Center*, 380 2nd Avenue (677 6474) or the *Women's Counseling Project* at Barnard College (see p.28).

DATES Written the other way round to

what Europeans are used to. 4.1.87 is not the 4th of January but the 1st of April.

DISABLED VISITORS Well catered for as far as public buildings (all re-fitted) and sidewalks (most are now ramped) go. Less so in terms of **getting around**: the subway is impossible unless you have someone to help you, whilst only the old 'checker' cabs tend to be big enough for wheelchairs, and many cab drivers are unwilling to stop for anyone who looks likely to cause them problems. Buses are better, since the modern ones are fitted with a lowering platform which considerably eases getting on and off, and drivers are obliged to – and generally do – help out. Further info on NYC for disabled people can be had from the *Center for the Handicapped*, 52 Chambers Street, Office 206 (566 3913).

Outside of New York City you'll find most places well adapted to the needs of disabled travellers. Many hotels have rooms set aside for handicapped people; Greyhound Bus and many airlines allow an escort to travel free with a disabled passenger; and Amtrak lay on special compartments on long-haul trains.

DOGS Dog shit on the sidewalk is much less a problem than it was, since it's now illegal not to clear up after your mutt. This law is firmly enforced, and wherever you go in the city you'll see conscientious dog owners scraping up after their pets with makeshift cardboard shovels and dumping the evidence in the nearest litter bin. So if you're doing your New York friend a favour and walking the dog, you know what to do.

DRUGS Though cannabis is now decriminalised in a few American states – Alaska for example – it's most definitely not in New York and if you're caught with any you'll incur at least a $100 fine. Harder drugs are, of course, illegal too and so best avoided. If anyone offers you a 'nickel bag' in the street, they're not selling sweeties (probably not even selling drugs), but touting a $5 deal of a hard drug. The urgent whispers of the traders around Washington Square and many other parts of the city of 'Sens, sens' are short for sensamilia (a particular type of marijuana) – though again whether that's what you'd actually end up with if you handed over any money is debatable. Latest substance to hit the streets is *crack*, a refined form of cocaine that's cheap, potent and highly addictive. As well as stewing brains it can also make the user extremely violent and aggressive: just what the city needed...

ELECTRIC CURRENT 110V AC: all plugs two-pronged and rather primitive.

EMERGENCIES For Police, Fire or Ambulance dial **911**.

FLOORS In the States, the ground floor is known as the first floor, the first floor the second...so if someone you know lives on the third floor you only have to walk up two flights of stairs.

ID Carry some at all times, as there are any number of occasions on which you may be asked to show it. Two pieces of ID are preferable and one should have a photo – passport and credit card are the best bets.

LAUNDRY Hotels do it but charge the earth. You're much better off going to an ordinary launderette (here called a *laundromat*) or dry cleaners, both of which you'll find plenty of in the Yellow Pages under 'Laundries'. Of them, the *West Side Disco Laundry*, 204 8th Ave (242 5219) sounds most fun, though we're not sure how clean it gets your clothes. The *East 49th Street Coop*, 302 E 49th St (759 2524) is handiest for most midtown hotels. Remember also that the YMCAs have coin-op washing machines.

LEFT LUGGAGE Two of the most likely places to dump your stuff are Grand Central Station (42nd St and Park Ave) and Port Authority Bus Terminal (41st St and 8th Ave). Grand Central's luggage department is open Monday-Friday 7am-8pm, Saturday & Sunday 10am-6pm, and charges $1 an item, $2 for a rucksack, $3 for a bike; and Port Authority's office is open daily 7am-12pm and has rates of 80c per item, $1.60 for a backpack.

LIBRARIES The real heavyweight is the central reference section of the New York Public Library on 5th Ave at 42nd St (see p.104). However, as the name suggests, while this is a great place to work and its stock of books is one of the best in America and indeed the world, you can't actually take books home at the end of the day. To do this you need to go to one of the branches of the NYC Public Library (for a full list ask in the reference library) and produce proof of residence in the city.

LOST PROPERTY Things lost on buses or on the subway: *MTA Lost Property Division*, 370 Jay St, Brooklyn (718 625

6200). Things lost in a cab: *Taxi & Limousine Commission Lost Property Information Dept.*, 211 W 41st St (869 4513). Otherwise, the nearest police station, particularly if you think they may have been stolen.

NOTICEBOARDS For contacts, casual work, articles for sale, etc. it's hard to beat the noticeboard just inside the doorway of the *Village Voice* office at 842 Broadway (near Union Square). Otherwise there are numerous noticeboards up at Columbia University, or in the Loeb Student Centre of NYU on Washington Square.

MEASUREMENTS AND SIZES The US has yet to go metric and measurements of length are for the moment in inches, feet, yards and miles, of weight in ounces, pounds and tons. Liquid measures are slightly more confusing in that an Imperial pint is roughly equivalent to 1.25 American pints, and an American gallon thus only equal to about four-fifths of an Imperial one. Clothing and shoe sizes are easier: women's garment sizes are always two figures less than they would be in Britain. For example, a British size 12 will be a size 10 in the States, a size 14 a size 12. To calculate shoe sizes in America, simply add 1½ to your British size – thus, if you're normally size 8 then you'll need a size 9½ shoe in New York.

PUBLIC HOLIDAYS You'll find most offices, some stores and certain museums closed on the following days: *1st January*; *Martin Luther King's Birthday* (26th January); *Washington's Birthday* (third Monday of February); *Memorial Day* (last Monday in May); *Independence Day* (4th July); *Labor Day* (first Monday in September); *Columbus Day* (second Monday in October); *Veterans Day* (11th November); *Thanksgiving* (last Thursday in November); *Christmas Day* (25th December). Also, New York's numerous parades mean that on certain days – *Washington's Birthday, St Patrick's Day, Easter Sunday*, and *Columbus Day* – much of 5th Avenue is closed altogether.

PUBLIC LOOS Don't really exist as such, and bars and restaurants like to put casual users off with forbidding signs like 'Restrooms for patrons only'. This can be overcome with the right degree of boldness and lack of care for appearances – and if you're desperate you're not going to be that worried

anyway. Among centrally located places you can steal into without feeling too guilty are the glossy Grand Hyatt Hotel; the Trump Tower, where there are public loos on the Garden level; the Waldorf Astoria, where the Ladies is sumptuous in the extreme; the New York Public Library at 42nd St and 5th Ave; and the Lincoln Center's Avery Fisher Hall and Library, both of which have several bathrooms.

ROLLER SKATES For hire from the Mineral Springs Pavilion, northwest corner of Sheep Meadow at 69th St, Central Park (861 1818): 10am-5pm weekdays, 10am-6.30pm weekends. $4 for first hour, $1.50 for each additional half hour. Or from *US Roller World*, 160 5th Ave (691 2680).

SUBWAY GRAFFITI One of the most recognisable features of modern-day New York is its subway trains, which are daubed with the squiggles and slogans of numerous graffiti artists. The quality of the designs varies, but for all graffiti writers – often young blacks living in the Outer Boroughs where the subway yards are – it's a very serious business. Started, urban legend has it, by a writer named Taki who lived up on 183rd Street in Washington Heights – the famed *Taki 183* – it's the aim of the graffiti writers (known as 'bombers') to leave their chosen mark or signature on as many trains as possible, thereby achieving a recurring split-second of fame all day every day until it is removed. Some of the artists have been pretty astute and have given up decorating trains and transferred their skills to canvas, showing regularly in downtown galleries where critics can muse on the social implications of their art – while several thousand dollars a time helps the artist out of the ghetto. But most New Yorkers hate the graffiti, believing it despoils the face of their city: Mayor Koch is currently waging a determined battle against it, employing painters to erase graffiti seven days a week, bringing in graffiti-proof subway cars and guard dogs (the Mayor originally wanted wolves) to patrol the subway yards. 'Make your mark in society, not on society' is Koch's slogan – as yet not exactly a winner.

SWIMMING POOLS See p.35 but watch out for places that bill themselves as baths but are in fact sex emporia for gay men.

TAMPONS Available in all pharmacies,

department stores and, most cheaply, from branches of *Duane Reed* (see p.211).

TAX Within New York City you'll pay an 8¼ per cent sales tax on top of marked prices on just about everything but the very barest of essentials, a measure brought in to help alleviate the city's 1975 economic crisis, and one which stuck.

TIME Five hours behind Britain.

TELEPHONE SERVICES AND HELP-LINES Crime Victims Hotline (577 7777 – 24 hours); Drugs Anonymous (874 0700); Free events (755 4100); Herpes Hotline (838 3691); Horoscopes (976 1000); Jokes (976 3838); Missing Persons Bureau (374 6913); Rape Hotline (777 4000); Road conditions (594 0700); Suicide Prevention League (736 6191); Time (976 1616); Traffic report (830 7666); Travelers Aid Society (944 0013); VD Hotline (734 6010); Weather (976 1212).

TERMINALS George Washington Bridge Terminal, W 179th St and Broadway (564 1114); Grand Central Terminal, 42nd St and Park Ave (532 4900); Pennsylvania Station, 31st-33rd St and 7th-8th Ave (868 8970); Port Authority Bus Terminal 41st St and 8th Ave (736 4700).

TIPPING It won't be long before you realise that tipping, in a restaurant, bar, taxi cab, hotel lobby or toilet, is an accepted part of life in the States – and that anyone who doesn't join in is regarded as 'cheap': the ultimate American insult. There's not really any way around this, and in most cases you're going to find that it's a great deal easier to simply cough up the minimum (double the tax) than brave the withering gaze of the staff, or worse, the horror-struck looks of your American friends. The secret is to save as much cash as possible by refusing all offers of help in public places – ie carry your own bags up to your room, open all doors yourself,

and most importantly, never accept handouts of after shave or perfume in posh washrooms.

TRAVEL AGENTS *Council Travel*, America's principal student/youth travel organisation, have offices at 205 E 42nd St (661 1450) and in the *William Sloane YMCA* at 356 W 34th St (239 4527), and deal in airline and other tickets, inclusive tours, car rental, international student cards, guidebooks and work camps. Bear in mind, though, that Greyhound and Trailway passes etc. are better value if you purchase them before you leave. For the full picture on travel through the rest of the country, see p.7.

TRAVELLER'S CHEQUES If you happen to lose yours the numbers to ring are: *American Express* (248 4584); *Visa* (406 4200); and *Thomas Cook* (921 3800). See p.14 for more on this.

TURKISH BATHS *Tenth Street Turkish Baths* 268 E 10th St (473 8806). Manhattan's longest-established Turkish bath, where you can use the steam rooms, pool and get a massage for just $10.

TV SHOWS There are always tickets on offer (free of charge) for certain TV game and chat shows, so if you want a taste of the tackier side of the American media first-hand, just enquire within NBC's Rockefeller Center studios on 5th Ave and there's a good chance you'll be offered some.

WHAT'S ON Any number of ways to pick up information. These include popping into the *Convention and Visitors Bureau* (see p.11), who have up-to-date leaflets, buying *New York Magazine*, the *New Yorker* or *Village Voice*, or getting hold of one of several free weekly magazines (*Key, Where* and *Broadway* are just three), which you can find in hotel lobbies and the like. If your appetite for absolutely fresh data still isn't sated, phone 755 4100 for a rundown of the day's cultural events.

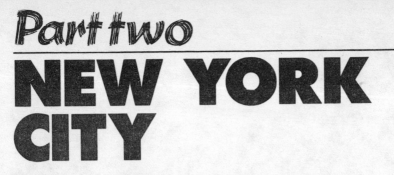

Part two
NEW YORK CITY

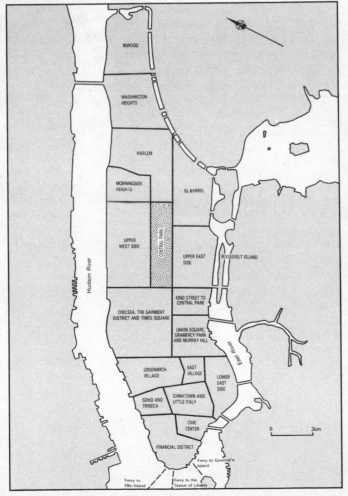

POINTS OF ARRIVAL

The airports

Two **international airports** serve New York: for *Virgin* arrivals, **Newark** (201 961 2000) in New Jersey, and **John F.Kennedy (JFK)** (718 656 4250) in Queens for all other airlines. **La Guardia** airport (718 476 5000), also in Queens, handles **domestic flights**.

Wherever you arrive, the most straightforward way into Manhattan is by **coach**; **taxis**, unless your flight is at some extreme and antisocial hour, are an unneccessary expense ($25 plus from JFK or La Guardia – $40 or more from Newark). If you do have money to throw around, better to spend it on a **helicopter ride** (around $50), which will deposit you within minutes at the East Side 34th Street or World Trade Center heliports.

The two Manhattan **coach terminals**, used by all airport coaches, are Grand Central and Port Authority. For most hotels, **Grand Central** (at Park Ave and 42nd St) is the more convenient: well poised for taxis to midtown Manhattan and with a subway station if you're heading towards the east of the city. **Port Authority** (on 8th Ave and 42nd St) isn't as good a bet for Manhattan (there's a lot of humping lugggage from coach to street) though you may find it handier if you're heading for the West Side of the city (via the A train), out to New Jersey (by bus) or on to other parts of America from nearby Pennsylvania railroad station.

Newark

Olympia Trails coaches leave for Manhattan every 15-30 minutes (5am-1am), stopping at the World Trade Center and outside Grand Central. The journey takes 25-40 minutes depending on traffic; fare $4. Details: Airport (201 981 2015), New York (964 6233), New Jersey (201 589 1188).

New Jersey Transit Coaches run to the Port Authority Terminal every 15-30 minutes (24 hrs). Journey time around 25-50 minutes; fare $4. Details: 201 762 5100.

JFK

Carey Coaches (632 0500) leave every 15-30 minutes (5am-1am) for Grand Central and Port Authority. Journey time 35-75 minutes; fare $8 one way, $10 for a round trip. Details: Airport (718 656 4444), New York (632 0500).

JKF Express. Bus/subway link from each of the JFK terminals. Leaves every 20 minutes (6am-1am), stopping at lower and midtown Manhattan subway stations (principally, World Trade Center, 14th St, 34th St, 42nd St and Rockefeller Center). Journey time: allow at least an hour to central Manhattan: fare $6.50 (collected on the train).

When you come to **leave**, *remember that JFK is large and very spread out: if your terminal is last on the coach route (like TWA or BA) you should allow a further 15 minutes to get there.*

La Guardia

Carey Coaches leave every 15-30 minutes for Grand Central (7.30am-12.30am) and Port Authority (7.30am-10pm). Journey time around 25-45 minutes; fares for both services are $6 one way, $10 round trip. Details: 476 5001.

Rock-bottom alternatives

For those whose stay has left them financially embarrassed, there are a couple of cheaper alternative routes out from the city to JFK and La Guardia – though not to Newark. They're real last resorts, however, and not options you'd want to consider for getting into Manhattan after an eight-hour flight.

For **JFK**, take the **E** train to the Union Turnpike-Kew Gardens station and then catch the **Q10** green bus to the airport: this will cost $1 for the subway, $1.50 for the bus and take around 90 minutes.

For **La Guardia**, take the **7** train to 82nd Street-Jackson Heights stop and a **Q33** bus to the airport: total $1.50.

Arriving by bus or train

If you're coming to New York by **Trailways** or **Greyhound bus**, you will arrive at the Port Authority Bus Terminal (see above).

By **train**, you will come in at either **Grand Central** or **Penn Station**. Grand Central takes arrivals from the Hudson Valley, the North and West US and Canada. Penn serves Long Island and New Jersey. Trains from Boston, Chicago, Washington and Florida may arrive at either station.

ORIENTATION

New York City comprises the central island of **Manhattan** along with four **outer boroughs** – **Brooklyn**, **Queens**, **The Bronx** and **Staten Island**.
Manhattan, to many, *is* New York. And certainly, whatever your interest in the city, it's here that you'll spend most time, and, unless you have friends elsewhere, are likely to stay. Understanding the intricacies of Manhattan's layout, and above all getting some grasp of its subway and transport system (see the following section, p.47), should be your first priority. If at all possible, try to master at least some of the following before arrival – if needs be on the flight over.

Manhattan's layout

Despite its grid-pattern arrangement, **Manhattan** can seem a wearyingly complicated place to get around: blocks of streets and avenues, apparently straightforward on the map, can be uniquely confusing on foot and the psychedelic squiggles of the subway map impenetrably arcane. Don't let subways and buses overawe you, though, as with a little know-how you'll find them efficient and fast. And if you're at all unsure just ask – New Yorkers are the most helpful and accurate of direction givers, and have seemingly infinite interest in initiating visitors into the great mysteries of their city.

From north to south **the island** of Manhattan is about 13 miles long and from east to west around 2 miles wide. Whatever is north of where you're standing is *uptown*, whatever south *downtown*; east or west is *crosstown*. As far as **districts** go, there are three major divisions:

● **Downtown** (below 14th St)
● **Midtown** (from 14th St up as far as Central Park)
● **Upper Manhattan** (north of Central Park).

The **southern (downtown) part of Manhattan** was first to be settled, which means that its streets have names and that they're somewhat randomly arranged. **Uptown, above Houston St on the east side, 14th St on the west**, the streets are numbered and follow a strict grid pattern. The numbers of these streets increase as you move north.

Downtown, the main **points of reference** are buildings: the World Trade Center and Woolworth Building are unmistakable landmarks. Uptown, just look out for the big north-south **avenues**. **Fifth Avenue**, the greatest of these, cuts along the east side of Central Park and serves as a dividing line between east streets (the **'East Side'**) and west streets ('the **West Side'**). **House numbers** increase as you walk away from either side of Fifth Avenue; numbers on avenues increase as you go north.

Locations are easily pinpointed by giving the nearest intersection of avenue and street: the Chrysler Building for example is at Lexington Avenue and 42nd Street – 'Lex and 42nd' in conversational shorthand. If you know the number of an address on an avenue there's a formula to work out the nearest street; this is complicated but useful and is printed below. If you ask directions the unit of distance always quoted is the **block**, the rectangle of land marked out by the lattice of streets and avenues. As they're rectangles, remember that walking east-west blocks will take about three times longer than the same number of north-south blocks.

When **cycling, driving or looking for a bus**, it's useful to know that traffic on **odd**-numbered streets runs from east to west, on **even**-numbered streets from west to east, and in both directions on major crosstown streets. Apart from Park, Broadway and 11th (which are two-way), all avenues run in alternate directions.

Walking, count on around 15 minutes for every 10 north-south blocks – rather more at rush hour. And keep in mind that however you plan your wanderings you're going to spend much of your time slogging it out on the streets. **Footwear** is important (trainers are good for spring/summer; winter needs something more waterproof). So is **safety**: a lot more people are injured in New York carelessly crossing the road than are mugged. Pedestrian crossings don't give you automatic right of way unless the *WALK* sign is on – and even then be prudent.

Address Locator

To find the nearest approximate cross-street when you know the number of a building on an avenue, follow this formula:

Cancel the last figure of the building's number, divide by 2, then add or subtract the key number below. The resultant number is the nearest street.

Ave A Add 3
Ave B Add 3
Ave C Add 3
Ave D Add 3
1st Ave Add 3
2nd Ave Add 3
3rd Ave Add 10
4th Ave Add 8
5th Ave
　　Up to 200 Add 13
　　201 to 400 Add 16
　　401 to 600 Add 18
　　601 to 775 Add 20
　　775 to 1286 Subtract 18
　　1287 to 1500 Add 45
　　Above 2000 Add 24
6th Ave Subtract 12
7th Ave
　　Up to 110th St Add 12
　　Above 110th St Add 20
8th Ave Add 10
9th Ave Add 13
10th Ave Add 14
Amsterdam Ave Add 60
Audubon Ave Add 165
Broadway (23rd St to 192nd St) .Subtract 30
Columbus Ave Add 60
Convent Ave Add 127
Central Park West Divide by 10 and add 60
Edgecombe Ave Add 134
Ft. Washington Ave Add 158
Lenox Ave Add 110
Lexington Ave Add 22
Madison Ave. Add 26
Manhattan Ave Add 100
Park Ave Add 35
Pleasant Ave Add 101
Riverside Drive Divide by 10 and add 72 up to 165th Street
St. Nicholas Ave Add 110
Wadsworth Ave Add 173
West End Ave Add 60

TRANSPORT

The Subway

The **New York subway** is dirty, noisy, intimidating and initially incomprehensible. But it's also the fastest and most efficient method of getting from A to B throughout Manhattan and the boroughs, which means that sooner or later you'll have to use it. Here are the basics...

● Broadly speaking, **train routes** run uptown or downtown, following the great avenues and targetting in on the downtown financial district: crosstown routes are limited.

● Trains and their routes are identified by a **number** or **letter**; though the subway is open 24 hours a day, most routes operate at certain times of day only.

● There are two types of train: **Expresses**, which stop only at major stations, and **Locals**, which stop at every station. If your destination is an Express stop the quickest way to get there is to change from Local to Express at the first Express station, either by walking across the platform or taking the stairs to another level.

● Any subway journey costs a **flat fare of $1**, bought in the form of a **subway token** from a token booth. There's no discount for buying several, but stocking up means less queueing and spare tokens are easily resold.

● **Subway maps** can be obtained from a token booth (at any subway station – though many run out) or, more reliably, from the concourse office at Grand Central; as a stopgap we've printed the map (in black and white) overleaf. Take time to study it before you set out – there are few on the platforms, it'll make travel much easier, and prevent the sign saying 'Tourist – Please Mug' that hangs around the neck of those who study maps on trains.

● **A special treat** is to stand right at the front next to the driver's cabin and watch stations hurtle by and rats fleeing along the track: the A train from 125th to 59th is best for this.

Perhaps the main source of confusion

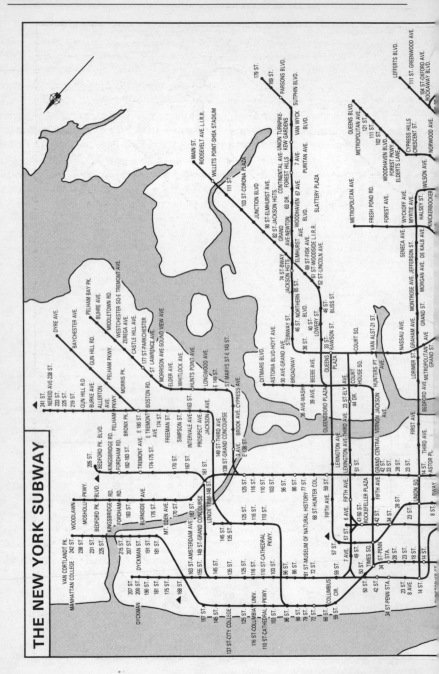

THE NEW YORK SUBWAY

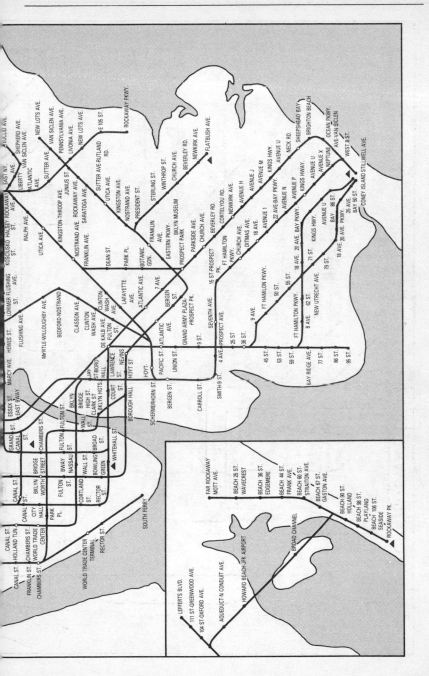

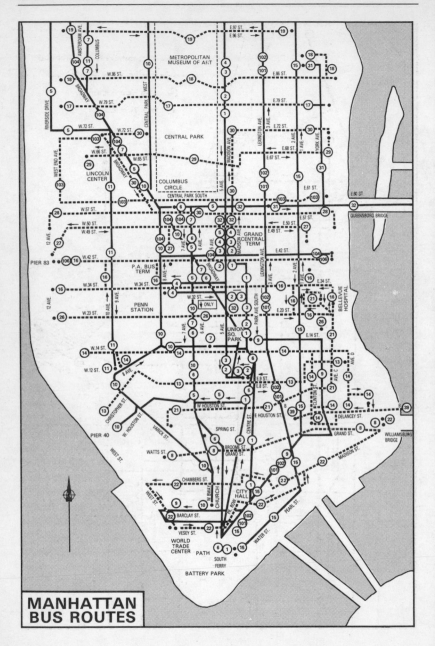

MANHATTAN BUS ROUTES

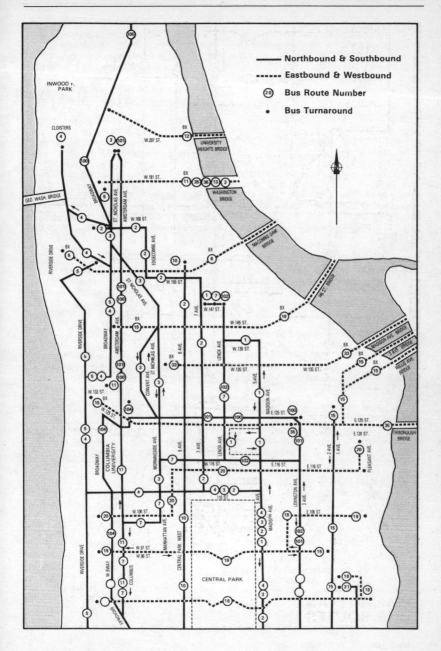

is the multiplicity of **line/train names**. The line names on the subway map will be recognised by most people but the old line names (the IRT, the IND and the BMT) are still very much in use, as are popular 'direction names'. Just to give one example: the West Side IRT, Broadway Local, Seventh Avenue Local and Number 1 train are all the same thing.

The **main lines and directions**, however, are these:

• **IRT** (Interborough Rapid Transport). Runs north and south on the East and West Sides of Manhattan. Train numbers **1 (local), 2 and 3** all follow Broadway and 7th Avenue; numbers **4, 5 and 6 (local)** follow Lexington Avenue.

• **Grand Central-Times Square Shuttle**. Connects the east and west sides of the IRT.

• **L** Connects the east and west sides of the IRT at 14th street.

• **A and K (local)** Follows 8th Avenue through midtown Manhattan and cuts through lower Manhattan to connect with Brooklyn.

• **N and R (local)** Follows Broadway through Manhattan and connects with Brooklyn and Queens.

Lastly, **safety**. Everyone has different views on this and everyone, too, has their horror stories. Many are exaggerated – and the subway definitely feels more dangerous than it actually is – but it's as well to follow a few established rules:

• **At night** always try to use the **centre cars**, as they are more crowded...and while you're waiting, keep to the area marked in yellow where you can be seen by the booth attendants (more subway crime occurs on the platform than in the trains).

• **By day** the whole train is theoretically safe, **but don't go into near-empty carriages** if you can help it.

• Keep an eye on bags at all times, especially when sitting/standing near the doors, a favourite snatching spot.

Buses

New York's bus system is a lot simpler than the subway, and a lot more frequent; you can also see where you're going and hop off when you pass anything interesting. Its one disadvantage is that it can be extremely slow – in peak hours almost down to walking pace.

Bus maps, like subway maps, can be obtained either from a subway token booth or from the main concourse of Grand Central. Again, we've printed a small size one to tide you over.

A quick glance at the **routes** will reveal that they run along all the avenues and across major streets. There are three **types of bus**: **regular**, which stop every two or three blocks arriving at 5-10 minute intervals; **limited stop**, which travel the same routes though stopping at only about a quarter of the regular stops; and **express**, which stop hardly anywhere, shuttling commuters in and out of the suburbs for a $3 fare. In addition, you'll also find small private buses running in from New Jersey.

Bus stops are marked by yellow curbstones and signs indicating bus routes, times and intersections. Buses **display their number, origin and destination** up front. If a bus arrives that isn't going the whole way to your intended destination ask for a **transfer** when boarding: this enables you to change to another service within one hour of the ticket's issue, a facility designed so that a single fare lets you make any one-way trip in Manhattan. It's always worth asking for a transfer when you get on a bus, just in case...

Anywhere in Manhattan the **fare** is $1, payable on entry with either a subway token (the most convenient way) or with the correct change – the driver won't give you any, nor accept pennies or dollar bills.

Buses and subway information 330 1234

Lost and Found 625 6200

Taxis

Taxis come expensive but are worth considering if you're in a hurry or a group, or if it's late at night.

There are two types: **Medallion Cabs**, immediately recognisable by their yellow paintwork and medallion up top, and **gypsy cabs**, unlicensed, uninsured operators who tout for business where the tourists arrive. Avoid gypsy cabs like the plague as they're rip-off merchants – their main hunting grounds are outside Grand Central and the East Side Airline Terminal on East 38th Street and 1st Avenue.

Up to **four people** can travel in an ordinary Medallion Cab, **five** in the chunky, old-fashioned *Checker* cab. **Fares** are inclusive of suitcases, etc. Charges rise, however, after 8pm and on Sundays; and by 100% if you're foolish enough to take one outside New York City limits (eg to Newark). Trips off Manhattan additionally incur toll fees (which the driver pays and then charges at the end of the trip).

The **tip** should be around 15% of the fare, though drivers generally don't seem too concerned about this. More likely to cause a problem is change: drivers don't like splitting anything bigger than a $10 bill, and anything bigger than a $20 will produce invective.

Before you hail a cab, it's always a good idea to work out exactly where you're going and if possible the quickest route there, since NY taxi drivers don't have The Knowledge of their London equivalents and often speak little English. If you feel the driver doesn't seem to know your destination, don't hesitate to point it out on a map.

Officially there are certain **regulations** governing taxi operators. A driver can ask your destination only when you're seated – and must transport you (within the city limits), however undesirable your destination. Also, if you request it, a driver must pick up or drop off other passengers, open or close the windows, and stop smoking (they can also ask you to stop). If you have any **problems** with a driver get the licence number from the right-hand side of the dashboard, or medallion number from the rooftop sign or on the print-out receipt for the fare, and phone the *NYC Taxis and Limousine Commission* on 382 9301. Should you leave something in a cab try the commission's **lost and found office** – 869 4513.

Driving
In a word, don't. Car hire is expensive and parking almost laughably so. Far better to keep your American driving fantasies to upstate excursions (for more on which, including car hire addresses, etc., see p.283).

If you do need to drive, though, bear in mind NYC's particular **driving rules**, which include compulsory seat belts for those in front, a 35 mph speed limit within the city, and a breathalyser – the *alcotest* – to weed out drunken drivers. When you can find somewhere to **park** don't do so in front of a fire hydrant, and check which side of the street it's permitted: traffic alternates daily on many streets, so follow the signs or the crowds. Private parking is expensive, extremely so at peak periods, but it makes sense to leave your car somewhere legitimate: if it's towed away you'll need to liberate it from the **car pound** (239 2533): expect to pay around $100 and waste the best part of a day.

Cycling
Pulling away from the lights on a bike in Manhattan can mean a replay of the Monaco Grand Prix, and it's just about as dangerous. To enjoy it – and it can be a viable form of transport once you're confident enough – do as the locals and go for all possible hireable equipment: pads, a helmet, goggles and a whistle to move straying pedestrians. Also, when you stop, be sure to chain your machine to something totally immovable if you'd like it to be there when you return.

Bike **hire** starts at $3 per hour (more for racing models). You'll need two pieces of ID (passport and credit card) and a deposit (usually $100, though some firms will take your credit card details instead). The *Yellow Pages* have full listings of firms but among good value, central suppliers are:
Bicycle Discount House, 351 E 14th St (228 4344).
Metro Bicycles, 1311 Lexington Ave at 88th St (427 4450). Open all week and good for Central Park.
6th Avenue Bicycles, 546 6th Ave at 15th St (255 5100). Open all week and handy for Greenwich Village.
Midtown Bicycles, 360 W 47th St (581 4500).

FINDING A PLACE TO STAY

There's no way round it. People pay stupid prices for a **room in Manhattan**, and if you haven't managed to procure a

slice of floor from a friend you're going to have to do the same. All that the recommendations below can do is cut a few corners...and steer you towards the better value places and the more interesting locations.

Whatever price range you decide to plump for, **booking ahead** is very strongly advised. At certain times of the year – Christmas and early summer particularly – you're likely to find *everything* (and we mean this) choc-a-bloc full. You can book a room yourself, by phoning direct to the hotel (0101 212 before the listed number, if you're dialling from Britain) or, often more cheaply, by going through a specialist **travel agent**. *STA Travel*, for instance, will reserve you a room at a reduced rate if you do this when buying your flight – and they handle everything from the youth hostels to mainstream hotels. See *Basics* for their (and other) addresses – and bear in mind, too, the possibilities of all-in flight and hotel package holidays.

As a last option, one of the most reliable **booking services** is *Meegan's*, which guarantees a room (though this may be limited to upmarket places only) at no extra charge. Phone 718 995 9292; or from outside the city, 800 221 1235.

Bottom line: Hostels, B & B, Camping
There aren't many alternatives at the **dirt cheap** end of the market: New York's bottom line is represented by the two so-called **International Student Centers**, which sound very official but are in fact little more than a few grubby, roach-ridden dorms. Rates are around $8 a bed, phoning ahead is advised, and keeping an eye on your belongings essential (NY dorms don't go in for the luxury of lockers for your gear). Addresses are:
Hotel Woodward ISC, W 55th St at Broadway (757 8030).
ISC, 38 W 88th St (787 7706).

Next up in terms of cost are the **YMCAs** (*Ys*, as they're known) which, despite the name, are mixed sex. These have rooms, not dormitories, but at present they're the nearest thing the city comes to a youth hostel. Rates are approximately $25 single, $38 double, dropping to $14 per person at Sloane House for those with a YHA card; rooms and security are reasonably good (if not exactly glamorous). Addresses are:
William Sloane House, 356 W 34th St (760 5860). The largest, with around 1500 rooms, several restaurants, a launderette, gym, swimming pools, student

travel shop and loads more.
Vanderbilt YMCA, 224 E 47th St (755 2410). Smaller and quieter than the Sloane House, and neatly placed in midtown Manhattan, just five minutes' walk from Grand Central Station. Inexpensive restaurant, swimming pool, gym and launderette.
West Side YMCA, 5 W 63rd St (7887 4400). Well-placed for the Upper West Side, Lincoln Center and Central Park – and with a similarly impressive range of facilities.
Chelsea Center Hostel, 511 W 20th St. Small, clean and safe downtown private hostel, with prices from $14. A useful alternative for downtown, but you'll need to book in high season.

Bed and Breakfast has taken off in a big way in America of late, particularly in New York where Manhattanites need all the cash possible to find their astronomical rent money. For the visitor to the city, it can be a good way of staying bang in the centre of Manhattan at (by New York standards) a reasonably affordable price. Don't expect to socialise with your temporary landlord/lady – chances are you'll have your own self-contained room and hardly see them – and don't go looking for street signs or adverts – all rooms are let out via official **agencies**. Among these, addresses include:
Urban Ventures, PO Box 426, NY 10025 (662 1234). The first and still probably the best registry in the city. Their budget double rooms go for $35 upwards, 'comfort range' rooms (with private bath) from about $60. If you wish, you can rent an entire apartment – minus hosts – from $50 a night.
New World Bed and Breakfast, 150 5th Ave, Suite 711, NY 10011 (675 5600). Much the same options at much the same rates.
Colby International, 139 Round Hey, Liverpool L21 1RG (051 220 5848); in New York phone 752 7473. If you want guaranteed B&B accommodation, Colby International can fix it up from the UK. Double rooms start at $55, studios from $70: book at least a fortnight ahead to be sure of a room in high season.

You won't save a great deal on any of the above options by **camping**. All of the campsites that could conceivably serve New York City are situated so far out as to make travel in and out a major cost. For the dedicated, though, these are the

most accessible:
Old Bethpage, Claremont Road, Long Island. The nearest site to the city – a short way up Long Island. Prices range from $6-12 depending on tent size and numbers sharing.
East Islip, Hecksher State Park. Beautiful situation and easier to reach on public transport – on the Long Island Railroad from New York City's Penn Station. Prices around $8 for a tent and two campers.

Hotels
Most of New York's hotels tend to be in midtown Manhattan – which is as good a **location** as any. You'll find only a handful (the *Washington Square* is a rare cheapie) downtown. **Selections** below are divided into two price categories: 'Inexpensive' ($40-60 for a double) and 'Moderate to Expensive' (mainly $60-100 but with a couple of big names thrown in at $120-150). All places listed are to some degree recommended, either for price, location or novelty. For full hotel listings, if you can't get a room at any of them, consult the NY Conventions & Visitors Bureau leaflet *Hotels in New York City*, available from either one of their offices (p.11) – or before you leave from the *USTTA*. See also the introduction (above) for *Mcogan's* reservation agency.

INEXPENSIVE

Aberdeen, 17 W 32nd St (736 1600). Double rooms for around $50.
Beacon, 2130 Broadway at 75th St (787 1100). Neatly placed Upper West Side hotel. Doubles from $50.
Carlton Arms, 160 E 25th St (679 0680). A strong contender for the city's latest Bohemian doss-house, with a characterful location near its sixties equivalent, the Chelsea. Interior decor by contemporary artists and clientele made up of down-at-heel artists, Europeans and long-stay guests. Doubles $40-50.
Clinton, 19 W 31th St (279 4017). Rather less salubrious but if you can stand the rooms (and the hustley crowd that always seems to be hanging about outside) some of the cheapest hotel rates in New York. Doubles from about $35.
Diplomat, 108 W 43rd St (921 5666). Good value, unpretentious hotel with doubles from $40.
Mansfield, 12 W 44th St (944 6050). The real value alternative to both the nearby

Algonquin and the Royalton (see 'Moderate to Expensive'), with doubles hovering around $50, three-person suites at $70 and six-person deals for about $90.
National, 7th Ave at 42nd St (947 3800). There are better places, in nicer parts of town, but if you're desperate or just plain broke, they'll do you a double here for $35, triples and quads for $50-60.
Pickwick Arms, 230 E 51st St (355 0300). For the price, one of the best deals you'll get. Doubles from about $55.
President, 234 W 48th St (246 8800). Standard downbeat hotel in an area full of them. Seedy but not unpleasant, and above all cheap, with doubles weighing in at about $50.
Remington, 129 W 46th St (221 2600). About as near as this category of hotel gets to luxury. Excellent value, with doubles from about $50.
Stanford, 43 W 32nd St (563 1480). Good value and location, with doubles for around $50.
Washington Square, 103 Waverley Place (777 9515). One of very few downtown hotels, bang in the heart of Greenwich Village. Basic but clean and offering double rooms at $55 up.
And two **women-only** hotels:
The Martha Washington Hotel, 30 E 30th St (689 1900). Doubles at $45 up. Friendly, safe location and recommended.
Allerton House, 130 E 57th St (753 8841).

MODERATE TO EXPENSIVE

Algonquin, 59 W 44th St (840 6800). New York's classic literary hangout (see p.117), as created by Dorothy Parker and her Round Table associates, and perpetuated by Noel Coward, Bernard Shaw, Irving Berlin and most names subsequent. Decor remains little changed; prices, if you've the $100 necessary for the cheapest double, compare very well with many much more mundane 'moderate' and expensive places.
Century-Paramount, 235 W 46th St (764 5500). A pleasant hotel nicely distanced from the worst of the Times Square sleaze. Doubles from about $65.
Chelsea, 222 W 23rd St (243 3700). One of New York's most noted landmarks (see p.109), both for its ageing Neo-Gothic building and, more importantly, its vivid folk history. For just about everyone has stayed at the Chelsea:

Thomas Wolfe and Dylan Thomas lived here; Bob Dylan and Leonard Cohen wrote songs here; and, in the Chelsea's last dramatic entry into the pop Hall of Fame, it was the scene of the final few days of a doomed Sid and Nancy. Despite all of which, ordinary people can actually afford to stay here with rooms (not, incidentally, renowned for luxury) at more or less standard New York prices. Doubles from $60, triples from $65 and quads from $75.

Edison, 228 W 47th St (840 5000). The most striking thing about this hotel is its size, with 1000 rooms at around $75 for a double, four-bedded rooms for just a little more. Good value.

Empire, 44 W 63rd St (265 7400). Unexciting but handy for the Lincoln Center, Midtown and the Upper West Side. Doubles from $85.

Gorham, 136th W 55th St (245 1800). Centrally placed and pleasant. Doubles in the $80-100 price range.

Gramercy Park, 2 Lexington Ave at 21st St (475 4320). Excellent downtown alternative, popular with Europeans. Doubles at $90-100.

Iroquois, 49 W 44th St (840 3080). Same street as the Algonquin, Mansfield (see 'Inexpensive') and Royalton (see below). Doubles $60 upwards.

Morgan's, 237 Madison Ave (686 0300). Owned by Steve Rubell and Ian Schrager of Studio 54 and Palladium fame, this is self-consciously – and quite successfully – the chicest doss-house in town. Discreet furnishings are by André Putnam, good-looking young staff clothed in Klein and Armani. Boy George holes up here when he's in town, as do a

whole entourage of other famous pop people. At around $150 for the average double (there are cheaper ones, down to about $120), you may not decide to join them, but for the price you do get a jacuzzi, a great stereo system and cable TV in your room.

Roger Smith, 501 Lexington Ave at 47th St (755 1400). Solid midtown hotel with doubles at about around $100.

Royalton, 44 W 44th St (730 1344). The traditional 'budget' alternative to the Algonquin, from which aspiring literary types could nip across the road to the hallowed Algonquin bar and pretend they were staying in the hotel. This itself has given the place cachet, though it remains relatively inexpensive. Doubles from about $75.

Salisbury, 123 W 57th St (246 1300). For the location – at the very hub of the 57th Street shopping scene – not an overpriced hotel, and quite cosy too. Doubles $90.

Seville, 22 E 29th St (532 4100). Useful if you want to be a little further downtown. $60-75 for doubles (though reduced rates for students).

Tudor, 304 E 42nd St (986 8800). Comfortable and convivial, despite the brash and noisy 42nd St location. Doubles from $80.

Wales, 1295 Madison Ave at 92nd St (876 6000). Almost in Spanish Harlem – though very definitely Upper East Side in feel. Fair prices and handy for the museums. Doubles start at a little over $60.

Westpark, 308 W 58th St (246 6440). A beautiful hotel just off Columbus Circle – and one of the city's few real bargains. Doubles $60 and up.

Chapter one

LOWER MANHATTAN

LOWER MANHATTAN harbours its extremes in close proximity. For some it's the most spectacular, most glamorous skyline in the world, for others a run-down and seedy home. But whatever your final perspective, it is undeniably archetypal New York: an area that encompasses Greenwich and the East Village, Chinatown and Little Italy, and, at the skyscraper heart of things, the startling corporate identity of the Financial District.

As a prelude to neighbourhood wanderings, the **Statue of Liberty** provides an obvious focus. Not so much for the vaunted symbol (though this is hard to ignore) as for the views of southern Manhattan. This lower part of the island begins with the shoreline **Financial District** – Wall Street at its centre – and then drifts, within half a mile, into the first of the city's ethnic districts. **Chinatown** here is still solidly a community (often Chinese-speaking only) and seemingly oblivious of nearby real estate wealth. It's a part of the city well worth getting to know, not least for the astonishingly cheap lunchtime food. **Little Italy**, adjacent, is in contrast an early warning of New York's irresistible tide – a quarter now largely overrun by slick cafés and restaurants.

Over to the west, quite different again in population and feel, are **SoHo** and **TriBeCa**, one-time industrial areas, now up-and-coming residential blocks and home to Manhattan's (and the world's) art scene, . Further north, a less radical shift, are traditionally politicised/literary **Greenwich Village** (touristed now but fun) and the **East Village**, which has taken on much of Greenwich's alternative/arts/political mantle. All of which makes for enjoyable and rewarding walking and café browsing. Walk beyond, though, into the **Lower East Side**, and the riches fade fast – New York's very real poverty quite unhidden and not a little unthreatening.

At the end of each section in this and the subsequent two chapters, you will find listings of cafés, bars and restaurants. These are laid out alphabetically for cross-referencing with the entries in the Drinking and Eating *chapter.*

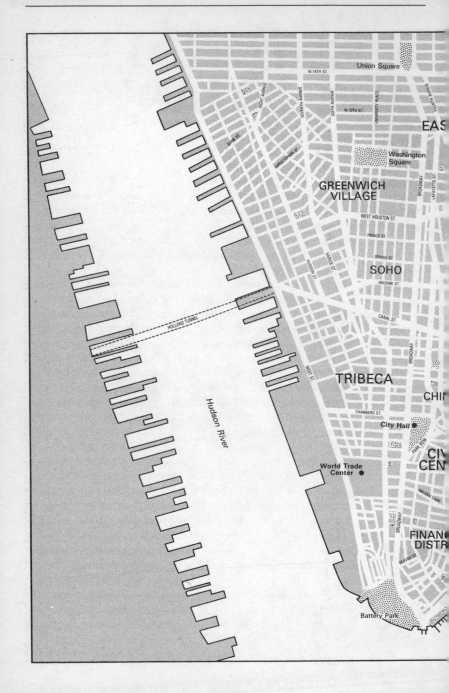

Union Square

W. 14TH ST.

W. 10TH ST.

EAS

Washington
Square

GREENWICH
VILLAGE

WEST HOUSTON ST.

PRINCE ST.

SPRING ST.

SOHO

BROOME ST.

CANAL ST.

Hudson River

HOLLAND TUNNEL

TRIBECA

CHI

CHAMBERS ST.

City Hall ●

CIV
CEN

World Trade
Center ●

FINAN
DISTR

Battery Park

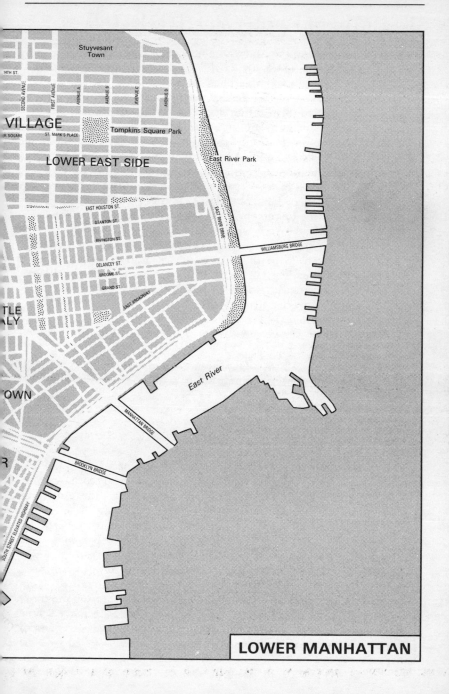

Stuyvesant
Town

14TH ST.

SECOND AVENUE
FIRST AVENUE
AVENUE A
AVENUE B
AVENUE C
AVENUE D

VILLAGE

R SQUARE

ST. MARK'S PLACE

Tompkins Square Park

LOWER EAST SIDE

East River Park

EAST RIVER DRIVE

EAST HOUSTON ST.

STANTON ST.

RIVINGTON ST.

WILLIAMSBURG BRIDGE

DELANCEY ST.

BROOME ST.

GRAND ST.

EAST BROADWAY

TLE
LY

East River

OWN

MANHATTAN BRIDGE

R

BROOKLYN BRIDGE

SOUTH STREET ELEVATED HIGHWAY

LOWER MANHATTAN

THE STATUE OF LIBERTY AND ELLIS ISLAND

Of all the many symbols of America, none has proved more enduring or evocative than the **STATUE OF LIBERTY**. This giant figure, torch in hand and clutching a stone tablet, has for a century acted as a kind of figurehead for the American Dream, and it's a measure of the global power of the United States that there is today probably no more immediately recognisable profile in existence. It's worth remembering, also, that the statue is – for Americans at least – a potent reminder that the USA is a land of immigrants: it was New York harbour where the first big waves of European immigrants arrived, their ships entering through the Verrazano Narrows to round the bend of the bay and catch a first glimpse of 'Liberty Enlightening the World' – for them the end of their journey into the unknown and symbolic beginning of a new life. Now, although only the very wealthy can afford to arrive here by sea these days, and a would-be immigrant's first (and possibly last) view of the US is more likely to be the customs check at JFK airport, Liberty remains – notwithstanding US foreign policy – a stirring sight, Emma Lazarus's poem, written originally to raise funds for the statue's base, no less quotable than when it was written...

Here at our sea-washed, sunset gates shall stand
A mighty woman with a torch, whose flame
Is the imprisoned lightning, and her name
Mother of Exiles. From her beacon-hand
Glows world-wide welcome; her mild eyes command
The air-bridged harbour that twin cities frame.
'Keep ancient lands, your storied pomp!' cries she
With silent lips. 'Give me your tired, your poor,
Your huddled masses yearning to breathe free,
The wretched refuse to your teeming shore.
Send these, the homeless, tempest-tost to me,
I lift my lamp beside the golden door.

The statue, which depicts Liberty throwing off her shackles and holding a beacon to light the world, was the creation of the French sculptor Frédéric Auguste Bartholdi, crafted 100 years after the American Revolution in recognition, apparently, of some fraternity between the French and American people (though it's fair to add that Bartholdi originally intended the statue for Alexandria in Egypt). Bartholdi built Liberty in Paris between 1874 and 1884, starting with a terracotta model and enlarging it through four successive versions to its present size, a construction of thin copper sheets bolted together and supported by an iron framework designed by Gustave Eiffel. The arm carrying the torch was exhibited in Madison Square Park for seven years, but the whole statue wasn't officially accepted on behalf of the American people until 1884, after which it was taken apart, crated up and shipped to New York.

It was to be another two years before it could be properly unveiled: money had to be collected to fund the construction of the base, and for some reason Americans were unwilling – or unable – to dip into their pockets. Only through the campaigning efforts of newspaper magnate Joseph Pullitzer, a keen supporter of the statue, did it all come together in the end. Richard Morris Hunt built a pedestal around the existing star-shaped Fort Wood, and Liberty was formally dedicated by President Cleveland on October 28th 1886 in a flag-waving shindig that has never really stopped. The statue was recently closed for extensive renovation – once more paid for by a fervently patriotic public – but now the whole thing is accessible again, opened in July 1986 with more back-patting ceremonial to commemorate the statue's centennial. Fifteen million people descended on Manhattan for the celebrations, well over half a million of them piling into Central Park to hear a special Liberty performance by the New York Philharmonic.

You can today take a lift up to the **crown**, though the torch, to which there is a cramped stairway, is sadly to remain closed to the public. In the **base** of the statue is a **Museum of Immigration**, not especially imaginative and at times dubious in its historical slant. But its photographs – browbeaten families being herded through the cavernous halls of the Ellis Island immigration station – are moving enough: all the more so as you move outside to Liberty Park and its spectacular views of the Lower Manhattan skyline, the twin towers of the World Trade Center lording it over the jutting teeth of New York's financial quarter. For while undeniably impressive, there is little on Wall Street that is designed to ease the lot of New York's present poor – its new and unwelcomed influx of Hispanic immigrants above all.

Ferries to the statue, run by *Circle Line*, leave from the pier in Battery Park, on the hour between 9am and 4pm; fare is $3.25 for the round-trip, half-price for children (tickets from Castle Clinton). The last ferry back leaves at 5pm so go over on the 3pm at latest: Liberty Island needs a good couple of hours to explore, and if the weather's good and there aren't too many people it can be a nice place to spend an afternoon.

Just across the water, **ELLIS ISLAND** was where the immigrants first arrived and were processed. Long closed to the public, it awaits the completion (in 1990) of a plan to turn it into a museum tribute to America's patchwork of peoples and cultures. In some ways this will be a pity, for the buildings, currently decayed and evocative, are likely to become bland and sanitised. The story, however, is undeniably promising material for the display. The island, known as Gibbet Island by the English (who used it for punishing unfortunate pirates), became an immigration station in 1894, just when the numbers coming into the country were beginning to reach their peak. In the first decade of this century around 2000 immigrants passed through its doors each day – and when closed in 1954 it had seen over 16 million prospective new Americans.

The immigrants who arrived here were all steerage class passengers; richer immigrants were processed at their leisure on board ship. The scenes on the island were horribly confused: most families arrived hungry, filthy and penniless, rarely speaking English, and invariably overawed by the beckoning metropolis across the water. Con men preyed from all sides, stealing their baggage as it was checked and offering rip-off exchange rates for whatever money they had managed to bring. The official procedures the immigrants were put through took place in the Grand Hall. First was a medical inspection – those who failed were chalked with a white cross; next an aptitude test – 38 simple questions and a passage from the Bible. Those who passed proceeded quickly by barge to Manhattan or the New Jersey shore; those who didn't were either remaindered on the island awaiting a decision, or simply sent straight back to the ships on which they arrived. Perhaps surprisingly, most did get through, and in a matter of hours: only 2 per cent of arrivals were refused in all, and many of those jumped into the sea and tried to swim to Manhattan rather than face going home.

The last of the three small islands which lie just south of Manhattan, **GOVERNOR'S ISLAND** is home these days to the US Coast Guard and only visitable if you must write first for a permit from the *USCG Support Center* (Governor's Island, NY 10004; 668 7255). In summer tours run quite regularly, the ferries are free and it makes for a close-by escape from the city if you've an hour or two to spare. 'Nowhere in New York is more pastoral', Jan Morris wrote of the island in *The Great Port*. Sights include a handful of colonial and 19C houses, and Fort Jay and Castle Williams – the former put up in 1789 by zealous and ever-vigilant revolutionary volunteers. Otherwise it's once again the views of downtown Manhattan that steal the show: from the peaceful, almost villagey environment of the island, more impressive than ever.

THE FINANCIAL DISTRICT

The skyline of Manhattans's **FINANCIAL DISTRICT** is the one you see in all the movies – dramatic skyscrapers pushed into the narrow southern tip of the island and framed by the monumental elegance of the Brooklyn Bridge. Heart of the nation's wheeler-dealing, this is the place where Manhattan (and indeed America) began – though precious few leftovers of those days remain, shunted out by big business eager to boost corporate image with HQs in the right places. Like the City of London the Financial District has a nine-till-five existence: don't go expecting life out of these times or at weekends.

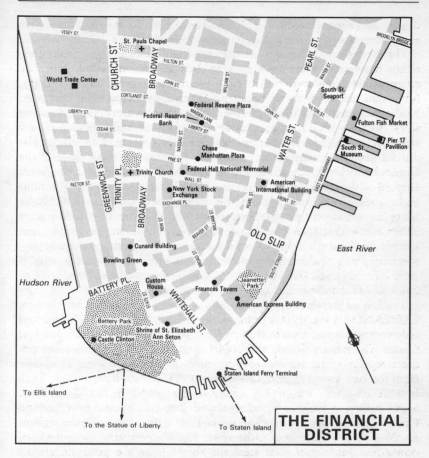

THE FINANCIAL DISTRICT

The Dutch arrived here first, building a wooden wall at the edge of their small settlement as protection from pro-British settlers to the north. Hence the narrow canyon of today's **Wall Street** gained its name, and it's here, behind the thin Neo-Classical mask of the **New York Stock Exchange**, that the purse strings of the capitalist world are pulled. From the **Visitors' Gallery** (Monday-Friday 10am-3.45pm; free) the exchange floor appears a mêlée of brokers and buyers, all scrambling for the elusive fractional cent on which to make a megabuck. Sit through the glib introductory film, though, and the hectic scurrying and constantly moving hieroglyphs of the stock prices make more sense. Along with the film, there's a small exhibition on the history of the Exchange – notably quiet on the more spectacular cock-ups. The most disastrous, the notorious *Black Tuesday* of 1929, is mentioned almost in passing, perhaps because it was so obviously caused by the greed and short-sightedness of the money men themselves. In those days shares could be bought 'on margin', which meant the buyer needed to pay only a small part of their total cost, borrowing the rest using the shares as security. This worked fine so long as the market kept rising – share dividends came in to pay off the loans, investors' money bought more shares. But it was, as Alistair Cooke put it, 'a mountain of credit on a molehill of actual money' and only a small scare was needed to start the avalanche. When the market slackened punters had to find more cash to service their debts and make up for the fall in value of their stocks, which they did by selling off shares cheaply. A panicked chain reaction began, and on October 24th 16 million shares were traded; five days later the whole Exchange collapsed as $125 million was wiped off stock values. Fortunes disappeared overnight: millions lost their life savings, banks, businesses and industries shut their doors, unemployment spiralled helplessly. The Great Depression began.

The **Federal Hall National Memorial**, at Wall Street's canyon-like head, can't help but look a little foolish, a Doric temple that woke up one morning and found itself surrounded by skyscrapers. The building was once the Customs House, later a bank, but the exhibition inside (Monday-Friday 9am-5pm; free) relates the headier days of 1789 when George Washington was sworn in as America's first President from a balcony on this site. It was a showy affair for a great if rather pompous man: 'I fear we may have exchanged George III for George I,' commented one senator observing Washingtons's affectations. The documents and models of the event repay a wander, as does the daintily rotunded hall. Washington's statue stands, very properly, on the steps.

At Wall Street's other end, **Trinity Church** (guided tours at 2pm, daily) waits darkly in the wings, an ironic onlooker to the street's dealings. There's been a church here since the end of the 17C, but this one in knobbly Neo-Gothic went up in 1846, and for fifty years was the city's tallest building, a reminder of just how recently high-rise Manhattan has sprung up. It's got much of the air of an English church (Richard Upjohn, its architect, came from Dorset), especially in the sheltered **graveyard**, resting place of early Manhattanites and lunching office workers. A search round the old tombstones rewards with such luminaries as first Secretary to the Treasury Alexander Hamilton.

Trinity Church is an oddity amid its office-block neighbours, several of which are worth nosing into. **One Wall Street**, immediately opposite the church, is among the best, with an Art Deco lobby in sumptuous red and gold that naggingly suggests a bankers' bordello. East down Wall Street, the **Morgan Guaranty Trust Building**, at number 23, bears the scars of a weird happening of 1920. On September 15th a horse-drawn cart pulled up outside and its driver jumped off and disappeared down a side street. A few seconds later the cart blew up in a devastating explosion that knocked out windows half a mile a way. Thirty-three people were killed (many literally blown to bits) and hundreds injured, but to this day the explosion remains unexplained. One theory holds that it was a premeditated attack on Morgan and his vast financial empire; another that the cart belonged to an explosives company and was illegally travelling through the city. Curiously, or perhaps deliberately, the pock-mark scars on the building's wall have never been healed.

The most impressive leftover of the confident days before the Wall Street crash is the old **Cunard Building** at 25 Broadway, whose marble walls and high dome housed the steamship's booking office – hence the elaborate, whimsical murals of sea travel and nautical gods splashed all around. As the large liners gave way to jet travel, Cunard could no longer afford such an extravagant shop window. Its sorry fate today is to house a post office, one that's been fitted out with little feeling for the exuberant space it occupies.

Broadway comes to a gentle end at the **Bowling Green**, an oval of turf used for the game by 18C colonial Brits on a lease of 'one peppercorn per year'. The encircling iron fence is an original of 1771, though the crowns that once topped the stakes were removed in later revolutionary fervour, as was a statue of George III, to be melted down and put to more practical use in cannonballs. Earlier still the green was the site of one of Manhattan's more memorable business deals, when Peter Minuit, first director general of the Dutch colony of New Amsterdam, bought the whole island from the Indians for a handful of baubles worth 60 guilders: but the other side of the story, the bit you never hear, was that these Indians didn't actually own the island; no doubt both parties went home smiling. Today the green is a spot for office people picnicking in the shadow of Cass Gilbert's **US Customs House**, which forms a grandiose plug to the south. With its back firmly to the sea the Customs House is a heroic monument to New York the port; four statues at the front represent the four continents (sculpted by Daniel Chester French, who also did Washington's Lincoln Memorial) and the twelve near the top personify the world's commercial centres, all fixed in homage to the maritime market. Inside, on the rotunda, are some rumbustious murals by Reginald Marsh, closed for some time for restoration but due to re-open soon.

Beyond the Customs House, Lower Manhattan lets out its breath in **Battery Park**, a bright and blowy space with **Castle Clinton** at one side. Before landfill closed the gap this 19C fort was an island, protecting Manhattan's southern tip. Later it found new life as a prestigious concert venue – in 1850 the enterprising P.T. Barnum threw a hugely hyped concert by soprano Jenny Lind, the 'Swedish Nightingale', with tickets at $225 a throw – before doing service (pre-Ellis Island) as the drop-off point for arriving immigrants. Today the squat castle isn't that interesting, though if you're curious it's generally open (Monday-Friday 9am-5pm) from around mid-March through to September; bear in mind that it's also the place to buy ferry tickets to the Statue of Liberty.

Back on State Street a dapper Georgian facade identifies the **Shrine of Elizabeth Ann Seton,** the first native-born American to be canonised. St Elizabeth lived here briefly before moving to found a religious community in Maryland. The shrine – small, hushed and illustrated by pious and tearful pictures of the saint's life – is one of a few old houses that have survived the modern onslaught. On the corner of Pearl and Broad Streets is another, **Fraunces Tavern,** set dramatically against a backdrop of skyscrapers. The three-storey Georgian brick house has been almost totally reconstructed to mimic the day of the incident that ensured its survival: on December 4th 1783, the British conclusively beaten, a weeping George Washington took leave of his assembled officers, intent on returning to rural life in Virginia: 'I am not only retiring from all public employments,' he wrote, 'but am retiring within myself' – with hindsight a hasty statement as six years later he was to return as the new nation's President. The second floor recreates the simple colonial dining room where this took place – all probably as genuine as the relics of Washington's teeth and hair in the adjacent museum. Admission is free, Monday-Friday 10am-4pm.

Turn a corner by the tavern and you're on **Water Street,** in its southern reaches a thinned-out agglomeration of skyscrapers developed in the early 1960s when the powers-that-were took it into their heads that Manhattan's business was stagnating because of lack of room for growth and so tore down the Victorian brownstones and warehouses that lined the waterfront. They thus missed a vital chance to let the old give context to the new, and if you stand on the barren plaza of the **American Express Building** at 2 New York Plaza, you're a long way from feeling anything other than windswept and alone. But not all of Water Street's development is quite so faceless: turn east down Old Slip and a pocket-size palazzo that was once the **First Precinct Police Station** slots good-naturedly into the narrow strip, a cheerful throwback to a different era.

Cross Water Street, take the next left to Pine Street and you'll find a skyscraper that's one of Manhattan's most joyful. In 1916 the authorities became worried that the massive buildings looming up around town would shield light from the streets, turning the lower and midtown areas into grim passages between soaring monoliths. The result of their fears was the first *zoning ordinance*, which ruled that a building's total floor space couldn't be any more than 12 times the area of its site. This led to the 'setback' style of skyscraper, and the **American International Building** at 70 Pine Street is the ultimate Art Deco cutaway wedding cake: light, zestful and with one of the best – and most overlooked – Deco interiors. Like other lobbies, no one minds you going in, and recent demolitions mean you can get a good view of the whole building – which might have been almost as well-known as the Empire State or Chrysler had it been more visible. Almost opposite, I. M. Pei's gridiron **88 Pine Street** stands coolly formal in white, a self-confident and self-contained modern descendant.

Around the South Street Seaport

At the eastern end of Fulton Street the **South Street Seaport** comes girded with the sort of praise and publicity that generally augurs a commercial bland-out. In fact it's a thoroughly likeable project that's attempting to preserve one of Lower Manhattan's few surviving industrial-historic areas. A fair slice of commercial gentrification was needed to woo developers, but the presence of a working fish market has kept things real in a way that should be a lesson for the likes of London's Covent Garden. For a hundred years this stretch of the waterside was New York's sailship port: it began when when Robert Fulton started a ferry service from here to Brooklyn, and left his name on the street and then its market. The harbour lapped up the trade brought by the opening of the Erie Canal, and, by the end of the 19C, was sending cargo ships on regular runs to California, Japan and Liverpool. Trade eventually moved elsewhere, though, and the blocks of warehouses and ship's chandlers, gradually and secretively being bought up by property speculators, were left to rot. Their rescue – by a historical monument order – was probably only just in time.

Best place to start looking round is the market's so-called **Museum Block**, an assembly of chi-chi shops hidden behind Water Street's hotchpotch of Greek Revival and Italianate facades. Apart from their upmarket attractions, offerings include a walking tour of the area and a 'voyage through time' at the **South Street Venture Cinema**. These multiscreen historical extravaganzas can be a bit cloying, but this one manages to entertain cleverly and imaginatively without embarrassing. Whether it's worth shelling out to the tune of $3.25 is up to you to decide.

The **New Fulton Market**, despite outward appearances, went up in 1983. Essentially it's a food emporium, and if prices aren't bargain basement they're certainly within reach, especially for the eclectic variety of fast food on the second floor, which other than the nearby *Jeremy's Pub* (see p.253) is the best bet for a cut-price lunch. Across the way the cleaned-up **Schermerhorn Row** has the 'English' North Star Pub at one end and *Sloppy Louie's* restaurant around the corner. Other guidebooks will tell you this is *the* cheap eatery in Lower Manhattan – fish fresh from the market, bare tables, no booze. But sadly, inevitably, the glossing-up of the area has meant the end of such straightforward grub, and today Sloppy Louie's has its insignia of American Express stickers like the rest of them.

The elevated East Side Highway forms a suitably grimy portico to the **Fulton Fish Market**, a tatty building that wears its 80 years as the city's wholesale outlet with no pretensions. If you can manage it, the time to be here is around 5am (organised tours run each second and fourth Thursday; $12, reservations needed – 669 9416) when buyers' lorries park up beneath the highway to collect the catches, the air reeks of salt and scale and there's lots of nasty things to step in. But it's invigorating stuff, a twilight world that probably won't be around that much longer – the adjacent **Pier 17 Pavilion**, a hypercomplex of restaurants and shops, could be one nail in its coffin. Next door, around piers 15 and 16, is the **South Street Museum** (Monday-Friday 11.45am-3pm, Saturday-Sunday 11am-4pm; $4.50 admission includes all tours, films and visits), a collection of nimble sailships and chubby ferries slowly being refitted to former glories. In the summer, the schooner *Pioneer* will coast you round the harbour for an additional consideration, though unless sailing is your passion I'd skip the ships; better to freeload at the outdoor **jazz concerts** on Friday and Saturday evenings (8pm throughout July and August).

From just about anywhere in the seaport you can see one of New York's most celebrated delights, the **Brooklyn Bridge**. This is now just one of several spans across the East River – and the Gothic slabs of the bridge's gateways are dwarfed by lower Manhattan's skyscrapers. But in its day the Brooklyn Bridge was a technological quantum leap: it towered over the low brick structures around and for 20 years was the world's largest suspension bridge, the first to use steel cables and for many more the longest single span. To New Yorkers it was an object of awe, the massively concrete symbol of the Great American Dream: 'All modern New York, heroic New York, started with the Brooklyn Bridge,' wrote Kenneth Clark, and indeed its meeting of art and function, of romantic Gothic and daring practicality, became a sort of spiritual model for the next generation's skyscrapers.

It didn't go up without difficulties. John Augustus Roebling, its architect and engineer, crushed his foot taking measurements for the piers and died of gangrene three weeks later; his son Washington took over only to be crippled by the bends from working in an insecure underwater caisson, and subsequently directed the work from his sick bed overlooking the site. Twenty workers died during the construction and, a week after the opening day in 1883, twelve people were crushed to death in a panicked rush on the Bridge's footway. Despite this (and innumerable suicides), New Yorkers still look to the Bridge with affection: for the 1983 centennial it was festooned with decorations – 'Happy Birthday Brooklyn Bridge' ran the legends – and the city organised a party.

Whether the Bridge has a similar effect on you or not, the view from it is undeniably spectacular. Walk across, near sunset if possible, from City Hall Park and don't look back till you're midway: the Financial District's giants clutter shoulder to shoulder through the spidery latticework, the East River pulses below and cars scream to and from Brooklyn. It's a glimpse of the 1980s metropolis, and on no account to be missed.

Back on the island, Fulton Street arcs right across Lower Manhattan with **Maiden Lane** as its southern parallel, an august and anonymous rollercoaster of finance houses, with **Nassau Street** linking the two in a downbeat precinct of on-offer goods and fast food. Where Nassau and Maiden Lane meet, Johnson and Burgees' toybox castle of **Federal Reserve Plaza** resounds like a witless joke over the original **Federal Reserve Bank**, whose fortressy walls supplied their Post-Modernist idea. The loggia of the plaza isn't all bad though, and it's worth poking your head inside for the **Whitney Museum Downtown**, changing collections of modern American art – for more on which see p.196. There's good reason for the Reserve Bank proper's iron-barred exterior: stashed 80 feet below the street are most of the 'free' world's gold reserves – 11,000 tonnes of them, occasionally shifted from vault to vault as wars break out or international debts are settled. It is possible – but tricky – to tour the piles of gleaming bricks; write to the *Public Information Department*, Federal Reserve Bank, 33 Liberty Street, NY 10045 or phone 791 6130 at least a week ahead, as tickets have to be posted. Upstairs, dirty money and counterfeit currency are weeded out of circulation as automated checkers shuffle dollar bills like unending packs of cards. Assistants wheelbarrow loads of cash around ('How much there?' I asked one: '$8½ million,' he replied) and, as you'd imagine, the security is just like in the movies.

When you've unboggled your mind of high finance's gold you can see some of its glitter at **One Chase Manhattan Plaza** immediately to the south on Pine Street. Prestigious New York headquarters of the bank, its boxy International style tower was the first in Lower Manhattan and brought downtown the concept of the plaza, an open forecourt at the entrance. Unfortunately Chase Manhattan's plaza has all the soul and charm of a car park, and even Dubuffet's *Four Trees* sculpture can't get things going. Continue to the end of Cedar Street and you'll find the **Marine Midland Bank** at 140 Broadway, a smaller, more successful tower by the same design team, with a tiptoeing sculpture by Isamu Noguchi. More sculpture worth catching lies behind Chase Manhattan Plaza on **Louise Nevelson Plaza**. Here a clutch of Nevelson's works lie like massive shrapnel on an island of land: a striking ploy of sculpture in the urban environment.

Back down Liberty Street to Church Street and at **One Liberty Plaza** stands the **US Steel Building**, a threatening black mass all the more offensive since the famed **Singer Building** was demolished to make way for it. Ernest Flagg's 1908 construction was one of the most delicate on the New York skyline, a graceful Renaissance-style tower of metal and glass destroyed in 1968 and replaced with what has justly been called a 'gloomy, cadaverous hulk'.

The World Trade Center and Battery Park City

Wherever you are in Lower Manhattan, two buildings dominate the landscape. Critics say the twin Ronson lighters of the **World Trade Center towers** don't relate to their surroundings and aren't especially pleasing in design – and spirited down to a tenth of their size they certainly wouldn't get a second glance. But the fact is they're *big*, undeniably and frighteningly so, and a walk across the plaza in summer months (closed in winter as icicles falling from the towers can kill) can make your head reel.

Perhaps the idea of so huge a project similarly affected the judgment of the Port Authority of New York and New Jersey, the Center's chief financier, which for several years found itself expensively stuck with two half-empty white elephants. Now the Trade Center, whose towers are the best part of a five building development, is full and successful, as the bustling concourses and ritzy *Windows on the World* restaurants can vouch. With courage, a trip to the 107th floor **observation deck** of the World Trade Center 2 (daily 9.30am-9.30pm; $2.95) gives a stupendous view from a height of 1350 feet – over a quarter of a mile. From the open-air rooftop promenade (closed during bad weather) the silent panorama is more dramatic still: everything in New York is below you, including the planes gliding into the airports. Even Jersey City looks exciting. As you timidly edge your way around, ponder the fact that one Philippe Petit once walked a tightrope between the two towers: nerve indeed. Best time to ascend is towards sunset when the tourist crowds thin and Manhattan slowly turns itself into the most spectacular light show this side of the Apocalypse.

The hole dug for the towers' foundations threw up a million cubic yards of earth and rock which were dumped into the Hudson to form the 23-acre base of **Battery Park City**. This, more than anything else, will change the character of the Financial District, with more office blocks and luxury apartments designed to turn the area into a place where the fortunate few can live as well as work. Originally, ten per cent of the housing was to be set aside for low-income groups, but with the recession of the 1970s that plan was scrapped: now the city has promised to invest just under half of the $1 billion it will receive in profits back into housing schemes for the poor. Architecturally, though, the Park is one of the better events of recent years: traditional themes are picked up throughout, and the whole scheme has a loose conformity that echoes much of the rest of Manhattan. Even before completion it was being lauded as the new Rockefeller Center. Using Rector Park as a starting-point, wander through the glassy Wintergarden and Dow Jones lobby, and wonder if such praise is justified.

Straight across from the World Trade Center on Vesey Street and Broadway, **St Paul's Chapel** comes from a very different order of things.

It's the oldest church on Manhattan, dating from 1766 – 80 years earlier than Trinity and almost prehistoric by New York standards. The church's architect was from London – St. Martin-in-the-Fields was his model – though his building seems quite American in feel, an unfussy 18C space of soap bar blues and pinks. George Washington worshipped here and his pew, zealously treasured, is much on show.

CITY HALL PARK AND THE CIVIC CENTER

Broadway and Park Row form the apex of **City Hall Park**, a noisy, pigeon-splattered triangle of green with the **Woolworth Building** as a venerable and much venerated onlooker. Some think this is New York's definitive skyscraper, and it's hard to disagree – money, ornament and prestige mingle in Cass Gilbert's 1913 'Cathedral of Commerce', whose soaring, graceful lines are fringed with Gothic decoration more for fun than any portentous allusion: if the Trade Center towers railroad you into

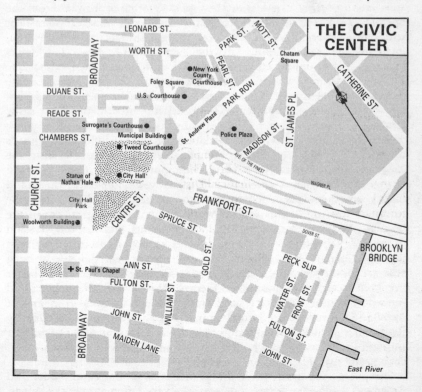

wonder by sheer size, then the Woolworth charms with good nature, and the famous lobby is one of the musts of the city. Frank Woolworth made his fortune from his 'five and dime' stores – everything cost either 5 or 10c, strictly no credit. True to his philosophy he paid cash for his skyscraper, and the whimsical reliefs at each corner of the lobby show him doing just that, counting out the money in 5c and 10c bits. Facing him in caricature are the architect (medievally clutching a model of his building), renting agent and builder. Within, vaulted ceilings ooze honey-gold mosaics and even the mailboxes are magnificent. The whole building has a well-humoured panache more or less extinct in today's architecture – have a look at the Citibank next door to see what recent years have come up with.

At the top of the park, marking the beginning of the CIVIC CENTER and its incoherent jumble of municipal offices and courts, stands City Hall. Finished in 1812 to a good-looking design that's a marriage of French Château and American Georgian, its first sorry moment of fame came in 1865 when Abraham Lincoln's body lay in state for 120,000 New Yorkers to file past. Later, after the city's 1927 fêting of the returned aviator Charles Lindbergh, it became the traditional finishing point for Broadway tickertape parades given for triumphant baseball stars, poets and astronauts, and, more recently, returned Iranian hostages. Inside it's an elegant meeting of arrogance and authority, with the sweeping spiral staircase delivering you to the precise geometry of the Governor's Room and the self-important Board of Estimates Chamber; admission (Monday-Friday, 10am-4pm) only when they're not sitting.

If City Hall is the acceptable face of municipal bureaucracy, the Tweed Courthouse behind is a reminder of a seamier underbelly of corruption. William Marcy 'Boss' Tweed worked his way from nowhere to become chairman of the Democratic Central Committee at Tammany Hall in 1856, and by a series of adroit and illegal moves manipulated the city's revenues through his own and supporters' pockets. He consolidated his position by registering thousands of immigrants as Democrats in return for a low-level welfare system, and by handouts and pay-offs to the queues of critics waiting to be bought. For a while Tweed's grip strangled all dissent (even over the budget for the Courthouse itself, which rolled up from $3 to $12 million, possibly because one carpenter was paid $360,747 for a month's work, a plasterer $2,870,464 for nine) until a political cartoonist, Thomas Nast, and the editor of the New York Times (who'd refused a half-million dollar bribe to keep quiet) turned public opinion against him. With suitable irony Tweed died in 1878 in Ludlow Street gaol – a prison he'd built when Commissioner of Works.

City Hall Park is dotted with statues of worthier characters, number one in whose pantheon is Nathan Hale. In 1776 he was captured by the British and hanged for spying, but not before he'd spat out his gloriously and memorably famous last words: 'I regret that I only have but one life to lose for my country.' These, and his over-swashbuckled statue, are his epitaph.

The same year and same place saw George Washington order the first reading of the **Declaration of Independence** in the city. Thomas Jefferson's eloquent, stirring statement of the new nation's rights had just been adopted by the Second Continental Congress in Philadelphia, and it no doubt fired the hearts and minds of the troops and people assembled.

We hold these truths to be self-evident, that all men are created equal, that they are endowed by their creator with certain unalienable rights, that among these are Life, Liberty and the pursuit of Happiness; that to secure these rights Governments are instituted among Men, deriving their just powers from the consent of the governed; that whenever any form of Government becomes destructive of these ends, it is the Right of the People to alter or abolish it, and to institute new Government...

Back on Center Street the **Municipal Building** stands like an oversized chest of drawers, its shoulders straddling Chambers Street in an attempt to embrace or engulf City Hall. Atop, an extravagant pile of columns and pinnacles signals a frivolous conclusion to a no-nonsense building. Walk through and you reach **Police Plaza,** a concrete space with the russet-hued **Police Headquarters** at one end and a rusty-coloured sculpture at its centre. One side of the plaza runs down to the glum-grey **Foley Square** where, with some pomp, reside the United States and New York County **Courthouses,** grand though underwhelming buildings after what has preceded. The County Court is the more interesting and accessible (Monday-Friday, 10am-4pm), its rotunda decorated with story-book WPA *murals* (see p.356) illustrating the history of justice. If there's time take a look too at the Art Deco **Criminal Courts Building** (known as *The Tombs* from a funereal Egyptian-style building that once stood on this site) on Center Street, and the unapologetically modern **Family Court** across the way; but by and large civic dignity begins to fade north of here, as ramshackle electrical shops mark the edge of **Chinatown.**

BARS *Jeremy's Alehouse, Blarney Inn.*

RESTAURANTS Cheap *John Street Restaurant, South Street Seaport Market*; **Greek** *Delphi.*

CHINATOWN AND LITTLE ITALY

With close on 100,000 residents (about half of New York's Chinese population), seven Chinese newspapers, around 150 restaurants and over 300 garment factories, **CHINATOWN** is unique in that it's Manhattan's only truly thriving ethnic neighbourhood, over recent years pushing its boundaries north across Canal Street into Little Italy, and sprawling east as far as the nether fringes of the Lower East Side.

On the face of things Chinatown is prosperous – a 'model slum', some have called it – with the lowest crime rate, highest employment and least juvenile delinquency of any city district. Walk through its crowded streets at any time of day, and every shop is doing a brisk and businesslike trade, restaurant after restaurant booming, and the foodstores' glorious displays of shiny squids, clawing crabs and clambering bucketfuls of lobster, and all manner of exotic green vegetables, give this part of the city the feel of a land of plenty. The reason why lies with the Chinese themselves, who, even here, in the very core of downtown Manhattan, have been careful to preserve their own way of dealing with things, keeping affairs close to the bond of the family and allowing few intrusions into what is, in effect, New York's most secretive ethnic group.

The Chinese began to arrive in the mid-19C, following in the wake of a trickle of Irish and Italians. Most had previously worked out west, building railways and digging gold mines, and few intended to stay: their idea was simply to make a nest-egg and retire to a life of leisure with their families (99 per cent were men) back in China. Some, a few hundred perhaps, did go back, but on the whole the big money took rather longer to accumulate than expected, and so Chinatown as a permanent settlement began. Which is not to say that they were welcomed by the authorities. The Mafia-style Tong Wars, towards the end of the 19C, made the quarter's violence notorious, and in 1882 the government passed an act forbidding entry for ten years to any further Chinese workers. It wasn't until the 1960s that specifically anti-Chinese restrictions were finally abolished, and immigration again surged. Today, beneath the neighbourhood's blithely prosperous facade, sharp practices apparently continue to flourish, with traditional extortion, protection rackets and non-union sweatshops. But the community is so concerned with being cloistered that you'd need long residence to detect any hint of it. And any kind of unpleasantness is certainly not directed towards the customer or tourist.

All of which is in any case academic, at least for most New Yorkers, who come to Chinatown not to get the lowdown on the Chinese but to eat. For nowhere in this city can you eat so well, and so much, for so little. **Mott Street** is the area's main thoroughfare and along with the streets around – Canal, Pell, Bayard, Doyers and Bowery – hosts a positive glut of restaurants, tea and rice shops and grocers. Cantonese cuisine

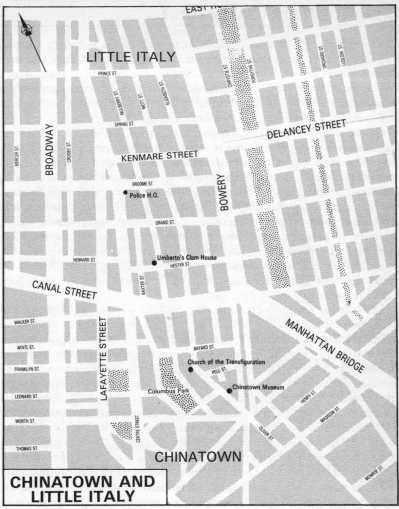

LITTLE ITALY

PRINCE ST.

MULBERRY ST.
MOTT ST.
ELIZABETH ST.

SPRING ST.

CHRYSTIE ST.
FORSYTHE ST.

ORCHARD ST.
LUDLOW ST.

DELANCEY STREET

MERCER ST.
BROADWAY
CROSBY ST.

KENMARE STREET

BROOME ST.
● Police H.Q.

BOWERY

GRAND ST.

HOWARD ST.
● Umberto's Clam House
HESTER ST.

CANAL STREET

BAXTER ST.

WALKER ST.

LAFAYETTE STREET

MANHATTAN BRIDGE

WHITE ST.

BAYARD ST.

FRANKLIN ST.

Church of the Transfiguration
● PELL ST.

LEONARD ST.

Columbus Park
● Chinatown Museum

HENRY ST.

MADISON ST.

WORTH ST.

CENTRE STREET

OLIVER ST.

THOMAS ST.

CHINATOWN

MONROE ST.

**CHINATOWN AND
LITTLE ITALY**

predominates but there are also many restaurants that specialise in the
spicier Szechuan and Hunan cuisines. Anywhere you care to walk into is
likely to be good, but if you're looking for specific recommendations
(especially for lunchtime *Dim Sum*) some of the best are detailed on
p.245.

The lure of Chinatown lies largely in this – eating and wandering amid
the exotica of the food and goods shops, and absorbing the neighbour
hood's vigorous streetlife – though there are a few interesting routes if you
want to set structure to your explorations. Mott Street, again, is the
obvious starting point, and you may want to detour from here to
Mulberry Street, which runs parallel, and its flanking **Columbus Park**.

Back on Mott there's the **Chinatown Museum** (see p.204) at the far end, on the site of the district's first Chinese shop. Next door a dim-lit arcade lists amongst its star attractions a live dancing chicken. Further up, a rare building predates the Chinese intake, the early 19C **Church of the Transfiguration**; right from here the corner of Pell and Doyers Streets was once known as 'Bloody Angle' for its miserable reputation as dumping ground for dead bodies during the Tong Wars. Though rather less sinister now, it's still no place to linger – and really, once you've made this circuit (or at least a rough approximation of it), you've seen more or less all there is of Chinatown's nucleus. Moving on, stroll over **Bowery** and wander the streets leading down to the estates that flank the East River, most of which are nowadays indigenous Chinese and where you'll encounter rather more local than tourist traffic. Then double back by way of East Broadway or Henry Street to where the **Manhattan Bridge**, its grand Beaux Arts entrance slightly ridiculous these days, mounts its assault on the East River. From here you could head north up Chrystie Street, which forms the nominal border between Chinatown and the Lower East Side, or west down Canal Street, back into the turmoil of Chinatown and the area known as Little Italy, long regarded as the hub of the city's considerable Italian community.

Little Italy
While many New Yorkers refuse to admit it, and many guidebooks continue to witter on about little old Signoras and elderly men sitting on street corners sipping Espresso, **LITTLE ITALY** is light years away from the solid ethnic enclave of old. It is also a lot smaller than it was, and the area settled by New York's huge 19C influx of Italian immigrants – who (like their Jewish and Chinese counterparts) cut themselves off clannishly to recreate the Old Country – is encroached upon a little more each year by Chinatown. Few Italians still live here and the restaurants (of which there are plenty) tend towards the valet-parking and exorbitant. In fact, it is this quantity of restaurants, more than anything, that gives Little Italy away: go to the city's true Italian areas, Belmont in the Bronx, or Carroll Gardens in Brooklyn, and you'll find very few genuine Italian eateries, since Italians prefer to consume their native food at home. It's significant, too, that when Martin Scorsese came to make *Mean Streets* – though the film was about Little Italy – it was in Belmont that he decided to shoot it.

But that's not to advise missing out on Little Italy altogether. Some original delis and bakeries do survive, and there are still plenty of places to indulge yourself with a cappuccino and pricey pastry, not least *Ferrara's* on Grand Street, the oldest and most popular, with a vibrant street-life in summer. If you're here in September the annual **Festa di San Gennaro** is a wild and typically Italian splurge to celebrate the saint's day, when Italians from all over the city turn up and **Mulberry Street**, Little

Italy's main strip, is transformed by street stalls and numerous Italian fast-snack outlets. Of the **restaurants**, *Umberto's Clam House* on Mulberry Street remains most famed, not for the food but for the fact that it was the scene of a vicious gangland murder in 1972, when Joe 'Crazy Joey' Gallo was shot dead while celebrating his birthday with his wife and daughter. Gallo, a big-noise keen to protect his business interests in Brooklyn and as provenly ruthless as the rest of them, was believed to have offended a rival family and so paid the price. For full listings on Umberto's and the cheapest of Little Italy's other restaurants, see p.245.

Slightly west of here, at the corner of Center and Broome Streets and in striking counterpoint to the clandestine lawlessness of the Italian underworld, the old **Police Headquarters** rears grandiosely out of the gloom, a palatial Neo-Classical confection meant to cow would-be criminals into obedience with a high-rise dome and lavish ornamentation. It's disused now, the police HQ long since moved to a bland modern building in Civic Center, and there's a question-mark over what it could be used for. They won't knock it down that's for sure, and it has been suggested that a community centre for what's left of the Italian population here might not be a bad idea. But for the moment it stands very much left alone, stocky, solid and empty – an overbearing palace on the edge of Little Italy. Walk beyond and you're already in **SoHo**, like Chinatown a booming district bursting its borders from the further side of Broadway.

RESTAURANTS Chinese *Hee Sung Fung, Loong Lau, Mon Bo, New Lin Heong, Non-Wah, Phoenix Garden, Silver Garden, Sun Say Gay*; **Fish** *Umberto's Clam House*. **Italian** *La Luna, Puglia*;

SOHO AND TRIBECA

Since the mid-1960s, **SOHO**, the grid of streets that runs *South of Houston* Street, has meant art. Squashed between the Financial District and, further north, Greenwich Village, it had long been a raggy no-man's land of manufacturers and wholesalers, but as the Village declined in hipness, SoHo was suddenly 'in'. Its loft spaces were ideal for cheap-rental studios, and galleries quickly attracted the city's art crowd, while boutique and restaurant hangers-on converted the ground floors. Like the Village, gentrification quickly followed – most of the artists left, the galleries stayed – and what remains is a mix of chi-chi antique, art and clothes shops, earthy industry and high living. Today a loft in SoHo means money (and lots of it) but no amount of gloss can cover up SoHo's quintessential appearance, its dark alleys of paint-peeled factories fronted by some of the best cast-iron facades in America.

Houston Street (pronounced *How*ston rather than *Hew*ston) marks the top of SoHo's trellis of streets, any exploration of which necessarily means criss-crossing and doubling back. **Greene Street** is as good a place to start as any, highlighted all along by the cast-iron facades that, in part if not in whole, saved SoHo from the bulldozers. Their origins are 19C, a time when the quarter fringed New York's liveliest street, Broadway marking a fashionable run of hotels, shops and theatres, and the streets to the west a seamier backdrop of industrial and red light areas cheerfully known as 'Hell's Hundred Acres.'

The technique of **cast-iron architecture** was utilised simply as a way of assembling buildings quickly and cheaply, with iron beams rather than heavy walls carrying the weight of the floors. The result was the removal of load bearing walls, greater space for windows, and, most noticeably, remarkably decorative facades. Almost any style or whim could be cast in iron and pinned to a building, and architects indulged themselves in Baroque balustrades, forests of Renaissance columns and all the effusion of the French Second Empire to glorify SoHo's sweatshops. Have a look at **72-76 Greene Street**, a neat extravagance whose Corinthian portico stretches the whole five storeys, all in painted metal, and at the strongly composed elaborations of its sister building at no.**28-30**. These are the best, but from Broome to Canal Street most of the fronts on Greene Street's west side are either real (or mimicked) cast-iron. Ironically, what began as an engineering trait turned into a purely decorative one as stone copies of cast iron (you'd need a magnet to tell many apart) came into fashion. At the north east corner of Broome Street and Broadway the magnificent **Haughwout Building** is perhaps the ultimate in the cast-iron genre. Rhythmically repeated motifs of colonnaded arches are framed behind taller columns in a thin sliver of a Venetian palace – the first building ever to boast a steam-powered Otis elevator. In 1904 Ernest Flagg took the possibilities of cast iron to their conclusion in his **'Little Singer' Building** at 561 Broadway (at Prince Street), a design whose use of wide window frames points the way to the glass curtain wall of the 1950s.

SoHo celebrates all this architecture in Richard Haas's smirky **mural** at 114 Prince Street (corner of Greene Street), also the venue of one of SoHo's affordable **markets** (there's another at the meeting of Spring and Wooster St). Many, probably most, of the clothes and antique shops around are beyond reasonable budgets, though the junkier bric-a-brac places may provide a bargain – search around Wooster and Thompson Streets, and see the listings on p.219 for details.

What you'll find in the innumerable **galleries** is similarly overpriced but makes for fascinating browsing, with just about every variety of contemporary artistic expression on view. No one minds you looking in

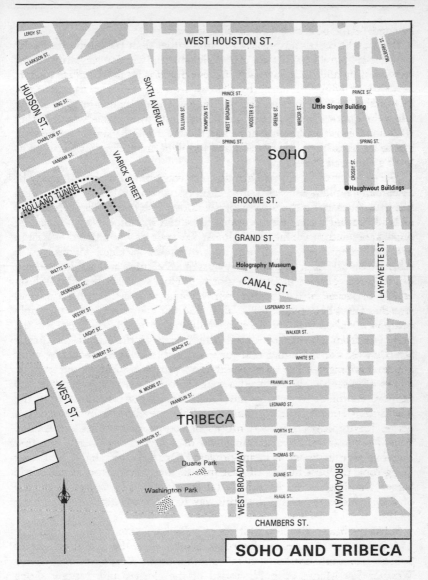

SOHO AND TRIBECA

for a while and doing this is also a sure way of bumping into the more visible eccentrics of the area. Most of the galleries are concentrated on **West Broadway**, in a patch that fancies itself as an alternative Madison Avenue. They're generally open Tuesday-Saturday 10/11am-6pm, Saturdays being most lively; for listings of galleries (and details of gallery tours) see p.228.

Loosely speaking, SoHo's diversions get grottier as you drop south. The highly touted and highly missable **Holography Museum** (p.207) at 11 Mercer is the last stop before SoHo hits **Canal Street**. This is SoHo's open bazaar, brash shop fronts loaded with fake Cartiers, dismembered torsos of electrical gear, books, cameras, records, the lot. Most people come here for the clothes – places like the *Canal Jean Co.* at 504 Broadway and a host of others – but the army surplus and discarded technology stores crave most attention. Like the signs say it's all 'as seen' – mainly trash, but good affordable fun. As TriBeCa to the south skips up the social ladder it's reckoned that Canal Street will be 'cleaned up'; which will be a pity.

TRIBECA, the *Triangle Below* Canal Street, has caught the fall-out of SoHo artists, and retains a lived-in, worked-in feel. Less a triangle than a crumpled rectangle – the area bounded by Canal and Chambers Streets, Broadway and the Hudson – it takes in spacey industrial buildings whose upper layers sprout plants and cats behind tidy glazing, the apartments of TriBeCa's new gentry. Like 'SoHo' the name TriBeCa was a 1960s invention to label the newly found scramble of warehouses, and like SoHo it's slowly creeping up in status and price. Best place to get a feel of TriBeCa's old and new is **Duane Park** between Hudson and Greenwich Streets, a tiny wedge of green trapped by old depots of egg and cheese distributors and new smart residential apartments, with the World Trade Center, Woolworth and Municipal Buildings peering over their shoulders. A block or two away, with less character but more space, there is also **Washington Park**, one of the few downtown patches you can stretch out on unintimidated, looking up to views of the Trade Center and Woolworth Building. Get here soon, though: it's only a matter of time before TriBeCa becomes just another piece of juicy real estate.

BARS *Barnabus Rex, Fanelli's, Kenn's Broome St Bar, Manhattan Brewery Company, Puffy's.*

RESTAURANTS Cheap *Prince St Bar, Spring Street Market*; **American** *Exterminator Chili, Tennessee Mountain*; **Vegetarian** *Food.*

GREENWICH VILLAGE

If you're a New Yorker, it's fashionable to dismiss **GREENWICH VILLAGE** (or 'the Village' as it's most widely known). There's so much more happening in SoHo, people say; the East Village is *sooo* much more funky and real; TriBeCa will soon be where it's at; or further uptown there's the Upper West Side... And it's true that while the Bohemian image of Greenwich Village endures well enough if you don't actually live in New York, it's a tag that has long since ceased to hold genuine currency. The only writers that can afford to live here nowadays are copywriters, the only actors those that are starring regularly on Broadway, and as for politics – the average Village resident long since dismissed them for the more serious pursuit of making money. Greenwich Village is firmly for those who have Arrived. Not that the Village is no longer exciting: to a great extent the neighbourhood still sports the attractions that brought people here in the first place. It's quiet, residential, but with a busy street-life that lasts later than any other part of the city; there are more restaurants per head than anywhere else, and bars, while never cheap, clutter every corner. If interesting people no longer live in the Village, they do hang out here – Washington Square is a hub of aimless activity throughout the year – and as long as you have no illusions about the 'alternativeness' of the place there are few better initiations into the city's life, especially at night.

Greenwich Village grew up as a rural retreat from the early and frenetic nucleus of New York City, first becoming sought after during the yellow fever epidemic of 1822 as a refuge from the infected streets downtown. When the fever was at its height the idea was mooted of moving the entire city centre here. It was spared that dubious fate, and left to grow into a wealthy residential neighbourhood that sprouted elegant Federal and Greek Revival terraces and lured some of the city's highest society names. Later, once the rich had moved uptown and built themselves a palace or two on Fifth Avenue, these large houses were to prove a fertile hunting ground for struggling artists and intellectuals on the lookout for cheap rents, and by the turn of the century Greenwich Village was well on its way to becoming New York's Left Bank. Of early Village characters, one Mabel Dodge was perhaps most influential. Wealthy and radical, she threw parties for the literary and political cognoscenti – parties to which everyone hoped, sooner or later, to be invited. Just about all of the well-known names who lived here during the first two decades of the century spent some time at her house on Fifth Avenue, just north of Washington Square. Emma Goldman discussed anarchism with Margaret Sanger, Conrad Aiken and T. S. Eliot dropped in from time to time, and John Reed – who went on to write *Ten Days That Shook the World*, the official record of the Russian Revolution – was a frequent guest.

Best way to see the Village is to walk, and much the best place to start is its natural centre, **Washington Square**, commemorated as a novel title by Henry James and haunted by most of the Village's illustrious past names. It is not an elegant- looking place – too large to be a square, too small to be a park, and not helped by the shacky toilet structures that group around its concreted centre. But it does retain its northern edging

of redbrick rowhouses – the 'solid, honourable dwellings' of Henry James'
novel – and, more imposingly, Stanford White's famous **Triumphal Arch**,
built in 1892 to commemorate the centenary of George Washington's
becoming President. James wouldn't, however, recognise the south side of
the square now: only the fussy **Judson Memorial Church** stands out amid
a messy blend of modern architectures, its interior given over these days
to a mixture of theatre and local focus for a wide array of community-
based programmes.

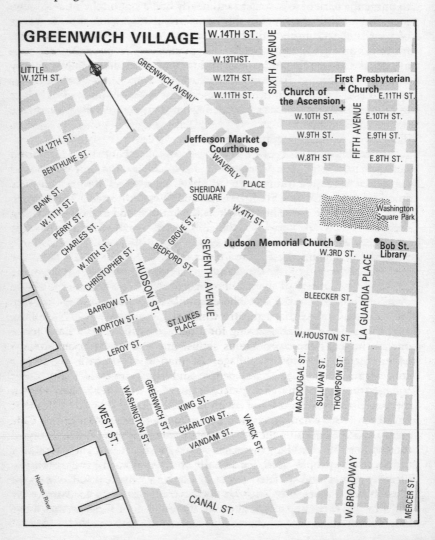

GREENWICH VILLAGE

W.14TH ST.

SIXTH AVENUE

GREENWICH AVENUE

LITTLE
W.12TH ST.

W.13TH ST.
W.12TH ST.
W.11TH ST.

Church of
the Ascension

First Presbyterian
Church
E.11TH ST.

FIFTH AVENUE

W.10TH ST.   E.10TH ST.

W.12TH ST.

BENTHUNE ST.

Jefferson Market
Courthouse

WAVERLY

PLACE

W.9TH ST.   E.9TH ST.

W.8TH ST   E.8TH ST.

BANK ST.
W.11TH ST.
PERRY ST.

CHARLES ST.

SHERIDAN
SQUARE

W.4TH ST.

Washington
Square Park

W.10TH ST.

CHRISTOPHER ST.

HUDSON ST.

BEDFORD ST.

GROVE ST.

SEVENTH AVENUE

Judson Memorial Church

W.3RD ST.

Bob St.
Library

BARROW ST.

MORTON ST.

ST.LUKES
PLACE

LEROY ST.

BLEECKER ST.

LA GUARDIA PLACE

W.HOUSTON ST.

WEST ST.

WASHINGTON ST.

GREENWICH ST.

KING ST.

CHARLTON ST.

VANDAM ST.

VARICK ST.

MACDOUGAL ST.

SULLIVAN ST.

THOMPSON ST.

W. BROADWAY

MERCER ST.

Hudson River

CANAL ST.

Most importantly, though, Washington Square remains the symbolic heart of the Village and its radicalism – so much so that when Robert Moses, that tarmaccer of great chunks of New York City (see p.286), wanted to plough a four-lane motorway through the centre of the square there was a storm of protest which resulted not only in the stopping of the road but also the banning of all traffic from the park, then used as a turnaround point by buses. And that's how it has stayed ever since, notwithstanding some battles in the 1960s when the authorities decided to purge the park of folk singers and nearly had a riot on their hands. You may find it a little threatening at times, particularly after dark when gangs of youths cluster intimidatingly at the junctions of its many paths. But, frankly, nothing's likely to happen to you (this is Greenwich Village after all, not the Lower East Side) and if things look hazardous it's just as easy to walk around. And, as soon as the weather gets warm, the park becomes sports field, dance floor, drug den and social club, boiling over with life as frisbees fly, skateboards flip and ghetto blasters crash through the urgent cries of dope peddlers and the studied patrols of police cars. Times like this there's no better square in the city.

Eugene O'Neill, probably the Village's most acclaimed resident, lived (and wrote *The Iceman Cometh*) at 38 Washington Square South and consumed vast quantities of ale at **The Golden Swan Bar**, which once stood on the corner of Sixth Avenue and West 4th Street. The Golden Swan (variously called The Hell Hole, Bucket of Blood and other enticing nicknames) was best known in O'Neill's day for the dubious morals of its clientele, a gang of Irish hoodlums known as the Hudson Dusters. O'Neill was great pals with this lot, and drew many of his characters from the personalities in this bar. It was nearby, also, that he got his first dramatic break, with a company called the Provincetown Players who on the advice of John Reed had moved down here from Massachusetts and set up shop on Macdougal Street, in a theatre which still stands (see p.272). Follow **Macdougal Street** south, pausing for a detour down Minetta Lane (once one of the city's most prodigious slums) and you hit **Bleecker Street** – Main Street, Greenwich Village in many ways, with a greater concentration of shops, bars, people and restaurants than any other Village thoroughfare. This junction is also the area's best-known meeting-place, a vibrant corner with mock-European sidewalk cafes that have been literary hangouts since the beginning of this century. The **Café Figaro**, made famous by the Beat writers in the 1950s, is always thronged throughout the day: far from cheap though still worth the price of a cappuccino to people-watch for an hour or so. Afterwards, you can follow Bleecker Street one of two ways – **east** toward the solid towers of Washington Square Village, built with typical disregard for history by NYU in 1958, or **west** right through the hubbub of Greenwich Village life.

Sixth Avenue itself is mainly tawdry shops and plastic eating-houses, but just the other side, across Father Demo Square and up Bleecker Street (until the 1970s an Italian open marketplace on this stretch, and still lined by a few Italian stores) are some of the Village's prettiest residential streets. Turn left on Leroy Street and cross over Seventh Avenue, where, confusingly, Leroy Street becomes St Luke's Place for a block. The houses here, dating from the 1850s, are among the city's most graceful, one of them (recognisable by the two lamps of honour at the bottom of the steps) the ex-residence of Jimmy Walker, mayor of New York in the twenties. Walker was for a time the most popular of mayors, a big spending, wise-cracking man who gave up his work as a songwriter for the world of politics, and lived an extravagant lifestyle that rarely kept him out of the gossip columns. Nothing if not shrewd, at a time when America had never been so prosperous, he for a time reflected people's most glamorous, big-living aspirations. He was, however, no match for the hard times to come, and once the 1930s Depression had taken hold he lost touch and – with it – office. South of Leroy Street, the Village fades slowly into the warehouse districts of SoHo and TriBeCa, a bleak area where nothing much stirs outside working hours, and the buildings are an odd mixture of Federal terraces juxtaposed against grubby-grey rolldown entranced packing houses. There's a neatly preserved row from the 1820s on Charlton Street; the area just to its north, Richmond Hill, was George Washington's HQ during the Revolution, later the home of Aaron Burr and John Jacob Astor. But those apart, you may just as well continue on up to Morton Street, which curves tranquilly round to Seventh Avenue a block north of St Luke's Place. Connecting with Seventh Avenue, Bedford Street, with Barrow and Commerce Streets nearby, is one of the quietest and most desirable Village addresses. Edna St Vincent Millay, the young poet and playwright who did much work with the Provincetown Playhouse, lived at no. 75½, said to be the narrowest house in the city, 9 feet wide and topped with a tiny gable. Another superlative: the clapboard structure next door claims fame as the oldest house in the Village, built in 1799, but much renovated since and probably worth a considerable fortune now.

Further up Bedford Street, past the former speakeasy Chumley's (see p.235), recognisable only by the metal grille on its door, is Grove Street. There, if you've time, peer into one of the neighbourhood's most typical and secluded little mews, Grove Court. Back on Seventh Avenue look out for Marie's Crisis Café (p.239), now a gay bar but once home to Thomas Paine, English by birth but perhaps *the* most important and radical thinker of the American revolutionary era, and from whose *Crisis Papers* the cafe takes its name. Paine was significantly involved in the Revolution, though afterwards regarded with suspicion by the government, especially after his active support for the French Revolution. By the time of his death here, in 1809, he had been condemned as an atheist and stripped of citizenship of the country he helped found. Grove Street meets Seventh Avenue at one of the Village's busiest junctions, **Sheridan Square** – not in fact a square at all unless you count Christopher Park's slim strip of green, but simply a wide and hazardous meeting (the Mousetrap, some call it) of several busy streets. **Christopher Street**, main artery of the west Village, leads off from here – traditional heartland of the city's gay community. The Square was named after one General Sheridan, cavalry commander in the Civil War, and holds a pompous-looking statue to his memory, but it's better known as scene of one of the worst and bloodiest of New York's Draft Riots, when a marauding mob assembled here in 1863 and attacked members of the black community. It's said that if it hadn't been for the protestations of local people they would have strung them up and worse; as it was they made off after sating the worst of their blood-lust.

Not dissimilar scenes occurred in 1969 when the gay community wasn't quite as established as it is now. The violence on this occasion was down to the police, who raided the **Stonewall gay bar** and started ejecting its occupants – for the local gay community the latest in a long line of petty harassments from the police. Spontaneously they decided to do something about it: word went round the other bars in the area, and before long the Stonewall was surrounded, resulting in a siege which lasted the best part of an hour and ended with several arrests and a number of injured policemen. Though hardly a victory for their rights, it was the first time that gay men had stood up *en masse* to the persecutions of the police, and as such represents a turning point in their struggle, formally instigating the Gay Rights movement and remembered still by the annual **Gay Pride march** (held on the anniversary of the riot, June 28th). Nowadays, too, the gay community is much more a part of Greenwich Village life, indeed for most the Village would seem odd without it, and from here down to the Hudson is a tight-knit enclave – focusing on Christopher Street – of bars, restaurants and bookshops used specifically, but not exclusively, by gay men. The scene on the Hudson itself, along and around West Street and the river piers, is considerably raunchier, and only for the really committed or curious (native New Yorkers, gay ones included, warn against going there at all), but this far east things crack off with the accent less on sex, more on a camp kind of humour. Among the more accessible gay bars, if you're strolling this quarter, are *The Monster* on Sheridan Square itself, *Marie's Crisis* on Grove Street (see above), and *Ty's*, further west on Christopher Street; for full gay listings, see p.238.

At the eastern end of Christopher Street is another of those car-buzzing, life-risking Village junctions where Sixth Avenue is met by **Greenwich Avenue**, one of the neighbourhood's major shopping streets. Hover for a while at the romantic Gothic bulk of the **Jefferson Market Courthouse**, voted fifth most beautiful building in America in 1885, and built with all the characteristic vigour of the age. It hasn't actually served as a courthouse for 40 odd years now, indeed at one time – like so many buildings in this city – it was branded for demolition. But it was saved thanks to the efforts of a few determined Villagers, and now lives out its days as the local library. Walk around behind for a better look, perhaps pondering for a moment on the fact that the adjacent well-tended allotment was, until 1974, the **Women's House of Detention**, a prison known for its abysmal conditions and numbering among its inmates Angela Davis. Look out, also, for **Patchin Place**, a tiny mews whose neat grey terraces are yet another Village literary landmark, home to e e cummings for many years and at various times also to John Masefield, the ubiquitous Dreiser and O'Neill and John Reed (who wrote *Ten Days that Shook the World* here).

Across the road, *Balducci's* forms a downtown alternative to its uptown deli rival, *Zabar's*, its stomach-tingling smells pricey but hard to resist. Nearby, **Bigelow's Pharmacy**, is possibly the city's oldest chemist and apparently little changed; and, south a block and left, **West 8th Street** is an occasionally rewarding strip of brash shoe shops and cut-price clothes stores. Up **West 10th Street** are some of the best preserved early 19C townhouses in the Village, and one of particular interest at **no.18**. The facade of this house, which juts anglewise into the street, had to be rebuilt after the terrorist Weathermen had been using the house as a bomb factory and one of their devices exploded. Three of the group were killed in the blast, but two others escaped and remained on the run until just a few years ago.

For anyone not yet sated on architecture, a couple of imposing churches are to be found by following 10th Street down as far as the Fifth Avenue stretch of the Village, where the neighbourhood's low-slung residential streets give on to some eminently desirable apartment blocks. On the corner stands the 19C **Church of the Ascension**, a small, light church built by Richard Upjohn (the Trinity Church architect), later redecorated by Stanford White and currently appealing desperately for funds to complete a much-needed restoration. Inside is a gracefully toned La Farge altarpiece and some fine stained glass but otherwise, unless the refurbishment is over, much of what you'll glimpse will be covered in brickdust and scaffolding. A block away, Joseph Wells's bulky, chocolatey-brown Gothic revival **First Presbyterian Church** is decidedly less attractive than Upjohn's structure, less soaring, heavier, and in every way more sober, with a tower said to have been modelled on the one at Magdalen College Oxford. To look inside, you need to enter through the discreetly added Church House (ring the bell for attention if the door's locked). Afterwards you're just a few steps away from the pin-neat prettiness of **Washington Mews**.

BARS *Badlands* (gay), *Be-Bop Café*, *Boots and Saddles* (gay), *Cedar Tavern*, *Chumley's*, *The Cubbyhole* (women's/lesbian), *Fifty Five*, *Garbo's* (women's/lesbian), *The Grove Club* (women's/lesbian), *Lion's Head*, *Marie's Crisis* (gay), *The Monster* (gay), *Peculiar Pub*, *Revolution*, *Ty's* (gay), *White Horse Tavern*,

RESTAURANTS Cheap *BBQ, Burger Boys of Brooklyn, Carmella's Garden Village, Cottonwood Café, The Front Porch, Jimmy Day's, Little Mushroom Café, Riviera Café, Triumph Restaurant, VG Restaurant, Waverley Restaurant*; **American and Mexican** *Betty Brown's Broadway Diner, Caramba, The Sazerac House*; **Chinese** *Szechuan Taste*; **Fish** *Janice's Fish Place*; **French** *Chez Brigitte*; **Indian and Middle Eastern** *Mitali West, Pitaria*; **Italian** *Arturo's Pizza, Cucina Stagionale, John's Pizzeria,Pizzeria Uno, Ray's Pizza, Trattoria Alfredo*; **Spanish and Greek** *Café Espanol, Granados, Original Souvlaki Restaurant*; **Vegetarian** *Arnold's Turtle, Bitable, Boostan, Eva's, Macie's Mad Dog Café.*

THE EAST VILLAGE

The **EAST VILLAGE** is quite different in look, feel and tempo to its western counterpart, Greenwich Village. Once, like the Lower East Side proper which it abuts, a refuge of immigrants and always a solidly working-class area, it became home to New York's non-conformist fringe in the earlier part of this century when, disenchanted and impoverished by rising rents and encroaching tourism, they left the city's traditional Bohemia and set up house here. Today the differences persist: where Greenwich Village is the home of Off-Broadway, the East Village plays stage to Off-Off; Tompkins Square Park is a more sinister rectangle of green than Washington Square could ever be, prowled by dispossessed residents rather than cheerful dope-dealers and tourists; and rents, while rising fast as the district becomes trendier and more sanitised, are said to be about a third of what you'll pay further west.

The East Village has seen its share of famous artists, politicos and literati: W. H. Auden lived at 77 St Mark's Place, the neighbourhood's main street, and from the same building the Communist Journal *Novy Mir* was run, numbering among its more historic contributors Leon Trotsky, who lived for a brief time in New York. Much later the East Village became the New York haunt of the Beats – Kerouac, Burroughs, Ginsberg *et al*, who, when not jumping trains across the rest of the country, would get together at Alan Ginsberg's house on East 7th Street for declamatory poetry readings and drunken shareouts of experience. Later, Andy Warhol debuted the Velvet Underground; the Fillmore East played host to just about every band you've ever heard of – and forgotten about; and, more recently, Richard Hell noisily proclaimed himself the inventor of punk rock. One thing the East Village has never been short of is movements...

That's not to say things are the same now as they were, and sadly, perhaps inevitably, a lot has changed over the last decade or so. Escalating rents have forced many people out and although the art scene is flourishing, if you're looking for a hotbed of dissidence and creativity you'd probably do better to look elsewhere – say, downtown in TriBeCa. But St Mark's Place is still vibrant, it's still fun, and if the thrift shops and panhandlers and political hustlers have given way to a range of ritzy boutiques selling punk chic, it remains one of the city's most vital and exciting enclaves.

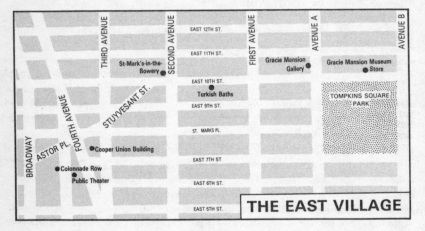

THE EAST VILLAGE

To explore the East Village best use **St Mark's Place** as a base and branch out from there. Start at the western, more peopled end, between Second and Third Avenues, where radical bookstores compete for space with offbeat clothiers, and, just beyond, young self-proclaimed priests of funky Manhattan chic mill around sucking on pizzas or gazing lazily at the mildewed items for sale at the unofficial flea market across the road on **Cooper Square**. This, a busy crossroads formed by the intersection of the Bowery, Third Avenue and Lafayette Street, is dominated by the 7-storey brownstone mass of the **Cooper Union Building**, erected in 1859 by a wealthy industrialist as a college for the poor, and the first New York structure to be hung on a frame of iron girders. It's best known as the place where, in 1860, Abraham Lincoln wowed an audience of top New Yorkers with his so-called 'might makes right' speech, in which he boldly criticised the pro-slavery policies of the southern states and helped propel himself to the White House later that year. For all its history, however, the Cooper Union remains a working college, recently and sensitively restored to 19C glory with a statue of the benevolent Cooper just in front.

Just beyond, feeding through to Broadway, is **Astor Place**, named after **John Jacob Astor** and, for a very brief few years, just before high society moved west to Washington Square, one of the city's most desirable neighbourhoods. In the 1830s Lafayette Street in particular was home to the city's wealthiest names, not least John Jacob, one of New York's most hideously greedy tycoons, notorious for having won his enormous fortune by deceiving everybody right up to the President. When old and sick in his house here – no mean affair by all accounts but long since destroyed – it's said that although so weak he could accept no nourishment except a mother's milk, and so fat he had to be tossed up and down in a blanket for exercise, his greed for money was such that he lay and dispatched servants daily to collect his rents.

It's hard to believe this was once the home of money and influence, though, for today **Lafayette Street** is an undistinguished sort of thoroughfare, steering a grimy route through the no-man's land between the East Village and, further down, SoHo. All that's left to hint that this might once have been more than a down-at-heel gathering of industrial buildings is **Colonnade Row**, a terrace of four monumental houses, now home to the Colonnade Theater. Opposite, the stocky brownstone and brick building is Joseph Papp's **Public Theater**, something of a legend as forerunner of Off-Broadway theatre, and original venue of hit musicals like *Hair* and *A Chorus Line* and still run by the man who pioneered Shakespeare in the Park (see p.271). From the Public Theater you can either follow Lafayette Street down to Chinatown, or cut down Astor Place, past the trendy **Astor Place Haircutters** where people queue ten deep in the street, and turn right into Broadway. Two minutes away, the **corner of Washington Place and Greene Street** is significant. It was here in 1911 that one of the city's most notorious sweatshops burned to the ground, killing about 150 women workers and spurring the state to institute laws forcing employers to take account of their workers' safety. Even now, though, there are sweatshops in New York in which safety conditions are probably little better.

Back on Broadway, look north and the lacy marble of **Grace Church** fills a bend in the street, built and designed in 1846 by James Renwick (of St Patrick's Cathedral fame) in a delicate Neo-Gothic style. Dark and aisled, with a flattened, web-vaulted ceiling, it's one of the city's most successful churches – and, in many ways, one of its most secretive escapes. Walk east from here cross back over Third Avenue. and you come to another, quite different church: **St Mark's-in-the-Bowery**, a box-like structure originally built in 1799 but with a neo-Classical portico added half a century later. In the 1950s the Beat poets gave readings here, and it remains an important literary rendezvous with regular readings and music recitals, as well as a traditional gathering point for the city's down-and-outs, desperately hanging on to their can collections, (passport to a frugal meal that night), or slumped half-dead on drugs.

Cross Second Avenue, on this stretch lined with Polish and Ukranian restaurants, and you're on **10th Street**, heart of the **East Village art scene** and in many ways now the New York City art business itself. Here there's plenty for sale for a few hundred dollars, and, compared to SoHo, there's a lot more worth buying – though you may have to wade through a sea of dross to find it. This will of course change, and as the East Village grows more upmarket so its art will doubtless become less exciting. But for the moment at least, the East Village art scene is recent, real and vigorous, 10th Street lined with small galleries with names like *Area X*, *Nature Mort* and *PPOW* selling work by mainly local artists. See p.229 for a full rundown.

Follow 10th Street east, past the old redbrick **Tenth Street Turkish Baths**, its steam and massage services active back into the last century, and you will reach Avenue A, Tompkins Square, and what is in effect the eastern fringe of the East Village. **Tompkins Square Park**, the woody dungeon which fills the central part of the square, isn't one of the city's most inviting spaces, but has long acted as focus for the Lower East Side/East Village community and its reputation as the city's centre for political demonstrations and home of radical thought. It was here in 1874 that the police massacred a crowd of workers protesting against unemployment, and here too in the 1960s that protests were organised and made themselves heard. The Yippie leader Abbie Hoffman lived nearby, and it's residents like him, along with many incidents in the square and down St Mark's Place (which joins the square on its west side), that have given the East Village its maverick name.

Just off the north-west corner of Tompkins Square, beyond 10th Street, is **Gracie Mansion Gallery**, one of the East Village's better-known galleries, run by the woman who took her name from the mayor's official residence and began by exhibiting work in her bathroom. Whatever's on when you're here, look inside for a glance at Frank O'Hara's **poem**, which winds itself around the top of each wall, whispering fondly of the days of the East Village Beat Scene. Still on 10th Street and facing the north side of the square is the **Greathouse Gallery** with a fine and funky sculpture garden ringed by gutted tenements. Next door the **Gracie Mansion Museum Store** sells small-scale original works from across the country, and for those pockets not quite up to the heady world of art collecting, a bright assemblage of earrings, trinkets and t-shirts.

BARS *Boy Bar* (gay), *Dan Lynch's* (music), *Downtown Beirut* (music), *Grassroots Tavern*, *Girl Bar* (women's/lesbian), *Holiday Cocktail Lounge*, *McSorley's*, *The Bar* (gay).

RESTAURANTS **Cheap** *Around the Clock*, *Astor Riviera*, *Kiev*. *La Ociandia di Giotto*, *Life Café*, *103 2nd*, *Phebe's*, *Rapid Algebra*; **East European** *Christine's*, *Jolanta*, *KK*, *Odessa*, *Ukrainian*, *Veselka*; **Fish** *Hisae's Place*; **Indian and Middle Eastern** *Caffe Kabul*, *Pita Cuisine*, *Mitali*, *Purborag*; **Italian** *Daro Café*; **Japanese** *Dojo*, *Hisae's Place*; **Spanish** *National Café*; **Vegetarian** *Dojo*, *Spring Street Natural Restaurant*

THE LOWER EAST SIDE

I don't wanna be buried in Puerto Rico
I don't wanna rest in Long Island cemetery
I wanna be near the stabbing shooting
gambling fighting and unnatural dying
and new birth crying
So please when I die...
Keep me nearby
Take my ashes and scatter them thru out
the Lower East Side...

Miguel Piñero *A Lower East Side Poem*

The **LOWER EAST SIDE** is one of Manhattan's least changed and most unalluring downtown neighbourhoods, a little-known quarter which began life towards the end of the last century as an insular slum for over half a million Jewish immigrants. They came here from Eastern Europe via Ellis Island, refugees in search of a better life, scratching out a living in a free-for-all of crowded, sweatshop competition. Since then the area has become considerably depopulated, and the slum-dwellers are now Puerto Rican rather than Jewish, but otherwise, at least on the surface, little has visibly changed.

The area's lank brick tenements, ribbed with blackened fire escapes and housing rundown bargain basements, must have seemed a bleak kind of pot of gold for those who saw themselves at the end of their rainbow, crammed into a district which daily became more densely populated, and where low standards of hygiene and abysmal housing made disease rife and life expectancy horribly low. It was conditions like these which spurred local residents like Jacob Riis and, later, Stephen Crane, to record the plight of the city's immigrants in their writings and photographs, thereby spawning not only a whole school of realistic writing but also some notable social reforms. Not for nothing – and not without some degree of success – did the Lower East Side become known as a neighbourhood where political battles were fought.

Today the Lower East Side splits neatly into two distinct parts. **South of East Houston Street** is the most respectable: wholesomely seedy and much of it still firmly Jewish. **North of East Houston** is part trendy Bohemia, abutting the East Village, but for the rest predominantly ruined and derelict, its houses either boarded up or serving as slum residences for the local Puerto Rican population.

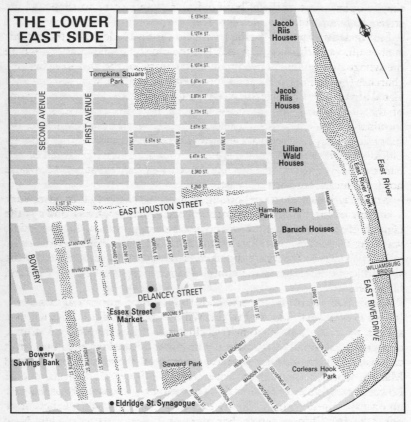

South of Houston

This is the most explorable part of the Lower East Side – and the more rewarding. In the streets south of Houston, the Jewish immigrants indelibly stamped their character, with their own shops, delis, restaurants, synagogues and, latterly, community centres. Even now, with a broader ethnic mix, it feels uniquely Jewish and a place apart from the rest of

Manhattan: geographically isolated, too, set out on the island's heel and served by few subway stations. If outsiders come here at all it's for the **bargain shopping**. You can get just about anything at cut-price in the stores down here: clothes on Orchard Street, lamps and shades on the Bowery, ties and shirts on Allen Street, underwear and hosiery on Grand Street, textiles on Eldridge. And, whatever you're buying, people will if necessary still haggle down to the last cent. The time to come is **Sunday morning**, for the **Orchard Street Market**, when you'll catch the vibrancy of the Lower East Side at its best. Weekdays the stores are still there, and they're open, most of them, but far fewer people come to shop and the streets have a forbidding, desolate feel.

East Broadway used to be the Jewish Lower East Side's hub, though this is now almost exclusively Chinese. For the old feel of the quarter – where the synagogues remain active (many in the north of the area have become churches for the Puerto Ricans) – best explore north of here, starting with **Canal Street. The Eldridge Street Synagogue** is worth a look: in its day one of the neighbourhood's grandest, though now the main doors of its formidable facade have been sealed shut and only the basement left for the sporadic get-togethers of a much-dwindled congregation. Carry on up Eldridge Street, though, and there is a little more activity: **Grand Street**, particularly, is lined with shops like the **Kossars Bakery**, at no.367, whose hot fresh *bialys* are hard to resist.

Grand leads east, through housing projects to the messy **East River Park** – not one of the city's most attractive open spaces. Halfway down is the **Church of St Mary**, elderly Jewish couples sitting on the benches outside, watching the world go by. The church bills itself as the oldest Neo-Gothic building (1832) in the city, a dignified claim somewhat diminished by the sign adjacent, advertising the church's current crowd-puller of weekend bingo sessions.

Essex Street, north from here, leads to **Delancey**, horizontal axis of the Jewish Lower East Side, and to the **Williamsburg Bridge** – adopted as a shelter by New York's homeless, clustered below around oil drums, emerging occasionally to browbeat a motorist into risking their makeshift carwashes. Either side of Delancey sprawls the **Essex Street Covered Market**, worth a quick peep, with *Ratner's Dairy Restaurant*, one of Lower East Side's most famous dairy restaurants, across the road. Further up on Essex is the exotic culinary experience of *Bernstein's*, believe it or not, a kosher Chinese eatery. For more on Lower East Side – and New York – Jewish eating, see p.251.

The atmosphere changes abruptly east of Essex Street. Here the inhabitants are mainly Puerto Rican, and the language spoken pre dominantly Spanish – the Jews having got rich long ago and moved into middle-income housing further uptown or in the other boroughs. **Clinton Street**, a mass of cheap Hispanic retailers, restaurants and travel agents, is in many ways the central thoroughfare of the Puerto Rican Lower East Side. Otherwise, if you are here on a Sunday, check out the free wine tours and tastings at **Schapiro's Winery** at 124 Rivington Street (11am-4pm, on the hour), the neighbourhood's – and probably the city's – only kosher wine and spirits warehouse where wine is made on the premises. Afterwards, head over to **Orchard Street**, again best on a Sunday when most of it becomes pedestrianised and filled with stalls selling off designer togs for hefty discounts. The rooms above the stores here used to house sweatshops, clothes factories so called since whatever the weather a stove had to be kept warm all the time for pressing the clothes when completed. The (reformed) garment industry moved uptown ages ago, but the buildings are little more salubrious now, slummy apartments at the end of dank unlit hallways occupied by poor, again mainly Hispanic, families. At the top end of Orchard, East Houston Street forms the northern border of this part of the Lower East Side.

Walk east from here and it's for the most part burnt-out tenements interspersed with a scattering of Spanish-style grocery stores; to the west things aren't much better. **Bowery** spears north out of Chinatown as far as Cooper Square on the edge of the East Village. This wide thoroughfare has gone through many changes over the years: it took its name from 'Bouwerie', the Dutch word for farm, when it was the city's main agricultural supplier; later, in the closing decades of the last century, it was flanked by music halls, theatres, hotels and middle-market restaurants, drawing people from all parts of Manhattan. Currently it's a skid row for the city's drunk and derelict, flanked by a long and demoralising line of boarded-up shops and SRO hotels near which few New Yorkers venture of their own accord. If you do, it may be intimidating and uneasy, but rarely dangerous – the people who crash down here are mostly long past acts of physical violence. The one – bizarre – focus, certainly a must for any Lower East Side wanderings, is the **Bowery Savings Bank** on the corner of Grand Street. Designed by Stanford White in 1894, it rises out of the neighbourhood's debris like a god, much as its sister bank on 42nd Street, a shrine to the virtue of saving money. Inside, the original carved cheque writing stands are still in place, and the coffered ceiling, together with White's great gilded fake marble columns, couldn't create a more potent feel of security. An inscription above the door as you exit leaves you in no doubt: 'Your financial welfare is the business of this bank.' Quite so, but back on the Bowery, stepping over the drunks and avoiding the pan-handlers, you can't help pondering what went wrong.

North of Houston

Cross East Houston Street and the Lower East Side takes on another different mantle, veering from downbeat (but trendy) Tompkins Square and the East Village to, further east and in marked contrast, what ranks as one of the most serious and unchecked pieces of urban blight in Manhattan. Here the island bulges out beyond the city's grid structure, the extra avenues being named A to D, and the area, by its devotees, **Alphabet City** (*Loisada* to the Puerto Ricans). Until a very few years ago, this was a notoriously unsafe corner of town, run by drug pushers and the hoodlums that controlled them. People told of cars queuing up for fixes in the street, and the terraces here were well-known safehouses for a brisk and businesslike heroin trade. All of this was brought to a halt in 1983 with *Operation Pressure Point*, a massive police campaign to clean up the area and make it a place where people would want to live. Which has to some extent happened, with crime figures radically down, although appearances remain much the same: the people who live here are poor Puerto Ricans; their houses, what's left of them, bombed-out shells amid fields of flattened rubble, next to which gangs of tramps have erected makeshift shelters. Half the houses aren't lived in at all, and many are plastered with graffiti protesting their misuse ('Property of the People of the Lower East Side', some say), while over on Avenue D posses of blacks and Puerto Ricans idle the day away outside grimy Spanish cafés.

Come down here and you'll certainly get hassled, but – during the day at least – you're unlikely to be mugged. And it's worth a quick circuit around this part of the Lower East Side just to see how bad things can get through lack of effective city money or control. Oddly enough it's also the best illustration of the absurdity of the Manhattan housing issue: here there is astounding poverty, filth, neglect, even danger. Yet the area is on the verge of a huge gentrification, and its apartments, though they may be next door to some rat-infested ruin, are going for ever-rocketing rents. What Alphabet City offers the average yuppie is hard to imagine, but it's well on its way up in the world nonetheless. There is, however, a long way to go – and for the moment, it's a lot more than four blocks from Avenue D to St Mark's Place...

RESTAURANTS Jewish *Bernstein-on-Essex, Katz's Deli, Ratner's, Sammy's Roumanian Restaurant, Yonah Schimmel's.*

Chapter two
MIDTOWN MANHATTAN

You're likely to spend a fair amount of time in **MIDTOWN MANHATTAN**. It's here most of the city's hotels are situated, here too that you'll arrive — at Penn or Grand Central Station or the Port Authority. And the area is in many ways the city's centre. Cutting through its heart is **Fifth Avenue**, New York's most glamorous (and most expensive) street, with the theatre strip of **Broadway**, an increasingly disreputable neighbour, just to its west.

The character of Midtown undergoes a rapid and radical transformation depending on which side of Fifth you find yourself. **East** are the corporate businesses, a skyward wave that creates Manhattan's rollercoaster appearance. If you've any interest in architecture (or simply sensation) you'll want to stroll this sector, looking in and up at such delights as the **Chrysler**, **Citicorp** and **Seagram Buildings** and the magnificent **Rockefeller Center**. **Fifth Avenue** itself, and its fashion-orientated counterpart, **Madison**, should be experienced too, if only to take measure of how much wealth a large number of Americans have accrued. And of course this is also a big museum strip, with the **Museum of Modern Art** and a host of lesser collections grouped together on **53rd Street** (see p.176 for accounts of these).

West of Fifth Avenue, and in particular west of Broadway, the area takes a dive — both in status and interest. The **theatre districts** are a natural entertainments focus, though these days more than a little sleazy, especially around **Times Square**. The **Garment District** has a certain throwback interest as a 19C foil to the corporate skyscrapers across the way — and a startling nearby landmark in the **Empire State Building**. However, the residential districts are frankly dull: **Chelsea** is long established but downbeat, **Clinton**, further up the west side, is gentrifying slowly but remains more than a little rough down by the West Side Highway; and **Murray Hill**, on the other side of town, has little to offer beyond some semi-elegant brownstones.

FIFTH AVENUE AND EAST: UNION SQUARE TO 42ND STREET

Downtown Manhattan ends with 14th Street, which slices across the island from the housing projects of the east side to the cut-price shops and eventually the meat-packing warehouses on the banks of the Hudson. In the middle, where Broadway and Fifth meet, is **Union Square**, one-time elegant centre of the city's theatrical and shopping scene (*May's* department store remains on the southern side), better known more recently as gathering-point for political demonstrations. Up until a couple of years ago this was a seedy haunt of dope pushing and street violence, but it's more inviting now, the spill of shallow steps enticing you in to stroll the paths, feed the squirrels, and gaze at its array of statuary — something no one would have dared do a couple of years back. As for the statues, they include an equestrian figure of *George Washington*, a *Lafayette* by Bartholdi (more famous for the Statue of Liberty) and, at the centre of the park, a massive *flagstaff base* whose bas-reliefs symbolise the forces of Good and Evil in the Revolution.

The square itself is flanked by quite a mixture of buildings, not least the **American Savings Bank** on the eastern edge, of which only the grandiose columned exterior survives. But it's the **Consolidated Edison** structure which dominates, its campanile an odd premonition of the Metropolitan Life Building a few blocks further north. Inside the Con Edison Building (HQ of the company responsible for providing the city with energy and those famous steaming manholes) there's a museum devoted to the city's power supplies through the ages: strictly for energy buffs, if such people exist...

The stretch of **Broadway** north of here was known once as 'Ladies' Mile' for its fancy stores and boutiques (*Lord and Taylor* started trading here), but notwithstanding a few sculpted facades and curvy lintels, it's now hard to imagine as an upmarket shopping mall. Turn right on East 20th Street for **Theodore Roosevelt's Birthplace** or at least a reconstruction of it: a rather grim brownstone mansion that's not at all exciting, just a few rooms with their original furnishings, some of Teddy's hunting trophies and a small gallery documenting the President's life. If you're mildly interested, the obligatory guided tour costs little enough.

Past here Manhattan's clutter breaks into the ordered open space of **Gramercy Park**, a former swamp reclaimed in 1831. Residential London in spirit, this is one of the city's best squares, its centre clean, tidily planted and, most noticeably, completely empty for much of the day — principally because the only people who can gain access are those rich or fortunate enough to live here. To the east **Peter Cooper Village** and **Stuyvesant Town** are perhaps the city's most successful examples of dense-packed

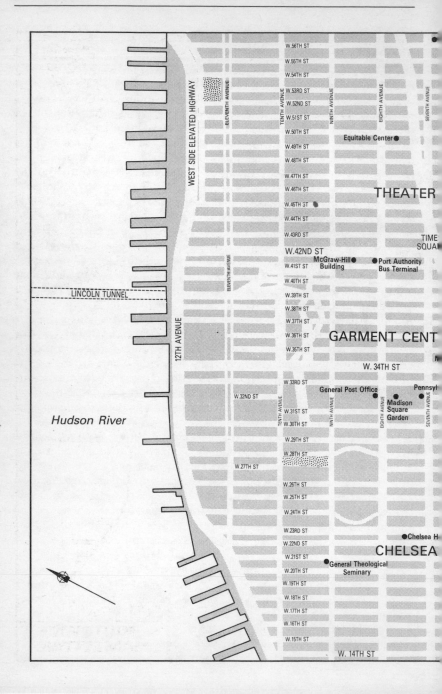

WEST SIDE ELEVATED HIGHWAY

ELEVENTH AVENUE

TENTH AVENUE

NINTH AVENUE

EIGHTH AVENUE

SEVENTH AVENUE

W.56TH ST
W.55TH ST
W.54TH ST
W.53RD ST
W.52ND ST
W.51ST ST
W.50TH ST

Equitable Center●

W.49TH ST
W.48TH ST
W.47TH ST
W.46TH ST
W.45TH ST ●
W.44TH ST
W.43RD ST

THEATER

TIME
SQUA

W.42ND ST

ELEVENTH AVENUE

W.41ST ST   McGraw-Hill● ●Port Authority
Building   Bus Terminal

W.40TH ST
W.39TH ST
W.38TH ST
W.37TH ST
W.36TH ST
W.35TH ST

GARMENT CENT

LINCOLN TUNNEL

12TH AVENUE

W. 34TH ST

W.33RD ST

General Post Office●   Pennsyl

W.32ND ST

TENTH AVENUE

NINTH AVENUE

EIGHTH AVENUE

SEVENTH AVENUE

W.31ST ST   ●Madison
W.30TH ST   Square
                  Garden

Hudson River

W.29TH ST
W.28TH ST
W.27TH ST
W.26TH ST
W.25TH ST
W.24TH ST
W.23RD ST

●Chelsea H

W.22ND ST
W.21ST ST

CHELSEA

W.20TH ST   ●General Theological
              Seminary

W.19TH ST
W.18TH ST
W.17TH ST
W.16TH ST
W.15TH ST

W. 14TH ST

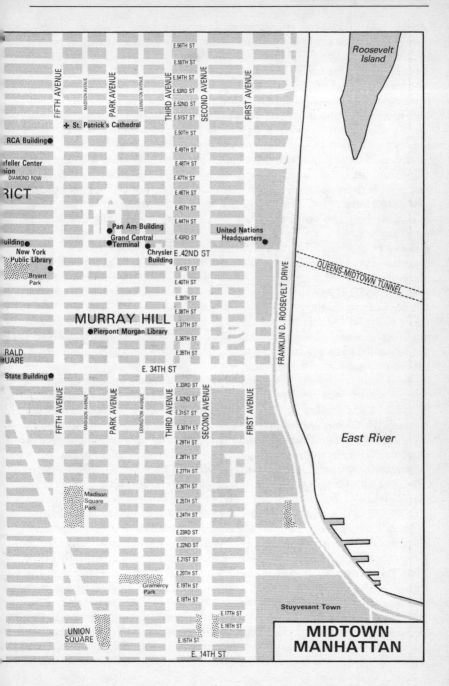

Roosevelt Island

E.56TH ST
E.55TH ST
E.54TH ST
E.53RD ST
E.52ND ST
E.51ST ST
E.50TH ST
E.49TH ST
E.48TH ST
E.47TH ST
E.46TH ST
E.45TH ST
E.44TH ST
E.43RD ST
E.42ND ST
E.41ST ST
E.40TH ST
E.39TH ST
E.38TH ST
E.37TH ST
E.36TH ST
E.35TH ST
E. 34TH ST
E.23RD ST
E.32ND ST
E.31ST ST
E.30TH ST
E.29TH ST
E.28TH ST
E.27TH ST
E.26TH ST
E.25TH ST
E.24TH ST
E.23RD ST
E.22ND ST
E.21ST ST
E.20TH ST
E.19TH ST
E.18TH ST
E.17TH ST
E.16TH ST
E.15TH ST
E. 14TH ST

FIFTH AVENUE
MADISON AVENUE
PARK AVENUE
LEXINGTON AVENUE
THIRD AVENUE
SECOND AVENUE
FIRST AVENUE

St. Patrick's Cathedral

RCA Building
efeller Center
sion
DIAMOND ROW

RICT

uilding
New York
Public Library
Bryant
Park

Pan Am Building
Grand Central
Terminal
Chrysler
Building

United Nations
Headquarters

FRANKLIN D. ROOSEVELT DRIVE

QUEENS MIDTOWN TUNNEL

MURRAY HILL
Pierpont Morgan Library

RALD
UARE

State Building

East River

Madison
Square
Park

Gramercy
Park

UNION
SQUARE

Stuyvesant Town

MIDTOWN MANHATTAN

urban housing, their tall, angled apartment blocks siding peaceful tree-lined walkways. It's worth knowing, though, that this is private not public housing, and the owners, Metropolitan Life, were accused of operating a colour-bar when the projects first opened. Certainly, the contrast with the immigrant slums a little way downtown isn't hard to detect... A block over, the land that makes up **Stuyvesant Square**, was a gift to the city from its governor and, like Gramercy Park, the park space in the middle was modelled on the squares of London's Bloomsbury. Though partially framed by the buildings of **Beth Israel Medical Center** and cut down the middle by the bustle of Second Avenue, it still retains something of its secluded quality, especially on the western side. Here there's a smatter of elegant terrace, the strangely colonial-looking **Friends Meeting House**, and, next door, the weighty brownstone **Church of St George** – best known as the place where financier J.P. Morgan used to worship.

Lexington Avenue begins its long journey north from Gramercy Park, past the lumbering **69th Regiment Armory** – site in 1913 of the notorious *Armory Show* which brought modern art to New York for the first time (see p.356) – to Manhattan's most condensed ethnic enclave, **Little India**. Blink, and you might miss this altogether: most of New York's 100,000 Indians live in Queens and all that's here is a handful of restaurants and fast-food places – far out-numbered by those down on East 6th Street – and a pocket of sweet and spice stores (*Kalyustan's*, on the east side of the street, is a good one).

Broadway and Fifth Avenue meet at **Madison Square**, by day a maelstrom of dodging cars and cabs, buses and pedestrians but, mainly because of the quality of the buildings and the clever park-space in the middle, with a monumentality and neat seclusion that Union Square has long since lost. The **Flatiron Building**, set cheekily on a triangular plot of land on the square's southern side, was (hard to believe now) the city's first true skyscraper, hung on a steel frame in 1902 with its full 20 storeys dwarfing all the other structures around. Not for long though: the **Metropolitan Life Company** soon erected their clock tower on the eastern side of the square which put, height-wise at least, the Flatiron to shame.

Next door is the corinthian columned marble facade of the **Appellate Division** of the NYS Supreme Court, resolutely righteous with its statues of Justice, Wisdom and Peace turning their weary backs on the ugly black glass New York Life Annexe behind. The grand structure behind that, the **New York Life Building** proper, was the work of Cass Gilbert, creator of the Woolworth Tower downtown. It went up in 1928 on the site of the original **Madison Square Garden** – renowned scene of drunken and debauched revels of high and Broadway society. This was the heart of the theatre district in those days and the place where the Garden's architect, Stanford White, was murdered by Harry Thaw. White was something of

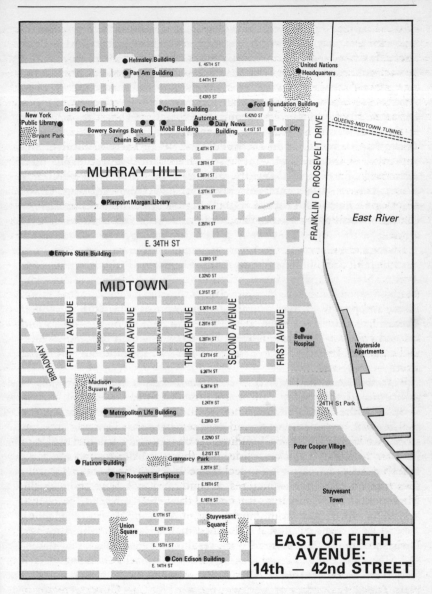

EAST OF FIFTH
AVENUE:
14th — 42nd STREET

a rake by all accounts, with a reputation for womanising and fast living, and his affair with Thaw's wife Evelyn Nesbit, a Broadway showgirl, had been well publicised – even to the extent that the naked statue of the goddess Diana on the top of the building was said to have been modelled on her. Millionaire Thaw was so humiliated by this that one night he burst into the roof garden, found White, surrounded as usual by doting women and admirers, and shot him through the head. Thaw was carted away to spend the rest of his life in mental institutions, and his wife's showbusiness career took a tumble: she resorted to drugs and prostitution somewhere in Central America.

So ended one of Madison Square's more dramatic episodes. Madison Square Garden has moved twice since then, first to a site on Eighth Avenue and 50th Street, finally to its present location in a hideous drum-shaped eyesore on the corner of 32nd Street. There is, however, one reminder of the time when this was New York's theatreland – the **Episcopal Church of the Transfiguration** just off Fifth Avenue on 29th Street. This, a dinky rusticated church set back from the street, brown brick and topped with copper roofs, has since 1870 been the traditional place of worship of showbiz people. It was tagged with the name 'The Little Church Around the Corner' after a devout but understanding priest from a nearby church had refused to marry a theatrical couple and sent them here. It's an intimate building, furnished throughout in warm wood and with the figures of famous actors (most notably Edwin Booth as Hamlet) memorialised in the stained glass. Further up Fifth is New York's prime **shopping territory**, home to most of the city's heavyweight department stores. *Macy's* is just a short stroll away on Herald Square; the old *Ohrbach's* building cowers beneath the bulk of the Empire State Building on 34th Street; opposite, there's *Altman's*, more upmarket and faintly stuffy; and, further up, filling the space between 38th and 39th Streets, the lavish headquarters of *Lord and Taylor* (for all of which see *Shopping*, p.210).

The **Empire State Building** – overshadowing by far the lure of such consumer items – occupies what has always been a prime site. Before it appeared this was home to the first Waldorf Astoria Hotel, built by William Waldorf Astor as a ruse to humiliate his formidable aunt, Caroline Schemmerhorn, into moving uptown. The hotel opened in 1893 and immediately became focus for city's rich – in an era, the 'Gay Nineties', when 'Meet me at the Waldorf' was the catchphrase to conjure with.* However, though the reputation of the Waldorf – at least for its prices – endures to this day, it didn't remain in its initial premises for very long, moving in 1929 to its current Art Deco home on Park Avenue.

---

*It was the consort of Mrs Schemmerhorn Astor, Ward Macallister, who coined the label 'The Four Hundred' to describe this lot. 'There are only about 400 people in fashionable New York society.' he asserted. 'If you go outside that number you strike people who are either not at ease in a ballroom or else make other people not at ease. See the point?'

Few would dispute the elegance of what took its place. The Empire State Building remains easily the most potent and evocative symbol of New York, and has done since its completion in 1931 – well under budget and after just two years in the making. Soon after, King Kong clung to it and distressed squealing damsels while nonchalantly grabbing at passing planes; in 1945 a plane crashed into the building's 79th storey; and most recently two Englishmen parachuted from its summit to the ground, only to be carted off by the NY police department for disturbing the peace. Its 102 storeys and 1472 feet – toe to TV mast – make it the world's third tallest building, but the height is deceptive, rising in stately tiers with steady panache. Inside, its basement serves as an underground marbled shopping precinct, lined with newstands, beauty parlours, cafés, even a post office, and is finished everywhere with delicate deco touches. After wandering around you can visit the *Guinness World of Records Exhibition* – though, frankly, you'd be better advised to save your money for the assault on the top of the tower.

The first lift, alarmingly old and rickety if you've previously zoomed to the top of the World Trade Center, takes you to the 86th floor, summit of the building before the radio and TV mast was added. The views from the outside walkways here are as stunning as you'd expect – better than the Trade Center since Manhattan spreads on all sides. On a clear day visibility is up to 80 miles, but given the city's pollution, on most it's more likely to be between 10 and 20. If you're feeling brave, and can stand the queues for the small single lift, go up to the Empire State's last reachable zenith, a small cylinder at the foot of the TV mast which was added as part of a hare-brained scheme to erect a mooring post for airships – a plan subsequently abandoned after some local VIPs almost got swept away by the wind. You can't go outside and the extra 16 storeys don't really add a great deal to the view, but you will have been to the top. (Daily 9.30am-midnight; $3)

Back down to earth, Fifth Avenue carves its way up the island. East down 34th Street lies **MURRAY HILL**, a tenuously tagged residential area of statuesque canopy-fronted apartment buildings, but with little apart from its WASPish anonymity to mark it out from the rest of midtown Manhattan. Like Chelsea further west, it lacks any real centre, any sense of community, and unless you work, live or are staying in Murray Hill, there's little reason to go there at all; indeed you're more likely to pass through without even realising it. Its boundaries are indistinct, but most agree they lie somewhere between Fifth Avenue and Third and, very roughly, 32nd to 40th Street, where begins the rather brasher commercialism of the midtown office block district.

When Madison Avenue was on a par with Fifth as *the* place to live, Murray Hill came to be dominated by the Morgans, the crusty old financier J.P. and his offspring, who at one time owned a clutch of property here. Morgan junior lived in the **brownstone** on the corner of 37th Street and Madison (now HQ of the American Lutheran Church), his father in a house which was later pulled down to make way for an extension to his **library** next door, the mock but tastefully simple Roman villa that still stands and is commonly mistaken for the old man's house. (If you've read the book or seen the film *Ragtime*, you'll remember that Coalhouse Walker made this fundamental mistake when attempting to hold Piermont Morgan hostage.) In fact, Morgan would simply come here to languish amongst the art treasures he had bought up wholesale on his trips to Europe: manuscripts, paintings, prints and furniture. Here during a crisis of confidence in the city's banking system in 1907, he entertained New York's richest and most influential men night after night until they agreed to put up the money to save what could have been the entire country from bankruptcy, giving up $30 million himself as an act of good faith. You can visit the library's splended interior and priceless collection; see p.201.

As you continue up Madison Avenue the influence of the Morgans rears its head again in the shape (or at least the name) of **Morgan's Hotel** between 37th and 38th Streets – founded and run by Steve Rubell, who made his pile out of Studio 54 and then went to prison for tax evasion. With the Palladium downtown (p.266) the hotel is Rubell's latest venture, last word in ostentatious discretion, not even bothering to proclaim its presence with the vulgarity of a sign. Look in on its elegant bar for a drink if you've got the cash, and for details on how much it costs to sleep here, see p.56.

East 42nd Street

After Morgan's you've more or less exhausted Murray Hill, so follow 38th Street back to Fifth Avenue and turn north. Before long you're standing on the corner of **42ND STREET**, one of the few streets in the world to have an entire musical named after it. With good reason too, for you *can* do anything on 42nd Street, highbrow or low, and it's also home to some of the city's most characteristic buildings, ranging from great Beaux Arts palaces like Grand Central Station to vulgar chargecard traps like the Grand Hyatt Hotel.

The **New York Public Library** (Central Research Library) on the corner of 42nd and Fifth is the first notable building on 42nd Street's eastern reaches: Beaux Arts in style and faced with white marble, its steps acting as a meeting point and general hangout for pockets of people throughout the year. To tour the library either walk around yourself or take one of the regular *tours* (Monday-Saturday at 11am and 2pm) which are free, last an hour and give a good all-round picture of the building. The main thing to see is the large coffered *Reading Room* at the back of the building. Trotsky worked here on and off during his brief sojourn in New

York just prior to the 1917 Revoution, introduced to the place by his friend Bukharin, who was bowled over by a library you could use so late in the evening. The opening times are considerably less impressive now, but the library still boasts a collection among the five largest in the world, stored in eight levels beneath this room, which alone covers half an acre. And while Trotsky may have been, with hindsight, a far less prestigious customer than Karl Marx, the computerised technology, with which you can find a book and have it delivered in a matter of minutes, makes the reading room of the British Library seem primitive by comparison.

Back outside, push through the crush crossing Fifth Avenue and walk east down Manhattan's most congested stretch to where Park Avenue lifts off the ground at Pershing Square to weave its way around the solid bulk of **Grand Central Station**. This, for its day, was a masterful piece of urban planning: after the electrification of the railways made it possible to re-route trains underground, the rail lanes behind the existing station were sold off to developers and the profits went towards the building of a new terminal – constructed around a basic iron frame but clothed with a Beaux Arts fake skin. Since then Grand Central has taken on an almost mythical significance, and though with the insidious eating away of the country's network its major traffic is now mainly commuters speeding out no further than Westchester County, it remains in essence what it was in the 19C – symbolic gateway to an undiscovered continent.

You can either explore Grand Central on your own or take one of the **tours** run by the *Municipal Arts Society* (see *Tours*); these leave from under the Kodak hoarding every Wednesday at 1pm and are excellent. But for the efforts of a few dedicated New Yorkers (and, strangely enough, Jackie Onassis, whose voice was no doubt a godsend) Grand Central wouldn't be here at all, or at least it would be much uglified. For it was only deemed a National Landmark in 1978, after the railroad's plan to cap the whole lot with an office tower was quashed. The most spectacular aspect of the building is its size, now cowed by the soaring airplane wing of the Pan-Am building behind but still no less impressive in the main station **concourse**. This is one of the world's finest and most imposing open spaces, 470 feet long and 150 feet high, the barrel-vaulted ceiling speckled like a Baroque Church with a painted representation of the winter night sky, its 2500 stars shown back to front: 'As God would have seen them', the painter is reputed to have remarked. It's a pity about the broad advertising hoardings, which can't help but obscure the enormous windows, but stand in the middle and you realise that Grand Central represents a time when stations were seen as appropriately dwarfing preludes to great cities. ' A city within a city,' as it has been called.

For the best view of the concourse climb up to the catwalks which span the 60-feet-high windows on the Vanderbilt Avenue side; then explore the terminal's more esoteric reaches: places like the **Tennis Club** on the third floor, which used to be a CBS studio but now punts out court-time for a membership fee of around $2000 a year; and the **Oyster Bar** in the vaulted bowels of the station – one of the city's most highly regarded seafood restaurants, serving something like a dozen varieties of oyster and cram-packed every lunchtime with the midtown office crowd. Just outside is something that explains why the Oyster Bar's babble is not solely the result of the big-mouthed business people that eat there: you can stand on opposite sides of any of the vaulted spaces and hold a conversation just by whispering, an acoustic fluke that makes this the loudest eatery in town.

Across the street, the **Bowery Savings Bank** echoes Grand Central's grandeur – like its sister branch downtown, extravagantly lauding the twin shibboleths of sound investment and savings. A Roman-style basilica, the floor is paved with mosaics, the columns are each fashioned from a different kind of marble, and, if you take a look at the elevator doors (through a door on the right) you'll see bronze bas-reliefs of bank employees hard at various tasks. But then, this kind of lavish expenditure is typical of the buildings on this stretch of 42nd Street, which is full of lobbies worth popping inside for a glimpse as you're passing. The **Grand Hyatt Hotel** back on the north side of the street is a notable one, if nothing else probably the best example in the city of all that is truly vulgar about contemporary American interior design, its slushing waterfalls, lurking palms and gliding escalators, representing plush-carpeted bad taste at its most meretricious.

The **Chrysler Building**, across Lexington Avenue, is a different story, dating from a time (1929) when architects could carry off prestige with grace and style. This was for a fleeting moment the world's tallest building – until it was usurped by the Empire State in 1931 – and since the rediscovery of Art Deco a decade or so ago has become easily Manhattan's best loved, its car-motif friezes, jutting gargoyles and arched stainless steel pinnacle giving the solemn midtown skyline a welcome touch of fun. Chrysler moved out some time ago, and for a while the building was left to degenerate by a company that didn't wholly appreciate its spirited silliness, but now a new owner has pledged to keep it lovingly intact. The **lobby**, once a car showroom, is for the moment all you can see (there's no observation deck), but that's enough in itself, with opulently inlaid elevators, walls covered in African marble and on the ceiling a realistic, if rather faded, study of work and endeavour, showing aeroplanes, machines and brawny builders who worked on the tower.

Flanking each side of Lexington Avenue on the southern side of 42nd Street are two more buildings worthy of a studied walk past. The **Chanin Building** on the right is another Art Deco monument, cut with terracotta carvings of leaves, tendrils and sea creatures. More interestingly, the design on the outside of the weighty **Mobil Building** across the way is deliberately folded so as to be cleaned automatically by the movement of the wind.

The Mobil Building fills the block as far as Third Avenue, across which, recently restored to pristine 1950s splenour, stands the **Horn and Hardart Automat**, 'the last of a great breed,' wrote Paul Goldberger, and still serving up lukewarm ready meals out of chrome and glass drawers. Goldberger makes inflated claims for the romance of this place, and in some ways he's right: it's the only remaining example of a fast food idea that used to be all over the city. But having tasted the mysterious items in those tiny drawers, or even from the newly-added self-service counter, I'd frankly recommend Horn and Hardart's as period-piece only.

East of here, beyond the deceptively modern HQ of the **New York Daily News** – whose foyer holds blown-up prints of the paper's more memorable front pages – 42nd Street grows more tranquil. And on the left, between Second and First Avenue, is one of the city's most peaceful spaces of all – the **Ford Foundation Building**. Built in 1967, this was the first of the city's long chain of atriums and is probably the best: a giant greenhouse gracefully supported by soaring granite columns and edged with two walls of offices from which workers can look down on to a sub-tropical garden which changes naturally with the seasons. It's astonishingly quiet: 42nd Street is no more than a murmur outside, and all you can hear is the burble of water, the echo of voices and the clipped crack of feet on the brick walkways, mingled with the ripe smell of the atrium's considerable vegetation: all in all making for one of the great architectural experiences of New York City.

At the east end of 42nd Street, steps lead up to **Tudor City**, which rises behind a tree-filled parklet and with its coats of arms, leaded glass and neat neighbourhood shops, is the very picture of self-contained dowager respectability. Trip down the steps from here and you're plum opposite the building of the **United Nations**, which rose up after the last war on the site of what was once known as Turtle Bay. Some see the United Nations complex as one of the major sights of New York; others, usually those who've been there, are not so complimentary. For whatever the symbolism of the UN there can be few buildings that are quite so dull to walk round. What's more, the self-congratulatory nature of the (obligatory) guided tours – in the face of UN impotence in war and hunger zones the world over – can't help but grate a little.

For the determined, the complex consists of three main buildings – the thin glass-curtained slab of the **Secretariat**, the sweeping curve of the **General Assembly Building**, and, just between, the low-rise connecting **Conference Wing**. It went up immediately after the war and was finished in 1963, the product of a suitably international team of architects which included Le Corbusier – though he pulled out before the building was completed. Daily **tours** leave every 15 minutes from the monumental

General Assembly lobby (First Avenue at 45th Street; 754 7713. 9.15am-4pm; $4.50, students $2.50) and take in the main conference chambers of the UN and its constituent parts, foremost of which is the General Assembly Chamber itself, expanded a few years back to accommodate up to 179 members' delegations (though there are at present only 159). It's impressive certainly, but can't help but seem wasted on a body that only meets for a few months each year. Other council chambers, situated in the Conference Building, include the Security Council Chamber, the Economic and Social Council and the Trusteeship Council. Once you've been whisked around all these, with the odd stop for examples of the many artefacts that have been donated to the UN by its various member states – rugs, paintings, sculptures, etc. – the tour is more or less over, and will leave you in the basement of the General Assembly Building, where a couple of **shops** sell ethnic items from around the world and a **post office** will flog you a UN postage stamp to prove that you've been here – though bear in mind it's only valid on mail posted from the UN.

BARS *Company* (gay), *Louis East, Molly Malone's, South Dakota* (gay), *Uncle Charlie's South* (gay).

RESTAURANTS Cheap *Bagel Palace, Gemini Diner, Horn and Hardart Automat, Jackson Hole Wyoming, RJ's, Sarge's Deli;* **American and Mexican** *America, El Rio Grande;* **Fish** *Oyster Bar;* **Japanese** *Genroku Sushi;* **Indian** *Annapurna, Curry in a Hurry, Madras Palace, Shaheen;* **Vegetarian** *Tibetan Kitchen.*

THE WEST SIDE: CHELSEA, THE GARMENT DISTRICT AND TIMES SQUARE

Few visitors bother with Chelsea and the Garment District, the two areas that fill the land between 14th and 42nd Streets. Chelsea is a low-built surly-seedy grid of tenements and row houses of so mixed a character as to be almost characterless. To the north, the Garment District muscles in between Sixth and Eighth Avenues on 34th to 42nd Streets taking in the dual monsters of Penn Station and Madison Square Garden. The majority of people who come here do so for a specific reason – to catch a train or bus, to watch wrestling or to work in factories, and it's only a wedge of stores between Herald and Greeley Squares that attract the out-of-towner.

CHELSEA took shape in 1830 when its owner, Charles Clarke Moore, laid out his land for sale in broad lots. Enough remains to indicate

Chelsea's middle-class suburban origins, though in fact the area never quite made it onto the short-list of desirable places to be. Stuck between Fifth Avenue and Hell's Kitchen and caught between the ritziness of the one and the poverty of the other, Manhattan's chic residential focus leapfrogged Chelsea to the East 40s and 50s. These days the dreary facades quickly establish Chelsea's atmosphere of run-down residentialism; the grid plan seems too wide, the streets too bare to encourage you to linger.

But that's not to say Chelsea doesn't have its moments. Moore donated an island of land to the **General Theological Seminary** on Chelsea Square at 20th Street and Ninth Avenue, an assembly of ivy-clad gothicisms seemingly dropped in from rural Oxfordshire. It's possible to explore inside – the entrance is via the modern building on Ninth Avenue – but the countrified feel is what makes it special, not any particular architectural feature.

During the 19C this area, especially West 23rd Street, was a centre of New York's theatre district before it moved uptown. Nothing remains of the theatres now, but the hotel which put up all the actors, writers and Bohemian hangers-on remains a New York landmark. The **Chelsea Hotel** has been undisputed watering-hole of the city's harder-up literati for decades: Mark Twain and Tennessee Williams lived here and Brendan Behan and Dylan Thomas staggered in and out during their New York visits. Thomas Wolfe assembled *You Can't Go Home Again* from thousands of pages of manuscript he had stacked in his room, and in 1951 Jack Kerouac, armed with a specially adapted typewriter (and a lot of Benzedrine) typed the first draft of *On the Road* non-stop on to a 120-foot roll of paper. In the 1960s the Chelsea took off again when Andy Warhol and his doomed protégé Edie Sedgwick walled up here and made the film *Chelsea Girls* in (sort of) homage; Bob Dylan wrote songs in and about it, and most recently Sid Vicious stabbed Nancy Spungen to death in their suite, a few months before his own pathetic life ended with an overdose of heroin. With a pedigree like this it's easy to forget the hotel itself, which has a down-at-heel Edwardian grandeur all of its own and, incidentally, is an affordable place to stay and an interesting one to drink.

Sixth Avenue forms Chelsea's eastern perimeter, around 28th Street becoming Manhattan's **Flower Market**: not really a market as such, more the warehouses where pot plants and cut flowers are stored before brightening offices and atriums across the city. Nothing marks the strip and you come across it by chance, the greenery bursting out of drab blocks, blooms spangling shopfronts and providing a welcome touch of life to an otherwise dull neighbourhood. For the record West 28th Street was the original **Tin Pan Alley**, where music publishers would peddle songs to artists and producers from the nearby theatres. When the theatres moved, so did the publishers.

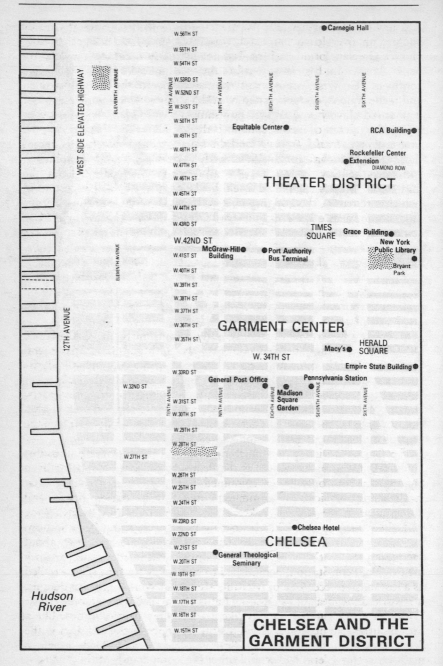

CHELSEA AND THE
GARMENT DISTRICT

A few streets north, Sixth Avenue collides with Broadway at **Greeley Square,** an overblown name for what is a trashy triangle celebrating Horace Greeley, founder of the **Tribune** newspaper. Perhaps he deserves better: known for his rallying call to the youth of the 19C to explore the continent ('Go West, young man!') he also supported the rights of women and trade unions, commissioned a weekly column from Karl Marx and denounced slavery and capital punishment. Sadly his paper no longer exists (though one of its descendants is the bored travellers' last resort, the *International Herald Tribune*) and the square named after him is one of those bits of Manhattan that looks ready to disintegrate at any moment.

Across the way is **Macy's,** the all-American superstore. Until the mid-1970s Macy's contented itself by being the world's largest store (which it remains), then, in response to the needs of the maturing Yuppie (and Bloomingdale's success) it went fashionably and safely upmarket, somewhere in the realm of Harrods and Heals. Like all great stores it's worth exploring – there's an amazing food emporium plus a recon-struction of P. J. Clarke's bar in the basement – though leave all forms of spending power at home. Nearby, the thoroughly unlikeable **Herald Center** names each of its seven glossy floors after an area of the city, something that didn't seem to be cutting much ice with the shoppers when last I was there.

In a way this part of Broadway is the shopfront to the **GARMENT DISTRICT,** a loosely defined pool between 34th and 42nd Streets and Sixth and Eighth Avenues. From this patch three-quarters of all the women's and children's clothes in America are made, though you'd never believe it: outlets are strictly wholesale with no need to woo customers, and the only giveaways to the industry inside are the racks of clothes shunted around on the street and occasional skips of offcuts that give the area its look of an open-air jumble sale.

The Garment District is something to see in passing: the unmissable landmark in this part of town is the **Pennsylvania Station** and **Madison Square Garden** complex, a combined box and drum structure that swallows up millions of commuters in its train station below and accommodates the *Knicks* basketball and *Rangers* hockey teams (along with their fans) up top. There's nothing memorable about Penn Station: its subterranean levels seem to have all the grime and just about everything else that's wrong with the subway, and to add insult to injury the original Penn Station, demolished to make way for this, is now hailed as a lost masterpiece. One of McKim, Mead and White's greatest designs, it reworked the ideas of the Roman Baths of Caracalla to awesome effect: 'Through it one entered the city like a god... One scuttles in now like a rat.' mourned an observer. A whimsical reminder of the old days is the **Penta Hotel** on the corner of Seventh Avenue and 33rd Street: a main venue for Glenn Miller and other big swing bands of the 1940s, it keeps the phone number that made it famous – 736 5000: under the old system PENNsylvania 6-5000, title of Miller's affectionate hit.

Immediately behind Penn Station the **General Post Office** is a McKim, Mead and White structure that survived, a relic from an era when municipal pride was all about making statements – though to say that the Post Office is monumental in the grandest manner still seems to underplay it. The old joke is that it had to be this big to fit in the sonorous inscription above the columns – 'Neither snow nor rain nor heat nor gloom of night stays these couriers from the swift completion of their appointed rounds' – a claim about as believable as the official one that the Manhattan postal district handles more mail than Britain, France and Belgium combined.

The **Port Authority Terminal Building** at 40th Street and Ninth Avenue is another sink for the area: a Dantesque version of a British concrete-and-glass bus station. Coaches strain, waiting to escape the city to all points in America, and though initially confusing it's efficiently run. *Greyhound* and *Trailways* leave from here as do regional services out to the boroughs and (should you arrive in the early hours) it's a remarkably safe place, station staff keeping the winos and weirdos in check.

Back to Broadway and **Herald Square** faces Greeley Square in a headlong replay of the battles between the *Herald* newspaper and its arch-rival Horace Greeley's *Tribune*. During the 1890s this was the **Tenderloin** area, dance halls, brothels and rough bars thriving beside the Elevated Railway that ran up Sixth Avenue. When the *Herald* arrived in 1895 it gave the square a new name and dignity, but it's perhaps best remembered as the square George M. Cohan said Hello to in the famous song. These days it wouldn't fire anyone to sing about it, saved only from unkempt sleaziness by Macy's on the corner below.

Cross **42nd Street** and you find Broadway at its worst. The excitment and *élan* of the street's eastern section are gone, and all that's left is a clutch of honky-tonk sex shops and porno cinemas. Neither do things improve if you turn west: 42nd Street here is a sordid corner of prostitution and petty vice you'll really do better to skip altogether – and that goes for much of Eighth Avenue north of 42nd. Head straight on and at 330 42nd Street is the **McGraw-Hill Building**, a greeny-blue radiator that architects have raved over: 'proto-juke box modern' Vincent Scully called it. The lobby should be seen.

Ninth Avenue makes amends of sorts for Eighth's unsavouriness, a long slash of ethnic delis and greengrocers of all kinds that come into their own in May when the **Ninth Avenue Food Festival** closes the run between 34th and 57th Streets. This stretch down to the Hudson was once known as **Hell's Kitchen**, a descriptive name for one of New York's poorest and most violent areas. Impoverished Irish immigrants settled here, quickly followed by Greeks, Italians and Hispanics: by the end of the 19C the tenements were the most overcrowded in the world, gangs roamed the rubbish-filled streets, and disease and infant mortality were rife. (It wasn't until 1867 that the city officially prohibited the indigenous herds of pigs that brushed with the gentry of Broadway.) With the *Tenement Housing Act* of 1901 things started to get better, and since then the old tenements have been flattened and the area renamed as **Clinton** to hide its past. In 1977 **Manhattan Plaza** went up on 42nd and 43rd Streets between Ninth and Tenth, in an attempt to draw the monied classes into the area. But prices were high and takers few for apartments irreparably sullied by nearby Times Square, and in a fit of innovation the buildings were let to actors, artists and the like who could prove a low income and would enhance the theatre district's 'creative feel'. Welfare families, needless to say, were deemed not to provide the right 'class'. Now Hell's Kitchen is gradually gentrifying against a background of raggy, multi-ethnic neighbourhoods, at its centre safe enough, but west of Ninth Avenue in the 40s and 50s bombed out and intimidating – a prelude to the out-and-out sleaze of the bars on the West Side Highway. There's no reason to go there, especially not at night, but if you do, take care.

Eventually Broadway runs into **TIMES SQUARE**, a pinched strip that in its excess and brashness is a distillation of the city itself. Centre of the Great White Way, it's tawdry, exciting, hostile, dirty and romantic in about equal doses, a place where you feel the grandness of the 1890s meeting the already dated glitter of the 1980s, with lurid enticements to sex shows alongside theatres only a touch more reputable and vastly more expensive. The smells of unending fast food houses colour the air, tourists mill in crocodiles and queue for cut-price tickets. Here, the new is a brash overlay on the old heart of the theatre district, and only a sentimentalist could despise it.

Which isn't to say that Times Square is wholly – or even halfway – likeable. Most important of its attributes is that it can be dangerous, particularly in the streets off the square itself, where hoards of out-of-towners offer easy pickings for petty criminals, drug dealers and women working as prostitutes. You're more likely to be hassled here than anywhere in the city, though there's too much going on when the theatres empty to make street crime viable: at other times beware – and keep to the main drag.

Like Greeley and Herald Squares, Times Square took its name from a newspaper connection when the *New York Times* built offices here in 1904. While the *Herald* and *Tribune* fought each other in ever more vicious circulation battles, the *NYT* took the sober middle ground under the banner 'All the news that's fit to print', a policy that enabled the paper to survive and become one of the country's most respected liberal voices. **Times Tower**, the slim chip at the Square's southern end, was its original headquarters, though the paper itself has since crept off round a corner to 43rd Street. Dotted around are the New York Conventions and Visitors

Bureau (see *Basics*), good for free maps and information, and some of Broadway's great theatres (see the listings on p.268) – and it's these last that add flavour to the scene – the clock-and-globe topped **Paramount Building** is a favourite, and the **Lyceum, Schubert** and **Lyric** each have their original facades. It's the nifty canvas and frame stand of the **TKTS**, the cut-price ticket shop, that immediately catches the eye though, selling tickets for shows that no one could otherwise afford. A lifelike statue of Broadway's doyen **George M. Cohan** looks on – though if you've ever seen the film *Yankee Doodle Dandy* it's impossible to think of him other than as a swaggering Jimmy Cagney. Really, Times Square is a mess, and one that successive mayors have promised to clean up. The last attempt was by demolishing several majestic theatres for a new Marriot Hotel; a few years earlier the celebrated old Astor Hotel was itself demolished, for, the argument ran, who would pay to stay on sleazy Times Square? Last word on the scene to Henry Miller from *Tropic of Capricorn*:

It's only a stretch of a few blocks from Times Square to Fiftieth Street, and when one says Broadway that's all that's really meant and it's really nothing, just a chicken run and a lousy one at that, but even at seven in the evening when everyone's rushing for a table there's a sort of electric crackle in the air and your hair stands on end like an antennae and if you're receptive you not only get every bash and flicker but you get the statistical itch, the quid pro quo of the interactive, interstitial, ectoplasmic quantum of bodies jostling in space like the stars which compose the Milky Way, only this is the Gay White Way, the top of the world with no roof and not even a crack or a hole under your feet to fall through and say it's a lie. The absolute impersonality of it brings you to a pitch of warm human delirium which makes you run forward like a blind nag and wag your delirious ears.

The **West 50s** between Sixth and Eighth Avenues are emphatically tourist territory. Edged by Central Park and the Theatre District and with Fifth Avenue and the Rockfeller Center in easy striking distance, they've been invaded by overpriced restaurants and cheapo souvenir shops: should you want to stock up on *I Love New York* underwear this could be the place.

One sight worth searching out is the **Equitable Center** at 757 Seventh Avenue that's taken a branch of the **Whitney Museum of American Art** under its wing. The building itself is dapper if not a little self-important, but you should catch Thomas Hart Benton's *Murals* if nothing else: for more on these and the rest of the collection, turn to p.196.

Otherwise **Carnegie Hall**, an overblown and fussy warehouse-like venue for opera and concert at 154 West 57th Street, is the thing to see. Tchaikovsky conducted the programme on opening night and Mahler, Rachmaninov, Toscanini, Frank Sinatra and Judy Garland played here, and though it's dropped down a league since Lincoln Center opened, the superb acoustics still ensure full houses most of the year. If you don't fancy or can't afford a performance, sneak in through the stage door on 56th Street for a look at the building – no one minds as long as there's not a rehearsal in progress. A few doors down, the **Russian Tea Room** (see p.255) is one of those places to see and be seen at, ever popular with in-names from the entertainment business. Reservations are needed for lunch and dinner, but to get an idea of the sumptuous red and gold interior, its totally un-Russian atmosphere and its astronomical prices, just order a sandwich.

Sixth Avenue is properly named *Avenue of the Americas*, though no New Yorker ever calls it this: guidebooks and maps labour the convention, but the only manifestation of the tag are lamp-post flags of Central and South American countries which serve as useful landmarks. If nothing else Sixth's distinction is its width, a result of the Elevated Railway that once ran along here, now replaced by the Sixth Avenue subway. In its day the Sixth Avenue 'El' marked the borderline between respectability to the east and dodgier areas to the west, and in a way it's still a dividing line separating the glamorous strips of Fifth, Madison and Park Avenues and the less salubrious western districts.

Running north from Herald Square, **Bryant Park** is the first open space, once again named after a newspaper editor – William Cullen Bryant of the *New York Post*, also famed as a poet and instigator of Central Park. Recently the park benefited from a civic clean-up, and secondhand bookstalls keep a truce with the dope dealers that lurk around. This is for the good, as Bryant Park is by design attractive – a bit straitlaced and formal perhaps, but more welcoming than many small parks. From here you can't miss the **Grace Building** which swoops down on 42nd Street, breaking the rules by stepping out of line with its neighbours, though with a showiness that rings rather hollow – and which, in any case, is less well finished than its twin, the Solow Building, on West 57th Street. Much more approachable is the **American Radiator Building** (now the American Standard Building) on West 40th, its black Gothic tower topped with honey-coloured terracotta that lights up to resemble a glowing coal – appropriate enough for the HQ of a heating company.

One of the best things about New York City are the small hidden pockets abruptly discovered when you least expect them. West 47th Street between Fifth and Sixth is a perfect example: this is **Diamond Row**, a short strip of shops chock-full with wildly expensive stones and jewellery, managed by ultra-Orthodox Hasidic Jews who seem only to exist in the confines of the street. Maybe they are what gives the street its workaday feel – Diamond Row seems more like the Garment District than Fifth Avenue, and the conversations you overhear on the street or in a delicatessen are memorably Jewish. The Hasidim are followers of a mystical sect of Judaism – the name means 'Pious Ones' – and traditionally wear beards, sidelocks and dark old-fashioned suits. A large contingent live in Williamsburg and Crown Heights in Brooklyn.

By the time it reaches midtown Manhattan, Sixth Avenue has become a dazzling showcase of corporate wealth. True, there's little of the ground floor glitter of Fifth or the razzamataz of Broadway, but what *is* here, and in a way what defines the stretch from 47th to 51st Streets, is the **Rockefeller Center Extension**. Following the earlier **Time Life Building** at 50th Street three near-identical blocks went up in the 1970s, and if they don't have the romance of their predecessor they at least possess some of its monumentality. Backing on to the Rockefeller Center proper, by day and especially by night, the repeated statement of each block comes over with some power, giving the wide path of Sixth Avenue much of its visual excitement. At street level things can be just as interesting: the broad sidewalks allow pedlars of food and handbills, street musicians, mimics and actors to do their thing. The basement of the McGraw-Hill Building shelters the **New York Experience** ($4.75; Monday-Thursday on the hour 11am-7pm; Friday-Saturday 11am-8pm; Sunday 12am-8pm), a creakingly and rather embarrassingly dated multi-screen, multi-media extravaganza. Only if it's raining very heavily is this 50-minute celebratory day-in-the-life of the city worth catching.

Across the avenue at 49th Street **Radio City Music Hall** has far greater rewards (for a description see p.118). Keep an eye open too for the **CBS Building** on the corner of 52nd Street: dark and inscrutable, this has been compared to the monolith from 2001, and, like it or not, certainly forces a mysterious presence on this segment of Sixth Avenue.

The rack of streets below Central Park have some of the most opulent hotels, shops and apartments in America, which means you spend a lot of time gawping at windows and gasping at prices. Best place to do both is along **57th Street**, where antiquarian bookstores and galleries crowd alongside the dyspeptic wealth of *Van Cleef and Arpels* (jewellery) and *Bergdorf Goodman* (jewellery and just about every other fashion that big money can buy). 57th Street has also recently overtaken SoHo as *the* centre for upmarket art sales, and galleries here are noticeably snootier than their downtown relations, often requiring an appointment for viewing. Three that usually don't: the **Marlborough Gallery** (2nd floor, 40 West 57th) specialising in famous names both American and European; the **Kennedy Gallery** (same building 5th floor) of 19C and 20C American painting; and **Daniel Woolf** (4th floor West 57th) with photographs old and new.

BARS *Blue Fox, Chelsea Commons Eagle's Nest, Mulligan's Grill, Molly Mog's, Jimmy Ray's, Ramrod* (gay), *Rawhide* (gay), *Spike* (gay).

RESTAURANTS Cheap *J.J. Applebaum Deli, Carnegie Deli, Empire Diner, Landmark Tavern, O'Reilly's, Southern Funk Café, Wine and Apples*; **American and Mexican** *Arriba, Arriba, Caramba, Hard Rock Café*; **French** *Café Un, Deux, Trois, La Bonne Soupe, La Fondue West Bank Café*; **Jewish** *Dubrow's*; **Italian** *Prego*.

FIFTH AVENUE AND EAST: 42ND STREET TO CENTRAL PARK

FIFTH AVENUE bowls ahead from 42nd Street with all the confidence of the material world. It's been a great strip for as long as New York has been a great city, and its name is an automatic image of wealth and opulence. Here that image is very real: all that considers itself suave and cosmopolitan ends up on Fifth, and the shops showcase New York's most opulent and conspicuous consumerism. That the shopping is beyond the power of most people needn't put you off, for Fifth rewards with some of the city's best architecture: the boutiques and stores are just the icing on the cake.

In its lower reaches Fifth Avenue isn't really as alluring as the streets off. The only eye-catcher is the **Manufacturers Hanover Trust Bank** on the south-west corner of 43rd, an early glass 'n' gloss box that teasingly displays its safe to passers-by, a reaction against the fortress palaces of earlier banks. Around the next corner, West 44th Street contains three New York institutions. The Georgian style **Harvard Club** at no.27, easily spotted of an evening by the paparazzi hanging about outside, has interiors so lavish that lesser mortals aren't allowed to enter. But it's still possible to enjoy the **New York Yacht Club**, its playfully eccentric exterior of bay windows moulded as ship's sterns, and with waves and dolphins completing the effect of tipsy Beaux Arts fun. For years this was home of the Americas Cup, a yachting trophy first won by the schooner *America* in 1851 and held here (indeed bolted to the table) until lost to the Australians amid much loss of face in 1984. Now though, for the time being at least, it's back in its place.

'Dammit, it was the twenties and we had to be smarty.' So said Dorothy Parker of the group known as the Round Table who hung out at the **Algonquin Hotel** at no. 59, and gave it a name as *the* place for literary visitors to New York – a name which still to some extent endures. The Round Table used to meet regularly here, a kind of American-style Bloomsbury group of the city's sharpest-tongued wits which had a reputation for being as egotistical as it was exclusive. Times have changed considerably, but over the years the Algonquin has continued to attract a steady stream of famous guests, most of them with some kind of literary bent, not least Noel Coward (who's table someone will point out to you if you ask nicely), Bernard Shaw, Irving Berlin and Boris Karloff. The bar is one of the most civilised in town.

West 47th Street or Diamond Row (see p.115) is another surprise off Fifth Avenue, but the first building to strike out at street level is **Charles Scribner & Son's Bookstore**, whose black and gold iron and glass storefront seems to have fallen from an Edwardian engraving. Inside it's equally dignified, with a collection of books that's highly browseable –

though to pick up a bargain **Barnes and Noble** across the Avenue is the no-frills alternative.

Central to this stretch of Fifth is a complex of buildings that, more than any other in the city, succeeds in being utterly self-contained and at the same time in complete agreement with its surroundings. Built between 1932 and 1940 by John D. Rockefeller, son of the oil magnate, the **Rockefeller Center** marked a high spot in urban planning: office space with cafés, a theatre, underground concourses and rooftop gardens work together with an intelligence and grace rare in any building then or now. It's a combination that shows every other City centre shopping mall the way, leaving you thinking that Cyril Connolly's snide description – 'that sinister Stonehenge of Economic Man' – was way off the mark.

You're lured in to the Center from Fifth Avenue down the gentle slope of **Channel Gardens** (so named because they divide *La Maison Française* and the *British Empire Building*) to the **RCA Building**, focus of the Center. Rising 850 feet, its monumental lines match the scale of Manhattan itself, though softened by symmetrical setbacks to prevent an overpowering expanse of wall. At its foot the **Lower Plaza** holds a sunken restaurant in the summer months, linked visually to the downward flow of the RCA by Paul Manship's sparkling *Prometheus*, and in winter becomes an ice rink, giving skaters a chance to show off their skills to passing shoppers. More ponderously, a panel on the eastern side relates John D. Rockefeller's priggish credo in gold and black.

Inside, the RCA is no less impressive. In the lobby José Maria Sert's murals, *American Progress* and *Time*, are a little faded but eagerly in tune with the 1930s deco ambience – presumably more so than the original paintings by Diego Rivera which were unsurprisingly removed by John D.'s son Nelson when the artist refused to scrap a panel glorifying Lenin. A leaflet available from the lobby desk details a **self-guided tour** of the Center, and to get the most thorough view it's worth following this, combining it with a visit to the roof-top **observation deck** (take the elevator to the 65th floor, 10am-9pm summer, 10am-6pm other times; $3.25, students $2.75). If you climb only one skyscraper it should be this one, for the RCA's central position gives the finest views of all – and even more mind-blowing at night, with helicopters hanging like fireflies above the Financial District, and Central Park glittering to the north.

Among the many offices in the RCA Building are the **NBC Studios** and it's possible to tour these, (one-hour tours leave regularly, 10am-4pm Monday-Saturday, reservations from the desk in the RCA first; $5) though if you're an American TV freak you'll do better to pick up a (free) ticket for a **show recording** from the mezzanine lobby, Room 48 or out on the street. The most popular tickets evaporate before 9am.

Best known of the RCA's other interiors is the **Radio City Music Hall** on Sixth Avenue, an Art Deco jewel box that represents the last word in

1930s luxury. The staircase is regally resplendent with the world's largest chandeliers, the murals from the men's toilets are now in the Museum of Modern Art and the huge auditorium looks like an extravagant scalloped shell or a vast sunset; 'Art Deco's true shrine' as Paul Goldberger rightly called it. Believe it or not Radio City was nearly demolished in 1970: the outcry this caused left it designated a National Landmark. To explore, take a tour from the lobby: Monday-Saturday 10.15am-4.45pm; $3.95.

A further bit of sumptuous deco is the **International Building** on Fifth Avenue, whose black marble and gold leaf give the lobby a sleek, classy feel dramatised by the ritz of escalators and the view across Lee Lawrie's bronze *Atlas* out to **St Patrick's Cathedral**. Bone-white in the sullied streets, St Patrick's seems the result of a painstaking academic tour of the Gothic cathedrals of Europe – perfect in detail, lifeless in spirit. There's something wrong too in the way the cathedral slots ever-so-neatly into Manhattan's grid pattern; on the plus side, the Gothic details are perfect and the cathedral is certainly striking – and made all the more so by the backing of the sunglass-black **Olympic Tower**, whose exclusive apartments house notables like Jackie Onassis when she's in town.

North of 52nd Street Fifth Avenue's ground floors quickly shift from airline offices to all-out glitz, *Cartier*, *Gucci* and *Tiffany's* among many gilt-edged names. The window shopping is fine, but beware assistants, who seem to flip between the crawlingly obsequious and the downright rude according to how much they think you're worth. This isn't the case at **Steuben Glass**, 715 Fifth, a showcase of delicate glass and Steuben crystalware perfectly displayed; nor **Nat Sherman's** at 711, tobacconist to the stars and purveyor of some lethal smokes (see p.209 for fuller listings on shops).

Just when you thought all the glitter had gone about as far as it could, you reach the **Trump Tower** at 57th Street, whose outrageously over-the-top atrium is just short of repellent – perhaps in tune with those who shop in the glamorous boutiques here. Perfumed air, polished marble panelling and a five-storey waterfall are calculated to knock you senseless with expensive 'good' taste: as it is even some of the security people look faintly embarrassed. But the building is clever, a neat little outdoor garden is squeezed high in a corner, and each of the 230 apartments above the atrium gets views in three directions. Donald Trump, the property developer all New York liberals love to hate, lives here, along with other worthies of the hyper-rich in-crowd.

There's a choice of antidote to all this: **Rizzoli's**, a Thinking Person's bookstore loud with Thinking Person's music, across the road at 712; or **FAO Schwartz**, an unending emporium of children's toys. Fight the kids off and there's some great stuff to play with – once again, the best money can buy. Across 57th Street Fifth Avenue broadens to Grand Army Plaza and the fringes of **Central Park**.

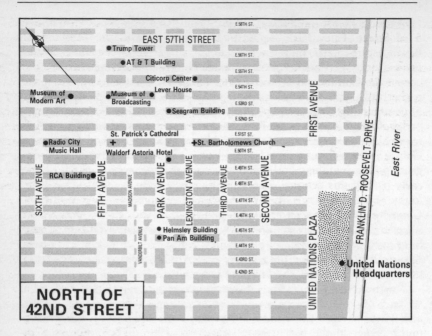

E.58TH ST.

EAST 57TH STREET
●Trump Tower   E.56TH ST.

●AT & T Building   E.55TH ST.

Citicorp Center●   E.54TH ST.
Lever House
Museum of ●   ●Museum of   E.53RD ST.
Modern Art   Broadcasting
●Seagram Building   E.52ND ST.

St. Patrick's Cathedral   E.51ST ST.
●Radio City   ✛   ✛St. Bartholomews Church
Music Hall   Waldorf Astoria Hotel   E.50TH ST.

RCA Building●   E.49TH ST.

E.48TH ST.

E.47TH ST.

E.46TH ST.

●Helmsley Building   E.45TH ST.
●Pan Am Building
E.44TH ST.

E.43RD ST.

E.42ND ST.
●United Nations
Headquarters

SIXTH AVENUE · FIFTH AVENUE · MADISON AVENUE · PARK AVENUE · LEXINGTON AVENUE · THIRD AVENUE · SECOND AVENUE · FIRST AVENUE · VANDERBILT AVENUE · UNITED NATIONS PLAZA · FRANKLIN D. ROOSEVELT DRIVE · East River

**NORTH OF
42ND STREET**

Madison, Park and Lexington Avenues

If there is a stretch that is immediately and unmistakably New York it is the area that runs east from Fifth Avenue in the 40s and 50s. The great avenues of Madison, Park, Lexington and Third reach their richest heights as the skyscrapers line up in neck-cricking vistas, the streets choke with yellow cabs and office workers, and Con Edison vents belch steam from old heating systems. More than anything else it's buildings that define this part of town, the majority of them housing anonymous corporations and supplying excitement to the skyline in a 1960s build-em-high glass box bonanza. Others, like the new AT&T headquarters and Citicorp Center, don't play the game; and enough remains from the pre-box days to keep variety.

MADISON AVENUE shadows Fifth with some of its sweep but less of the excitement. A few good stores sit behind the scenes here, like *Brooks Brothers*, on the corner of East 44th Street, traditional clothiers to the Ivy League and inventors of the button-down collar, but Madison doesn't have quite the prestige of Fifth or Park. Between 50th and 51st Streets the **Villard Houses** merit a serious walk past, a replay of an Italian palazzo (one that didn't quite make it to Fifth Avenue) by McKim, Mead and White. The houses have been surgically incorporated into the Helmsley Palace Hotel and the interiors polished up to original rococo splendours.

Madison's most interesting buildings come in a four-block strip above 53rd Street: **Paley Park**, squeezed in a gap next to the Museum of Broadcasting (p.207) on the north side of East 53rd between Madison and Fifth is a tiny vest-pocket park complete with mini-waterfall. Around the corner the **Continental Illinois Center** looks like a cross beween a space rocket and a grain silo. But it's the new **AT&T Building** between 55th and 56th streets that has grabbed all the headlines. Another Johnson-Burgee collaboration, it follows the Post-Modernist theory of eclectic borrowing from historical styles: a Modernist skyscraper sandwiched between a Chippendale top and a Renaissance base – the idea being to quote from great public buildings and simultaneously return to the fantasy of the early part of this century. The building has its fans – especially for the lobby which contains Evelyn Longman's sculpture *The Spirit of Communication*, removed from the old AT&T headquarters downtown – but in the main the tower doesn't wholly work. Perhaps Johnson should have followed the advice of his teacher, Mies Van der Rohe: 'It's better to build a good building than an original one.' More info is on hand from the lobby attendants.

Less flamboyantly, the **IBM Building** next door at 590 Madison has a stylish enclosed plaza of plants, water and tinkling classical music, achieving the effect the Trump Tower aimed for and missed, and scoring much higher in the user-friendly stakes than the AT&T. Across 57th Street, as the first of Madison's boutiques appear, the **Fuller Building** is worth catching – black and white Art Deco, with a fine entrance and tiled floor.

'Where wealth is so swollen that it almost bursts' wrote Collinson Owen of **PARK AVENUE** in 1929 and things aren't much changed: corporate headquarters jostle for prominence in a triumphal procession to capitalism, pushed apart by Park's broad avenue that once carried railtracks. Whatever your feelings it's one of the city's most awesome sights. Looking south, everything progresses to the high altar of the **New York Central Building** (now re-christened the Helmsley Building), a delicate, energetic construction with a lewdly excessive Rococo lobby. In its day it formed a skilled punctuation mark to the avenue, but had its thunder stolen in 1963 by the **Pan-Am Building** that looms behind. Bahaus guru Walter Gropius had a hand in designing this, and the critical consensus is that he should have done better. HQ of the international airline, the profile is meant to suggest an aircraft wing and the blue-grey mass certainly adds drama to the cityscape, though whatever success the Pan-Am scores it robs Park Avenue of the views south it deserves and needs, sealing 44th Street and drawing much of the vigour from the buildings all about. Another black mark was the rooftop helipad, closed in the 1970s after a helicopter misjudged a landing and slipped from the top, killing those in it and several on the ground.

Despite Park Avenue's power, an individual look at most of the skyscrapers reveals the familiar glass box, and the first few buildings to stand out do so exactly because that's what they're not. Wherever you placed the solid mass of the **Waldorf Astoria Hotel** (between 49th and 50th) it would hold its own, a resplendent statement of Art Deco elegance. If you're tempted, it's a smidgen cheaper than the comparable competition – between $160-$250 for a double. Crouching behind, **St Bartholomew's Church** is a low-slung Byzantine hybrid that by contrast adds immeasurably to the street, giving the lumbering skyscrapers a much-needed sense of scale. As you'd imagine, every so often property developers wave a huge cheque under the church fathers' noses for the land rights: so far they've managed to resist. The spikey-topped **General Electric Building** behind seems like a wild extension of the church, its slender shaft rising to a meshed crown of abstract sparks and lighting stokes that symbolises the radio waves used by its original occupier, *RCA*. The lobby (entrance at 570 Lexington) is yet another deco delight.

Amongst all this it's difficult at first to see the originality of the **Seagram Building** between 52nd and 53rd Sts. Designed by Mies Van der Rohe with Philip Johnson and built in 1958, this was the seminal curtain-wall skyscraper, the floors supported internally, allowing a skin of smokey glass and whisky-bronze metal (Seagram are distillers), now weathered to a dull black. In keeping with the era's vision every interior detail down to the fixtures and lettering on the mailboxes was specially designed. It was the supreme example of Modernist reason, deceptively simple and cleverly detailed, and its opening caused a wave of approval. The plaza, an open forecourt designed to set the building apart from its neighbours and display it to advantage, was such a success as a public space that the city revised the zoning laws to encourage other high-rise builders to supply plazas. The result was the windswept anti-people places now found all over down and midtown Manhattan, and a lot of pallid Mies copies, boxes that alienated many from 'faceless' modern architecture.

Across Park Avenue McKim, Mead and White's **Racquet and Squash Club** seems like a Classical continuation of the Seagram Plaza. More interesting is the **Lever House** across the way between 53rd and 54th, the building that set the Modernist ball rolling on Park Avenue in 1952. Then, the two right-angled slabs that form a steel and glass bookend seemed revolutionary compared to the traditional buildings that surrounded it. Nowadays it's overlooked and not a little dingy.

LEXINGTON AVENUE is always active, especially around the mid 40s, where commuters swarm around Grand Central and a well-placed post office on the corner of 50th Street. Just as the Chrysler Building dominates these lower stretches, the chisel-topped **Citicorp Center** (between 53rd and 54th Streets) has taken the north end as its domain. Finished in 1979, the graph paper design sheathed in aluminium is architecture become mathematics, and now one of Manhattan's most conspicuous landmarks. The slanted roof was designed to house solar panels and provide power, but the idea was ahead of the technology and Citicorp had to content themselves by adopting the distinctive top as a corporate logo. The atrium of stores known as *The Market* is also one of the city's best, with inexpensive food (try a *Healthwork's* salad) and live music at 6-8pm Saturdays, noon on Sundays. A more likeable meeting of commerce, culture and friendly mall you couldn't hope to find.

Hiding under the Center's skirts is **St Peter's**, a tiny church built to replace one demolished to make way for the Citicorp. Part of the deal was that the church had to stand out from the center – which explains the granite material. Thoroughly modern inside, it's worth peering in for sculptor Louise Nevelson's *Erol Beaker Chapel*, venue for Wednesday lunchtime jazz concerts, and a church hall-cum-theatre with a reputation of being one of the city's most innovative.

The Citicorp provided a spur for the development of Third Avenue, though things really took off when the old Elevated Railway that ran here was dismantled in 1955. Until then Third had been a strip of earthy bars and rundown tenements, in effect a border to the more salubrious midtown district. After the Citicorp gave it an 'official' stamp of approval, office blocks sprouted, revitalising the flagging fortunes of midtown Manhattan in the late 1970s. The best section is between 44th and 50th Streets – look out for the sheer marble monument of the **Wang Building** between 48th and 49th whose cross-patterns reveal the structure within.

All this office space hasn't totally removed interest from the street (there are a few good bars here, notably *P. J. Clarke's* at 55th, a New York institution – see p.237), but most life, especially at night time, seems to have shifted across to **Second Avenue** – on the whole lower, quieter, more residential and with any number of singles/Irish bars to crawl between. The area from Third to the East River in the upper 40s is known as **Turtle Bay** and there's a scattering of brownstones alongside chirpier shops and industry that disappear as you head north. Of course the UN HQ Building (see p.107) has had a knock-on effect, producing buildings like **1 UN Plaza** at 44th and 1st, a futuristic chess piece of a hotel that takes its design hints from the UN Building itself. Inside, its marbled, chromey lobby is about as uninviting as any other modern American luxury hotel. Should this be your cup of tea, a double room will set you back a few hundred dollars; if not, just pray that all New York hotels don't end up like this.

First Avenue has a certain raggy looseness that's a relief after the concrete claustrophobia of Midtown, and **Beekman Place** (49th-51st Streets between First Avenue and the river) is quieter still, a beguiling enclave of garbled styles. Similar, though not quite as intimate, is **Sutton Place**, a long stretch running from 53rd to 59th between 1st and the river.

Originally built for the lordly Morgans and Vanderbilts in 1875, Sutton increases in elegance as you move north and, for today's créme de la créme, **Riverview Terrace** (off 58th Street) is a (very) private enclave of five brownstones. The Secretary-General of the UN has a place here and the locals are choosy who they let in: disgraced President Richard Nixon was refused on the grounds he would be a security risk.

BARS *Bogart's* (gay), *Chaps* (gay), *Costello's, Green Derby, Kelly's Irish Bar, Last Call* (gay), *Murphy's, P.J. Clark's.*

RESTAURANTS Cheap *Showtime Deli, Stage Deli;* **French** *Brasserie, Magic Pan Creperie;* **Japanese** *Hatsuhana;* **Health Food** *The Great American Health Bar;* **Indian** *Nupur;* **Mexican and South American** *Via Brasil; The Yellow Rose.*

Chapter three
UPPER MANHATTAN

UPPER MANHATTAN begins above 57th Street, the corporate wealth of midtown giving way abruptly to the smug residentialism of the Upper East and West Sides. **Central Park** lies in between, the city's back garden, where people come to play and jog or in the summer months just stay sane, escaping midtown's crowds in one of the most intelligent pieces of urban landscaping ever.

The **Upper East Side** is at its most opulent in the mansions of **Fifth** and **Madison Avenues,** today taken over by the **Metropolitan** and other of the city's great museums. For the rest it's in part an elegant, mind-your-own-business residential area, a scattering of historical attractions towards its periphery, with to the north, still more or less identifiable, the old German neighbourhood of **Yorkville** – the only concession to ethnic presence.

The **Upper West Side** is a lot less refined, though it does have one building – the **Lincoln Center** – that carries considerable cachet, hosting New York's most prestigious arts performances. It is again predominantly residential, well-heeled on its southern fringe, especially along stretches of Columbus Avenue and Central Park, though considerably less so as you move north. At its top end, marked at the edge by the monolithic **Cathedral of St John the Divine,** is **Morningside Heights,** an area that is the last gasp of Manhattan's wealth before the decayed streets of **Harlem** and – much further east – its Hispanic counterpart **El Barrio.** Further north is **Inwood** and the city's least expected museum – the medieval arts collection of **The Cloisters** (see p.197).

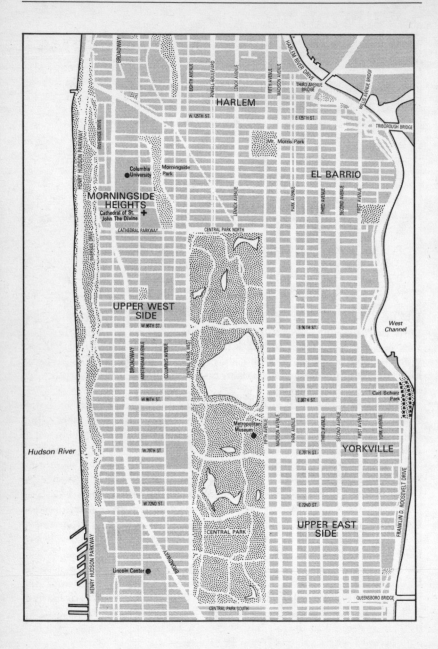

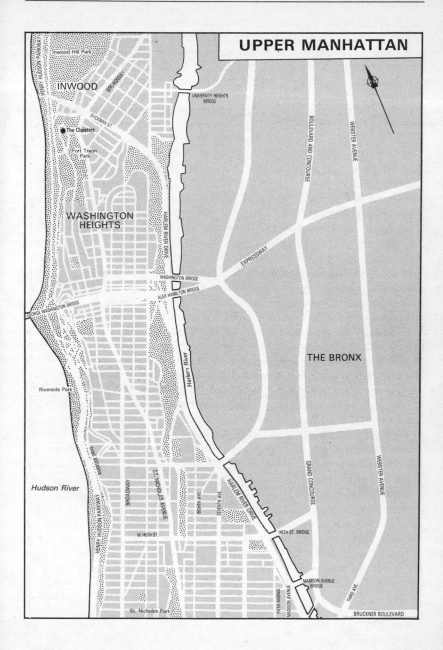

UPPER MANHATTAN

INWOOD

Inwood Hill Park

BROADWAY

DYCKMAN ST.

● The Cloisters

Fort Tryon
Park

WASHINGTON
HEIGHTS

HENRY HUDSON PARKWAY

UNIVERSITY HEIGHTS
BRIDGE

HARLEM RIVER DRIVE

WASHINGTON BRIDGE

ALEX HAMILTON BRIDGE

GEORGE WASHINGTON BRIDGE

EXPRESSWAY

BOULEVARD AND CONCOURSE

WEBSTER AVENUE

THE BRONX

Harlem River

Riverside Park

Hudson River

HENRY HUDSON PARKWAY

RIVERSIDE DRIVE

BROADWAY

ST. NICHOLAS AVENUE

BURR AVE.

SEVENTH AVE.

HARLEM RIVER DRIVE

GRAND CONCOURSE

WEBSTER AVENUE

W. 145TH ST.

145TH ST. BRIDGE

St. Nicholas Park

FIFTH AVENUE

MADISON AVENUE

MADISON AVENUE
BRIDGE

THIRD AVE.

BRUCKNER BOULEVARD

CENTRAL PARK

'All radiant in the magic atmosphere of art and taste.' So enthused *Harper's* magazine on the opening of **CENTRAL PARK** in 1876, and though it's hard to be quite so jubilant about the place today, few New Yorkers could imagine life without it. For whether you're into jogging, baseball, boating, botany or just plain walking, or even if you rarely go near the place, there's no question that it's Central Park which makes New York a just-about-bearable place to live. For many people here, it's their only contact with nature: they know it's spring because Central Park is turning green; winter must be coming when the trees start losing their leaves. Certainly, life without it would be a lot more unhinged.

Central Park came close to never happening at all. It was the poet and newspaper editor, William Cullen Bryant, who had the idea for an open public space back in 1844, and he spent seven years trying to persuade city hall to carry it out, while developers leaned heavily on the authorities not to give up any valuable land. But eventually the city agreed and an 840-acre space north of the city limits was set aside, a desolate swampy area then occupied by a shanty town of squatters. The two architects commissioned to design the landscape, Frederick Olmsted and Calvert Vaux, planned to create a rural paradise, a complete illusion of the countryside bang in the heart of Manhattan, which even then was growing at a fantastic rate. They also saw their scheme as a leveller, a democratic park where all would contribute 'to the greater happiness of each...rich and poor, young and old, Jew and Gentile'.

The park was finished in 1876, and opened with such publicity that Olmsted and Vaux were soon in demand as park architects all over the States. Locally they went on to design the Riverside and Morningside open spaces in Manhattan, and Prospect Park in Brooklyn. Working alone, Olmsted laid out the campuses of Berkeley and Stanford in California, and had a major hand in that most televised of American artificial landscapes – Capitol Hill in Washington.

Today, in spite of the advent of motorised traffic, the sense of disorderly nature Olmsted and Vaux intended largely survives, cars and buses cutting through the park in sheltered canyons originally meant for horse-drawn carriages. The skyline, however, has changed, buildings thrusting their way into view and detracting from the park's original pastoral intention. Worse still are Robert Moses' alterations, which turned large stretches of landscaped open space into asphalted playground. Lately, too, the success of Central Park has in a way been its downfall, for as the crowds have become thicker, so the park has become more difficult to keep up to scratch; its lawns have become muddied, the gardens weary-looking and patchy, and the quieter reaches, which the two architects imagined a haven of peace and solitude, sites of muggings and

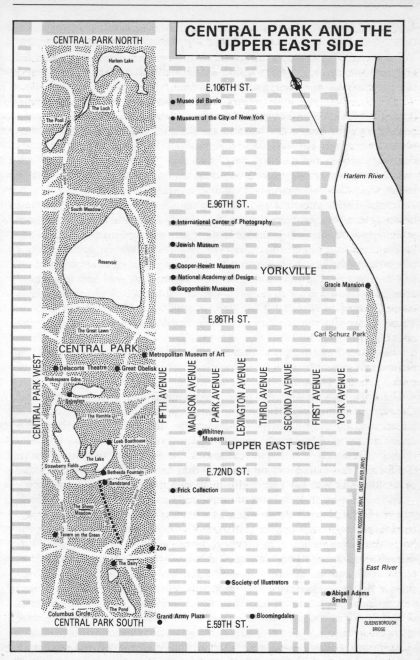

CENTRAL PARK AND THE UPPER EAST SIDE

CENTRAL PARK NORTH

Harlem Lake

The Loch

The Pool

E.106TH ST.

● Museo del Barrio

● Museum of the City of New York

Harlem River

South Meadow

E.96TH ST.

● International Center of Photography

● Jewish Museum

● Cooper-Hewitt Museum

Reservoir

YORKVILLE

● National Academy of Design

● Guggenheim Museum

Gracie Mansion ●

The Great Lawn

E.86TH ST.

Carl Schurz Park

CENTRAL PARK

● Metropolitan Museum of Art

● Delacorte Theatre   ● Great Obelisk

Shakespeare Gdns

Belvedere

The Ramble

CENTRAL PARK WEST

FIFTH AVENUE

MADISON AVENUE

PARK AVENUE

LEXINGTON AVENUE

THIRD AVENUE

SECOND AVENUE

FIRST AVENUE

YORK AVENUE

● Loeb Boathouse

The Lake

Strawberry Fields

● Bethesda Fountain

● Whitney Museum

UPPER EAST SIDE

● Bandstand

E.72ND ST.

The Sheep Meadow

● Frick Collection

● Tavern on the Green

FRANKLIN D. ROOSEVELT DRIVE (EAST RIVER DRIVE)

East River

● Zoo

● The Dairy

● Society of Illustrators

● Abigail Adams Smith

Columbus Circle

The Pond

Columbus Circle

CENTRAL PARK SOUTH

● Grand Army Plaza

● Bloomingdales

E.59TH ST.

QUEENSBOROUGH BRIDGE

attacks on women. To their credit, the city authorities have since 1980 mounted a determined assault on all these evils, renovating large portions, upping the park's policing, and greenifying it at the expense of the softball pitches and basketball nets. But it will some time before Central Park is looking anything like its best.

There's not really much else to say: the attractions of Central Park depend on the time of year, and the thing to do is explore it for yourself – and check out possible events at the Visitors' Center (see below).

Getting around in the park.
Much the best way is to hire a **bicycle** from either the *Loeb Boathouse* or *Metro Bicycles* (Lexington at 88th Street – see p.53) Both cost around $3 an hour plus deposit, a much better deal than the famed (and extortionate) **buggy rides** (about $15 for a half-hour's trot). **On foot**, there's little chance of getting lost since one glance at the skyline should provide the clue to where you are. To know exactly, just find the nearest lamp-post: the first two figures signify the number of the nearest street. As for **trouble**, should you run into anything serious best give up all you've got and make a dash for it. You should be all right during the day, though always be careful. After dark it's illegal to enter on foot, so if you want to look at the buildings of Central Park West lit-up, à la Woody Allen's *Manhattan*, best fork out for a buggy.

The park divides easily in two: the area south of the reservoir, and the rest; most things of interest lie in the south. Entering here from Grand Army Plaza, the **Pond** lies to your left and to your right Central Park **Zoo**, currently undergoing a fairly extensive restoration. First point to head for (unless you fancy a game of chess at the **Chess and Checkers Pavilion**) is the **Dairy**, a kind of dolly-Gothic ranch building originally intended to provide milk for nursing mothers and now the park's **Visitors' Center** (Tuesday-Sunday 11am-4pm), giving out free leaflets and maps, selling books and putting on sporadic exhibitions. There are two routes beyond. The first skirts the southern fringe of **Sheep's Meadow** past the **Carousel** (which kids can ride on for a pittance) to **Tavern on the Green**, actually planned as a sheep enclosure but now one of the city's most exclusive – and expensive – restaurants. The second, and more obvious, is north up the **Mall**, the park's most formal stretch, flanked by statues of an ecstatic-looking Robert Burns and a pensive Walter Scott, to the **Bandshell**, and, beyond that, to the terrace and sculpted birds and animals of the **Bethesda Fountain**. To your left, **Cherry Hill Fountain** provided a turnaround point for carriages, and has deliberately excellent views of the **Lake**, which sprawls a gnarled finger from here across the heart of Central Park. **Strawberry Fields** is just west of here, opposite the home of Yoko Ono in the Dakota Building on Central Park West. This is nothing special in itself, but is invariably crowded with those here to remember John

Lennon (see p.139).

To go **boating** on the lake, hire a vessel from the **Loeb Boathouse** on the eastern bank (9am-5pm; $20 deposit, $5 per hour); or cross the water by the elegant cast-iron **Bow Bridge** and delve into the wild woods of **The Ramble**. Take care though, as The Ramble provides notorious cover for muggers and rapists. On the other side, **Belvedere Castle** is a mock medieval citadel recently renovated, giving views over the northern half of the park and mounting small exhibitions. Just below, the **Shakespeare Garden** holds, they say, every species of plant or flower mentioned in the Bard's plays, and the **Delacorte Theater** is venue for the annual *Shakespeare in the Park* festival. Across the **Great Lawn** stand **Cleopatra's Needle** (from the Heliopolis in Egypt and 3000 years old) and the **Metropolitan Museum** (see p.178). Otherwise there's little beyond here – only the reservoir and, in the park's most northerly reaches, the **Conservatory Garden**. If you're planning on walking all the way to Harlem, this is a possible route.

THE UPPER EAST SIDE

A two-square-mile grid, scored with the great avenues of Madison, Park and Lexington, the **UPPER EAST SIDE**'s defining characteristic is wealth – as you'll at once appreciate if you've seen one of the many Woody Allen movies set here. It's the **west** of this area that sets this tone; **east** of Lexington Avenue was until recently a working-class district of modest houses, though not surprisingly gentrification is quickly changing its character.

The west East Side – Fifth and Madison avenues
Fifth Avenue has been the haughty patrician face of Manhattan since the opening of Central Park attracted the Carnegies, Astors and Whitneys to migrate north and build fashionable residences in the strip alongside. Gazing out over the park, most went up when Neo-Classicism was the rage, and hence the original buildings – those that survive – are cluttered with columns and Classical statues. A great deal of what you see, though, is third or fourth generation building: through the latter part of the 19C, fanciful mansions would be built at vast expense, to last only ten or fifteen years before being demolished for even wilder extravagances. Rocketing land values made the chance of selling at vast profit irresistible.

Grand Army Plaza is the introduction to all this, an oval at the junction of Central Park South and Fifth Avenue that marks the division between Fifth as a shopping district and residential boulevard. It's one of the city's most dramatic open spaces, flanked by the extended château of the **Plaza Hotel**, with the darkened swoop of the **Solow Building** behind. Across the plaza, no one has a good word to say for the **General Motors Building** or its sunken forecourt, especially since a much-admired hotel, the Savoy, was demolished to make way for it a few years back. Two more hotels, the high-necked **Sherry Netherland** and **Pierre** luxuriate nearby, mocked by the size of General Motors' marble clad monolith. Many of the rooms here are occupied by permanent guests – and they're not on welfare.

When **J.P.Morgan** and his pals arrived on the social scene in the 1890s, established society cocked a snook at the 'new money' by closing its downtown clubs on Morgan and anyone else it considered infra-dig. Morgan's response was the time-honoured all-American one: he commissioned Stanford White to design him his own club, bigger, better and grander than all the rest – and so the **Metropolitan Club** at 1 East 60th was born, an exuberant confection with a marvellously over-the-top gateway. Just the thing for arriving robber barons. On the corner of 65th Street America's largest reform synagogue, the **Temple Emanuel**, strikes a more sober aspect, a brooding Romanesque-Byzantine cavern that manages to be bigger inside than it seems out. The interior melts away into mysterious darkness, making you feel very small indeed.

East 65th and most streets of the East 60s are typical Upper East Side, a trim mix of small apartment houses which, not as valuable or coveted as the mansions on the avenues, escaped demolition as land prices escalated. Even so they've always been salubrious places to live: 45-49 East 65th was commissioned by Sara Delano Roosevelt as a handy townhouse for her son Franklin, 142 belonged to Richard Nixon, and 115 is the US headquarters of the PLO. Quite a neighbourhood.

Fifth Avenue's wall continues with Henry Clay Frick's house at 70th Street, marginally less ostentatious than its neighbours and now the tranquil home of the **Frick Collection**, one of the city's musts. This is the first of many prestigious museums that gives this stretch its name of *Museum Mile*. Along the avenue (or just off it) are the **Whitney** (modern American art), the **National Academy of Design**, the **Metropolitan Museum** (New York's British Museum and National Gallery rolled into one), the **Jewish Museum**, the **Guggenheim Collection** (20C painting housed in Frank Lloyd Wright's helter-skelter mustard pot), the **Cooper-Hewitt Museum of Design**, the **International Center of Photography** and, pushing further north, the **Museum of the City of New York**. Enough to be going on with for a week at least; the listings start on p.176.

Take away Fifth Avenue's museums and a resplendent though fairly bloodless strip remains. **Madison Avenue**, especially above 62nd Street, is totally different, lined with top-notch designer boutiques whose doors are kept locked, with security cameras to check you over before entry. **Park Avenue** is less developed and less extravagant yet still as stolidly comfortable – medium rise apartment blocks in anonymous dark brick with a little ornament at ground level to prove the worth of their owners. The occasional building stands out, like the self-glorifying **Colonial Club** at 62nd Street, but the best feature is the view as Park Avenue coasts down to the New York Central and Pan-Am buildings. Another landmark is the **Seventh Regiment Armoury** between 66th and 67th Streets, a Lego fortress bedecked with fairy-tale crenellations – yet just a little sinister all the same. It's the venue for a winter *antiques fair* each January, a good opportunity to gawp at the enormous drill hall inside, one that drew complaints from the locals not so long ago when it was used as a temporary shelter for the homeless.

The east East Side and Roosevelt Island

Lexington Avenue is Madison without the class, firmly **east East Side**. As the west became richer, property developers rushed to slick up real estate in the east, seldom with total success. Subsequently, apartment blocks have been repartitioned to cater to the growing demand for single accommodation. Much of the East 60s and 70s now house lone young upwardly mobile professionals wanting to play it safe with a conservatively modish address, as the number of singles bars on Second and Third Avenues gives away.

It's left to **YORKVILLE**, a German-Hungarian neighbourhood that spills out from 77th to 96th streets between Lexington and the East river, to try and supply character. Much of New York's German community arrived after the failed revolution of 1848-9, to be quickly assimilated into the area around Tompkins Square before the opening of the Elevated Railway forced a move uptown in the 1870s. Sadly the community here is greatly depleted, but the environs of 86th Street still have traditional German delicatessens like **Schaller and Weber** (1654 2nd Avenue between 85th and 86th Streets) or **Bremen House** (218-220 East 86th between 2nd and 3rd Avenues). Try also the Baroque cakes and pastries at **Cafe Geiger** (206 East 86th) or a meal at **Ideal** (238 East 82nd between Second and Third Avenues).

86th Street runs into a park named after **Carl Schurz**, a German immigrant who rose to fame as Secretary of the Interior under President John Quincy Adams and as editor of *Harper's Weekly*. It's a model park, a breathing space for elderly German speakers and East Siders escaping their postage-stamp apartments. FDR Drive cuts beneath, giving uninterrupted views across the river to Queens and the confluence of dangerous currents where the Harlem River, Long Island Sound and Harbour meet – not for nothing known as **Hell Gate**.

One of the reasons Schurz Park lacks the all-too-usual park weirdos is the high-profile security that surrounds **Gracie Mansion** at 88th Street nearby. Roughly contemporary with the Morris-Jumel Mansion (p.150), it has been much cut about over the years to end up as the official residence of the mayor of New York City – though 'Mansion' is a bit overblown for what is a rather cramped clapboard cottage. Present incumbent Ed Koch has opened the Mansion for walk-round **tours**, usually on Wednesday, though you need to book in advance (570 4751).

The streets south of Yorkville are again residential, mostly high-rise apartment blocks of zero interest, in the main with little to lure you. On the southern perimeter, **Bloomingdale's** at 59th and Third is the celebrated, definitive American store for clothes and accessories, skilfully aiming its wares at the stylish and affluent (see p.210). And nearby, at 421 East 61st Street between York and First Avenue, is the **Abigail Adams Smith Museum** (Monday-Friday 10am-4pm; $2) another of those 18C buildings that managed to survive by the skin of its teeth. This wasn't the actual home of Abigail Adams, daughter of President John Quincy Adams, just its stables, restored with Federal period propriety by the Colonial Dames of America as the dwelling house it became. In late years the Smith family fell on hard times, and there are interesting knick-knacks from that era, including the simple dress poor Abigail had to make for herself. The contents are more engaging than the house itself and there's an odd sort of pull if you're lucky enough to be guided around by a chatterly urbane Colonial Dame. The house is hemmed in by decidedly unhistoric buildings and overlooked by the **Queensboro Bridge,** which may stir memories as the 59th Street bridge of Simon and Garfunkel's *Feeling Groovy* or from the title credits of TV's *Taxi.* An intense profusion of clanging steelwork, it's utterly unlike the suspension bridges that elsewhere lace Manhattan to the boroughs; 'My God, it's a blacksmith's shop!' was architect Henry Hornbostel's comment when he first saw the finished item in 1909.

To get a view of and from the bridge, best way over is on the aerial tramway that connects with **ROOSEVELT ISLAND** across the water. For a subway token the trip is worth it in itself – and if you feel like exploring, Roosevelt Island rewards with some imaginative housing and eerie views. On paper this should long have been an ideal residential spot, but its history as 'Welfare Island', a gloomy quarantine block of gaol, poorhouse, lunatic asylum and smallpox hospital, for years put it out of bounds to Manhattanites. The stigma only started to disappear in the 1970s when Johnson and Burgee's masterplan spawned the Eastview, Westwood, Island House and Rivercross housing areas. The grim ruins remain – the octagonal **tower** at the island's north end is the insane asylum (it briefly housed Mae West after an unpalatably lewd performance in 1927) and to the south the **Smallpox Hospital** stands as a ghostly Gothic shell; currently both are off limits awaiting restoration. Maybe because no cars are allowed here, Roosevelt Island seems far away from New York City, a sort of post-Manhattan purgatory before the borough of Queens. Crossing back over the bridge gives a spine-tingling panorama of the city, the one Nick Carraway described in F. Scott Fitzgerald's *The Great Gatsby*.

Over the great bridge, with the sunlight through the girders making a constant flicker upon the moving cars, with the city rising up across the river in white heaps and sugar lumps all built with a wish out of non-olfactory money. The city seen from the Queensboro Bridge is always the city seen for the first time, in its wild promise of all the mystery and the beauty in the world...'Anything can happen now that we've slid over this bridge,' I thought; 'anything at all...'

BARS *Avenue One* (women's/lesbian), *Drake's Drum*, *Shescape* (women's/lesbian).

RESTAURANTS Cheap *Rathbone's*; **German** *Café Geiger, Ideal, Kleine Konditorei*.

THE UPPER WEST SIDE AND MORNINGSIDE HEIGHTS

North of 59th Street, paralleling the spread of Central Park, midtown Manhattan's tawdry west side becomes decidedly less commercial, less showy, and after the Lincoln Center fades into a residential area of mixed and multiple charms. This is the **UPPER WEST SIDE**, these days one of the city's most desirable addresses, though unlike its counterpart to the east of the park, a neighbourhood whose typical resident would be hard to pin down. The Upper West Side is an odd mixture of districts and faces: there's no shortage of money, as one glance at the statuesque apartment blocks of Central Park West will testify, but this exists alongside slum areas that, while they have been pushed north, have been little affected by any shifts in status.

First some **orientation**. The Upper West Side proper stretches west from Central Park as far as the Hudson river, and north from the bottom end of the park to Columbia University and Morningside Heights. Its main artery is Broadway, and generally speaking the further you get away from here either to the east or west the wealthier things become, until you reach Central Park West, or in the other direction Riverside Drive. Sandwiched between these most prestigious of Manhattan addresses are enclaves of public housing, SRO hotels and downbeat street hustle that increase the further north you go, until, on Amsterdam Avenue and Columbus Avenue in the 100s (streets that in the blocks around the 70s have become irreparably yuppified) you're walking through solid and very poor Puerto

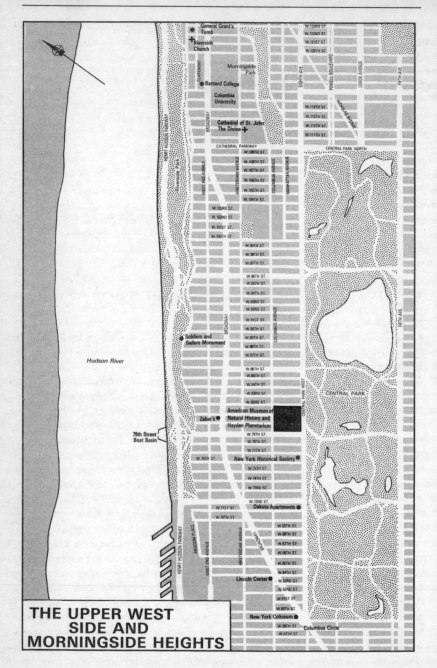

THE UPPER WEST
SIDE AND
MORNINGSIDE HEIGHTS

Rican neighbourhoods. These different lifestyles and incomes do co-exist – and for the most part happily. Give it a few years though, a handful more gourmet grocers, Japanese restaurants, sidewalk cafés, book and antique stores, and the Upper West Side may look quite different.

To explore, best start at **Columbus Circle**, an odd cast of buildings grouped around a roundabout at the Central Park's south- west corner. Christopher Columbus stands uncomfortably atop a column in the centre, and at the southern end, the city's *Department of Cultural Affairs* has recently found a home in a structure which, when it went up in 1965, was said to resemble a Persian brothel. From here the **NY Conventions and Visitors Bureau** gives advice and dispenses free leaflets, city, bus and subway maps seven days a week (9am-6pm, weekends 10am-6pm), while upstairs is venue for exhibitions of local and community art.

Broadway sheers north from the circle to **Lincoln Plaza** and, on the left, the **Lincoln Center for the Performing Arts**, a marble assembly of buildings put up in the early 1960s on the site of some of the city's most rancid slums. Home to the Metropolitan Opera and the New York Philharmonic, as well as a host of other smaller companies, this is worth seeing even if you're not into catching a performance, and the best way to do it is to go on an **organised tour**. These leave roughly every hour on the hour between 10am and 5pm each day, and take in the main part of the Center at a cost of $5.25 (students $4.75) for a one-and-a-half hour tour. Be warned that they can get very booked up; best phone ahead to be sure of a place.

The complex itself pulls you in by way of its neat central plaza and fountain, which focuses on the grand classical forms of the Opera House. Of the three principal halls, Philip Johnson's **New York State Theater** on the left is most imposing, at least inside, its foyer serried with balconies embellished by delicately worked bronze grilles, and with a ceiling finished in gold leaf. Johnson also had a hand in the **Avery Fisher Hall** opposite, called in to refashion the interior after its acoustics were found to be below par. The seating space here, though, has none of the magnificence of his glittery horsehoe-shaped auditorium across the way, and the most exciting thing about Avery Fisher Hall is its foyer, dominated by a huge hanging sculpture by Richard Lippold, whose distinctive style you may recognise from an atrium or two downtown.

The **Metropolitan Opera House** (aka 'the Met') is by contrast overdone, its staircases designed for the gliding evening wear of the city's élite. Behind each of the high windows hang **murals** by Marc Chagall. The artist wanted stained glass, but it was felt these wouldn't last long in an area still less than reverential towards the arts, so paintings were hung behind square-paned glass to give a similar effect. These days they're covered for part of the day to protect them from the morning sun; the rest of the time they're best viewed from the plaza outside. The left hand one, *Le*

Triomphe de la Musique, is cast with a variety of well-known performers, landmarks snipped from the New York skyline and a portrait of Sir Rudolph Bing, the man who ran the Met for more than three decades – here garbed as a gypsy. The other mural, *Les Sources de la Musique*,is reminiscent of Chagall's renowned Met production of *The Magic Flute*: the god of music strums a lyre while a Tree of Life, Verdi and Wagner all float down the Hudson River. As for performances, you'll find full details of what you can listen to and how to do it on p.274.

Each side of the Met broadens into two further piazzas, one centring on the **Guggenheim Bowl** where you can catch free summer lunchtime concerts, the other faced by the **Vivian Beaumont Theater**, a repertory stage which has been closed for some time due to lack of funds. This latter square is mostly taken up by a pool, around which Manhattan office workers munch their lunch; while mid-pond reclines a lazy Henry Moore figure, given counterpoint at the edge by a spidery sculpture by Alexander Calder.

Whatever people say about the whys and wherefores of the Lincoln Center, there can be little doubt of its impact on an area which before the 1960s was one of the city's most pitiful urban disasters. (It was here that the film of *West Side Story* was shot in 1960.) As well as creating an arts centre, the Lincoln scheme was an exercise in urban renewal, a grand plan intended to make this part of the Upper West Side a truly desirable neighbourhood – which has succeeded remarkably well, even if in typical New York style it has in effect replaced a poor ghetto with a rich one and simply dumped the slum dwellers further uptown. Up from Lincoln Plaza roads lead all ways, Broadway curving off north and Ninth Avenue becoming the increasingly sought-after **Columbus Avenue**. Not so long ago this too was rundown; now its shops are being upgraded and its restaurants – and there are plenty of them, especially in the 60s and 70s – battle it out for the upwardly mobile custom of the local residents.

A block east from here, however, has always been well-off – and as long as the monumental apartment blocks that line Central Park West continue to stand will remain so. Stroll down West 67th Street past the **Hotel des Artistes**, one-time Manhattan address of the likes of Noel Coward, Isadora Duncan and Alexander Woollcott, and do a left, following Central Park West as far as the junction of 72nd Street. More huge apartment blocks loom here, first the **Majestic**, yellow-brick and rectangular and topped with commanding twin towers; then, more famously, the **Dakota Building**, a grandiose German Renaissance-style mansion built in the late 19C to persuade wealthy New Yorkers that life in an apartment block could be just as luxurious as in a private house. Over the years there have been few residents here not publicly known in some way: current big-time tenants include Lauren Bacall and Leonard Bernstein, and not so long ago the building was used as the setting for

Polanski's film *Rosemary's Baby*. But most people now know the building as the former home of **John Lennon** – and (still) of his wife Yoko Ono, who owns a number of the apartments. It was outside the Dakota, on the night of December 8th 1980, that Lennon was murdered – shot by a man who professed to be one of his greatest admirers.

His murderer, Mark David Chapman, had been hanging around outside the building all day, clutching a copy of his hero's latest album, *Double Fantasy*, and accosting Lennon for his autograph – which he got. This was nothing unusual in itself – fans often used to loiter outside and hustle for a glimpse of the great man – but Chapman was still there when the couple returned from a late-night recording session and he pumped five bullets into Lennon as he walked through the Dakota's 72nd Street entrance. Lennon was picked up by the doorman and rushed to hospital in a taxi, but he died on the way from a massive loss of blood. A distraught Yoko issued a statement immediately: 'John loved and prayed for the human race. Please do the same for him.'

Why Chapman did this to John Lennon no one really knows; suffice to say his obsession with the man had obviously unhinged him. Fans may want to light a stick of incense for Lennon across the road in **Strawberry Fields**, a section of Central Park which has been restored and maintained in his memory through an endowment by Yoko Ono; trees and shrubs were donated by a number of countries as a gesture towards world peace. The gardens are pretty enough, if unspectacular, and it would take a hard-bitten sceptic not to be a little bit moved by the *Imagine* mosaic on the pathway and Yoko's handwritten note inviting passers-by to pay their respects.

Afterwards, keep on north up Central Park West, past the dull grey Beaux Arts slab of the **New York Historical Society**, which has a permanent museum (see p.202), and left by the **American Museum of Natural History**. Said to be the largest museum of any kind in the world, this fills four blocks with its bulk, a strange architectural mélange of heavy Neo-Classical and rustic Romanesque styles, that was built in several stages, the first by Calvert Vaux and Jacob Wrey Mould in 1872. For a full account of the museum and its exhibits, see p.208. South of here West 72nd Street leads west to Broadway, where several streets meet in a busy, hustly riot of fast food joints and downgrade bars. This is officially named **Verdi Square**; unofficially, and rather more accurately, it's known as *Needle Park* (as in 'Panic in...'), some say after the thin strip of gardens, others, less naively, because of its former function as a smack users' playground.

A short walk further west brings you down to the Hudson River and West Side Highway, where you can see the old **Penn Railroad Yards**, abandoned for close on two decades, though now earmarked for a new luxury housing project. Local residents, scared of yet another new influx

of people into an already crowded and increasingly gentrified neighbour
hood, whipped up a storm of protest over this, but the plan currently
looks set to go ahead regardless. North from here **Riverside Drive** weaves
its way up the western fringe of Manhattan island, the Upper West Side's
second best address after Central Park West and flanked by palatial
townhouses and multi-storey apartment blocks put up in the early part of
this century by those not quite rich enough to compete with the folks
down on Fifth Avenue. **Riverside Park**, following for fifty blocks or so,
provides a gentle break before the traffic hum of the Henry Hudson
Parkway, landscaped in 1873 by Frederick Olmsted of Central Park fame.
A few blocks away, through the park and down the steps under the road,
is a place few people know about: the **79th Street Boat Basin**, where a
couple of hundred Manhattanites live on the water. It's one of the city's
most peaceful locations, and while the views across to New Jersey aren't
exactly awesome, they're a tonic after the congestion of Manhattan
proper. Across the canyon of West End Avenue, turn left at the junction
of Broadway and 79th Street. Crossing 80th Street, the first thing you
notice is another area landmark, **Zabar's** – the Upper West Side's
principal and best gourmet shop. Here you can find more or less anything
connected with food, the ground floor given over to things edible, the first
to cooking implements and kitchenware, a collection which, in the
obscurity of some of its items, must be unrivalled anywhere. What yuppie
kitchen, for example, could do without a duck press?

The northern reaches

To the north, the Upper West Side gets rapidly more seedy, merging into
poor black and Puerto Rican neighbourhoods where people hang out
listlessly on street corners, hassling for small change. The transformation
is sudden, but like so many districts of New York it's not entirely
complete, and even here stately apartment blocks rub shoulders with SRO
hotels, and always the spiky towers of the luxury **Eldorado Building** on
Central Park West peak tantalisingly over the skyline.

A little further up, the **Cathedral Church of St John the Divine** rises out
of the burned-out tenements, dumped cars and hustlers of the southern
fringes of Harlem with a sure, solid kind of majesty – far from finished
but already one of New York's main tourist hotspots, and on the itinerary
of a steady stream of coach parties throughout the season.

The church was begun in 1892, to a Romanesque design that with a
change of architect became French Gothic. Work progressed quickly but
stopped with the outbreak of war in 1939 and has only resumed recently,
fraught with funding difficulties and hard questioning by people who
consider that, in an area of the city as impoverished as this, the money
might be better spent on something of more obvious benefit. That said,
St John's is very much a community church, housing a soup kitchen and

shelter for the homeless, studios for graphics and sculpture, a gymnasium, and (still to be built under the choir) an amphitheatre for the production of drama and concerts. And the building itself is being undertaken by local blacks trained by English stonemasons. Progress is long and slow: still only two-thirds of the cathedral is finished, and completion isn't due until around 2050 – even assuming it goes on uninterrupted. But if this happens it will be the largest cathedral structure in the world, its floor space – at 600 feet long and at the transepts 320 feet wide – big enough to swallow both the cathedrals of Notre Dame and Chartres whole, or, as tour guides are at pains to point out, two full-size American football pitches.

Walking the length of the nave, these figures seem much more than just another piece of American braggery. Though the cathedral appears a lot more finished here, it's not not until you reach the crossing, where the naked stone has still to be encased in the milk-white marble of the choir, that you realise how far it is from completion. Here too you can see the welding of the two styles, particularly in the choir which rises from a heavy arcade of Romanesque columns to high, light Gothic vaulting, the dome of the crossing to be replaced by a tall and delicate Gothic spire. For some idea of how the cathedral as a whole will look, glance in on the gift shop, housed, for the moment, in the north transept, where there's a scale model of the projected design. Afterwards, take a stroll out into the cathedral yard and workshop, in which you can watch Harlem's apprentice masons tapping away at the stone blocks of the future – and finished – cathedral.

West out of the church towards Broadway is fringed by cheap restaurants, bars and secondhand bookshops. No. 2911 is the **West End Café**, hangout of Kerouac, Ginsberg and the Beats in the 1950s – 'one of those nondescript places,' wrote Joyce Johnson, 'before the era of white walls and potted ferns and imitation Tiffany lamps, that for some reason always made the best hangouts.' It's little changed, and still serves the student crowd from **Columbia University**, whose campus fills seven blocks between Amsterdam and Broadway. This is one of the most prestigious academic institutions in the country, ranking with the Ivy League colleges of Boston and boasting a set of precincts laid out by McKim, Mead and White in grand Beaux Arts style. Of the buildings, the domed and colonnaded Low Memorial Library stands centre-stage at the top of a wide flight of stone steps, focus for demos during the Vietnam war; and the lawns hold sculptures by Moore and Rodin. If you want to know more, pick up one of the free guided **tours** which leave regularly Monday to Friday from the information office on the corner of 116th Street and Broadway. And for sustenance and some great views of Manhattan, go and eat in the restaurant on the top floor of the Butler Library.

Across the road **Barnard College** is no less pastoral in feel, but was until recently, when Columbia removed their men-only policy, the place where women were forced to study for their degrees. Just beyond, **Riverside Church** has a graceful French Gothic Revival tower, loosely modelled on Chartres and like St John's turned over to a mixture of community centre and administrative activities for the surrounding parish. Take the lift to the 20th floor and ascend the steps around the carillon for some classic spreads of Manhattan's jaggy skyline, New Jersey and the hills beyond – and the rest of the city well into the Bronx and Queens. Take a look too at the church, whose open and restrained interior (apart from the apse, which is positively sticky with Gothic ornament) is in stark contrast to the darkened mystery of St John the Divine.

Around the corner from the church is **Grant's Tomb**, a grubby, Greek-style memorial plastered with graffiti and surrounded by some bizarre, reptilian, mosaic-covered benches. The Grant in question is General Ulysses S., Yankee Civil War hero and miserable failure as US President in the latter years of the 19C. Perhaps not surprisingly, this memorial concentrates on the general's military successes rather than his term as President, the sarcophagi holding the general and his wife grandiosely based on Napoleon's in Paris.

This part of the city is known as **MORNINGSIDE HEIGHTS**, buffer zone for Harlem which sprawls forbiddingly below and with an academic, almost provincial air lent by its abundance of colleges and some fairly swanky properties on Riverside and Morningside Drives. **Morningside Park** was landscaped in 1887 by Frederick Olmsted, but it's never been especially appealing and is today a refuge of muggers and the dispossessed. If it's light it's quite feasible to walk north from here into Harlem; after dark you'd best turn south for the downtown crowds...

BARS *Dublin House, Emerald Inn, Lucy's Retired Surfers Bar, KCOU, McAleer's, McGlade's, Metropolis, Town and Country* (gay), *Wildwood* (gay), *The Works* (gay).

RESTAURANTS Cheap *Amsterdam's, Dallas Barbecue, J.G. Melon, O' Neal's Balloon, Teacher's, West End Café*; **American and Latin American** *Arriba Arriba, Caramba, Los Panchos, Victor's Café, Yellow Rose*; **Chinese** *Empire Szechuan, Hunan Balcony, Pez-Dorado*; **Fish** *Hisae's West*; **Italian** *Café Pacifico, Perretti*; **Japanese** *Cherry Restaurant, Hisae's West, Sakura*; **Middle Eastern and Indian** *At Our Place, Blue Nile, Indian Kitchen, Mughlai*.

HARLEM, HAMILTON HEIGHTS AND THE NORTH

HARLEM is the side of Manhattan that few visitors bother to see. Home of a declined and still declining black community, its name is synonymous with racial tension and urban decay, languishing under the bad reputation gained from riots of the 1940s, 1950s and 1960s. Yet Harlem is more a focus of black consciousness and culture than out-and-out ghetto. And, perhaps because of its near-total lack of support from Federal and Municipal funds (one example – there is no public high school here, the kids have to be shipped out), Harlem has formed a self-reliant and inward looking community. For many Manhattanites white and black, 110th Street is a physical and mental border not willingly crossed: but to understand New York, its problems and its strengths, it is necessary to understand – and visit – Harlem.

Harlem – hints and history

Practically speaking, Harlem's **sights** are too spread out to amble between. You'll do best to make several trips, preferably using one of the **guided tours** available (see *Basics*) to get acquainted with the area. Harlem's **problems** of poverty, unemployment and attendant crime mean that foreign visitors, especially whites, can be soft targets for trouble. Though it's unlikely you'll be in any danger during the daytime, 125th Street, 145th Street, Convent and Lenox Avenues and East 116th Street in Spanish Harlem are the places you're *least* likely be hassled – at night stick to the clubs only.

As the name suggests, it was the Dutch who founded the settlement of *Nieuw Haarlem*, naming it after a town in Holland. Until the mid-19C this was farmland and plantation, but when the New York and Harlem railroad linked the area with Lower Manhattan it attracted the richer immigrant families (mainly German Jews from the Lower East Side) to build elegant and fashionable brownstones in the steadily developing suburb. When work began on the IRT Lenox line later in the century, property speculators were quick to build good quality homes in the expectation of seeing Harlem repeat the success of the Upper West Side. They were too quick and too ambitious, for by the time the IRT line opened most of the buildings were still empty, their would-be takers uneasy at moving so far north. A black real estate agent saw his chance, bought the empty houses cheaply and rented them to blacks from the rundown, midtown districts. Very quickly Harlem became black, while remaining home to a mix of cultural and social communities: the western areas along **Convent Avenue** and **Sugar Hill** were for years the patch of the middle classes, and preserve traces of a well-to-do past. In the east the bulge between Park Avenue and the East River became **Spanish Harlem**, now largely peopled by Puerto Ricans and more properly called *El Barrio* – 'the Neighbourhood'. In between live the descendants of West Indian, African, Cuban and Haitian immigrants, often crowded into poorly maintained housing.

This cramping together of dissimilar cultures has long caused tensions and problems not easily understood by downtown bureaucracy. Dotted around Harlem are buildings and projects that attest to an uneasy municipal conscience, which have not in any real sense solved the problems of unemployment and urban decay. Sometimes, amid the boarded-up shopfronts and vacant lots, it's hard to believe you're but a mile or two away from the cosily patrician Upper East Side.

But there was a brief period when Harlem enjoyed a golden age. In the 1920s whites began to notice the explosion of black culture that had occurred here: jazz musicians like Duke Ellington, Count Basie and Cab Calloway played in nightspots like the Cotton Club, Savoy Ballroom, Apollo Theater and Small's Paradise; the drink flowed as if prohibition had never been heard of and the sophisticated set drove up to Harlem's speakeasies after downtown had gone to bed. Maybe because these revellers never stayed longer than the last drink, they and history seldom recall the poverty then rife in Harlem, the harshness of scraping a living even before the Depression finally put paid to the revels of the few and decline drove middle-class blacks out of Harlem. One of the most evocative voices heard in the clubs those days was of Ethel Waters, who sang in the Sugar Cane Club:

> Rent man waitin' for his forty dollars,
> Ain't got me but a dime and some bad news.
> Bartender give me a bracer, double beer chaser,
> 'Cause I got the low-down, mean, rent man blues.

And today? As midtown real estate prices continue to rocket, new interest is being shown in sprucing up Harlem's residential dereliction. Unlike many 'ghettos', the basic quality of the 19C houses here is excellent and ripe for renovation: what unsettles black activists is that 65% of the property in Harlem is owned by the City of New York, which assumed control after houses were abandoned by their owners. Mindful of historical precedent the downtown developers are viewed with suspicion, and renovation seen as a chance to attract young middle-class whites to the area and so signal the end of a black community that has won strength through long adversity. Others think that the arrival of whites would be a trickle at most, given the expense of renovation; and that integration in itself would be no bad thing. For Harlem, the future remains undecided...

Harlem and El Barrio
125th Street between Broadway and Fifth Avenue is the working centre

of Harlem, a flattened, shell-shocked expanse spiked with the occasional skyscraper. The subway throws you up here and the **New York State Office Building** on the corner of Seventh Avenue provides a looming modern landmark: commissioned after the last serious riots in 1968, it was intended to show state committment to the support of the community. Really, though, it's an intrusion on the earthy goings-on of 125th Street. Walk a little west from here and you reach the **Apollo Theater** at number 253, Not much from the outside, despite a recent cleaning up, it was for 20-odd years from 1913 the centre of black entertainment in New York City and north-eastern America: almost all the great figures of jazz and blues played here along with singers, comics and dancers. Since then it's served as a warehouse, movie theatre and radio station, and in its latest incarnation televises weekly rock concerts for cable TV. Across the way at 125th and Seventh Avenue the Theresa Towers office block was until the 1960s the **Theresa Hotel**. Fidel Castro was once a guest here, shunning midtown luxury in a popular political gesture.

125th Street rolls energetically eastwards: turn right at Lenox Avenue and you enter the **Mount Morris Park Historical District** and at 201 Lenox the **Mount Oliphet Church,** an American version of a Roman version of what they thought a Greek temple looked like, and one of literally hundreds of religious buildings dotted around Harlem. The sombre, bulky **St Martin's** at the south east corner of Lenox Avenue and 122nd Street is another, and both have been fortunate in avoiding falling into decay as church and community declined. Elsewhere the Mount Morris Park Historic District comprises some lovely **row houses** that went up in the speculative boom of the 1890s: take a look at the block on **Lenox Avenue** between 120th and 121st Streets or the Romanesque **Mount Morris Park West** for the best. When, a few years back, the city held a lottery to sell a dozen abandoned houses on Mount Morris Park there was an immediate outcry from the local people, who considered one of the prime slices of Harlem was being raffled off to faceless downtown concerns. A compromise was reached that ensured each prospective buyer who lived in Harlem would be entered three times, guaranteeing a 50-50 chance of a win. For these 12 houses, 2500 applications were received. Which is hardly surprising. Looking at Mount Morris Park West you can't help but feel that it too will go the way of Greenwich Village and the Lower East Side – the quality of building is so good, the pressures on Manhattan so great that it's just a matter of time.

The former Mount Morris Park is now **Marcus Garvey Park**, taking its name from the black leader of the 1920s, and altogether a decidedly odd urban space. Craggy peaks block off views, meaning you never get an idea of the square as a unity, and the jutting outcrops contradict the precise lines of the houses around. At the top an elegant octagonal climbing frame tames the high ground, a fire tower of 1856 that's a unique example of the early warning devices once found throughout the city. Spiral your way to the top for a great view.

Seventh Avenue becomes **Adam Clayton Powell Jr Boulevard** above 110th Street, a broad sweep pushing north between low-built houses that for once in Manhattan allow the sky to break through. Since its conception Powell Boulevard has been Harlem's main concourse, and it's

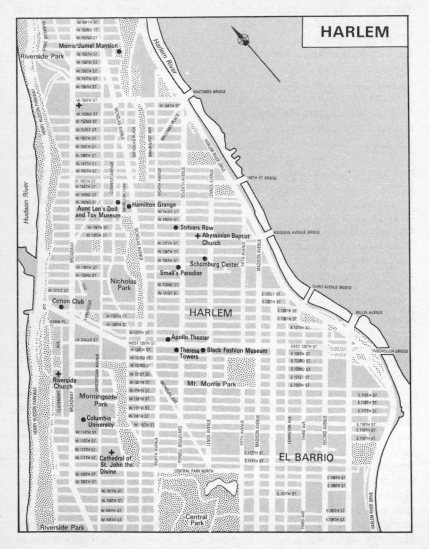

not difficult to imagine the propriety the shops and side streets had in their late 19C heyday, though now they're a chain of graffiti-splattered walls and storefronts punctuated with demolished lots. At 135th Street and Powell Boulevard the new **Small's Paradise** is also a reminder of that era, taking its cue from the famous club of the 1920s where monied downtowners, gangsters and bootleggers mingled with Small's dancing waiters to the sounds of jazz. The tradition is kept up in Friday and Saturday night jams and concerts; no cover and no minimum mean you can afford the laid-on taxi back home – see p.264 for the phone number. When here during the day it's worth checking out the **Schomberg Center for Research in Black Culture** at Lenox and 135th (Monday-Wednesday 12am-8pm, Thursday-Saturday 10am-6pm; free) for its occasional shows of black American and African art.

A few streets north at 132 West 138th Street is yet another church – though this one, the **Abyssinian Baptist Church**, is special not because it's architecturally interesting, but because of the career of its long-time minister, the **Reverend Adam Clayton Powell Jr**. In the 1930s Powell was instrumental in forcing the mostly white-owned, white-workforce shops and stores of Harlem to begin employing the blacks who ensured their economic survival. Later he became the first black on the city council, then New York's first black representative at Congress – a career which came to an embittered end in 1967, when amid strong rumours of the misuse of public funds he was excluded from Congress by majority vote. This failed to diminish his standing in Harlem, where voters twice re-elected him before his death in 1972. There's a small **museum** to Powell's life, the scandal of course unmentioned, but a more fitting memorial is the Boulevard that today bears his name.

The Abyssinian Baptist Church is also famed for its revival-style Sunday morning **services** and a gospel choir of gut-busting vivacity. Usually all are welcome to join in, though it's discreet to phone ahead (362 7474). An alternative, and a viable one, is to join the Penny Sightseeing Company's **Harlem Gospel Tour** (Thursday 10am, and Sunday 10.30am; $17, reservations at least two days in advance from the address in *Basics*).

These days no one is going to make grandiose claims for Powell Boulevard, but cross over to 138th Street between Powell and 8th Avenue (aka Frederick Douglass Boulevard) and you're in what many consider the finest, most articulate block of row houses in Manhattan – **Strivers' Row**. Commissioned during the 1890s housing boom, this takes in designs by three sets of architects – the best McKim, Mead and Whites' north side of 139th, a dignified Renaissance-derived strip that's an amalgam of simplicity and elegance. Within the burgeoning black community of the turn of the century this came to be *the* desirable place for ambitious professionals to reside – hence its nickname. Maybe it's an indication of Harlem's future that despite the presence of Strivers' row there's been no knock-on effect on the wasteland all around; if streets like these can't trigger redevelopment, cynics argue, then what can?

From Park Avenue to the East River is Spanish Harlem or **EL BARRIO**, dipping down as far as East 96th Street to collide head on with the affluence of the Upper East Side. The centre of a large Puerto Rican community, it is quite different from Harlem – the streets are dirtier, the atmosphere more intimidating. El Barrio was originally a working-class Italian neighbourhood (a small pocket of Italian families survives around 116th Street and 1st Avenue) and the quality of building here was nowhere as good as that immediately to the west. The occupants have had little opportunity to evolve Hispanic culture in any meaningful or noticeable way, and the only space where roots can be seen is **La Marqueta** on Park Avenue between 111th and 116th Streets, a five-block street market of tropical fruit and veg, sinister-looking meats and much shouting; brush up your Spanish and watch your change. To get some background on the whole scene **El Museo del Barrio** at Fifth Avenue and 104th Street (see p.204) is a showcase of Latin American art and culture.

Hamilton Heights and the North

Much of Harlem's western edge is taken up by the area known as **HAMILTON HEIGHTS**, like Morningside Heights to the south a mixed bag of campus, rubbishy streets and slender parks on a bluff above Harlem. Just one stretch, the **Hamilton Heights Historic District** that runs down Convent Avenue to City College, pulls Hamilton Heights up from the ranks of the untidily mediocre. Years ago the black professionals who made it up here and to Sugar Hill a little further north could glance down on lesser Harlemites with disdain: it's still a firmly bourgeois residential area – and one of the most attractive uptown.

But even if this mood of shabbiness around a well-heeled neighbour hood is to your liking, there's little in the way of specific sights. The 135th Street St Nicholas subway is as good a place to start as any, for up the hill and round the corner is Convent Avenue, containing the Heights' single historic lure – the house of Alexander Hamilton, **Hamilton Grange**.

Alexander Hamilton's life is as fascinating as it was flamboyant. An early supporter of the Revolution, his enthusiasm quickly brought him to the attention of George Washington, and he became the general's aide-de-camp, later founding the Bank of New York and becoming first Secretary to the Treasury. Hamilton's headlong tackling of problems made him enemies as well as friends: alienating Republican populists led to a clash with their leader Thomas Jefferson, and when Jefferson won the Presidency in 1801, Hamilton was left out in the political cold. Temporarily abandoning politics, he moved away from the city to his grange here (or rather near here – the house was moved in 1889) to tend his plantation and conduct a memorably sustained and vicious feud with

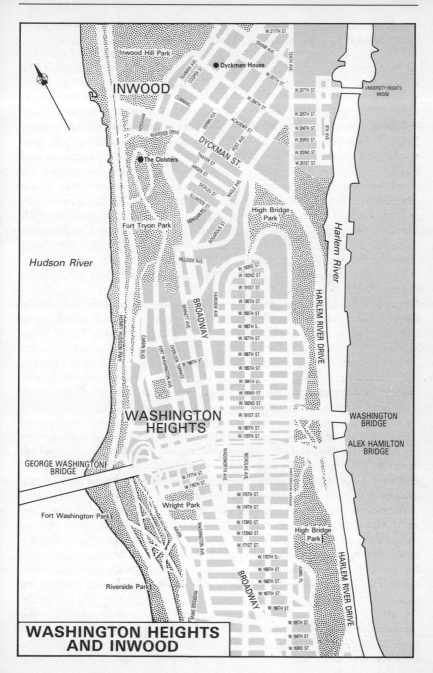

WASHINGTON HEIGHTS
AND INWOOD

one **Aaron Burr**, who had beaten Hamilton's father-in-law to a seat in the Senate and then set up the Bank of Manhattan as a direct rival to the Bank of New York. After a few years as Vice-President under Jefferson, Burr ran for the governorship of New York; Hamilton strenuously opposed his candidature and after an exchange of extraordinarily bitter letters, the two men fought a duel in Weehawken, New Jersey, roughly where today's Lincoln Tunnel emerges. Hamilton's eldest son had been killed in a duel on the same field a few years earlier, which may explain why, when pistols were drawn, Hamilton honourably discharged his into the air. Burr, evidently made of lesser stuff, aimed carefully and fatally wounded Hamilton. So died 'the most restless, impatient, artful, indefatigable and unprincipled intriguer in the United States' as President John Adams described him; you'll find his portrait on the back of a $10 note.

All of which is a lot more exciting than the **house** he lived in at 287 Convent Avenue (at 142nd Street, daily 9am-5pm; free) a Federal-style mansion today uncomfortably transplanted between a fiercely Roman esque church and an apartment block. To be honest I'd call in only if visiting the wonderful **Aunt Len's Doll and Toy Museum** nearby – for more on which see p.206.

If you've just wandered up from Harlem, **Convent Avenue** comes as something of a surprise. Its secluded, blossom-lined streets have a garden suburb prettiness that's spangled with Gothic, French and Italian Renaissance hints in the happily eclectic houses of the 1890s. Running south, the feathery span of the Shepard Archway announces **City College**, a rustic-feeling campus of Collegiate Gothic halls built from grey Manhattan schist dug up during the excavations for the IRT line and mantled with white terracotta fripperies. Founded in 1905, City College made no charge for tuition, so becoming the seat of higher learning for many of New York's poorest, and though free education came to an end in the 1970s, 75% of the students still come from minority backgrounds to enjoy a campus that's as warmly intimate as Columbia is grandiose.

The change from Convent Avenue to Broadway is almost as abrupt as it is up from Harlem. Broadway here is a once-smart, now raggy sweep that slowly lifts to the northernmost part of Manhattan island, **WASHINGTON HEIGHTS**. Even from Morningside or Hamilton Heights the haul up is a long one: but the first two good stop-offs are both easily reached from the number 1 train to 157th and Broadway or the AA to 155th or 163rd. **Audubon Terrace** at 155th and Broadway is an Acropolis in a cul-de-sac, a weird, clumsy 19C attempt to deify 155th Street with museums dolled up as Beaux Arts temples. Easily the best of these is the **Museum of the American Indian**, but as you might expect from something so far out of town, it's little known and little visited. For a full account of each museum, see p.203.

Within walking distance the **Morris-Jumel Mansion** (160th Street between Amsterdam and Edgecombe Avenues, Tuesday-Sunday 10am-4pm; $2) is another uptown surprise: cornered in its garden the mansion somehow survived the destruction all around, and today is one of the more successful house museums, its proud Georgian outlines faced with a later Federal portico. Inside, the mansion's rooms reveal some of its engaging history: built as a rural retreat in 1765 by Colonel Roger Morris, it was briefly Washington's headquarters before falling into the hands of the British. A leaflet describes the rooms and their historical connections, but curiously omits much of the later history. Wealthy wine merchant Stephen Jumel bought the derelict mansion in 1801 and refurbished it for his wife Eliza, formerly a prostitute and his mistress. New York society didn't take to such a past, but when Jumel died in 1832, Eliza still married ex-Vice President Aaron Burr – she for his connections, he for her money. Burr was 78 when they married, 20 years older than Eliza: the marriage lasted for six months before old Burr upped and left, to die on the day of their divorce. Eliza battled on to the age of 91, and on the top floor of the house you'll find her obituary, a magnificently fictionalised account of a 'scandalous' life.

From most western stretches of Washington Heights you get a glimpse of the **George Washington Bridge** that links Manhattan to New Jersey, and it's arguable that the feeder road to the bridge splits two distinct areas: below is bleakly rundown, above the streets relax in smaller, more diverse ethnic neighbourhoods of old-time Jews, Greeks, Central Europeans and especially the Irish, though a major Hispanic community has recently built up. A skilful, dazzling sketch high above the Hudson, the bridge skims across the channel in massive metalwork and graceful lines, a natural successor to the Brooklyn Bridge. 'Here, finally, steel architecture seems to laugh,' said Le Corbusier of the 1931 construction. To appreciate what he meant, grit your teeth and walk – midtown Manhattan hangs like a visible promise in the distance.

What most people come to visit in Washington Heights, though, is **The Cloisters**, the Metropolitan Museum's collection of medieval art housed in a Frankenstein's monster of a castle in **Fort Tryon Park**. Unequivocally, this is a must (see p.197 for persuasion), and should you plump for riding up on the subway you'll find an additional reward in the park itself, cleverly landscaped by Frederick Law Olmsted and a comfortable place to get lost for half an hour or so. Conceivably, you might want to venture further north to **INWOOD** whose rambling park was once the stamping-ground of Indian cave dwellers. Those were the exciting days, for now Inwood is essentially a green-belt pause before the Bronx, and its one stop-off is the **Dykman House** (4881 Broadway at 204th Street; Tuesday-Sunday 11am-5pm; free) an 18C Dutch farmhouse restored with period bits and bobs; pleasant enough, but hardly worth the journey.

RESTAURANTS Cheap *Sylvia's Restaurant.*

Chapter four

THE OUTER BOROUGHS

Manhattan is a hard act to follow, and the four **OUTER BOROUGHS** – **Brooklyn**, **Queens**, **The Bronx** and **Staten Island** – inevitably pale in comparison. They lack the excitement (and the mass money) of Manhattan's architecture; with a few honourable exceptions they don't have museums to compare with the Met or MoMA, nor galleries like SoHo's; and their life, essentially residential, is less obviously dynamic.

So why step off the island? The answer, perhaps, if you've just a few days in NYC, is 'don't' – or at least only do so for the fun of returning on the **Staten Island Ferry**. But if you're staying longer, you will probably be more receptive to the boroughs' attractions, not least among them the chance to escape the sometimes stifling environment of Manhattan. And there are definite, if modest, attractions. **Brooklyn** offers the beautiful **Prospect Park**, salubrious **Brooklyn Heights** and, for addicts of rundown seaside resorts, **Coney Island**. **Queens**, scarcely ever visited by outsiders, has the bustling Greek community of **Astoria**. As for **Staten Island**, the ferry is its own justification. Whether you choose to take a look at the fourth borough, **The Bronx**, is a more ambivalent exercise. The area is ordinarily residential at its north end but the south, as any number of New York stories will attest, is Hard Territory, as desolate and and bleak an urban landscape as you'll find anywhere.

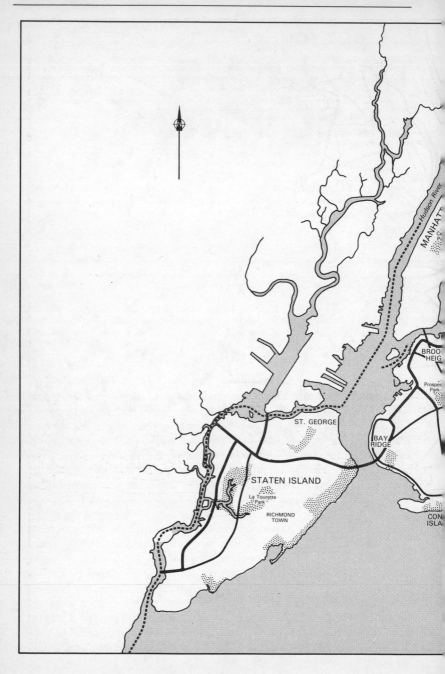

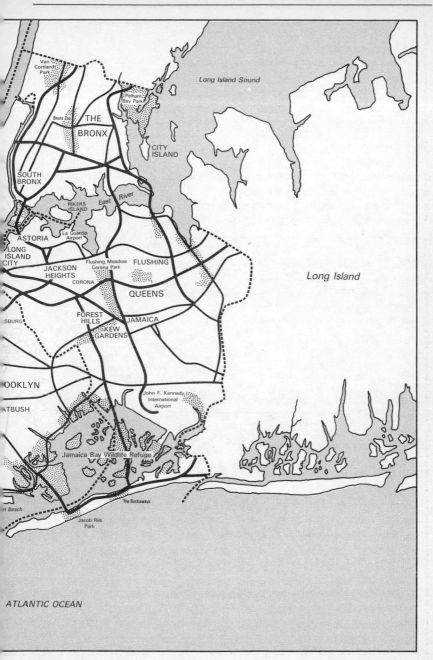

Van
Cortlandt
Park

Pelham
Bay Park

Bronx Zoo

THE
BRONX

Long Island Sound

CITY
ISLAND

SOUTH
BRONX

RIKERS
ISLAND

East *River*

ASTORIA

La Guardia
Airport

LONG
ISLAND
CITY

JACKSON
HEIGHTS

Flushing Meadow
Corona Park

FLUSHING

Long Island

CORONA

QUEENS

SBURG

FOREST
HILLS

JAMAICA

KEW
GARDENS

OOKLYN

TBUSH

John F. Kennedy
International
Airport

Jamaica Bay Wildlife Refuge

n Beach

The Rockaways

Jacob Riis
Park

ATLANTIC OCEAN

BROOKLYN

Duh poor guy! Say, I've got to laugh, at dat, when I t'ink about him! Maybe he's found out by now dat he'll neveh live long enough to know the whole of Brooklyn. It'd take a guy a lifetime to know Brooklyn t'roo an' t'roo. An' even den, you wouldn't know it at all.
Thomas Wolfe *Only the Dead Know Brooklyn*

'The Great Mistake'. So New York writer Pete Hamill summed up the 1898 annexation of his borough, and in a way, that's how most Brooklynites feel even today, traditionally seeing themselves as **Brooklyn** residents first, inhabitants of New York City a poor second. Though always the underdog to Manhattan, Brooklyn has a firm and individual identity, a definite feel which is embodied in a mass of urban folklore. The

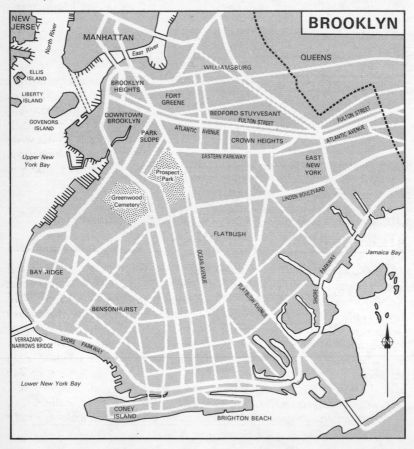

Brooklyn Dodgers, the accent, Woody Allen, Mel Brooks, W.C. Fields: all, in one way or another, are unmistakably Brooklyn – and all to some degree sum up this most diverse of the New York City's boroughs.

If it were still a separate city Brooklyn would be fourth largest in the United States, but until as recently as the early 1800s it was no more than a group of loosely connected towns and villages existing relatively autonomously from already thriving Manhattan across the water. It was with the arrival of Robert Fulton's steamship service, linking the two, that Brooklyn began to take on its present form, starting with the establishment of a leafy retreat at Brooklyn Heights. What really changed the borough, though, was the opening of the Brooklyn Bridge, and thereafter development began to spread deeper inland, as housing was needed for the increasingly large workforce necessary to service a more commercialised Manhattan. By the turn of the century, Brooklyn was fully established as part of New York City, and its fate as Manhattan's perennial kid brother was sealed.

Brooklyn Heights is the most obvious – and justly the most visited – district, but that's as far as most people get. Yet there are other neighbourhoods which are at least as picturesque, and in a way a lot more real. **Park Slope**, for example, has some of the city's best preserved brownstones, and Calvert and Vaux's **Prospect Park** is for many an improvement on their more famous bit of landscaping in Manhattan; **Coney Island** and **Brighton Beach** are worth the subway ride for their unique atmospheres if not as beach resorts; and the **Brooklyn Museum** has a collection which can compete with anything on Manhattan. Basically, treat Brooklyn not as a suburb but as a separate city, and you begin to appreciate it.

DOWNTOWN BROOKLYN: BROOKLYN HEIGHTS, ATLANTIC AVENUE AND SOUTH

BROOKLYN HEIGHTS is one of New York City's most beautiful and wealthy neighbourhoods, and as such it has little in common with the rest of the borough. From the early 18C on, bankers and financiers from Wall Street could live amongst its peace and exclusivity and imagine themselves far from the tumult of Manhattan, but still close enough to gaze across to the monied spires. Today the Heights are not far different, their tree-lined streets, perfectly preserved terraces and air of civilised calm extraordinarily lovely, and it's not hard to see why people want to live here. That is, though, give or take a handful of churches, all there is to see: students of urban architecture could have a field day, but for the rest of us there's little to do beyond wander and breathe in the neighbourhood's peace.

Assuming you're walking from Manhattan (and it really is the best way, for the views if nothing else), the Brooklyn Bridge is the most obvious place to begin a tour of the district. At its far end you'll find yourself in what's called the **Fulton Ferry District**. This, hard under the glowering shadow of the Watchtower (world HQ of the Jehovah's Witness organisation), was where Robert Fulton's ferry used to put in, and during the 19C it grew into Brooklyn's first and most prosperous industrial neighbourhood. With the coming of the bridge it fell into decline, but now is on the way up again: its ageing buildings are being slowly tarted up as loft spaces, and, down on the ferry slip itself, a couple of barges – *Bargemusic* and the *River Café* – entice die-hard Manhattanites across the bridge by night.

Camden Plaza West leads off beneath the elevated highway: follow this for a little way and a right up Henry Street will take you into the oldest

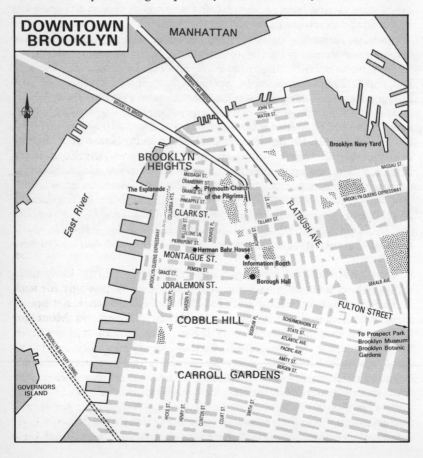

part of Brooklyn Heights proper. Middagh Street holds the neighbour hood's oldest house, no.24, dating from 1829 and built in the wooden Federal style – dubbed 'gingerbread' because of its elaborately carved details. On the next street up, Orange, stands the **Plymouth Church of the Pilgrims**, a simple church that went up in the mid-19C and became the preaching base of **Henry Ward Beecher**, under whom it grew to be one of the country's most talked-about churches. Beecher – liberal, abolitionist, campaigner for women's rights – was a great orator: he held mock slave auctions here and used the money to buy slaves' freedom, and toured the country persuading the rich to give to charitable institutions. This brought the famous to his church, and Horace Greeley, Mark Twain, even Abraham Lincoln, all worshipped here on more than one occasion. Sadly, though, Henry Ward remains less known outside New York than his sister, Harriet Beecher Stowe, author of *Uncle Tom's Cabin*, since his later years were marred by an adultery scandal of which he was acquitted but never finally cleared in public esteem. The church is kept locked most of the time, so the only chance you'll get to see its barn-like interior is when there's a service on. No great loss.

Clark Street leads down to the river and **The Esplanade** (called 'The Promenade' by the locals), home of notables like Norman Mailer (he lives in one of the creeper-hung palaces here) and with fine views of Lower Manhattan across the water. East is **Pierrepoint Street**, one of the Heights' main arteries and studded with delightful – and fantastic – brownstones. On the corner of Henry Street the **Herman Behr House** is a chunky Romanesque Revival mansion which has been, successively, a hotel, brothel, Franciscan monastery (it was the brothers who added the horrific canopy) and currently private apartments. Further down Pierrepoint, look in if you can on the **Church of the Saviour**, notable for its exquisite Neo-Gothic interior, and, across the road, the **Brooklyn Historical Society**, who present regular exhibits on aspects of the borough's social history. The society's walking tours of the Heights also leave from here (see *Basics*).

West, and you're on **Montague Street**, Brooklyn Heights' lively main thoroughfare, lined with bars and restaurants and, surprisingly for such an exclusive district, with a workaday atmosphere that makes it one of New York's pleasantest throughfares. At the far end, on **Montague Terrace**, Thomas Wolfe lived for while and wrote *Of Time and the River*. South of here are a couple of neat mews, **Grace Court Alley** and **Hunts Lane**, not unlike those off Washington Square in Manhattan, and just below, **Joralemon Street**, traditionally a street of artisans rather than brokers and consequently holding houses decidedly less grand. The far end of Montague is known as 'Bank Row' – downtown Brooklyn's business centre – and leads on to what is in effect the borough's Civic Center, the end of the residential Heights signalled by the tall Art Deco blocks of Court Street. Across the road the sober Greek-style **Borough Hall** is topped with a cupola-ed belfry; to its left there's the massive **State Supreme Court** and Romanesque **post office**, next to which stands a bronze of Henry Ward Beecher. There's little to linger for, and the buildings are ugly, but stop off at the **Information Booth/TKTS Office** just in front for a map and Brooklyn information pack.

Beyond the civic grandeur **Fulton Street** leads east, principal shopping street for the borough as a whole and here pedestrianised into a characterless shopping mall. There's another TKTS office, plentiful mainstream shops, and **Gage & Tollner**, Brooklyn's most famous restaurant that serves seafood and steaks in a setting determinedly left unchanged. If you can afford it – and the food doesn't come cheap – there are worse places to break for lunch.

South of Brooklyn Heights is **ATLANTIC AVENUE**, which runs from the East River all the way to Queens and is for a short stretch centre to New York's Middle Eastern minority. There are some fine and reasonably priced Yemeni and Lebanese restaurants here and a good sprinkling of Middle Eastern grocers and bakeries. Try the **Damascus Bakery** for pitta bread, and the **Sahadi Importing Co.** at no.187 for nuts, dried fruit, halva and the like; and see p.257 for our listings of the best restaurants. Crossing Atlantic Avenue, Cobble Hill, Boerum Hill and Carroll Gardens are some of Brooklyn's most up-and-coming neighbourhoods, though they're unlikely ever to challenge the respectability of the Heights. **COBBLE HILL** is most elegant, its main streets – Congress, Warren and Amity – a mixture of solid brownstones and colourful redbrick terraces, most of which have long been a haven of the professional classes. Really, the attraction is just in strolling the streets, but there are a couple of features you may want to base your walk around: Jenny Jerome, later Lady Randolph Churchill and mother of Winston, was born at **197 Amity Street** in a house now disfigured by aluminium windows and a modern rustic facing; and **Warren Place** is worth a quick peek for a tiny alley of workmen's cottages from the late 19C – a shelter of quiet just a stone's throw from the thunder of the Brooklyn-Queens Expressway. **BOERUM HILL** is scruffier and less architecturally impressive, home to a large Spanish population – as is **CARROLL GARDENS**, least yuppified of the three and still distinctly Italian. If it's lunchtime try the pizzas at *House of Pizza and Calzone* on Union Street, or the Sicilian specialities at *Ferdinando's* further down.

CENTRAL BROOKLYN: PARK SLOPE AND PROSPECT PARK

Fulton Street mall joins Flatbush Avenue opposite the **Brooklyn Academy of Music** – BAM to its friends and one of the borough's most cherished institutions, playing host over the years to a glittering – and innovative – array of names. Follow Fulton Street and turn south across Atlantic Avenue and you're in **CROWN HEIGHTS**: New York's largest West Indian neighbourhood, which bursts into life with an enormous carnival each Labor Day.

More interesting, though, is the route up Flatbush Avenue to **Grand Army Plaza**. This is where Brooklyn really asserts itself as a city in its own right – pure classicism, with the traffic being funelled around the central open space. It was laid out by Calvert and Vaux in the late 19C, who designed it as a dramatic approach to their newly completed Prospect Park just behind. The triumphal **Soldiers and Sailors Memorial Arch**, which you can climb (spring and autumn weekends only), was added 30 years later, and topped with a fiery sculpture of Victory in tribute to the Yankees' triumph in the Civil War. On the far side of the square the creamy smooth **Brooklyn Public Library** continues the heroic theme, its facade smothered with stirring declarations to its function as fountain of knowledge, and with an entrance showing the borough's home-grown poet, Walt Whitman. Behind, there's the **Brooklyn Museum** (see p.199)and the **Brooklyn Botanic Garden** (April-September Tuesday-Friday 8am-6pm, Saturday/Sunday 10am-4pm; October-March Tuesday-Friday 8am-4.30pm, Saturday/Sunday 10am-4.30pm).

This is one of the most enticing park spaces in the city, smaller and more immediately likeable than its more celebrated rival in the Bronx, and making for a relaxing place to unwind after a couple of hours in the museum. Sumptuously but not over-planted, it sports a Rose Garden, Japanese Garden, a Shakepeare Garden (laid out with plants mentioned in the bard's plays) and some delightful lawns draped with weeping willows and beds of flowering shrubs. There's also a conservatory which houses, among other things, the country's largest collection of bonsai trees.

The Botanic Garden is about as far away from Manhattan's bustle as it's possible to get, but if you can tear yourself away there's also **PROSPECT PARK** itself. Energised by their success with Central Park, Olmsted and Vaux landscaped this in the early 1890s, completing it just as the finishing touches were being put to Grand Army Plaza outside. In a way it's better than Central Park, having more effectively managed to retain its pastoral quality, and though there have been encroachments over the years – tennis courts, a zoo – it remains for the most part remarkably bucolic in feel. Focal points include the **Lefferts Homestead**, an 18C colonial farmhouse shifted here some time ago and now open for tours Wednesday-Sunday, the **Zoo** (though it's no better and no less cruel than Central Park zoo) and the lake in the southern half. The **boathouse** has maps and information on events in the park (dance, drama and music are performed in the bandshell most summer weekends) or you can pick up all kinds of park info on 718 788 0055.

The western exits of Prospect Park leave you on the fringes of **PARK SLOPE**, with some of New York's best preserved brownstones and, in an area currently building itself up as a serious rival to Brooklyn Heights, some of the city's fastest-soaring property prices. Main streets are **Seventh** and **Fifth Avenues**, both of which share new shops for the recent incomers and old-established stores in almost equal proportion – though of the two Fifth is more downmarket, still supporting a solid Hispanic community. There are any number of **places to eat** here, better and often at lower prices than you'd pay in Manhattan for similar quality. *Le Parc* is reliable and not over-expensive, or there's *Dominski's* (corner of 3rd Street and Seventh Avenue). More famously, *Charlie's*, the other side of Flatbush Avenue near Eighth, is a little pricier but friendly and fun. Plus there's a number of highly recommended vegetarian restaurants on Seventh Avenue (see p.257 for the full picture).

Walk down Fifth Avenue, across the Prospect Expressway, and you reach **Greenwood Cemetery**: larger even than Prospect Park and very much the place to be buried in the last century if you could afford to lash out on an appropriately flashy headstone – or better still mausoleum. Among the names buried here Horace Greeley, politician and campaign ing newspaper editor, lies relatively unpretentiously on a hill; William Marcy 'Boss' Tweed, 19C Democratic chief and scoundrel, slumbers deep in the wilds; and the Steinway family, of piano fame, have their very own 119-room mausoleum. Look out also for the tomb of one John Matthews, who made a fortune out of carbonated drinks and had himself a memorial carved with birds and animals, some fierce-looking gargoyles, and (rather immodestly) scenes from his own life. You can stroll around the cemetery and find all this for yourself; or take a **guided tour** (see *Basics*).

SOUTH BROOKLYN: CONEY ISLAND AND BRIGHTON BEACH

CONEY ISLAND, reachable direct from Manhattan on the B, D, F or N subway lines, was for years where generations of working-class New Yorkers came to relax, at its height visited by 100,000 people a day who idled away their weekends in an extended party of beach-lounging, hot dogs, candy floss and strolls down the boardwalk. By the 1950s, however, the resort was past its best, and now, although plenty of people still flock here when the weather's fine, the good-time carefree atmosphere is long gone. Coney Island is today one of Brooklyn's – and New York's – poorest districts, predominantly Hispanic and with a pervasive atmos phere of menace through which even the police travel in groups of three. The amusement park is peeling and rundown, until recently the boardwalk was cracked and broken, and *Nathan's*, Coney Island's once legendary and unique hot dog stand, now has franchises all over the city. Really, if you like rundown seaside resorts, there's no better place on earth.

The main street is **Surf Avenue**, above which run the gaudy subway trains on their way back to Manhattan. Weekdays here are a depressing sight – gangs of youths hanging about outside bars and souvenir-hung arcades that, whatever the weather, emit cringingly inappropriate fairground music. The **beach** at least is beautiful, a broad clean swathe of golden sand, and it's not difficult to see what once made people come here. But the rusty mecanno sprawl of the amusement park is an unwelcoming backdrop, and on hot weekends it's hard to find a space even now; dedicated bathers would be better off making for Long Island.

Further along, **BRIGHTON BEACH**, or 'Little Odessa', is home to the country's largest community of Russian emigrés, around 20,000 in all, together with a long-established and now largely elderly Jewish population. It's a livelier neighbourhood than Coney Island, more prosperous, less defeated. But out of season the boardwalk, lined with melancholy elderly Slavs, can seem just as sad.

Things cheer up on **Brighton Beach Avenue**, the neighbourhood high street which runs underneath the El in a hotpotch of foodshops and appetising restaurants. Russian souvenirs are everywhere, and any number of grocers offer a range of possibilities for lunch – maybe some caviar or smoked fish from *International Food* at no.249, as a topping to some heavy black bread. Or there's *Mrs Stahl's Knishes* on the corner of Brighton Beach and Coney Island Avenue, a remnant from more firmly Jewish days. **Sit-down food** is also readily available, though you'd be better off waiting until evening as it's then the restaurants really hot up, becoming a near parody of a rowdy Russian night out with loud live music, much glass clinking and the frenzied knocking back of vodka. All very definitely worth a trip: see p.257 for listings.

THE BRONX

The Bronx. There's no other part of New York about which people are so ready to roll out their latest and most gruesome horror stories. For this, the city's northernmost borough, represents in its decaying reaches one of the most severe examples of urban deprivation you're ever likely to see. But whatever they tell you in Manhattan, however many Bronx jokes you hear, it's not as unequivocally bleak as people would have you think. In fact, it's really only the South Bronx and a few isolated pockets which are in any way dangerous, and for the most part you can treat it much as you would any other part of New York.

The Bronx developed – and has since declined – more quickly than any other part of the city. First settled in the 17C by a Dutch landowner

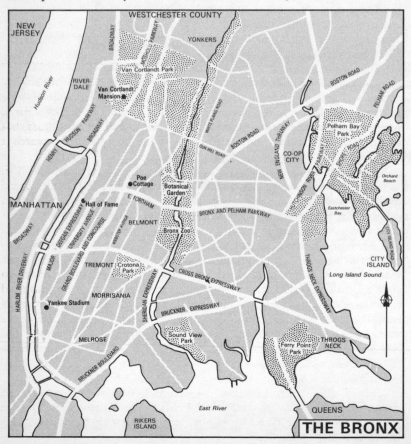

THE BRONX

named James Bronck, like Brooklyn it only became part of the city proper at the turn of the last century. 1900 onwards things moved fast and the Bronx became one of the most sought-after parts of the city in which to live, its main thoroughfare, **Grand Concourse**, becoming edged with increasingly luxurious Art Deco apartment blocks – many of which, though greatly rundown, still stand today. This avenue runs the length of the borough, and many places of interest lie on it or reasonably close by. Most people travel up for the **Zoo**, or bypass the greater part of the borough altogether for **Orchard Beach** or **City Island**. Other places besides these are worth seeing: the grotesqueries of **Woodlawn Cemetery** and smug **Riverdale** in the north; the **New York Botanical Gardens** – large enough to seem a really tangible escape from the city; and even the **South Bronx**, probably best experienced only as a passing cityscape from the relative comfort of the subway train. This is easy to do since the subway travels above ground after leaving Manhattan, cutting directly through the worst of the South Bronx decimation.

YANKEE STADIUM AND THE SOUTH BRONX

First stop the subway makes after leaving Manhattan is at **Yankee Stadium**, home to the New York Yankees baseball team and holding some of the best facilities for the sport in the country. Inside, Babe Ruth, Joe di Maggio and a host of other baseball heroes are enshrined by statues, but otherwise there's little reason to stop if you're not coming to watch a game (see *Sport* for details).

North and west stretches the awful wasteland of the **SOUTH BRONX**, first part of the borough to become properly urbanised but now scarred by huge squares of rubble, levelled apartments sprawling between gaunt-eyed tenements, and with streets dotted with huddled groups of young blacks and Hispanics. The sense of hopelessness is overwhelming, and without a massive injection of money, and some encouragement to businesses and the white middle classes (all of which have long since moved way up or downtown) to come back with their cash, there are no signs that the South Bronx will ever get back on its feet. Carter promised to do something about this and did nothing, and Reagan's withdrawal of employment support will make things even worse. This is the place where a city's dispossessed have been shovelled up, dumped, and left to rot – and no one, not even those who live in other parts of the Bronx, would seem to care. Somehow, the South Bronx jokes you heard back in Manhattan fall a little flat when you experience the neighbourhood for yourself.

Through all this, if you are on foot, **Grand Concourse** still manages to shine with some level of sanity. Stray either side, however, and you're getting into areas which most people – not all alarmists by any means – would consider dangerous.

CENTRAL BRONX: BELMONT, THE ZOO AND THE BOTANICAL GARDENS

Beyond 180th Street the Bronx improves radically. Turn north up Arthur Avenue and you're in **BELMONT**, a strange mixture of tenements and clapboard houses that is home to by far the largest segment of New York's Italian community. It's a small area, bordered to the east by the Zoo and the west by Third Avenue, and with 187th Street as its axis. And it's far enough away from Manhattan for the Italians to keep it their own. Few tourists come here but if you're on your way to the zoo, amble through to see its pungent grocery stores and pork butchers, cafés and sweet-smelling bakeries. There's also no better part of the Bronx if you want to **eat**: choose from swanky *Mario's* (where Al Pacino shot the double-crossing policeman in *The Godfather*) or the pizzas at *Ann & Tony's*, both on Arthur Avenue. Or there's the *Roma Luncheonette*, on the corner of Belmont Avenue and 187th Street, and the *Café Margharita* across the street. Listings p.258.

Follow 187th to the end and you're on the edge of the park which holds **Bronx Zoo**, (Daily 10am-5pm, Sundays and holidays 10am-5.30pm), accessible either by its main gate on Fordham Road or by a second entrance on Bronx Park South. This last is the entrance to use if you come directly here by subway (East Tremont Avenue stop).

The zoo, however, is a disappointment. Though the largest urban zoo in the country and one of the first to realise that animals both look and feel better in the open, it's still surprisingly traditional and caged, at least in the spring and winter months. During the summer some species – the big cats and other Asian and African mammals – are left to roam, separated from the public by a series of moats, but otherwise there's nothing that's all that special. Tuesdays, Wednesdays and Thursdays the zoo is free; other times entrance is $3.75.

Across the road from the zoo's main entrance is the back turnstile of the **New York Botanical Gardens** (Tuesday-Sunday 10am-5pm, last admission 4pm) which in their southernmost reaches are as wild as anything you're likely to see upstate. Further north near the main entrance (Pelham Parkway subway) are more cultivated stretches and the *Enid A. Haupt Conservatory*, where you'll find 11 galleries of palms, ferns, cacti and orchids in an airy iron-framed building of 1902. This costs $2.50, however, and unless you're loaded is just as good from the outside. The gardens themselves are enormous enough to wander around for hours; guides are available from the shop in the *Museum Building*.

Leave the gardens by their main entrance and walk west and you come eventually to Grand Concourse and the **Poe Cottage**. This tiny white clapboard anachronism in the midst of the Bronx's bustle was Edgar Allen

Poe's home for the last three years of his life, though it was only moved here recently when threatened with demolition. Poe came here in 1846 with his wife Virginia and his mother-in-law; Virginia suffered from tuberculosis and he thought the country air would do her good. Never a particularly stable character and dogged by problems, Poe was rarely happy in the cottage: he didn't write a great deal (only the short, touching poem, 'Annabel Lee'), there was never enough money, and his wife's condition declined until she eventually died, leaving Poe with a distraught mother-in-law and a series of literary ambitions that never seemed to come off. He left the cottage for the last time in 1849 to seal the backing for his longest-running dream – his own literary magazine – but got entangled in the election furore in Baltimore, disappeared, and was eventually found weak and delirious in the street, dying in hospital a few days later. What actually happened no one knows, and the house, with its few meagre furnishings spread thinly through half a dozen rooms, tells you little more about the man. (Wednesday-Friday 9am-5pm, Saturday 10am-4pm, Sunday 1pm-5pm; $1).

NORTH BRONX

The **NORTH BRONX** is the topmost fringe of New York City, and if anyone actually makes it up here it's to see the **Woodlawn Cemetery** (subway Woodlawn), which is worth a stroll around if only to see how money doesn't necessarily buy good taste. This has for many years been the top people's cemetery, and like Greenwood in Brooklyn (see p.162) brags some tombs and mausoleums which are memorable mainly for their hideousness. It's a huge place but there are some tombs which stand out: one Oliver Hazard Belmont, financier and horse dealer, lies in a dripping Gothic fantasy near the entrance, modelled on the resting place of Leonardo da Vinci in Amboise, France; F.W. Woolworth has himself an Egyptian palace guarded by sphinxes; while Jay Gould, not most people's favourite banker when he was alive, takes it easy in a Greek style temple. And that's not all. Pick up a guide from the office at the entrance and you can discover all kinds of famous names and disgusting mausolea.

West of the cemetery lies the **Van Cortlandt Park**, forested and hilly (dangerous say some) and used in winter by skiers and tobogganists. Apart from the sheer pleasure of hiking through its woods, the best thing here is the **Van Cortlandt Mansion**, nestled in its south-west corner not far from the subway station. This is an authentically restored Georgian building, very pretty, and with its rough-hewn grey stone really rather rustic. During the Revolutionary wars it changed hands a number of times, and was used as an operations HQ by both the British and the Patriots. On the hills above, George Washington had fires lit to dupe the

British that he was still here (he was in fact long gone) and it was in this house he slept before heading his victory march into Manhattan in 1783. Nowadays most of the rooms are open to the public, and kept up by the Society of Colonial Dames of America (Monday-Saturday 10am-5pm, Sunday 12am-5pm; $2).

Immediately west rise the monied heights of **RIVERDALE** – one of the city's most desirable neighbourhoods, and so far from the South Bronx in feel and income it might as well be on the moon. Venture up if you wish, but there's not a lot to see save **Wave Hill**, a small country estate donated to the city a couple of decades back and which in previous years was briefly home to Mark Twain and, later, Teddy Roosevelt. The grounds are botanical gardens, the 19C mansion a forum for temporary art installations, concerts and workshops: a great idea, but a pity it couldn't have been in a part of the city that needed it more badly (Daily 10am-5.30pm; greenhouses 10am-12am and 2pm-4pm; $2, students $1).

At the other side of the Bronx **Pelham Bay Park** gives onto **Orchard Beach** and, linked by a short causeway, **City Island**. This, reachable by taking subway 6 to the end and a Bx12 bus, is something of an oddity in this part of town: a small fishing village whose main street is lined with fish and seafood restaurants and whose harbour crammed with visiting yachtspeople. That it's so hard to get to is probably just as well...

QUEENS

Of New York City's four outer boroughs, **Queens**, named after the wife of Charles II, is the most consistently ignored. Even Staten Island, across the water and barely considered part of the city at all, has something to offer, even if it's only the ferry that takes you there. But Queens, despite being considerably more accessible than Staten Island, a great deal larger than Brooklyn, and immeasurably safer than the Bronx, simply lacks enough cachet to make it a desirable place to live. People who live in Queens, the thinking seems to run, are either excruciatingly dull or just can't afford to live anywhere else.

Assuming you're still reading, it's worth pointing out that Queens isn't in fact so terrible. Just that architecturally it's more semi-detached suburbia than tenements and brownstones, there are for the moment fewer immigrant areas than in either Brooklyn or the Bronx, and that if Queens has any historic buildings they tend to be clapboard. Do, however, check out Greek **Astoria**, both for its restaurants and foodstores and the film studios; **Jackson Heights**, which has the city's largest concentration of South Americans; and **Kew Gardens** and **Forest Hills**, which have any amount of yuppie chic.

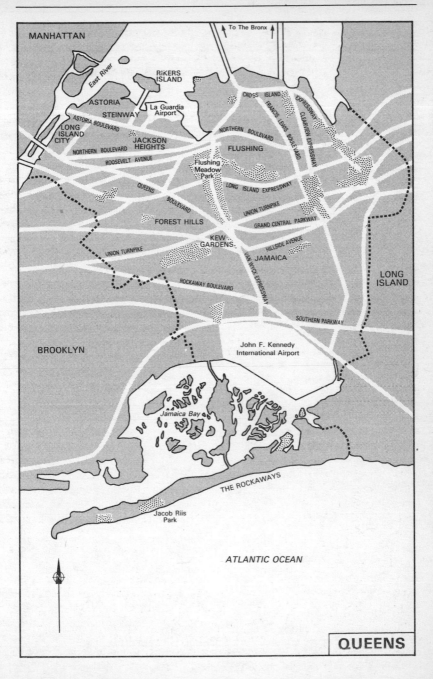

QUEENS

ASTORIA AND AROUND

Bleak industrial **LONG ISLAND CITY** is most people's first view of Queens, for it's through here that the subway train cuts above ground after crossing over from Manhattan. Unless it's a weekend and you fancy browsing through the **Queens Plaza Flea Market** on the corner of Queens and Northern Boulevard, there's no point in getting off as there's nothing to see. This might change, as Long Island City is on the verge of being colonised by artists escaping extortionate Manhattan rents and taking over the disused loft spaces here. But it's not exactly SoHo yet, and for the present it's **ASTORIA** that makes it worth crossing the river, one of Queens' original communities and famous for two things: film making and the fact that it's the largest single concentration of Greeks outside Greece itself (Melbourne included). Until the **movie industry** moved out to the West Coast in the early 1930s Astoria was the cinematic capital of the world. Paramount had their studios here until the lure of Hollywood's reliable weather left Astoria empty and disused by all except the US Army – which was how it remained until recently when Hollywood's stranglehold on the industry weakened. The new studios here now rank as the country's fourth largest and, encouraged by the success of films like *The Wiz*, *Ragtime* and others where the bulk of the filming was done in New York, are set for a major expansion. They're not open to the public at present but you can visit the **American Museum of the Moving Image** in the old Paramount complex at 34-31 35th Street, near Broadway, where there's an excellent display of posters, stills, sets and equipment both from Astoria's golden age and more recent times. Phone first for an appointment – 718 784 4520.

Greek Astoria stretches from Ditmars Boulevard in the north right down to Broadway, and from 31st across to Steinway Street. Between 80,000 and 100,000 Greeks live here (together with a substantial community of Italians) and the evidence is on display in a sizeable quantity of **restaurants and patisseries** that repay a closer look. There's not a great deal else to see, but check out our restaurant listings on p.258 before you write the area off.

East of Astoria lies **STEINWAY**, a district that was bought up by the piano manufacturer and used as housing for their workers. These were mainly Germans and the area had for a time a distinctly Teutonic feel, but the community has long since gone, and apart from the **piano factory** (phone 718 721 2600 for visits) there's little to keep you. Next door is the noise-trap of **La Guardia Airport** and, just offshore, **RIKER'S ISLAND**, which holds the city's largest and most overcrowded prison. Not surprisingly, this isn't New York City's most appealing corner.

JACKSON HEIGHTS, FLUSHING, FOREST HILLS AND BEYOND

Next door to Steinway is the South American enclave of **JACKSON HEIGHTS**, a small and largely self-contained community of 150,000 or so Columbians, half as many Ecuadorians and a good number of Argentinians and other South American peoples. The neighbourhood first turned Hispanic in the 1960s, when huge influxes of people came over – many illegally – to find work and escape from the poverty and uncertain politics of their own countries, and it's now the largest South American contingent in the States. Tighter immigration controls, however, have radically dwindled the intake and the community here is now more or less static.

Eating-wise, there's no better part of Queens for exotic, unknown and varied cuisines. Roosevelt Avenue and, running parallel, 37th Avenue between 82nd Street and Junction Boulevard, are focus for the district, and along both streets you'll find Argentinian steakhouses, Columbian restaurants, and pungent coffee houses and bakeries stacked high with bread and pastries. See p.258 for restaurant listings.

East of Jackson Heights you hit **CORONA**, its subway yards ringed by menacing barbed wire and patrolled by dogs to deter graffiti artists. A few steps away is the **Shea Stadium**, home of the New York Mets and the arena where Popes said mass to over 50,000 New Yorkers in both 1965 and 1979. The Beatles, too, played here in 1965 (though not at the same gig) and the stadium – presumably in anticipation of further such events – has recently been upgraded with a giant video screen. For details on the Mets and when they play, see *Sport*.

Shea went up as part of the 1964 World Fair, which was held in adjoining **Flushing Meadow Park**. This is now the site of the US Tennis Open Championships each summer, and boasts around 30 courts and seating for well over 25,000 people (again see *Sport*). The other side of the park, **FLUSHING** is a rather dull middle-income suburb which has picked up the tag 'birthplace of religious freedom in America' for its role as secret Quaker meeting place during the 17C, when anyone who wasn't a Calvinist was persecuted by the Dutch.

The Quakers met in the **Bowne House** which still stands, officially the oldest house in the city and open to the public on selected days of the week. It's a short walk from the Bowne Street subway station and if you're in Flushing you may just as well take a look. But be warned that the enthusiasm of the volunteers that show you around is not always mirrored by the excitement of the displays, which in the main consist of the drab furniture used over the years by the Bowne family; and, as symbolic centrepiece, the kitchen where the Quaker meetings took place. Outside stands **Kingsland House,** shifted here from its original site about a mile away and reputedly the first house in Flushing to release its slaves. All this and more is detailed in the Queens Historical Society's do-it-yourself walking tour of 'Historic Flushing', for details of which see *Tours*. Or go to their headquarters in the Kingsland House itself.

On the other side of Flushing Meadow Park – and a long walk or a bus ride from Flushing – **FOREST HILLS** is perhaps choicest of Queens neighbourhoods, home to Geraldine Ferraro and the West Side Tennis Club. This is snooty, a high-income suburb with a strong Jewish component, spectacularly pricey housing and a high street (Austin) of designer boutiques and chi-chi restaurants. Priciest bit of all is **Forest Hills Gardens,** a mock Tudor village that is interesting not for what it is but for what it might have been, since it was built originally as housing for the urban poor until the rich grabbed it for themselves. Another 'planned' neighbourhood, **KEW GARDENS,** to the south, was at the turn of the century a watering-hole popular with ageing New Yorkers, complete with hotels, lakes and a whole tourist infrastructure. All that has gone now but Kew remains, in a leafy and dignified kind of way, one of Queens' most visually enticing districts.

Just beyond is the city's other airport, **JFK International,** with to its right the wild, island-dotted indent of **JAMAICA BAY** – now an official wildlife refuge where you can observe around 300 varieties of birds, for free, seven days a week. Part enclosing the bay the narrowing spit of **THE ROCKAWAYS** is the largest beach area in the country, stretching for 10 miles back towards Brooklyn – most of it strollable by the boardwalk. At the far end **Jacob Riis Park** lays on another beach and assorted facilities, with **nude bathing** tolerated (if not officially allowed) in the eastern corner, haunt of predominantly gay naturists.

STATEN ISLAND

Until about 20 years ago **Staten Island,** the common name for what's officially Richmond County, was isolated – getting to it meant a ferry trip or long ride through New Jersey, and daily commuting into town was almost an eccentricity. Staten Islanders enjoyed an insular, self-contained life in the state's least populous borough, and the stretch of water to Manhattan marked a cultural as much as physical divide. In 1964 the opening of the Verrazano Narrows Bridge changed things; upwardly mobile Brooklynites found cheap property on the island and swarmed over the bridge to buy their parcel of suburbia. And today Staten Island has swollen into tightly packed residential neighbourhoods amid the rambling greenery, endless backwaters of tidy look-don't-touch homes.

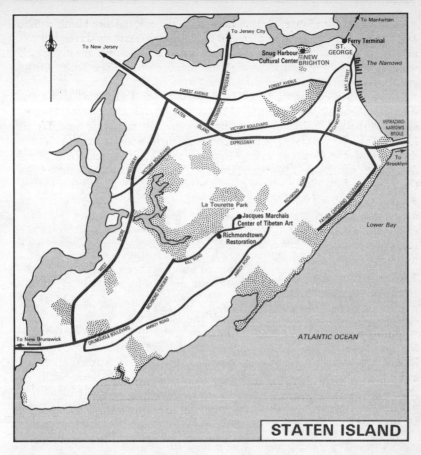

STATEN ISLAND

But most don't even see as much as this. Nine out of ten tourists who take the Staten Island ferry drool over the view and on arriving promptly turn back to Manhattan. What they miss are a couple of museums and a nerve-soothing break from the city, but that's about it: a few other bits and bobs lie scattered around but none are worth going out of the way for; thankfully either or both of the two museums repay the inland excursion.

THE FERRY, THE JACQUES MARCHAIS CENTER AND RICHMONDSTOWN RESTORATION

The **Staten Island ferry** sails around the clock with half-hourly departures between 9.30am and 4pm, and is famed as New York's best bargain: for

25c (return) wide-angled views of the city and Liberty are yours, becoming more spectacular as you retreat. By the time you arrive Manhattan's skyline stands mirage-like, filtered through the haze as the romantic, heroic city of a thousand and one posters. The Staten Island ferry terminal quickly dispels any romance: it's a dirty, disreputable sort of place, which serves as a mini-training ground for winos on their way to the Bowery. But if you're exploring the island it's easy enough to escape to the adjoining bus station and catch the 113 (connects with ferry so have $1 change or a token ready as they're unavailable at the terminal) which cuts down and across to the two central museums. Along the way the **Verrazano Narrows Bridge** flashes its minimalist message across the entry to the bay, a slender, beautiful span that was (until the Humber Bridge opened) the world's longest at 4260 feet – so long that the tops of the towers are 4cm out of parallel to allow for the curvature of the earth.

In the middle of Staten Island's residential heartland the **Jacques Marchais Center of Tibetan Art** (April-November Saturday and Sunday only 1pm-5pm; $2.50; phone 987 3478 for additional summer hours) is an unlikely find; the bus drivers don't know it's there, so ask to be let off at Lighthouse Avenue, walk up the hill and it's on the right at no.338. Jacques Marchais was the alias of Jacqueline Kleber, a New York art dealer who reckoned she'd get on better with a French name. She did, and combined with the advantages of a rich husband, used her wealth to indulge her passion for Tibetan art. Eventually she assembled the largest collection in the Western world, reproducing a *gompah* or Buddhist temple on the hillside in which to house it. Even if you know nothing about such things the exhibition is small enough to be accessible, with magnificent bronze Boddhistavas, fearsome deities in union with each other, musical instruments, costumes and decorations from the mysterious world of Tibet. Give it time – after a while the air of the temple and its gardens is heady. Best time to visit is in the first or second week of September when the Tibetan harvest festival takes place: Tibetan monks in saffron robes perform the traditional ceremonies, and Tibetan food and crafts are sold. Phone ahead for the exact date.

Back on the main Richmond Road, a short walk brings you to the **Richmondstown Restoration** (Wednesday-Friday 10am-5pm, Saturday/Sunday 1pm-5pm; $2, students $1.50), a gathering of a dozen or so old houses and miscellaneous buildings transplanted from their original sites and grafted on to the 18C village of Richmond. Starting from the **Historical Museum**, half-hourly tours negotiate the best of these – including the **Voorlezer's House**, oldest elementary school in the country, a picture-book **general store**, and the lovely, atmospheric **Guyon-Lake-Tyson House** of 1740. What brings it to life are the craftspeople using old techniques to weave cloth and fire kilns – in the summer conducted tours stop and the becostumed workers fill you in on the facts. It's all carried off to picturesque and ungimmicky effect in rustic surroundings: difficult to believe you're just 12 miles from downtown Manhattan.

And that's about it. For the committed explorer there's the up-and-coming area of **ST GEORGES** (near the ferry terminal), slightly more mixed in the people who live there than the firmly middle-income families further inland. Good antique shops abound: try the **Edgewater Hall Antique Center** – a bank that's been refurbished as a shopping mall. About a mile and a half away in New Brighton is the Greek Revival pile of the **Snug Harbour Cultural Center** – former home for retired sailors that now houses the galleries and studios of the island's swelling artists' community. In summer the Metropolitan Opera and New York Philharmonic give concerts here – good music in intimate outdoor surroundings – and each weekend there are guided tours of the center and nearby **Botanical Gardens** (March-November 2pm; free; phone 448 2500 for more info).

Chapter five
MUSEUMS

New York is not a city that lacks visual stimulation – and you may find there's enough on the streets without having to contemplate walking inside a museum. But you should at least be aware of what you're missing. For in the big two Manhattan museums – the **Metropolitan** and **Museum of Modern Art** – there are few aspects of Western cultural art left untapped. The Metropolitan, in particular, is exhaustive (mercilessly so, if you try to take in too much too quickly), with arguably the finest collection of European art anywhere in the world as well as superlative displays of everything from African artefacts to medieval sculpture. The Museum of Modern Art (MoMA) takes on where the Met leaves off, emphasising exactly why (and how) New York has become art capital to the world.

Among the other **major museums**, you'll find exciting collections of modern art, and invariably excellent temporary shows, at the **Guggenheim** and **Whitney**, a wide array of 17C and 18C paintings at the **Frick**, and – amid unexpectedly pastoral scenes – a glorious display of medieval art out at **The Cloisters** in Fort Tryon. All of which should, if time permits, be seen. So too, depending on personal interests and tastes, should some of the **lesser museums**, often quirkily devoted to some otherwise total obscurity. On a highly selective basis, highlights must include the **Pierpoint Morgan Library**, the **International Center for Photography**, the **Museum of the American Indian** (a neglected wonder of the city) and, for anyone less than enamoured with current New York TV screens, the public archives of the **Museum of Broadcasting**.

Opening hours don't fall into any fixed patterns: many museums close on Mondays (and national holidays), opening into the early evening one or two nights a week. **Admission charges** are almost always high, occasionally softened for those with student ID cards, but happily, certain museums are free or much reduced one evening a week. Otherwise you'll commonly find the 'voluntary donation' system in operation. This in theory means you're allowed to give as little or as much as you like to get in (hence enabling museums to keep their charitable status); in practice you'll need to be pretty hard-headed to give any less than the (not particularly low) recommended minimum.

The following museums are **free** at the stated times:
Tuesday. Whitney (6pm-8pm), Guggenheim (5pm-8pm), International Center of Photography (5pm-8pm), Cooper-Hewitt (5pm-9pm), Museum of American Folk Art (5.30pm-8pm) and National Academy of Design (5pm-8pm). **Thursday.** Museum of Modern Art (5pm-9pm pay what you wish).

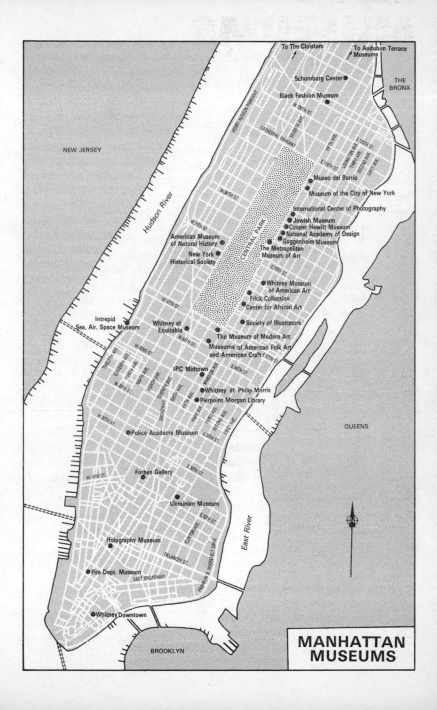

To The Cloisters
To Audubon Terrace Museums

THE BRONX

Schomburg Center

Black Fashion Museum

NEW JERSEY

Hudson River

Museo del Barrio
Museum of the City of New York
International Center of Photography
Jewish Museum
Cooper Hewitt Museum
National Academy of Design
Guggenheim Museum
The Metropolitan Museum of Art

American Museum of Natural History
New York Historical Society

CENTRAL PARK

Whitney Museum of American Art
Frick Collection
Center for African Art

Intrepid Sea, Air, Space Museum

Whitney at Equitable

Society of Illustrators

The Museum of Modern Art
Museums of American Folk Art and American Craft

IPC Midtown

Whitney at Philip Morris
Pierpoint Morgan Library

QUEENS

Police Academy Museum

Forbes Gallery

Ukrainian Museum

East River

Holography Museum

Fire Dept. Museum

Whitney Downtown

BROOKLYN

MANHATTAN MUSEUMS

THE MAJOR COLLECTIONS

THE METROPOLITAN MUSEUM OF ART

5th Ave at 82nd St. Lexington Avenue. Subway 86th St & Lexington. Tuesday 9.30am-8.45pm; Wednesday-Sunday 9.30am-5.15pm; closed Mondays. Admission by voluntary donation, suggested $4.50. $2.25 for students. Free conducted tours,"Highlights of the Met", daily; also highly detailed tours of specific galleries; recorded tours of the major collections $2.50.

The Met, as it's usually known, is the foremost museum in America. Its galleries take in over three and a half million works of art and span the arts and cultures not just of America and Europe (though these are the most famous collections) but also of China, Africa, the Far East, and the Classical and Islamic worlds. Any kind of overview of the museum is out of the question: it demands many and specific visits, or, at least, self-imposed limits.

Broadly, the Met breaks down into five **major collections**: *European Painting, American Painting, Medieval Art, 'Primitive' Art* and *Egyptian Antiquities*. You'll find the highlights of these detailed below. Keep in mind, however, that there is much, much more for which space forbids anything other than a passing mention. Among the **"lesser" Met collections** are *Greek and Roman galleries* (second only to those in Athens), *Islamic art* (possibly the largest display anywhere in the world), a *Far Eastern gallery* (with a reconstruction of a Chinese garden, assembled by experts from the People's Republic), a *Musical Instrument Collection* (the world's oldest piano, of course, included) and what would, anywhere else, be seen as essential *Modern Art galleries* (Picasso's *Portrait of Gertrude Stein* and Pollock's *Parsiphaë* are just two standouts).

There are two main **problems** in visiting, other than the obvious frustrations of size and time. The first is **scheduling**. Certain collections are open only on a rotating basis, so if you're intent on seeing anything less than obvious, phone ahead first (535 7710). The second difficulty is the piecemeal way the Met has developed. Its 19C multi-millionaire benefactors were often as intent on advertising their own taste as on setting America on the cultural highroad, and their bequests often stipulated distinct and **separate galleries** for their donations. If you're interested in one particular period or movement of art you won't neccessarily find it all in the same place.

Initial orientation, despite this, is not too hard. There is just one main entrance and once within you find yourself in the **Great Hall**, a deftly lit

Neo-Classical cavern where you can consult plans, check tours and pick up info on the Met's excellent lecture listings. Directly ahead is the **Grand Staircase** and what is for many visitors the single greatest attraction – the European Painting galleries.

European Painting galleries

The Met's European Painting galleries divide in two parts. The initial rooms start with a scattering of Italian works, move into a small but fine English collection, then Northern and Italian Renaissance and (probably the most significant) 17C Dutch. The André Meyer galleries *follow and are dominated by a tremendous core group of Impressionist painting. Ideally, try to take in each half in separate bouts, separated at least by a break in the museum's café: these are large collections.*

Though the Met's **ENGLISH GALLERY** is essentially a prelude to the major collections, it's an unusually brilliant and elegant one. At its heart are a group of portraits by **William Gainsborough** and **Thomas Lawrence**, the two great English portrait artists of the 18C. Gainsborough's *Mrs. Grace Dalrymple Elliott* is typical of his portrait style – an almost feathery lightness softening the monumental pose. Lawrence is best represented by his likeable and virtuoso study of *Elizabeth Farren*, painted at the precocious age of 21, and by *The Calmady Children*, a much-engraved portrait that was the artist's own favourite among his works.

Beyond, a drop back in time, are the **EARLY FLEMISH AND NETHERLANDISH PAINTINGS**, precursors of both the Northern and Italian Renaissance. Inevitably the first paintings are by **Jan Van Eyck**, who is generally attributed with beginning the tradition of North European realism. There are two definitely accepted works – *The Crucifixion and The Last Judgement* – painted early in the artist's career and, much like the minatures he painted for the Turin-Milan Hours; bright, realistic and full of expressive (and horrific) detail. *The Annunciation* nearby is probably by Jan too; its perspective is tidily if not totally accurately drawn, the Romanesque right-hand side of the portal and the Gothic left symbolising the transition from Old Testament to New. There's more allusion to things Gothic in **Rogier van der Weyden**'s *Christ Appearing to His Mother*, the apochryphal visit surrounded by tiny statuary depicting Christ's earlier and Mary's later life. It's one of the most beautiful of all van der Weyden's works, quite different in feel to Van Eyck with a warmth of design and feeling replacing the former's hard draughtsman's clarity. This development is continued through the third great Northern Gothic painter, **Gerhard David**, as is the vogue for setting religious scenes in Low Countries settings. The background to David's exquisite *Virgin and Child with Four Angels* is medieval Bruges; in *The Rest on the Flight to Egypt* landscape features are added to by Low

Country genre scenes. **Bruegel**'s *Harvesters*, one of the Met's most reproduced pictures, and part of the series of twelve paintings that included his (Christmas card familiar) *Hunters in the Snow*, shows how these innovations were assimilated.

Cutting left at this point brings you to the **SPANISH PAINTINGS** and the very different landscape of **El Greco**'s *View of Toledo*. This extraordinary picture – all brooding intensity as the skies seem about to swallow up the ghost-like town – is perhaps the best Greco anywhere in the world. Beside it is El Greco's *Portrait of a Cardinal*, and there is also **Velazquez**'s *Portrait of Juan de Parej* – 'All the rest are art, this alone is truth,' remarked a critic of the piercing, sombre portrait when it was first exhibited.

The **ITALIAN RENAISSANCE** is less spectacularly represented but there's a worthy selection from the various Italian schools, including an early *Madonna and Child Enthroned with Saints* by **Raphael** and a late **Botticelli**, the crisply linear *Three Miracles of Saint Zenobius*. Among the **Mannerists**, best of the Italian collections, is **Bronzino's** *Portrait of a Young Man*. Turning right from the main galleries takes you to a smaller series of religious paintings: **Michele de Verona**'s handsome *Madonna and Child with the Infant John the Baptist*, very much in the 15C Italian tradition with a marmorial surface bathed in soft light; Look ot to for **Crivelli**'s *Pietà* and **Mantegna**'s rigid and sculptural *Adoration of the Shepherds*.

With the **Robert Altman Collection**, here cleverly jigsawed into the main gallery, a small number of Dutch works, including **Memling**'s *Tommaso Portinari and his Wife* and a *Mystical Marriage of St Catherine*, prelude the main **DUTCH PAINTINGS** section. This, dominated by the major works of Rembrandt, Vermeer and Hals, is the culmination of the main European galleries – and arguably the finest single group of paintings in the museum.

Vermeer, genius of the domestic interior, is represented by five works. *Young Woman with a Water Jug* is a perfect example of his skill in composition and tonal gradation, combined with an uncannily naturalistic sense of lighting. *A Girl Asleep* is deeper in its composition – or at least appears to be, the rich fabric separating the foreground from the rooms beyond. Vermeer often used this trick, and you see it again in *Allegory of the Faith*, where the drawn curtain presents the tableau and separates the viewer from the lesson before him. Most haunting of all, however, is the great *Portrait of a Young Woman*, the artist at his most complex and the Met at its most fortunate.

Vermeer's pictures show the domestic harmony of 17C Holland. **Hals**'s early paintings reveal its exuberance. In *Merrymakers at Shrovetide* the figures explode out from the canvas in an abundance of gesture and richness. *Young Man and a Woman*, painted five years later, shows a more subdued use of colours (though not vitality). As do the individual portraits, with their capturing of fleeting, telling pointers: step back from his *Portrait of a Man* or *Claes Kuyst Van Voorhout* and the seemingly slapdash strokes melt into a bravura statement of spirit.

The best of **Rembrandt**'s works here are also portraits. There is a beautiful painting of his common-law wife, *Hendrikje Stoffels*, painted three years before her early death – a blow that marked a further decline in the artist's fortunes. In 1660 he went bankrupt, and the superb *Self-Portrait* of that year shows the self-examination he brought to later works. A comparison between the flamboyant 1632 *Portrait of a Lady* and the warmer, later *Lady with a Pink* reveals his maturing genius.

In addition to these big three names, the Dutch rooms also display a good scattering of their contemporaries, most memorably **Pieter de Hooch**, whose *Two Men and a Woman in a Courtyard of a House* is his acknowledged masterpiece, with its perfect arrangement of line, form and colour. At the same time as de Hooch was painting peaceful courtyards and Vermeer lacemakers and lute players, **Adrian Brouwer** was turning his eye to the seamier side of Dutch life. When he wasn't drunk or in prison he came up with works like *The Smokers*, typical of his tavern scenes. Traditionally *The Smokers* is a portrait of Brouwer and his drinking pals – he's the one in the foreground, in case you hadn't guessed.

The André Meyer Galleries

David's sternly didactic *Death of Socrates*, **Turner**'s *Grand Canal, Venice* and one of **Constable**'s *Salisbury Cathedral* paintings line the outer corridor of the André Meyer galleries. But once inside, you are straight to the heart of the collection, amid a startling array of **IMPRESSIONIST AND POST-IMPRESSIONIST** art.

The display, fittingly, starts with **Edouard Manet**, the movement's most influential precursor yet in his early style, contrasting light and shadow with modulated shades of black, firmly linked in tradition with Hals, Velazquez and Goya. The *Spanish Dancer*, an accomplished example of this style and heritage, was well received on Manet's debut at the Paris Salon in 1861. Within a few years, though, he was shocking the same establishment with 'Olympia', 'Le Déjuner sur l'Herbe' and the Meyer's striking *Woman with a Parrot* – the woman, incidentally, model for all three paintings. Later his style shifted again as he adopted the Impressionist lightness of handling and interest in perception. He worked for a time with Renoir and Monet, a period of which *Boating* is typical, a celebration of the middle classes at play.

Claude Monet, who was influenced by Manet's early style before Impressionism, was one of the movement's most prolific painters. He returned again and again to a single subject to produce a series of paintings, each capturing a different moment of light or atmosphere.

Three superb examples are on show here: *Rouen Cathedral, The Houses of Parliament from the Thames* and *Poplars* – in which you can detect the beginnings of his final phase of near-Abstract Impressionism.

Cézanne's technique was very different. He laboured long to achieve a painstaking analysis of form and colour, something clear in the *Landscape of Marseilles*. Of his few portraits, the jarring, almost cubist angles and spaces of *Mme Cézanne in a Red Dress* seem years ahead of their time. Take a look too at *The Card Players*, whose dynamic triangular structure thrusts out, yet retains the quiet concentration of the moment. **Renoir** is perhaps the best represented among the remaining Impressionists, though his most important work here dates from 1878, when he began to move away from the mainstream techniques he'd learned working with Monet. *Mme Charpentier and her Children* is a likeable enough piece, whose affectionate if unsearching tone manages to sidestep the sugariness that affected his later work. Better, or at least more real, is his *Waitress at Duval's Restaurant*.

The Post-Impressionists, logically enough, follow, with **Gaugin**'s masterly *Ia Orana Maria*. The title, the archangel Gabriel's first words to Mary at the Annunciation, is the key to the work: the scene was a staple of the Renaissance, here it is transferred to a wholly different culture in an attempt to unfold the dense symbolic meaning, and perhaps also to voice the artist's feeling for the native South Sea islanders, whose cause he championed. *Two Tahitian Women* hangs adjacent, a portrait of his lover Tehura – skilful, studied simplicity.

Toulouse-Lautrec delighted in painting the world Gauguin went to Tahiti to escape. *The Sofa* is one of a series of sketches he made in Paris brothels. The artist's deformity distanced him from society, and he identified with the life of the prostitutes in his sketches – he also hated posed modelling, which made the bored women awaiting clients an ideal subject.

Courbet and **Degas**, too, are well represented. Courbet especially, with examples of every phase and period of his career, including *Young Ladies from the Village*, a virtual manifesto of his idea of realism, and *Woman with a Parrot*, a superbly erotic and exotic work, and one that gave Manet the idea for his work of the same name. Degas constantly returned to the subject of dancers, and there are studies in just about every medium from pastels to sculpture. Unlike the Impressionists, Degas subordinated what he saw to what he believed, and his *Dancers Practising* shows this – the painting is about structure, alluded to in the way the dancer on the right picks up the form of the watering can used to lay the dust in the studio. Also here is a vaguely macabre casting of his *Little Dancer*, complete with real tutu, bodice and shoes.

All of which is little more than the surface of the André Meyer galleries. There's also work by **van Gogh**, **Rousseau** and **Seurat**, paintings from the

Barbizon School, sculpture by **Rodin** and a peripheral gallery of paintings that express the official taste of the 19C.

The Lehman Pavilion

The Lehman Pavilion was tacked on to the rear of the Met in 1975 to house the collection of Robert Lehman, millionaire banker and art collector. It breaks from the Met's usual sober arrangement of rectangular floor plans: rooms are laid out beside a brilliantly lit atrium, some in re-creation of Lehman's own home.

More importantly, Lehman's enthusiasms fill the gaps in the Met's account of **ITALIAN RENAISSANCE** painting. This was his passion, and the heart of the collection centres around a small **Botticelli** *Annunciation*, an exquisite celebration of the Florentine discovery of perspective. From the Venetian school comes a sculptural *Madonna and Child* by **Giovanni Bellini** and two unaffected portraits by **Jacometto Veneziano**, as well as an unusual *Expulsion from Paradise* by the Sienese **Giovanni di Paolo**, in which an angel gently ushers Adam and Eve from Eden, while a Byzantine God points to their place of banishment.

Left of this core collection are works from the **NORTHERN RENAISSANCE**, highlighted by a trio of paintings by Memling, Holbein and Petrus Christus. **Christus**'s vast canvas of *St Elegius*, patron saint of goldsmiths, shows an Eyckian attention to detail in its depiction of the saint's jewels and precious stones – a genre insight into the work of the 15C goldsmith. **Memling**, working around 30 years later, used a lighter palette to achieve the delicate serenity of his *Annunciation*, in which cool colours and a gentle portrayal of Mary and her attendant angels illuminate the Flemish interior. **Hans Holbein**'s *Portrait of Erasmus of Rotterdam* was one of three he painted in 1523 that established his reputation as a portraitist. Elsewhere in the Lehmann wing – and you could visit the Met rewardingly by just limiting yourself just to these halls – are works by artists as diverse as El Greco, Ingres, and Ter Bosch. But one painting that really stands out is **Rembrandt**'s *Portrait of Gerard de Lairesse*: by all accounts de Lairesse was disliked for his luxurious tastes and unpleasant character, but mainly for his face – which had been ravaged by congenital syphillis.

As the Lehman wing moves towards the **19C and 20C** it loses authority, but there are minor works by major artists, including Renoir, van Gogh, Gauguin, Cézanne and Matisse. Have a look at **Suzanne Valadon**'s *Reclining Nude*: Valadon is largely ignored today, and is best known as a model for Toulouse-Lautrec, Renoir and Degas (who encouraged her to become a painter in her own right). But her boldly coloured canvasses show her originality and also her influence on her son, **Maurice Utrillo**, whom she taught to paint as an attempt to wean him off the drink and drugs that were his downfall. Utrillo's *Rue Ravignon* here stands besides his mother's painting.

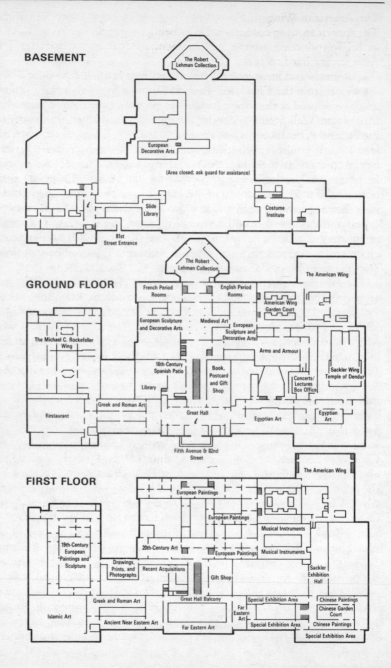

BASEMENT

The Robert Lehman Collection

European Decorative Arts

(Area closed; ask guard for assistance)

Slide Library

Costume Institute

81st Street Entrance

GROUND FLOOR

The Robert Lehman Collection

The American Wing

French Period Rooms

English Period Rooms

American Wing Garden Court

European Sculpture and Decorative Arts

Medieval Art

European Sculpture and Decorative Arts

The Michael C. Rockefeller Wing

Arms and Armour

Sackler Wing Temple of Dendur

16th-Century Spanish Patio

Book, Postcard and Gift Shop

Concerts/ Lectures Box Office

Library

Greek and Roman Art

Great Hall

Egyptian Art

Egyptian Art

Restaurant

Fifth Avenue & 82nd Street

FIRST FLOOR

The American Wing

European Paintings

European Paintings

Musical Instruments

19th-Century European Paintings and Sculpture

20th-Century Art

European Paintings

Musical Instruments

Drawings, Prints, and Photographs

Recent Acquisitions

Gift Shop

Sackler Exhibition Hall

Greek and Roman Art

Great Hall Balcony

Far Eastern Art

Special Exhibition Area

Chinese Paintings

Chinese Garden Court

Islamic Art

Ancient Near Eastern Art

Far Eastern Art

Special Exhibition Area

Chinese Paintings

Special Exhibition Area

The American Wing

The American wing comes nearest to being a museum in its own right, and as an introduction to the development of fine and decorative art in America it's hard to fault.

Galleries – and most immediately a series of **furnished historical rooms** – take off from the **Charles Engelhard Court,** a shrubby, restful sculpture garden enclosed at the lower end by the *Facade of the United States Bank*, lifted from Wall Street. Stepping through the facade would drop you in the **Federal Period Rooms** and the restrained Neo-Classical elegance of the late 18C. If you're approaching this section of the Met fresh, however, better to start at the third floor and work down to see the rooms in chronological order. You begin with the **Early Colonial period**, represented most evocatively in the *Hart Room* of around 1674, and end with **Frank Lloyd Wright**'s *Room from the Little House, Minneapolis*, originally windowed on all four sides, in key with Wright's concept of minimising interior-exterior division. On the second-floor balcony, an elegant accompaniment to all of this, be sure not to miss the iridescent *Favrile* glass of **Louis Comfort Tiffany** – Art Nouveau at its best.

THE COLLECTION OF AMERICAN PAINTINGS begins on the second floor with **18C** works by **Benjamin West**, an artist who worked in London and taught or influenced almost all American painters of his day. *The Triumph of Love* is typical of his Neo-Classical, allegorical works. More heroics come with **John Trumbull**, one of West's pupils, in *Sortie made by the Garrison of Gibraltar* and the fully-blown Romanticism of *Washington Crossing the Delaware* by **Emanuel Leutzes**. This last shows Washington escaping across the river in the winter of 1776, historically and geographically inaccurate but nonetheless a national icon.

Early in the **19C**, American painters gained the confidence to move away from themes solely European. **William Sidney Mount** depicted genre scenes on his native Long Island, often with a sly political angle – as with *Cider Makers* and *The Bet* – and the painters of the **Hudson Valley School** apotheosise that landscape in their vast lyrical canvasses. **Thomas Cole**, the school's doyen, is represented by *The Oxbow*, his pupil **Frederick Church** by an immense *Heart of the Andes* – combining the grand sweep of the mountains with minutely depicted flora. **Albert Bierstadt** and **S.R.Gifford** continued to concentrate on the American west – their respective works *The Rocky Mountains, Lander's Peak* and *Kauterskill Falls* have a near-visionary idyllism, bound to a belief that the westward development of the country was a manifestation of divine will.

Winslow Homer is allowed a gallery to himself – fittingly for a painter who was to influence greatly the late 19C artistic scene in America. Homer began his career illustrating the day-to-day realities of the Civil War – there's a good selection here that shows the tedium and sadness of those years – and a sense of recording detail carried over into his late, quasi- Impressionistic studies of seascapes. *Northeaster* is one of the finest of these, close to Courbet in its strength of composition and colour.

The mezzazine below brings the Met's account of American art into the 20C. Some of the initial portraiture here tends to the sugary, but **J.W. Alexander**'s *Repose* deftly hits the mark – a simple, striking use of line and light with a sumptous feel and more than a hint of eroticism. By way of contrast, there's **Thomas Eakin**'s subdued, almost ghostly *Max Schmitt in a Single Scull*, and **William Merritt Chase**'s *For the Little One*, an Impressionist study of his wife sewing. Chase studied in Europe and it was there that he painted his *Portrait of Whistler*. **Whistler** returned the compliment but destroyed the work on seeing Chase's (quite truthful) depiction of himself as a dandified fop – and in a teasing style that mimicked his own. Whatever Whistler's conceits, though, his portraits are adept: witness the *Arrangement in Flesh Colour and Black: Portrait of Theodore Duret* nearby.

The reputation of **John Singer Sargent** has suffered its ups and downs over the years – he now seems to be coming back into fashion. There is certainly a virtuosity in his large portraits, like that of *Mr and Mrs I. N. Phelps Stokes*, the couple purposefully elongated as if to emphasise their aristocratic characters. *Padre Sebastiano* is a smaller, more personal response. The *Portrait of Madam X* (Mme Pierre Gautreau, a notorious Parisian beauty) was one of the most famous pictures of its day: exhibited at the 1884 Paris salon, it was considered so improper that Sargent had to leave Paris for London. 'I suppose it's the best thing I've done,' he said wearily on selling it to the Met a few years later.

Medieval Art

You could – in theory at least – move straight on to the **MEDIEVAL GALLERIES** from the American wing. But this would be heavy-going – and in any case you'd be missing out on a carefully planned approach.

This is the **corridor** leading in from the Great Hall, an entrance gallery that displays the sumptuous **Byzantine metalwork and jewellery** that J.P. Morgan donated to the museum in its early days. At its end is the main **sculpture hall**, piled high with religious statuary and carvings (a tremendous *St Nicholas Saving Three Boys in the Brine Tub*) and split with a *reja* (altar screen) from Valladolid Cathedral.

Right from here the **medieval treasury** has an all-embracing – and magnificent – display of objects religious, liturgical and secular. And beyond are the **Jack and Belle Linski galleries**: Flemish, Florentine and Venetian painting, porcelain and bronzes.

Dotted throughout the medieval galleries are later **period rooms**, panelled Tudor bedrooms and Robert Adam fancies from England, florid

Rococo boudoirs and salons from France, and an entire Renaissance patio from Velez Blanco in Spain. It's all a bit much, leaving you with the feeling that Morgan and his robber baron colleagues would probably have shipped over Versailles if they could have laid their hands on it.

The Egyptian Collection
'A chronological panorama of ancient Egypt's art, history and culture,' boasts the blurb to the Egyptian collection, and the display is certainly lavish. Brightly efficient corridors steer you through the treasures of the digs of the 1920s and 1930s, art and artefacts from the Prehistoric to Byzantine periods of Egyptian culture.

The **statuary** are the most immediately striking of the exhibits, though after a while it's the smaller **sculptural** pieces that hold the attention longest. Figures like *Merti and his Wife* were modelled as portraits, but often carvings were made in the belief that a person's *Ka* or life force would continue to exist in an idealised model after their death. There's a beautifully crafted example in the *Carving of Senebi* in gallery 8; what was probably Senebi's tomb is displayed nearby. Also in this room is the dazzling collection of *Princess Sithathorunet's jewellery*, a pinnacle in Egyptian decorative art from around 1830 BC; the *Models of Mekutra's House* (around 1198 BC); and the radiant *Fragmentary Head of a Queen*, sensuously carved in polished yellow jasper.

At the end of all this sits the **Temple of Dendur,** housed in a vast airy gallery designed to give hints and symbols of its original site on the banks of the Nile. Built by the Emperor Augustus in 15 BC as an attempt to placate a local chieftain, the temple was moved here as a gift of the Egyptian people during the construction of the Aswan High dam – it would otherwise have been drowned. Sadly the gallery, rather than suggest the empty expanses of the Nile, dwarfs what is essentially an unremarkable building, one that might be more engaging if you could explore inside. The temple needs a helping hand, and gets it at night, illuminated on a corner of Central Park with at least some of the mystery that's missing during the day.

The Michael C. Rockefeller Wing
Son of governor Nelson Rockefeller, Michael C. Rockefeller disappeared during a trip to West New Guinea in 1961. The Rockefeller wing stands as a memorial to him, including many of his finds alongside the Met's comprehensive collection of art from Africa, the Pacific Islands and the Americas. It's a superb gallery, the muted, reassuring decoration throwing the 'PRIMITIVE' ART exhibits into sharp and often frightening focus. You don't need much knowledge of 'Primitive' cultures to feel the intensity of the work here: the blackened *reliquary heads* from Gabon once contained the skulls of a family's ancestors, and issued magical

protection; the elegant spared lines of terracotta *heads* from Ghana put you in mind of Modigliani portraits, and the rich geometry of the *South American jewellery and ornaments* too seems often startlingly contemporary.

THE MUSEUM OF MODERN ART

11 W 53rd St. Subway Rockefeller Center. Friday-Tuesday 11am-6 pm, Thursday 11am-9pm, closed Wednesday; $5, students $3.50, Thursday 5pm-9pm pay what you wish.

Instigated in 1929, moved to its present permanent home 10 years later, and only a couple of years ago extensively updated in a steel pipe and glass renovation that doubled its gallery space, **THE MUSEUM OF MODERN ART** (plain MoMA to the initiated) offers probably the finest and most complete account of late 19C and 20C art you're likely to find. Basically, if you're in New York for any length of time and you want to catch some museums, MoMA has to be top of the list of places not to miss.

The new building is designed to ease you as effortlessly and easily as possible into the collections – and, with ultra-modern glass-enclosed landings and gliding escalators, it's an enjoyable place just to walk inside. On the **ground floor** you'll find the usual pairing of restaurant and shop, as well as a video room and film theatre (pick up a leaflet for a rundown on what's currently showing), and outside a **Sculpture Garden** holding scattered works by Rodin, Matisse and Barnett Newman, to name only three. The museum proper begins upstairs, with the first and second floors devoted to the main **painting and sculpture galleries**, the **third** to **architecture and design**, and it's these, on the whole, that most people come to see. But in addition to these three main sections, MoMA also has galleries devoted to **photographs, prints and drawings**, all of which give rotating displays of the museums's collections. The **photographs**, in particular, are marvellous: one of the finest, most eclectic collections around and a vivid evocation of 20C America, from the dramatic landscapes of Ansel Adams to Stieglitz's dynamic views of New York and the revealing portraits of Man Ray.

1st floor Painting and Sculpture
Once on the first floor, **Cézanne's** *Bather* of 1885 pulls you inside, leading on towards further **POST-IMPRESSIONISTS**: principally works by **Gauguin, Redon, Ensor** and, most famously, **Van Gogh's** *Starry Night*. Left, off the Cubist galleries, **Monet's** *Water Lilies* begins a less figurative theme: stirring attempts to abstract colour and form which cover well over half their gallery's space, their swirling jades, pinks and purples making it faintly like sitting in a giant aquarium. Retracing your steps, the

CUBIST space includes a scatter of works by **Picasso** and **Braque**; and, most notably, Picasso's *Demoiselles d'Avignon*: a jagged, sharp, and for its time, revolutionary clash of tones and planes which some hold to be the heralder (and initial arbiter) of Cubist principles – though **Derain**'s *Bathers* in the previous room may have equal claim to the title.

Rooms encapsulating entire periods and movements follow, cursory glances but with a staggering quality of material. **Kirchner**'s *Dresden* and *Berlin* street scenes are the focus of a gallery devoted to the glaring realities of the **GERMAN EXPRESSIONISTS**; the whirring abstractions of **Boccioni** are mainstay of the **FUTURISTS**' paeans to the industrial age; and a room takes in the work of **DE STIJL**, or more accurately **Mondrian**, following the artist's development from early limp Cubist pieces to later works like *Broadway Boogie Woogie*. This, painted in 1940 after the artist had moved to New York, reflects the artist's love of jazz music – its short, sharp stabs of colour conveying an almost physical rhythm.

Amongst all this, **Matisse** has a large room to himself, centring on his *Dancers* of 1909, and taking in other lesser- known works like the pudgy series of *Heads of Jeanette*, where straight Impressionism becomes, in the final head, no more than series of disfiguring lines and lumps. Look out, also, for the *Red Studio*, a depiction of Matisse's studio in France in which all perspective is resolved in shades of rusty red. The next gallery holds late works by **Picasso**, in particular *The Charnel House* – like *Guernica* which used to hang here before it was removed to Spain's Prado, an angry protest against the horrors of war. Nearby hangs one of Modigliani's finest works – a *Reclining Nude*, drawn with sensitive, sensuous linearity. In contrast are the brooding skies of **de Chirico** and a handful of dreamlike paintings by **Magritte**, **Dali**, **Delvaux** and **Balthus**: illogical scenes but disturbing in their clarity and undercurrents of eroticism. Never more so than in Balthus's *The Living Room* – in which the static poses of the adolescent girls and carefully positioned guitar hint at notions of sexual awakening.

2nd floor Painting and Sculpture
The second Painting and Sculpture gallery continues chronologically, and (inevitably) with a more **AMERICAN** slant – suitably prefaced by **Frank Stella**'s anarchic epoxy and mesh *Kastura* at the top of the escalator. In the gallery proper is **Andrew Wyeth**'s *Christina's World*, one of the best known of all modern American paintings, along with a couple of typically gloomy canvasses by **Hopper**, *House by the Railroad* and *New York Movie*: potent and atmospheric pieces which give a bleak account of modern American life. Contrast these with **Sheeler**'s *American Landscape*: 'the industrial landscape pastoralised', a critic noted, and almost toytown in its neat vision of industrialisation, in which nothing moves and all gleams neat and clean.

More **abstract** pieces follow: early Jackson Pollocks, **Gorky**'s Miro-like doodles, some neat satires by **Dubuffet** and, at the end of the room, the anguished scream of **Bacon**'s *No.7 from 8 Studies for a Portrait*. What many come here for, however, is to see the paintings of the **NEW YORK**

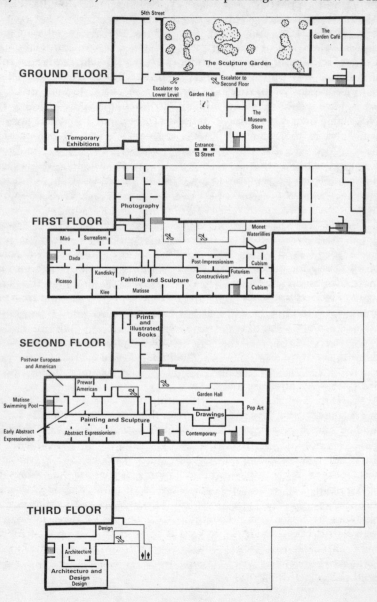

SCHOOL ARTISTS: large-scale canvases most of them, and meant to be viewed from a distance, as here, in large airy rooms. The paintings of **Pollock** and **de Kooning** – wild, and in Pollock's case textured, patterns with no clear beginning or end – mingle with the more ordered efforts of the Colour Field artists and the later works of artists like **Matisse** and **Miro**. Matisse's work here is mainly paper cutouts, most striking the bold blue shapes of his *Swimming Pool* which the ageing artist made to decorate the walls of his apartment in Nice. The work of the so-called **Colour Field artists** is more vivid but emphasises the importance of colour in a similar way – their paintings, in **Barnett Newman**'s words, 'drained of impediments of memory, association, nostalgia, legend, myth, and what have you': in short without anything but pure colour, as in Newman's own *Vir Heroicus Sublimus*, sheer red and huge against the wall, and in the radiating, almost humming blocks of colour of the paintings of **Mark Rothko**. **Robert Motherwell**'s *Elegy to the Spanish Republic*, one of a series of more than a hundred such paintings, is slightly different: colour is less important, and the broad splashes of black are meant to hint at the rituals of the corrida, the shapes roughly reminiscent of the testicles displayed at the finale of a bullfight.

The last of the painting and sculpture rooms is made up of 30 years of donations by Philip Johnson – **POP ART** mainly, and including **Jasper Johns**' *Flag*, a well-known piece in which the Stars and Stripes is painted on to newsprint, transforming America's most potent symbol into little more than an arrangement of shapes and colours. Look out also for the work of **Robert Rauschenberg**, thrown-together assemblies of urban junk, and **Claes Oldenburg**'s soft floor sculptures and papier-mâché represent-ations of cakes, hamburgers and gaudy fast foods.

(For more on the work and ideas of 20C American artists – specifically those of the New York school – see pp.356-358).

3rd floor – Architecture and Design

Architecture and design is, after painting and sculpture, MoMA's most important concern. The galleries on the third floor take in models of key modern buildings – **Frank Lloyd Wright**'s *Falling Water*, **Le Corbusier**'s *Ville Savoie* – and original drawings by architects. Among the latter are the sheer futuristic blocks of **Mies van der Rohe**, some beautifully accomplished studies by Wright and a loony sketch for the urbanisation of Algiers by Le Corbusier. Further aspects of modern design are traced through the swollen glasswork of **Tiffany**, **Guimard**'s flowery Art Nouveau furniture and, in addition to a couple of **Rietveld** chairs, a Rietveld sideboard which looks as if it could do with a spot of Rietveld paint. Look out too (indeed you can't miss them) for the spanking red *Pinin Farina* motor car and, dangling delicately over the escalator, a green Bell helicopter from 1945.

THE GUGGENHEIM MUSEUM

5th Ave at 89th St. Subway 86th St. Wednesday-Sunday 11am-5pm, Tuesday 11am-8pm, closed Monday; $3.50, students $2, Tuesday 5-8pm free.

Multi-storey car park or upturned beehive? Whatever you think of the **GUGGENHEIM MUSEUM**, it's the building which steals the show. Frank Lloyd Wright's purpose-built structure, 16 years in the making, caused a storm of controversy when it was unveiled in 1959, bearing little relation to the statuesque apartment blocks of this most genteel part of Fifth Avenue. Reactions, though Wright didn't live long enough to hear many, ranged from disgusted disbelief to critical praise and acclaim. And even now, though the years have given the building a certain respectability, no one seems to have quite made up their mind...

Solomon R. Guggenheim was one of America's richest men, his mines extracting silver and copper – and a healthy profit – all over the USA. Like other 19C American capitalists the only problem for Guggenheim was what to spend his vast wealth on, so he started collecting Old Masters – a hobby he continued half-heartedly until the 1920s, when various sorties to Europe brought him into contact with the most avant-garde and influential of European art circles. Abstraction in art was then considered little more than a fad but Guggenheim, always a man with an eye for a sound investment, started to collect modern paintings with fervour, buying up wholesale the work of Kandinsky, adding items by Chagall, Gleizes, Leger and others, and exhibiting them to a bemused American public in his suite of rooms in the Plaza Hotel. It's these works, enlarged with special purchases and the odd donation, which form the nucleus of the permanent collection. Don't, however, expect to see a great deal of it when you visit: most of the Guggenheim's space is these days given over to temporary exhibitions of 20C artists – a situation that may change if the much argued-over extension ever gets the go ahead.

Consequently, there's little you can say about the Guggenheim without predicting what's going to be on show. Rather it's the space itself which dominates – 'one of the greatest rooms erected in the 20C,' wrote Philip Johnson, and quite rightly: even if you hate the sight of the place from the outside it's hard not to be impressed by the tiers of cream concrete opening up above like the ribs of some giant convector fan as you go in. Most of the temporary exhibits are shown in the circular galleries, and the best way of seeing them is to zip straight to the top of the building (by way of the crescent-shaped lifts) and saunter down the gentle slope. On the way, two galleries offer a representative sample of the Guggenheim's **Permananent Collection**: the first, on the **fourth floor**, giving a quick glance at the Cubists, Chagall and, most completely, Kandinsky; the other, the **Tannhauser Wing**, offering a short résumé of modern movements in European painting up to, roughly, the Fauves. Highpoints here are a handful of late 19C paintings, not least the exquisite Degas *Dancers* and other Post-Impressionists, Van Gogh's *Mountains at St Remy* and some sensitive early Picassos.

THE FRICK COLLECTION

1 E 70th St. Subway 68th St and Hunter College. Tuesday-Saturday 10am-6pm, Sunday 1pm-6pm, closed Monday; $2, Sunday $3. Tuesday-Saturday students 50c. Daily introductory talks (Tuesday-Friday) at 2pm; lectures on aspects of European art on Thursday at 3 pm and Saturday at 4pm; and weekly concerts of classical music: all for no more than the regular admission ticket – pick up a leaflet for details.

Henry Clay Frick was probably the most ruthless of New York's robber barons. Vicious, uncompromising and anti-union, he broke strikes with state troopers, survived assassination attempts and instead of spending his millions on good deeds like his partner, Andrew Carnegie, surrounded himself with the best of Europe's art treasures. Today this forms the basis of **THE FRICK COLLECTION**- one of the most enjoyable of New York City galleries.

First opened in the mid-1930s, the museum has been kept largely as it would have looked when the Fricks were living there. It's in dubious taste for the most part, much of the furniture heavy 18C French, but the nice thing about it – and many people rank the Frick as their favourite New York gallery because of this – is that it strives hard to be as unlike a museum as possible. Ropes are kept to a minimum and even in the most sumptuously decorated rooms there are plenty of chairs you can freely sink into. When weary you can take refuge in the central closed courtyard, whose abundant greenery, fountains and marble are arranged with a classical attention to order, and whose echoey serenity you'd be hard pushed to find anywhere else in the city.

The **collection** itself was acquired under the direction of Joseph Duveen, notorious – and not entirely trustworthy – adviser to the city's richest and most ignorant. For Frick, however, he seems to have picked out the cream of Europe's post-First World War private art hoards, even if the opening ensemble of the **Boucher Room** is not to your taste, decorated with succulent representations of the arts and sciences. Next along, the **Dining Room** is more reserved, its Reynoldses and Hogarths overshadowed by the one non-portrait in the room, **Gainsborough**'s *St James's Park*: a subtly moving promenade under an arch of luxuriant trees – 'Watteau far outdone,' wrote a critic at the time. Outside there's more lusty French painting (Boucher again) and, in the next room, **Fragonard**'s *Progress of Love* series, which was painted for Madame du Barry in 1771 – and rejected by her soon after.

Better paintings follow, not least of them **Bellini**'s *St Francis*, which suggests his vision of Christ by means of pervading light, a bent tree and an enraptured stare. **El Greco**'s *St Jerome*, above the fireplace, reproachfully surveys the riches all around, and looks out to the South Hall, where hang one of Boucher's very intimate depictions of his naked wife – loaded with meaning – and an early **Vermeer**, *Officer and Laughing Girl*: similarly suggestive, and full of lewd allusions to forthcoming sex. In the opposite direction, the Library holds a number of British works, most notably **Constable**'s *Salisbury Cathedral*, and in the North Hall hangs an engaging and sensitive portrait of the *Comtesse de Haussonville* by **Ingres**.

But it's the **West Gallery**, beyond here, that's the Frick's major draw, and which holds some of its finest paintings. Two **Turners**, views of Cologne and Dieppe, hang opposite each other, both a blaze of orange and creamy tones; **Van Dyck** pitches in with a couple of uncharacteristic ally informal portraits of Frans Snyders and his wife – two paintings only reunited when Frick purchased them; and across the room **Frans Hals** reveals himself in a boozy and rare self-portrait. **Rembrandt**, too, is well represented, by the enigmatic *Polish Rider* – more fantasy-piece than portrait – and a set of piercing self-portraits. At the far end of the West Gallery **Whistler** shares the Oval Room with **Houdon**'s *Diana*, his portrait of fellow-artist *Rose Corder* posed to the point where she would have to faint before Whistler would stop painting. Past here, the East Gallery holds more paintings still, but more interesting is the tiny room on the other side of the West Gallery. This houses an exquisite set of Limoges **enamels**, mainly 16C, as well a collection of small-scale paintings that includes a *Virgin and Child* by **Jan van Eyck** – one of the artist's very last works, and among the rare few to have reached America.

THE WHITNEY MUSEUM OF AMERICAN ART

Madison Ave at 75th St, Subway 77th St and Lexington. Closed Mondays; Tuesday 1pm-8pm; Wednesday-Saturday 11am-5pm; Sunday 12am-6pm, $4; students with ID free; also free for all Tuesday 6-8pm. Excellent – and free – gallery talks on Tuesday (1.30pm, 3.30pm, 6.15pm), Wednesday/Thursday/Friday (11.30am, 1.30pm, 3.30pm).

A grey-faced Brutalist arsenal designed by Marcel Breuer, the **WHITNEY**'s oblique windows and cantilevered floors have an intimidating and suspiciously institutional air. Within, however, all such impressions are quickly dispelled. This is some of the best gallery space in the city and the perfect forum for the works that it owns – one of the pre-eminent collections of 20C American art. It is also a superb exhibition locale and, like the Guggenheim, devotes much of its time and rooms to this end. The majority of Whitney exhibitions are given over to retrospectives and debuts of lesser-known themes – Ed Keinholz and sculpture of the New York School are a couple of recent examples. Every other year, though, there is an exhibition of a wholly different nature – the **Whitney biennial** – designed to give a provocative overview of what's happening in contemporary American art. It is often panned by critics but always packed with visitors; catch it if you can between March and June on odd-numbered years.

Gertrude Vanderbilt Whitney founded the collection in 1930 around works by Hopper, Thomas Hart Benton, George Bellows and other living painters. Currently the gallery owns over 10,000 pieces of painting, sculpture and photography by artists as diverse as Calder, Nevelson, O'Keefe, de Kooning, Rauschenburg, Le Witt and Nam June Paik. The **Highlights of the Permanent Collection**, a somewhat arbitrary pick of the Whitney's best, are arranged by both chronology and theme. The works form a superb introduction to 20C American art, best evaluated with the help of the Gallery Talks, designed to explain and locate the paintings and sculptures in their various movements.

Gertrude Whitney's taste tended towards **Realism** and the paintings often tie in with the expectations of the genre. **George Bellows'** *Dempsey and Firpo* though is a sort of Neo-Mannerist view of a boxing match, full of movement and flesh – 'I don't know anything about boxing; I'm just painting two guys trying to kill each other,' said Bellows. The collection is particularly strong on **Edward Hopper** (his works were bequeathed to the museum) and several of his best paintings are here: *Early Sunday Morning* is typical, a bleak urban landscape, uneasily tense in its lighting and rejection of topical detail. The street could be anywhere (in fact it's Seventh Avenue) and, for Hopper, becomes universal.

As if to balance the figurative works that formed the nucleus of the collection, more recent purchases include much **abstraction**. **Marsden Hartley's** *Painting Number 5* is a strident, overwhelmed work, painted in the memory of a German officer friend killed in the early days of the Great War. **Georgia O'Keefe** called it 'a brass band in a closet', and certainly her own work is gentler, though with its darknesses: *Abstraction* was suggested by the noises of cattle being driven to the local slaughterhouse. Have a look too at O'Keefe's flower paintings: verging on abstraction but hinting at deeper organic forms.

The **Abstract Expressionists** feature particularly strongly, with great works by high priests **Pollock** and **De Kooning**, leading on to **Rothko** and the **Colour Field painters** – though you need a sharp eye to discern any colour in **Ad Reinhard's** *Black Painting*. In a different direction, **Warhol**, **Johns** and **Oldenburg** each subvert the meanings of their images. Warhol's silkscreened *Coke Bottles* fade into motif, Jasper Johns' celebrated *Three Flags* once again erases the emblem of patriotism, replacing it with ambiguity, and Claes Oldenburg's lighter-hearted *Soft Sculptures*, squidgy loos and melting motors, fall into line with his declaration, 'I'm into art that doesn't sit on its ass in a museum.' Finally, don't – you can't – miss **Ed Keinholz**'s *The Wait*, perhaps the best macabre joke in town.

The Whitney also exhibits in three other galleries:

The Whitney at Philip Morris
120 Park Ave. Subway Grand Central.
Two sections: a small **Picture Gallery** (Monday-Saturday 11am-6pm, Thursday 11am-7.30pm, free; gallery talks Monday, Wednesday and Friday 12.30pm) with changing exhibitions on just about any (modern) theme you care to mention. And a **Sculpture Court** (Monday-Saturday 7.30am-9.30pm, Sunday 11am-7pm; free) festooned with works: a great idea and a much better place to wait for a train than Grand Central across the road.

Whitney Museum at the Equitable
757 7th Ave. Subway 50th St. Monday-Friday 11am-6pm, Thursday 11am-7.30pm, Saturday 12am-4pm, Free. Gallery talks 12.30pm Monday, Wednesday, Friday.
Two collections of American art, one changed yearly, the other every couple of months. Expect striking works from big 20C names like O'Keefe, Rothko, Hopper and Johns – pick up the informative booklet for more details. Two thing you can't miss: **Roy Lichtenstein**'s 68-foot *Mural with Blue Brush Stroke*, which pokes you in the eye as you enter, and in a corridor **Thomas Hart Benton**'s *America Today* murals dynamically and magnificently portray ordinary American life in the days before the Depression.

Whitney Museum Downtown
Federal Reserve Plaza. 33 Maiden Lane at Nassau St. Subway Broad St. Monday-Friday 11am-6pm; free.
Five changing exhibitions of modern American art each year, with good free brochures and gallery talks.

THE CLOISTERS

Fort Tryon Park. Subway 190th St then M4 bus to museum. March-October Tuesday-Sunday 9.30-5.15pm. November-February Tuesday-Sunday 9.30-4.45pm. Suggested donation $4.50; $2.25 students. Free tours Tuesday-Thursday 3pm.

High above the Hudson in Fort Tryon Park, **THE CLOISTERS** stands like some misplaced Renaissance palazzo-cum-monastery. Which was presumably the desired effect. For this was the folly of collectors George Barnard and John D. Rockefeller, who in turn spent the early years of this century shipping over the best of medieval Europe that was going: Romanesque chapels and Gothic halls, transplanted brick by brick and now housing the best part of the **Metropolitan Museum's medieval collection**. If you're familiar with the type of buildings that have been cannibalised, then the place can't help but feel a Frankenstein's monster, an assemblage of parts to make a distorted whole. But it is all undeniably well carried off, not without atmosphere, and in detail superb.

The best approach – from the 190th Street subway – is directly across the park; Rockefeller thoughtfully bought up the land on the other side of the river so as not to spoil the views. Starting from the entrance hall, working anti-clockwise lays out the collection in a loosely chronological order. First off is the simple monumentality of the **Romanesque Hall** made up from French remnants and the frescoed Spanish **Fuentiduena Chapel**, both 13C and immediately inducing a reverential hush. They corner on perhaps the prettiest of the four sets of cloisters here, those from **St Guilhelm**, strong and busily carved capitals from 13C France. More or less contemporary, and again from France, is the nearby **Langon Chapel**, attractive enough in itself and enhanced by a 12C **ciborium** that manages to be formal and graceful in just the right proportions, and protects an emotive **Virgin and Child** beneath.

At the centre of the museum is the **Cuxa cloister**, from the 12C Benedictine monastery of Saint Michel de Cuxa near Prades in the French Pyrenees; its capitals are brilliant peasant art, many carved with weird, self-devouring grotesque creatures. Pastiche additions to the scene are the the gardens, planted with fragrant, almost overpowering, herbs and flowers, and (bizarrely in keeping) piped plainsong.

The museum's smaller **sculpture** is equally impressive. In the **Early Gothic Hall** are a number of carved figures, one a memorably tender and refined **Virgin and Child**, carved in England in the 14C, probably for veneration at a private altar. The collection of **tapestries** is special, too, including a rare surviving Gothic work showing the **Nine Heroes**. The heroes, popular figure of the ballads of the Middle Ages, comprise three pagans (Hector, Alexander, Julius Caesar), three Hebrews (David, Joshua,

Judus Macabeas) and three Christians (Arthur, Charlemagne, Godfrey of Bouillon). Five of the nine are here, clothed in the garb of the day (around 1385) against a rich backdrop. The **Unicorn Tapestries**, in the succeeding room, are even more spectacular – brilliantly alive with colour, observation and Christian symbolism.

Most of the Met's medieval painting is to be found downtown, but one important exception here is **Campin**'s *Merode Altarpiece*. Housed in its own antechamber, this tryptych depicts the Annunciation scene in a typical bourgeois Flemish interior of the day. On the left the donors gaze timidly on through an open door, to the right St Joseph works in his carpenter's shop; St Joseph was mocked in the literature of the day, which might account for his rather ridiculous appearance – making a mousetrap, a symbol of the way the devil traps souls. Through the windows behind life goes on in a 15C market square, perhaps Campin's native Tournai.

With the ground floor, you move into Gothic architecture. Or at least into a pseudo-Gothic chapel, built around the monumental **sarcophagus of Ermengol VII**, with its whole phalanx of family and clerics carved around to send him off. Two further cloisters are here to explore, along with an amazing downstairs **Treasury**. This is crammed with items but two can easily be singled out: the **Belles Heures de Jean, Duc de Berry**, perhaps the greatest of all medieval Books of Hours, executed by the Limburg Brothers with dazzling genre miniatures of seasonal life; and the 12C **altar cross** from Bury St Edmunds in England, a mass of tiny expressive characters from Biblical stories. Finally, hunt out a minute **rosary bead** from 16C Flanders: with a representation of the passion inside, it seems barely possible it could have been carved by hand.

SMALLER OR SPECIALIST MUSEUMS

ART AND VISUALS

Asia Society Gallery
725 Park Ave. Subway 68th St and Hunter College. Tuesday-Saturday 11am-6pm, Sunday 12am-5pm; $2, Students $1.
Small permanent display of the Rockefeller collection of Asian art. Worth the admission fee if the accompanying temporary exhibition looks promising. Asia House also holds interesting performances/lectures/films/ free events: phone 517 ASIA for details.

Alternative Museum

17 White St. Subway Franklin St. Wednesday-Saturday 11am-6pm, closed July and August; free.

Temporary exhibitions of contemporary art, emphasising international developments. Well-organised and adventurous, with displays supplemented by regular musical events and poetry readings. For information pick up their calendar, or simply give them a call – **966 4444**.

Bronx Museum of the Arts

851 Grand Concourse, the Bronx. Subway 161st St. Monday-Thursday 9.30am-5pm, Sunday 12.30pm-4.30pm; donations preferred.

Contemporary American art, none of any great note, plus changing exhibitions of Bronx-based artists.

The Brooklyn Museum

220 Eastern Parkway, Brooklyn. Subway Eastern Parkway Brooklyn Museum. Monday, Wednesday, Thursday, Friday 10am-5pm, Saturday 11am-6pm, Sunday 1pm-6pm, closed Tuesdays; pay what you wish, suggested $2.

When Judy Chicago's Dinner Party was exhibited here back in the early 1980s, the Brooklyn Museum had people queuing all the way round the block. Since then it's reverted to its former, little-visited status: a museum good in its own right but doomed to stand perpetually in the shadow of the Met. Which is a pity, for it's a likeable place, and a good reason for forsaking Manhattan for an afternoon.

It does, however, need considerable selectivity, for in terms of size this is most certainly a Major Museum. Highlights, depending on your personal interests, are likely to be the **Classical and Greek antiquities**, the **Ethnographic** department, the American **Period Rooms**, and the mainly 19C **American and European Picture Galleries** on the top floor. In the American picture galleries, the paintings of Eastman Johnson and John Singer Sargent stand out; the European galleries, on the other hand, are disappointing, and while there are a number of big names on show – Degas, Cézanne, Toulouse-Lautrec, Dufy, Modigliani – only in the small drawings gallery do you feel you're looking at anything like their best work. On the way out drop in on the museum's **Gift Shop**, which sells genuine ethnic items from around the world at not unreasonable prices.

City Gallery

2 Columbus Circle. Subway 59th St. Monday-Friday 10am-5.30pm, Saturday 10am-5pm; free.

Funded by the city, this is a showcase gallery for NYC artists and community-based arts associations. Exhibitions change monthly.

Fashion Moda
2803 3rd Ave at 147th St. Subway 3rd Ave/149th St. Tuesday-Saturday 2pm-7pm; free.
'Fashion Moda is impossible to define because by definition we have no definition.' Which goes some way to explaining what you're likely to see here: anarchic and always surprising temporary expositions of art that are a positive attempt to break with the at times chic safety of the Manhattan art scene. Its siting in the worst of the South Bronx's urban decay is deliberately intimidating, but if you can get someone to drop you on the doorstep, Fashion Moda's exhibitions rarely fail to entertain.

Forbes Galleries
62 5th Ave at 12th St. Subway Union Square. Tuesday, Wednesday, Friday and Saturday, 10am-4pm; free.
The world's largest collection of Fabergé Easter Eggs – Malcolm Forbes' favourite playthings, after the magazine that bears his name.

Grey Art Gallery
33 Washington Place. Subway 8th St. Tuesday/Thursday 10am-6.30pm, Wednesday 10am-8.30pm, Friday 10am-5pm, Saturday 1pm-5pm; free.
Display gallery of NYU's art department, mounting exhibitions of variable quality throughout the year. The permanent collection, when on display, is known for its post-1940s American works.

IBM Gallery of Science and Art
Madison Ave at 56th St. Subway 5th Ave and 53rd. Tuesday-Friday 11am-6pm, Saturday 10am-5pm; free.
Unfairly ignored, this basement gallery exhibits more art than science – and sometimes a cross-over.

International Center of Photography
1130 5th Ave. Subway 96th & Lexington. Tuesday 12am-8pm, Wednesday-Friday 12am-5pm, Saturday-Sunday 11am-6pm; $2, students $1. Free on Tuesday after 5pm.
Founded and directed by Cornell Capa, brother of Robert, the ICP exhibits on photography in all its aspects. The Center's permanent collection features most of the great – Cartier-Bresson, Adams, Kersetz, Eugene Smith – and in addition there are usually three temporary shows on at any given time. At least one of these is bound to be worthwhile, often featuring the city's most exciting avant-garde and experimental work. All in all, an excellent adjunct to MoMA's static collection.

ICP Midtown
77 W 45th St (International Paper Plaza). Subway Grand Central.
Monday-Friday 11am-6pm, Saturday 12am-4pm; $1, students 50c.
Smaller, changing exhibitions of photographs from the main collection.

National Academy of Design
1083 5th Ave. Subway 86th St. Tuesday 12am-8pm, Wednesday-Sunday
12am-5pm; $2.50, students $2. Free Tuesday 5pm-8pm.
Samuel Morse founded the National Academy of Design along the lines
of London's Royal Academy, and though 1083 Fifth Avenue is nothing
so grand as Burlington House, similarities remain: a school of fine art,
exclusive membership and regular exhibitions which, as you'd imagine,
are usually (though not exclusively) American. There's a tradition that
academicians and academics give a work of art on their election here:
associates a self-portrait, academicians a 'mature work'. One hundred and
fifty years' worth of these pictures are now held by the Academy and form
the mainstay of the Selection from the Permanent Collection – varied
throughout the year but always with a strong slant towards portraiture.

Icing on the cake is the building itself: a faintly snooty Beaux Arts
townhouse donated to the academy by the husband of sculptor Anna
Hyatt Huntingdon; her *Diana* gets pride of place below the cheerful
rotunda.

New Museum of Contemporary Art
583 Broadway. Subway Prince St. Wednesday-Sunday 12am-6pm,
Wednesday until 8pm; $2.50, students $1.50.
Regularly changing exhibitions by contemporary American artists.
Offbeat, eclectic and worth checking out. Pick up the museum's calendar
for details on current and forthcoming exhibits and lectures.

The Pierpoint Morgan Library
29 E 36th St. Tuesday-Saturday 10.30am-5pm, Sunday 1pm-5pm, closed
Sundays in July and August; pay what you wish, suggested $3.
Built by McKim, Mead and White for J Pierpoint Morgan in 1917, this
gracious Italian-style nest, feathered with the fruits of the financier's
magpie-ish trips to Europe, is one of New York's best small museums –
though many of the exhibits are changed regularly so it's difficult to say
precisely what you'll see. Focal points are usually a fine assortment of
Rembrandt prints, the **East Room** or library, a sumptuous three-tiered
cocoon of rare books, autograph musical manuscripts and various trinkets
culled from European households and churches; and to its right the **West
Room**. This last served as Morgan's study and has been left much as it was
when he worked here, with the carved 16C Italian ceiling, a couple of
paintings by Memling, and, among the few items contemporary with the

building, a desk custom-carved to a design by McKim. Portraits of JP and his son look on, JP Junior having narrowly survived an assassination attempt in 1920 when a bomb meant for him killed 38 innocent bystanders. Here, swathed in academic finery, he sports the self-satisfied grin of the man who escaped without a scratch.

Society of Illustrators' Museum
128 East 63rd St. Monday-Friday 10am-5pm, Tuesday 10am-8pm; free.
Changing selections from the Society's permanent collection of illustrations – wartime propaganda to slick contemporary adverts, with all manner of cartoons and drawings in between. The exhibitions centre on theme or illustrator – designed primarily for aficionados but always accessible, well-mounted and topical.

CITY HISTORY

Fraunces Tavern
Pearl and Broad Streets. Subway Bowling Green. Monday-Friday 10am-4pm; free.
Odds and sods from the Revolutionary era likeably housed in an historic building; see p.66.

Museum of Bronx History
3266 Bainbridge Ave the Bronx. Subway 205th St/Bainbridge Ave. Monday-Friday 9am-5pm by appointment (881 8900); $1.
Bronx-related artefacts from Indian times to the Depression.

Museum of the City of New York
5th Ave at 103rd St. Subway 103rd St. Tuesday-Saturday 10am-5pm, Sunday 1pm-5pm; free.
Spaciously housed in a purpose-built Neo-Georgian mansion on the fringes of Spanish Harlem, this gives a competent if unexciting rundown on the history of the city from Dutch times to the present day. Paintings, furniture and a slide show – plus the museum runs Sunday walking tours of New York neighbourhoods (see *Basics*).

The New York Historical Society
Central Park West at 77th St. Subway 81st St. Tuesday-Friday 11am-5pm, Saturday 10am-5pm, Sunday 1pm-5pm; $2, Tuesday pay what you wish.
More a museum of American than New York history, but another venue well worth keeping an eye on for its temporary exhibitions, and with a

permananent collection that repays a visit in its own right. Focus of this are the paintings of **James Audubon,** the Harlem artist and naturalist who specialised in lovingly detailed watercolours of birds – all very similar, and unless you're a keen ornithologist, not exactly attention-grabbing. Other galleries hold a broad sweep of **19C American painting:** principally portraiture (a slobbish Aaron Burr and the picture of Alexander Hamilton that found its way on to the $10 bill) and Hudson River School landscapes (among them Thomas Cole's famed and fanatically pompous *Course of Empire* series). More rewarding is the glittering display of **Tiffany glass,** providing an excellent all-round view of Louis Tiffany's attempts 'to provide good art for American homes'. On a more historical note, and for a small additional fee, you can look round the museum **library,** which boasts such diverse items as the original Louisiana Purchase document and the correspondence between Aaron Burr and Alexander Hamilton that led up to their duel. All in all an interesting museum, and one often overlooked.

Queens Museum
Flushing Meadows-Corona Park. Subway Willets Point. Tuesday-Saturday 10am-5pm, Sunday 1pm-5pm; donation required.
Primarily worth the trip for its one and only permanent item: an 18,000-square-foot model of the five boroughs of New York City, spectacularly lit, constantly updated and originally conceived for the 1964 World's Fair by Robert Moses. Great fun if you know the city well, and useful orientation if you don't.

COMMUNITY AND ETHNIC

Center for African Art
54 E 68th St. Subway 68th St and Hunter College. Tuesday-Friday 10am-5pm, Saturday 11am-5pm, Sunday 12am-5pm; $2.50, students $1.50.
Changing exhibitions of the best of traditional African art. An eye-opener compared to the static/junky collections that are usually found.

The Museum of the American Indian
Audubon Terrace, Broadway at 155th St. Subway 157th St or 155th St Tuesday-Saturday 10am-5pm, Sunday 1pm-5pm. $2, students $1.
Way the finest of the Audubon Terrace collections, this languishes up in Harlem almost totally ignored. When a few of its prize exhibits were shown downtown for a couple of weeks, more people went to look than turned up at the museum that year. Don't follow this pattern, for you'll miss out on a superb and fascinating assemblage of daily artefacts from

almost every tribe native to the Americas. Ordinarily this might sound a little overpowering but the display here is skilful and backed up with an intelligent range of informational aids. Highlights include assorted scalps, the personal knick-knacks of Sitting Bull and Geronimo, shrunken human figures from Ecuador and some amazing eskimo scrimshaw. There's also a very reasonably priced museum shop selling various authentic items. Every so often plans are mooted to move the whole collection downtown: wherever it is, catch it.

Museo del Barrio
1230 5th Ave. Subway 103rd St. Tuesday-Friday 10.30am-4.30pm, Saturday/Sunday 11am-4pm; donation requested.
Literally 'the neighbourhood museum', this place was founded in the 1960s by a group of Puerto Ricans from Spanish Harlem who wanted to educate their children and remind them of their roots. Now, although the emphasis remains largely Puerto Rican, the museum has come to embrace the whole of Latin America, with five major loan exhibits of painting, photographs and crafts each year. Supplementary events include talks, summer concerts and kid's puppet theatre – all free.

Chinatown Museum
8 Mott St. Subway Canal. Monday-Saturday 10am-6pm, closed Sunday.
A hoard of Chinese costumes, Buddhas and religious accoutrements located at the end of a sleazy amusement arcade (which itself includes a devastatingly cruel contraption caging a 'live, dancing chicken'). A neat stop-off on any tour of Chinatown were it not for the fact that it's open only to groups of eight or more.

Hispanic Museum
Audubon Terrace (see Museum of the American Indian, above). Tuesday-Saturday 10am-4.30pm, Sunday 1pm-4pm; free.
Inevitably this is overshadowed by the adjacent Museum of the American Indian, but it's worth sticking your nose round the door of the Hispanic for the chocolatey terracotta interior, a scattering of Spanish masters, and, best of all, the joyful *Murals of Spain* by Joaquin Sorolla Y. Bastida.

Jewish Museum
1109 5th Ave. Sunday 11am-6pm, Monday, Wednesday, Thursday 12am-5pm, Tuesday 12am-8pm , Friday 11am-3pm; $4, students $2. Subway 86th and Lexington or 96th St.
The Jewish Museum in New York City – you expect something pretty good. But as it is the museum fails to deliver: there's a dessicated account of the wanderings of the tribes of Israel and a stultifying collection of religious bric-a-brac, but all the chances of showing the history of the

Jewish community in the city are missed. Visit only if temporary exhibitions sound promising.

Schomburg Center for Research in Black Culture
515 Lenox Ave at 135th St. Subway Lenox and 135th St. Monday Wednesday 12am-8pm, Thursday-Saturday 10am-6pm; free.
Thought-provoking exhibitions on the history of blacks in the US.

Studio Museum of Harlem
144 W 125th St. Subway Lenox and 125th St. Wednesday-Friday 10am-5pm, Saturday 1pm-6pm; $1.50, students 50c.
Exhibitions of contemporary (and often local) art, photography and sculpture.

Ukrainian Museum
203 2nd Ave. Subway Astor Place. Wednesday-Sunday 1pm-5pm; $1. students 50c.
Situated in the heart of the Ukrainian East Village, there's little to entice outsiders into this small collection. On two tiny floors, it divides itself between recounting the history of immigration to the US from the Ukraine and showing (more interestingly) ethnic items from the Ukraine itself. Look out for the hand-painted Easter eggs or *pysanky* – a craft that's still kept up since, according to Ukrainian folklore, when production ceases the world will end.

CRAFTS, FASHION AND DESIGN

Museum of American Craft
40 W 53rd St. Monday-Saturday 10am-5pm; $1.50.
A showcase of modern crafts as chosen by the American Craft Council. Bright, brash and good fun.

Museum of American Folk Art
49 W 53rd St. Tuesday 10.30am-8pm, Wednesday-Sunday 1.30pm-5.30pm. $2; free after 5.30pm Tuesday.
Changing exhibitions of traditional handicrafts with the emphasis on the domestic; could be just the place if the splendours the Met offers aren't your cup of tea.

Black Fashion Museum
155 W 126th St. Subway 125th St. Lenox. Monday-Friday 12am-8pm; phone 666 1320 for an appointment; suggested donation $1.50.
It's on the premise that the contribution of the black fashion designers has

gone largely unrecognised that the Black Fashion Museum organises its exhibits, a wide variety of costumes designed and made by blacks from the 18C on. The second floor has a quirky group of robes and gowns, including a slave dress of finely stitched cotton, and Mary Todd Lincoln's velvet inaugural gown designed by Elizabeth Keckley, a freed slave. The Lenox site, sadly, makes for specialist interest only.

Cooper-Hewitt Museum
2 E 91st St. Tuesday 10am-9pm, Wednesday-Saturday 10am-5pm, Sunday 12am-5pm; $2, students $1. Free Tuesday 5pm-9pm.
When he decided to build at what was then the unfashionable end of Fifth Avenue, millionaire industrialist Andrew Carnegie asked for 'the most modest, plainest and most roomy house in New York'. And that's nearly what he got – a series of wood-panelled boxes too decorative to be plain, too large to be modest. But they provide good gallery space today for the Cooper-Hewitt collection of design, shown off here in three floors of changing exhibitions. Themes vary so check what's on first – the Cooper-Hewitt is as good as its exhibitions, which tend to be excellent.

MAINLY FOR KIDS

Aunt Len's Doll and Toy Museum
6 Hamilton Terrace (141st St) 281 4143. Phone first for an appointment, Donation appreciated.
'Aunt Len' is a scholarly and charming retired schoolteacher whose collection of 3000-plus dolls and teddy bears is amusing and interesting – and made all the more so by her infectious enthusiasm.

Brooklyn Children's Museum
145 Brooklyn Ave. Subway Eastern Parkway/Brooklyn Museum. Monday-Friday 1pm-5pm, Saturday/Sunday 10am-5pm, closed Tuesday; free.
Participatory museum stacked full of scientific and natural artefacts with which to play. Fun for both children and adults.

Children's Museum of Manhattan
314 W 54th St. Subway 57th St. Tuesday-Sunday 11am-5pm; weekdays child $2, adult $1, weekends child $3, adult $2.
Another participatory museum centring on science and nature exhibits. Primarily directed at ages up to 12 years.

Fire Department Museum
104 Duane St. Subway Chambers St. Monday-Friday 9am-4pm, closed weekends; free, but phone before visiting – 570 4230.
Something of a surprise this: nothing spectacular but a pleasing homage to New York City's firefighters, and indeed firepeople everywhere. On display are fire engines from the last century (hand-drawn, horse-drawn and steam-powered), helmets, dog-eared photos and a host of motley objects on three floors of a disused fire station. A neat and endearing display.

OTHERS

Intrepid Sea-Air-Space Museum
Far western end of 46th St at Pier 86. Wednesday-Sunday 10am-5pm; $4.75.
This worn-out aircraft carrier had a distinguished history, including hauling Neil Armstrong and Co. out of the ocean following the Apollo 11 moonshot. Today it holds a celebration of the nation's military might of the very worst kind – fighter planes clustered with bombs and emblazoned with 'World's Greatest Dad' stickers, prototype models for the evil-looking B-1B fighter housed in a cavernous ship that reeks of gunmetal and regimented sweat.

Museum of Broadcasting
1 E 53rd St. Subway 5th Ave. Tuesday-Saturday 12am-5pm; suggested $3, $2 students. Tuesday 12am-8pm; pay what you wish. Phone 752 4690 for details of lectures by artists and directors.
An archive of American TV and radio broadcasts, unusually accessible to the public, whose excellent card reference system allows you to trace 1950s comedies, old newsreels and other oddities. Be warned though that there are only a couple of dozen video consoles and someone before you may well be getting down to a day's worth of 'I Love Lucy'. Arrive, if possible, at opening.

Museum of Holography
11 Mercer St. Subway Canal or Prince St. Wednesday-Sunday 12am-6pm, Thursday 12am-9pm; $3.
Give this a miss: surprisingly there's nothing innovative and what exhibits there are have a tired, dusty feel.

The American Museum of Natural History/Hayden Planetarium
Central Park West at 79th St. Subway 81st St. Daily 10am-5.45pm,
Wednesday, Friday, Saturday until 9pm; pay what you wish: suggested
$3.50, Planetarium $4.
According to the *Guinness Book of Records*, this is the largest museum
in the world bar none, and once you've paced the length of its ageing
exhibition hall and witnessed a fair number of its 34 million exhibits,
you'll know it. Which is basically to say be selective: anthropologists
could have a field day here, but for anyone else a highly discriminating
couple of hours should be ample.

The main entrance on Central Park West is the one to make for, leaving
you well placed for a loop of the more interesting halls on the first floor:
principally intelligently mounted artefacts from Asia and Africa, backed
up with informal commentary and lent atmosphere with drums and ethnic
music. These are sandwiched between dusty dioramas of the two
continents' mammals. Upstairs there's a wilting array of dinosaurs,
downstairs a static display of fish, both really only of interest to kids.
Better to miss these altogether and check out the Hall of Meteorites
instead: better laid-out and including some strikingly beautiful crystals –
not least the *Star of India*, the largest blue sapphire ever found.

The museum's astronomy department is installed in the adjacent
Hayden Planetarium – accessible from the first floor of the Natural
History Museum or from a separate entrance on 81st Street. Here you can
view a variety of astronomical displays and gadgetry, hear Henry Fonda,
Walter Kronkite and assorted celebrities relate an impassioned tale of
space endeavour, or watch a soporifically dull history of the universe
(narrator Vincent Price) in the theatre. All of which are cloyingly dull –
and, again, primarily directed at children. You may instead prefer to fork
out for the planetarium's **laser light shows**, held on Friday and Saturday
evenings to provide visuals and sound for teenage stoners to freak out to
their favourite Led Zep or Floyd tracks. If conventional New York
nightlife is beginning to pale, it's always a thought...

Police Academy Museum
235 E 20th St. Subway 23rd St. Monday-Friday 9-3pm; free,
A collection of memorabilia of the New York Police Department, the
largest and oldest in the country. It's used to inculcate reverence for the
force in young cadets, and just about merits itself to anyone not wildly
interested in law and order. Really, it's not about crime or punishment so
much as the personal effects of New York's Finest: night sticks, uniforms,
photos and the like. There's a copper badge of 1845 as worn by the
sergeants of the day, earning them the sticking nickname of 'coppers'. If
you are into firepower, search out the tommy gun in a violin case –
original gangster issue.

Chapter six
SHOPS AND GALLERIES

New York is consumer capital of the world. Its shops cater for every possible taste, preference, creed or perversity, in any combination and in many cases at any time of day or night – and as such they're as good a reason as any for visiting the city. To enjoy them to the full you obviously have to have money, and lots of it, but even if you can't afford to buy, the city's shop windows, department stores, gourmet grocers, ethnic and oddity stores are still there for the browsing.

As in most large cities, New York stores are concentrated in specific neighbourhoods, so if you want something particular you invariably know exactly where to head. **Midtown Manhattan** is mainstream shopping territory – department stores, big-name clothes designers and the large chains. **Downtown Manhattan** plays host to a wide variety of more offbeat stores: small boutiques, secondhand bookshops and almost pedantically specialised stores selling nothing but candles or a hundred different types of caviar. **Uptown**, the Upper East Side is an upmarket continuation of midtown Manhattan, with – on Madison especially – a greater concentration of exclusive clothiers, antique and art dealers, while the Upper West Side has a quite different personality and an array of off-the-wall stores that can compare to anything in SoHo or the Village. Bear in mind, too, that New York's **ethnic** enclaves have some of the city's most exciting and colourful places to shop, and – the Outer Boroughs included – some of its most specialised. For full details on specific shopping neighbourhoods see the relevant part-headings in this chapter.

As regards **when to shop**, most parts of the city are at their least oppressive early weekday mornings, and at their worst around lunchtimes and on Saturdays. There are few days of the year when everything closes (really only Thanksgiving, Christmas and New Year's Day) and many shops, including the big midtown department stores, regularly open on Sundays. Remember, however, that certain (usually ethnic) communities close their shops in accordance with religious and other holidays. Don't bother to shop on the Lower East Side on Friday afternoon or on Saturday, for example, though you can on Sunday. By contrast, Chinatown is open all day every day, while the stores of the Financial District follow the areas's nine-to-five routine and for the most part are shut all weekend.

Opening hours in midtown Manhattan are roughly 9am-6pm Monday-Saturday with late closing on (usually) Thursdays; downtown shops tend to stay open later, at least until 8pm and often until about midnight. Unless we've stated otherwise the stores listed follow broadly these hours. As far as **payment** goes, credit cards rule as ever and even the smallest of shops will take *Visa, American Express, Access* (here called *Mastercard*) and *Diners Club*: many also run their own credit schemes. *Traveller's Cheques* are widely accepted too, though they must be in US Dollars and you may have to provide ID. All the time, be careful. Manhattan's stores, crowded frenzied places that they are, are ripe territory for **pickpockets and bag-snatchers**: keep a firm eye on your belongings.

DEPARTMENT STORES

In *Saks, Bloomingdale's* and others less well known across the Atlantic, New York has some of the great department stores of the world. However, while their range might often be superlative, most aren't really places to stock up on essentials. With New York stores the accent is these days on designer clothes and chi-chi accessories, and if you want to buy something in a hurry without turning it into a real NYC shopping experience, you'd often do better to use a more specialised store. Prices too, out of sale times, can be prohibitive. (*During* sale-times, though, you may well find some unprecedented bargains: visit on and around holiday periods and watch the newspapers for timings).

Alexander's, 731 Lexington Ave (593 0880); 4 World Trade Center Plaza (466 1414). Often the same goods you'll find in more upmarket stores (designer 'labels' minus the labels) but at much lower prices. If you're looking for something at Lord & Taylor's or Bloomingdale's, check out Alexander's first: you may turn up a bargain.

B. Altman, 5th Ave and 34th St (689 7000). The building says it all: solid and traditional, like the values which form the bedrock of Altman's reputation. Quirks include an art and rare book department – an oddity perfectly in keeping with the store's stalwart columns and crystal chandliers.

Bergdorf Goodman, 754 5th Ave (753 7300). The name, the location, the thick pile carpets and discreetly hidden escalators – everything about Bergdorf's speaks of its attempt to be New York City's most gracious department store. Lucky that most of the folk who shop here – wrinkled old dowagers from Fifth Avenue on Central Park mainly – have purses stacked with chargecards. The rustle of money would utterly ruin the feel.

Bloomingdale's, 1000 3rd Ave (355 5900). New Yorkers are proud of

Bloomingdale's: somehow it's an affirmation of their status, their sense of style, and they not surprisingly flock here in droves. You may not be so impressed. Bloomingdale's isn't especially cheap, and it has more the atmosphere of a large, bustling bazaar, packed with concessions to perfumiers and designer clothes. You can, however, be sure that whatever you want, Bloomies — as the store is popularly known — is likely to stock it.

Bonwit Teller, 4 E 57th St (593 3333). An old-established store, now housed amid the vulgar nouveau decor of the hideous Trump Tower. Adornments for wealthy women.

Henri Bendel, 10 W 57th St (247 1100). Deliberately more gentle in its approach than the biggies, and with a name for exclusivity and top-line designers.

Lord & Taylor, 424 5th Ave (391 3344). The most establishment of the New York stores, with classic designer fashions, household goods and accessories — and no surprises.

Macy's, Broadway at 34th St, Herald Square (695 4400). The best way to describe Macy's is in figures: for with 2 buildings, 2 million square feet of floor space, 10 floors (4 for women's garments alone) and $5m gross turnover every day, it is truly what it claims to be — the biggest department store in the world, and these days a serious designer fashion rival to Saks and Bloomingdale's. Wander round even if you don't want to buy: you'll be sprayed with the latest fragrances from France or Beverly Hills, smeared with virulent lipsticks and fed on tasters in the cellar foodhall. If you see only one of the city's large department stores, it should really be this.

May's, Broadway at 14th St (677 4000). Solidly proletarian in feel and quite a change from the status-seeking emporia further uptown. Honest value.

Saks Fifth Avenue, 611 5th Ave (753 4000). The name is virtually synonomous with style and elegance. Basically, with the glittering array of celebrities that use the place regularly, Saks can't fail.

F.W. Woolworth. Some 20 branches dotted around Manhattan. Check the phone book for addresses.

PHARMACIES AND DRUGSTORES

You'll find a complete list of places selling medicines and toiletries under 'pharmacies' in the *Yellow Pages*; most are open roughly Monday-Saturday 9am-6pm. Also, the department stores sell toiletries and cosmetics; though cheaper are **Duane Reed**, who seem to have cornered the market on discount drugs, toiletries, cigarettes and basic stationery over much of Manhattan, especially midtown where branches lurk on every street. Below are listed some of the better or more specialised pharmacies, as well as a selection of those open longer hours in case of need.

24 Hour Pharmacy
Kaufman, 557 Lexington Ave (755 2266).

Lower Manhattan
Bigelow Pharmacy, 414 6th Ave (533 2700). Established in 1832, this is one of the oldest chemists in the city – and that's exactly how it looks, with the original Victorian shopfittings still in place. Open 7 days a week.
Kiehl Pharmacy, 109 3rd Ave (475 3400). Another ancient pharmacy but with goods more in keeping with its age: the stock includes herbs, roots, dried flowers and spices.
Tak Sun Tong, 11 Mott St (374 1183). Herbal Chinese remedies: snake skin, shark's teeth and the like.

Midtown Manhattan
Caswell-Massey Ltd, Lexington Ave at 48th St (755 2254). The oldest in America, selling a shaving cream created for George Washington and a cologne blended for his wife, as well as more mainstream items.
Edward's Drug Store, 225 E 57th St (753 2830). General pharmacy open 7 days a week.
Freeda Pharmacy, 225 E 41st St (685 4980). Kosher drugs. Closed weekends.
Martin's Drugstore, 451 3rd Ave (680 5230). Open until 10pm , 8pm weekends.
Westerly Pharmacy, 911 8th Ave (757 6289). Open 7 days a week.

Uptown Manhattan
Alexander Pharmacy, 1751 2nd Ave (410 0060). Open 7 days.
Arnowitz Pharmacy, 1551 York Ave (737 3305). Open 7 days.
Carvia Chemists, 1540 1st Ave (570 2100). Open 7 days.
Jaros Drug Inc, 25 Central Park West (247 8080). Open 7 days.
Tower Chemist Inc, 1257 2nd Ave (838 1490). Open 7 days.
Windsor Pharmacy, 1419 6th Ave (247 1538). Open 7 days.

FOOD AND DRINK

Food – buying it as much as consuming it – is a New York obsession. Nowhere do people take eating more seriously than Manhattan, and consequently there's no better place to shop for food. Where to buy the best bagels, who stocks the widest – and weirdest – range of cheeses: these are questions that occupy New Yorkers a disproportionate amount of time. The shops themselves are mouth-watering, and even the simplest street-corner deli should be enough to get your taste-buds jumping; more sophisticated places, gourmet or speciality shops for example, will be enough to make you swoon. The listings below, while comprehensive, are by no means exhaustive. Wander the streets and you'll no doubt uncover plenty more besides. If you're after **drink**, remember that you can only buy liquor – ie wines, spirits, or anything else stronger than beer – at a specialist liquor store.

General: Supermarkets, Delis and Gourmet Shops

There are a number of **supermarket** chains which pop up all over the city: *Big Apple*, *Sloan's* and *Grand Union* are ubiquitous; *D'Agostino* and *Gristedes* tend to keep to the smarter neighbourhoods. *The Food Emporium*, again all over Manhattan, opens at all of its locations (most centrally on 42nd St between 9th and 10th Ave) **all night**. In addition, many of the **department stores** listed above – principally *Macy's*, *Bloomingdale's* and *B. Altman* – have food halls.

Delis are basically grocery stores but with a more serious attitude to food. You should never have to walk more than a couple of blocks to find one, most are open late and some, like the *Smiler's* chain (not cheap), stay open all night; for specific locations see the *Yellow Pages*. Obviously they sell groceries, but most delis will also make you a sandwich and a coffee, plus they often offer hot ready meals and the chance to dip into a copiously provided salad bar.

Gourmet shops are glorified and more widely stocked delis. Each of the more gentrified neighbourhoods will have its local gourmet store; here's a rundown of the best and the best known:

Balducci's, 424 6th Ave (673 2600). Perennial rival of Zabar's (see below); slightly more expensive.
Caviarteria, 29 E 60th St (759 7410). Mainly caviar – over a dozen varieties – and a stock of smoked fish and pates.
Dean & Delucca, 121 Prince St (254 7774). Last of the big three neighbourhood food emporia. Very chic, very SoHo, very expensive.
DDL Foodshow, 444 Columbus Ave (787 6644). Owned by Dino de Laurentis and with a branch in Beverley Hills, this place is pure Hollywood, consciously taking the voyeuristic gluttony of New York's foodshops to its logical extreme. Everything about DDL, especially its prices, is totally over the top.
EAT, 867 Madison Ave (772 1586); 1064 Madison Ave (879 4017). Eli Zabar's bid to capture the custom of Upper East Siders. Pricey.

Fine & Schapiro, 138 W 72nd St (877 2874). Long established, with excellent, principally kosher, meals to go and renowned sandwiches.

Murray's Sturgeon Shop, 2429 Broadway (724 2650). Specialises in smoked fish.

Russ & Daughters, 179 E Houston St (475 4880). Technically, this store is known as an *appetizing*, a term which refers to the Lower East Side foodshops set up at the turn of the century to sate the homesick appetites of immigrant Jews, and selling smoked fish, caviar, pickled vegetables, cheese and bagels. This is one of the oldest: basically the original Manhattan gourmet shop.

Schaller & Weber, 1654 2nd Ave (879 3047) and other stores in the Outer Boroughs. Culinary heart of the Upper East Side's now sadly diminished German-Hungarian district of Yorkville, this shop is a riot of cold cuts, salami and smoked meats. Not for vegetarians.

Zabar's, 2245 Broadway (787 2000). The apotheosis of New York food-fever, Zabar's is still the city's most eminent foodstore. Choose from an astonishing variety of cheeses, cooked meats and salads, fresh baked bread and croissants, excellent bagels, and cooked dishes to go. Upstairs stocks implements to help you put it all together at home. Not to be missed.

Speciality Foodstores

Bakeries and patisseries

Damascus Bakery, 195 Atlantic Ave (855 1456). Syrian bakery, long established, with the city's best supply of different pita breads, as well as a dazzling array of pastries.

David's Cookies. A chain, with numerous branches all over the city (see the phone book for exact locations) selling excellent cookies.

The Erotic Baker, 117 Christopher St (989 8846); 73 W 83rd St (362 7557); 246 E 51st St (752 9790). The name says it all really, and if you're imagining all kinds of crusty phalluses and full frontal crotch arrangements, you'd be absolutely right. The last thing you come here for is the quality of the food.

Ferrara, 195 Grand St (226 6510). Little Italy cafe-patisserie with branches in Milan and Montreal.

Fung Wong, 30 Mott St (267 4037). Chinese pastries.

HBH Pastry Shop, 29-28 30th Ave, Astoria, Queens (718 274 1609). Greek pastry shop selling *baklava* plus numerous less well-known Balkan sweetmeats. Sit-down café too.

H&H Bagels, 2239 Broadway & 1551 2nd Ave (799 9680). Open 24 hours, 7 days a week, this is the home of New York's finest bagel.

Hungarian Pastry Shop, 1030 Amsterdam Ave (866 4230). Though far from Yorkville, and not actually run by Hungarians, this place is good either for an afternoon snack or to round off a meal at the Hungarian restaurant next door. Popular with Columbia students.

Kleine Konditorei, 234 E 86th St (737 7310). Yorkville German patisserie with a restaurant serving up all manner of honest Teutonic stodge.

Kossar's, 367 Grand St (473 4810). Jewish baker specialising in *bialys*.

Moishe's, 181 E Houston St (475 9624) & 115 2nd Ave (673 0708). New York's most authentic Jewish bakery.

Veniero's, 342 E 11th St (674 7264). Century-old Italian style patisserie.

Vesuvio, 160 Prince St (925 8248). SoHo's most famous Italian bakery.

Yonah Schimmel's, 137 E Houston (477 2858). More Jewish treats, this time in the shape of home-made *knishes*, with a variety of fillings (*kasha*, potato, cheese and others, but no meat), which you can either take away or consume on the premises. Even if you've tried the knishes sold by street vendors and didn't like them, it's worth giving this place a go. Yonah's knishes taste nothing like the mass-produced kind.

Zaro's, Grand Central Station. Croissants, bagels, and all good things.

Zito's, 259 Bleecker St (929 6139). Downtown's other Italian baker, renowned for its fine round *pane de casa*. Open every day.

Cheese and dairy

Alleva Latticini, 188 Grand St (226 7990). Italian cheesery.

Ben's Cheese Shop, 181 E Houston St (254 8290). Next door, and a nice complement to, Russ & Daughters on the Lower East Side. The greater part of the cheese sold here is still made on the premises.

Cheese of all Nations, 153 Chambers St (732 0752). Cheese from all over the world. Upstairs, a small restaurant serves substantial cheesey lunches for around $5, and there's a plentifully stocked wine cellar to help wash it all down.

Cheese Unlimited, 1259 2nd Ave (861 1306). No less a selection in this, the Upper East Side's favourite cheese emporium. And with the added attraction of potted histories of the different cheeses. More a cheese gallery than shop.

Fruit and veg

Most of the city's **greengrocers** are run by Koreans and usually have a salad bar as well as a healthy array of fruit and veg from leeks to papaya. Many stay open all night. If you got up early enough you could also try one of the city's **greenmarkets**, which open early morning a couple of days a week at about a dozen locations over Manhattan. These are run by the city authorities, roughly between June and November, and act as a forum for market gardeners and small farmers from Long Island or the Hudson Valley who come into New York to sell their produce direct. When they've sold everything they leave, so if you're interested in buying, make an early start.

Locations can vary, but very broadly you should find Greenmarkets at the following places on at least one day a week: World Trade Center, *Tuesday* and *Thursday*; Southbridge Towers between Beekman and Pearl, *Saturday*; City Hall, *Friday*; St Mark's-in-the-Bouwerie, *Tuesday*; Tompkins Square, *Saturday*; Independence Plaza at Greenwich and Harrison St, *Wednesday and Saturday*; Union Square, *Wednesday*, *Friday*, *Saturday*; 67th St between 1st and 2nd Ave, *Saturday*; 87th St between 1st and 2nd Ave, *Saturday*; 102nd St at Amsterdam Ave, *Friday*.

Health food, vegetarian and spice shops
For herbs and spices it's hard to beat **Aphrodisia**, 282 Bleecker St (989 6440). As far as health food shops go, the **General Nutrition Center** is the largest chain (check the phone book for addresses) – though often the one-off downtown health shops are rather better:
Brownies, 91 5th Ave (242 2199). NYC's first health food store and still one of the best in town.
Good Earth Foods, 1334 1st Ave (472 9055) & 182 Amsterdam Ave (496 1616). Not cheap but one of the best-equipped health food outlets in the city. Has a worthy juice and food cafe.
Gramercy Natural Food Center, 387 2nd Ave (725 1651). Best known for its fish, poultry and organic dairy products.
Prana, 148A 1st Ave (228 3632). Wholefood shop, again pricey.
Whole Foods in SoHo, 117 Prince St (673 5388). Health food supermarket, open 7 days with a very wide selection.

Ethnic Foods
Not surprisingly, you'll find the best ethnic foodstores in the areas where those communities live. Try the following:
British: *Myers of Keswick*, 634 Hudson St (691 4194), is the place to go if you're pining for Marmite, pork pies and the like.
Chinese: Best Chinese supermarket in Chinatown is *Kam-Man*, 200 Canal St (571 0330). A marginally cheaper alternative, though with a greatly reduced selection, is *Chinese American Trading*, 91 Mulberry St (267 5224).
Greek: Astoria in Queens – try *Kalamata Foods*, 38-01 Ditmars Boulevard (718 626 1250).
Indian: *Kalustyan's* 123 Lexington Ave (685 3416) is best of the small gang of fooderies that make up the tiny Little India district of Manhattan. Failing that, *Spice and Sweet* is just up the block at no. 135 (683 0900), *Foods of India* across the road at 120 Lexington Ave (683 4419).
Italian: Little Italy or the Italian district of Belmont in the Bronx.
Jewish: still going strong down on the Lower East Side – though Jewish cuisine tends to appear all over the city.

Middle Eastern: on Atlantic Avenue in Brooklyn; **Sahadi**, at no. 187, is best.
South American: Jackson Heights, Queens.
West Indian: Crown Heights, Brooklyn.

Ice cream
Two chains have largely carved up the city's appetite for ice cream between them: **Baskin-Robbins**, who have about half a dozen outlets spread between Wall St and Harlem, and the considerably better **Haagen-Dazs**, who trade from about 10 locations across Manhattan; again, the phone book has details.

While their ice cream is excellent, and comes in myriad different flavours, there are a few smaller operators which die-hard New York ice cream freaks swear by. Of these **Steve's**, 444 6th Ave (677 4221), incurs the most violent loyalties; and the **Chinatown Ice Cream Factory**, 65 Bayard St (577 9701), the most bemused reactions, since it's the only place that serves up mango, green tea and lychee flavours.

Sweets, nuts and chocolates
For **sweets, nuts and dried fruit** you could do worse than wander around the Lower East Side, where any number of unpretentious stores flog great tubs of all three: try *Mutual* at 127 Ludlow St, or *Economy Candy* at 13 Essex St, near Bernstein's restaurant.
If you are into designer chocolate try **Teuscher**, 256 E 61st St (751 842), whose truffles are renowned; or, in the Village, **Li-Lac**, 120 Christopher St (242 7374), who make delicious chocolates on the premises and don't overcharge for them. Uptown, the best place to go is **Elk**, 240 E 86th St (650 1177), a Yorkville candy store selling Yorkville-style candies – rich and marzipanned – or failing that **Treat Boutique**, 200 E 86th St (737 6619), for six different kinds of home-made fudge and a broad selection of dried fruit and nuts.

Tea and coffee
Zabar's (see above) is good for coffee if not tea; or there's **Gillies 1840**, 160 Bleecker St (260 2131), America's oldest coffee shop; **McNulty's**, 109 Christopher St (242 5351), which also carries a wide selection of teas; or **Porto Rico**, 201 Bleecker St (477 5421) – which has a coffee bar for tasting.

Liquor Stores

Prices for all kinds of liquor are controlled in New York State and vary little from one shop to another. There are, however, a number of places which either have a particularly good selection or where things tend to be a touch less expensive. It's those which are listed here. Bear in mind are there's a state law forbidding the sale of strong drink on Sundays so liquor stores are closed.

Astor Wines and Spirits, 12 Astor Place (674 7500). Manhattan's best selection and most competitive prices.
Beekman Liquor Store, 500 Lexington Ave (759 5857). Good, well-priced midtown alternative to Astor.
Columbus Circle Liquor Store, 1780 Broadway (247 0764). Ditto for uptown.
Garnett Wine & Liquor, 929 Lexington Ave (772 3211). Another good value liquor store.
Schapiro's, 126 Rivington St (475 7383). Kosher wines made on the premises. Free tours of the cellars, with wine tasting, Sunday 11am-4pm on the hour.
Sherry-Lehman, 679 Madison Ave (838 7500). New York's top wine merchant.

MARKETS

New York doesn't really go in for markets in a big way: those that there are, are mostly highly organised, wholesale-only affairs with retail stores attached, or simply neighbourhoods devoted to a specific items. As for street markets, they can't compare with Europe.

Fleamarkets, junk and bargains
Flea markets, certainly, have yet to catch on in the States, and New York has no one large market where you can pick up old clothes or antiques. There are, however, clutches of streets known for bargains in certain fields, and odd places – parking lots, playgrounds, or maybe just an extra-wide bit of sidewalk – where people set up regularly to sell their wares. These can vary from organised stalls flogging pricey homespun woollies to someone squatting down on a blanket peddling an ancient winter's coat and a few dog-eared paperbacks: either way, it's the nearest New York ever gets to a flea market. Here's a rundown of likely locations, but bearing in mind that it's illegal to sell anything in the street without a licence, the more impromptu affairs may have disappeared by the time you read this.

Orchard Street, main artery of the Jewish Lower East Side, is pedestrianised on a Sunday when its cheap clothes shops and stalls hold sway. Lively, vibrant and stacked full of bargains, it attracts people from all over the city. The rest of the **Lower East Side** is similarly well stocked with bargains all week: **Allen Street**, just below Houston, is good for shirts and, especially, ties; sections of **Grand Street** are given over to hosiery, underwear, fabrics and bedlinen; while **Bowery** below Houston is mainly lamps and lighting fixtures stores; above Houston, catering and kitchen items. North of here **Cooper Square** usually turns up a scattering of junk objects turned out from various Manhattan attics and wardrobes; on and around St Mark's Place and — more so — on **First Avenue** from around 12th Street down to Houston, are good neighbourhoods for secondhand clothing stores – as is, further uptown, **Columbus Avenue** in the 70s. The corner of **Spring and Wooster Street** in SoHo sells more upmarket clothes and jewellery most days of the week; as does the small **Prince and Greene Street** market and, in the Village, a larger affair on the corner of **Broadway and East 4th Street** – the latter one of the better of its kind in New York. Obscure electrical and household goods spill onto the sidewalk of **Canal Street** between Sixth Avenue and Lafayette Street; and **14th Street**, roughly from Union Square to Seventh Avenue, sports a wide array of discount houseware shops.

Look out, too, for neighbourhood **block fairs**. Organised by the local tenants' association, these are like urban village fêtes, cropping up most frequently in midsummer and giving residents the chance to turn out their unwanted junk. You'll see them advertised locally, on noticeboards and in newspapers, and depending on the neighbourhood it can be well worth going along. The kind of thing that counts as unwanted junk on Madison Avenue can be well worth having. More significantly, block fairs are a good way of getting a taste of real, neighbourhood New York, beyond the sirens and skyscrapers.

General and food markets

For details on the city-sponsored **greenmarkets**, which sell fruit and veg from various locations in the city, see p.215. More generally, you can buy most types of food at the **Essex St Covered Market**, as well as gaudy jewellery, cheap lace and wigs. Uptown, there's **La Marqueta**, on Park Avenue between 111th and 116th St in the heart of El Barrio, which sells sweets, spices, vegetables, fruits and all things Latin American. Or a few ranks of stalls along **Ninth Avenue** between 37th and 42nd St sell foods from just about every country that has any kind of ethnic representation in New York, however small. Mid-May, this blossoms into the **Ninth Avenue Festival**, in which the length and breadth of the avenue is taken up with foodstalls; see *Parades and Festivals*. If you're up early enough (5am – see *Tours*) the daily **Fulton fish market** is a lively affair; for New York's freshest fish at any time of day, use the market's **Retail Store** at 18 Fulton St (952 9658).

Finally, the **Flower District**, in west Manhattan on 6th Avenue between 26th and 30th St, isn't strictly a market but it is worth a look. If you can't find what you want here, be it houseplant, tree, dried, cut or artificial flower, then it's a fair bet you won't anywhere else in New York.

CLOTHES AND FASHION

Dressing right is as important in Manhattan as how much you earn – indeed, it's usually the best indication of it. Which is not to say that fashion here is ahead of its time. On the contrary, while New York may be streets in front of the rest of the country fashion-wise, compared to Europe it's pretty staid: clothes here are more about dressing to fit the neighbourhood you live in and the people you mix with than blazing any kind of trend-setting trails.

If you are prepared to search the city with sufficient dedication you can find just about anything, but it's **designer clothes** ('drop dead chic') and the snob values that go with them that predominate. **Second-hand clothes**, here referred to as 'vintage' or 'antique' clothing, have caught on of late but never seem to have developed the chic they picked up in Britain; plus, the 'antique' or 'vintage' label tends to have made them ridiculously overpriced. Basically, if you want *real* secondhand stuff go to a thrift shop, roughly akin to a charity shop in Britain.

For secondhand and/or trendy clothes the best place to look is downtown, and particularly the East Village and parts of SoHo; designer items, from the better known international designers, can be found on Fifth Avenue, in the larger and more reputed department stores and along Madison Avenue in the 60s and 70s. For a note on clothing sizes see p.40.

New and designer clothes

Fashion focus of America, and, they'd have you believe, the world, the **Garment Center** is one of the best places for picking up designer clothes at a discount. Occupying the blocks between Sixth and Seventh Avenues in the 30s, there's an office here for every women's garment retailer and manufacturer in the country, and though some are wary of selling to one-off, non-wholesale customers, you can pick up some enviable bargains if you have enough front, carry cash and are not prepared to take no for an answer. There's no point in giving an exhaustive list of establishments here: things change, and much depends on how pushy you are. But if you're into making a full-blooded assault on the Garment District, Gerry Frank's *Where to Find it, Buy it, Eat it in New York* gives a full rundown. Bear in mind, too, that the many of **department stores** listed on p.210 generally stock as good a selection of the (more mainstream) designer fashions as you're likely to find.

Agnes B, 116 Prince St (925 4649). Downtown trendy clothes store.

Banana Republic, branches at 87th St and Broadway; Bleecker St and 6th Ave; South Street Seaport (1 800 527 5200). Expensive clobber for the chic traveller: boots, bags, designer safari suits etc. The basement holds a copiously-stocked travel bookshop.

Barney's, 117 7th Ave (929 9000) 'The World's Largest Men's Store'.

Betsey Johnson, 130 Thompson St (420 0169). SoHo outlet of the New York designer. Functional clothes at almost affordable prices.

Black Market, 307 9th St (677 6266). All things black.

Brooks Brothers, 346 Madison Ave (682 8800). Something of an institution in New York, priding itself on its non-observance of fashion and still selling the same tweeds, gaberdines, quietly striped shirts and ties it did 50 years ago. It's a formula that seems to work.

Burberry's, 9 E 57th St (371 5010). If you're still not sure how to identify a yuppie, take a look at the clothes they sell here.

Canal Jean Co., 504 Broadway (226 1130). Enormous warehousey store sporting a prodigious array of jeans, jackets, t-shirts, hats and more, new and second-hand. Young, fun and reasonably cheap.

Capezio, 755 7th Ave (245 2140); 136 E 61st St (758 8833); 177 Macdougal St (477 5634). Basically a dancewear outfitters, the Village branch now sells a range of New York's best designers. Expensive.

Charavari. 'Sports' clothes from Europe. Branches for men at 2339 Broadway at 85th St (873 7242); for women at 2307 Broadway at 83rd St (873 1424); for all at 257 Columbus Ave (787 7272) and 18 W 57th St (333 4040).

Fiorucci, 125 E 59th St (751 5638). Large, well-stocked New York branch of the Italian clothes chain.

Flip, 46 W 8th St (254 9810). Another well-known world-wide clothing group, with a fine assortment of no-nonsense, classic US youth garb.

Gucci, 685 5th Ave (826 2600). Manhattan's snootiest clothes store.

Laura Ashley, 714 Madison Ave (371 0606). Like Burberry, Laura Ashley has scored a major hit with upwardly mobile Americans.

Parachute, 121 Wooster St (925 8630). Nice stuff, well cut and imaginative, but nothing for under $100. If that seems cheap, or you're after something just a touch more chic, **Comme des Garcons** across the road at 116 Wooster (219 0660) should be able to oblige.

Patricia Field, 10 E 8th St (254 1699). Touted as Manhattan's most inventive clothes store, Pat Field's was one of the first NYC vendors of 'punk chic', and has since blossomed into one of the few downtown emporia that yuppie uptowners will actually visit.

Trash 'n' Vaudeville, 4 St Mark's Place (982 3590). Famous to the extent that it advertises its wares in British magazines like *ID*. Great clothes, new and 'antique', in the true East Village spirit.

Unique Clothing Warehouse, 718 Broadway (674 1767). Canal Jean's rival in the affordable youth clothes market – and there's not much to choose between them. In the tee-shirt corner you can create your own design with a set of permanent, washable paints and a plain shirt.

Urban Outfitters, 20 University Place (475 0009). As well as kitchen and household items, a good range of stylish clothing.

Antique and second-hand clothes

Antique Boutique, 712 Broadway (460 8830). Self-proclaimed 'largest and best vintage clothing store in the world'.

Cheap Jack's, 167 1st Ave (473 9599). Large vintage clothing store.

Civilian Clothing, 164 9th Ave (243 9160). A few years back this was awarded the title of 'best shop in Chelsea' by the *Daily News*. 1950s styles.

Love Saves the Day, 119 2nd Ave (228 3802). Probably the only one of Manhattan's vintage clothes shops that could be described as anything like cheap.

Richard Utilla, 112 Christopher St (929 7059) and 244 E 60th St (737 6673). 1930s to 1950s clothing, and tons of bargains a bit *too* secondhand for the average New Yorker.

Thrift shops are scattered all over the city, but the best concentration is on the Upper East Side. A selection, by no means comprehensive, might include those at 1577 3rd Ave; 1430 3rd Ave; 1642 3rd Ave; 1496 3rd Ave and 330 E 59th St. All of these are run by deserving causes, from local youth clubs to the New York City Opera, but you won't be paying Oxfam prices.

Discount clothing

Bolton's. Designer clothes at vast reductions. Locations include: 43 E 8th St (475 6626); 53 W 23rd St (924 6860); 1180 Madison Ave (722 4419); 225 E 57th St (755 2527); 27 W 57th St (935 4431); 2251 Broadway (873 8545).

Gabay's, 225 1st Ave (254 3180). Over-ordered, flawed or returned goods from the upmarket midtown department stores. Well worth a rummage.

Loehmann's. New York's best-known store for designer clothes at knock-down prices. No frills, no refunds, no exchanges, but people still flock here with almost religious fervour. Next time you're deep in designer labels on Fifth Ave in the 50s, bear in mind that most of the garments probably came from Loehmann's. Branches at: 19 Duryea Place, Brooklyn (718 469 9800); 60-06 99th St, Rego Park, Queens (718 271

4000); 9 West Fordham Road, The Bronx (295 4100).
S&W, 287 7th Ave (924 6656). American designer sportswear at considerable discounts.

Finishing touches: shoes, hair, specs

There's really only one place to go for a **haircut** in New York City: the *Astor Place Haircutters* at 2 Astor Place (475 9854) – so trendy that people queue six deep on the pavement outside while a doorman calls names from a clipboard. It's by no means Vidal Sassoon, but they'll do any kind of style and, most importantly, don't cost the earth – around $8 for a straight cut, which by NYC standards is extremely cheap. Give your name to the doorman on arrival and however long the queue seems you should be seen in under half an hour. If you don't fancy Astor bear in mind that hairdos elsewhere cost upwards of $25.

As for **shoes**, for bargains the greatest concentration of shops is on West 8th Street between Fifth and Sixth Avenues in the Village. If it's designer labels you're after you'll have to head way uptown – on and around Fifth Ave in the 50s.

Glasses are considerably cheaper here than in Europe. If you break yours, or simply need a new pair to go with the new Armani outfit, take a look at the vast array at *Cohen's Optical,* 117 Orchard St (674 1986). Nicaragua's Daniel Ortega supposedly spent $3000 here on a pair of bullet-proof ones.

BOOKS AND MAGAZINES

Books are just one more thing of which there's a fantastic selection in New York. New or second-hand, US or foreign, there's little which isn't available somewhere. If there's a particular book you want to look at but not buy, don't forget the New York Public Library at 42nd Street and Fifth Avenue.

General Interest and New Books

B. Dalton. A nationwide chain, and overall the city's best-stocked and most reliable bookstore for general titles, with a main branch in Manhattan at 666 5th Ave (247 1740); others at 109 E 42nd St (490 7501); 396 6th Ave (674 8780); 170 Broadway (349 3560).
Barnes & Noble. New Yorkers feel cheated if they pay full price for anything: here they can pick up new hardbacks and paperbacks for a

fraction of their published price. Branches at 105 5th Ave (807 0099); their sale annexe opposite; Rockefeller Center; 56 W 8th St; 3rd Ave and 47th St; 57th St and 7th Ave; 3rd Ave and 59th St; Broadway at 73rd St; 45th St and Broadway; 86th St near Lexington; and at Penn Plaza. Many more in the Outer Boroughs.

Book Forum, 2955 Broadway (749 5535). Good on politics, poetry and academic subjects.

Books and Co., 939 Madison Ave (737 1450). Delightful bookshop with a 'literary' bias and information on readings, events, etc.

Coliseum Books, 771 Broadway (757 8381). Large, good on paperbacks and academic books.

Doubleday. The American arm of W.H. Smith, and a passable general store but no more. Main branches at 673 5th Ave (953 4805) and, larger, at 724 5th Ave (3997 0550). Otherwise in the Citicorp Center on E 53rd St (953 4714).

Endicott Booksellers, 450 Columbus Ave (787 6300). Believe it or not, this place was here before the arthouse gang colonised Columbus, and certainly it tries hard to give the impression it has been here since the city began, providing helpful service and a wonderful range of titles.

Gotham Book Mart, 41 W 47th St (719 4448). Just a short step away in case Scribner's hasn't got what you're after. Owner Frances Steloff, who's 95 years old, still lives upstairs having made her name as patron of authors like Henry Miller, James Joyce and Gertrude Stein in the 1920s: it was she who had the courage to publish *Ulysses* after it had been rejected by everybody else on grounds of obscenity, and she too who once smuggled 25 copies of Miller's *Tropic of Cancer* into the US from Paris via Mexico. Needless to say, the shop enjoys a legendary reputation. Good on drama and theatre publications, and excellent for the more obscure 'literary' stuff. A noticeboard downstairs advertises readings and literary functions, and a gallery puts on sporadic exhibitions.

Greenwich Books, 127 Greenwich Ave (242 3095). Bookshop of the Beat generation, with a range of titles by Kerouac, Ginsberg and the rest, as well as a host of less prolific names.

Papyrus, 2915 Broadway (222 3350). New and used titles, especially good on political and radical literature.

Scribner's, 597 5th Ave (758 9797). 'Purchasing a book here is like a great ceremonial event' wrote Paul Goldberger, and it's hard to disagree. Long established, central, and, as far as stock goes, hard to beat. One of the city's most beautiful bookshops.

Shakespeare & Co., 2259 Broadway (580 7800). New and used books, paper and hard cover, neatly placed to capture the Upper West Side yuppie trade.

Spring Street Books, 169 Spring St (219 3033). SoHo's most wide-ranging

yuppie trade.
Spring Street Books, 169 Spring St (219 3033). SoHo's most wide-ranging and pleasant bookshop, good on paperbacks, magazines and newspapers from home and abroad.

Secondhand Books

Abbey Bookshop Inc, 61 4th Ave (260 5740). Mainly hardback.
Argosy Bookstore, 116 E 59th St (753 4455). Unbeatable for rare books, also sells clearance books and titles of all kinds, though the shop's reputation means you may well find the mainstream works cheaper elsewhere.
Bryant Park. Secondhand bookstalls Monday-Friday whenever the temperature hits 40°f or more. Excellent bargains if you're prepared to rummage.
Burlington Bookshop, 1082 Madison Ave (288 7420). Secondhand and new books.
Mendoza Book Co., 15 Ann St, off City Hall Park (227 8777). Old books on every subject under the sun.
Pageant Book & Print Shop, 109 E 9th St (674 5296). Large selection of secondhand books and prints.
Ruby's Book Sale, 119 Chambers St (732 8676). Civic Center's other used bookstore, dealing especially in paperbacks and ancient dog-eared magazines. Excellent value.
Strand Bookstore, 828 Broadway (473 1452). With around 8 miles of books and a stock of over two million, this is the largest book operation in the city – and the sole survivor in an area once rife with secondhand book stores. As far as recent titles go, you can pick up review copies for half price; more ancient books go for anything from 50c up.

Special Interest Bookstores

Travel
The Complete Traveler, 199 Madison Ave (6779 4339). Manhattan's premier travel bookshop, excellently stocked, secondhand and new. See also the Bleecker St branch of **Banana Republic,** listed on p.000.
Rand McNally Bookstore, 10 E 53rd St (751 6300). Bookshop of the map and guide publishers: brilliant on maps, particularly of the US, average on other people's guides.
New York Bound Bookshop, 43 W 54th St (245 8503). Most city bookshops are copiously stacked with books about New York, but this one specialises in them. Living homage to New York City.

Art, photography, cinema and the theatre

Metropolitan Bookstore, 38 E 23rd St (254 8609). General bookshop with a wide selection of art books.

999 Bookshop, 999 Madison Ave (288 9439). High-cost glossy art books.

Wittenborn Art Books, 1018 Madison Ave (288 1558). Probably the best stocked art bookshop in the city, new and antiquarian.

A Photographer's Place, 133 Mercer St (431 9358). Lovingly run bookshop specialising in all aspects of photography.

Drama Bookshop, 723 7th Ave (944 0595). Theatre books, scripts and publications on all manner of drama-related subjects.

Crime

Foul Play, 10 8th Ave (675 5115). Books for mystery and detective buffs.

Murder Ink, 271 W 87th St (362 8905). This bookstore was the first to specialise in mystery and detective fiction in the city, and it's still the best, billed as stocking every murder, mystery or suspense title in print, and plenty out.

Mysterious Bookshop, 129 W 56th St (765 0900). Run by a weekly columnist from *Ellery Queen* magazine; especially good on used and out-of-print titles.

SF and comics

Forbidden Planet, 821 Broadway (473 1576). Science fiction, fantasy and horror fiction and comics.

Science Fiction Shop, 56 8th Ave (741 0270). New and used science fiction records and books.

Supersnipe Comic Book Art Euphorium, 222 E 85th St (879 9628). For collectors and dilettantes, *Superman*, *Marvel* comics, *2000 AD* etc.

Kids

Eeyore's Books for Children, 2252 Broadway (362 0634) and 1066 Madison Ave (988 3404). Not the only specialist children's bookshop in Manhattan but easily the best, with a broad selection of titles and story-telling sessions on Sunday mornings and Monday afternoons.

Language and foreign

Librairie de France/Libreria Hispanica/The Dictionary Store, 115 5th Ave (673 7400). Massive complex housing New York's French and Spanish bookshops, a dictionary store with over 8000 dictionaries of more than 100 languages, and a department of teach-yourself language books, records and tapes.

Rizzoli, 712 5th Ave (397 3700). Bookshop of the prestigious Italian

publisher, specialising in European publications and with a good selection of foreign newspapers and magazines. Also in SoHo at 454A W Broadway (674 1616).
Liberation Bookstore, Lenox Ave and 131st St (281 4615). Works from Africa and the Carribean.

Mind and body
East West Books, 78 5th Ave (243 5994). Bookshop with a mind, body and spirit slant.
Samuel Weiser Inc., 132 E 24th St (777 6363). Occult and oriental books: witchcraft, eastern religions, satanism and spiritualism.

Radical, feminist and gay
Four Continent Book Corporation, 149 5th Ave (533 0250). Despite the name, primarily devoted to books and periodicals from the Soviet Union.
Revolution Books, 13 E 16th St (691 3345). New York's major left-wing bookshop and contact point. Books, pamphlets, periodicals and info on current action and events.
St Mark's Bookshop, 13 St Mark's Place (260 7853). Probably the largest and best-known 'alternative' bookstore in the city, with a good array of titles on obscure subjects. Good postcards too, and one of the best places to get hold of radical and art NYC magazines. Open late.
Womanbooks, 210 W 92nd St (873 4121). Bookstore, record shop and community centre run by women and stocking a wide array of feminist and lesbian titles as well as more general stuff. See p.00.
A Different Light, 548 Hudson St (989 4850). Excellent gay/lesbian bookstore, as well as a centre for contacts and further information. See *Basics*.
Oscar Wilde Memorial Bookshop, 15 Christopher St (255 8097). Principally a gay men's bookstore.

Magazines and newspapers

Hotalings, Times Square at 142 W42nd St (840 1868) stocks newspapers from around the world, as does the **newsstand** on 42nd St outside the NY Public Library. For **radical publications from abroad**, try the newsstand a little further along 42nd towards 6th Avenue.
The Magazine Store, 30 Lincoln Plaza (397 3061). Best for British publications and foreign magazines generally.
The midtown branch of **Rizzoli**, 712 5th Ave, also has a fair selection of foreign papers and periodicals.

ART: GALLERIES, SUPPLIES, POSTERS AND PRINTS

Art, and especially contemporary art, is big in New York: a fact reflected in the number and variety of private galleries. Even if you have no intention of buying, many of these are well worth seeing. They broadly fall into **four areas**: along Madison Avenue in the 60s and 70s for antique works and the occasional (minor) Old Master; 57th Street between Sixth and Park Avenues for contemporary big names; SoHo for whatever is currently fashionable; and the East Village for the same, but less establishment and cheaper. A few of the more exclusive places are invitation only. Excellent conducted tours of the galleries are run by *Manhattan Art Tours* (see *Tours*). If your budget can't stand the prices, the shops of the larger museums are the best places to go for cards, prints and posters.

Commercial Galleries

Below are listed some of the more interesting options in the cheaper and generally more exciting locations, **SoHo and the East Village**. Opening times are roughly 11am-6pm Tuesday-Saturday, and the best time to gallery-hop, especially in SoHo, is a Saturday, or wherever you spy an opening. These are identifiable by the crowds and are generally free for those with enough bluff.

SoHo Galleries
A.I.R. Gallery, 63 Crosby St (966 0799). Women's co-op exhibiting work by members and others.
DIA Art Foundation, 393 West Broadway; 77 Wooster St; 2nd Floor 141 Wooster St. Non-profit organisation which commissions and exhibits work by ne w artists. Always worth a look.
The Drawing Center, 137 Greene St (982 5266). Specialises in oversized painting/sculpture/construction.
Dyansen Gallery, 122 Spring St (226 3384). Contemporary painting and sculpture, plus an Erté sculpture collection.
Edward Thorp, 419 West Broadway (431 6880). Mainstream figurative painting.
49th Parallel, 4th Floor, 420 West Broadway (925 8349). Canadian art; sponsored by the Canadian Government.
John Weber, 3rd floor, 142 Greene St (966 6115). Conceptual, Minimal and highly unusual works.
Jordan Volpe Gallery, 457 West Broadway (505 5240). Specialities include the American Arts and Crafts movement; the furniture of Gustav Stickel; Rookwood Pottery; and Louis Tiffany lamps.

Leo Castelli, 2nd Floor 420 West Broadway (431 5160). One of the original dealer/collectors, instrumental in aiding the careers of Rauschen berg and Warhol. Big names at big prices.
Louis Meisel, 141 Prince St (677 1340). The place to find out what Abstract Illusionism looks like. Meisel claims to have invented the term, along with Photorealism, also well in evidence here.
Mary Boone, 420 and 417 Broadway (966 2114). Leo Castelli's protégé, specialising in up-and-coming European and American artists.
O.K.Harris, 383 West Broadway (431 3100). A lively, unpredictable gallery run by Ivan Karp, champion of Super-realism. One of the first SoHo galleries.
Paula Cooper, 155 Wooster St (674 0766). Minimal and Abstract works, and much more.
SoHo Center for Visual Artists, 114 Prince St (226 1995). Non-profit exhibition gallery sponsored by the Aldrich Museum, Connecticut.
Susan Caldwell, 2nd floor, 383 West Broadway (966 6500). Non-figurative and abstract painting/sculpture in a typically airy SoHo loft.
Sonnabend, 3rd floor, 420 West Broadway (966 6160). Across the board painting, photography and video.
Sperone Westwater Fisher, 2nd floor, 142 Greene St (431 3685). Flashy European and American painting.
Vorpal, 465 West Broadway (777 3939). Chiefly the tiresome conundrums of Max Escher's prints.

East Village Galleries
A&P Gallery, 215 E 4th St (254 7060). Thursday-Sunday 1pm-6pm.
Area X Gallery, 200 E 10th St (477 1177).
Avenue B Gallery, 167 Ave B (473 4600). Painting and sculpture.
B-Side Gallery, 543 E 6th St (477 6792). Figurative painting.
Civilian Warfare, 155 Ave B (475 7498). Trail-blazer.
Eastman-Wahmendorf, 216 E 10th St (420 9019). Wednesday-Sunday 1pm-6pm. Summer group shows.
Executive Gallery, 632 E 11th St (598 9421). Designer furniture from 1930s to 1970s.
Gracie Mansion Gallery, 167 Ave A (477 7331). Displays 'post-contemporary art'.
Gracie Mansion Gallery Museum Store, 337 E 10th St (677 9037). Affordable works by US artists.
Greathouse, 335 E 10th St (460 0016). Sculpture and photography.
Limbo Gallery, 647 E 9th St (475 5621).
Piezo Electric, 437 E 6th St (505 6243).
PPOW, 216 E 10th St (477 4084). All media.
Semaphore East, 157 Ave B (475 2130). Represents many well- known East Village artists.

Sensory Evolution Gallery, 525 E 6th St (505 9144).

Prints, Posters and Cards

The Fourth Street Card Shop, 177 W 4th St (675 5464). Marvellous collection of postcards and greetings cards.
Postermat, 37 W 8th St (982 1946). Reproduction posters.
Poster Originals, 924 Madison Ave (861 0422). Original (and as such expensive) prints from the States and Europe.
Metropolitan Museum of Art, 5th Ave (570 3726). Considering the size and breadth of the museum, its shop is disappointing: a fair selection of mainstream art books, posters, cards and general paraphernalia.
Museum of Modern Art Shop, 11 W 53rd St (708 9700). The city's best collection of modern art books, cards and posters.
Untitled, 159 Prince St (982 2088). Art books, posters and the world's largest selection of postcards. Smaller branch, **Untitled II**, at 680 Broadway, near Washington Square (982 1145).

Art supplies

Arthur Brown Inc, 2 W 46th St (575 5555). America's largest art suppliers, with a pen department that claims to stock every pen in the known universe.
Eastern Artists, 352 Park Ave South (725 5555).
New York Central 62 3rd Ave (473 7705).
Pearl Paint Company, 308 Canal St (431 7932). Five floors of artist supplies including one for house painting. Another contender for title of the country's largest art shop.
Sam Flax. Branches at 15 Park Row (620 3040); 25 E 28th St (620 3040); 55 E 55th St (620 3060); 747 3rd Ave (620 3050); and 12 W 20th St (620 30380).
Tay's Art Supplies, 27 3rd Ave (475 7365). Artists materials for the East Village.

MISCELLANEOUS

The things listed below fit easily into none of the foregoing categories. They're either shops which might be interesting to visit simply for themselves; or they sell items which are cheaper in New York than at home; or they're places which deserve a mention just for being weird.

Antiques

Much the cheapest place to browse is **Brooklyn**, along Atlantic Avenue between Hoyt and Third streets. But you'd be pretty crazy to come to New York actually to buy antiques: prices are outrageous. The following are worth a look anyway.

American Hurrah, 316 East 70th St (535 1930). Aged Americana mainly: furniture, quilts, paintings and bric-a-brac. A wonderful selection but prohibitive prices.

Antique Supermarket, 84 Wooster St (226 2880). Antique Wurlitzer jukeboxes, one-armed bandits, roulette wheels and neon signs.

Bolero, 134 Spring St (219 8900). The city's most beautiful display of Art Deco furniture and accessories.

Depression Modern, 135 Sullivan St (982 5699). A lesson in how to make money out of things people previously discarded as junk.

Manhattan Art and Antiques Center, 1050 2nd Ave (355 4400). Around 70 shops and stalls, stocking a vast assortment.

Sideshow, 184 9th Ave (675 2212). More memorabilia than antiques, featuring items like ancient tins (tea, tobacco, etc.) and old kitchen implements.

Urban Archeology, 137 Spring St (431 6969). Large-scale accessories and furniture mainly American turn-of-the-century, so authentic that the shop rents them out for film sets.

Ethnic crafts

General: *Folklorica*, 89 5th Ave (255 2525), the *United Nations Gift Center*, in the basement of the UN Building on 1st Avenue (754 7700), and the *Brooklyn Museum shop* (see p.199) all sell a variety of crafts from different nations.

American: *Made in America*, 1234 Madison Ave (289 1113), serves a diet of Americana, antique and contemporary; the *Museum of American Folk Art*, 125 W 55th St (245 8296), stocks American crafts and applied arts, though little that can't be found cheaper elsewhere.

Chinese: numerous places in Chinatown; try *Orienthouse*, 242 Broadway (431 8060), or *Quons, Yuen, Shing and Co.* on Mott St.

Irish: The *Irish Pavilion*, 130 E 57th St (759 9041).

Japanese: *Japanese craft shop* at E 6th St and 2nd Avenue.

Latin American: *Tianguis Folk Art*, 284 Columbus Ave (799 7343); *Putamayo*, 857 Lexington Ave (734 3111).

Russian: *Samovar*, 209 E 14th St (677 2307).

Ukrainian: *Surma*, E 11th St (477 0729).

Music, records and electrical equipment

Record shops

Tower Records, the city's largest record shop, has branches in the Village at 692 Broadway (505 1500) and near the Lincoln Center at 1965 Broadway (7699 2500) for all new records, tapes, CDs and videos. Other good record chains include **Sam Goody** and **King Karol** – locations from the phone book. For more specialist tastes there are...

Bleecker Bob's, 118 W 3rd St (475 9677). Secondhand, punk and new wave, anything recorded over the last 10 years or so.

Dayton's, 824 Broadway (254 5084). Rare records, old reviewer's copies and deleted show and film soundtracks.

Discophile, 26 W 8th St (473 1902). Specialises in classical music.

99 Records, 99 Macdougal St (777 4610). Good selection of independent label bands, English imports and reggae.

J&R Music World, 23 Park Row (732 8600). Good discounts; J&R's jazz and classical section is a few doors along at no. 33.

Musical instruments

New York's heaviest concentration of musical instrument stores is located on one block of W 48th St between Sixth and Seventh Avenue: **Manny's**, at 156 (819 0576), and **Alex** at 164 (765 7738), are the best known in a row of many. A treat for guitar lovers, though slightly harder to get to, is **Mandolin Brothers** at 629a Forest Avenue on Staten Island (981 8585), which has one of the world's best collection of vintage guitars.

Electrical equipment and cameras

Electrical goods of almost any description are cheap in America. Best place for discount shopping is on Seventh Avenue a little north of Times Square in the 50s, or try one of the major chains. These include *Crazy Eddie*, whose main branch at 405 6th Ave (929 4242) also stocks a good supply of discount records, videos and computer software, and *47th St Camera* and *The Wiz*, both with branches around the Manhattan. Don't be tempted by US TVs or videos – they won't work on the British system – and make sure that anything you buy is dual voltage. For **cameras** midtown from 30th and 50th Streets between Park and 7th Avenues is the patch: shop around as prices vary wildly – a little sharp-nosed bargaining is the order of the day.

For both cameras and electrical items (along with many other goods) you'll be expected to pay **VAT and import duty** when returning to the UK. Duty on most electrical/optical equipment is less than 10% of the UK retail price, but phone Customs and Excise on 01 626 1515 for precise figures.

Toys, games and sports

Athlete's Foot. Jogging gear at affordable prices. Ten Manhattan branches, most centrally at 500 5th Ave at 42nd St (575 1680). See the Yellow Pages for the rest.

F.A.O. Schwarz, 745 5th Ave (644 9400). Showpiece of a nationwide chain sporting three floors of everything a child could want.

Gingerbread House, 9 Christopher St (741 9010). Smaller and more intimate.

Herman's. Sporting goods chain with branches at 135 W 42nd St (730 7400); 845 3rd Ave (688 4603); 110 Nassau St (233 07033); 39 W 34th St (279 8900).

Hudsons 97 3rd Ave at 12th St (473 7320). Good value camping equipment.

Modell's. Army surplus and outdoor equipment plus straight sporting items. 280 Broadway, 200 Broadway, 243 W 42nd St and 111 E 42nd St. Telephone for each of these – 962 6200.

Paragon, 867 Broadway (255 8036). Giant bargain-priced sports good store.

Play it Again Sam, 171 E 92nd St (876 5888). Second-hand toys.

Tents and Trails, 21 Park Place (227 1760). Three floors of camping and hiking equipment.

Victor Fliegelman, 535 8th Ave, 21st floor (868 9155). Century-old family business supplying most Manhattan games shops and selling direct to the public at wholesale prices.

Village Chess Shop, 230 Thompson St (475 9580). Every kind of chess set for every kind of pocket and usually packed with people playing.

Trivia and oddities

The Last Wound-Up, 290 Columbus Ave (787 3388). Wind-up toys of every shape and size. Other branches in the Herald Center, South Street Seaport and Broadway at 19th St.

Mythologies, 370 Columbus Ave (874 0774). Sells a gamut of weird – and useless – items.

99 Cent Shops. All over Manhattan, downtown to midtown, with everything marked at 99c.

Only Hearts, 281 Columbus Ave (724 5608). Everything heart-shaped.

Pop Eye Gallery, 130 Thompson St (777 3500). Anything over-sized.

Chapter seven
DRINKING AND EATING

A full rundown on **New York food and drink** – including ethnic (and American) dish directories – appears in the Basics chapter. What follows are essentially reviews, designed for use with the area listings in the Manhattan and Outer Boroughs chapters.

MANHATTAN

It's in **Manhattan** – and more specifically Downtown, Lower Manhattan – that you're likely to spend most time drinking and eating. You'll find this part of the chapter divided into three main sections: *Bars, Diners, delis burgers and budget eats* and *Restaurants*. You can **eat** in any of these – including most bars. As for **drinking**, you'll find some of the bars listed here (music and gay-orientated places, most obviously) cross over into the Nightlife chapter that follows (see pp.260-267), both in terms of feel and in often escalating prices.

24-hour eateries, coffee shops and delis are detailed at the end of the Manhattan restaurants section on p.256.

BARS

Loosely speaking, Manhattan's **bars** fall into one of two categories: roughish places that consider themselves **male-only** territory, and more upmarket, considerably **more mixed** hangouts, which New Yorkers tend to use to pick up a member of the opposite (or same) sex. The latter are sometimes known – and refered to here – as singles bars.

Selections below are personal favourites. The choice, obviously, is a lot wider – in Lower Manhattan it's hard to walk more than a block without finding a bar – and takes in the whole range of taste, budget and purpose. With the exception of the Financial District, the best hunting grounds are downtown and it's here that you'll find the best value **bar food**. **Hours of opening** are generally mid-morning through to 1 or 2am; some stay open later but by law all must close by 4am. Bar kitchens usually stop operating around midnight or a little before. Wherever you go you'll be expected to **tip**: the going rate is 50c for a single drink, a couple of dollars per person for an evening's boozing.

Groupings – as with the restaurant reviews that follow – are by the three main chapter **divisions** (Lower, Mid and Upper). For ease of reference, however, all specifically **gay** bars are gathered together in a single section on p.238.

Almost everywhere

Blarney Stone. Chain of Irish (and essentially male-only) bars with branches all over Manhattan. Nothing too wild, and often filled with downbeat drunks slumped into their bourbon, but the city's cheapest drinks and some excellent value food.
McCann's. Another Irish chain serving affordable booze and a broad selection of food. Their biggest, best (and for women most accessible) branch is the E 45th St basement, between 5th and Madison.

Lower

Barnabus Rex, 155 Duane St (963 9693). Friendly bar, popular with the local TriBeCa crowd and revolving around the pool-table and a good country jukebox. More reminiscent of Tucson, Arizona than downtown Manhattan.
Be-Bop Café, 28 W 8th St (982 0892). An active bar: motorised chic sprouting out of the floor and clinging to the walls, loud music and a youthful clientele. Good fun if your pocket can take the drink prices; food is less wildly priced at $4 upwards for burgers, pasta and suchlike.
Blarney Inn, 122 Water St (825 9765). Cheap Irish bar rare for this part of town.
Cedar Tavern, 82 University Place (929 9089). Beat meeting-point in the 1950s and now a cosy student bar with food (burgers for around $4 and other entrées $6 up) and reasonably priced drinks. Summertime you can sit and eat in their covered roof garden.
Chelsea Commons, corner of 24th St and 10th Ave (929 9424). Not only a personable bar but a great place to eat – outside meals for under $6. Very much a local hangout.
Chumley's, 86 Bedford St (675 4449). Not easy to find and with good reason, for this place used to be a speakeasy and is obviously so well known now it doesn't need to advertise its presence. Not especially cheap, but high on atmosphere and with a good choice of beers and food from $7. Best arrive before 9pm to be sure of one of the battered tables – at which, incidentally, James Joyce put the finishing touches to *Ulysses*.
Dan Lynch's, 221 2nd Ave near 14th St. (677 0911). Low on charm and

high on sleaze, this East Village watering-hole has blues and R&B bands from 10pm every night of the week. Drinks aren't as cheap as you might expect from the decor but there's no cover for the music. Good for honest, sweat-it-all-out nights on the town.

Downtown Beirut, 158 1st Ave at E 9th St (777 9011). Mega-sleaze East Village punk bar with music, live and recorded.

Fanelli's, 94 Prince St (226 9412). SoHo's oldest established bar, cosy and informal. Food — homecooked, unpretentious fare — weighs in at about $6.

Fifty Five, 55 Christopher St (929 9883). Almost next door to the more renowned Lion's Head, but cheaper, and with a great jazz jukebox and regular performances of live jazz.

Grassroots Tavern, 20 St Mark's Place (475 9443). Basement bar at the centre of the East Village hum: not expensive, with a good oldies jukebox and two dartboards.

Holiday Cocktail Lounge, 75 St Mark's Place (777 9637). Offbeat Village Bar that attracts a mixed bag of customers. Quite safe, but Bohemia with an edge nonetheless.

Jimmy Day's, 186 W 4th St (929 8942). Dimly lit bar-restaurant serving some of the most inexpensive food and drink in the city — solid American fare for under $5.

Jimmy Ray's, 729 8th Ave (246 8562). Despite a disreputable looking exterior, one of the better bars of the area. Popular with actors, good food.

Kenn's Broome Street Bar, 363 West Broadway (925 2086). These days more restaurant than bar, Kenn's is a blatant symbol of gentrified SoHo, transformed over the years from spit-and-sawdust pub to murkily lit trendspot. An amicable place though, and serving reasonably priced food.

Lion's Head, 59 Christopher St (929 0670). Small bar in the heart of the Village, traditionally patronised by a literary clientele that has plastered its book covers all over the walls. Nothing too alternative, but a lively place for a drink, especially at weekends. Food too — burgers, steaks, etc. — though you'll find the same thing cheaper elsewhere.

Manhattan Brewery Company, 40 Thompson St (219 9250). Started by an Englishman with an eye to a money-spinner, this cavernous bar-restaurant brews and sells its own English-style beer and doles out good simple food at fair prices. A hectic, crowded place, patronised by the after-hours office bunch.

McSorley's, 15 E 7th St (473 8800). NYC's longest-established watering-hole ('We were here before you were born' reads a window plaque) and a male-only bar until just over a decade ago. These days it retains a saloon look, though, with a youthful gang indulging themselves on the cheap strong ale. There's no trouble deciding what to drink — you can have beer, and you can have it dark or lite.

Peculier Pub, 182 W 4th St (691 8667). Popular local bar whose main claim to fame is the number of beers it sells – over 200 in all from any country you care to mention.

Puffy's; 81 Hudson St (766 9159). Small, funky TriBeCa bar in the midst of the resounding streets near the river. Lunchtime food, very cheap booze, and a great jukebox.

Revolution, 1 University Plaza, Washington Square (254 7555). More of a restaurant than a bar, but go to drink and people-watch rather than eat.

White Horse Tavern, 567 Hudson St at W 11th St (243 9260). Convivial and inexpensive Village bar where Dylan Thomas supped his last before being carted off to hospital with alcoholic poisoning, and where today you can buy burgers, chilli and the like for under $5. Bareboards Bohemia, little changed, apart from the excellent jukebox, since Dylan fell off his barstool.

Midtown

Costello's, 225 E 44th St (599 9614). Journalists' bar, once, legend has it, frequented by Ernest Hemingway. These days quiet except early evening, when (during the week) Costello lays on free hors d'oeuvres. Food in the restaurant out back starts at around $5.

Green Derby, 978 2nd Ave (688 1250). Just opposite Murphy's, this tries hard to be Irish through and through. Basically though it's a singles hangout, convivial if not especially cheap.

Kelly's Irish Bar, 131 E 45th St. By our reckoning this serves New York's cheapest ale.

Landmark Tavern, 626 11th Ave: see *Burgers, Delis and diners* p.243.

Molly Malone's, 287 3rd Ave (725 8375). Accessible (mixed) Irish bar with solid, if unexciting, food.

Molly Mog's, 65 W 55th St (581 5436). Midtown bar and restaurant, best visited early evening when the hot hors d'oeuvres are on offer. About as inexpensive as you could reasonably expect from this part of Manhattan.

Mulligan's Grill, 857 7th Ave (246 8840). There's nothing particularly stunning about this place, except that it offers a welcome and affordable escape from the costlier reaches of theatreland, both for drink and food.

Murphy's, 977 2nd Ave (751 5400). Irish bar which attracts the midtown singles set. Drinks are costly but food prices less so – a rarity and useful standby in this part of town.

P.J. Clark's, 915 3rd Ave (759 1650). One of the city's most famous watering-holes, this is a spit-and-sawdust alehouse with a not so cheap restaurant out the back. You may recognise it as the location of the film *The Lost Weekend,* or, if you've been to Macy's, from its duplicate in the basement there.

Upper

Between 60th and 85th Streets, Amsterdam and particularly Columbus Avenues offer a string of restaurants and bars mostly similar in character and price; hopping from one to the next is the best way to explore. Much of 2nd and 3rd Avenues between 50th and 70th Streets on the Upper East Side is singles bar territory.

Drake's Drum, 1692 2nd Ave (988 2826). Easy-going pub selling burgers, fish and chips, etc. for around $5.

Dublin House, 225 W 79th St (874 9528). Brash Irish bar with a young crowd, good jukebox and inexpensive drinks. Definitely recommended if you're up this way.

Emerald Inn, Columbus at 68th St. Amiable pub with food.

KCOU, 430 Amsterdam Ave (580 0556). Straightforward upmarket bar with jukebox. Not expensive, despite appearances, yet a little more rarified than **McAleer's** across the street.

Lucy's Retired Surfers Bar, 503 Columbus Ave at 84th St. Strictly a restaurant, but with a lively crowd at the small bar.

McGlades 154 Columbus Ave (595 9130). Cheerful bar with reasonably priced food and drink.

Metropolis, 444 Columbus Ave (769 4444). Laid-back, chi-chi hangout for beautiful people. The booze doesn't come cheap, and don't even think about eating in the restaurant.

Gay and Lesbian bars

NYC's **gay men's** bars cover the spectrum: from relaxed, mainstream cafes to some very heavy numbers indeed – the recommendations below are geared firmly towards the former. Most of the better established places are in **Greenwich Village,** with the **East Village** and **Murray Hill-Gramercy Park** areas (the east 20s and 30s) up-and-coming, the East Village having a more lesbian identity. Things tend to get raunchier further west as you reach the bars and cruisers of the West Side Highway and meat-packing (literally – this is not gay slang) districts, both of which are hard-line and, at times, dangerous. For further listings and details, see *The Native* newspaper.

Lesbian and **women-only** bars are, in comparison, thin on the ground – often operating only on one or two nights a week at one of the gay men's bars. *Womannews* – as well as *The Native* – can be a useful supplement for listings and events.

Mainly for men
GREENWICH VILLAGE
Badlands, 8 West St (741 9236). One of the most popular and most enjoyable Village bars, especially in summer.
Boots and Saddle, 76 Christopher St (929 9684). Middle-of-the road leather action. A little sleazy.
Marie's Crisis, 59 Grove St (243 9323). Enjoyable bar which features old-time singing sessions on Friday and Saturday nights. Often packed, always fun.
The Monster, 80 Grove St (924 3558). Large, campy bar with a drag cabaret, piano and video.
Ty's, 114 Christopher St (741 9641). Relaxed but convivial.

ELSEWHERE
The Bar, 68 2nd Ave at 4th St (674 9714). Neighbourhood bar for the East Village. Relaxed, pool table.
The Blue Fox, 131 8th Ave (929 7183). Easy-going. Good for both food and drink.
Bogart's, 320 E 59th St (688 8534). Piano bar with a wide mix of custom.
Boot Hill, 317 Amsterdam Ave (874 8068). Well-established Upper West Side gay bar.
Boy Bar, St Mark's Place between 2nd and 3rd. (674 7959). Crowded and costly trend-spot.
Chaps, 1558 3rd Ave (860 9829). Western-style bar/restaurant. Reliable and not too expensive.
Company, 365 3rd Ave (532 5222). Glittering decor and clientcle to match.
The Eagle's Nest, 142 11th Ave (929 9304). A fairly serious leather bar.
Last Call, 975 2nd Ave (753 0789). Nothing special – but then there's not a lot of choice uptown...
Ramrod, 394 West St (929 9718). Leather bar. More mainstream than the above.
Rawhide, 212 8th Ave. Don't let the name put you off: this is an accessible and enjoyable bar.
South Dakota, 405 3rd Ave (684 8376). One of the friendliest spots in the city, and with excellent food. Recommended.
Spike, 120 11th Ave (243 9688). Another very popular leather bar.
Town and Country, 656 9th Ave at 46th St (307 1503). Clientele reflects the neighbourhood – Hispanic/Irish. Unpretentious and downmarket.

The Tunnel Bar, 116 1st Ave at 7th St (777 9232). Cruisy leather bar.
Uncle Charlie's South, 550 3rd Ave (684 6400). Flashy and fun, in a part
of the east 20s and 30s that's second only to the Village as a desirable gay
area.
Wildwood, 308 Columbus Ave (874 8325). Dependable uptown hangout.
The Works, 462 Columbus Ave at 81st. (799 7365). Laid-back theme bar.
Cool and pleasant and about the only option for this part of town

Mainly for women
Avenue One, 1189 1st Ave (535 6423). Bar with a regular weekly
women-only slot. Phone for details.
The Cubbyhole, 438 Hudson St (243 9079). A lesbian yuppie bar;
clientele tend to be rich, well-dressed and cliquey.
Garbo's, 255 Broadway (431 1810). Separate bar and dance floor areas,
popular with black lesbians. Great fun if a little costly.
Girl Bar, 15 St Mark's Place between 2nd and 3rd (674 9684).
Wednesday nights only. A chi-chi lesbian bar filled with straight looking
women. Wear your best togs.
The Grove Club, 70 Grove St (242 1408). Formerly known as the
Duchess, this is a legendary lesbian dive – small, tacky and over-priced but
with a devoted following.
The Saint (See *Mainly for men*). Women's Sunday afternoon tea dances
most weeks – phone ahead to check and bring ID.
Shescape, 41 E 58th St (758 6336). A high-energy uptown bar –
lip-synching contests here are not to be missed – and with a dance floor
that's usually packed.

BURGERS, DELIS AND BUDGET EATS

Bars are often the cheapest places to eat in New York – but they're by no
means the only budget option. Any number of **diners**, **cafés** and **burger
joints** will serve you straight American food for $3-$7 and for a little
variety of taste there are the ubiquitous **delis**, most of which do hot
takeaway meals as well as snacks and bumper sandwiches.

Detailed here, too, are a couple of useful New York institutions: happy
hour hors d'oeuvres and weekend brunch. **Happy hour** is one of the city's
best scams: hors d'oeuvres, laid out around 5pm-7pm by numerous
Midtown bars, and all consumable for the cost of a drink. **Brunch** is a
more regular activity but one that can still set you in good store for the
day, with cocktails (sometimes unlimited champagne) thrown in with the
modest cost of a meal.

For further cheap eating options, see also the Chinese restaurants (and
above all the *dim sum* lunch places), detailed in the following *Restaurants*
section.

Burgers, delis and diners

Most of these listings are for **diners** or basic **café-restaurants**, which tend to serve standard American food (burgers, steak and seafood) for $5-$7, plus drinks and tip. The rest are **burger chains** and a selection of the more interesting **delis** that offer sit-down meals.

Lower Manhattan
Around the Clock, 8 Stuyvesant St (598 0402). Centrally situated East Village restaurant serving crêpes, omelettes, burgers and pasta at reasonable prices. Open 24 hours.
Astor Riviera, 452 Lafayette St (677 4461). Inexpensive East Village 24 hour restaurant serving a broad coffee shop menu.
BBQ, 21 University Place (674 4450). Barbecue chicken and burgers for $3-$7. Also, Early Bird specials: two meals for the price of one before 6.30pm. Another branch at 27 W 72nd St (873 2004).
Burger Boys of Brooklyn, 149 Bleecker St (677 7630). Burgers, kebabs, omelettes and baked potatoes for $4-6. One of Bleecker's best bargains.
Carmella's Village Garden, 49 Charles St (242 2155), a little way up from the *Little Mushroom* is cheaper still.
Empire Diner, 210 10th Ave (243 2736). With its gleaming chrome-ribbed Art Deco interior this is one of Manhattan's original diners, still open 24 hours and still serving up plates of simple American food. The food is very average, the plate is a beauty.
The Front Porch, 253 W 11th St (675 8083). Across-the-board menu – steaks, salad, seafood – that is reliable value at around $7 a plate. Also at 2272 Broadway (at W 82nd St; 877 5220) and 119 E 18th St, Irving Plaza (473 7940).
Jimmy Day's, 186 W 4th St (929 8942). Dimly lit bar-restaurant serving some of the most inexpensive food and drink in the city – solid American fare for under $5.
Jolanta, 119 1st Ave: *see Eastern European*, p.252
Kiev, 117 2nd Ave: *see Eastern European*, p.252
La Ocandia di Giotto, 25 Cleveland Place – continuation of Lafayette St between Spring and Kenmore. Small, popular meeting-place for in-the-know SoHo dwellers. Drop in for conversation rather than the meal of a lifetime.
Life Café, 343 E 10th St at Tompkins Square (477 8791). Trendy East Village haunt which hosts sporadic classical music recitals. Food is burgers, Tex-Mex or vegetarian – plates all around $5.
Little Mushroom Café, 183 W 10th (242 1058). Fish, pasta and omelettes at $5-12, and Thai food in the evening. One of the cheaper places along this stretch of the Village, catering to a mixed gay/straight crowd. Bring your own booze from the deli opposite.

Odessa, 117 Ave A at Tompkins Square: *see Eastern European*, p.252

103 2nd, 103 2nd Ave (533 0769). 24-hour, people-watching coffee shop – trendy and a little on the expensive side.

Phebe's, 361 Bowery at E 4th St (473 9008). Good value food – including weekend brunch and a 3-hour 'happy hour' during the week. Opening hours till 4am make it a regular off-off Broadway hangout.

Prince Street Bar, 125 Prince St (228 8130). SoHo bar and restaurant used by the local arthouse clique. Broad array of different foods, and for SoHo, not terribly expensive.

Rapid Algebra, 65 St Mark's Place (673 7159). A café-restaurant that tries hard for cool, with a consciously modern decor bathed in purple light. Good though somewhat pricey food: entrées around $8, stuffed pitta sandwiches $3.

Riviera Café, 225 W 4th St (242 8732). Central Village restaurant serving acceptable food at low prices. In the 1960s this was very much the place to be seen.

South Street Seaport Market, east end of Fulton St. The market's second-floor selection of fast food chains are among the least expensive places to eat in the area.

Spring Street Market, 111 Spring St (226 4410). Wonderful deli. The best sandwiches downtown.

Ukrainian Restaurant, 140 2nd Ave at St Mark's Place: *see Eastern European, p.250*

Midtown

J.J. Applebaum's Deli, 34th St at 7th Ave (563 6200). Huge and excellent deli with two sitdown floors. Good for refortifying after Macy's.

Bagel Palace 36 Union Square, Corner of 16th St and Park Ave South (673 0452). Bagels topped with just about anything, plus a hundred different omelettes.

Carnegie Deli, 854 7th Ave (757 2245). This place is known for the size of its sandwiches – by popular consensus the most generously stuffed in the city, and a full meal in themselves.

Hard Rock Café, 221 W 57th St (489 6565). A quality burger restaurant which for some reason (perhaps the fact that the loud music prevents all talk) continues to pull in celebrity New York, or at least the odd rock star. Full to bursting most nights, especially at weekends, but only the famous can book ahead – everyone else stands in line outside.

Horn and Hardart Automat, 220 E 42nd St at 3rd Ave (599 1665). New York's last remaining automat – once a great American institution with their convenience meals kept in little chrome drawers. The food here explains why the rest died out but the decor, restored a few years back, is full fifties splendour. Main courses $3-5.

Jackson Hole Wyoming, 521 3rd Ave (679 3264). Midtown burger chain with a reputation for obscenely large burgers. Good value for dyed-in-the-wool carnivores. Another branch at 1633 2nd Ave (737 8788).

Landmark Tavern, 626 11th Ave (757 8595). Long-established Irish bar-restaurant popular with the midtown yuppie crowd. Good food, huge portions.

Mulligan's Grill, 857 7th Ave: see *Bars* p.235.

O'Reilly's, 56 W 31st St (684 4244) Posh Irish pub/restaurant with standard American dishes at $6-12. Good value for this part of town.

Paul and Bob's Mashed Potato, 400 3rd Ave. Plates of 'regular' or 'diabetic' mash with various topping, ranging from bolognese to curried vegetable. Friendly and cheap – around $4.

RJ's, 220 Madison Ave (889 5553). A rare midtown budget diner. Burgers and barbecue items mainly, $6-$10.

Sarge's, 548 3rd Ave (679 0442). Large coffee shop serving standard American food. Open 24 hours a day.

Showtime Deli, 930 2nd Ave (759 3880). Well-placed deli with seating and a huge menu.

Southern Funk Cafe, 330 W 42nd at 9th Ave – in the McGraw-Hill building (564 6560). Cheap'n'cheerful cafeteria with steak, jambalaya and other Southern specialities at $5 and up. Recommended.

Stage Deli, 834 7th Ave (245 7850). Another reliable all-night standby.

Wine and Apples, 117 W 57th St (246 9009). A kind of hybrid Greek-Hungarian diner with meals from $5-$8 and inexpensive booze. A life-saver in this part of town.

Upper

Amsterdam's, 428 Amsterdam Ave (874 1377). Bar-restaurant serving burgers, ribs and the like for under $10. Downtown branch at 454 Broadway (925 6166).

Arriba Arriba, 440 Amsterdam Ave at 41st St (580 8206). Cheap take-out branch of the Tex-Mex chain. $3 and up.

Dallas Barbecue, 27 W 72 St (873 2004). Spare ribs, chicken and chilli for under $5. For this part of town, just off Central Park West, marvellous value. Main branch at 336 E 86th St (772 1616).

JG Melon, 340 Amsterdam Ave (874 8291). Burgers and straight American fare for $4-$10. Another branch at 1291 3rd Ave (744 0585)

O'Neal's Baloon, 48 W 63rd St (399 2352). A somewhat trendy gathering point, handy for Lincoln Center across the way. Burgers, chilli and the like for $5-10.

Papaya King, 179 E 86th St (369 0648). By popular – and *New York Times* – consent, the best hot dogs in the city.

Rathbones, 1702 2nd Ave (369 7361). Opposite *Elaine's* (see *Expense Account,* p.255) and an excellent alternative for ordinary humans. Take a window seat and watch the stars arrive, and eat for a fraction of the price. Burgers, steak, fish from $4 – and a wide choice of beers.

West End Café, 2911 Broadway (666 9160). Hep 1950s Beat joint now patronised mainly by Columbia students and addicts of live jazz. Rough and ready dishes, most for under $5, and a good choice of international beers. See p.264 for the music angle.

Happy hours and free food

Happy hour hors d'oeuvres are essentially a midtown phenomenon – and the hour(s) in question are generally 5pm-7pm, Monday-Friday only. Since the idea is to draw in well-heeled clientele, just out from their offices, you'll do well to dress in similar fashion. Places below, however, are all pretty accessible so long as you perform with confidence and don't obviously clear the tables. The cost of a regular drink or cocktail at any should work out around $3. For happy hour devotees, there are additional possibilities in addition to those below: just check out the more upmarket midtown hotels.

Biff's Place, downstairs at the *Halloran House Hotel*, 525 Lexington Ave (755 5000). One of the most popular happy hours, with excellent hors d'oeuvres disappearing rather quickly. Don't arrive much after 6pm.
Café 31, 449 3rd Ave (686 4250). Hot hors d'oeuvres until 8pm and all drinks $2.
The Cattleman, 5 E 45th St (661 1200). Swish, low-lit bar with a pianist crooning old Broadway standards. Good, plentiful food.
Jimmy Weston's, 131 E 54th St (838 8384). Wide selection of food, though pricier than usual drinks (reckon on $4). Men must wear jacket and tie.
Molly Mog's, 65 W 55th St (581 5436). Another good standby, though again, don't get here too late as the food moves fast.
Tandoor, 40 E 49th St (752 3334) Indian-style snacks and delicacies.
Trattoria, ground floor of the Pan-Am Building, E 45th St (661 3090). Pasta, pizzas and Italian dainties in relatively unintimidating surroundings. Recommended.

Brunch bargains

Brunch is a real money spinner in New York and the number of restaurants offering it is constantly expanding. Selections below all do a good **weekend** menu for an all-in price that includes either one or two free cocktails or unlimited champagne – but don't regard this as a definitive list. Further brunches are to be had along Third Avenue, especially between 20th and 40th Street, and there are always numerous ads in the *TV Shopper* (which you can pick up at supermarkets), or in most newssheets.

Biltmore Garage, 1 Mitchell Place/1st Ave at 49th St (832 8558). Around $7 with cocktail or unlimited champagne.
Café 31, 449 3rd Ave (686 4250). Around $8 with two free cocktails.
Marmalade Park, 222 E 39th St (687 7803). Around $7 with a cocktail or unlimited (though this time begrudgingly poured) champagne.
Mitchell's, 122 E 27th St (689 2058). $8 brunch with cocktail or unlimited champagne.

RESTAURANTS

New York's ethnic make-up is at its most obvious and accessible in the city's **restaurants**. Somewhere in Manhattan you can eat just about any world cuisine – and often a lot better than you'd find in its natural habitat. Don't, however, make the mistake of assuming ethnic food is necessarily inexpensive. Usually it's not: you pay Manhattan's highest prices for the better Italian, French and Japanese eateries; Greek and Spanish food, too, often works out expensive; and only Chinese is dependably low-budget. Despite which, **selections** below shouldn't break the bank – most serve entrées at around $10, some much lower, and at lunchtime you'll often find special deals or set menus. Listings are by country of origin, with closing sections on *Fish and seafood*, *Vegetarian and wholefood* and last and most certainly least, *Expense account*.

American, Mexican and Latin American

Grouped together for simplicity, these are all filling and good value options. Regional **American** restaurants can be fairly sedate but will always be generous; similarly with **Mexicans** and **Tex-Mex** restaurants – though they're often livelier hangouts serving cocktails.

Lower
Betty Brown's Broadway Diner, Broadway and West Houston (490 9633). Fluorescent-lit storehouse of American cuisine. Has just about everything you might desire. $5-$15.
Caramba 684 Broadway (420 9817), and, in order of current yuppie chic rating, at 8th Ave and 54th St, and 2567 Broadway. No, this place doesn't come cheap, but its three locations were at time of research among the most fashionable places to eat in town. That said, you can get one of their

combination Mexican platters for $7-8, after which, washed down by one of their notorious Margaritas, you're unlikely to be able to manage (or be capable of) much more.

Cottonwood Café, 415 Bleecker St (924 6271). Noisy Village restaurant with almost exclusively young custom, mainly NYU students. Texan cuisine (chicken, chops, okra and mash) – good, filling and not over-priced at $6 up. Live music every night (except Sunday) from 10.30pm.

Exterminator Chilli, Church St and Walker St (219 3070). The best place for chilli: masses of varieties, including vegetarian. $5-$8.

Tennessee Mountain, 143 Spring St (431 3993). Substantial southern-style food at moderate prices ($8 up). Try the ribs.

Midtown

America, 9 E 18th St (505 2110). Cavernous restaurant with menu to match; despite which, really rather dull.

Arriba Arriba, 762 9th Ave at 51st St (489 0810). The less frenetic alternative to *Caramba*.

El Rio Grande, 160 E 38th St (867 0922). A bit ritzy: you can eat Mexican, or if you prefer, Texan, by simply crossing the 'border' and walking through the kitchen. Not cheap but personable and fun – and the Margaritas are earth (and brain) shattering.

Pete's Tavern, Irving Place at 18th St (473 7676). Intimate restaurant with good American-Italian food for $7-10.

Southern Funk Cafe, 330 W 42nd at 9th Ave: see *Budget Eats* p.243.

Via Brasil, 34 W 46th St (997 1158). Excellent, though pricey, Brazilian food. Not much for under $10.

The Yellow Rose, 839 2nd Ave (687 6131). Good value midtown Mexican.

Upper

Los Panchos, 71 W 71st St (874 7336). Moderate to expensive Mexican restaurant serving a good value weekend brunch. Tables outdoors in summer.

Sylvia's Restaurant, 328 Lenox Ave at 125th St (534 9414). Legendary southern soulfood in Harlem. For more adventurous eating.

Teacher's, 2249 Broadway (787 3500). Pasta and fish for about $6. Nice atmosphere and a useful noticeboard.

Victor's Café, 240 Columbus Ave (595 8599). Cuban food at affordable prices on Columbus's central restaurant strip.

Yellow Rose, 450 Amsterdam Ave (595 8760). As the name suggests, meaty Texan food. Burgers, ribs and steaks from $5-10.

Chinese

Chinese cuisine provides one of the city's best bargains, particularly if you pick up on *Dim Sum* (see *Food and Drink*) and other lunchtime specials. As far as areas go, **Chinatown** not surprisingly has the highest restaurant concentration, but there's another good contingent in the **Upper West Side 90s**.

Lower
Hee Sung Feung, 46 Bowery (374 1319). Renowned Dim Sum restaurant where you pick what you want from a moving trolley. An adventure for the uninitiated.
Loong Lau, 206 Canal St (513 0255) and **Sun Say Gay**, 220 Canal St (964 7256). Two obvious Chinatown lunchtime choices, both serving up huge plates of meat and rice for around $3.
Mon Bo, 65 Mott St (964 6480). Bright cheery Cantonese serving incapacitating rice and noodle dishes for under $5, more exotic fare for just a little more.
New Lin Heong, 69 Bayard St (233 0485). Mon Bo's sister restaurant – and similarly substantial.
Non-Wah, 13 Doyers St (962 6047). Hong Kong-style Dim Sum.
Phoenix Garden, 46 Bowery Arcade (233 6017). Tucked away from the tourists but well known to New Yorkers for the quality and authenticity of its (Cantonese) food. Great value.
Silver Palace, 50 Bowery (964 1204). Another predominantly Dim Sum restaurant.
Szechuan Taste, 189 Bleecker St (260 2333). One of the city's best value Szechuan restaurants.

Upper
Empire Szechuan, 2581 Broadway (666 0555). Szechuan food from $6.
Hunan Balcony, 2596 Broadway (865 0400). Hunan-style food from $6.
Pez-Dorado, 2492 Broadway (595 8195). Ultra inexpensive Cuban-Chinese. Full meals around $5-$7, but you could eat for a lot less.

French, Spanish and Greek

French restaurants tend to trade on their names in New York – those that are good know it and make you pay accordingly. A handful, though, have slipped through with value for money intact and in Greenwich Village you'll find a number of enjoyable restaurants with a **Mediterranean** flavour. **Greek** food is generally best out in Astoria (see Queens, in the Outer Boroughs section, p.258).

Lower
Café Español, 172 Bleecker (475 9230). Hole-in-the-wall restaurant serving sumptuous Spanish fare for around $10 a plate. Try the *Mariscada* – a filling seafood dish that can easily feed two.
Chez Brigitte, 77 Greenwich Ave (929 6736). Tiny restaurant that fits only eleven, but with an all-day roast meat dinner for about $6 as well as other bargains from a simple menu.
Delphi, 109 West Broadway (227 6322). Accommodating Greek restaurant with good menu, great portions and unbeatable prices. The antipasti and fish are excellent value at $5-$10 or there's gyros and the like from $2.50. Best Manhattan choice for bargain Greek eating.
Granados, 125 Macdougal St (673 5576). Solid Spanish food with live music on selected nights.
National Café, 210 1st Ave (473 9345). Maybe the cheapest Spanish cooking in town. Closes at 10pm.

Midtown
Café Un, Deux, Trois, 123 W 44th St (354 4148). French brasserie-style restaurant. Consistently good food, and as a bonus, crayons for table-top doodling while you wait for your order. $10-$20.
La Bonne Soupe, 48 W 55th St (586 7650). Traditional French food at reasonable prices. Steaks, omelettes, snails and fondues from $6.
La Fondue, 43 W 55th St (581 0820). Fondues for under $10.
Magic Pan Crêperie, 149 E 57th St (371 3266). Relatively inexpensive and filling alternative to 57th Streets's chargecard traps. Wide selection of crêpes, sweet and savoury, for around $8.
West Bank Café, 407 W 42nd at Manhattan Plaza (695 6909). Some French, some American, all delicious and not as expensive as you'd think – upwards of $7.

Indian and Middle Eastern

Best place to look for **Indian** food is midtown Manhattan – and more specifically Lexington Avenue, between 28th and 30th Streets. Other than a handful of places serving pitta-related snacks, **Middle Eastern** food is thin on the ground in Manhattan though widely available along Atlantic Avenue in Brooklyn – for which see the Outer Boroughs section below.

Lower
Khyber Pass, 32 St Mark's Place (677 1490). Afghan food – which, if you're unfamiliar, is filling and has plenty to offer vegetarians (pulses, rice, aubergines are frequent ingredients). Excellent value for around $7. No liquor licence.
Gandhi, 345 E 6th St (614 9718). Excellent and inexpensive downtown Indian.

Indians. Another branch across town: **Mitali West,** 296 Bleecker St (989 1367).
Pitaria, 230 Thompson St (473 8847). Village eatery offering wholesome pitta sandwiches to take out or eat in.
Pita Cuisine, 65 Spring St (966 2529). Much the same though with a better range and the emphasis more on sitting down.
Purborag, 124 4th Ave (677 7073). Not very appealingly situated – just off Union Square – but a reasonable quality and inexpensive Indian.

Midtown
Annapurna, 108 Lexington Ave (679 1284). Northern Indian cuisine from around $8.
Curry in a Hurry, 130 E 29th at Lexington Ave (889 1159). Fast and inexpensive – eat for around $5.
Madras Palace, 104 Lexington Ave at 27th St (532 3314). More upmarket at around $10.
Nupur, 819 2nd Ave (697 4180). Solid value Indian, above average quality for Manhattan, serving meals for $6-$10.
Shaheen, 99 Lexington Ave (683 2139). Good value meals around $5.

Upper
At Our Place, 2527 Broadway at 94th St (864 1410). Middle Eastern cuisine at its best and least expensive, and including an extensive vegetarian menu. Most dishes around the $6 mark.
The Blue Nile, 103 W 77th at Columbus Ave (580 3232). Actually an Ethiopian, but the food has affinities with Indian – highly spiced and very filling. A good option to playing it safe: vegetarian dishes too. $6-$10.
Indian Kitchen, 2200 Broadway (362 8760). Small greasy-spoon Indian where you can get a substantial and palatable plate of curry and rice for about $3 and bring your own drink to wash it down.
Mughlai, Columbus Ave at 75th St (724 6363). Uptown, upmarket Indian with prices about the going rate for this strip – $10-$15.

Italian

Little Italy, the most obvious location, is now mainly tourist traps or very upmarket restaurants: pick with care. For the real thing it's again best to head for the Outer Boroughs – Belmont in the Bronx or Caroll Gardens in Brooklyn (see p.258) – or content yourself with pizza, either from *Ray's* (or a similar snack joint), or a regular sit-down restaurant.

Everywhere
Ray's Pizza. NYC's most ubiquitous pizza chain, with branches all over

midtown (and other districts) of Manhattan. Reckon on a dollar or so for a slice, $8 upwards for the whole thing.

Lower
Arturo's Pizza, 106 W Houston St (475 9828). Excellent entrées at around $10, coal-oven pizzas big enough to share for a little less. While-you-eat entertainment includes live music. Convivial, if not the cheapest feed in town.
Cucina Stagionale, 275 Bleecker at Jones St (924 2707). Enormously popular pasta place – possibly because most dishes are around $6. Expect to queue.
Daro Café, 95 St Mark's Place (777 8027) Pricey entrées but some tasty pasta dishes large enough to eat as main courses for around $4. Plus, after 9pm, live classical music. Homely and comfortable, and you can bring your own drink.
John's Pizzeria, 278 Bleecker St (242 9529). No slices, no takeaways, but one of the city's best (thin crust) pizzas. Be prepared to queue. Another uptown branch at 408 E 64th St.
La Luna, 112 Mulberry St (226 8657). Surrounded by the valet-parked limos and eating palaces of Little Italy, this must be one of the city's cheapest Italian restaurants: honest and unassuming in every way, from the vast peasant portions of pasta they serve to the gruff Brooklyn manner of the waiters and the fact that you have to walk through the kitchen to sit down. If you like Italian food and are budgeting, a must.
Puglia, 189 Hester St (226 8912). Little Italy's other affordable Italian, where they cut costs and sharpen the atmosphere by sitting everyone at the same long trestle tables. Consistently good food, consumed loudly and raucously.
Pizzeria Uno, 391 6th Ave (242 5230). Solid value pizzas and again frequent queues. It's a good idea to book.
Ray's Pizza, 465 6th Ave (243 2253). Long-time rival to John's, and not to be confused with the chain you see all over the city. Thick crusts.
Trattoria da Alfredo, 90 Bank St (929 4400). This tiny restaurant enjoys a reputation second to none – if you want to find out why, you'd best book a week or more ahead. No drinks licence so bring your own.

Midtown
Prego, 1365 6th Ave (307 5775). Pasta joint with a wide choice of generously spooned dishes for a flat $6 but an off-puttingly bathroom-like interior. Not for the hungover – and no liquor licence either. Fill up and move on.

Upper
Café Pacifico, 384 Columbus (724 9187). Mainly pasta – but you come

here for the luridly self-indulgent decor. Overpriced at $10-$15.
Perretti, 270 Columbus Ave at 72nd St (362 3939). Neighbourhood Italian with below average prices.

Japanese

Since sushi arrived in the city a few years back **Japanese** food has taken off in a big way. Apart from the *Dosanko* chain, most restaurants are in midtown.

Everywhere
Dosanko. Chain of fast food restaurants serving Japanese food at prices that everyone can afford. The food isn't the best in the city, and the surroundings are pure McDonald's, but there's no better way to try Japanese food if you're on a shoestring.

Lower
Dojo, 24 St Mark's Place (674 9821). Popular East Village hangout, with reasonably priced vegetarian and Japanese food in a brash, fun environment. One of the best value restaurants in the city, and certainly one of the cheapest Japanese menus you'll find.

Midtown
Genroku Sushi, 365 5th Ave (947 7940). Sushi and other Japanese-Chinese food. You pick what you fancy off a moving conveyor belt.
Hatsuhana, 17 E 48th St (355 3345). Every sushi lover's favourite sushi bar. Not cheap.

Upper
Cherry Restaurant, 335 Columbus Ave (874 3630). An inexpensive coffee shop which serves a wide selection of Japanese food.
Sakura, 2298 Broadway (769 1003). Another highly elegant Sushi bar.

Jewish, East European and German

The city's large Jewish Community, most of whom originated in Eastern Europe, means that **kosher** restaurants (either serving dairy or non-dairy menus – see *Basics*) are found all over town, with the highest concentration
on the Lower East Side. They cover all price ranges but average out at good, and very filling, value – as do the various and consistently delicious **Polish, Hungarian** and other **East European** restaurants.

Lower
Bernstein-on-Essex, 135 Essex St (473 3900). Small Jewish restaurant serving orthodox menu and (believe it or not) kosher-Chinese food.
Jolanta, 119 1st Ave (473 9936). Small Polish restaurant where you can eat sumptuously for well under $5. Try also the other Polish eateries further up 1st: **KK**, between 11th and 12th Streets, and **Christine's** – just across 12th Street on the same side.
Katz's Deli, 205 E Houston St (254 2246). More a fully-fledged restaurant than deli and a fine option for lunch. Their pastrami or corned beef sandwiches, doused with mustard and with a side pile of pickles, should keep you going for about a week.
Kiev, 117 2nd Ave (674 4040) Eastern European dishes and burgers. Great and affordable food at any time of the day or night.
Odessa, 117 Ave A at Tompkins Square (473 8916). The customary scramble for a seat may put you off, but the food here – a filling array of dishes from the Caucasus – and prices (under $5 for a meal) are impressive. Coffee shop decor, loud, plastic and brightly lit: not the sort of place to chew the fat.
Ratners, 138 Delancey St (677 5588). Massive dairy restaurant, crowded at all times of the day. High on atmosphere though on the pricey side – the same food costs much less at, say, the *Grand Dairy Restaurant* on Grand St.
Sammy's Roumanian Restaurant, 157 Chrystie St (673 0330). Surround ed by the boarded-up shopfronts and rotting garbage of Chrystie Street, Sammy's is some indication of just how far the Upper East Side will come to get a good meal – or at least how far they're swayed by a restaurant's reputation. For this is one of the most sought-after eating-places in New York, its walls plastered with the calling cards and photos of past customers. The food, if you've $25 so to burn for a full meal, is undeniably a treat.
Ukrainian Restaurant, 140 2nd Ave at St Mark's Place (533 6765). An East Village institution, recently spruced up but still serving staggering portions of Slav fare for around $5. Very popular though large enough to cope.
Veselka, 144 2nd Ave (228 9682). Ukrainian-Polish restaurant that offers a fine borscht for $3. Likeable snackery in an unlikeable area.
Yonah Schimmel's, 137 E Houston St (477 2858). Knishes, baked on the premises, and some wonderful bagels. Unpretentious and patronised by a mixture of wrinkled old men wisecracking in Yiddish and – on Sundays especially – young uptowners slumming it while they wade through the *New York Times*.

Upper

Café Geiger, 208 E 86th St (734 4428). Famed German eatery in Yorkville. Around $7-$14.

Green Tree Restaurant, 1034 Amsterdam Ave (864 9106). Hungarian restaurant, serving up a mixture of spicy Magyar and conventional American dishes primarily for the Columbia student trade. Go more for the prices than the food: from $5.

Ideal Restaurant, 238 E 86th St (650 1632). The genuine Germanic item: a small luncheonette serving wursts, sauerkraut and suchlike in huge portions for paltry prices.

Kleine Konditorei, 234 E 86th St (737 7310). German patisserie and restaurant serving all manner of Teutonic stodge.

Fish and seafood

Budget **fish restaurants** are a rarity in the city since the area around its fish market was dolled up into the South Street Seaport. Here's the best of what remains...

Lower

Hisae's Place, 35 Cooper Square (228 6886). A little pricey, though the varied range of dishes on offer should be enough to tempt most palates inside. Fish mainly, but with a good choice of Japanese, including a sushi menu. Entrées $7-$10.

Janice's Fish Place, 570 Hudson St at 11th (243 4212). Excellent Village restaurant with prices to match at $10-$15. Save for a treat.

Jeremy's Alehouse, 259 Front St (964 3537). Till recently a waterside sleaze bar in the shadow of the Brooklyn Bridge: now noticeably more trendy with the aggrandisement of the nearby Seaport, but still serving up well-priced pint mugs of beer and excellent fish (fresh from the adjacent Fulton St Market). Expect to spend $8-10, all told.

Umberto's Clam House, 129 Mulberry St (431 7545). As renowned for its role as famous Mafia execution spot (see p.77) as for the food. Cooking though is good – seafood, hot, medium or mild and always delicious.

Midtown

Oyster Bar, Grand Central Terminal (490 6650). Wonderfully atmospheric old place, down in the vaulted dungeons of Grand Central, where midtown office workers break for lunch. Fish, seafood, and of course oysters, though none of it exactly budget rated. If you're hard up, settle for the clam chowder with bread – delicious, quite ample and just a couple of dollars.

Upper
Hisae's West, 20 W 72nd St (787 5656). Uptown branch of Hisae's (see above).
Lucy's Retired Surfers Bar and Restaurant, 503 Columbus at 84th St. Seafood oddities for washed up West Siders. Good bar.

Vegetarian and wholefood

Surprisingly, exclusively vegetarian restaurants are a rarity: most places serve fish and poultry along with meatless dishes – which is useful for mixed dining. And unless you're in a real carnivores' haven, it's unusual to find a regular restaurant that doesn't have something meat-free

Everywhere
Amy's. Healthful fast food – veggie burgers, quiches and pitta sandwiches – at a number of locations over mid- and uptown Manhattan. Good value.

Lower
Arnold's Turtle, 209 Spring at 6th Ave (431 0414). 'Natural' foods – a term embracing wholewheat pizza and other substantial offerings. The upmarket clientele haven't yet bumped up the prices, which range between $5 and $10.
Bitable, 647 Broadway at Bleecker. (505 5663). Standard veggie grub from $5-$10. Not exclusively vegetarian, and less pretentious than other places in this area.
Boostan, 85 Macdougal St (533 9561). Intimate Village vegetarian: good food, and you can take your own booze. Inexpensive.
Eva's, 11 W 8th St (677 3496). The Meatless Combination Platter is the best bet from a mainly meaty menu.
Food, 127 Prince St (473 8790). Again not exclusively vegetarian, but serving a good array of wholesome dishes without meat. Around $7 a plate.
Macie's Mad Dog Café, W 4th St (242 5623). Probably the best vegetarian in the city: imaginative cooking with a wide choice of carefully considered entrées – for example, low-sodium vegetarian options. Small, popular and a must.
Spring Street Natural Restaurant, 62 Spring St at Lafayette (966 0290). Pricier and not wholly vegetarian but very good. $9 and up.

Midtown
The Great American Health Bar, 154 E 43rd St (682 5656). Comes well praised, but rather bland and uninviting.
Tibetan Kitchen, 444 3rd Ave (679 6286). Vegetarian food from the Himalayas – at just $3 up. Bring your own drink. Closed Sundays.

Expense account

Should you win the lottery or have rich relatives, New York has some superb restaurants to choose from, usually ladling out **French-tinged** American food or **nouvelle cuisine**. Go expecting to pay $50-$100 a head, don't wear the same gear you would for CBGB's, and phone first.

Elaine's, 1703 2nd Ave (534 8103). Remember the opening shots of Woody Allen's Manhattan ? That was Elaine's, and today her restaurant is still a favourite with NYC media types, celebs and literati. If you want to star-gaze there's no better place to come; if you're hungry or watching the pennies I'd go somewhere else.
Lutece, 249 E 50th Street (752 2225). The best restaurant in the country they say, or at least they used to. Now devotees claim Lutece's fame has led to the relative demise of its kitchen.
Maxwell's Plum, 1181 1st Ave (628 2100). Once a major uptown singles venue and now one of the most favoured NYC restaurants, people visit Maxwell's as much for the Art Nouveau interior as for the food. One way of cutting costs is to sit in the café section by the window where things are that much cheaper, though after you and your food have been ogled by a whole evening's worth of passers-by, you begin to understand why.
The Quilted Giraffe, 955 2nd Ave (753 5355). Nouvelle cuisine at astronomical prices: don't leave home without your credit card and, if you're a man, a tie.
The Rainbow Room, RCA Building, 65th Floor (757 9090) The city's best views, most over-priced food, and tackiest entertainment. Early evening, though, you might find it worth the price of a cocktail to take in the city skyline in comfort. Once again, Sunday best only.
Russian Tea Room, 150 W 57th Street (265 0947). There's hardly a better place to eat in the city if you want to spot a celebrity. Again, though, rates are through the roof – and if the outside menu doesn't put you off, the garish interior certainly will.
Sardi's, 234 W 44th St (221 8440). More celebrities competing for space in the gossip columns.
Windows on the World, World Trade Center, 107th floor (938 1111) The views, obviously, are the main attraction. But if you've money to burn the food's supposed to be quite edible too, and the wine cellar is said to be the best in New York.

24 HOUR EATS

This is simply a checklist for **late night** (and mainly budget-constrained) hunger. For review details, check respective listings in the *Diners, delis etc* and *Restaurants* sections.

If you're nowhere near any of the addresses below, don't despair. There are numerous additional all-night delis (for takeaway food) and in most neighbourhoods of the city you'll also find at least one 24 hour Korean greengrocer – good for most food supplies.

Lower
Around the Clock, 8 Stuyvesant St and 9th (598 0402).
Astor Riviera, 454 Lafayette (677 4461).
Empire Diner, 210 10th Ave (243 2736).
John Street Restaurant, 135 John St (248 8880).
Kiev, 117 2nd Ave (674 4040).
103 2nd, 103 2nd Ave (533 0769).
Triumph Restaurant, 148 Bleeker St (228 3070).
Waverley Restaurant, 385 6th Ave (675 3181).
West Side Diner, W 31st and 9th Ave (560 8407).

Midtown
Brasserie, 100 E 53rd St (751 4840).
Gemini Diner, 641 2nd Ave (532 2143).
Sarge's Deli 548 3rd Ave (679 0442).
Stage Deli 834 3rd Ave (245 7850).
Market Diner, 572 11th Ave (244 6033).

THE OUTER BOROUGHS

If you decide to explore the **Outer Boroughs,** food could be as good a motivation as any. The ethnic communities here have for the most part retained close character — and their **restaurants** are similarly authentic, generally run by and for the locals. It is in **Brooklyn** that you'll find New York's best Middle Eastern and (an unexpected delight) Russian food; in **Queens,** Greek; and in **Belmont** (the more inviting centre of the Bronx), Italian.

BROOKLYN

Brooklyn Heights/Atlantic Avenue
Clark Street Station, Clark St and Henry St (718 797 2096). Good neighbourhood hangout.
Hannah, Montague St. Best bet for sushi this side of the river.
Dar Lebnan, 151 Atlantic Ave (718 596 9215). Lebanese food.
Jimmy's Falafel, 11 Court St (718 875 9137). Falafel, shawerma (kebab) and other good things in pitta bread. Inexpensive.
Montague Street Saloon, 122 Montague St (718 522 6770). Burgers and salads for around $5.
Son of the Sheik, 165 Atlantic Ave (718 625 4023). Rough and ready Syrian restaurant with meals for around $7. Recommended.
Mr Souvlaki, 147 Montague St (718 858 8997). Greek basics for $4-$5.
Steve's, 515 Atlantic Ave at 3rd Ave (718 625 0984). Good value coffee shop.
Tripoli, 160 Atlantic Ave (718 596 0461). Lebanese restaurant serving fish, lamb and some vegetarian dishes for a low $7-$8.

Park Slope
Charlie's, 348 Flatbush Ave at 8th Ave (718 857 4585). Bar serving traditional American fare.
Dominski's, 7th Ave at 3rd St. Inexpensive bar-restaurant.
Le Park, 7th Ave and Carroll St. Standard American menu.

Coney Island/Brighton Beach
Kavka's, 405 Brighton Beach Ave. Good value Russian restaurant.
Nathan's Famous, Surf and Stillwell Ave (718 266 3161). New York's most famous hot dogs (and most other American snacks). Not the ultimate in gastronomy but legend nonetheless.

Odessa, 1113 Brighton Beach Ave (718 769 2869). Excellent and varied Russian menu at unbeatable prices.

Sadko, 205 Brighton Beach Ave (718 934 8204). Russian food and folk music. Authentic.

Mrs Stahl's, 1001 Brighton Beach Ave. Long-standing Brighton Beach knishery.

QUEENS

Astoria

Kalyva, 36-15 Ditmars Boulevard (718 932 9229). Home-style Greek food for between $6 and $10.

Roumeli, 33-04 Broadway, between 33rd and 34th Sts. (718 278 7533). Excellent Greek — a little upmarket but very popular locally.

Tavgetos, 30-13 30th Ave. Good basic Greek food. Finish your meal with a sweet across the road at the **HBH Pastry Shop.**

Jackson Heights

Inti-Raymi, 89-10 37th Ave (718 424 1938). Unpretentious restaurant serving substantial low-priced Peruvian food.

Las Americas, 89-28 37th Ave at 90th St (718 458 1638). Columbian cakes, pastries and full meals. Good for inexpensive lunches.

THE BRONX

Belmont

Ann and Tony's, 2407 Arthur Ave, corner of 187th St (364 8250). Good pizzas.

Dominick's, 2356 Westchester Ave (822 8810). All you could hope for in a Belmont Italian: great atmosphere, wonderful food and low(ish) prices.

Mario's, 2342 Arthur Ave (548 1188). This is pricey but very impressive cooking, enticing even die-hard Manhattanites out to the Bronx.

STATEN ISLAND

La Fosse aux Loups, 11 Schuyler St (718 442 9111). Once an inexpensive Mexican eatery, now a fairly expensive Belgian restaurant — though still serving good value Mexican food.

Chapter eight

NIGHTLIFE: ROCK, JAZZ AND CLUBBING

Considering New York's everyday energy and diversity, its **music scene** is on the whole disappointing. There is excellent **jazz**, traditional and contemporary and still concentrated in Greenwich Village, and around the venues you'll find a scattering of blues and Latin American music. But **rock music** is currently something of a write-off – at least as far as originality goes. Since the early days of punk, which found an American focus here at Max's Kansas City (since closed) and the legendary CBGBs, American bands have drifted; if you see anyone interesting, they're likely to be a British import.

With **nightclubs**, New York is much more in its element. The disco palaces are spectacular and taken very seriously, often furnished for a year or so of fame on multi-million dollar budgets, and with sound and light systems that are nowhere rivalled. Art too plays an important role: clubs are often venues for performance artists and many are decorated by such figures as Andy Warhol or graffitist Keith Haring, themselves frequent attenders. The general focus, though, as in London, is on costume and image, and the most interesting clubs are by definition the most exclusive, their doors guarded against the unhip by fashion-wary bouncers. The sections that follow give account of the best current venues. Keep in mind however that the music, and especially the club, scenes change continually; for the current **background**, check out the magazine *Details*, the city's eloquent and interesting manual of fashion and style. And for the best **listings**, check the *Village Voice* (still the chronicler of anything slightly 'alternative') and the more mainstream *New York Magazine*.

ROCK MUSIC

New York's rock music scene has changed quite radically over recent years. It's more diffused now, and rising rents and closing venues have (as in just about every other field) forced many musicians off Manhattan and into the Outer Boroughs and New Jersey: if there is a scene at all nowadays, it's one that has no clear centre. That said, there are still plenty of bands around, playing many different kinds of music: there's an exciting off-Manhattan hub in Hoboken, New Jersey, centring on Maxwell's (see below); rap and hip hop are still – and probably will remain – big, both in the streets and the recording studios, which put out a regular diet of cultish 12 inch singles; and, in Brooklyn and Queens at least, there's a huge Latin/South American and reggae contingent – though the venues themselves are way off the average tourist circuit. In Manhattan itself – principally in the East Village and Lower East Side – most of the energy is provided by a growing assortment of neighbourhood bars which host a variety of new wave and (often) blues talent. Basically the listings below should point you to the more major venues; if you want to get more involved or listen to something more obscure, the *Village Voice* or *East Village Eye* are once again hard to beat.

For music-orientated bars see also the preceding chapter, and for clubs that host sporadic live music nights, see the Nightclubs *section below.*

Venues
Abilene Café, 359 2nd Ave (473 8908). Blues acts nightly. $10 cover.
Beacon Theatre, 2124 Broadway (787 1477). Live bands most nights.
The Bitter End, 147 Bleecker St. (673 7030). Mainstream acts in an intimate cabaret club setting. Don't expect to see anyone famous. Entrance around $5.
The Bottom Line, 15 W 4th St (228 7880). Not New York's most adventurous venue but one of the better known – and the place where you're most likely to see established name bands. Cabaret set-up, with tables crowding out any suggestion of a dance floor. Claim to fame: Bruce Springsteen is said to have first turned heads here. Entrance around $10.
CBGB's, 315 Bowery (982 4052). Deliberately sleazeville and, despite its relative demise over recent years, still a great place to see (if not actually listen to) a band. Entrance $5-10.
Dan Lynch's, 221 2nd Ave (677 0911). Blues and R&B bands nightly from 10pm. Free entrance.
The Dive 257 W 29th St (695 4516). Small and convivial, but again, more local than international talent.
Lone Star Café, 5th Ave (242 1664). Billed as the 'official Texas embassy', but don't let this put you off: the Lone Star puts on a good variety of acts, big name bands included, and there's no better, no sweatier place to get down to some honest good-time R&B, country and homegrown American vibes. Though the clientele aren't going to win any prizes for trail-blazing fashion ideas, they always, but always, have a good time. Drinks are quite cheap and food (burgers, chicken and the like) starts at around $5. Two shows a night. Entrance $10.

Maxwell's, Washington and 11th St, Hoboken, NJ (201 656 9632). Neighbourhood club hosting up to a dozen bands a week: some big names but really one of the best places to check out the current tri-state scene.
Nightingale, 2nd Ave at 13th St (673 0487). Blues bar.
Pyramid, 101 Ave A (420 1590). The downbeat East Village scene at its funky, friendly best, with custom ranging from tuxedos and party frocks newly arrived from chic Upper East Side dinner parties to stud-ridden bikers fresh off gruesome machines parked in lines outside. Live bands every night (from around midnight) and a good disco; come before nine and entrance is free.
The Ritz, 119 E 11th St (254 2800). Cavernous Art Deco ballroom that's the Bottom Line's main rival for name acts – generally more contemporary. Admission $8-10.
SOB's ('Sounds of Brazil'), 204 Varick St (243 4390). Latin American disco/club/restaurant, with regular jazz and salsa-tinged bands. Lively and fun, popular with a predominantly yuppie crowd. Two performances a night.
Tin Pan Alley, 220 W 49th St (582 9367). Bar with regular live bands.

Other **venues** worth a visit include several on Bleecker Street – the **Back Fence**, **Kenny's Castaways**, the **Other End** – all of which lay on a loud diet of R&B and pub-style rock most nights of the week, at no extra cost than a slight mark-up on drinks. Remember, too, that at the other end of town the legendary Harlem **Apollo Theatre** is again sporadic host to an assortment of entertainers.

JAZZ AND FOLK

There are few cities anywhere that are home to quite so many **jazz** clubs, venues, festivals, jazz-related organisations or, indeed, musicians – and if you're serious about jazz then this itself could be a good reason for visiting (even moving to) Manhattan.

Most clubs are located downtown, most often in **Greenwich Village** or **SoHo**; midtown clubs tend on the whole to be slick dinner-dance joints for the hotel-business-people and as such are expensive and largely unexciting. To find out what's happening week-to-week, complement usual listings sources with the jazz **monthly**, *Downbeat*, and listen to some of the city's jazz-orientated **radio stations**. Two of the best of these are *WBGO* (88.5 FM) and *WKCR* (98.7 FM) – the latter Columbia University's radio station. Price policies vary from club to club, but at most there's a hefty **cover** (around $10) and always a **minimum** charge for food and drinks. An evening out at a major club will set you back at least $15 per person, $25-$30 if you want to eat. Piano bars – usually small and atmospheric – come cheaper with neither admission fee nor a minimum, though drinks are obviously still hiked up.

Jazz venues

Angry Squire, 216 7th Ave (242 9066). Nightly jazz and solid and affordable food and drink – including unlimited champagne brunch at weekends. Nights $5 cover. Highly recommended.

Arthur's Tavern, 57 Grove St (675 6879). Small, amiable piano bar with some inspired performers and no cover or minimum – though drinks are predictably pricey. A good place for a night out as long as you're not into getting wrecked.

The Blue Note, 131 W 3rd St (475 8592). Big names mainly and with high prices – but good music and atmosphere. For all shows there's a $5 drinks minimum per person plus $25 cover charge per table, $15 if you sit at the bar. Come later, though, around 2am, and the jam sessions (most nights of the week) are free entry.

Bradley's, 70 University Place (228 6440). Neighbourhood bar that features well-known bass/piano duos and acts as meeting point of local jazz musicians. Best to arrive late, as early evening the bar is too crowded with locals to actually hear anything. $5 minimum per person at the tables; no cover.

Burgundy Café, Amsterdam Ave (787 8300). Chic Upper West Side wine bar with bass-horn duos and good food. No cover charge but a two drink minimum per set. Good for Sunday brunch.

Eddie Condon's, 144 W 54th St (267 8277). Unexciting midtown jazz bar-restaurant with uninspired bands and over-priced food.

Erol Beaker Chapel, St. Peter's Church, beneath the Citicorp building at 3rd Ave and 53rd St. Jazz concerts Sunday and Wednesday at 5.30.

Fat Tuesday's, 190 3rd Ave (533 7902). Another of New York's principal jazz venues, small and atmospheric in a mirrored basement with low ceilings. Prices vary according to who's on, but generally hover around the $10 cover, $5 minimum mark.

Greene Street Café, 101 Greene St (925 2415). Huge converted warehouse, split between two levels and with dreadful acoustics. The music is generally excellent but views from the bar are so restricted you'll need either to pay for a balcony seat ($5 cover plus $5 minimum) or splash out on a dinner table.

Jazz Cultural Theater, 368 8th Ave (244 0977). Jazz workshops are run here throughout the week, with open jam sessions Tuesday, Thursday or Sunday, plus name attractions at around 10pm Friday and Saturday nights, 6pm Sundays. Admission $10 on the door, $7 in advance.

Knickerbocker's, 9th St and University Place (228 8490). Just down the street from Bradley's, this is an excellent restaurant with high calibre bass/piano duos. $7 minimum at the tables – nothing at the bar (which has a better view of the performers); no cover.

Michael's Pub, 211 E 55th St (758 2272). This slick midtown bar isn't so much known for the quality of its jazz as for the fact that Woody Allen plays clarinet here on occasional Monday nights.

Seventh Avenue South, 21 7th Ave (242 4694). Small, unwelcoming venue worthwhile only if you go for a particular bill.

Small's Paradise, 2294 7th Ave (234 6330). Legendary Harlem jazz club with no cover and no minimum – which means you'll be able to afford the laid-on taxi to whisk you back to midtown.

Sweet Basil, 88 7th Ave (242 1785). One of New York's major – and most crowded – jazz spots, particularly at weekends, when there's brunch and free jazz through the afternoon. For the best of the music, though, stick to weekday evenings. Shows usually start at 9pm. $10 cover and a $6 minimum at the tables, per set.

Universal Jazz Coalition, Jazz Center of NY, 380 Lafayette St (505 5660). Jazz musicians' collective which produces its own concerts and runs a series of workshops. Variable prices ($5-8) depending on who's on. No alcohol. Jazz ascetics only.

Village Corner, Bleecker St at La Guardia Place (473 9762). Pleasant smoky bar with free admission – though don't go for the music which is generally lost in the din of conversation.

Village Gate, Bleecker St at Thompson (475 5120). One of New York's oldest and largest surviving jazz clubs and still one of the best. Monday salsa nights are the current highlight, well worth the $10 entrance; other times, you can cut costs by taking a seat in the downstairs sidewalk cafe and listening to regular bass/piano duos for a $5 minimum.

Village Vanguard, 178 7th Ave (255 4037). An NYC jazz landmark that celebrated its fiftieth anniversary last year. Big names still come here and the original owner, Max Gordon, can usually be seen dozing in the bar. Admission $10; $5 drink minimum at weekends.

West End Café, 2911 Broadway (666 9160). Just across the road from Columbia University this was a beat haunt in the fifties but is now patronised mainly by students – lured not least by the good cheap food and wide range of beers. For jazz too it's recommended, particularly for catching older, more established names that don't work in the commercial clubs downtown. Cover charge $5, plus a $7.50 drink or food minimum per set.

Folk venues

Eagle Tavern, 355 W 14th St (475 7092). Local and imported Irish folk on Wednesday evenings. $5 cover.

Folk City, 130 W 3rd St (254 8449). Casual and smokey – like the archetypal 1960s Greenwich Village hangout. An enjoyable, intimate, place. Book ahead for major name gigs. Normal entrance around $5.

The Speakeasy, 107 Macdougal St (598 9670). The only folk club in NYC with music seven nights a week. Something of a hangout for musicians and folkies. $3-$7 minimum; bland health-food menu.

NIGHTCLUBS AND DISCOS

As stressed earlier, **clubs** in this city can (and must if they want to survive) change rapidly. The rundown below − and particularly the line-up in the 'exclusive' section − would be a fun one right now, but within weeks it's bound to have serious omissions. Keep an ear to the ground and an eye to *Details* magazine.

The **procedure** of clubbing in New York is less likely to change its ways. Assuming you're curious (and rich) enough, these are the main points:

● Hippest (and cheapest) time to club is during the week. Weekends are favoured by out-of-towners and so shunned by serious nightpeople.

● Style is vital: don't expect to get into any of the 'exclusive' places below just because you can afford it.

● Nothing gets going much before 1am. Don't go before this. And when you do eventually stagger out (most clubs close around 4am), keep your wits about you.

● Don't reckon to beat bar prices by smuggling in a hipflask − the mixers are the same price as everything else: around $5. A night at any NYC club needs money.

Note that most of the city's exclusively gay or lesbian *nightspots are detailed under Bars (see* p.238).

EXCLUSIVE

Nell's, 246 W 14th St (675 1567). The city's most genuinely exclusive club, small and with a notoriously stringent door policy administered by the formidable Nell. You may be lucky, but it's debateable how long Nell's will last anyway, for as the glitterati point out, the novelty of having to pay to get in (strictly no guest list here) is already wearing a bit thin. $5 weekdays, $10 weekends.

Palladium, 126 E 14th St (473 7171). Biggest and in many ways still among the best of the city's nightclubs − though Palladium's original exclusivity has taken a nose-dive of late. Housed in an enormous old theatre, the dance floor, sound system and light show are second to none, and the Mike Todd room and other nooks and crannies provide plenty of corners to explore. For an honest, sweaty night's dancing, hard to beat. $15 ($20 weekends).

Private Eye's, 40 W 21st St (206 7770). More videoclub than disco, since the dancefloor is little larger than a sixpence and most of the clientele seem to entranced by the flickering video screens coating the walls to care. Great sound system though, and it's nice just to hang out watching the Beautiful People arrive and gazing at those insidious screens. Though basically a mixed venue, there's often a large gay presence – and specifically gay nights on Wednesdays and Sunday. $15.

The Tunnel, 12th Ave at 27th St (244 6444). NYC nightbird Haoui Montaug reckons this is the best club in town, but then he would – he's on the door sorting out the freeloaders from the paying punters. By any accounts, though, the Tunnel is impressive, a converted railway tunnel that is part packed dance floor, part mocked-up stately home, with the old rail-lines stretching far into a blackness illuminated by shifting laser lights. If you only have the time – or money – for one New York club, it should really be this. $12-15 weekdays, $20 weekends.

LESS SO

Big Kahuna, Broadway at Houston St (460 9633), Surfing chic bar-club, with giant waves sprouting out of the walls, sand on the floors and a bar made up like a beach hut. Just the job if you yearn for the days of Good Vibrations; and even if you don't, at $5 entrance it's still a good place – especially if you can't afford a fully-fledged club but want to dance.

The Cat Club, 76 E 13th St (505 0090). Disco club which puts on live bands and hosts the occasional special or benefit. Enjoyable enough, though even the management wouldn't pretend their club was exactly trend-setting.

4D, 605 W 55th St (274 0628). Housed in the old *Visage* club building, this place isn't as exclusive – or exciting – as it makes out. Indeed, for $15 ($20 at weekends), there are much better places to go. Wierd sci-fi interior and very crowded.

Heartbreak, 179 Varick St (691 2388). This is in fact a restaurant but after 10pm each night it pushes back the tables, rolls up the carpet and becomes a dance floor, treating its punters to a mixture of old stuff, new stuff, and, on some nights, purely 1950s rock'n'roll. There's basic food and a lengthy bar (not overpriced by NYC club standards), but Heartbreak scores most points for its lack of bullshit: a place where you can just let your hair down and have a good time. $15 admission.

Kingfisher Room, 67 Bleeker St (529 1477). Up-and-coming nightspot whose decor resembles an ersatz boardroom of a midtown bank. Off the main club circuit, and consequently a little more approachable. Admission $5.

Limelight, 666 67th Ave (807 7850). Housed in a converted Gothic church, this caused a storm of outrage when it opened. However, though still streets ahead of its dull London clone, it's much less chic than it used to be, with a door-policy relaxed to the point of non-existent.

The Red Parrot, 617 W 57th St (247 1530). A massive old-style nightclub that likes to see itself as one of the city's more exclusive – an attitude reflected in the meat-headish demeanour of the thugs on the door. The novelty is swing music, with a fifteen-piece big band and a whole heap of tacky revivalism. $15 admission.

Reggae Lounge, 285 West Broadway (226 4598). Weeknights hard-core reggae music, weekends more mainstream and danceable. $10 admission.

Roseland, 239 W 52nd St (247 0200). More swing but this time the real thing: ballroom dancing from lunchtime to midnight, Thursday to Sunday, just as it's been for the last 65 years. $10 admission.

The Saint, 233 E 6th St (477 0866). Cavernous mega-disco with multi-level dancing and live music. Only open Saturdays, however, when it'll cost you $15 to get in.

Save the Robots, Avenue B near 2nd St. Late-night club that gets going about 4am – when all the others are just closing.

Shout, 124 W 43rd St (869 2088). Rock 'n' Roll revival meetings for Manhattan's chicest Brylcreams and bobtails. Increasingly popular with those who remember the records from the first time round. Opens early evening, admission $10.

1010, 515 W 185th St (645 5157). A gentrification of an old roller/hip hop disco. Less intimidating now, certainly, but boring. $15.

Chapter nine

THE PERFORMING ARTS AND FILM

Broadway, the Met, the New York Philharmonic – New York City can still supply glittering venues and glamorous events. But you may need to take out a mortgage to attend. **Theatre** is fabulous, but fabulously expensive, with Broadway prices crippling and even off-Broadway seats going for well over London's West End prices. If you know where to look, though, there are a variety of ways to get tickets cheaper, and on the fringe prices approach the realistic. We detail the better of these options below. **Dance, music** and **opera** are also superbly catered for: again the big mainstream events are extremely expensive: smaller ones are often more interesting as well as far cheaper. If you must see the New York Philharmonic you can always catch one of their free concerts in Central Park. **Cinema**, though New Yorkers treat it with almost as much reverence, is surprisingly unexciting: new American films get here long before they reach Europe of course, but there aren't too many places showing anything else.

What's on listings can be found in a number of places. Perhaps the best general source, clear and comprehensive, is *New York* magazine, though the *Village Voice* is better for things downtown and anything vaguely 'alternative'. The Sunday *New York Times Weekly Guide* is also good, especially for mainstream events: the paper's *Weekend* section, on Fridays, lists 'ticket availability' – ie those major shows not sold out for the weekend. Specific Broadway listings can be found in the free *Official Broadway Theater Guide*, available from theater and hotel lobbies or either of the New York Convention and Visitor's Bureaux.

THEATRE

New York is one of the great **theatre** centres of the world. You can find just about any kind of production here, from lavish, over-the-top musicals to experimental productions in converted garages: the variety is endless. But it's not cheap. Indeed the big budget Broadway blockbusters seem to be pricing themselves out of existence – with prices steadily spiralling and audience levels dropping, theatreland is in trouble. What follows is a guide to where to find the various types of production – and how to avoid paying the earth for them.

Venues in the city are referred to as **Broadway, Off Broadway,** or **Off-Off Broadway,** groupings which represent a descending order of ticket price, production polish, elegance and comfort (but don't necessarily have much to do with the address). They also represent an ascending order of innovation, experimentation, and theatre for the sake of art rather than cash. **Broadway** offerings consist primarily of large-scale musicals, comedies and dramas with big-name actors; the occasional classic, the occasional one-person show. **Off Broadway** theatres also tend to provide polished production qualities, but combine them with a greater willingness to experiment. It's in Off Broadway you'll find social and political drama, satire, ethnic plays and repertory; in short anything that Broadway wouldn't consider a sure-fire money-spinner. Lower operating costs also mean Off Broadway often serves as the try-out locale for what end up as big Broadway productions. **Off-Off Broadway** is the fringe: drama on a shoestring, sometimes on subjects that other theatres would find too sensitive or too unprofitable to mount. Unlike Off Broadway, Off-Off doesn't have to use professional actors.

For the record, it's the size of the theatre which technically determines the category it falls into: under 100 seats and a theatre is Off-Off; 100 to 500 and it's Off. Most Broadway theatres are located in the blocks just east or west of Broadway between 40th and 52nd Streets: Off and Off-Off Broadway theatres are sprinkled throughout Manhattan, with a concentration in the East and West Villages, Chelsea, and several in the 40s and 50s west of the Broadway theatre district.

TICKETS AND VENUES

Nowhere are regular **tickets** cheap on Broadway – a couple of orchestra seats for something like *Cats* will set you back a cool $100. Off-Broadway prices have risen recently, too, to as much as $35 in some cases, but most seats remain considerably cheaper than anything you'll find along the Great White Way. If you know where and how to look even these prices can be cut considerably. Basically there are two straightforward and well practised methods of **cutting costs**, the first of which requires a little patience...

• Queue up on the day of performance at the **TKTS booth** at Times Square, where at least one pair of tickets for every performance of every Broadway and Off Broadway show is available at half price (plus a $1.25 ticket service charge – altogether between $15 – $20). There's a single queue for all shows, and the most popular sell out soonest: get here early if you're after hit of the month. TKTS hours are 3pm-8pm Monday-Saturday; 12am-2pm for Wednesday and Saturday matinees, but the booth opens as early as 10.30am if a long queue forms; on Sundays, matinee and evening performance tickets are on sale from noon until they run out. There's another TKTS booth in the lobby of 2 World Trade Center (useful to know if it's raining, even more useful in that certain matinee tickets are sold here on the day *before* the performance) and one at Court and Montague Streets near Borough Hall in Brooklyn, reputedly with the shortest queues of all. Both these booths close at 5.30pm daily; all three take cash or traveller's cheques only; best days for availability and short queues are Tuesday, Wednesday and Thursday.

● Look for **twofer discount coupons** in either of the New York Convention and Visitor's bureaux and many shops, banks, restaurants and hotel lobbies. These entitle two people to a hefty discount (though the days when they really offered two-for-the-price-of-one are long gone) and unlike TKTS it's possible to book ahead, though don't expect to find coupons for the latest shows. If you can't find a coupon for the production you want, *Hit Show Club* (300 West 43rd St, NY 10036) will send a pair of discount slips for every Broadway show going on receipt of a stamped addressed envelope; useful if you're around for any length of time.

● If you're prepared to pay **full price** you can, of course, go directly to the theatre, but rather easier *Tickets Central*, 406 West 42nd St, sell tickets for 50 Off and Off-Off Broadway theatres from 1pm-8pm daily: expect to pay upwards of $15 Off Broadway, $6 Off-Off. Finally, if queuing up for tickets is below your dignity and your credit rating, *Ticketron* (977 9020) and *Chargit* (944 9300) will book seats for those with credit cards; pick up the tickets at the theatre on production of your card. A charge of $2.50 is added to the top-whack ticket price you'll pay.

Off-Off Broadway and Repertory

AMAS Repertory, 1 E 104th St (369 8000). Multi-racial showcase.

American Jewish Theater of the 92nd St Y, 1395 Lexington Ave (427 4410). Classical and contemporary plays in English on Jewish themes.

American Place Theater, 111 W 46th St (247 0393). New works by living Americans.

Circle In The Square Uptown, 1633 Broadway (581 0720). Classics and 'potential classics'.

Circle Repertory Company, 99 7th Ave South (924 7100). Contemporary: has premiered many award winners.

Jean Cocteau Repertory, *Bouwerie Lane Theatre*, 330 Bowery (677 0060). Aims at 'dramatic poem' production style. Genet, Sophocles, Shaw, Strindberg, Sartre, Wilde, Williams, etc, along with unknowns.

Hudson Guild Theater, 441 W 26th St (760 9810). Introduces new American and European playwrights.

Negro Ensemble Company, 424 W 55th St (246 8545). Plays about the black experience.

New Federal Theater of the Henry Street Settlement, 466 Grand St (598 0400). Outlet for minority playwrights, performers and production staff. Has premiered some award-winners.

New York Deaf Theatre, 620 E 13th St (741 5126/620 7448). Performances signed and spoken.

New York Shakespeare Festival, *The Public Theater*, 425 Lafayette St (598 7150). Year-round, six performing areas stage new American plays and accommodate visiting artists and companies. In summer the Shakespeare Festival proper takes off at the open air *Delacorte Theatre* in Central Park (861 7277) performances are free but come early for the best places.

Ontological-Hysteric Theater Company, no permanent premises (243 6153). Avant-garde/destructionist productions.

Palsson's Forbidden Broadway, 155 W 72nd St (595 7400). Cabaret – satire and spoofs of Broadway hits.

Playwrights Horizons, 416 W 42nd St (279 4200). New works and new writers. Originated the controversial 'Sister Mary Ignatius Explains It All to You', and 'Sunday In The Park With George'.

Royal Court Repertory, 301 W 55th St (997 9582). Many mystery plays; other drama and comedy.

Theater For the New City, 162 2nd Ave (254 1109). Known for following the development of new playwrights and presenting integration of dance, music, and poetry with drama.

Theater Of The Open Eye, 270 W 89 St (534 6363). New and adapted works with a mythic or poetic quality.

West Side Repertory, 252 W 81st St (666 3521/874 9400). Small basement theatre that puts on four productions a year: Shaw, Wilde, Pirandello. Professional producer-director; performers and staff are pros and talented amateurs.

The Wooster Group (Performing Garage), 33 Wooster St (966 3651). Experimental/Multi-media/Abstract.

WPA Theater, 138 5th Ave (691 2274). Neglected American classics and American Realist plays, acted in a style described as 'derived from Stanislavski'.

Off Broadway

Worth checking out for interesting production are:

American Theater of Actors, 314 W 54th St (581 3044).

Apple Corps Theater Company, 336 W 20th St (929 2955).

Cherry Lane Theater, 38 Commerce St (989 2020).

Chicago City Limits, 351 E 74th St (772 8707).

Clurman Theater, 412 W 42nd St (594 2370).

Cubicolo Theater, 414 W 51st St (265 2138).

Douglas Fairbanks Theater, 432 W 42nd St (239 4321).
Jan Hus Theater Company, 351 E 74th St (288 6743
La Mama Theater Club, 74A E 4th St (475 7710).
Lucille Lortel Theater, 121 Christopher St (924 8782).
Manhattan Theater Club, 321 E 73rd St (288 2500).
Meat & Potatoes Theater Co., 306 W 38th St (564 3293).
Meridian Gay Theater, 137 W 22nd St (924 0077).
Off Center Theater, 436 W 18th St (929 8299).
Orpheum Theater, 126 Second Ave (239 6200).
Park Royale Theater, 23 W 73rd St (279 4200).
Promenade Theater, 2161 Broadway (580 1313).
Provincetown Playhouse, 133 Macdougal St (777 2571).
Ridiculous Theater Company, 1 Sheridan Square (691 2271).
Roundabout Theater Company, 100 E 17th St (420 1360).
Samuel Beckett Theater, 410 W 42nd St (594 2826).
Second Stage Theater, 2162 Broadway (787 8302).
78th Street Theater Lab, 238 W 78th St (595 5240).
SoHo Repertory Company, 401 E 29th St (679 8828).
St Clements Theater, 423 W 46th St (246 7277).
Theater at St. Peter's Church, Lexington and 54th St (223 6440).
13th St Theater, 50 W 13th St (675 6677).
Westbeth Theater Center, 155 Bank St (691 2272).

DANCE

New York has five major ballet companies, dozens of modern troupes and untold thousands of soloists. You would have to be very particular indeed in your tastes not to find something of interest. Events are listed in broadly the same places as for music and theatre – if this is your particular interest, though, you might want also to pick up *Dance Magazine*. Half-price tickets, on a day-to-day basis only, are available from **The Music & Dance Booth** in Bryant Park (42nd St between 5th and 6th Avenues). This is open Tuesday-Friday noon-2pm and 3pm-7pm; Wednesday and Saturday 11am-2pm and 3pm-7pm; Sunday (for Monday tickets) noon-6pm: call 382 2323 for details of ticket availabilty.

Venues and Companies

American Ballet Theatre. Under the direction of Mikhail Baryshnikov, the ABT is big, glamorous and the epitome of the standard idea of ballet. The company has its studios and offices downtown near Union Square but performs at the *Metropolitan Opera House* (in the Lincoln Center) from early May into July.

Brooklyn Academy of Music, 30 Lafayette St, Brooklyn (718 636 4100).

Universally known as BAM, this is America's oldest performing arts academy and one of the busiest and most daring producers in New York. In the autumn, BAM's *Next Wave* festival showcases the hottest international attractions in avant-garde dance and music; in winter visiting artists appear, and each spring there's a *Festival of Black Dance* – everything from ethnic authenticity to tap and body popping. A great venue and one definitely worth crossing the river for.

City Center, 131 W 55th St (246 8989). Rivalling Radio City Music Hall for tinges of exotic kitsch, five resident dance troupes hold seasons here lasting from two weeks to a month. Companies include modern ensembles led by America's two undisputed choreographic giants, the *Merce Cunningham Dance Company* and the *Paul Taylor Dance Company*. Also here are the *Alvin Ailey American Dance Theater* (glossy contemporary pizzazz with an emphasis on black dance), the *Joffrey* and *Dance Theatre of Harlem* (see above), and occasionally the *Martha Graham Dance Company*. What's left of the year is devoted to a mix of visiting artists from the USA and abroad.

The Cunningham Studio, 11th Floor, Westbeth, 463 West St (691 9751). The home of the *Merce Cunningham Dance Company*, this rooftop studio is used as an evening performance space by young choreographers. The night-time views of the Manhattan skyline provide a stunning backdrop to performances.

Dance Theatre of Harlem. The mostly black ensemble founded in 1971 has rapidly developed into a company of major standing. They perform annually at *City Center* (see above) in a mixed repertory that includes many classics along with short works devised specifically for their own company.

Dance Theater Workshop, down the block and around the corner from the Joyce at 219 W 19th St (924 0077). Alternative dance is king at DTW, with varied programmes featuring the broadest range of the newest and brightest. The small space is located on the second floor of a former warehouse, has an unintimidating relaxed atmosphere, low ticket prices and performances virtually every night of the year.

Emanu-El Midtown YM/YWHA, 344 E 14th St (673 2207). Has been presenting dance for decades. The facility is actually a gymnasium and can be stifling on even moderate days. Still, the range of talents seen here (and the budget-priced admission) make it a space to know about.

The Joffrey Ballet. At the *City Center* (see above). Famed for its interpretations of 20C classics and contemporary works by the likes of Twyla Tharp and resident choreographer Gerald Arpino, the Joffrey divides its time between New York and Los Angeles.

The Joyce Theater, 175 8th Ave (242 0800). Probably the most important middle sized dance space in Manhattan, the Joyce has the *Eliot Feld Ballet* in residence plus short seasons of other top-notch companies.

The Kitchen, 512 W 19th St (255 5793). Innovatory dance, performance art and experimental music space.

New York City Ballet. Performs half of each year at the Lincoln Center's *New York State Theater* (see below) and is considered by many to be the greatest dance company in existence.

P.S. 122, 150 1st Ave (228 4249). A converted school in an unfashionable downtown section of the city: tends to the radical and the new.

Riverside Church has a small theatre in its complex on Riverside Drive at 122nd St (864 2929). The annual *Riverside Dance Festival* (phone for dates) presents both ethnic and traditional modern dance.

CLASSICAL MUSIC AND OPERA

New Yorkers take serious music seriously. Long queues form for anything popular, a good many concerts sell out, and summer evenings can see a quarter of a million people turning up in Central Park for free performances by the New York Philharmonic. The range of what's on offer is wide, but it's big names at big venues that pull the crowds, leaving you with a good number of easily attended selections. Tickets for these are available half price (on the day) from the *Music and Dance Booth* in Bryant Park (see p.272 for details).

Opera venues
The Lincoln Center (Broadway at 64th St; see p.137), New York's powerhouse of highbrow art, very much dominates the city's operatic scene. Its star turn is **The Metropolitan Opera House** ('The Met'; 362 6000) with the *Metropolitan Opera Company* playing from September to late April and the *American Ballet Theatre* (see Dance) taking over in the spring. Tickets are outrageously expensive and difficult to get hold of, and while last minute cancellations and standing room tickets *can* be picked up from the box office, a line is likely to form the night before if the performance is a popular one. A much better option, still in the Lincoln Center, is **The New York State Theater** (970 5770) where Beverley Sills' *New York City Opera* plays David to the Met's Goliath. Its wide and adventurous programme varies wildly in quality – sometimes startlingly innovative, occasionally failing totally. Seats go for less than half the Met's prices, and standing room tickets are available if a performance sells out.

Away from the Lincoln Center productions come on a smaller scale with ticket prices to match. Quality will vary wildly from production to production, but the companies listed here are all pretty good and, importantly, often schedule works which are neglected in the Met's roster of familiar 'top-of-the-charts' classics.

Amato Opera Theater, 319 Bowery (228 8200). This downtown group presents an ambitious and varied repertory of classics. Singers, designers and conductors are young professionals on the way up. Weekends only.
Bel Canto, 220 E 76th St (535 5231). Another weekend operation offering Mozart, Rossini and some modern works.
Light Opera of Manhattan, P.O. Box 1253, FDR Station, NY 10150 (532 6180). Specialists in Gilbert and Sullivan.

Concert Halls
The Avery Fisher Hall, in the Lincoln Center, p.137 (874 2424). Permanent home of the *New York Philharmonic* under Zubin Mehta, and temporary one to visiting orchestras and soloists. Ticket prices range from $6 to $30. An often fascinating bargain are the **NYP open rehearsals** at 9.45am on concert days. Tickets for these, non-reservable, cost just $3.
The Alice Tully Hall (362 1911), also in the Lincoln Center, is a smaller venue for chamber orchestras, string quartets and instrumentalists. Prices similar to those in the Avery Fisher Hall.
Brooklyn Academy of Music, 30 Lafayette St, Brooklyn (636 4100). See Dance.
Bargemusic, Fulton Ferry Landing, Brooklyn (718 624 4061). Jazz and chamber music. Admission around $10.
Carnegie Hall, 154 W 57th St (247 7800). The greatest names from all schools of music performed here in the past, from Tchaikovsky and Toscanini to Gershwin and Billie Holiday. The acoustics remain superb, and a patching-up operation is under way to amend years of structural neglect and restore the place to former glories. Expect music of just about any sort, and low to moderate prices.
Cooper Union, 3rd Ave at 7th St (254 6374).
Kaufman Concert Hall, in the 92nd Street Y at Lexington Avenue.
Lehman Center for the Performing Arts, Bedford Park Boulevard, the Bronx (960 8833).
Merkin Concert Hall, Abraham Goodman House, 129 W 67th St (362 8719).
Town Hall, 123 W 43rd St (840 2824).

CABARET AND COMEDY

Comedy clubs and **cabaret spots** are rife in New York and often of an extraordinarily high standard. What you'll see varies from stand-up comics and improvised comedy (amazing if you've never been before – quick-fire wit is part of the city psyche) to singing waiters and waitresses, many of whom are professional performers waiting for their big break. Most clubs have shows every night, often two at weekends (at 9pm and about midnight) and they usually charge a cover and a minimum on drinks. There are quite a few – check *New York Magazine* for the fullest listings – but those below are usually worth trying:

Catch a Rising Star, 1487 1st Ave (794 1906). New talent showcase nightly. Alumni include Pat Benatar.

Comedy U, 55 Grand St (431 4022). Cabaret bar with new talent Wednesdays; all women comedians Thursdays; Friday-Sunday stand-up comics and improvisation. Two shows Friday, three on Saturday.

Comic Strip, 1568 2nd Ave (861 9386). Famed showcase for stand-up comics and young singers going for the big time. Nightly shows from 9pm. Admission $5-$10, two drink minimum.

Dangerfield's, 1118 1st Ave (593 1650). New talent Sundays; established entertainers Monday to Saturday.

Duplex, 55 Grove St (255 5438). Village cabaret popular with gays. Two shows a night, mainly comedy, previewing yet more up-and-coming New York talent. Tuesday-Sunday until 4am: $6-$10 cover, 2 drink minimum. The rowdy piano bar downstairs is worth catching.

Folk City, 130 W 3rd St (254 8449). Best known for music (see p.264) but with excellent stand-up and improvised comedy sessions at weekends. With $2-3 admission, and drinks not too hopelessly priced, this could be the best comedy deal in town.

Improvisation, 358 W 44th St (765 8268). Nightly new comic and singing talent – most, as the name suggests, improvised.

Manhattan Punch Line 410 W 42nd St, 3rd floor (239 0827). October-June. Satire, comedy, stand-up gagsters, revues.

Something Different, 1488 1st Ave (570 6666). Cabaret club which serves desserts and sodas brought to your table by singing staff. Open seven days, weekends until 3am.

FILM

New Yorkers treat **film** with an enthusiasm which borders on obsession: people queue hours to see obscure foreign movies; being literate in movie trivia is taken as a sure sign of cultured sophistication; and Revival cinemas do brisk business. Talk to a New Yorker and sooner or later the conversation will get around to their favourite line from a favorite scene of a favourite movie. Fortunately it's not difficult to get wise to the flavour of the month, since the city catches the **latest releases** way before London. If you want to be ahead of the crowds back home, flip though any newspaper (most critically Andrew Sarris in *Village Voice* or Pauline Kael in the *New Yorker*) for details of which film is showing where, and be warned that for the newest movies you'll need to queue up to an hour just to buy your ticket, usually some time before the film starts. Be sure you're in the right queue for the showing you want, and expect to pay around $6.

The only surprising thing about New York cinema is just how mainstream it is: most European cities could offer a better selection of obscure/cult movies. If you're here mid-September to early October the **New York Film Festival** at the Alice Tully Hall, Lincoln Center, is well worth catching: a showcase of serious cinema from around the world. Otherwise there are far fewer specialist movie theatres than you might expect, though at those which do exist the choice is good. Bills change daily, so you'll need a keen eye to spot a favourite from what's on offer. The following regularly feature **Revival and Art movies**:

Cinema Village, 22 E 12th St (924 3363). Modern films (1950 onwards) are the standard bill here, plus the occasional festival.

Metro Cinema, Broadway at 99th St (222 1200). Screens old favourites.

The Museum of Modern Art, 11 W 53rd St (708 9490). Two new theatres devoted to a vast array of classic films. Archival material is available in MoMA's film library.

Regency, Broadway at 67th St (724 3700). Runs films in series packages: Bette Davis flicks, the films of Katherine Hepburn, Alfred Hitchcock, and so forth.

Thalia, Broadway at 95th St (222 3370). The grand-daddy of 'art cinemas'. This theatre has been showing daily double bills of great European and American movies for decades.

Thalia SoHo, 15 Vandam St (675 0498). An off-shoot of its popular uptown parent.

Theatre 80 St Marks, 80 St Mark's Place (254 7400). Also schedules classics. Don't miss the mini-Grauman's Chinese Theatre collection of star footprints and autographs in the sidewalk outside.

Part three
NEW YORK STATE

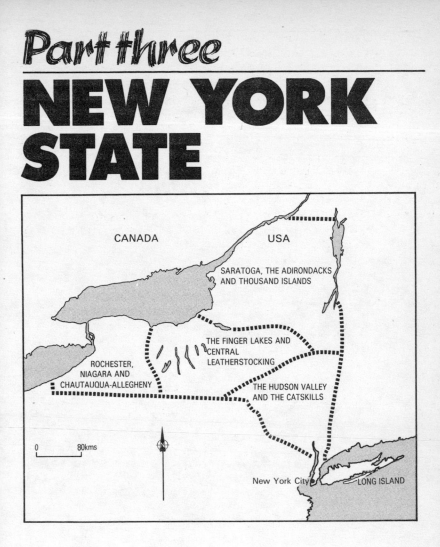

CANADA USA

SARATOGA, THE ADIRONDACKS
AND THOUSAND ISLANDS

THE FINGER LAKES AND
CENTRAL
LEATHERSTOCKING

ROCHESTER,
NIAGARA AND
CHAUTAUQUA-ALLEGHENY

THE HUDSON VALLEY
AND THE CATSKILLS

0   80kms

New York City LONG ISLAND

NEW YORK STATE: AN INTRODUCTION

New York is one of the largest and most scenically varied states in the USA. Yet despite some hefty promotion by the tourist authorities it remains relatively unknown even to Americans. With characteristic chauvinism New Yorkers view the idea of travelling further north than the Bronx with horror, and Europeans barely realise New York State exists at all.

Which is a pity, but not altogether surprising. Inevitably, in such a confusing clash of names it's the city seen on TV and sung about in musicals that's going to come out on top. And while upstate New York, as it's usually called, may have any number of natural attractions to tempt the visitor – mountains, lakes, waterfalls, forests for the asking – they're for the most part spread out and appeal primarily to more seasoned travellers. The rest stop over in Manhattan to taste some glitzy high-life and then, for untainted scenery and the great outdoors, it's off to the Grand Canyon or Yellowstone Park. Particularly if you're on a budget, though, upstate's enticements are right on your doorstep and well worth considering.

The most obvious target if you don't want to leave the city for more than a day or two is **Long Island**, which unfurls east of the city in over a hundred miles of lush farmland and broad sandy beaches. This is where the city's wealthy (the **South Fork**), not so wealthy (**Jones Beach**) and gay (**Fire Island**) head at weekends, and it's not surprisingly crowded in places, particularly in high season. But there are stretches that serve fewer trippers, the unfashionable **North Fork** for example; and ferry links

with Connecticut mean you're well poised to travel on to New England.

North of the city, the **Hudson Valley** is no less accessible and certainly more beautiful, its wooded banks winding a way north to the state capital **Albany** – itself not of much interest but providing a possible overnighter before the sharper angles of the **Catskill Mountains**. On from Albany the spa and horse-racing centre of **Saratoga Springs** is probably the chicest upstate hangout after the Hamptons, and another handy stopover before taking on the increasingly wild terrain beyond. This, the **Adirondack National Park**, is America's largest national park and in winter as inhospitable an environment as you'll find. In summer, though, there's no better country for climbing and walking, and come the autumn its foliage compares with anything you'll see in New England.

But it's the top west corner of New York which holds its most avidly visited spot: **Niagara Falls**. If you *have* to see these go ahead: they are magnificent. But bear in mind that unless you're heading on into Canada there's little else of interest this far out and the countryside, while pleasant enough, is much less spectacular than in the other regions. Nearby **Buffalo**, the state's second largest city, is dull, and its close neighbour **Rochester** has only mild appeal. One way of working things is to fly up to see the Falls (Buffalo is the nearest airport) and wend a lazy route back via the **Finger Lakes** – gentle, relatively empty and home to New York's best wineries – and **Central Leatherstocking**, stopping off at towns like **Ithaca** and **Cooperstown** on the way.

Practicalities

Information
Wherever you are in New York State the best place to pick up information and maps is from the **Chamber of Commerce**. All towns have one, usually with an office open to the public at least Monday-Friday and often at weekends. We've included addresses and phone numbers in the guide.

Getting About
The best way to get around upstate is to **rent a car**: the public transport network is less than comprehensive and even if you are going somewhere that has a bus or train station it will often be several miles outside town, making a certain amount of walking unavoidable. Petrol is relatively cheap in the States and the

hire charge itself needn't break the bank. Cheapest way to do it is to pick up a **fly-drive package** before you leave (see *Basics*). Hiring a car in Manhattan, you'll need to be 18 with a credit card, 21 without, and hand over the card as security or leave a hefty deposit. The Manhattan *Yellow Pages* are the best place to find cheap deals – try *Rent a Wreck* (1 800 221 8282) or others specialising in used car rental. Rates are around S34 a day plus $8 collision damage insurance (which you have to pay whoever you use) and a small mileage charge after the first 100 miles; weekly prices start at about $180 plus $50 collision insurance, with the mileage rate levied after 850 miles. Alternatively there are the big chains: *Avis*, 217 E 43rd St and elsewhere (1 800 331 1212); *Budget*, 225 E 43rd St and elsewhere (807 8700); *Hertz*, 310 E 48th St and elsewhere (1 800 654 3131); *National* 252 W 40th St (1 800 328 4567): phone around for the best rates. There are car hire outlets in the larger upstate towns too.

As regards breakdown and other **driving problems/information**, the *AAA* (*American Automobile Association*) offer their services free of charge to AA or RAC members (and members of most other national motoring organisations) though time limits on validity vary. Details from the principal branch of the New York City *AAA* at 28 E 78th St (586 1166), open Monday-Friday 9am-5.30pm. Upstate, most towns have an *AAA* branch and an emergency phone number; check with the local Chamber of Commerce for details.

If travelling by car is beyond your means don't despair: both *Greyhound* and *Trailways* **buses** serve most of the major targets – from where, if you want to reach somewhere obscure, there's often a local connection. Costs are low (relatively) and services can be relied upon to leave and arrive on time. There are also a number of smaller operators who travel from New York City to various destinations state-wide, tending to stop off at smaller towns: these include *Hampton Jitney*, who serve Long Island, and *Shortline*, who also cover Long Island, travel up the Hudson Valley to Albany and the Catskills, and through the Finger Lakes to Syracuse and Buffalo. For timetables and routings contact the appropriate office: *Greyhound* 625 8th Ave (971 0492) or the Port Authority Terminal (635 0800); *Trailways* Port Authority Terminal (730 7460); *Shortline* (736 4700); *Hampton Jitney* (895 9336 or 516 283 4600).

Trains on the other hand are best avoided. Though quite comfortable, they're expensive (often more than flying), aren't as reliable as buses and don't cover a very wide network. The trip up to Albany, though, is worth doing by train for the scenery, and on Long Island the **Long Island Railroad** is a feasible way of getting around. If you want to **fly** anywhere in the state see *Basics* for details of domestic airlines.

Accommodation

As in the rest of America you'll find accommodation a major expense, though much less so than in New York City. Bottom-line are **youth hostels** (YHAs) and **YMCAs** (Ys), which are, where relevant, listed in the text. These vary in quality and price, but broadly speaking if you're a YHA member you can expect to pay $5-$10 for a dormitory bed, anything up to $25 if you're not. In all cases, booking in advance is more or less essential. There are youth hostels or YMCAs in Albany, Lake George, Lake Placid, Niagara Falls, Palmyra, Syracuse, Trumansburg and other places. See the *American Youth Hostels Handbook* for details. Otherwise the cheapest option is a **motel**, never difficult to find and charging an average of $30-35 per night for a double room. Call in at the Chamber of Commerce for a list of the cheapest and most accessible ones, or pick up the leaflet produced by *I Love NY*. Inexpensive **hotels** vary from the recently invented 'Country Inns' (smaller, more like British guesthouses) to regular corporate chains like *Holiday Inn* or *Howard Johnsons*, prices starting at around $50 a night and levelling out at about $80; once again in most instances the Chamber of Commerce has full details of what's on hand or the chains produce their own booklets. Another recent phenomenon in New York – indeed in America – is that of **bed & breakfast**, bookable through local agencies and costing around $50 a night. Each region has its own agency; get in touch before you set out and find out what's on offer:

● **Long Island** *Alternate Lodgings*, Box 1782, E Hampton, NY 11937 (516

324 9449; 212 686 7847); *A Reasonable Alternative*, 117 Spring St, Port Jefferson, NY 11777 (516 928 4034); *Bed & Breakfast of Long Island*, PO Box 312, Old Westbury, NY 11568 (516 334 6231); *Hampton Bed & Breakfast Registry*, Box 695, E Moriches, NY 11940 (516 878 4439).

● **Hudson Valley & Catskills, Saratoga, Finger Lakes & Central Leatherstocking** *Bed & Breakfast USA*, PO Box 528, Croton-on-Hudson, NY 10521 (914 271 6228).

● **Adirondacks** *North Country Bed & Breakfast*, The Barn, Box 286, Lake Placid, NY 12946 (518 523 3739).

● **Niagara and Buffalo** *Rainbow Hospitality*, 9348 Hennelpin Ave, Niagara Falls, NY 14304 (716 283 4794).

Finally, there are plenty of **campsites**, usually pleasantly sited and well equipped, all over New York State, or **dude ranches**: ranch type holiday camps which lay on facilities for riding, swimming and other sports in a kitschy Frontier-style atmosphere. New York State has about 20, with prices ranging from $150-$200 for a week. *I Love NY* have comprehensive lists of both.

Chapter ten
LONG ISLAND

Long Island, reaching some 125 miles to the east of Manhattan, is the obvious target for a quick break from the city. The western end, which includes the urban boroughs of Brooklyn and Queens, is little more than an extension of NYC. But as you head east, the settlements begin to thin out and a countryside takes over which, especially in the duney reaches of the South Shore and the far-off North Fork, can get surprisingly remote. The **North and South Shores** differ greatly too – the former more immediately beautiful, its cliffs topped with mansions and estates built by wealthy New Yorkers in America's boom years, while the South Shore is fringed by an almost continuous stretch of beach and dune, and in many places populous pockets of vacationers to match. **Jones Beach** and – for gays especially – **Fire Island** are the major resorts here. At its far end Long Island splits in two, the **North Fork** retaining a marked rural aspect while the **South Fork**, much of which is known as **The Hamptons**, has long been an enclave of New York's richest and finest.

For most of these places **transport** is no problem, and while as ever a

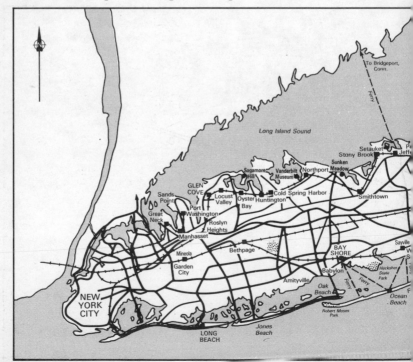

car is the best way of getting around, the Long Island Railroad provides a reliable if rather grubby alternative. *Greyhound* plys longer routes or, for local connections, there are the *Hampton Jitney, Suffolk County* and other bus services. Pick up schedules at local Chambers of Commerce or, for the LI Railroad, from Penn Station.

If you're driving there are a number of regulations to bear in mind regarding Long Island's **beaches**. Permits for parking are issued only to residents of the nearby towns, and without these you face a stiff daily rate or even steeper fine if you want to leave your car in any of the ordained car parks. On the whole it works out cheaper to head down to the beach on foot, or, if you have a car and want to use it, to either find a beach at which you can park for free or somewhere really out of the way where no one's likely to disturb you. For full information contact the local Chamber of Commerce.

THE SOUTH SHORE AND FIRE ISLAND

The suburbs of Brooklyn and Queens straggle their way eastwards, merging without break into the drab dormitory towns of western Long Island. **GARDEN CITY** is as green (and as bland) as its name suggests, made up of long shady boulevards lined with grandiose stockbroker

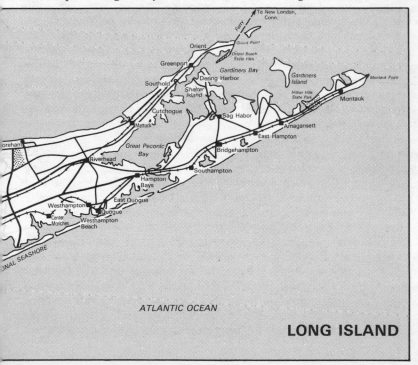

dwellings sitting behind hoovered lawns. Its 7th Street has been tagged 'the Fifth Avenue of Long Island', dotted with fashion and speciality shops, and the town as a whole has the exclusive feel of a Surrey suburb. Other than the pricey *Garden City Hotel* there's nowhere **to stay**, and apart from the **Cradle of Aviation Museum** out at Mitchel Field, little reason to stop at all. But if you do find yourself out here, **eating and drinking** are best done at *Leo's* on the corner of Franklin Avenue and 7th Street. Five miles away, just off the Northern State Parkway, **OLD BETHPAGE VILLAGE** forms the only possible target on this part of the island aside from the sea. A restored pre-Civil War village painstakingly assembled here from a variety of sites, it's billed as 'a trip back in time', with craft demonstrations, animals and the like helping to suspend your disbelief. Personally, I'd keep straight on for the beach.

Long Island's **South Shore** merges gently with the wild Atlantic, shallow and open and slicked with slithers of creamy sand that spawn luscious duney beaches throughout its entire 125 -mile length. First beach proper is **LONG BEACH**, easy to reach by regular train from Penn Station and consequently well-favoured by New Yorkers eager to escape the summer city heat. **JONES BEACH STATE PARK** (actually a series of beaches) lines a skinny spit of land a little further along, the brainchild of Robert Moses who single-handedly masterminded so many of New York's parks, both in and out of the city, and whose desire to cover everything with asphalt has left him with a rather ambiguous reputation today. Jones Beach is probably his most successful creation, primarily because he decided to leave well alone and to simply make it more accessible with a boardwalk and a handful of car parks. Come here on warm summer weekends and you'll find yourself fighting for a space; edge along a few hundred yards and the crowds begin to thin out, especially if you stroll up as far as **GILGO** or **OAK BEACH**, or cross the water to the **Robert Moses State Park** on the western tip of Fire Island. Unless you bring your own, the only alternative to fast **food** is the *Boardwalk Restaurant*, hard by the most populous section of Jones Beach, where you can eat seafood for $6 up and take in great views of the Atlantic at the same time. Those driving pay $3 for the privilege of a parking space; otherwise the best way of reaching Jones Beach from the city is to take a train from Penn Station to **FREEPORT** and a connecting bus from there.

From Jones Beach follow Ocean Parkway along the island to **CAPTREE**, best base for early morning fishing trips or whale-sighting expeditions (516 785 1600 if you're interested), and cross back to Long Island proper by way of the Robert Moses Causeway to **BAY SHORE** — of no interest for itself but much the best of the ferry terminals for FIRE ISLAND (which you can reach for around $4 one-way). This way you miss out the sprawling mess of **BABYLON** and **AMITYVILLE**, the latter with a reputation founded on its famous 'horror' of a decade or so ago – an event since popularised in a book and film of the same name. The house on the hill, from which the family were driven in terror by some mysterious supernatural force, still stands.

In many ways **FIRE ISLAND**, a slim spit of land lying parallel to the south shore, is a microcosm of New York City. In summer half of Manhattan heads up here for the weekend, holing up in a series of tiny settlements that mirror the city in minature. These days it's primarily a gay resort: young gays make for **CHERRY GROVE**; older and wealthier ones for **FIRE ISLAND PINES**; **KISMET** is the hangout of older Jews, **OCEAN BAY PARK** yuppie and jappie; while **POINT O WOODS** is probably the most exclusive enclave on the island, ringed by fences to keep out the riff-raff. Whatever you think about this kind of strict demarcation, it's typically New York, and it's as well to remember that Fire Island isn't the kind of place people visit to experience something different; they go because they know what to expect.

Few people live on Fire Island in winter, when it's a blustery strip of desolation buffetted by Atlantic storms and only connected with the mainland by infrequent ferries. Most houses are holiday homes, or timeshare apartments bought up by syndicates of people so they can have at least one weekend in two out on the beach. Ferries dock at a number of villages but most frequently at trendy **OCEAN BEACH**, where the trippers dump supplies of groceries on boldly marked trollies (cars aren't allowed on the island) and set off for their vacation pads. The season is as rigidly defined as the people: Memorial Day onwards Fire Island hums with activity and is swamped with crowds; after Labor Day, though the weather may still be very warm, the throngs diminish dramatically and you may be able to find a space on the beach or a table in one of the restaurants. Needless to say it's better out of season, but if you can't come then it's still worth a trip, if only to taste the bizarre spirit of hedonism that infects the place for these few months. Bear in mind, too, that even when Fire Island is packed to the gills, it's still long enough to throw off the bulk of the crowds and offers some gorgeous wild walks along the dunes and beaches.

Accommodation is best booked in advance whenever you're coming, and reservations are essential in high season: *Jerry's*, 620 Bay Walk, Ocean Beach (516 583 8870) doles out rooms, and you can expect to pay roughly $30 per person, double that at weekends; or *Flynn's*, in nearby Ocean Bay Park (516 583 5000), has doubles from $50-60. In Fire Island Pines – and thus more specifically for gays – best place to stay is the *Botal* (516 597 5600), or, much cheaper, *Buck 'n' Beau's Bed 'n' Board* (516 597 6833); and in Cherry Grove there's the *Cherry Grove Beach Hotel* (516 597 6600) – home also to the hi tech and very popular *Ice Palace* discotheque. *Giovanni's*, directly opposite the Ocean Beach ferry terminal, is the best and most convivial **place to eat** for under $5; *Flynn's* is frequented with almost ritualistic determination by the younger summer residents – Fridays above all – while on Saturdays, *Leo's* on Bay Walk is good for riotous boozing and eating. *Skimmer's*, in Ocean Bay Park, is *the* place to go for hot hors d'oeuvres.

Bay Shore onwards route 27 hurries through a series of sprawly settlements, none of special interest. (Unless you're following an **alternative route to Fire Island**, in which case ferries leave from SAYVILLE – to Cherry Grove, Fire Island Pines – and PATCHOGUE – to Davis Park, Watch Hill. All cost around $4 one-way.) Beaches continue all along here, emptier the further you get away from the city, but if you're not intent on swimming or sunbathing, don't stop until you near the southern fork of Long Island and the area known as THE HAMPTONS.

THE NORTH SHORE AND NORTH FORK

The **North Shore** is Long Island at its most rugged, dropping into the sea in a series of bluffs, coves and wooded headlands, less developed than the South Shore and in many places with a more tangibly rural feel, especially up on the distant North Fork. Come off the Long Island Expressway beyond Queens and you're already on top of that part of the North Shore known as the **Gold Coast** – hunting-ground in the 1920s and 1930s of the rich and elegant, and even now dotted with palatial mansions hiding away in trees which sweep graciously down to the deeply indented shoreline. The first jut of land you reach – with the uninteresting town of GREAT NECK at its centre – became Scott Fitzgerald's *West Egg* in *The Great Gatsby*, home of the narrator Nick and Gatsby himself. To this day it harbours some of the most expensive real estate in the country – so expensive that nowadays few people can afford to live here, and many of the large houses have either been demolished or stand empty and disused.

SANDS POINT, on the sharp tip of the next peninsula, is one such place, a collection of turn-of-the-century buildings once owned by the Guggenheim family and now open to the public as a park and museum. It's a mixed estate, part Tudor revival, part turreted castle (**Castlegourd**), with at its centre the Normandy-style manor house of **Falaise**. You can walk around the house, check out a display on American folk and applied art in the Castlegourd section of the complex, or just browse around the 209 acres of parkland – it's deliberately unkempt, and offers great views over what Fitzgerald called 'the most domesticated body of salt water in the Western hemisphere, the great barnyard of Long Island Sound'. (May-October Saturday-Wednesday 10am-5pm. Tours – non-obligatory – of the park cost 50c and take 40 minutes; obligatory escorted tours of Falaise run all day Monday-Wednesday and take an hour, fee $2. Admission to estate $1).

If Sands Point represents an attempt to recreate an entire pageant of past European architectural styles, then the estate of OLD WESTBURY GARDENS a few miles inland, is more definite in its aims – a conscious and not entirely unsuccessful stab at reproducing an English country estate complete with stately mansion and acres of imaginatively ordered gardens. Built by one John S. Phipps, to keep his English wife in the style to which she was accustomed, the English feel is enhanced by the furnishings of the house – oak panels, gilded mirrors and crystal chandeliers – and a collection of paintings that is dominated by the works of Reynolds, Constable and Gainsborough. All in all, a convincing charade, and a vivid indication of the degree of wealth it was possible to amass in America's boom years. (April-October Wednesday-Sunday 10am-5pm. Admission to gardens $3; house and gardens $5. Look out for the jazz concerts on the lawns during the summer months.)

After Westbury Gardens you'll want to get away from Long Island's freeway-girded centre and head back to the coast. ROSLYN HEIGHTS is the first town you'll hit, quaintly centring on a dipping main street and flanked by towered and gabled clapboard houses. From here a road heads coastwards via the newly refurbished town of GLEN COVE – an ugly combination of industrial estate and pedestrianised shopping mall – and some lushly wooded countryside. This is LOCUST VALLEY, home for many years to a localised accent that was distinguished by its lazy, rather affected drawl. Non-speakers claimed it was borne out of the snobbery of the people who lived here and referred to it as 'Locust Valley Lockjaw', and even now to a small extent it's said that you can identify the languid tones of someone who has lived in Locust Valley all their life.

It's SAGAMORE HILL, though, that makes the road worth taking – ex-country retreat of Teddy Roosevelt and today one of Long Island's major tourist hangouts, swarmed over by thousands of eager crocodiling schoolkids every year (May-October daily 9.30am-5pm, November-April 9.30am-4.30pm; 50c). Roosevelt lived here for 30 odd years – after cowboying for a while in the Dakotas and in between big game hunting in Africa – and the house has been very largely kept as it was then: 23 rooms in all, cosily furnished and adorned everywhere by the great man's trophies sprouting horns from walls or grinning toothily up from the firesides. All of the furnishings, even the books, are original to the house, in a sensitive and not over-ostentatious piece of preservation. The laughable price and gorgeous grounds, springy lawns falling down to Oyster Bay and the sea, make it a detour well worth making – though you'll need a car. Before you leave, be sure to take a look in at the Old Orchard Museum across the far side of the car park. This displays artefacts relating to Teddy's political and personal life, and shows a short biographical film.

Push south from here to OYSTER BAY and Raynham Hall (20 West

Main Street; Tuesday-Sunday 1pm-5pm; 50c), a heavily restored 18C mansion that was the Townsend family home during the Revolutionary wars. British troops were quartered here for a time, and Townsend, who was Washington's chief spy in New York City, was able through some smart eavesdropping to foil Benedict Arnold's plot to betray West Point. These days it's a great deal less intriguing, but worth the entrance fee for the carefully renovated rooms and some tidy formal gardens. Just outside town the **Planting Fields Arboretum** (Monday-Friday 9am-5pm) on Planting Fields Road is an extensive set of botanical gardens that repays a look if you're interested in such things, and includes the **Coe Mansion**, a mock-Tudor monstrosity which the marine-insurance magnate William Robertson Coe called home (daily 10am-5pm; entrance fee May-September and weekends, other times free).

COLD SPRING HARBOUR lies across from here, one of Long Island's most attractive small towns though long since despoiled by a burgeoning tourist industry. It grew up as a whaling port, and the **Whaling Museum** on Main Street (Tuesday-Sunday, 11am-5pm) recaptures that era better than the town ever could now, its major features a fully equipped whaleboat and a 400-piece assembly of scrimshaw work. Hourly films give the lowdown on the industry which flourished here in the mid-19C and died almost as soon as it had begun. A few miles on, **HUNTINGTON** is a bustling little provincial town with a couple of minor excitements which could conceivably hold you for an hour or two. **Walt Whitman's birthplace** (weekends 10am-4pm), out at Huntington Station, has a handful of the poet's manuscripts; the **Historical Society** (Tuesday-Friday 10am-4pm) shows a set of 18C period rooms, and the **Hekscher Museum** holds a rather ordinary potpourri of American and European fine art (Tuesday-Friday 10am-5pm, weekends 1pm-5pm).

Less modest is the **VANDERBILT MANSION** (May-October Tuesday-Saturday 10am-4pm; $1) just outside CENTREPORT, a country estate once home to William K. Vanderbuilt II and showing about as much taste as you will have come to expect if you've seen a Vanderbilt residence before. This one, in the style of a Baroque Spanish palace, is heavily ornate both outside and in, with marble-encased galleries, swirling staircases and gaudily carved fireplaces. William K. hadn't the business brain of his great-grandfather Cornelius (the railway tycoon) and he devoted himself instead to living it up and indulging his great passion, natural history. The fruits of this enthusiasm (all 17,000 of them) are on show in a building in another part of the grounds.

The Vanderbilt Mansion holds a commanding view of **NORTHPORT BAY**, where the town of the same name – 'achingly all-American' wrote Joyce Johnson in *Minor Characters* – sits bright and ordered by the water's edge. Its main street runs straight and wide to the placid harbour, a long stretch of wooden-fronted shops and houses that looked authentic enough to be used as a backdrop for shoot-out westerns in the 1920s and 1930s. A small **historical museum** (Tuesday-Sunday 1pm-4pm), giving a résumé of the town's shipbuilding past, may provide an excuse for the briefest of stopovers, but otherwise head straight on to **SUNKEN MEADOW**, which emerges through the trees as a free **beach**, nature and recreation reserve that's more remote and far less crowded than, say, Jones or Long Beach.

Beyond, you pass through some of the most beautiful countryside on the island, leafy glades enfolding a road that winds its way around the tranquil incuts of Long Island Sound. **STONY BROOK** is generally regarded as the historic and cultural heart of the region, home to a *SUNY* campus and with a reconstructed centre that stands as testament to the dream of wealthy 1940s philanthropist Ward Delville, who rescued the place from chronic decay and rebuilt it in its original federalist splendour. It's neatly done, and there's no denying the prettiness of the white clapboard houses, but for all the attention to detail you can't help but feel you're seeing a reconstruction, and its timbered shopfronts remind more of a laundered shopping precinct.

You have to stroll half a mile or so down the road to find the town's real pull – **The Museums at Stony Brook,** a concoction of three museums, one showing paintings and drawings, another a collection of carriages and a third a historical collection. The *Art Museum* is largely made up of the work of **William Sidney Mount**, an artist who lived in a house up the road (at present open to the public just once a year but which the museum plans to restore when funds permit) and painted most of his life along the North Shore between here and Setauket. Mount is widely considered America's first true genre painter: he began painting European-influenced religious scenes but soon graduated to more original portrayals of local street and rural life, incorporating blacks and ethnic groups centrally and uncritically into pictures for the first time. Contemporary critics found this mildly outrageous but applauded Mount's skill, and his paintings were snapped up avidly in Europe, where aristocrats were delighted with what they saw as an exotic and faintly risqué subject-matter. Among the best pictures in the museums's vast collection (they own virtually everything of Mount's) are the sensitive *Banjo Player* (1855), probably Mount's best-known painting, *Dance of the Haymakers* (1845), and *Farmers Nooning* (1836) – one of the most ambitious of his works, with a highly original attention to detail and landscape. Look out, too, for some of his local scenes – *The Mill at Stony Brook* (1855) for example, the model for which you can see by the pond in the centre of town (daily 10am-5pm, closed Mondays; $2.75).

From Stony Brook route 25a follows the coast to Port Jefferson, taking in the ravishingly pretty village of **SETAUKET** on the way, where you could do worse than take a stroll around the churchyard of the 18C

Caroline Church or just stop off to soak up the tidy peace of the manicured village green. **PORT JEFFERSON** is a mix of industrial working harbour and jazzed-up waterside buildings housing seafood restaurants and souvenir shops – pleasant enough, but too much a museum-piece to enjoy for very long. Basically the reason for coming here is twofold: to call in at the **Mather Museum** on Prospect Street, which puts on a convincing show of local artefacts and Indian finds, and to wait for one of the frequent (four times daily in spring, more in summer) **ferries** to Bridgeport, Connecticut. The journey takes an hour and a half and costs $6 one-way for foot passengers.

SHOREHAM, further down the coast, has been for some time focus of a local controversy: nestling sinisterly behind the exuberant green, it's one of the largest nuclear reactors on the East Coast, finished a couple of years back but yet to produce any electricity. Pressure groups campaigned against the siting of the reactor from the beginning and now seem confident it will never go into operation, not least because – since construction went a cool $4 billion over budget – no one can afford its energy. Inland from Shoreham the leafy gentleness of the North Shore gives way to the sweeping ploughland plains of Suffolk County's agricultural heartland – believe it or not, the North East's largest arable producer, with a climate mild enough to grow peaches, tomatoes and grapes out in the open. At **RIVERHEAD**, an unattractive town where you branch south for the designer-chic of the Hamptons and Montauk, or take a more rustic path up Long Island's North Fork.

The **North Fork** has a strikingly different feel to its southern neighbour, and, indeed, to the rest of the island: not only is it more rural, but its landscapes are a great deal wilder. There are also far fewer tourists. Of its towns, **CUTCHOGUE** is the first of any real interest, a set of pre- and post-colonial houses grouped around a village green. It makes a good base for tours around the **Hargrave Vineyard** at the junction of Route 25 and Alvan's Lane – Long Island's only winery. These run regularly throughout the day between Memorial and Labor Day, at weekends only from Labor Day until Christmas.

Heading west, the North Fork takes on a markedly New England air, primarily due to the fact that this region, together with a number of towns across Long Island Sound, once formed an independent colony. Its principal centre is **SOUTHOLD**, where there's an **Archaeological Museum** which houses the most complete set of Indian finds of Long Island. Drop in between Thursday and Sunday 1.30pm-4.30pm and you'll find it open; otherwise carry straight on – the town has little else to detain you.

GREENPORT, 5 miles on, is probably this area's most picturesque town, a clutter of narrow streets and alleys leading down to a harbour pierced by the masts of visiting yachts. It also forms much the best base for exploring this end of the island, with **accommodation** easy to find and relatively cheap (try *Bartlett House*, 503 Front Street (516 477 0371) which has double rooms for as little as $35 in season). There are regular 15 minute **ferry connections** to Shelter Island and hence the South Fork.

ORIENT POINT, just a few miles east, offers access to the gloriously untouched **Orient Point State Park** and frequent **ferries** (in summer six a day; last one leaves 2pm) to New London, Connecticut – a journey which takes 1½ hours and costs $6 one-way, $9 for a day return.

THE SOUTH FORK: THE HAMPTONS, SAG HARBOUR AND MONTAUK

Chic riviera or staid stockbroker country? Whatever you think of **The Hamptons** they're still very much the place to see and be seen. A string of small towns set in the green countryside of Long Island's fashionable South Fork, there are few more wealthy – or status-ridden – parts of America than this: huge palaces lurk in the trees or stand boldly on the flats behind the dunes, much of the property bought up greedily by affluent New Yorkers eager for a weekend retreat; cars are consciously prestigious British or German models; clothes, designer labels of the safest and most sedate kind. Nowhere, but nowhere, is consumption as deliberately conspicuous as in The Hamptons...

Even though the money-tag is less than a century old, the Hamptons have always been sought-after, and the towns here are among the oldest in the state, settled by incomers from New England in the mid-1650s. Until the late 19C they remained relatively isolated farming communities, but as the rich became more mobile, turning up here in their motor cars, this grew into their playground. In the 1920s and 1930s celebrities and ritzy New Yorkers flocked here in force, starting a fashion that has never really died. Pollock and De Kooning came up in the 40s, Betty Friedan still lives in Sag Harbour, Gloria Vanderbilt has a house in Southampton, and Woody Allen and other big names are either residents or frequent visitors, all giving the area a gossip column cachet that you'll either love or hate. That it's expensive there can be no doubt, and the crowds that congregate here in summer may alone be enough to put you off. But if you come up on the Long Island Railroad, put up somewhere relatively cheap (for all the chic country clubs there are still plenty of shoestring motels) and use local buses for getting around, you'll find you can survive without spending a fortune. And the beaches which fringe the nearby Atlantic are everywhere long enough to grab some space for yourself.

The Hampton furthest west, **WESTHAMPTON**, attracts a crowd markedly less studded with celebrities than its eastern counterparts and is, as a result, more commercial: discos jostling for space with loud pizza restaurants, and the singles set – 'Groupers' to the locals – flooding into timeshares to swap sexual experiences. There's little to do but swim by day and eat and drink by night, but if you're here in the first week of August you may be interested in catching the annual open-air art show in nearby **WESTHAMPTON BEACH**. Quieter, and a good base for the 15-mile-long swathe of beach that rings nearby Shinnecook Bay, is **QUOGUE**, a mile or two further on and accessible by bus. The same goes for **HAMPTON BAYS**, essentially a family-geared resort but neatly placed for the nearby sheltered expanses of Shinnecook and Beconic Bays – both of which, if you're prepared to walk, have beach space for the asking. If, however, you want somewhere with a touch more style, best forge on to Southampton.

Largest of the towns, and best situated for seeing the rest of the region, **SOUTHAMPTON** is one of the most famous havens of the rich on the entire eastern seaboard. And though it hasn't been totally overwhelmed by money, long association with the Long Island Smart Set has left it unashamedly twee: one glance at the boutiques, galleries and jewellery shops lining its pristine streets should be enough to give you some idea of the kind of people who visit here. That said, even if it isn't cheaper, accommodation is easier to find than in the other Hamptons, and the nearby beaches are quite superb – though like the town itself they can be obliterated with bodies at the season's height. If you haven't a car they're just a short walk away and ideal for a day or so's basking; if you have, try somewhere more remote – like most of the beaches around here, only town residents are allowed to use the car parks.

Things to see in town include an excellent local **Historical Museum** (17 Meeting House Lane; June-September, Tuesday-Sunday 11am-5pm), which gives a rundown on Southampton history from Indian times onwards; the **Parish Art Gallery** (25 Job's Lane; Tuesday-Saturday 10am-5pm, Sunday 1pm-5pm), which puts on changing exhibitions and whose permanent collection takes in a large set of works by William Merrit Chase; and the **Halsey Homestead**, the oldest English frame house in the state, built in 1648 and furnished in period style (South Main Street; June-September Tuesday-Sunday 11am-4.30pm).

For **information**, the *Chamber of Commerce* (daily 9am-5pm) is at 76 Main Street and gives out walking tours of the town and lists of B&B **rooms**; otherwise the cheapest bed in town is at the *Hill Guest House*, 535 Hill Street (516 283 9889). For **food**, *Joe's*, 23 Hill Street, does pizzas and pasta at rock-bottom prices, or, if you want something a little more exciting, try *Barrister's* on Main Street for marvellous soft-shell crabs; alternatively, the *Driver's Seat*, on Job's Lane, is younger, trendier and marginally less expensive. **Bikes** can be hired by the hour or day from *Rotations* (516 283 2890), at the junction of Job's Lane and Hill Street. If you're here at the end of the summer season, Labor Day weekend is highlighted by the **Pow-Wow** at the **Shinnecook Indian Reservation** on the outskirts of town, when the tribe opens its allotted lands to public gaze and sells ethnic foods and handicrafts and performs traditional dances. Other times, best steer clear of the reservation; the Shinnecooks are said to discourage visitors.

The next Hampton east is **BRIDGEHAMPTON**, a migrant black workers' community turned comfortable escape for successful New York literary and artistic types, who have more or less banished the original locals by buying up all the property – a familiar tale around here. A drive down the main street will show you just about all there is to see. *Cato's* and *Bobby Van's* are the laid-back hangouts where Bridgehampton's novelists and playwrights drift in to eat after a hard day over a hot word processor. Give them a go if you're here for any length of time – you might even see someone famous (Kurt Vonnegut, Malcolm Morley and Alan Alda are all local residents). And before you head on, do a right at the war memorial, where a few miles down the road is another fine stretch of sandy **beach**, one that stays far less crowded than Southampton's.

Five miles further on, **EAST HAMPTON** was once voted the prettiest village in the entire USA by a newspaper poll, and it's easy to see why. Dark clapboard houses set around a wedge of village green, backed by a stolid Norman-style church and small cemetery make this small-town America at its most endearing. One of the houses was the subject of John Howard Payne's *Home Sweet Home*, a song the actor-dramatist wrote from Paris in the 1820s when homesick, and is now open to the public as a **museum** (Monday-Saturday 10am-4pm Sunday 2pm-4pm). A sharp précis of the town's history is given at an 18C **town house** on Main Street, but that aside there's little to keep you – only a still-working **Hook Mill** at the far end of Main Street and the palace-studded estates just south of town.

If you want to stay, beware that rooms in East Hampton can work out prohibitively expensive. Far better to bed down in adjacent **AMAGANSETT** – less pretentious than East Hampton and another gathering-place for the singles set, who swarm down to strut their stuff along the nearby **Atlantic Avenue Beach**. There's a good museum too, the **East Hampton Town Marine Museum** (Tuesday-Saturday 10.30am-5.30pm, July-September only), dedicated to the maritime history of this part of Long Island and with displays and dioramas on fishing, whaling and other nautical activities. At bedtime try the *Gansett Green Manor* (516 267 3133) on Main Street, where you should be able to find doubles for around $50.

North of here, and administratively part of East Hampton, **SAG HARBOUR** is one of the most historic of the South Fork towns, once a harbour second only to that of New York, and designated first Port of Entry to the New Country by George Washington; the state's first **custom**

house was established here and still stands (June-September Tuesday-Sunday 10am-5pm). Nowadays Sag Harbour is becoming heavily touristed but, despite the encroaching boutiques, it retains a feel which marks it out strikingly from its rather more sanitised neighbours to the south and west.

The town's prosperity was founded, albeit for a short period only, on whaling, and as at Cold Spring Harbour on Long Island's north shore, there are a number of relics from those years. Best of these is the **Whaling Museum** on Main Street (May-September 1pm-5pm, Sunday 2pm-5pm), housed in an overblown Greek Revival mansion and containing whaling equipment and a collection of guns and scrimshaw. Nearby the **Whaler's Presbyterian Church** dates from the same era, once topped with a telescope-shaped spire (since lost) and crenellated with jutting rows of whale blubber spades. A more touching monument to the town's whaling antecedents is the **Oakland Cemetery**, where memorials remember young whalers, most of whom died in their twenties: one, in the shape of a broken mast, stands out in particular – beautifully reliefed and recalling horrific encounters with 'the monsters of the deep'.

There's no whaling done nowadays, of course, and the town focuses on a peaceful main street which curves elegantly down to a harbour where pleasure boats rock gently at their moorings, looking over to the privately owned estates of **NORTH HAVEN**. From here one Colonel Meigs routed the unfortunate English in the Revolutionary wars, destroying a dozen ships and making off with copious supplies of food and drink – a feat for which he's remembered in a monument on Union Street. Now the only reason to go to North Haven is to take one of the frequent ferries to **SHELTER ISLAND**, a short $4 ride across the bay. There's not much here unless you're into the wholesome joys of outdoor activities, but Route 114 takes you straight to DERING HARBOUR from where you can catch another ferry to GREENPORT on Long Island's North Fork.

John Steinbeck lived in Sag Harbour for many years – it was from here he set out on his *Travels with Charley* – and he's remembered by a plaque on the windmill in the harbour, which offers **tourist information** in the summer months. There's hardly anywhere to **stay** - only the *Baron's Cove Inn* (516 725 2100) has rooms, and they're not cheap – but if you're after **something to eat** Main Street is lined with reasonably priced restaurants. Try the burgers at *Ryerson's* or the *Sandbar*, and have a drink in *The Corner* near the harbour, a well-frequented local haunt. The only other possibility of a room at realistic rates is the *Ram's Head Inn* (516 749 0811), overlooking Coecles Bay on Shelter Island, where you can sleep for around $25 per person.

MONTAUK, up beyond Amagansett on the farthest tip of Long Island, is quite different from the rest of The Hamptons – indeed, few people ever lump them together. Untainted by social climbers, it sits bleakly among the dunes, a blustery, wind-battered place which, but for a hurricane and the Wall Street Crash of 1929, would have been a resort of some size. As it is, the entrepreneur who wanted to develop the place lost his money and, a weird Florentine tower in the centre of town apart, Montauk stayed as it was – a not particularly attractive town with easy access to some enticingly undisturbed country, not least the dunes and free beaches of the **Hither Hills State Park**, and the rocky toe of **Montauk Point** itself.

This area was originally, in the 18C, little more than a summer pasture for grazing cattle, and the town's oldest buildings date from that time. Later it became better known as a quarantined campground for diseased veterans of the Spanish-American War – Teddy Roosevelt's Rough Riders & Co. – who were forced to bivouac on the wilds of Montauk Point after being refused entry by a hygiene-conscious New York City. Today this cape has a rare beauty that figures in all the tourist brochures, its **Lighthouse** (which you should be able to visit) forming an almost symbolic finale to this stretch of the American coast. Back in the town centre there are a number of **motels** offering fairly priced rooms: try the *Oceanside Beach Resort* (516 668 9825), on the junction of the Old Montauk Highway and Main Street, whose doubles flicker between $30 and $60 depending on the time of year. For **sustenance** you'll do no better than *The Lobster Roll* on the Montauk Highway, a famous eatery in these parts, where you can feed on excellent fish and seafood, all freshly caught, for between $5 and $10.

Chapter eleven
THE HUDSON VALLEY AND THE CATSKILLS

To the average New Yorker, the **Hudson River Valley** is a wide, dirty stretch either passed under en route to Jersey City or over to reach Hackensack. But travel a few miles north, leaving Manhattan under its smoggy blanket, and you're in some of the most beautiful and easily accessible countryside in the state, a region lionised in the paintings of Thomas Cole and Frederick Church. The **Catskill Mountains** often formed the subject of their pictures and the wooded peaks of the Catskill Park are still one of the most attractive, most visited spots upstate. In the autumn the region comes into its own with a brilliant variety of colours in the thick woodlands that rivals anything to be seen in New England. And always, below, is the Hudson, treacly brown as it forges its way to the ocean. Henry Hudson discovered the river in 1609, searching for the north-west passage – he failed, but the Dutch, French and English settlements that sprung up in his wake have left a corridor of historic towns at the river's edge. If you're heading onwards to the Adirondacks there's much to see here – otherwise a circuit of the Hudson Valley will take about three days.

First stop on most explorations are the three **Tarrytown Restorations**, about 25 miles out of Manhattan: Washington Irving's former home is here, in idyllic surroundings which can be visited by train as a day trip from the city. Elsewhere the US Military Academy at **West Point** is an undying attraction and beyond, the **West Bank** of the river leads through mountainsides of maple and a string of small towns like **New Paltz** and **Kingston,** both on *Trailways* bus routes. *Amtrak* travel up the **East Bank** to **Albany,** the brutally if imaginatively modernised state capital, though this eastern rail route isn't going to help you see the mansions around **Hyde Park**: for these you just have to have a car.

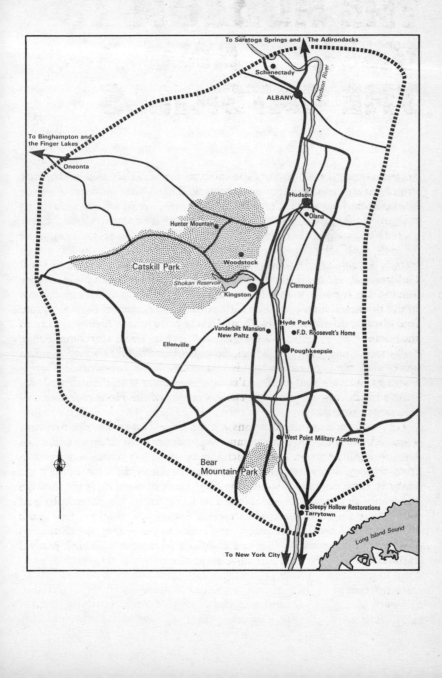

LOWER HUDSON VALLEY: THE SLEEPY HOLLOW RESTORATIONS AND LYNDHURST

Centring on **TARRYTOWN**, the **Sleepy Hollow Restorations** (Sunnyside, the Philipsburg and Van Cortland Manors) and the National Trust's **Lyndhurst** form the first stops on an exploration of the Hudson valley, an easy day trip from NYC either by car or, less conveniently, the Hudson-Harlem commuter train from Grand Central. Tarrytown, leafy and residential, straddles the eastern end of the Tappan Zee Bridge and was made mildly famous as the village around which **Washington Irving** spun the tale of *The Legend of Sleepy Hollow*. Irving moved just south of the town in 1835, and rebuilt a farm cottage there as **Sunnyside**, 'a little old fashioned stone mansion,' he wrote, 'all made up of gable ends, and as full of angles and corners as an old cocked hat.' Tours squeeze around the rooms, and are enjoyable even if you've never read a word of Irving. To get there, turn off US 9 (Broadway) on to West Sunnyside Lane; tours run daily 10am-5pm, tickets $4, $7 for this and one other restoration, $10 for all three.

About a mile north of Sunnyside, **Lyndhurst** is as dapper a piece of 19C Gothic revivalism as you'll find anywhere, spikily crenellated and washed round by landscaped lawns. The conducted tours (April 14th-November 14th Wednesday-Sunday 10am-4.15pm; admission charge) fill you in on Lyndhurst's collection of Victoriana and the lives of its previous owners, who included the much hated Jay Gould. At the northern end of town the **Philipsburg Manor and Mill** was home to the Philipse family, Dutch settlers of 1600 who milled grain here and shipped it down river to New York and abroad. This made them a fabulous fortune, and their only mistake was to put their money on the wrong side in the Revolutionary war, after which their holdings were summarily confiscated. The **Manor House** restoration mimics that era in a too-good-to-be-true combination of bare floors and elegant furniture, though the **mill** itself is still real enough, grinding grain and lending the setting a Constabley charm. Sometimes it's possible to join group tours of the **Old Dutch Church of Sleepy Hollow**, across the road from the Manor House; or you can pick up a leaflet and explore the cemetery and its tombs of Washington Irving and Andrew Carnegie for yourself.

Unlike the Philipse family, the Van Cortlands were staunch revolution aries, and so hung on to the **Van Cortland Manor** at **CROTON-ON-HUDSON** until 1945. This is the largest and most elaborate of the restorations, and the most ambitious – the house an immaculate representation of life in the late 18C, with a pleasing contrast between the fripperies of the manor itself and the down-to-earth practicalities of its **Ferry House**. There are demonstrations of domestic arts and an ornamental garden, plus added ornaments in the shape of the becostumed staff. To get here, head north from Tarrytown on Route 9 for about 8 miles, exit on to Croton Point Avenue, then go one block east to South Riverside Avenue and turn right for the main entrance. Admission as Sunnyside.

Next stop for most will be West Point Military Academy, for which you cross the river at PEEKSKILL; alternatively, if you're driving from Tarrytown it's possible to head over the bridge there and up through the closely wooded mountains of the **PALISADES INTERSTATE PARK** and **BEAR MOUNTAIN**: a gorgeous area for walking and sailing in summer, skiing in winter. Facilities congregate around the *Bear Mountain Inn* (914 786 2731) whose moderately priced rooms fill very quickly.

WEST POINT

Some years after the end of the Revolutionary war, Congress realised that the ragged troops who had won the battles of the 1770s had been knocked into shape by officers and expertise almost exclusively European, and that homegrown skills needed to be cultivated in case foreign help wasn't so readily forthcoming again. Thus the **UNITED STATES MILITARY ACADEMY AT WEST POINT** was founded in 1802, and has been supplying the country with officers ever since – Generals Custer, Robert E. Lee, Douglas, MacArthur, Eisenhower and Patton to name but a famous few. Today 4000-odd candidates fill the place, as smart and showpiece-tidy as the campus itself, protectively overlooking the river from a wide bluff. A tough four-year regime of intensive sports accounts for the frighteningly fit physiques around, and the academic training is equally stiff. In the **Visitors' Information Centre** (8.30am-4.15pm daily) a model cadet room and film detail the rigours of West Point Life, and the **West Point Museum** (10.30am-4.15pm daily) shows their spoils: weapons, uniforms and trophies from wars at home and abroad include General MacArthur's bath robe, Hitler's pistol, Frank Borman's space suit and, disturbingly, the removed safety catch from the Nagasaki atomic bomb. Root out the Vietnam section and all you find is a sub-Action Man Viet Cong uniform – army chiefs always felt the war could have been won, had the politicians not 'tied their hands'. No one's celebrating that war here.

Most of West Point's visitors come in search of patriotism rather than war memorabilia, and it's readily supplied on the **Parade Ground** where trainee officers and gentlepersons do their drilling, with much pomp and circumstance and a great deal of shouting. If this is your kind of thing – and it is impressive – phone 914 938 2638 or 938 5621 for a schedule of events, which are at their most frequent in spring and autumn. Other than this there's not that much to see: a dismal cadet chapel styled in military

Gothic, and the remains of **Fort Putnam** (May-October 10.30am-4pm daily), one of several built to keep control of the Hudson against the British, are all that might detain you.

If you're **coming from New York City** the *Day Line Ferry* leaves Pier 81 at the end of West 41st Street at 9.30am Wednesday, Thursday, Saturday and Sunday between late May and mid September and returns at 3.30pm, arriving back in New York at 6.30pm. Costs for the round trip, via Bear Mountain, are $12 per person.

Pushing **north** from West Point you're confronted with a choice: to the west of the river is a string of pleasant towns along Thruway 87; on the east side historic houses are the pull – the homes of the Vanderbilts, Roosevelts, Livingstones and the painter Frederick Church point to just how long this has been a desirable stretch of riverside real estate. It's possible to zig-zag from one side to the other, but easier and more satisfying to attack each side individually – say the west bank heading north, the east coming back.

THE WEST BANK: NEW PALTZ, KINGSTON AND CATSKILL

Distinguished by what is carefully called 'The oldest street in America with its original houses', **NEW PALTZ** sits prettily between Mohonk Mountain and the Hudson. In 1677 a small community of exiled Huguenots bought the land here from an Indian tribe, and named it after Pfalz in the Rhineland where they'd found temporary refuge. At first they built log huts, but soon made lasting homes of stone, and it's these everyone comes to see today: six of the houses date from before 1720, and they're arranged around a village green worthy of any chocolate box. The oldest, the **Jean Hasbrouk Memorial House** is a folksy example of the simple Flemish style imported by the refugees, one that became increasingly elegant as the community thrived. A comprehensive **guided tour** traces the history of each house and shows the remodelled interiors, starting from the **Deyo House** at 10.30am and 1.30pm. A 2¼ hour tour costs $4, a 1¼ hour tour $2, and the site is open Wednesday-Sunday from Memorial Day to the end of September.

For **food and a room**, KINGSTON further on is a better bet, though there's no shortage of fast food joints and delis in New Paltz: of the restaurants, *Barnaby's* has cheapish burgers and salads, and the *Wildflower Café* (914 255 0020) covers the health food/vegetarian market. Further out – and the closest chance of a cheapish room – is the antique-furnished *Schoonmaker's House* (914 687 7946), on Route 213 between High Falls and Rosendale, $50 double; or *Brodhead House* in

High Falls itself (914 687 7700), $50 double.

Cut west out of New Paltz on Route 299 and you're heading through the pink and white laurels that blanket **Mount Mohonk**, whose outdoor facilities have been monopolised by the huge *Mohonk Mountain House*. But drive on to **Lake Minnewaska** and there's a relative wilderness to explore around the hemlock-rimmed lake. Admission is $5.

KINGSTON comes billed as 'the Williamsburg of the north', and while nothing so elaborate it lives up to the hype and expectations of a place that prides itself on its history. Dutch settlers had a trading post here only seven years after Hudson discovered the river, enjoying a peaceful relationship with the local Indians, which ended when they rose against the settlers, burning down the post and massacring most of its inhabitants. Governor Peter Stuyvesant ordered a stockade built, and a few of the farmhouses from this period survive, ensuring the town's popularity with tourists today. The **stockade** area at the end of town is the picturesque part that everyone comes to see, and **Green** and **Crown Streets** are cluttered with well-preserved houses of the 17C and 18C in a mix of styles. Pride of place goes to the low, rough-hewn **Senate House** (312 Fair Street, April-December Wednesday-Saturday 10am-5pm, Sunday 1pm-5pm; free). During the Revolutionary battles the Hudson Valley was the scene of much of the fighting, and as the British pushed the patriots and their embryonic government north, Kingston was hurriedly declared capital of the state. The state Senate met here from September until October, when the British troops began to get too close for comfort (eventually they sacked and burned much of the town). Inside the Senate House is a restoration of how the building might have looked then, and outside is an equally modest garden and museum (times as Senate House). The Senate House is also the place to find out about the **walking tours** given by the *Friends of Historic Kingston* (914 338 5100) for a wider view of the old stockade and its architecture. While you're here, poke your head round the door of the **Volunteer Firemen's Hall and Museum** (265 Fair Street, Friday 11am-3pm, Saturday 10am-4pm; free) for some intricate and highly polished devices.

The early 19C saw the completion of the Delaware-Hudson canal a few miles out of town, which in its turn led to the development of **Roundout's Landing** nearby. Coal, bricks and produce went down river to New York City, and ever-increasing numbers of tourists responded by heading into the Catskills via Kingston. The canal has long since fallen into disuse, but the **Hudson River Maritime Center** (Wednesday-Sunday 12am-5pm; $1) preserves some of this history, with a selection of antique and antiquated boats, a working shipbuilding yard and weekend trips to a lighthouse. When I was here the place was in chaotic reorganisation, but by now it should be worth checking out, along with the remodelled waterfront buildings below the old Route 9 bridge.

For **accommodation** the choice is between the *Holiday Inn* at 503 Washington Avenue (914 338 0400) – doubles around $50 – or there's a *Howard Johnson's Motor Lodge* (914 338 4200) at Route 28 North (exit 19 off Thruway 87). Inexpensive **food** isn't difficult to find: two restaurants are *Dallas Hot Weiners* at 51 North Street, for hamburgers, sandwiches, etc., or the *Pizza Place* at the corner of John and Wall Streets. For a dearer blow-out *Scheller's Restaurant*, 61 John Street, has German/Austrian grub with home-made wursts, hams and strudels.

It's about 27 miles from Kingston to **CATSKILL** – a prim, quaintish residential place along classic Main Street: what goes on in town goes on along this strip, and that probably doesn't amount to very much. Nearby, the leafy **Catskill Creek** draws a good number of the boating and fishing crowd into town, and though there's nothing in the way of 'sights' the Federal, Gothic and Greek Revival houses of the centre are worth an amble; for a detailed account of the more characterful buildings – including the house of artist Thomas Cole, founder of the Hudson Valley School – pick up *A Guide to Catskill's Archictectural History* from the County Court House (319 Main Street) or the **Green County Promotion Department** (290 Main Street; 518 622 3934) who can also help with accommodation.

From Catskill it's an easy hop across the Rip Van Winkle Bridge to OLANA and HUDSON – for which see p.308 – or west into the Catskill National Park.

THE CATSKILLS

Whoever has made a voyage up the Hudson must remember the Kaatskill mountains. They are a dismembered branch of the great Appalachian family, swelling up to a noble height, and lording it over the surrounding country. Every change of season, every change of weather, indeed, every hour of the day, produces some change in the magical hues and shapes of these mountains, and... sometimes, when the rest of the landscape is cloudless, they will gather a hood of gray vapours which, in the last rays of the setting sun, will glow and light up like a crown of glory.

So wrote Washington Irving at the beginning of *Rip Van Winkle*, and beneath the purple his prose isn't far wrong. **The Catskills**, magnificent heights wooded with maple and beech which turn to shuffled embers of orange, gold and bronze each autumn, have a rich and ravishing beauty – one that can absorb any number of weekending Manhattanites. It's inspiring country, and filled with all the amenities – campsites, hiking trails, canoeing, fishing and, especially, skiing: both **Catskill** town and **Ellenville** are home to numerous ski-resort-cum-night club pleasure palaces. If you're not here for the sport, though, or the high prices scare you off, just stick within the delimits of the Catskill Park and its majestic mountain heights – it is, as Thoreau said, 'a landscape fit to entertain a travelling god'.

Through the mountains

It's difficult to suggest any single route through the mountains: from Catskill Route 23/23A forms a neat circle, easily managed (easier still if you detour across Route 296) and giving breath-taking views across the mountains and the dramatic **gorge** between Hunter and Catskill – the mythical spot where Rip nodded off for 20 years. Out of Kingston you can loop past the lovely **Ashokan Reservoir** and **Woodstock** and head through the bosky uplands to pick up Route 23A at Lexington. Really, there's an unlimited variety of byways to explore if you have time and transport on your side. A drive-through taster can be managed in a day, but if you're touring the region in detail pick up the Green County Promotion Department's *Scenic Tours Map* in Catskill for a thorough selection of planned-out routes.

Though each of the Catskill's small villages has its charms, **WOODSTOCK** is the only town to spend any time in. It's not the place of the famed psychedelic picnic of the 1960s – that was about 60 miles west of here – nor is it the hippy hangout usually imagined. Yet since the 1969 concert Woodstock has become a part of the international lexicon; people use the terms 'before Woodstock' and 'after Woodstock' with the hushed air of a religious event. The town that lent its name to the jamboree has itself become a cultural landmark – and one of the prettiest and most agreeable spots upstate.

Founded in the 1700s, Woodstock first gained fame as a major arts and crafts centre at the turn of this century, when the Byrdcliffe Crafts Studios and the summer school of New York's Art Students' League were established here. The art connection flourished, and today's village abounds in artists of all disciplines, both struggling and successful. To the visitor it's a sort of drive-in arts colony, but many of New York's best and brightest now live in Woodstock or have second homes here. To be honest, with a few exceptions you'll need to search hard beneath the tourist facade to truly original or even artistic – but that's half the fun.

Best time to visit is a weekday, when the town is a lot less crowded. Perhaps surprisingly, it's possible to find **rooms** without busting your budget, but they're limited and in the busy season an advance reservation is more or less essential. In the centre of the village the *Twin Gables Guest House*, 77 Tinker Street (914 679 9479), is Woodstock's best bargain – from $17.50 single, $27.50 double – but has a devoted following so reserve well ahead. Down by the Old Mill Stream the *Millstream House*, 38 Tannery Brook Road (914 679 8211), is a neat and trim place with doubles at $45 including breakfast, and the *Pinecrest Lodge*, Country Club Lane (914 679 2814), at the edge of the village has doubles for $55, again with breakfast.

Budget **eating** is also well served: *Duey's*, 50 Mill Hill Road is a good, inexpensive hangout, and the *News Shop* on the Village Green excellent for a bargain breakfast. For pizza, heroes, salads and lasagne, *Woodstock Pizza*, also on the Green, is a nifty choice, and the deli section of the *Grand Union Supermarket* on Mill Hill Road offers rock-bottom prices on sandwiches and takeout hot meals. Though not the cheapest place to eat, *Marty's Café Espresso*, 59 Tinker Street, was a hub during the 1960s and is still going strong with live music at weekends year round. What's more there's no cover charge, which makes the burgers and Italian dinner specialities quite reasonable.

Along with Marty's, *The Joyous Lake* on Mill Hill Road (914 679 9300) started life as one of Woodstock's choice **venues**: it still features up-and-coming bands, first-rate disco and modest admission charges. **Theatre** is mainly a summer event, with the noted *Woodstock Playhouse* on Mill Hill Road (914 679 2436) offering a lengthy season of drama and dance, and the *River Arts Repertory* at the *Birdcliffe Theater* on Byrdcliffe Road (914 679 2100) presenting sometimes stellar productions. There's **classical music** at the *Maverick Chamber Music Concerts* every summer Sunday on Maverick Road (914 679 8746). **Galleries** are littered throughout Woodstock and vary as much in style as quality: in addition to numerous commercial places, take in the *Art Gallery of the Woodstock Artist's Association*, 28 Tinker Street; the gallery/shop of the *Woodstock Guild of Craftsmen*, 34 Tinker Street; and the *Catskill Center for Photography*, 59A Tinker Street. And don't miss *Garden of Eve's*, a junk/bookshop at 5 Tannery Brook Road. For **listings** of events (and much more) the *Woodstock Times* is packed with information on and insights into the community. Tuning in to *WDST* (100m FM), Woodstock's radio station, is another good way of finding out what's happening.

Skiing, Walking and Sleeping – some practical details
The Catskill Park's facilities don't always come cheap: **Hunter Mountain Resort**, ski centre of the region, draws in New York City's crowds to its 37 trails and slopes from the end of November till Easter – it can, and does, handle 14,000 skiers an hour. Use of the extensive facilities costs $17 a day (2-, 3-, and 5-day reduced tickets available), plus there's full equipment hire. The *very* cheapest rooms go from $56 a double – ask at the *Hunter Mountain Lodging Bureau* opposite the entrance to the resort (10am-6pm daily; 518 263 4208).

Cross country and mountain **walking** is understandably popular, and there are miles of well-organised trails to follow. Best way to start is with the Department of Environmental Conservation booklet, *Catskill Trails*, available from 439 Main Street, Catskill, which details 30-odd routes and contains much useful advice. Whether you're walking or not the Catskills offer excellent **camping**. State campgrounds include the *Devil's Tomb stone Ground* 4 miles south of Hunter on Route 214 (914 688 7160); the

North and Shore Lake Ground 3 miles north-east of Haines Falls off Route 23A (518 589 5058); the *Kenneth Wilson Campground* 5 miles west of Woodstock on County Route 40 off Route 28, (914 679 7020); and, in the heart of the trails, the *Woodland Valley Ground*, 6 miles south-west of Phoencia.

THE EAST BANK: HYDE PARK, CLERMONT AND OLANA.

The Hudson's eastern bank rises and falls in the low hummocks and parkland that side the *Taconic State Parkway*, fastest if not most rewarding road to Hyde Park. Slower but more scenic is Route 9; and a good compromise is to take the Parkway and cross over to Route 9 via Route 84.

Finding a room on the east bank isn't as easy as on the west, something to bear in mind as you make your plans. For HYDE PARK best choice is a **motel**: most, like the *Colonial Motel*, 38 Albany Post Road (914/229 2444), start at around $35 for a double; the nearest **campsite** is in the *Mills-Norrie State Park* (914/889 4646), 4 miles north of Hyde Park on Route 9. In RHINEBECK *Kallop's Bed and Breakfast* is small but inexpensive: $15 single, $25 double.

HYDE PARK is a peaceful plateau of land with magnificent views of the river and, signposted off the Albany Post Road, the **homes of Franklin and Eleanor Roosevelt**. Though it's nothing like so rural as the home of the other President Roosevelt at Sagamore Hill, Long Island, the **house** (daily 9am-5pm, closed Tuesdays and Wednesdays from December to February; $2, ticket includes entrance to the Vanderbilt Mansion) where Franklin Delano Roosevelt was born and spent much of his adult life is pleasingly sited and well documented. It's not possible to see the whole place as it was badly damaged by fire a few years ago, but the newish **museum** more than makes up for this with extensive information, documents and photos of FDR's career. He was struck by polio in 1920, and the specially adapted car he drove is on show, along with photos from the war years, the plans for the New Deal and the letter from Einstein that led to the development of the first atomic bomb.

Roosevelt lies buried in the grounds of his home beside his wife **Eleanor**, a gifted and influential politician without whose aid it's unlikely his political career would have survived. Born Anna Eleanor Roosevelt, she was the niece of Theodore and a distant cousin of Franklin, and became active in liberal Democratic affairs after her husband contracted polio. In the early 1930s she toured the country, reporting to FDR on the living conditions of the unemployed and poor − an act that influenced the framing of the New Deal. After Franklin's death in 1945 Eleanor moved to **Val-Kill**, a nearby retreat she had had built 20 years earlier, from here carrying on her work as US delegate to the United Nations General Assembly and Chairman of the Human Rights Commission, and receiving dignatories such as Khrushchev, Tito, Haile Selassie and John F. Kennedy until her death in 1962. To tour the simple home of this remarkable woman, catch the half-hourly shuttle bus from the FDR house (open 10am-6pm daily from April to October; $1.95).

If the Roosevelt homes are examples of urbane humility, then the **VANDERBILT MANSION** further up Route 9 shows just how little taste big money can buy. Believe it or not, this was the smallest of the various Vanderbilt residences, built for Frederick, grandson of the railroad baron 'Commodore' Cornelius. From the entrance to the extensive grounds, McKim, Mead and White's Beaux-Arts building is pompously commanding. Inside, the mansion is gloomily elaborate, from the gilt and frills of the Rococo reception room to Louise Vanderbilt's gross recreation of a Louis XV boudoir. Because Frederick's marriage to Louise, a divorcee and socialite 12 years his senior, was disapproved of, he received the least inheritance among his siblings. On Louise's death he hid himself away in a small sanctuary here and set about increasing his inheritance to a fortune of $80 million. Regular tours of the mansion run from 10am to 5.30pm daily; admission is $1.95.

After these excesses you need some relief, and **CLAREMONT**, 22 miles north on Route 9 (turn west onto Route 6: the grounds are open 8am-sunset, the house Wednesday-Saturday 10am-5pm, Sunday 1-5pm, last tour 4.20pm; free) is just the thing. Home to several generations of the Livingstone family, Claremont's dignified Federal interior is one of genteel restraint, and the surrounding park, rich with fragrant lilacs and locusts, a delight. Inside the house is a portrait of **Robert Livingstone**, the man who negotiated one of the great bargain land deals of all time, the **Louisiana Purchase**. Back in 1803 Louisiana was the name given to a vast and vague territory covering roughly one-third of North America. These lands were controlled by the French, but Napoleon had already had his fingers burnt attempting to put down a revolt in the colonies, and realised that the combined strength of a native and American fighting force would be impossible to match, so he sold Louisiana – for $16 million. Livingstone and President Thomas Jefferson could hardly believe it: the land area of the United States had effectively been doubled, and for a fraction of the price they'd been prepared to pay. It worked out at 4 cents an acre: no wonder Livingstone looks so pleased with himself.

Claremont is pretty, no argument; but the real treat comes just one mile south of the Rip Van Winkle bridge, hidden away on a hillside.

'About one hour this side of Albany is the center of the world. I own it'. wrote the artist **Frederick Church** of **OLANA**, the home he designed and built. It's arguably the most attractive and certainly the best sited of all the Hudson Valley mansions: Church chose the spot above a bend in the river for its superlative views and the peculiar quality of light that he repeatedly sketched and painted. To improve on nature he re-landscaped Olana's hillside, placing an artificial lake to balance and reflect the Hudson, choosing and siting every tree. And the house itself was Church's almost obsessive passion. Built in a jokey Persian style with the help of Calvert Vaux and Richard Morris Hunt, he made 200 sketches of the staircase alone to fit it into his vision of a combined home, studio and gallery. Much of the inspiration came from his trips to Persia and the Middle East (the name *Olana* is Arabic for 'house on the hill') and the colours and rich motifs all have an enthusiastic eastern feel. An (obligatory) conducted tour takes in the various rooms filled with the bric-a-brac Church accumulated on his travels and a good proportion of his romantic canvasses: 'Pictures as vivid and mellow as if painted by sunbeams,' as one contemporary put it. The house is open from May 28th-September 5th, Wednesday-Saturday 10am-5pm, Sundays 1pm-5pm; September 7th-October 30th, Wednesday-Saturday 12am-5pm, Sunday 1-5. Tours are popular so phone in advance for a reservation – 518 828 0135. Tickets cost $1, 50c students.

Heading north from Olana you pass through **HUDSON**, and to be honest that's the best thing to do – its restored clapboard Victorian houses can easily be taken in without making a stop. Alternatively, if you're making for ALBANY it's quicker to cross over the Rip Van Winkle bridge to CATSKILL and pick up the 87 Thruway.

ALBANY

ALBANY made its money by controlling the east-west trade route of the Erie canal, and its reputation by being capital of the state. The governor's official residence is here, and the wheelings and dealings of the state bureaucracy roll on in the glassy Empire State Plaza that gives the city its futuristic skyline and contemporary identity. It's not a place to spend more than half a day or so (all you'll need to see are the civic buildings and a fine museum), but it forms a handy stop-off when heading up to Saratoga Springs and the Adirondacks, or Vermont and New England.

Arrive by *Greyhound* or *Trailways* and it's a bearable walk or bus ride to the centre; arrive by train and you're in RENSSELAER about 2 miles out of town – don't try and walk it, but catch a regular bus straight to the Plaza. Other than the small *youth hostel* at 46 Elm Street (518 434 4963), what budget **rooms** exist start at around $35 a double in out-of-centre hotels: contact the **Albany Conventions and Visitors' Bureau**, 600 Broadway, 518 434 1217 or 474 2418 (closed at weekends), who may also know of vacancies in the State University halls of residence in the summer. Bear in mind too that Albany's hotels fill almost as swiftly as Saratoga's in the racing season (August). Cheap central **food** is on offer from snack bars in the concourse, burgers etc. from *Jack's Diner*, 547 Central Avenue, pizzas from the *Little Antony* chain, 1095 Central Avenue or 128 Madison Avenue.

Piercing like an arrowhead into the confusion of downtown Albany, Nelson A Rockefeller's **Empire State Plaza** stands like an echo of the earlier Rockefeller Centre in New York City, the 42 storey **Corning Tower** supported by a bodyguard of four subsidiary buildings. The billion-dollar blocks went up in the 1960s and 1970s to house the offices of the State Legislature – and, no doubt about it, add architectural prestige to a workaday town centre. Ninety-eight acres of 19C Albany were torn down for this, and whatever you may think of that the Empire State Plaza is a well-conceived piece of urban planning, marginally more likeable than most. Come here by bus or car and you'll be delivered into the underground concourse, a sort of subterranean Main Street splattered with modern art. Information desks hand out maps and the *Visitors' Assistance Centre* (at the Capitol end of the concourse) co-ordinates conducted tours, but it's easy enough to follow the signs. For a lie of the land, the Corning Tower **observation deck** (daily 9am-4pm) seems

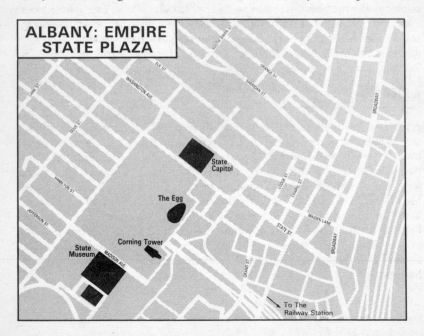

ALBANY: EMPIRE
STATE PLAZA

designed to make you feel like the conqueror of an invaded country, looking out across Albany's flyover to the Adirondack foothills, the Catskills and the Massachusetts Berkshires.

For the locals, at least, Albany's number one target is the **New York State Museum** (10am-5pm daily, hourly tours; free), the whole state revealed in imaginative if static natural history tableaux. There's an excellent section on New York City – better in fact than anything you'll find in Manhattan itself – with histories of immigration and skyscraper building, storefronts and period rooms, the original set of *Sesame Street* and a 1940 subway car to show you how much things haven't changed.

At the other end of the strip the **Capitol** building adds a little soul to the anti-human Plaza. A sandwich of Italian, French and Flemish Gothic, it's a reminder of an earlier period of civic grandeur, built at the end of the 19C for the then fantastic sum of $24 million – twice the bill for the Capitol building in Washington DC. The **conducted tours** (on the hour 9am-4pm daily, half-hourly in summer; free) pick out the opulent highlights: the Senate Chamber rich in Siena marble and carved mahogany, and the 'Million Dollar Staircase', festooned with carvings of governors, Presidents and sundry national heroes. Less ornate but more bizarre, another staircase busily interprets Darwin's theories of evolution.

A short walk from the Capitol the **Performing Arts Center** adds the only curves to the rigid angularity of the Plaza. Known as 'The Egg', there's not a straight line in it. Even if you don't catch a play, it's worth peeking inside; ask at the concourse information desk for tour details.

Other than this Albany has but a couple of mainstream attractions. A 20-minute walk or an 8 bus from the centre, **Historic Cherry Hill** (5321/2 South Pearl Street – walk down Broadway and turn left on to South Pearl Street; Tuesday-Saturday 10am-3pm, Sunday 1pm-3pm, tours on the hour; $2, students $1) is a better-than-average mansion that housed five generations of the Van Rensselaer family from 1787 to 1963, a continuity that makes for some interesting leftovers in the house's decoration. Back toward town, the **Shuyler Mansion** (bus 6 or 8; 27 Clinton Street, April-December, Wednesday-Saturday 10am-5pm, Sunday 1pm-5pm; free) was the house of Revolutionary notable General Philip Shuyler and his daughter Elizabeth, until she married Alexander Hamilton here in 1780. All this is enough for anyone in a single day, but for devotees of the Hudson Valley school of painting the **Albany Institute of History and Art** at 125 Washington Avenue (one block east of the Capitol; 9am-5pm, closed Thursday) has the best collection outside the Metropolitan Museum.

Chapter twelve
SARATOGA, THE ADIRONDACKS AND THOUSAND ISLANDS

With a few exceptions, the region stretching from Albany to the Canadian border is little explored except by mountaineers, hikers and those in search of specifically outdoor pursuits. Yet the area has plenty to offer beyond that. Above all there's the elegant spa and resort town of **Saratoga Springs**, whose genteel enticements are surrounded by delicate country

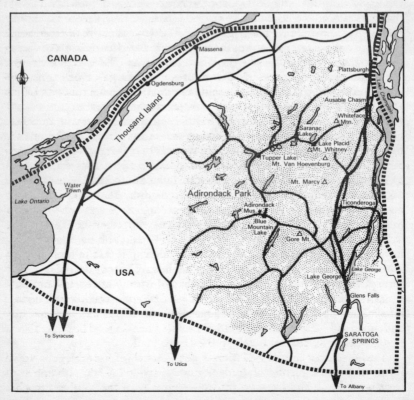

side which before long puckers into the wooded foothills of the **Adirondack National Park** – a mountainous area of startlingly wild, elemental beauty. On the way it's worth a stop at **Glens Falls** for the **Hyde Collection** of fine art, and at **Lake George** for the lake if not the town, which remains unashamedly tourist-smothered. From here buses either push straight up Route 87 to **Lake Champlain** and the Canadian border, or fork left for a loop of the Adirondack Park, taking in **Lake Placid**, centre of the region's considerable winter sports industry, and – beyond – the **Thousand Islands**: another nature area and popular haunt of water-sports enthusiasts.

SARATOGA SPRINGS

'At Saratoga,' wrote Henry James, 'you linger under passionate protest.' Maybe so, but it wasn't like that for America's wealthiest tycoons, and for well over a century being seen at **SARATOGA SPRINGS** was *de rigueur* for the north east's richest and most glittering names. The town first became known as a summer watering-hole in the days when its curative springs were medically fashionable; then, after a newly rich Irish boxer opened a casino and racecourse, it blossomed into a gambling and racing centre that brought the wealthy here in droves. The Morgans, the Vanderbilts, the Whitneys all had houses in Saratoga at one time, and Diamond Jim Brady, with his socialite and much-married mistress Lillian Russell, was one of the town's most ostentatious visitors.

Today, despite some alterations (notably the pulling down of the plush Grand Union Hotel and the closure of the casino), Saratoga retains the feel of a graceful summer resort. And while it may have at last deigned to admit the plebs, you get the impression it doesn't feel it has to make them *too* welcome. Bear in mind, also, that in August – the racing season – its population still increases threefold, so if you're shy of throngs of monied people, high prices (rates rocket upwards in August) or just don't want the hassle of trying to find a room, best keep away altogether then. The centre is fairly compact, but the town's attractions – the racecourse, the baths, its museums – are dispersed across a wide area so if you're on foot it's a good idea to orientate yourself with a **Saratoga Circuit tour**. These leave through the day in the summer months from the Drink Hall opposite Congress Park, take two hours and cost $8. For a full schedule and further information on the town the **Chamber of Commerce** is at 494 Broadway and open all year round Monday-Friday 9am-5pm. There is also a July/August **information booth** in the Drink Hall.

Outside August **accommodation** is not as much of a problem as you'd think: there are plenty of budget motels around – the Chamber of Commerce has a full list with prices – especially in the southern reaches of Broadway, with rates hovering around $30 for a double for most of the year; or try the *Spa Motel* at 73 Ballston Avenue (518 587 5280). For a touch more style and a central location, check in at the *Adelphi* (518 587 4683), bang in the centre of Broadway, where you can luxuriate in a nostalgic double room for $45 upwards, more in July and August. **Camping**, too, is easy: follow Route 9N out of town and you stumble across a number of sites, among them *Moskos*, about a mile out of town, and *Lake Tuckaway* and *Whispering Pines*, both at GREENFIELD CENTER some 4 miles from Saratoga. **Bikes** can be hired from the *Gideon Putnam Hotel* for around $10 a day, and **mopeds** from *Saratoga Moped Rentals* at 133 Broadway. Caroline and Phila Streets are the best places to look for **restaurants**, with a good concentration of downbeat eateries used by local students. Of these, *Hattie's Chicken Shack* is best, a soulfood hangout popular with ballet dancers from SPAC (see below) where you can eat excellently well for under $5. Alternatives are *Café Lena*, on the same street, or the *Court Bistro* on Court Street.

Broadway is Saratoga's main axis, and it takes in just about every aspect of the modern town, from the uglified shopping precincts, parking lots and motel signs of its southern end to the Victorian Gothic and Renaissance revival palaces of North Broadway, built by the very wealthiest of Saratoga's part-time residents and even now shuttered for the greater part of the year. **Congress Park**, which flanks part of Broadway, was carefully cultivated for the *curistes* who flocked here for the waters in the 19C, and it remains a shady retreat from the bustle of the main street. Look out for the old **casino**, a grandiose structure where Willie Vanderbilt once lost a cool $130,000 while waiting for the ladies to dress for dinner. It's one of the few of Saratoga's past attractions not to serve its original purpose, turned into a complex of **museums** showing off the local Historical Society's collection of sumptuous furniture drawn from the finest nearby houses.

The **Racetrack**, however, still functions very much as it did in the old days, and though somewhat engulfed by modern additions the grand old **clubhouse** can still be seen. Even if the races aren't on it's worth a look; if they are, better don your glad-rags. Should you find the races just a little intimidating – and you wouldn't be the first – try the **Harness Track** down on Crescent Avenue: White City to the racecourse's Ascot. The harness meetings here run several times a week between May and November and cost only $1.75 to get in. In case you don't get to either, make do with the **National Museum of Racing** on Union Avenue (Monday-Friday 9.30am-5pm, Saturday 12am-5pm, later during August), whose array of paintings, trophies and racing memorabilia are beautifully displayed and worth seeing even if you hate the sport.

The other side of South Broadway **Saratoga State Park** was planned as a spa resort along European lines, finished in 1935 with three sets of

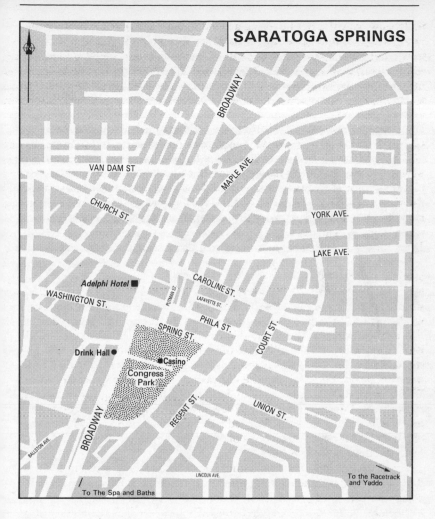

SARATOGA SPRINGS

baths, a couple of golf courses, a de luxe hotel – the *Gideon Putnam*, named after the man who built the first hotel here – and plenty of other healthy attractions. **Springs** are scattered all over, as they are in the city, but their high sulphorous content makes them best avoided unless you're here for a cure. Probably the most interesting feature of the park is **SPAC** (The Saratoga Performing Arts Center), home to the New York Ballet in July, the Philadelphia Orchestra in August, and with a host of other events throughout the summer season – check at the Chamber of Commerce for details, or phone 518 584 9330. Of the **baths**, only two are still open, the *Lincoln* in July and August and the *Roosevelt* all year round. A soak and massage costs $13 ($9 off-season) and is an ultra-relaxing way to spend 90 minutes. For an appointment call 518 548 2000/2010.

Finally there's **Yaddo**, a Georgian mansion set in some overgrown parkland near the racecourse where writers and artists have retreated to finish/start/rewrite novels, songs and creative works since 1926. Truman Capote wrote *Other Rooms, Other Voices* here, and Saul Bellow, Philip Roth and Leonard Bernstein are just a few of those who have used Yaddo's facilities to impose discipline on their muse. You can't visit the mansion – the artists who stay here observe a very strict routine and complete isolation is seen as essential – but you can explore the grounds to your hearts content. Open daily – 8am till dusk.

HEADING NORTH: GLENS FALLS AND THE HYDE COLLECTION

From Saratoga it's a short 30 mile or so jump up Route 87 to **GLENS FALLS** – 'a remarkably pretty town,' wrote Henry James, but really worth a mention only for the surprisingly good art gallery just outside town. This is the **Hyde Collection**, 161 Warren Street (June-August Tuesday-Wednesday/Friday-Sunday 11am-5pm, other months 2pm-5pm; closed January; $2, students $1, Wednesdays free), a clutter of paintings and sculpture gathered together by a couple of local paper magnates and housed in their antique-stacked pseudo-Italian villa. Plenty of well-known artists get a look in, though it has to be said that you rarely feel you're looking at their very best work. Among the better pieces are a couple of Winslow Homer watercolours, a tiny Botticelli *Annunciation*, soft, delicate and temptingly handbag size, and Picasso's *Boy Holding a Blue Vase* – a late Rose period study that smirks at two sugary Renoirs opposite. But the museum's pride, and justifiably so, are two paintings on the ground floor: the first, a *Head of a Negro* by Rubens, and, more strikingly, a *Portrait of Christ* by Rembrandt, painted in 1657 with all the characteristics of the artist's powerful later style – dark, with a vivid use of chiaroscuro, and pervaded by an overwhelming sense of sadness and loss. To see the collection you can either take a guided tour or just walk around on your own. Personally I'd go for the latter: when I was last there the guides were abysmal.

THE ADIRONDACKS

A region of mystery, over which none can gaze without a strange thrill of interest and wonder at what might be hidden in that vast area of forests, covering all things with its deep repose.

Fanciful perhaps, and over a century old, but these words, declaimed by one of the men responsible for preserving the wild beauty of the **Adirondack Mountains**, could just as easily be said today. Certainly the rugged grandeur of this region is hard to deny: 43 peaks of over 4000 feet cover an area that on its own could swallow Connecticut whole, much of which has since 1885 been turned over to a national park that ranks as America's largest. In summer there's nowhere more beautiful, the mountains purple-green and stretching far to the distance in shaggy tiers, in autumn the trees forming a gorgeous russet-red kaleidoscope that can leave you woozy with awe of the place.

Although the Adirondacks cover such an enormous area there are few towns of any size to plan your journey around, and it's difficult to recommend one single **route**. The more important targets – Lake George, Lake Placid, Plattsburgh – are linked by either *Trailways* or *Greyhound* bus, but you'll find it hard going and probably less rewarding without your own transport. Basically there are two options: either travelling by car, using Route 87 as an axis and branching off at will, or bussing it to a main town and, if you're into **hiking**, exploring the mountains from there. Hiking trails, campsites and the like are well-documented: pick up the two *I Love NY Camping* and *Accommodation* booklets; and, for trails, the Department of Environmental Conservation in Albany do an excellent series of *trail-guides*. (They have regional offices in Warrensburg, Northville and Ray Brook.)

The Eastern Fringes
LAKE GEORGE is a gentle introduction to the Adirondacks, a slim, knuckly finger of water dotted with islands and surrounded by curvy low mountains frosted with a soft sheen of birch and pine. Its beauty is a mild one compared with the fiercer terrain further north, but though much of the land around the lake remains almost impenetrable wilderness, you'll be surprised how its relative accessibility to excursionists from the south has left parts at least irreparably spoilt by some appallingly thoughtless exploitation. **LAKE GEORGE VILLAGE** is the worst offender, clasping the south-west corner of the lake in an ugly sprinkle of motels, gift shops and loud amusement parks. Its main street is good ground for cheap **rooms**, and there's a *youth hostel* a block away from the bus station. But really, unless you want to take a **boat excursion** around the lake (there are a variety of regular cruises, costing roughly $5-$10; call 518 668 5777 for a schedule), I'd push straight on north.

The village peters out into steep banks of pencil-thin birches scattered here and there with tiny wooden holiday homes and, on the right side of the road, grander summer mansions hiding out through the trees – relics of a time when the Adirondacks were a favourite destination with those Manhattan millionaires eager to rough it a bit. You can choose one of two routes from here; either pushing straight on up Route 87 or branching off on Route 9N, which follows the west bank of the lake up to **FORT TICONDEROGA**, straddling the gap between Lakes George and Champlain. This makes valiant efforts to recall its glorious record in the Revolutionary wars (it was attacked six times and only defeated three, the literature boasts), with daily drum and musket demos and a neat assembly of Revolutionary mementoes. (May-October daily 9am-5pm; July-August 9am-6pm).

From here the road edges up the slender southern reaches of Lake Champlain (across which you can take ferries from ESSEX – half-hourly in summer), joining up with Route 87 again a few miles south of **AUSABLE CHASM** (May 14th-October 16th daily 9am-4pm, July-August daily 9am-5pm; $9.95). It's worth the trip up here just to see this, a dead sheer gorge carved out in a series of tree-hung steps and rock drawers by the Ausable river as it flows into Lake Champlain. Tours, highly organised affairs that they are, don't come cheap but are well worth it, exploring the first half of the canyon on foot by means of gouged-out steps and steel gantrys, and the second part by boat. The most exciting part of the tour is the *Grand Flume*, where the boat squeezes between a gap scarcely more than 20 feet wide and later through some hair-raising rapids, at the end of which a bus ferries you back to the start. If you're staying, **rooms** come cheapest in neighbouring KEESVILLE: try the *Grand Prix*, *Rippling River* or *Villa Motel*, all on Ausable Street and none costing more than $30 for a double.

Nearby **PORT KENT** is a second terminal for ferries to the far side of the lake and the state of Vermont. Otherwise, continue north to **PLATTSBURGH**, a historic town that makes much the best base for exploring this part of New York State. **Rooms** are well-priced and easy to come by (there are any number of motels on Margaret Street, few costing more than $30 double, some as low as $15) and there's a stretch of sandy beach to bask on if the weather permits. When you've lounged long enough **boats** will show you the lake twice a day (phone 518 563 1000 for details) or **ferries** leave every 20 minutes from adjacent CUMBERLAND HEAD for Grand Isle, Vermont. Costs are $1.45 one-way for foot passengers, $5.95 for a car with driver.

Central Adirondacks
Route 28 leads north from Lake George into the forested heart of the Adirondack Park. Here the countryside has taken on a more savage

aspect, the mountains exposing shoulders of jaggy rock over which rivers tumble and cascade. Before long the road cuts a trail past GORE MOUNTAIN – a favourite ski resort (see p.321) – eventually reaching **BLUE MOUNTAIN LAKE**, where the **Adirondack Museum** sits snugly among the trees on the lake's northern bank.

This museum comes heavily plugged by the regional tourist authorities and repays a stop, if only for its comprehensiveness. Twenty buildings house a variety of exhibits which give the lowdown on every aspect of the Adirondacks, from surviving and getting about (by stagecoach or motorlaunch) to the native art of the region – the museum holds paintings by Cole and Homer in its broad collection. Try to see everything: some bits are more interesting than others but most is so lovingly displayed as to rouse even the most hardened townie. (June 15th-October 15th daily 10am-6pm).

From Blue Mountain Lake you can either continue west on route 28, through OLD FORGE and dropping down to UTICA and the main New York State Thruway, or push north on Route 30 to **TUPPER LAKE**, where there are some reasonably-priced **campsites** and a couple of **motels** if you feel you've gone far enough for the day. Try the *Park* (518 359 3600) or *Top Notch Motel* (518 359 9467), both on Park Street. After here Route 3 heads east to Saranac Lake – one of the most delightful small towns in the Adirondacks.

Set at the very centre of this desolate, depopulated region, **SARANAC LAKE** comes as something of a surprise: a small provincial centre which began as a lumbering village but rose to prominence as a health resort after one Edward Trudeau recovered from a fatal illness here and founded an institute so that others could do the same. The town has pulled in the rich and famous over the years – Albert Einstein, Robert Louis Stevenson and Somserset Maugham are just a few of the big names said to have stayed here – but these days it's something of a tourist trap, and you can expect to pay that little bit more for your **accommodation**. If you stay, the motels on Lake Flower Avenue are about the cheapest you'll get (try *Flint's* or the *Sara-Placid*), or there are a number of campsites on the islands in the lake. Alternatively, make the short journey to Lake Placid, just 10 miles or so down the road.

LAKE PLACID TOWN, so named although it actually rims the aptly tagged Mirror Lake, seems to be very much resting on its Olympic laurels. It's still a major winter sports centre, and if you walk the length of its short main street you'll find the references to its month or so of glory as venue of the 1980 Winter Olympics come thick and fast. You can't miss the **Olympic Center** where the principal ice events were held, though the **Intervale Ski Jumps**, a little way out of town on Route 73, are probably more exciting: take the elevator to the 90 metre summit and look out on the Adirondacks rucking far into the distance. You can take the Center and the ski jumps in on an **all-in tour** (details from the Chamber of Commerce), a high-thrill, high altitude affair which includes a two-stage **chairlift** ride to the top of nearby Little Whiteface Mountain and a close-up look at the so-called 'Champagne of Thrills' **bobsleigh run** on Mount Hoevenburg. Also, and even more dramatically, the tour takes you up the 8-mile-long **Veterans Memorial Highway** and through the core of Whiteface by elevator (if you can't stand lifts there are stairs). All this fills the best part of a day and at $10 a head works out pretty good value. But if you want to see just a couple of sights all are open individually: rates and times for the high season – *Intervale Ski Jumps* (daily 9am-5pm,; $3.50); *Bobsleigh Run* (daily 9am-4pm; $1); *Little Whiteface Chairlift* (daily 9am-4pm; $3.50); *Whiteface Memorial Highway* (daily 8am-6pm; $3).

The Olympics aside, there's not much else to Lake Placid, and you wonder what it must have been like before 1980. It's a pleasant enough base for the region though, smaller and less developed than, say, Lake George, its lakes – Mirror and Placid – with a more tranquil sort of wooded beauty. **John Brown's Farm** (Wednesday-Saturday 10am-5pm, Sunday 1pm-5pm), out on the road to the Olympic sites, is the only other thing to see. The famous abolitionist brought his family to this house in 1849 to aid a small colony of black farmers, and from here fought his campaign against slavery, organising terrorist forays into the southern states until he was hanged with six of his followers in 1859, and thus elevated, in verse and song, to the status of martyr and champion of liberty. His house is somewhat less interesting than his story, but it is free, and you may well like to make the pilgrimage here before ascending the giddy heights of the ski jumps next door.

If you are staying, there's a summer **youth hostel** (518 668 2634) on the corner of Main Street and Park Street, and a good scatter of **motels** on Wilmington Road, which leads from the Olympic Center towards Whiteface Mountain – try the *Cobble Mountain Lodge* (518 523 2040) or *Hi-Ridge Motel* (518 523 3938), both around $25 for a double. Or, if you're prepared to pay extra for a lakeside view, the *Mirror Lake Inn*'s (518 523 2544) cheapest doubles go for a little over $50 most of the year. Those **camping** can either use *Michaud's Motor Court*, out on the Cascades Road, or the *Adirondack Loj* (which also has rooms) out of town in the brooding shadow of 5344 metre-high Mount Marcy, the state's highest mountain. **Places to eat** and spend evenings are plentiful – *Gilligan's* seemed liveliest when I was around. For infor mation on all these things and more the **Chamber of Commerce** is at 90 Main Street.

A note on skiing and whitewater rafting
Obviously, **LAKE PLACID** is the best and most variably equipped centre

for winter sports, especially **skiing**, with Whiteface Mountain offering 28 slopes and trails at a cost of $17 per person per day, $19 at weekends. State-wide, the way to distinguish the relative difficulty of each slope is to look at the signs – green for easy, blue for moderate, and black for the experienced only. **GORE MOUNTAIN**, to the south-east, is the Adirondacks' second ski centre, with 41 slopes and rates broadly the same as Whiteface. There are, of course, numerous other smaller centres: for more information and details on the inclusive packages offered by motels, pick up a copy of the *I Love NY Skiing and Winter Sports* booklet.

More adventurously and, hour for hour, more expensively, **whitewater rafting** is fast becoming one of the area's most popular sports, shooting river rapids on rafts under the careful control of experts – an exhilarating business. Trips are run seasonally, dependent on weather and water levels, but most take place in spring and autumn when the rivers are high but not overly so. *Adirondack River Outfitters* (Box 649, Old Forge, NY13420; 315 369 3536) offer one of the best and most reliable ranges, from one-hour samplers to all-day expeditions, for anything between $10 and $70 per person. Similar companies include *Hudson River Rafting Co.* (Cunningham's Ski Barn, North Creek, NY 12853; summer 518 251 2964; rest of the year 518 251 3215) and *American River Expeditions* (Manchester, NY 14504; 716 289 6099). Write or call for brochures and full details.

THE THOUSAND ISLANDS

The slender strand of land known as **The Thousand Islands** – so called for the 1800 hunks of land which dot the broader stretches of the St Lawrence River – forms the north-western rim of New York State. This is about as far away from New York City as it's possible to get, which is the main reason few foreign travellers ever make it – and the fact that attractions, if you're not into water sports, are few.

In the south **OSWEGO** may tease you up from Syracuse for the day, a long-standing American naval base whose **fort** puts on some tired musket demonstrations and parading uniforms. Better to head north up Route 81, which forms a. spine for much of the Thousand Island region, to **WATERTOWN**, the area's principal settlement. This, though industrial and gloomy for the most part, is on the way to **CLAYTON**, starting point for cruises around the **Thousand Islands State Park**. These last 2¾ hours and run hourly between 9am and 4pm during the summer.

OGDENSBURG, the next town along, has the fine **Remington Art Museum**, which brags the world's largest single collection of paintings and bronzes by Frederick Remington – prolific recorder of the Old West. Beyond here there's almost nothing before you reach Canada, only

MASSENA, headquarters of the **St Lawrence Seaway Project**, in which a Visitors Centre gives a modernistic interpretation of the river and dam developments as well as inspiring views across the islands from an information deck. Once you've seen this, Canada is within spitting distance; or there's ample room for some straightforward lazing on the numerous islands.

Chapter thirteen

THE FINGER LAKES AND CENTRAL LEATHERSTOCKING

Stretching all the way from Rochester on Lake Erie to Albany at the head of the Hudson Valley, the Finger Lakes and Central Leatherstocking make up the rich agricultural heart of New York State – a region still comparatively unknown to foreign tourists but long popular with native New Yorkers. It's a large and disparate area, ranging from the fertile flatlands of the north towards Lake Ontario, to rugged low mountains enclosing the lakes further south and the green, pastoral heart of Central Leatherstocking to the east. **The Finger Lakes** fan out north to south, a series of narrow land-locked channels which, according to Iroquois legend, were formed when the Great Spirit placed his hand on the land in blessing and left behind a huge water-filled imprint. In fact, they were gouged out by glaciers during the Ice Age, a period from which there are tell-tale signs all over the region, in the form of drumlins, steep gorges and any number of waterfalls. There are eleven lakes in all, but six at most need figure prominently on your travels – **Canandaigua, Keuka, Seneca, Cayuga, Owasco** and **Skaneatles**. Travelling, because of the lakes, can be difficult if you want to cross east to west, and everywhere you'll find routes that much more circuitous than anywhere else. One way of doing things is to take the New York State Thruway as an axis and drop down to explore each lake and its environs individually. Generally speaking, major settlements – those that there are – are to be found at the heads and bottoms of the lakes, wooded wildernesses encasing the banks in between.

This is big **wine country** too, and the areas around Hammondsport on Keuka Lake, and on Seneca Lake, produce what are widely held to be excellent quality grapes and wines; you can visit most of the wineries and sample their wares, either indulging a week-long binge of touring and tasting or just taking in one or two. Most of the major wineries are listed in the text. Otherwise, there are few large towns to speak of: **Corning**, home to a couple of good museums, and **Ithaca**, site of Cornell University, are both good bases for the south of the region. Those apart you'll find most interest in the smaller centres and the gentle appeal of the landscape.

Central Leatherstocking – named after the protective leggings the frontiersmen who first settled here wore – unfolds west into the state's lushest farmland, bordered roughly by Route 81, which runs from Syracuse to Binghampton, the NYS Thruway and Route 88, all of which join up at Schenectady on the outskirts of Albany. Within this rough triangle **Cazenovia** and the **Musical Museum** at Deansboro are the most recommended stop-offs, with **Cooperstown** the best overnighter.

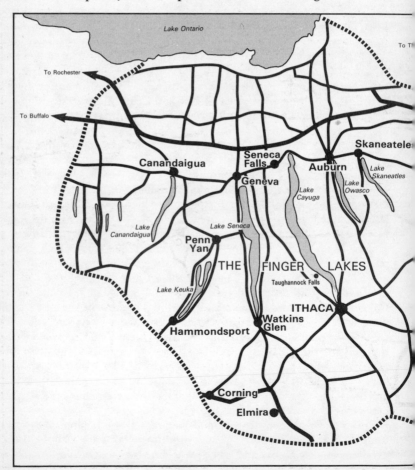

THE FINGER LAKES

First important town, and first turn off the Thruway, is **CANAN-DAIGUA**, which sits dignified at the top of the lake of the same name, a collection of statuesque Victorian houses fringing wide, tree-lined boulevards. Most people come here to see the grandest of these, the **Sonneberg Mansion and Gardens**, recently restored 19C home of a wealthy New York banker. Unfortunately, it's a sterile renovation, the house no more than a set of wearily furnished downstairs rooms, sectioned off behind forbidding braided ropes. The garden is better:

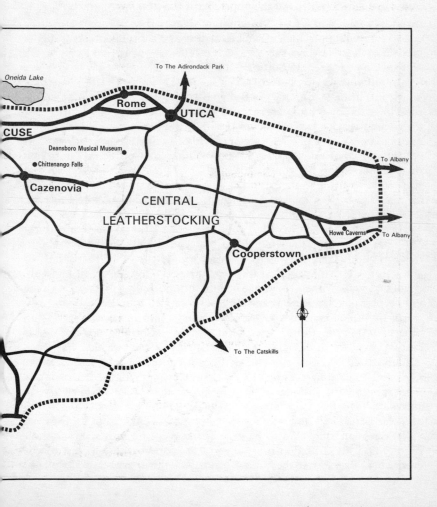

Italian colonnades edge French fleur-de-lys patterned flower beds, there are Chinese willow pattern gardenettes and Japanese landscapes planted in accordance with ancient Buddhist principles. But most looks slightly tatty and there seems little chance of the grounds ever being fully restored to their former glory. Frankly, and in spite of the free wine-tasting on the way out, it's barely worth the entrance price. (Daily 9.30am-6pm; $4.25; guided tours at 10am, 1pm and 4pm).

The road south from Canandaigua takes you to the next lake along, the rugged catapult of **Lake Keuka** with at its head the administrative centre of **PENN YAN**. Other than a classic American provincial high street there's not much here, and you'd do well to push on south to **HAMMONDSPORT**, centre of the Finger Lakes wine industry. There are five wineries in Hammondsport, and all offer free tours, but most people take the **Taylor and Great Western Tour**, easily the largest wine making concern in the state, which as well as tasting and a display of memorabilia lays on a short film on the local wine industry, which you can watch seated in a converted 35,000-gallon wine barrel.

Not all wineries are, however, the size of Taylor's, and for something a little less like a factory try the **Bully Hill Vineyard** a few miles down the road. It is run by a fifth generation Taylor (Walter S.) who restored this, the original Taylor family vineyard, with his father in the early 1950s, so becoming entangled in a legal dispute with Taylor's up the road which is still running. Basically, Taylor's – now owned by Coca-Cola – insist on their monopoly of the family name and have done everything possible to stop Walter S. from using it; forcing him at first to substitute blank labels on his wine bottles, and then, when this wasn't enough, to change the name of his wine altogether – hence Bully Hill.

The dispute goes on, but as you'll find out if you take a tour, Walter has other gripes with the wine industry. If you're lucky he'll be around to tell you about them personally – bitter though he is, he rarely fails to entertain. After you've tasted the wine stroll around the small museum, decorated with Walter Taylor's angry paintings. Bully Hill is open to the public Monday-Saturday 10am-3pm, with guided tours on the hour.

Twenty miles south lies **CORNING**, where two museums provide an otherwise undistinguished town with a good reason to stop. Corning is best known for its glass, especially *Steuben Glass*, which has been manufactured here since Frederick Carder started making his character istic art nouveau pieces in 1903. The **Corning Glass Center** (daily 9am-5pm; $2.50), includes an excellent *Museum of Glass*, which gives a complete history of glass, from ancient heads and amulets to the works of Tiffany and Galle and later more abstract pieces. Look out for the head of an Egyptian king (said to be the earliest piece of glass sculpture ever found), and the collection of 19C and 20C paperweights. Glass, too, is everywhere the motif in the building: external mirrors are carefully placed to angle the outside landscapes for indoor consumption, at the same time cleverly shielding the interior from direct sunlight. Adjacent is the *Hall of Science and Industry*, full of pushbutton exhibits on the wondrous properties of glass and its related technical breakthroughs, and, beyond that, the *Steuben Glass Factory* itself, where from behind a screen every stage of the production process can be seen. Outside, if you can afford it, buy some at the Steuben *Shop*, or content yourself with cheaper objects at the cut-price factory outlet alongside.

Corning's other star act is the **Rockwell Museum** (Monday-Saturday 9.30am-8.30pm, Sunday 9am-5pm; $2.50), 10 minutes' stroll away on the other side of Market Street, the town's hub and focal point for shopping and nightlife. This museum, assembled by a local entrepeneur and friend of Frederick Carder, has a larger collection of Steuben than the Glass Center (the world's largest in fact), an array of Victorian toys and, most interestingly, perhaps the best collection of Western American art you'll see this far east of the Rockies. Some of these are the visionary landscapes of Albert Bierstadt – his evocations of Yosemite and Mount Whitney painted with a studied grandiosity – others portrayals of primitive heroes and their relationship with the animal world. Best are the quiet reflective studies of native Indians by Joseph E. Sharp and E. Irving Couse; most striking the work of Frederick Remington, whose frontiersmen and cowhands, bucking broncos and gunslingers, sum up in heroic style the winning of the Wild West. A great collection, and if you never realised this era had been so well documented outside of John Wayne & Co., an education too.

That's about all there is to Corning, and if it's not too late I'd recommend you move on. If, however, you find yourself stuck, **rooms** are cheapest and most cheerful at the *Valley Lodge Hotel* (607 962 3518), a couple of miles out of town on Route 414, and evening **meals** best at either *Sorge's* (Italian/American) or *Wet Goods*, both on Market Street.

Continuing on Route 17 it's not long before you hit **ELMIRA**, which but for its fame as Mark Twain's summer home you could miss out altogether. Twain wrote most of his classic books here, and even if you're not a special fan it's worth taking a little time off for the exhibit on him in the local **Historical Society Museum** and his octagonal **study** relocated on the Elmira College campus. Look in, too, on the **Arnot Museum**, which houses minor works by European painters from Bruegel and Claude to Courbet and Picasso.

Heading north from Elmira it's a short ride up to **WATKINS GLEN**, known most widely for its championship motor racing circuit, rather less so for its spectacular **Gorge and State Park** All things considered it's this that steals the show, a cavernous gorge layered into glacier-cut strata and leading like a scene from Herzog's *Nosferatu* to 19 waterfalls, grottoes and overhangs, and above, some stupendous Finger Lakes views. For up-to-date details on prices, opening times, etc. phone 607 535 4511.

From Watkins Glen you can skirt **Seneca Lake** as far as **GENEVA** – a stately small town with a main street once described as 'the most beautiful in America' – or edge east to the next lake over, **Cayuga Lake**, and Ithaca at its southern end.

ITHACA is one of the most attractive towns of this region, piled San Francisco-like above Lake Cayuga and culminating in the towers of Cornell University. The university has been here since 1865, and it still provides the town's main and all-pervading feature. Take a walk around the campus and look in on the boxy **Herbert Museum**, worth visiting as much for its situation and views across the lake as for the mediocre collection of pictures inside. The rest of the university precincts you can either see on your own or take a guided tour, for information on which go to the **Chamber of Commerce** in the town centre at 122 West Court Street. As far as a **place to sleep** goes, there's a *youth hostel* (607 387 6716) just outside TRUMANSBURG, 13 miles from Ithaca, or the *Hillside Hotel* (607 273 6864), hard by the university at 518 Stewart Avenue, has doubles from $30. For **food**, use *Oliver's Deli* (415 College Avenue) or the *Chariot* (420 Eddy Street), although the heavy student presence means, as ever, that cheap eating, drinking and action are rarely hard to find.

Pick up Route 89 north from here and you soon run into one of the most impressive of the state parks that surround Ithaca – the **TAUGHANNOCK FALLS**. It's worth stopping off to admire the falls themselves, a slender body of water crashing through a chink on the curvy end of the canyon: higher than Niagara they say, and though not nearly so impressive, with a subtle kind of beauty nonetheless. You can pitch a tent here if you have one; if not carry on up Route 89 until you reach the top of Cayuga Lake and branch off left for **SENECA FALLS**, birthplace of women's suffrage in America and site of the first Women's Rights Convention back in 1848. The place where it all happened is currently (and ironically) a launderette, but the authorities plan to restore it as a shrine in the not-too-distant future. For the moment, make do with the **Women's Hall of Fame**, 76 Fall Street (Monday-Friday 10am-4pm, Saturday/Sunday 12am-4pm), which honours female achievements in a range of disciplines, and the **Women's Rights Visitors Center** at 116 Fall Street (Monday-Friday 9am-5pm, summer weekends 10am-4pm), through whom you can take a **walking tour** of the important related landmarks. These include the **houses** of Elizabeth Cady Stanton, ringleader of the original movement, and Amelia Bloomer, whose battle to get women out of their cumbrous underclothes is well documented.

AUBURN, a few miles east at the head of **Owasco Lake**, was home to another famous woman, Harriet Tubman, who led 300 slaves to freedom during the Civil War and whose **house** (315 253 2621) you can visit by appointment. Stop off also at the **Seward House**, one-time dwelling of the man who purchased Alaska and helped to form the Republican Party, with a set of period rooms peopled by mannikins making a brave attempt to recapture the lifestyle of an American statesman in the early days of the Union.

Lastly **SKANEATLES**, which crouches prettily at the neck of the last lake of any size, is the best and least crowded of the Finger Lakes resorts, and makes for a good spot to rest up and do some serious bathing. A mile or so down the western side of the lake is a good, relatively uncrowded **beach** and cove; a few miles further on there's a **marina** where you can hire water sports equipment. One problem is that **accommodation** is fairly sparse, but there are a number of motels dotted within a few miles of town, and the **Sherwood Inn** (315 685 3405), bang in the centre of Skaneatles, is not as expensive as you'd think – a double can be had for as little as $40.

ALONG THE NEW YORK STATE THRUWAY: SYRACUSE AND UTICA

SYRACUSE heralds the end of the Finger Lakes and the beginning of Central Leatherstocking, a lively modern city that made its name first for the production of salt and, more importantly, for its central position on the **Erie Canal**, which after a long battle between politicians and anxious taxpayers was finally opened in 1825. The canal was designed to link the Great Lakes with New York City via the Hudson, so cutting what until then had been hefty transport costs in half and facilitating the easy movement of goods along this all-important trading route. At first not everyone was in favour: Jefferson called the idea 'little short of madness'; other critics spoke of 'a big ditch' in which 'would be buried the treasure of the state, to be watered by the tears of posterity', and it took one man, De Witt Clinton, son of the former governor, to have enough faith in the project and drum up the money needed to dig the trench. The whole thing took 15 years, cost over a thousand lives and ended a good $3m over budget, but with it was spawned America's first generation of engineers, and the prosperity of New York City and the towns alongside rose almost overnight. A **museum** in the Weighlock Building on East Water Street tells the story of the canal and the **Erie Canal Center**, on Cedar Bay Road, has plenteous info on the resultant state park.

The canal apart, there's little else to Syracuse, but the presence of the university gives its downtown area a youthful feel worth taking in even if you don't want to stay. If you do, the *Downing International Hostel* at 459 Westcott Street (315 472 5788) offers the most central and inexpensive chance of a **bed**, and *Phoebe's* 900 East Genesee Street the closest you'll get to a budget meal. More information from the **Conventions and Visitors Bureau** at 100 E Onondaga St.

UTICA forms the next and, frankly, only worthwhile stop along the thruway, an industrial city with a large Italian minority and a pleasantly scruffy town centre. If you stop, call in at the **Munson-Williams Procter Institute** (Tuesday-Saturday 10am-5pm, Sunday 1pm-5pm) with works by Pollock, Gorky, Rothko, Klee and assorted items by Hopper and Malcom Morley in a sympathetic modern building – though it's Thomas Cole's characteristically stirring *Voyage through Life* series which stands out. Next door, and in stark contrast, the 19C **home** of the Munson, Williams and Procter families, whose collection this is, has been restored in period fashion (times as above). Give it five minutes before you disappear off to the other main attraction, the **FX Matt Brewery**, where you can join one of the free tours throughout the day in the summer months (winter 12am-4pm only). These take in the brewing and bottling plants and, though not exceptionally spectacular, do include a free mug of ale before you leave.

THE HEART OF CENTRAL LEATHERSTOCKING: CAZENOVIA AND COOPERSTOWN

Route 92 out of Syracuse takes you through the verdant heart of the Leatherstocking region, a gently undulating landscape of lush pasture and ploughland punctured with small orchards and copses. It's not long before you hit **CAZENOVIA**, where the main treats on offer are a pretty tree-ringed lake and another ancestral home, **Lorenzo**, furnished as ever in period style and set in some beautifully kept grounds. Afterwards, detour briefly to the **Chittenango Falls**: delightfully low-key and, in a countryside well-served by equally well-touted torrents of water, refreshingly picturesque – tumbling haphazardly over almost perfectly landscaped rocks. Climb down to the first overlook for the best view.

Another diversion worth taking if you've got wheels and the time is to the **Musical Museum** at **DEANSBORO** (April-December daily 10am-4pm; $3), a few miles off Interstate 20 on Route 12B. This is one of the state's best-kept secrets, a comprehensive display of musical instruments from grind organs, cylinder-operated musical boxes and more modern contraptions, all of which you can play. Don't miss the 1950s juke boxes out the back in a simulated ice cream parlour, fully functioning and packed with golden oldies; and Morgan's Bar, drinkless but with walls lined with some hilarious player pianos. An excellent, ear-ringing way to pass an hour.

But it's **COOPERSTOWN**, 40 miles further on, which forms Central Leatherstocking's most enticing target – an almost aggressively pretty village which sits graciously on the wooded banks of tranquil **Lake Otsego**. Its beauty was first spotted by William Cooper, father of James Fenimore, who planned the village out in 1790 and brought his family here to live. His more famous son, since tagged America's first novelist, later immortalised the place in his *Leatherstocking Tales*; he also, somewhat astutely for 1838, predicted the fate of Cooperstown today 'as one of resort for the inhabitants of the large towns during the warm months'.

That Cooperstown is well-touristed these days there's no question, but unless you're here at the height of the August onslaught you're unlikely to find the crowds too offputting. Its most obvious feature is the **National Baseball Hall of Fame** (daily 9am-6pm), housed in a tidy neo-Georgian building on Main Street just down the road from Doubleday Field where the game is said to have originated. It's an inspired musem: everything is displayed in such an attention-grabbing manner that even if you're not a fan of the sport (or know nothing about it) it's difficult to remain uninterested. Babe Ruth, probably the greatest baseball hero, gets an exhibit to himself, with a selection of personal effects arranged around his Yankee Stadium locker, and more of the game's greats are shown in action in a series of life-sized photographs that depict unforgettable baseball moments.

At $4 a time the Baseball Museum is fairly expensive, but it is possible to cut costs by buying a **combination ticket** for $9 that gets you into the baseball hall and Cooperstown's other two main attractions – the Fenimore House and Farmer's Museum, which lie opposite each other a short walk out along Lake Street (Route 80). The **Farmer's Museum** (May-November daily 9am-5pm, November-April Tuesday-Saturday 9am-5pm, Sunday 1pm-5pm) is a concoction of original rural buildings assembled from within a 100-mile radius of Cooperstown, attempting (and such attempts are common in America) to recreate 'the sounds, the sights, even the smells of yesteryear'. It's a bold try, and the buildings themselves – peopled by craft demonstrators in period dress and some bored-looking livestock – do well not to appear too contrived. When you've tired of this, pop across the road to the **Fenimore House** (May-November daily 9am-5pm, rest of the year variable; closed January-March), a Greek-revival mansion that was once home of the illustrious Coopers and now serves as a museum and general HQ of the New York State historical association. It mounts some enterprising exhibitions, mainly of American art, and numbers amongst its permanent collection a large and folksy set of 19C paintings, some by leading members of the Hudson School, and, less interestingly, Cooper memorabilia in rooms adorned with Cooper furniture.

Once you've seen this you've really seen Cooperstown, but the place itself is so inviting you may want to rest up for a bit. One-hour **cruises** of the lake leave from an office at the end of Fair Street, a block away from the Hall of Fame, and you can swim from the **beach** at the *Glimmerglass State Park* at the top end of the lake. The nearest **campsite** (and **youth hostel**) is *Beaver Valley*, 4 miles south on Route 28; for the closest and most realistically priced **bed** try the *Baseball Town Motel* on Main Street or, 3 miles away on Route 28, the *Major League Motor Inn*. **Evenings**, you can either fill up on burgers, chicken and the like at *Beeffees*, or Italian nosh at the *Glimmerglass Restaurant*, both on Main Street. There's a **Chamber of Commerce** office on Chestnut Street, near Main Street.

Pushing east, the only thing that might conceivably detain you before you reach Albany is **HOWE CAVERNS** (daily 9am-6pm; $7), a dark, drippy warren of caves which you can visit on guided tours; part on foot, part by boat across an underground lake. It's OK, but bearing in mind the cost, fairly predictable, and not really worth a special trip. If time is getting on you can **stop over** at the nearby *Howe Caverns Motel* for $35 a night. Otherwise it's a quick half-hour run down to Albany, the state capital.

Chapter fourteen

ROCHESTER, NIAGARA AND CHAUTAUQUA-ALLEGHENY

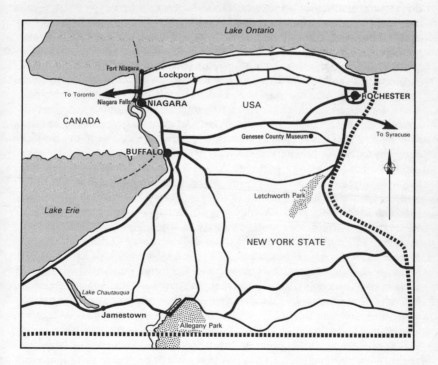

The thin end of New York State's wedge, the Niagara Frontier swallows up millions of tourists who venture nowhere else upstate – the **Niagara Falls** have been a fixture on grand tours of America for years, and inevitably dwarf the frontier's other places. Downtown **Rochester** is a smugly prosperous home to Kodak and a great photographic museum. **Buffalo** plays business headquarters to the state and is salvaged from mediocrity by one of the best art galleries outside Manhattan, and by its role as most convenient springboard for Niagara. **Chautauqua-Allegheny** has reminders of the original population of this part of North America, the Iroquois Indians. The Falls, though, overshadow all else with some justification: they're one of the most spectacular sights on the continent.

ROCHESTER

In contrast to the industrial mess that surrounds it, downtown **ROCHESTER** is a salubrious place. Loosely corralled by an inner ring road, the central office-block area is bordered by well-heeled mansions on spacious tree-lined boulevards. All in all it seems that Rochester is doing very nicely, thank you.

The money comes from the giant **Eastman Kodak** corporation, whose success has been the town's: the philanthropic ventures of George Eastman are all over the place – Kodak Park and the Eastman Theater, heading a seemingly endless list. Things haven't always been so rosy, however, for in the 1960s riots by dispossessed blacks shook the city and led to a rethink in urban planning. Today it looks as though the town has learned its lesson: coming over as a rich uncle eager to please, spoiling its charges with smart civic amenities. What's of interest lies in or around the downtown centre and can be seen in a day – which is for the best as accommodation is nowhere cheap.

After George Eastman had made his fortune with the Kodak camera, the first simple mass market device, he retired to a good looking Georgian-style mansion at 900 East Avenue. This has become the **International Museum of Photography** (Number 1 Park Avenue bus, get off at Barrington Street: Tuesday-Sunday 10am-4.30pm, conducted tours at 2pm; $2, students $1) and, as you'd expect with Kodak clout and finance behind it, is one of the best of its kind. The first floor has been left much as it was, all roomy grandeur and Georgian frills, with the *Mees Gallery* of cameras obscure, ancient and modern tacked on behind. Upstairs, the museum has a first-rate exhibition of photographs since the year dot: extensive *19C galleries* include work by Julia Margaret Cameron, David Octavius Hill, and Lewis Carroll's portrait of (the) Alice, along with five *20C galleries* that form an A to Z of modern greats – Steiglitz, Hine, Atget, Weston, Cartier-Bresson and loads of others.

You don't have to be mad about photography to enjoy the museum, but tours of the **Kodak factories** require a bit more dedication. There's a choice of two: the film and paper plant at 200 West Ridge Road, or the camera and equipment works, 900 Elmgrove road. Both are free and kick off daily at 9.30am and 1.30pm; 716 722 2465 for more details.

Susan B. Anthony isn't generally known outside the States, possibly since her life's work was aimed at the single domestic purpose of securing women the vote, possibly because male historians have chosen to exclude her. Throughout her life she championed the cause of woman's suffrage from her **house** at 17 Madison Street, whose exhibition today respectfully recounts a life for the most part scorned and slandered. In the Presidential election of 1872 Anthony led 16 women to vote, then a highly illegal and provocative act. The ensuing trial was a mockery, but the publicity it generated gave a considerable boost to the cause of universal suffrage, though this wasn't actually to be achieved until 1919. Related paperwork and memorabilia fill the house, which is open Wednesday through Saturday 11am-4pm.

Rochester's newest crowd-puller is a sleek blockbuster on Manhattan Square: the **Margaret Woodbury Strong Museum** (Tuesday-Saturday 10am-5pm, Sunday 1pm-5pm; $2, students $1.50). This documents middle-class life in 19th century America in exhibitions showing growth and industrialisation through the domestic arts and crafts that were produced. It's all here in copious detail – Margaret Woodbury Strong collected omnivorously, with unlimited funds to help. Perhaps that's why, despite the excellence of the pieces, the museum doesn't always come off – one exhibition is titled '*Collecting: the endless quest*', which in a way defines Strong's undirected philosophy. On the second floor thousands upon thousands of toys and dolls sit card-filed and crammed into display cases. For me there was just too much to see: afficionados of Victoriana will have a field day.

Staying and leaving

From the **Amtrak station** and **Greyhound drop-off** it's possible to walk to the **city bus station** near the shopping centre (*Trailways* conveniently take you straight there). From here buses run to the museums; there's a flat fare of 70c in the city. Chances are you won't have time to move far from Rochester's centre: if so the cheapest **accommodation** option is the *Holiday Inn* at 120 Main Street East (716 564 6400) with doubles at around $70; otherwise you're stuck with the **youth hostel** (315 597 5553) out at PALMYRA, 20 miles from Rochester on Route 21 and reachable by bus. There's a lively if mainstream **music scene** to check out – pick up a copy of the giveaway *Freetime* for excellent listings, plus restaurant bargains and happy hours. *Shatzees*, 21 Richmond Street (716 454 4612) and *Scorgies*, 150 St Andrews Street (716 232 9661) are the most interesting venues, with a slant towards new wave.

Leaving Rochester, a choice of roads takes you west towards Buffalo and Niagara, the slow routes 104 and 31/31A dipping through wide sweeps of wheat and pasture, and a succession of one-horse-towns with names like *Clarkson*, *Johnson's Creek* and *Model City*. The faster way west is out on US 490 to pick up the US 90 thruway which runs to Buffalo. En route, the **Genesee County Museum** (May-October, 10am-4pm daily, 10am-5pm in summer; $6.75) has yet another gathering of 18C and 19C houses spread around a park. It's as pretty and interesting as any other – and consequently a pricey day out for the inflated admission price. Conceivably, you could also continue south to **LETCHWORTH PARK**, stopping off, if time's no problem, to gaze over the 600-foot drop of the 17-mile-long **Genesee River Gorge**.

BUFFALO

As the thruway sweeps down into **BUFFALO** the town centre rises up in a looming cluster of Art Deco spires and glass box skyscrapers – Manhattan in miniature on Lake Erie. But that's a slight comparison: despite the impressive City Hall and shavings of park scattered about, Buffalo smacks of much money and precious little soul. A great art gallery goes some of the way to redeem things, but first and foremost Buffalo is a business town: most people visit because they have to, and expense accounts pay the way. Give it a day at the most.

The **Albright-Knox Art Gallery** (1285 Elmwood Avenue, bus from station, Tuesday-Saturday 11am-5pm, Sunday 12am-5pm; donation required) at the northern end of town is what in the end makes Buffalo worth a visit. The museum gives a good account of American painting from the 19C on, but is strongest in American and European art of this century and especially the last thirty years: the Colour Field painters, Abstract Expressionism, Pop, Op and Kinetic Art are on show, Rothko, Pollock, Lichtenstein and Rauschenberg among the names. The diverse movements and styles of the 1960s and 1970s get a good look in, gallery information is first-rate, and there's a fine, selective group of sculptures. This is one of the best museums in the state and would hold its own in New York City. Don't miss it.

For the rest, the **Theodore Roosevelt Inaugural National Historic Site** at the **Wilcox Mansion** (641 Delaware Avenue, Monday-Friday 10am-5pm, Saturday – Sunday 12am-5pm; 50c) hark back to the one notorious episode in Buffalo's history. In 1901 **President McKinley** was shot and wounded while attending an exhibition here, and though he quickly recovered, the surgeons had botched the operation and the unfortunate President contracted gangrene and died. McKinley had been a guest at the Wilcox Mansion and it was here that Roosevelt was sworn in as his successor, beginning his eight-year career of waving America's big stick and assassinating the wildlife of three continents. Scrappy odds and ends relate to both men, but if you've visited Sagamore, Long Island (see p.289), there's nothing really new. If you're interested, the Wilcox house is also starting point for architectural **walking tours** of the city – phone 716 884 0095 for more details.

The other site you're steered to is the **Naval and Servicemen's Park** off Marine Drive (April-November Monday-Friday 10am-5pm, Saturday-Sunday 10am-6pm; $3.50) a museum 'of naval history containing memorabilia of the sea, sailors and naval engagements of yesteryear' which wasn't my cup of tea at all, though the cruiser *Little Rock* was almost worth it for the grotesque mannikins within. Navy freaks only need apply.

A few essentials

Downtown Buffalo untangles itself as a cobwebby mesh with City Hall landmarking the centre. It's the second largest city in the state and too big to negotiate on foot – the **bus station** at the north division of Church and Ellicott Streets links the centre with outlying places. For **food** the usual fast joints are dotted about, but much more interesting (and not much more expensive) is the *Broadway Market* area (999 Broadway, closed Wednesday and Sunday) with its Balkan, Polish and German restaurants. *Garcia's Irish Pub* at 74-76 Pearl Street (716 856 0111) also comes recommended. Two further drinking possibilities are the *Continental*, 212 Franklyn, near Court Street (716 842 1292) which boasts punk bands five nights a week, or the more sedate *Anchor Bar*, 1047 Main Street (716 886 8920), where the local specialities – chicken wings and blue cheese dressing – are said to have originated, and with jazz each weekend. For **accommodation** downtown the *Lenox Hotel*, half-an-hour from the station at 140 North Street at Delaware (716 884 1700) is the only possibility this side of extravagance: doubles from $42. In the suburbs prices cheapen out – doubles at $30 at the *Sheridan Park Motor Hotel*, 40 Grand Island Boulevard, Tonawanda (716 873 8776).

From Buffalo it's a 20-mile drive on route 190 to what the publicity people always call the 'most accessible wonder of the world'.

NIAGARA FALLS

It is merely a great deal of water falling over some cliffs. But it is very remarkably that.

Rupert Brooke *Letters from America*

You hear it before you see it. Three-quarters of a million gallons of water a second exploding as it drops with awesome power, crushing and fracturing on the knife-edge rocks below. By any standards the **Niagara Falls** are impressive, and made more so by the variety of methods laid on to get you closer: boats, catwalks, observation towers and helicopters push you as near to the curtain of water as they dare, and the simple enormity of it all is mind-blowing. It's not difficult to see why the Falls are one of America's top tourist attractions, neither is it difficult to envisage the crowds that flock here as a result. You can take in the Falls from both the US and Canadian towns (they're most impressive from the Canadian side, reachable by direct bus from Buffalo), though don't expect much more from either – no one ever came here to enjoy downtown Niagara.

Arriving and staying

Turn up at or near the **bus station** and you're next door to the **Welcome Center** on Niagara Street, who can help with **rooms**. Worth trying are the *Uptown Motel*, 492 Main Street (716 285 8366) with doubles from $28; the *Coachman Motel*, 523 3rd Street (716 285 2295), doubles at $30; or the *Big Tree Tourist Home*, 40 Niagara Street (near Rainbow Bridge; 716 285 9258), some doubles below $30. Unless you have a YHA card these prices aren't much above what you'll pay at the *Frontier Youth Hostel*, 1101 Ferry Avenue, corner of Memorial Parkway (716 282 3700) or the *YMCA*, 1317 Portage Road (716 285 8491) though the YMCA does reductions for women with their own sleeping bags. Failing this, Route 62 east of 190 has a near endless chain of **motels** with doubles from $20 if you shop around. The nearest **campsites** are further out still with *KOA Niagara Falls North* at 1250 Pletcher Road, Lewiston (716 754 8013). Be warned that the other site on Grand Island Boulevard comes described as 'Fantasy Island'.

For cheap **eats** there's a 24-hour *Howard Johnson's*, a *Burger King* and *Dante's Pizzeria* all on Main Street; picnicking on Goat Island is a good alterative; and though it's out of the way, *The Bakery and Ports of Call Restaurant*, 3004 Niagara Street, is a great place to drink and meet the locals.

The Falls

Niagara's Falls were formed about 12,000 years ago when the retreat of melting glaciers allowed water trapped in Lake Erie to gush north to Lake Ontario. As the water spilled over the ridge it cut away at the rock, spawning the first falls 7 miles downstream. On the US side the **American Falls** and the **Bridal Veil Falls** stretch straight in a drop of 194 feet, while across the border the **Horseshoe Falls** curve round slightly lower. You can get the best view of both from the **Prospect Point Observation Tower** (daily; 25c) or from **Goat Island** and its park in between. On the island you're within spitting distance of the rapids, and the daring of the various nutcases who attempted to go over in barrels seems even more suicidal. This practice was prohibited some years ago, though in 1960 Roger Woodward, a 7-year-old, went over and survived to tell the tale. Just how remarkable this was comes home if you take the half-hour *Maid of the Mist* **Boat trip** (from the foot of the observation tower, mid-May-mid-October, Monday-Friday 10am-5pm, Saturday-Sunday 10am-6pm;

$4.25), a deafening circuit in the swirling waters. As you stand dripping, reflect that you're only seeing about half the flow of water – the rest is diverted to hydro-electric power stations. At night the falls are illuminated, the coloured waters dramatically tumbling into blackness; and, should you come here in winter, the whole scene changes as the falls freeze in fantastic razor-tipped megaliths.

Town and country
You can only look at a waterfall for so long, and though they've tried to tart **NIAGARA TOWN** up with a tropical winter-garden and convention/ shopping centres, it's still pretty grotty. The single thing worth turning your back to the Falls for is the **Native American Center**, 25 Rainbow Mall (May-September 9am-6pm; other months Tuesday-Friday 9am-5pm, Saturday-Sunday 12am-5pm; $3, students $1) symbolically shaped as a turtle: Indian cosmology describes the earth being created on a turtle's back. As well as an exhibition of Indian crafts and life there are daily dancing displays by Iroquois Indians, which – though laid on for the tourists – are well worth it.

With your own transport it is possible to trace the **Niagara Valley** along the Robert Moses Parkway to the **Whirlpool**, a violent maelstrom of broken timbers and flotsam slowly being crushed in the circling waters.

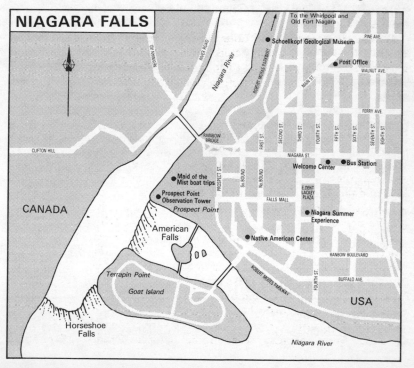

Every so often canoeists try to shoot the rapids here (the breakers are much bigger than you might think): the last lot to do so had to be rescued by helicopter.

A few miles further on the **Niagara Power Project Visitors' Center** might tempt the curious, though really the best thing about it is the view across the deep valley to Canada. I'd head on for **Old Fort Niagara** at Youngstown (July 1st-Labor Day daily 9am-7.30pm; $3: for other hours phone 716 745 7611), a likeable restoration of fortifications manned variously by the French, British and Americans since 1726, when the fort controlled the route from the St Lawrence river to the Great Lakes and the west. On summer weekends costumed enthusiasts give musket demonstrations and re-enact their favourite battles, and the mill pond of Lake Ontario can be swum in if you're circumspect. Good fun and about half an hour's slow drive from Niagara.

Alternatively it's quite straightforward to **cross the border** by foot to **NIAGARA, ONTARIO**. Simply take your passport and pay a small charge to go across the Rainbow Bridge: the rewards are arguably better views and a lot more tawdry commercialisation. Prices are no cheaper than on the other side, and you don't even get a stamp in your passport.

Niagara Listings
Airport Buffalo airport is an hour from the Falls by *Niagara Scenic Buses*. Hourly pick-ups from the bus station, fare $8.
Amazing fact If the Niagara Falls were beer, enough would spill over in a second to supply you with a pint a day for the next 15,342 years.
Amtrak Information 1 800 523 5270
Cave of the Winds Or the Cave of the Drips. A passage leading to the base of the Bridal Veil Falls (daily in summer, $3.50). For those without the nerve to go on the *Maid of the Mist*.
Greyhound Bus Stop Main Street and Pine Avenue.
Helicopter flights From the Rainbow Bridge end of Main Street. The most exciting way to see the Falls – prices $12 up and worth every cent.
Niagara Summer Experience Free concerts and theatre plus enthusiastically 'ethnic' evenings. July and August weekends at the E. Dent Lackey Plaza.
Post office Corner of Walnut Avenue and Main Street.
Schoelkopf Geological Museum Audio-visual explanation of the Falls for geology buffs. Off the Robert Moses Parkway, open daily.

CHAUTAUQUA-ALLEGHENY

CHAUTAUQUA-ALLEGHENY forms the south-west corner of New York State, running between the Niagara frontier and the ruler line of the

Pennysylvania border. This is way off the tourist track, visitors being put off by the distance and lack of specific 'sights'. In all fairness, they're probably right – nothing you can put your finger on is a must, though the incidentals are appealing enough. **CHAUTAUQUA** itself stands by the lake that takes its name, a thin trigger reaching down to **JAMESTOWN**, whose claim to fame is its **Heritage Museum of Childhood** (dolls, toys, etc.) at 314 West 5th Street.

Picking up Route 17 in Jamestown leads to **SALAMANCA**, which without any apparent irony brags of being 'the only city in the world located on an Indian reservation'. This is the starting point for trips into the **Allegheny State Park** and, in the other direction, the **Seneca-Iroquois National Museum** (off Route 17 on the Indian Reservation, May-October Monday-Saturday 10am-5pm, Sunday 12am-5pm). As you'd imagine from the place and river names all around this was once the Iroquois homeland, and the museum traces their history, including the humiliating defeat inflicted on the Delaware tribe when all their warriors were made 'honorary women'. It's also possible to go on **tours** of the reservation which include an Indian foods dinner: contact *Tribal Public Relations* on 716 945 3895 for more details.

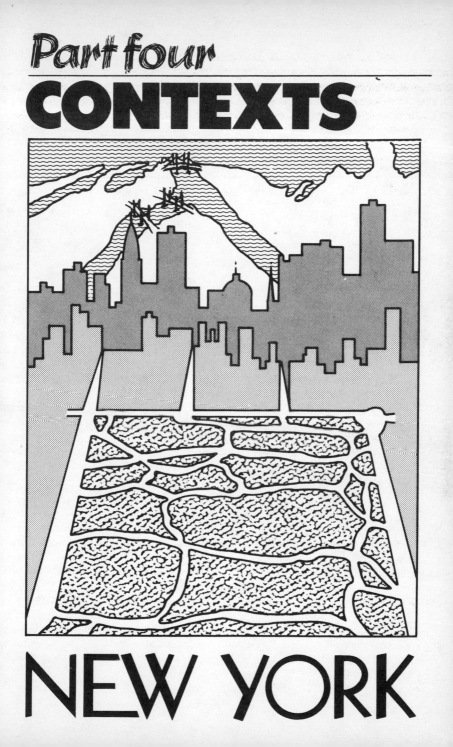

Part four
CONTEXTS

NEW YORK

THE HISTORICAL FRAMEWORK

*To Europe she was America, to America
she was the gateway of the earth. But to
tell the story of New York would be to
write a social history of the world.*
                              H.G.Wells

Early Days – and Colonial Rule

In the earliest times the area that is today
New York City was populated by Native
Americans. Each tribe had its own territory and lived a settled existence in
villages of bark huts, gaining a livelihood
from crop planting, hunting, trapping
and fishing. In the New York area the
Algonquin tribe was the most populous.
Survivors of this and other tribes can still
be seen at Long Island's **Shinnecook
reservation** – as well as remnants of
native culture at the upstate Turtle Center for the Native American Indian.

The native lifestyle represented a continuum of several thousand years, one
that was to end with the arrival of
European explorers. In 1524 **Giovanni
da Verrazano**, an Italian in the service of
the French King Francis 1, arrived, following the footsteps of Christopher Columbus thirty two years earlier. On his
ship, the *Dauphane*, Verrazano had set
out to find the legendary North West
Passage to the Pacific; instead he discovered **Manhattan**. 'We found a very
agreeable situation located within two
small prominent hills, in the midst of
which flowed to the sea a very great
river, which was deep within the mouth;
and from the sea to the hills, with the
rising of the tide, which we found eight
feet, any laden ship might have passed'.
Verrazano returned, 'leaving the said
land with much regret because of its
commodiousness and beauty, thinking it
was not without some properties of
value', to woo the court with tales of
fertile lands and friendly natives, but
oddly enough it was the best part of a
century before the powers of Europe
were tempted to follow him.

In 1609 **Hendrik Hudson**, employed
by the **Dutch East India Company**,
landed at Manhattan and sailed his ship,
the *Half-Moone*, as far as Albany. Hudson found that the river did not lead to
the North West Passage he had been
commissioned to discover – but in
charting its course for the first time gave
his name to the mighty river. 'This is a

very good land to fall with', noted the
ship's mate, 'and a pleasant land to see'.
In a series of skirmishes Hudson's men
gave the native people a foretaste of
what to expect from future adventurers.
Hudson sailed home to England, where
he was promptly ticked off for working
for the Dutch and sent on another
expedition under the British flag: arriving
in Hudson Bay, the temperature falling
and the mutinous crew doubting his
ability as a navigator, Hudson, his son
and several others were set adrift in a
small boat on the icy waters – where,
presumably, they froze to death.

The British fear that the Dutch had
gained the upper hand in the new found
land proved well justified, for they had
the commercial advantage and wasted
no time in making the most of it. In the
next few years the Dutch established a
trading post at the most northerly point
Hudson had reached, **Fort Nassau**. In
1624, four years after the Pilgrim Fathers
had sailed to Massachusetts, thirty families left Holland to become New York's
first European settlers, most sailing up to
Fort Nassau but a handful – eight families in all – staying behind on a small
island they called Nut Island because of
the many walnut trees there; today's
Governor's Island. Slowly the community
grew as more settlers arrived, and the
little island became crowded; the decision was made to move to the limitless
spaces across the water, and **the settlement of Manhattan**, an Indian word
whose meaning is uncertain, began.

The Dutch gave their new outpost the
name **New Amsterdam** and in 1626
Peter Minuit was sent out to govern the
small community of just over three hundred. Among his first, and certainly more
politically adroit, moves was to buy the
whole of Manhattan Island from the
Indians for trinkets worth 60 guilders
(about £20 today); though the other side
of the anecdote is even better – for the
Indians Minuit dealt with didn't even
come from Manhattan, let alone own it.
As the colony slowly grew, a string of
governors succeeded Minuit, the most
famous of them **Peter Stuyvesant** –
'Peg Leg Pete', a seasoned colonialist
from the Dutch West Indies who'd lost
his leg in a scrap with the Portuguese.
Under his leadership New Amsterdam

doubled in size and population, protected from British settlers to the north by an encircling wall (**Wall Street** today follows its course) and defended by a rough-hewn fort on what is now the site of the Customs House. Stuyvesant also built himself a farm (a *bowerie* in Dutch) a little to the north, that gave its name to the **Bowery**.

Meanwhile the **British** were steadily and stealthily building up their presence to the north. Though initially preoccupied by Civil War at home, they maintained their claim that all of America's East Coast, from New England to Virginia, was theirs, and in 1664 sent a Colonel Richard Nicholls to claim the lands around the Hudson that King Charles II had granted to his brother, the Duke of York. To reinforce his sovereignty Charles sent along four warships and landed troops on Nut Island and Long Island. The Dutch settlers had by then had enough of Stuyvesant's increasingly dictatorial rule, especially the high taxation demanded by the nominal owners of the colony, the Dutch West India Company, and so refused to defend Dutch rule against the British. Captain Nicholls' men took New Amsterdam, renamed it **New York** in honour of the Duke and settled down to a hundred-odd years of British rule, interrupted but briefly in 1673 when the Dutch once more managed to gain the upper hand.

During this period not all was plain sailing. When King James III was forced to abdicate and flee Britain in 1689, a German merchant called **James Leisler** led a revolt against British rule. Unfortunately for Leisler it mustered little sympathy, and he was hanged for treason. Also, by now black slaves constituted a major part of New York's population, and though laws denied them weapons and the right of assembly, in 1712 a number of slaves set fire to a building near Maiden Lane and killed nine people who attempted to stop the blaze. When soldiers arrived, six of the incendiaries committed suicide and twenty one others were captured and executed. In other areas primitive civil rights were slowly being established: in 1734 **John Peter Zenger**, publisher of the *New York Weekly Journal*, was tried and acquitted of libelling the British government, establishing freedom for the press that would later bring about the First Amendment to the Constitution.

Revolution

By the 1750s the city had reached a population of 16,000, spread roughly as far north as Chambers Street. As the new community became more confident, so it realised that it could exist independently of the government in Britain. But in 1763 the **Treaty of Paris** concluded the Seven Years' War with France, and sovereignty over most of explored North America was conceded to England. British rule was thus consolidated and the government decided to try throwing its weight about. Within a year, discontent over British rule escalated with the passage of the punitive **Sugar, Stamp and Colonial Currency Acts**. Further resentment erupted over the **Quartering Act**, which permitted British troops to requisition private dwellings and inns, their rent to be paid by the colonies themselves. Ill-feeling steadily mounted and skirmishes between soldiers and the insurrectionist **Sons of Liberty** culminated in January 1770 with the killing of a colonist and the wounding of several others. **The Boston Massacre**, in which British troops fired upon taunting protestors, occurred a few weeks later and helped formulate the embryonic feelings of the Revolution.

In a way, New York's role during the **War of Independence** was not crucial, for all the battles fought in and around the city were generally won by the side that lost the war. But they were the first military engagements between the British and American forces after the **Declaration of Independence**, proclaimed to the cheering crowds outside the site of today's **City Hall Park**, who then went off to tear down the statue of George III that stood on the Bowling Green. The British, driven from Boston the previous winter, resolved that New York should be the place where they would reassert their authority over the rebels, and in June and July of 1776 some two hundred ships under the command of **Lord Howe** arrived in New York Harbour. The troops made camp on Staten Island while the commander of the American forces, **George Washington**, consolidated his men, in the hope that the mouth of the harbour was sufficiently well defended to stop British ships from entering it and encircling his troops. But Howe managed to slip two frigates past Washington to moor north of the city and decided to make his assault on the city by land. On August 22nd he landed 15,000 men, mainly Hessian mercenaries, on the south west corner of Brooklyn. His plan was to occupy Brooklyn and launch an attack on Manhattan from there. In the **Battle of Long Island**, Howe's men penetrated the American forward lines at a number of points, the most important engagement taking place at what is today Prospect Park.

The Americans fell back to their positions and as the British made preparations to attack the fortifications, Washington could see that his garrison would be easily defeated. On the night of August 29th, under cover of rain and fog, he evacuated his men safely to Manhattan from the ferry slip beneath where the Brooklyn Bridge now stands, preserving the bulk of his forces. A few days later Howe's army set out in boats from Green Point and Newtown Creek in Brooklyn to land at what is now the 34th Street heliport site. The defenders of the city retreated north to make a stand at Harlem Heights, but were pushed back again to eventual defeat at the **Battle of White Plains** in Westchester County (the Bronx), where Washington lost 1400 of his 4000 men. More tragic still was the defence of **Fort Washington**, perched perched on a rocky cliff 230 feet above the Hudson, near today's George Washington Bridge. Here, rather than evacuate the troops, the local commander made a decision to stand and fight: trapped by the Hudson to the west it was a fatal mistake, and upwards of 3000 men were killed or taken prisoner. Gathering more forces Washington retreated, and for the next seven years New York was occupied by the British as a garrison town. During this period many of the remaining inhabitants and most of the prisoners taken by the British slowly starved to death.

Lord Cornwallis's **surrender** to the Americans in October 1783 marked the end of the War of Independence, but it was not until two years later, in November 1785, that New York was finally relieved. Washington, the man who had held the American army together by sheer will power, was there to celebrate, riding in triumphal procession down Canal Street and saying farewell to his officers at **Fraunces Tavern**, a building that still stands at the end of Pearl Street. It was a tearful occasion for men who had fought through the worst of the war

years together: 'I am not only retiring from all public employments,' he declared, 'but am retiring within myself'.

But that was not to be. New York was now the fledgling nation's **capital** and, as Thomas Jefferson *et al.* framed the Constitution and the role of President of the United States, it became increasingly clear that there was only one candidate for the position. On April 30th 1789 Washington took the oath of President at the site of the **Federal Hall National Memorial** on Wall Street. The federal government was transferred to Philadelphia a year later.

Immigration and Civil War

In 1790 the first official census of Manhattan put the population at around 33,000: business and trade were on the increase, with the market under a buttonwood tree on Wall Street being a forerunner to the New York Stock Exchange. A few years later, in 1807, **Robert Fulton** launched the *Clermont*, a steamboat that managed to splutter its way up the Hudson River from New York to Albany, pioneering trade with upstate areas. A year before his death in 1814 Fulton also started a ferry service between Manhattan and Brooklyn, and the dock at which it moored became a focus of trade and eventually a maritime centre, taking its name from the inventor.

But it was the opening of the **Erie Canal** in 1825 that really allowed New York to develop as a port. The Great Lakes were suddenly opened to New York, and with them the rest of the country; goods manufactured in the city could be taken easily and cheaply to the American heartlands. It was on this prosperity, and the mass of **cheap labour** that flooded in throughout the nineteenth and early twentieth centuries, that New York – and to an extent the nation – became wealthy. The first waves of **immigrants**, mainly **German** and **Irish**, began to arrive in the 1830s, the latter forced out by the Potato Famine of 1846, the former by the failed Revolution of 1848-9, which had left many German liberals, labourers, intellectuals and businessmen dispossessed by political machinations. The city could not handle people arriving in such great numbers and epidemics of yellow fever and cholera were common, exacerbated by poor water supplies, insanitary conditions and the poverty of most of the newcomers. But in the 1870s large-scale **Italian** immigration began, mainly of labourers and peasants from southern Italy and Sicily, whilst at the same time refugees from **Eastern Europe** started to arrive – many of them Jewish. The two communities shared a home on the **Lower East Side**, which became one of the worst slum areas of its day. On the eve of the Civil War the majority of New York's 750,000 population were immigrants; in 1890 one in four alone of the city's inhabitants was Irish.

During this period life for the well-off was fairly pleasant and development in the city proceeded apace. Despite a great fire in 1835 that destroyed most of the business district downtown, trade boomed and was celebrated in the opening of the **World's Fair** of 1835 at the Crystal Palace on the site of Bryant Park – an iron and glass building that fared no better than its London namesake, burning down in 1858. In the same year work began on clearing the shanty towns in the centre of the island to make way for a newly landscaped open space – a marvellous design by Frederick Law Olmsted and Calvert Vaux that became **Central Park**.

Two years later the **Civil War** broke out, caused by growing differences between the northern and southern states, notably on the issue of slavery. New York sided with the Union (north) against the Confederates (south), but had little experience of the hand-to-hand fighting that ravaged the rest of the country. It did however form a focus for much of the radical thinking behind the war, particularly with **Abraham Lincoln**'s influential 'Might makes Right' speech from the **Cooper Union Building** in 1860. In 1863 a conscription law was passed that allowed the rich to buy themselves out of military service. Not surprisingly this was deeply unpopular, and New Yorkers rioted, burning buildings and looting shops: over a thousand people were killed in these **Draft Riots**. A sad addendum to the war was the assassination of Lincoln in 1860: when his body lay in state in New York's City Hall, 120,000 people filed past to pay last respects.

The Late 19th Century: Wealth and the Rise of the Robber Barons

The end of the Civil War saw much of the country devastated but New York intact, and it was fairly predictable that the city would soon become the wealthiest and most influential in the nation. Broadway developed into the main thoroughfare, with grand hotels, restaurants and shops catering for the rich; newspaper editors **William Cullen Bryant** and **Horace Greeley** respectively founded the *Evening Post* and the *Tribune*; and the city became a magnet for writers and intellectuals, with **Washington Irving** and **James Fenimore Cooper** among notable residents. By dint of its skilled immigrant workers, its facilities for marketing goods, and the wealth to build factories New York was also the greatest business, commercial and manufacturing centre in the country. **Cornelius Vanderbilt**'s controlled a vast shipping and railroad empire, and **J.P.Morgan**, the banking and investment wizard, was instrumental in organising financial mergers that led to the formation of prototype corporate business. But even bigger in a way was a character who was not a businessman but a politician: **William Marcy Tweed**. From lowly origins Tweed worked his way up the Democratic Party ladder to the position of alderman at the age of twenty one, eventually becoming Chairman of the party's State Central Committee. Surrounded by his own men – the **Tweed Ring** – and aided by a paid-off mayor, 'Boss' Tweed took total control of the city's government and finances. Anyone in a position to endanger his money-making schemes was bought off by cash extorted from the huge bribes given by contractors eager to carry out municipal services. In this way $160,000,000 found its way into Tweed and his friends' pockets. Tweed stayed in power by organising the speedy naturalization of aliens, who, in repayment, were expected to vote in Tweed and his sidekicks every so often. For his part, Tweed gave generously to the poor, who knew he was swindling the rich but saw him as a Robin Hood figure. As a contemporary observer remarked, 'The government of the rich by the manipulation of the poor is a new phenomenon in the world'. Tweed's swindles grew in audacity and greed until a determined campaign by **George Jones**, editor of the *New York Times*, and **Thomas Nast**, whose vicious portrayals of Tweed and his henchmen appeared in *Harper's Weekly*, brought him down. The people who kept Tweed in power may not have been able to read or write, but they could understand a cartoon and Tweed's heyday was over. A committee was established to investigate corruption in City Hall and Tweed found himself in court. Despite a temporary escape to Spain he was returned to the US, and died in Ludlow Street Gaol – by pleasing irony a building he had commissioned as Chief of Works.

The latter part of the nineteenth century, however, was for some the city's golden age: elevated railways (the **Els**) sprung up to ferry people quickly and cheaply across the city, **Thomas Edison** lit the the streets with his new electric light bulb, powered from the first electricity plant on Pearl Street, and in 1883, to the wonderment of New Yorkers, the **Brooklyn Bridge** was opened, Brooklyn itself along with Westchester and the Bronx becoming part of the city in 1898. All this commercial expansion stimulated the city's cultural growth and **Walt Whitman** eulogised the city in his poems, **Henry James** recorded its manners and mores in novels like *Washington Square*. **Richard Morris Hunt** built palaces for the wealthy Robber Barons along Fifth Avenue, who plundered Europe to assemble art collections to furnish them – collections that would, eventually find their way into the newly opened Metropolitan Museum. For the 'Four Hundred', the wealthy élite that revelled in and owned the city, New York in the 'gay nineties' was a constant string of lavish balls and dinners that vied with each other until opulence became obscenity. At one banquet the millionaire guests arrived on horseback and ate their meals in the saddle; afterwards the horses were fed gourmet-prepared fodder.

At the same time, emigration of Europe's impoverished peoples continued unabated, and in 1884 new immigrants from the orient settled in what became known as **Chinatown**; the following year saw a huge influx of southern Italians to the city. As the Vanderbilts, Astors and Rockefellers lorded it over the mansions uptown, overcrowded tenements led to terrible living standards for the poor. Working conditions were little better, and were compassionately described by police reporter and photographer **Jacob Riis**, whose book *How the Other Half Lives* detailed the long working hours, exploitation and child

labour that kept the city's coffers full. More Jewish immigrants arrived to cram the Lower East Side and in 1898 the population of New York amounted to over 3 million – the largest city in the world. Twelve years earlier Augustus Bartholdi's **Statue Of Liberty** had been finished, holding a symbolic torch to guide the huddled masses; now pressure grew to limit immigration, but still people flooded in. **Ellis Island**, the depot which processed arrivals, was handling 2000 people a day, a total of 10 million by 1929, when laws were passed to curtail immigration. By the turn of the century, around a half of the city's peoples were foreign-born, and a quarter of the population was made up of German and Irish migrants, most of them people living in slums. The section of Manhattan bounded by the East River, East 14th Street and Third Avenue, the Bowery and Catherine Street was probably the most densely populated area on earth, inhabited by a poor who lived under worse conditions and paid more rent than the inhabitants of any other big city in the world. Yet, in 1900, J.P.Morgan's United States Steel Company became the first billion dollar corporation.

The early 1900s saw some of this wealth going into adventurous new architecture. SoHo had already utilised the **cast iron building** to mass produce classical façades, and the **Flatiron Building** of 1902 announced the arrival of what was to become the city's trade mark – the skyscraper. On the arts front **Stephen Crane**, **Theodore Dreiser** and **Edith Wharton** used New York as the subject for their writing, **George M.Cohan** was the Bright Young Man of Broadway and in 1913 the **Armory exhibition** of Modernist painting by Picasso, Duchamp and others caused a sensation. Meantime the skyscrapers were pushing higher and higher, and in the same year a building that many consider the *ne plus ultra* of the genre, the **Woolworth Building**, was formally opened. Also that year **Grand Central Terminal** celebrated New York as the gateway to the continent.

The first two decades of the century saw a further wave of immigration, made up chiefly of Jews. In that period one third of all the Jews in Eastern Europe arrived in New York and upwards of 1½ million of them settled in New York City, primarily in the Lower East Side. Despite advances in public building, caused by the outcry that followed Jacob Riis's reports, the area could not cope with a population density of 330,000 per square mile, and the poverty and inhuman conditions reached their worst as people strove to better themselves by working in the sweatshops of Hester Street. Workers, especially those in trades dominated by Jewish immigrants from socialist backgrounds, began to strike to demand better wages and working conditions. Most of the garment manufacturers, for example, charged women workers for their needles and the hire of lockers, and handed out swingeing fines for spoilage of fabrics. Strikes of 1910-1911 achieved only limited success, and it took disaster to rouse public and civic conscience. On March 25th 1911, just before the **Triangle Shirtwaist Factory** at Washington Place was about to finish work for the day, a fire broke out. The workers were trapped on the tenth floor and 146 of them died (125 were women), mostly by leaping from the blazing building. Within months the State had passed 56 factory reform measures, and unionisation spread through the city.

The Great War, the Jazz Age and World War Two
With America's entry into the First World War in 1917 New York benefited from wartime trade and commerce. At home, perhaps surprisingly, there was little conflict between the various European communities crammed into the city. Although Germans comprised roughly one fifth of the city's population, there were few of the attacks on their lives or property that occurred elsewhere in the country.

The post-war years saw one law and one character dominating the New York scene: the law was **Prohibition**, passed in 1920 in an attempt to sober up the nation; the character was **Jimmy Walker**, elected mayor in 1925 and who led a far from sober lifestyle. 'No civilised man', said Walker 'goes to bed the same day he wakes up', and during his flamboyant career the Jazz Age came to the city. In speakeasies all over town the bootleg liquor flowed and writers as diverse as **Damon Runyon**, **F. Scott Fitzgerald** and **Ernest Hemingway** portrayed the excitement of the times. With the **Wall Street** crash of 1929 (see p.63),

however, the party came to an end. The Depression began and mayor Walker was flushed away with the torrent of civic corruption and malpractice that the changing times had uncovered and unleashed.

By 1932 approximately one in four New Yorkers were unemployed, and shanty towns, blackly known as 'Hoovervilles' after the then President, had sprung up in Central Park to house the workless and homeless. Yet during this period three of New York's most opulent – and most beautiful – skyscrapers were topped out: the **Chrysler Building** in 1930, the **Empire State** in 1931 (though it was to stand near-empty for years) and in 1932 the **Rockefeller Center** – all very impressive, but of little immediate help to those in Hooverville, Harlem or other depressed parts of the city. It fell to **Fiorello La Guardia**, Jimmy Walker's successor as mayor, to take over the running of the crisis-strewn city. He did so with

lisation programmes that, surprisingly, won him the approval of the people in the street: Walker's good living had got the city into trouble, reasoned voters, hard-headed straight-talking LaGuardia would get it out. Moreover President Roosevelt's **New Deal** supplied funds for roads, housing and parks, the latter undertaken by the controversial Parks Commissioner **Robert Moses**. Under LaGuardia and Moses, the most extensive public housing programme in the country was undertaken; the Triborough, Whitestone and Henry Hudson bridges completed; 50 miles of new expressway and 5000 acres of new parks opened. And, in 1939, mayor LaGuardia opened the airport that carries his name.

LaGuardia ran three terms as mayor, taking the city into the **war years**. The country's entry into the Second World War in 1941 had few direct effects on New York City: lights were dimmed, 200 Japanese were interned on Ellis Island and guards placed on bridges and tunnels. But, more importantly, behind the scenes experiments taking place at Columbia University split the uranium atom, giving a name to the **Manhattan Project** – the creation of the first atomic weapon.

The Post-War Years
Though the beleagured black community of Harlem erupted into looting and

violence in 1943, the city maintained its pre-eminent position in the fields of finance, art and communications, both in America and the world, its intellectual and creative community swollen by refugees escaping the Nazi threat to Europe. When the **United Nations Organisation** was seeking a permanent home, New York was the obvious choice: lured by Rockefeller-donated land the building of the Secretariat began in 1947.

The building of the United Nations, along with the boost in the economy that followed the war, brought about the development of midtown Manhattan. First off in the race to fill the once-residential Park Avenue with offices was the **Lever House** of 1952, quickly followed by skyscrapers like the **Seagram Building** that give the area its distinctive look. Downtown, the **Stuyvesant Town** and **Peter Cooper Village** housing projects went ahead, along with many others all over the city. As ever, there were plentiful scandals over the financing of the building, most famously concerning the **Manhattan Urban Renewal Project** on the Upper East Side.

A further scandal, this time concerning organised crime, ousted mayor **William O'Dwyer** in 1950: he was replaced by a series of uneventful characters who did little to stop the gradual **decline** that had begun in the early 1950s as a general stagnation set in among the country's urban centres. New York fared worst: immigration from Puerto Rico had once more crammed East Harlem and the Lower East Side, and the nationwide trend of black migration from poorer rural areas was also magnified here. Both groups were forced into the ghetto area of Harlem, unable to get a slice of the city's wealth. Racial disturbances and riots occurred in what had for two hundred years been one of the more liberal of American cities. One response to the problem was a general exodus of the white middle classes – the **Great White Flight** as the the media gleefully labelled it – out of New York. Between 1950 and 1970 over a million families left the city. Things went from bad to worse during the 1960s with **race riots** in Harlem, Bedford-Stuyvesant and East Harlem.

The **World's Fair** of 1964 was a white elephant to boost the city's credit in the financial world, but on the streets the call for civil liberties for blacks and protest against US involvement in Vietnam were, if anything, stronger than in the rest of the country. What little new building went up during this period seemed to willfully destroy the much of the best of earlier traditions: a new **Madison Square Garden** was built on the site of the grandly Neo-Classical **Pennsylvania Station** and the **Singer Building** in the Financial District was demolished for an ugly skyscraper. In Harlem municipal investment stopped altogether and the community stagnated.

Manhattan reached **crisis point** in 1975. By now the city was spending more than it received in taxes – billions of dollars more. In part, this could be attributed to the effects of the White Flight: companies closed their headquarters in the city when offered lucrative relocation deals elsewhere, and their white collar employees were usually glad to go with them, thus doubly eroding the city's tax base. Even after municipal securities were sold, New York ran up a debt of $13,000,000,000. Essential services, long shaky through underfunding, were ready to collapse. The mayor who oversaw this farrago, **Abraham Beame**, was an accountant.

Essentially, three things saved the city: the **Municipal Assistance Corporation** (aka the *Big Mac*), which was formed to borrow the money the city could no longer get its hands on; the election of **Edward I. Koch** as mayor in 1978; and, in a roundabout way, the plummeting of the dollar on the world currency market following the oil price rises of the 1970s. This last effect, combined with cheap transatlantic airfares, brought European tourists into the city *en masse* for the first time, and with them came money for the city's hotels and service industries. Mayor Koch, cheerfully saying 'Isn't it terrible ?' to whatever he could not immediately put right, and asking 'How am I doing ?' each time he scored a success, gained the appreciation of New Yorkers, ever eager to look to their civic leaders for help or blame.

The slow reversal of fortunes coincided with the completion of two face-saving building projects: though, like the Empire State Building it long remained half empty, the **World Trade Center** was a gesture of confidence by the Port Authority of New York and New Jersey, which financed it; and in 1977 the **Citicorp Center** added modernity and prestige to its environs on Third Avenue.

Since the mid-Seventies slump the city has in some respects gone from strength to strength. Ed Koch, now in his third term of office, has managed simultaneously to offend liberal groups and win the electoral support of ethnic groups, and despite the death of his friend and supporter Queens Borough president **Donald Manes**, (who committed suicide when an investigation into the city's various debt collecting agencies was announced) he is probably the most popular mayor since LaGuardia – some measure of just how adroit a politician he is. A spate of building has given the city yet more fabulous architecture, notably **Battery City Park** downtown. Yet the problems of homelessness, crime and violence, of unemployment, particularly among blacks and Hispanics, and of a decaying social fabric that the New Right under Reagan will do little to improve, mean that in the 1980s the flip side of New York's glittering coin is still a tarnished face that few care to see.

ARCHITECTURAL CHRONOLOGY

1625 First permanent **Dutch settlement** on Manhattan.

No buildings remain of the period. **Wall Street** marks the defensive northern boundary of the settlement in 1653.

Late 18C New York under **British colonial rule**.

St Paul's Chapel (1766) built in Georgian style.

1825 Opening of **Erie Canal** increases New York's wealth.

Fulton Street dock and market area built. Greek Revival row houses popular – eg **Schermerhorn Row, Colonade Row, St Mark's Place, Chelsea**. Of much Federal Style building, few examples remain: The **Abigail Adams Smith House**, the **Morris-Jumel Mansion** and **Gracie Mansion** the most notable.

1812 British blockade of Manhattan.

City Hall built.

1830-50 First wave of **immigration**, principally German and Irish.

The **Lower East Side** developed. **Trinity Church** built (1846) in English Gothic style, **Federal Hall** (1842) in Greek revival.

1850-1900 **More immigrants** (Irish and Germans, later Italians and East European Jews) settle in Manhattan. **Industrial development** brings extreme wealth to individuals. The **Civil War** (1861-65) has little effect on the city.

Cast iron architecture enables buildings to mimic grand Classical designs cheaply. Highly popular in the shops and factories of SoHo, eg the **Haughwout Building** (1859). Large, elaborate mansions built along Fifth Avenue for the country's new millionaires. **Central Park** opened (1876). The **Brooklyn Bridge** (1883) links Gothic with industrial strength; **St Patrick's Cathedral** (1879) and **Grace Church** (1846) show it at its most delicate. The **Statue of Liberty** is unveiled (1886).

Early 20C

The **Flatiron Building** (1902) is the first skyscraper. Much civic architecture in the Beaux Arts Neo-Classical style: **Grand Central Terminal** (1919), **New York Public Library** (1911), **US Customs House** (1907), **General Post Office** (1913) and the **Municipal Building** (1914) are the finest examples. The **Woolworth Building** (1913) becomes Manhattan's 'Cathedral of Commerce'.

1915

The **Equitable Building** fills every square inch of its site on Broadway, causing the first zoning Ordinances to ensure a degree of setback and allow light to reach the streets.

1920 **Prohibition** law passed. Economic confidence of the 1920s brings the **Jazz Age**.

1929 **Wall Street Crash**. America enters the **Great Depression**.

1930s The **New Deal** and **WPA** schemes attempt to reduce unemployment.

1941 America enters the **war**.

1950 **United Nations Organisation** established.

1960s **Protest Movement** stages demonstrations against US involvement in Vietnam.

1970s Mayor Abraham Beame presides over **New York's decline**.

Art Deco influences show in the **American Standard Building** (1927) and the **Fuller Building (1929)**.

Many of the lavish buildings commissioned and begun in the 1920s reach completion. Skyscrapers combine the monumental with the decorative: **Chrysler Building** (1930), **Empire State Building** (1930), **Waldorf Astoria Hotel** (1931) and the **General Electric Building** (1931). The **Rockefeller Center**, the first exponent of the idea of a city-within-a-city, is built through the decade. The **McGraw-Hill Building** (1931) is self-consciously modern.

Little new building is commissioned other than housing estates. WPA Murals decorate buildings around town, notably in the **New York Public Library** and the **County Courthouse**.

New zoning regulations encourage the development of the setback skyscraper: but little is built during the war years.

The **UN Secretariat** (1950) introduces the glass curtain wall to Manhattan. Similar Corbusier-influenced buildings include the **Lever House** (1952) and, most impressively, the **Seagram Building** (1958), whose plaza causes the zoning regulations to be changed in an attempt to encourage similar public spaces. The **Guggenheim Museum** (1959) opens.

Much building of the early 1960s is pallid imitation of the glass box skyscraper. The **Pan-Am** (1963) B**uilding** attempts something different, but more successful is the **Ford Foundation** (1967). In the hands of lesser architects, the plaza becomes a liability. A new **Madison Square Garden** (1968) is built on the site of the old Penn Station. The minimalist **Verrazano-Narrows Bridge** (1964) links Brooklyn to Staten Island .

The **World Trade Center Towers** (1970) add a soaring landmark to the lower Manhattan skyline. **The Rockefeller Center Extensions** (1973-4) clone the glass box skyscraper.

1975 City financing reaches **crisis point** as businesses leave Manhattan.

Virtually no new corporate development until the **Citicorp Center** (1977) adds new textures and profile to the city's skyline. Its popular atrium is adopted by later buildings.

1978 Investment in the city increases. **Ed Koch elected mayor**.

One UN Plaza adapts the glass curtain wall to skilled ends.

1980s **Corporate wealth returns** to Manhattan.

The **IBM Building** (1982) shows the conservative side of contemporary architecture; Post Modernist designs like the **AT&T Building** (1983) and **Federal Reserve Plaza** (1985) depart from convention to mix historical styles in the same building.

1986 **Ed Koch returned as mayor**.

The mixed-use **Battery City Park** opens to wide acclaim

20C AMERICAN ART: A BRIEF SURVEY

This is no more than a brief introduction to a handful of American painters; for more detailed appraisals, both of the century's major movements and specific painters, see the Books *listings on p.363.*

20C American art begins with **The Eight**, otherwise known as the **Ashcan School**, a group of artists who were painting in New York in the first decade of this century. Led by Robert Henri, many of them worked as illustrators for city newspapers and they tried to depict modern American urban life — principally in New York City — as honestly and realistically as possible, in much the same way as earlier painters had depicted nature. Their exhibitions, in 1908 and 1910, were, however, badly received, and most of their work was scorned for representing subjects not seen as fit for painting. Paralleling the work of the Ashcan School was that of the group that met at the **Photo-Secession Gallery** of the photographer Alfred Stieglitz on Fifth Avenue. They were more individual, less concerned with social themes than expressing their own individual styles, but were equally unappreciated. Art, for Americans, even for American critics, was something that came from Europe, and in the early years of the 20C attempts to Americanise it were still regarded with suspicion.

Change came with the **Armory Show** of 1913: an exhibition, set up by the remaining Ashcan artists (members of the new *Association of American Painters and Sculptors*), to bring more than 1800 European works together and show them to the American public for the first time. The whole of the French 19C was represented at the show, together with Cubist and Expressionist painters, and, from New York, the work of the Ashcan painters and the Stieglitz circle. It was visited by over 85,000 people in its month-long run in New York, and plenty more caught it as it toured America. The immediate effect was uproar. Americans panned the European paintings, partly because they resented their influence but also since they weren't quite sure how to react; the indigenous American artists were criticised for being afraid to adopt a native style; and the press

fanned the flames by playing up to public anxieties about the subversive nature of modern art. But there was a positive effect: the modern art of both Europe and America became known all over the continent, particularly abstract painting. From now on American artists were free to develop their own approach.

The paintings that followed were, however, far from abstract in style. The Great Crash of 1929 and subsequent Depression led to the school of **Social Realism** and paintings like **Thomas Hart Benton**'s *America Today* sequence (currently in the Whitney Museum at the Equitable): a vast mural that covered, in realistic style, every aspect of contemporary American life. The New Deal and the resultant **Federal Art Project** of the WPA supported many artists through the lean years of the 1930s by commissioning them to decorate public buildings, and it became widely acknowledged that not only were work, workers and public life fit subjects for art, but also that artists had some responsibility to push for social change. Artists like **Edward Hopper** and **Charles Burchfield** sought to recreate, in as precise a way as possible, American contemporary life, making the particular (in Hopper's case empty streets, lone buildings, solitary figures in diners) 'epic and universal'. Yet while Hopper and Burchfield can be called great artists in their own right, much of the work of the time, particularly that commissioned as public works, was inevitably dull and conformist, and it wasn't long before movements were afoot to inject new life into American painting. It was the beginning of abstraction.

With these ideas so the centre of the visual art world gradually began to shift. The founding of the **Museum of Modern Art**, and also of the **Guggenheim Museum** some years later, combined with the arrival of many European artists throughout the 1930s (Gropius, Hans Hofmann, the Surrealists) to make New York a serious rival to Paris in terms of influence. **Hans Hofmann** in particular was to have considerable influence on New York painters, both through his art school and his own boldly Expressionistic works. Also, the many American artists who had lived abroad came back armed with a set of European experiences which they could couple with their native spirit to produce a new, indigenous and wholly original style. First and most prominent of these was **Arshile Gorky**, a European-born painter who had imbibed the influences of Cézanne and Picasso – and, more so, the Surrealists. His technique, however, was different: not cold and dispassionate like the Europeans but expressive, his paintings textured and more vital. **Stuart Davis**, too, once a prominent member of the Ashcan School, was an important figure, his paintings using everyday objects as subject matter but jumbling them into abstract form – as in works like *Lucky Strike*, which hangs in the Museum of Modern Art. Another artist experimenting with abstract forms was **Georgia O'Keefe**, best known for her depictions of flowers, toned in pastelly pinks and powder blues. These she magnified so they became no more than unidentified shapes, in their curves and ovular forms curiously erotic and suggestive of fertility and growth. The Whitney Museum holds a good stock of her work.

The **Abstract Expressionists** – or **The New York School** as they came to be known – were a fairly loose movement, and one which splits broadly into two groups: the first creating abstractions with increasing gusto and seemingly endless supplies of paint, while the rest employed a more ordered approach to their work. Best known among the first group is **Jackson Pollock**, a farmer's son from Wyoming who had studied under Thomas Hart Benton in New York and in the 1930s was painting Cubist works reminiscent of Picasso. Pollock considered the American art scene to be still under the thumb of Europe, and he deliberately set about creating canvasses that bore little relation to anything that had gone before. For a start his paintings were huge, and it was difficult to tell where they ended; in fact Pollock would simply determine the edge of a composition by cutting the canvas wherever he happened to feel was appropriate at the time – a large-scale approach that was much imitated and in part determined by the large factory spaces and lofts where American artists worked. Also, it was a reaction against bourgeois (and therefore essen-

tially European) notions of what a painting should be: the average Abstract Expressionist painting simply couldn't be contained in the normal collector's home, and as such was at the time impossible to classify. Often Pollock would paint on the floor, adding layers of paint apparently at random, building up a dense composition that said more about the action of painting than any specific subject matter: hence the term 'action painting' which is invariably used to describe this technique. As a contemporary critic said: with Pollock the canvas became 'an arena in which to act – rather than as a space in which to reproduce...'

Similar to Pollock in technique, but less abstract in subject matter, was the Dutch-born artist **Willem de Kooning**, whose *Women* series clearly attempts to be figurative – as do a number of his other paintings, especially the earlier ones, many of which are in the Museum of Modern Art. Where he and Pollock are alike is in their exuberant use of paint and colour, painted, splashed, dripped or scraped on to the canvas with a palette knife. **Franz Kline** was also of this 'gestural' school, though he cut down on colour and instead covered his canvas with giant black shapes against a stark white background: bold images reminiscent of Chinese ideograms and Oriental calligraphy. **Robert Motherwell**, who some have called the leading light of the Abstract Expressionist movement (in so far as it had one), created a similar effect in his *Elegies to the Spanish Republic*, only here his symbols are drawn from Europe not the East – and unlike Abstract Expressionist paintings they gain their inspiration from actual events. Again, for his work the Whitney and MoMA are good sources.

Foremost among the second group of Abstract Expressionists was **Mark Rothko**, a Russian-born artist whose work is easy to recognise by its broad rectangles of colour against a single- hued background. Rothko's paintings are more controlled than Pollock's, less concerned with exuding their own painterliness than with expressing, as Rothko put it, 'a single tragic idea.' Some have called his work mystic, religious even, and his paintings are imbued with a deep melancholy, their fuzzy-edged blocks of colour radiating light and, in spite of an increasingly lightened palette, a potent sense of despair. Rothko, a deeply unhappy man, committed suicide in 1970, and it was left to one of his closest friends, **Adolf Gottlieb**, to carry on where he left off. With his *pictographs* Gottlieb spontaneously explored deep psychological states, covering his canvasses with Red Indian signs. He also used a unique set of symbols of cosmos and chaos – discs of colour above a blotchy earth – as in his *Frozen Sounds* series of the early 1950s, at present in the Whitney collection.

The Abstract Expressionists gave native American art stature worldwide and helped consolidate New York's position as centre of the art world. But other painters weren't content to follow the emotional painting of Pollock and Rothko *et al.*, and toned down the technique of excessive and frenzied brushwork into impersonal representations of shapes within clearly defined borders – **Kenneth Noland**'s *Target* and the geometric (and later 3-dimensional) shapes of **Frank Stella** being good examples. **Ad Reinhardt**, too, honed down his style until he was using only different shades of the same colour, taking this to its logical extreme by ultimately covering canvasses with differing densities of black.

Barnett Newman is harder to classify, though he is usually associated with the Abstract Expressionists, not least because of the similarities to Rothko of his bold 'fields' of colour. But his controlled use of one striking tone, painted with only tiny variations in shade, and cut (horizontally or vertically) by only a single contrasting strip, give him more in common with the trends in art that followed. **Helen Frankenthaler** (and later **Morris Louis**) took this one stage further with pictures like *Mountains and Sea*, which by staining the canvas rather than painting it lends blank areas the same importance as coloured ones, making the painting as if created by a single stroke. With these two artists, colour was the most important aspect of painting, and the canvas and the colour were absorbed as one. In his mature period Louis began – in the words of a contemporary critic – 'to think, feel and

conceive almost exclusively in terms of open colour'. And as if in rejection of any other method, he destroyed most of his work of the previous two decades.

With the 1960s came **Pop Art**, which turned to America's popular media for subject – its films, TV, advertisements and magazines – and depicted it in heightened tones and colours. **Jasper Johns**' *Flag* bridges the gap, cunningly transforming the Stars and Stripes into little more than a collection of painted shapes, but most Pop Art was more concerned with monumentalising the tackier side of American culture: **Andy Warhol** did it with Marilyn Monroe and Campbell's Soup; **Claes Oldenburg** by recreating everyday objects (notably food) in soft fabrics and blowing them up to giant size; **Robert Rauschenberg** by making collages or 'assemblages' of ordinary objects; **Roy Lichtenstein** by imitating the screen process of newspapers and cartoon strips; and **Ed Kienholz** through realistic tableaux of the sad, shabby or just plain weird aspects of modern life. But what Pop Art really did was to make art accessible and fun. With it the commonplace became acceptable material for the 20C artist, and as such paved the way for what was to follow. **Graffiti** has since been elevated to the status of art form, and New York painters like Keith Haring and **Kenny Scharf** are celebrities in their own right, regularly called in to decorate Manhattan nightclubs.

Ironically, over the last decade or so there has been a return to straight figurative depictions, either suprarealistically as in the poignant acetate figures of **Duane Hanson** and the more conventional nude studies of **Philip Pearlstein**, or in a minimal way as with the quasi-abstractions of **Robert Moskowitz**. There has even been a return by some artists to the conventions of 19C portraiture and history painting, seen in the work of **Mark Tansey** and **Robert Arneson**. Most exciting is the work of the KOS group, from the South Bronx. As for the future, things have never been more fluid. But New York remains, at least in terms of the market-place, centre of art world-wide – and the city to which everyone continues to look for inspiration.

TWO VIEWS OF NEW YORK CITY

Now York City is about reaction: its devotees are committed, so are its critics. Below are two views of the city by native-born British writers: the first by resident New Yorker, **Quentin Crisp**, the second by **David Widgery**, who lives in London.

Quentin Crisp

*There are few more active devotees of New York City than **QUENTIN CRISP**. He has lived here — in a seedy boarding house in the East Village — for five years, making a living from writing and reviewing films and filling up on peanuts and champagne at literary launches, lunches and previews across America: all part of what he calls the smiling and nodding racket. He's a well-known figure in his neighbourhood, and he recently achieved his greatest ambition — to be given full American citizenship after four years as a 'resident alien'. 'Now', says Crisp, 'I am beyond deportation and able to commit my first murder.' Though nearing 80 years of age, he has no desire to return to Britain: he would, he claims, rather live in New York than anywhere else in the world. What follows is a brief personal view of the city, specially written for this book, by one its most diehard fans.*

I am now a twilight American.

In the days when I was only English, a full-time American, curling his lip as he spoke, said to me, 'You British think that where the suburbs of New York end, the suburbs of Los Angeles begin.' Actually our ignorance is even more profound than that. When we say 'America' we mean New York and, when we say 'New York', we are referring not to the state nor even to the Bronx or Brooklyn but only to Manhattan. Furthermore, if shown a map of The United States, we mistake Long Island for Manhattan whereas in fact the latter is merely a tiny rock, the shape of a date stone, crushed between Long Island and the rest of the continent. Nevertheless, in spite of its cramped situation and its relatively limited size, it cannot be denied that, when you are in this city, you feel you are at the heart of the world.

At a time when most people who crossed the Atlantic Ocean did so by boat, it was the skyline of New York that made the deepest impression. Returning home, the first things a traveller mentioned were the skyscrapers. They are still spectacular but nowadays, when most capital cities bristle with very tall buildings, this aspect of New York is no longer so remarkable. Indeed it would not be difficult to photograph London or Sydney to look like any American metropolis. For an English person, though not necessarily for an Australian, the uniqueness of New York lies not in its architecture nor in its climate but in its people.

Everybody here is your instant friend.

Strange to relate, it is the natives themselves who issue dire warnings concerning the coldness and the dangers of the place. Ignore what they say. Take exactly the same safety precautions that you would use as a visitor to any big modern city. Do not stroll, swaddled in furs and bristling with diamonds, along dim side streets after midnight. At all other times, wander whither you please. Even those denizens who wish to praise their habitat misguidedly tell you that you will love the bustle of New York. In truth, except during rush hours, it is a leisurely city in which anything goes. I have seen elderly gentlemen meandering through mid-Manhattan wearing nothing but their running shorts. In fact there is almost nothing that anyone could wear or say or do here that would cause anything like the shocked reaction that in England greets the slightest deviation from traditional dress or behaviour.

See the sights if you must; go to the top of the Empire State Building or the World Trade Center if you are a born tourist, but spend most of your time in the streets where you will find you are perpetually welcome as though this teeming city were a village. It is not a good idea to travel on the subway. The system is very complicated and the situation is made worse by the fact that all maps have been disfigured beyond recognition. Moreover, the stations are bleak and the trains so noisy that conversation of any kind is impossible. Unless you are desperate, try not to take taxis. They are amazingly plentiful but the drivers, though friendly, have no more idea of the whereabouts of your destination than you do. English cabbies, if you try to give them instructions, interrupt you angrily with the words, 'D'yer wanna drive the damn thing yerself?' Their American counterparts expect a guided tour and, to complicate matters further, may not understand anything you say. As you look through the thick pane of glass that separates you from them, you will see they have names like Ascencio or Rodriguez so, if communications break down, try Spanish.

When your feet give out, take buses. They are frequent, air cooled in summer and warm in winter but unfortunately you must pay your fare (a dollar at the moment) in exactly the right amount of silver coinage. Bus drivers give no change. This is almost the only annoying quirk that mars the joy of metropolitan life.

Feel free to ask for street directions from anybody; you will get their life story. And though they look like gangsters, even the policemen are cozy.

New York is one vast carnival. The splendour and the squalor are woven together more closely and more conspicuously than in any other city that I, at any rate, have ever visited. At one moment you are treading sidewalks paved with the names of famous people; the next you are bouncing down avenues in such a state of disrepair that, if you are in a fast-moving vehicle, your head hits the roof. It is also a gloriously noisy place in which ambulances, police cars and fire engines never seem to sleep. Being in New York is like taking part in a Frank Capra movie – crazy, human, beautiful. You will notice as soon as you arrive that everyone is handsome, probably because of the dazzling mixtures of races that have made their homes here.

If there are any drawbacks to this earthly paradise, they are climatic and financial.

At a distance most parts of the world seem to have a climate; when you are in them, they only have weather. This is true of New York. Occasionally the seasons are as unpredictable as those of Southern England but I am happy to tell you that they are never as dreary. Speaking generally, the winters are short, as bright and bitter as one of Dorothy Parker's epigrams, but the summers seem long because they are so hot. Some years for most of July and all of August the temperature hovers at ninety degrees. If, during this time, there is a thunderstorm, do not expect any relief. Hot water pours from the sky, a torrid wind blows through the concrete canyons and the next day is as humid as the one before. To enjoy the city at its best, come in the autumn – like Mr. Columbus. This time of year is almost always clear, beautiful and dry.

The rigours of the financial climate are harder to evade. When you visit America, stay with friends however much you may come to dislike them before the end of your stay. Hotels are staffed by very obliging people and their managers make a great fuss of you but accommodation is far from cheap. All this happiness has to be paid for.

However, do not allow these minor disadvantages deter you for a moment. Pack tonight; leave home tomorrow.

Books by Quentin Crisp include The Naked Civil Servant (Fontana £2.50); How to become a Virgin (Fontana £1.95); *and, most recently,* Manners from Heaven (Flamingo £2.95).

David Widgery

DAVID WIDGERY combines a career as a general practitioner in London's East End with that of a writer and critic. He is a closet New York afficianado, and regards riding the Circle Line, sunbathing on top of the World Trade Center and eating in Little Italy during the San Gennaro Festival as among the greatest pleasures of civilised life. 'I love the United States', he says, 'but it's the America of radicalism, muckraking and rhythm and blues which the establishment is at present so keen to deny.'

I first went to Manhattan nearly 20 years ago; a terrified teenager clutching a '99 Day, $99' coach ticket. America seemed to be curling open like an old tin can before my eyes, the civil rights movement was spilling into the northern city ghettoes, the Berkeley students were discovering pot and 'organising within the knowledge factory' and a huge plume of smoke hung above Los

Angeles from the gleeful riot in Watts. Sixties New York was fast, belligerent and scared. My strongest memories were the poster over the Students for a Democratic Society's HQ saying 'No Vietnamese ever called me Nigger'; the smell of hot oil and rubber inside Greyhound Stations and queues of poor people with their parcels wrapped up with infinite patience and newly achieved dignity.

Back again in 1974, New York still felt, to a European, a radical city, a place of imminence, a mix of the older 1960s possibilities and the new spirit of the women's and gay movement which still meant change. The Watergate Tapes were on sale in supermarket checkouts, Vietnam was in every other sentence and the Movement was still moving. Political optimism was only temporarily stalled, the Empire was uneasy.

So the first shock of New York deep into the Reign of Reagan is its platitudinous self-confidence, its intellectual conformism and a social conservatism so profound it has ceased to be a cosmetic and has been absorbed into the very civic skin. Never mind the homeless sleeping out in the public parks, subways unfit for cattle, the poor hawking secondhand goods on the street corners and the plummeting stock exchange; there is a tennis clip on every mountain bike, a new restaurant on every intersection and if you don't *enjoy*, it's your own damn fault.

Typical is what's happened to the poor old Statue of Liberty, spruced up for its Centennial as the new brand image of capitalism, another product from the people who gave you freedom.. The statue was a democratic gesture, its catchline was written by the socialist poet Emma Lazarus, and the French fund-raising effort was an act of defiance against absolutism. But its incessantly produced image now beams benignly over the aerial bombardment of Tripoli and the rolling up of the Contras, or whatever wheeze comes next from the patriots who now direct US foreign policy.

Inside Liberty's tower, a Museum of Immigration is now housed (rather tough on black Americans, who mostly arrived in shackles at the plantation posts), which even includes Samuel Gompers, George Grosz and Helen Keller. But the Museum is deserted while thousands stand in a queue to photograph themselves looking out from Liberty's flame. While I read a panel on the rise of the No-Nothing-Party before the First World War and its campaign against dope fiends and alien gunmen, someone strides past in a studied 'Don't Mess with the US' T-shirt shouting 'All this history bores me'. Indeed.

History is now New York's enemy and if you enquire about Watergate, let alone Stonewall, people brought up on TV and leisure magazines look back with alarm. Being a European sentimentalist, I trot off to the usual shrines, eating a cold turkey sandwich on the spot John Lennon got shot; gawping at the Apollo and the Cedar Bar and visiting Trotsky's old print shop in St Mark's Place. While wading through throngs of New Yorkers queueing for 'Vienna 1900' (a kind of Habitat catalogue for the Franz-Josef era) at the Museum of Modern Art to see the Pollocks and De Koonings I hear the gallery guide announcing that 'the Post-Impressionists were like the European Romantics. That is they were alchoholics and committed suicide.' But the real New York is a another time-space continuum. Now.

As a city it has lost none of its architectural exuberance and manic energy. The taxis still swerve rather than drive, the sign language is still imperative and muscular ('Don't block the box', 'Touchbank Here', 'Stop Cheap Steaks') and people throw frisbees as if their life depended on it. There is less English spoken, more babies with bald fathers and a lot more purple prose in the delis which now stick reviews over their midget vegetables and lake sturgeons and offer varietal grape juices. *Enjoy* is the supreme injunction.

If you think gentrification is people sticking brass door knockers on their Stoke Newington front doors, you should see the gentry in operation in New York. There a neighbourhood can be razed, and replaced by yuppie lego in a matter of months and gourmetified and art-galleried in the process.

Which is not to say all the cultural landmarks have been built over by sushi bars and designer bike shops. Despite AIDS, people still strip for charity, organise telephone sex link-ups which are shown on your telephone bill as long distance calls, and queue to see 'My Beautiful Launderette' which, along with

Laura Ashley, muffins and antique clocks, was one of the few signs that the United Kingdom exists.

The US labour movement, once mighty but now organising only 17% of the workforce, soldiers on, thank God, and the best day I spent in New York was being shown around the back of a power plant, Mafia-disposed toxic waste and all, by a rank and file organiser. And there is a Left, although in comparison with the movement of the 1960s and 1970s it is microscopic.

So I was delighted to meet Victor Navasky, the editor of the *Nation*, an organ of sensible liberalism which, in current circumstances, seems crypto-Bolshevik; to come across writers for the post-Murdoch *Village Voice* who are as appalled by Reaganism as most Europeans; and to meet people who are, ahem, Marxists.

What is surprising is the degree of self-delusion among those tyros of empiricism, the bankers themselves. Banker availability is a New York speciality, they are young, they are noisy and they are everywhere: restaurants, gallery openings, night clubs and all younger than oneself. I interrupt one who is discussing the investment potential of a Jamie Reid Sex Pistols daub at Reid's New York opening at the Josh Bauer Gallery.

'Does it matter to you that since Reaganomics, the USA is not only a net debtor, but the biggest debtor in the world? And why are all the farms going bust?'

He isn't worried, his art collection will see him through; if the Exchange busts, he has a Schnabel under the table.

Steve Mass, founder of the Mudd Club, is also delighted by the ironies of yuppies shelling out for Situationist off-cuts, but equally off-beam. 'What we really needed in New York was someone like David Hebridge to tell us what it all *meant.*' Hmmm. Was it like this in 1928, I wonder?

At the Palladium, which has less style than Stoke Newington's Three Crowns on Friday night, more bankers are waiting to meet the Eurythmics, whose co-leader's birthday we are celebrating. 'Do you know any good bands in Britain? Up and coming and with investment potential?' asks one. I take a deep breath, 'Well, there's this group called the Redskins. You seem to have plenty of statues that need kicking down.'

This article was originally published in City Limits Magazine *in October 1986; thanks to them for letting us reprint. David Widgery's most recent book is* Beating Hearts, *a study of racism and anti-racism centring on the East London Bangladeshi community where he practises. He also wrote the introduction to the photobook,* A Day in the Life of London.

BOOKS

Travel/Impressions
Mike Marqusee and Bill Harris (ed.)
New York: an Anthology (Cadogan
£15.95). Pricey, but the best and most
neatly packaged collection of writings on
New York – from Walt Whitman to Kathy
Acker – that you'll find.
Stephen Brook *New York Days, New
York Nights* (Picador £3.95). A witty and
fairly penetrating account of the city,
marred only by some remarkably sexist
passages.
Jan Morris *Manhattan '45* (Faber
£12.50). Morris's latest, and best, writings on Manhattan, reconstructing New
York City as it greeted returning GIs in
1945. Effortlessly written, fascinatingly
anecdotal. See also *The Great Port* (OUP;
£4.95).
Brendan Behan *Brendan Behan's New
York* (Hutchinson £4.95). Behan's journey through the underbelly of New York
City in the early 1960s, readably re-
counted in anecdotal style – and with
some characterful sketches by Paul
Hogarth.
Jerome Charyn *Metropolis* (Abacus
£4.50). A native of the Bronx, Charyn
dives into current-day New York from
every angle and comes up with a book
that's sharp, sensitive and refreshingly
real: one of the best things you can read
on the city, from one of its better contemporary writers. See *New York in fiction*,
below.
Florence Turner *At the Chelsea* (Ham-
ish Hamilton £12.95). 1960s memoir of
the famed hotel and its various arty (and
artless) transients, by a woman who
lived there for a decade.
Edmund White *States of Desire: Travels
in Gay America* (Picador £3.95). This, a
revealing account of life in gay communities across America, contains an
informed if slightly dispassionate chapter on New York. Good on Fire Island
and the more lurid aspects of NYC gay
bars.
Henry James *Lake George to Burlington*
(Tragara Press 1981). Travels through
the peaceful and often wild backwaters
of New York State in the late 1800s. As
ever, elegantly written.
Paul Theroux *Sunrise with Seamonsters*
(Penguin £4.95). A collection of travel
pieces which includes a sensational
chapter on the New York subway: al-

ways a good subject for some hysterical
writing, but Theroux should really know
better.

History, Politics and Society
Edward Robb Ellis *The Epic of New
York City* (Coward-McCann o/p).
Popularised history of the city in which its
major historical figures – Peter Stuyvesant, William Tweed and the rest –
become a cast of characters as colourful
as any historical novel. Interesting, but
you sometimes wonder where Ellis gets
his facts from.
Alistair Cooke *Alistair Cooke's America*
(BBC £7.75). TV spin-off history with a
few quirky touches. Available in most
libraries, it's useful background reading.
Hugh Brogan *Pelican History of the
United States* (Penguin £5.95). Good,
up-to-date and very complete general
history of America.
Howard Zinn *A People's History of the
USA* (Longmans £8.95). Traces the history of America's peoples, especially its
black and ethnic groups, taking broad
swipes at the establishment along the
way. See too *The Free and the Unfree*
(Pelican £4.95), which also tells the story
from a minorities angle.
Edmund Fawcett and Tony Thomas
America and the Americans (Fontana
£2.95). A wide-ranging, up-to-the-minute
and engagingly written rundown on the
USA in all its aspects, from politics to
sport to religion. Essentially a beginner's
guide to the nation.
Hunter S.Thompson *The Great Shark
Hunt* (Picador £5.95). This collection of
essays on contemporary American life
and politics is thought-provoking and
hilarious.
Tom Wolfe *The Purple Decades* (Penguin o/p). Recent compendium of essays
on the US by the chronicler of American
style.
Studs Terkel *Working* (Penguin £7.95)
and *American Dreams* (Paladin £3.95).
Though not specifically pertaining to
New York, Terkel's interviews with ordinary American citizens are as illuminating
a guide to US life you could hope for.

Art, architecture and photographs
Paul Goldberger *The City Observed: A
Guide to the Architecture of Manhattan*

(Penguin £5.95). If you're looking for an up-to-date, well-written and erudite run-down on New York's premier buildings look no further. Goldberger's book is hard to fault.

Gerard R. Wolfe *New York: A Guide to the Metropolis* (McGraw-Hill $12.95). Only available in the States, this is more academic – and less opinionated – than Goldberger's book, but it does include some good stuff on the Outer Boroughs. Also informed historical background.

N. White and E. Willensky (ed.) *AIA Guide to New York* (Macmillan). Standard guide to the city's architecture, more interesting than it sounds.

Mark Girouard *Cities and People* (Yale UP £16.95). Glossy book of urban sociology which contains a good account of the social history of New York City in the 19C.

W. Brown *American Art* (Harry N. Abrams £32.50). Encyclopedic account of movements in the visual and applied arts in America from Colonial times to the present day.

Les Krantz *American Artists* (Facts on File £10.95). Alphabetic guide to American art after World War Two. An attractive and indispensable reference.

Barbara Rose *American 20C Painting* (Skira/Rizzoli £12.95). Full and readable, with prints that more than justify the price.

Lucy R. Lippard *Pop Art* (Thames & Hudson £4.95). Broad critical analysis of (mainly) American art of the 1960s.

Jacob Riis *How the Other Half Lives* (Dover). Republished photo-journalism reporting life in the Lower East Side. The original awakened many to the plight of New York's poor.

Philip S. Foner and Reinhard Schultz *The Other America* (Journeyman £7.95). Art and images of poverty and the labour movement in the USA. Includes photographs of early 20C New York by Jacob Riis (see above) and Lewis W. Hine.

American Images Exhibition Catalogue (Penguin £14.95). For post-war American photography this is hard to beat.

Specific guides

Toby & Gene Glickman *The New York Red Pages* (Praeger $7.95). Radical guide to the city taking in politically significant sites and points of interest. Covering Lower Manhattan only and

again solely available in America, if you can get hold of it it's an informing read.

Zelda Stern *The Complete Guide to Ethnic New York* (St Martin's Press $7.95). Everything you ever wanted to know about New York's ethnic neighbourhoods, large and miniscule, from restaurants to ethnic shops, markets and festivals. Well worth investing in.

Deborah Jane Gardner *New York Art Guide* (Art Guide Pubs. £2.95). Pocket book detailing city galleries, museums, performance spaces, art and architectural associations and much more. Useful if you're touring private galleries.

James Stevenson *Uptown Local, Downtown Express* (Viking $15.75). Line drawings and droll commentary on some of the minutiae of New York's urban landscape by the *New Yorker* writer and cartoonist.

Barbara McMartin *Fifty Hikes in the Adirondacks* (Backcountry $9.95). Hiking guide to the national park. Backcountry also publish hiking guides to the Hudson Valley and the Finger Lakes. On sale only in the US.

R. & P. Albright *Short Walks on Long Island* and **Phil Angellino** *Short Bike Rides on Long Island* (Globe-Pequot $6.95). Apart from our own, much the best books to buy if you're spending any length of time on Long Island.

New York in fiction

Paul Auster *The New York Trilogy: City of Glass, Ghosts* and *The Locked Room* (Faber £10.95). Three Borgesian investigations into the murders, mystery and madness of contemporary NYC. Using the conventions of the crime thriller Auster unfolds a disturbed and disturbing picture of the city.

William Boyd *Stars and Bars* (Penguin £2.95). Set partly in New York, part in the deep South, a well-observed novel that tells despairingly and hilariously of the unbridgeable gap between the British and Americans. Full of ringing home truths for the first-time visitor to the States.

Jerome Charyn *War Cries over Avenue C* (Abacus £4.95). Alphabet City is the derelict backdrop for this novel of gang warfare among the Vietnam-crazed coke barons of New York City. An offbeat tale of conspiracy and suspense.

James Cochrane (ed.) *The Penguin Book of American Short Stories* (Penguin £3.95). Lead story in this is Washington

Irving's classic *Legend of Sleepy Hollow*, set in the Catskills and the Hudson Valley.

E.L. Doctorow *Ragtime* (Picador £2.50). America, and particularly New York, before World War One: Doctorow cleverly weaves together fact and fiction, historical figures and invented characters, to create what ranks as biting indictment of the country and its racism. See also the earlier and equally skilful *Book of Daniel; Loon Lake*, much of which is set in the Adirondacks; and *World's Fair* – a beautiful evocation of a Bronx boyhood in the 1930s. All are available in Picador.

J.P. Donleavy *A Fairy Tale of New York* (Penguin £4.95). Comic antics through the streets of New York in the well-worn Donleavy tradition.

Andrea Dworkin *Ice and Fire* (Secker & Warburg £9.50). An unpleasant and disturbing romp through the East Village by one of America's leading feminist writers.

Ralph Ellison *Invisible Man* (Penguin £3.95). The definitive if sometimes long-winded novel of what it's like to be black and American, using Harlem and the 1950s race riots as a background.

F. Scott Fitzgerald *The Great Gatsby* (£2.25). Fitzgerald's best and best known novel, set among the estates, the parties and hedonism of Long Island's Gold Coast in the twenties. Good evocative detail on the city too.

Oscar Hijuelos *Our House in the Last World* (Serpent's Tail £5.50). A warm evocative novel of immigrant Cuban life in New York from before the war to the present day.

Chester Himes *The Crazy Kill* (Alison & Busby £2.95). Himes writes fast-moving thrillers set in Harlem, of which this is just one. A&B also publish a number of others. Among other New York detective writers, **John Franklin Bardin** is the most original, using the city as a vivid backdrop for his intricate plots; **Jerome Charyn** the most bizarre, in both plot and character; and **Rex Stout** the most entertaining, also with much enjoyable locational detail.

Henry James *Washington Square* (Penguin £1.95). Skilful examination of the codes and dilemmas of New York genteel society in the 19C.

Tama Janowitz *Slaves of New York* (Picador £3.50). Written by one of the so-called 'brat-pack' of young American writers, a collection of short stories that pokes gentle fun at New York in the eighties. Janowitz's recurring cast of characters is colourful, shocking, sad and endearing.

Joyce Johnson *Minor Characters* (Picador £2.50). Women were never a prominent feature of the Beat generation; its literature examined a male world through strictly male eyes. This book, by the woman who lived for a short time with Jack Kerouac, redresses the balance superbly well. And there's no better novel on the Beats in New York.

William Kennedy *The Albany Trilogy* (Penguin, 3 volumes £2.95-£3.95). The binding thread of these novels is Albany and the Catskills, in the first adeptly recreated during the Prohibition era and following the fugitive tracks of gangster Jack 'Legs' Diamond.

Stephen Koch *The Bachelor's Bride* (Marion Boyars £10.95). Readable but slightly affected novel of art society in sixties New York.

Larry Kramer *Faggots* (Methuen £3.95). Parody of the New York City gay scene, lewdly honest and raucously funny, by the author of the AIDS play *The Normal Heart*.

Edward Limonov *It's Me, Eddie* (Picador £2.95). The Jewish-Russian emigré on welfare in New York City and ambivalent about why he ever came. Tries hard to be at once funny and meaningful but rarely succeeds on either level.

Mary McCarthy *The Group* (Penguin £3.95). Eight Vassar graduates making their way in the New York of the thirties. Sad, funny and satirical.

Jay McKirney *Bright Lights, Big City* (Flamingo £2.75). A cult book, and one which made first-time novelist McKirney a mint, following a struggling New York yuppie from one cocaine-sozzled nightclub to another. A good, racey read, if slightly banal.

Ann Petry *The Street* (Virago £3.95). The story of a black woman's struggle to rise from the slums of Harlem in the 1940s. Convincingly bleak.

Marge Piercy *Braided Lives* (Penguin £3.95). More a novel of Detroit than New York but an excellent one, and with much 1950s detail on the city, its neighbourhoods and embryonic movements.

Thomas Pynchon *V* (Picador £4.50). First novel by one of America's greatest living writers. The settings shift from Valletta to Namibia, but New York's

Lower East Side is a key reference point. And there's a fantastic crocodile-hunt through the city sewers. Recommended.

Judith Rossner *Looking for Mr Goodbar* (Coronet £2.25). A disquieting kind of book, tracing the progress – and eventual demise – of a woman teacher through volatile and permissive New York in the sixties. Good on evoking the feel of the city in the sixties era, but on the whole a depressing read.

Henry Roth *Call It Sleep* (Penguin £4.95). Roth's only work of any real note traces – presumably autobiographically – the awakening of a small immigrant child to the realities of life among the slums of the Jewish Lower East Side. Read more for the evocations of childhood than the social comment.

Paul Rudnick *Social Disease* (Penguin £3.50). Hilarious, often incredible send-up of Manhattan night-owls. Very New York, *very* funny.

Damon Runyon *First to Last* and *On Broadway* (Picador £3.50 and £4.95). Two collections of short stories drawn from the chatter of Lindy's Bar on Broadway and since made into the successful musical *Guys 'n' Dolls*.

J.D. Salinger *The Catcher in the Rye* (Penguin £2.50). Salinger's brilliant novel of adolescence, following Holden Caulfield's sardonic journey of discovery through the streets of New York City. If you've never read it, a must.

Sarah Schulman *The Sophie Horowitz Story* (Naiad Press $7.95). A lesbian detective story set in contemporary New York: dry, downbeat and very funny. See also *Girls, Visions and Everything* (Seal Press $8.95), a stylish and, again, humorous study of the lives of Lower East Side lesbians.

Hubert Selby Jr *Last Exit to Brooklyn* (Marion Boyars £6.95). When first published in Britain in 1966 this novel was tried on charges of obscenity and even now it's a disturbing read, evoking the sex, the immorality, the drugs, the violence of downtown Brooklyn in the 1960s with fearsome clarity. An important book,

but to use the words of David Shepherd at the obscenity trial, you will not be unscathed.

Dyan Sheldon *Dreams of an Average Man* (Penguin £3.95). Dense, typically mordant novel of deceit, social manners and mid-life crises among NYC yuppies Insightful and disturbing.

Madison Smartt Bell *The Year of Silence* (Chatto £11.95). The story of Upper West Side suicide, and the effects it has on everybody connected, from the woman's lover to the Broadway panhandler who discovers the body. Controlled, delicately paced writing, structured (almost) as a set of separate stories, and unsentimentally revealing the city and its people from all angles. See also Bell's collection of short stories, *Zero db*, also published by Chatto.

Betty Smith *A Tree Grows in Brooklyn* (Pan £1.95). Something of a classic, and rightly so, in which a courageous Irish girl makes good against a vivid pre-war Brooklyn backdrop. Totally absorbing.

Edith Wharton *Old New York* (Virago £3.95). A collection of short novels on the manners and mores of New York in the mid-19C, written with Jamesian clarity and precision. Virago also publish her *Hudson River Bracketed* (£4.95) and *The Mother's Recompense* (£3.95), both of which centre around the lives of women in 19C New York.

Tom Wolfe *The Bonfire of the Vanities* (Cape £12.95). Wolfe's first novel, and one which uses his skills of social observation to the full. Sherman McCoy is a Wall Street bond dealer who finds he can't live on $1 million a year, and who meets his match when – while swooning at the monied spires of Manhattan – he inadvertently drives his Mercedes into the South Bronx. It's no literary masterpiece, but is the best top-to-toe revelation of New York in the eighties you could wish for – and a fine racy read to boot.

Howard Moss (ed.) *New York: Poems* (Avon $5.95). Anthology of poems relating, sometimes tenuously, to New York.

NEW YORK ON FILM

'There are eight million stories in the Naked City.' So goes the line in the 1948 movie of the same name. Ever since the silent era, filmmakers have been mining some of those stories, hoping to turn them into cinematic gold. What follows is a selection, biased by our own tastes, of some of the more representative films set and/or shot in the city and its environs.

After Hours (Martin Scorsese: 1985). Scorsese trades grimness for a grin in feverish nightmare comedy of young computer programmer's overnight descent into hell – downtown NY. Lightweight but entertaining, thanks to game cast and Scorsese's at-his-fingertips technique.

All About Eve (Joseph L. Mankiewicz: 1950). Terrifically talky, overripe egos in Manhattan theatre world. A script peppered with brilliantly artificial dialogue, delivered from the guts by Bette Davis as ageing Broadway star Margo Channing.

All That Jazz (Bob Fosse: 1979). Broadway choreographer Roy Scheider's life and death viewed as a running, Felliniesque production number in Fosse's autobiographical ego-trip. What can be said about a musical whose highpoint is an open-heart surgery extravaganza?

Angel Heart (Alan Parker: 1987). Mickey Rourke runs up against destiny and one Louis Cyphre (Robert De Niro) in the New York of the 50s: atmospheric shots of Harlem and Coney Island add to the ambience of evil, violence and guilt.

Angels with Dirty Faces (Michael Curtiz: 1938). Action, comedy and sentimentality expertly whipped up by Warner Brothers. Archetypal role for James Cagney as gangster who goes to the chair pretending to be a coward for the sake of idolising slum boys (The Dead End Kids).

Angelo My Love (Robert Duvall: 1983). Actor-turned-director Duvall's neo-realist portrait of young city gypsy (a motion picture natural) and his milieu.

Annie Hall (Woody Allen: 1977). Oscar-winning autobiographical comic romance between neurotic Allen and scatty Diane Keaton is a Valentine to her and to the city. Simultaneously clever, bourgeois and very winning. For place-spotters, Annie's apartment was on 70th

Street between Lexington and Park.

Blackboard Jungle (Richard Brooks: 1955). Idealistic teacher Glenn Ford tames violent young thugs in studio-bound NYC high school. Watchable, even though it's largely contrived Hollywood social realism. The sensation it caused had something to do with the use of Bill Haley and the Comets' 'Rock Around the Clock'.

Breakfast at Tiffany's (Blake Edwards: 1961). Truman Capote's sophisticated novella somewhat softened to accommodate Audrey Hepburn as charmingly loose Manhattanite Holly Golightly.

Broadway Danny Rose (Woody Allen: 1974). Warm, engaging little showbiz fable with Allen as good-hearted, small-time agent on the run from loony Mafia family. Mia Farrow is the blond floozie catalyst. Scenes shot at Carnegie Deli, 55th and Broadway.

Coogan's Bluff (Don Siegel: 1968). First teaming of *Dirty Harry* director and Clint Eastwood, as upright Arizona lawman showing NY's Finest how to corral criminals. Siegel's **Madigan**, made the same year, contrasts detective Richard Widmark's routine with police commissioner Henry Fonda's problems. Both pictures are stylish, tough character studies.

The Cool World (Shirley Clarke: 1964). This arty documentary-style scan of Harlem teen who longs to be gun-toting gang member doesn't coalesce, despite grippingly 'real' moments. Three years earlier Clarke experimented with film forms in **The Connection**, in which a group of addicts awaiting their pusher are recorded by docu-filmmaker. Three years later she trained her camera on a monologuing black hustler in **Portrait of Jason**.

The Cotton Club (Francis Ford Coppola: 1984). Jazz and gangsters in costly, overplotted musical melodrama starring Richard Gere.

The Crowd (King Vidor: 1928). Downbeat ,influential silent study of day-to-day lives of hard-luck office worker and wife. Mixes pathos, realism and humour in just the right amounts.

Cruising (William Friedkin: 1980). Cop Al Pacino goes underground to ferret out killer of gays in tasteless, unbalanced thriller filmed on location. Salaciously stylised 'realism'.

Cry of the City (Robert Siodmak: 1948). Ruthless gangster Richard Conte pursued by boyhood friend turned cop Victor Mature. Made at a time when police sirens and rainsoaked sidewalks were the stuff of poetry.

Dead End (William Wyler: 1937). Highly entertaining, stage-derived tragedy of the East Side's teeming poor, set on an impressive studio-built street set. With Humphrey Bogart as a mother-obsessed small-time gangster, and a pack of lippy adolescents who earned their own movie series as *The Dead End Kids*.

Desperately Seeking Susan (Susan Seidelman: 1985). Bored suburban housewife Rosanna Arquette becomes obsessed with mysterious Madonna in off-the-wall comedy. Effervescent and unpretentious with a feel for modern New York.

Dog Day Afternoon (Sidney Lumet: 1975). Outlandish but true story of man (Al Pacino, perfect) robbing bank so his lover (Chris Sarandon, ditto) can have a sex change. One of the best NY movies ever.

Easter Parade (Charles Walters: 1948). Fred Astaire came out of retirement to partner Judy Garland in a musical festooned with 17 Irving Berlin songs. The title tune – featuring a stroll on Fifth Avenue – was, like everything else, shot on a Hollywood backlot.

Escape From New York (John Carpenter: 1981). In 1997 Manhattan has become a maximum security prison from which anti-hero Kurt Russell must rescue the hijacked US President. Visually explosive thriller promises more than it delivers.

Eyes of Laura Mars (Irvin Kershner: 1978). Chic terror in surprisingly effective pulp thriller that uses NY locations cannily. Faye Dunaway is riveting as vulnerable fashion photographer with psychic vision.

Eyewitness (Peter Yates: 1981). Unsuccessfully updated 1940s-style melodrama benefits from Manhattan setting and comic-romantic by-play between janitor William Hurt and Sigourney Weaver as TV reporter investigating a murder he supposedly saw.

Fame (Alan Parker: 1980). Collective, contemporary puttin'-on-a-show sort of musical-drama set against the background of Manhattan's High School for the Performing Arts. Some good scenes and acting, but end result is neither fish-nor-fowl.

Fort Apache, The Bronx (Daniel Petrie: 1981). Paul Newman in handsome form as veteran cop based in the city's most crime-infested and corrupt precinct. Tense, entertaining and totally unbelievable.

42nd Street (Lloyd Bacon: 1933). Milestone backstage musical from Warner Bros, starring Ruby Keeler as the young chorine who has to replace the ailing leading lady: she goes out onstage as an unknown and, guess what, comes back a star. Corny and cheerful.

The French Connection (William Friedkin: 1971). Plenty of juicy atmosphere in extremely tense, sensationally made Oscar-winning cop thriller starring Gene Hackman, whose classic car chase takes place under the Bensonhurst Elevated Railroad.

The Godfather (Francis Ford Coppola: 1972) Oscar-winning epic about Mafia family, friends and enemies is superb movie opera. **Part Two**, two years later, developed and deepened its predecessor's themes and strengths. A great double bill.

The Group (Sidney Lumet: 1966). A bevy of fine acting talent on display in ambitious, episodic adaptation of Mary McCarthy's novel about the personal/professional careers of a 1930s Vassar College clique. See *Books*.

Guys and Dolls (Joseph L. Mankiewicz: 1955). Marlon Brando sings and dances in this overblown version of Broadway musical about Damon Runyon-derived low-lifes. Jean Simmons is fetching as Salvation Army lass he woos, while Frank Sinatra walks amiably through.

Hannah and Her Sisters (Woody Allen: 1986). Allen in mellowed, Chekhovian mood. The human comedy on view is exceptionally well-played and wryly observed, but it lacks depth.

Hello Dolly! (Gene Kelly: 1969). This elephantine nail in the movie musical's coffin was an extravagant showcase for Barbara Streisand, too young but dynamic anyway as widowed matchmaker Dolly Levi.

Hester Street (Joan Micklin Silver: 1975). Young, tradition-bound Russian-Jewish immigrant Carol Kane joins her husband in turn-of-the-century Lower East Side to find he's cast off Old World ways. Simple but appealing, independently made tale with splendid period feeling.

Insignificance (Nicholas Roeg: 1985). Marilyn Monroe, Albert Einstein and Eugene McCarthy lookalikes play stagey games in the Roosevelt Hotel. Essentially empty, Roeg's movie is worth watching for Tony Curtis's boozy senator and the lyrical, terrifying last few minutes.

It's Always Fair Weather (Gene Kelly, Stanley Donen: 1955). *On the Town* gone sour. Trio of wartime buddies reunite ten years later and discover they loathe each other and themselves. Smart, cynical and satirical musical that was – undeservedly but unsurprisingly – a box office flop.

King Kong (Meridan C. Cooper/Ernest B. Schoedsack: 1944). A giant ape runs amok when taken from his jungle home to far less hospitable New York by a film producer. The scene where King Kong stands astride the Empire State Building, swatting passing planes while tending Fay Wray, has become part of city myth.

King of Comedy (Martin Scorsese: 1983). Quirky, biting satire set on the fringes of the New York entertainment world mixes the familiar with the bizarre in the tale of talentless autograph hound Rupert Pupkin (Robert De Niro) who wants to be celebrity on par with his Johnny Carson-like idol Jerry Lewis.

Klute (Alan J. Pakula: 1971). Oscar winner Jane Fonda as Manhattan callgirl Bree Daniel, ably supported by titular detective Donald Sutherland, in taut, well above-average damsel-in-distress thriller with modern twists. Fonda's is one of the best performances on film.

Looking For Mr Goodbar (Richard Brooks: 1977). Diane Keaton plays Upper West Side school teacher by day, promiscuous coke-sniffing club-goer by night, until she winds up in the evil hands of Richard Gere. Violent and frightening – even more so once you know it was based on a true story. See *Books*.

The Lost Weekend (Billy Wilder: 1945). Strong, enduring drama about dipso writer Ray Milland's delirium tremens-strewn path to Bellevue. One of the most famous scenes is his long trek down Third Avenue trying to sell his typewriter. Shot on location, including P.J. Clarke's bar (see p.123).

The Manchurian Candidate (John Frankenheimer: 1962). Enormously skilful critique of American politics (from Richard Condon's novel) culminates with brainwashed Laurence Harvey turning assassin in Madison Square Garden. With Frank Sinatra, Angela Lansbury and Janet Leigh.

Manhattan (Woody Allen: 1979). A black-and-white masterpiece of middle-class intellectuals' self-absorptions, lifestyles and romances, cued by a Gershwin soundtrack in what is probably the greatest eulogy to the city ever made. Essential viewing.

Manhattan Melodrama (W.S. Van Dyke; 1934). Clark Gable and William Powell as boyhood pals from the slums who grow up on opposite sides of the law. Mickey Rooney plays Gable aged 12, Myrna Loy is the love interest. The movie earned notoriety when Public Enemy no.1 John Dillinger was shot down as he emerged from seeing it in a Chicago cinema.

Marathon Man (John Schlesinger: 1976). Ex-Nazi deathcamp doctor Laurence Olivier goes after student Dustin Hoffman's teeth – and life – in incredible, botched-up and brutal thriller.

Marty (Delbert Mann: 1955). Modest Oscar winner from Paddy Chayefsky's teleplay about fat, mother-dominated Bronx butcher Ernest Borgnine meeting equally shy schoolteacher Betsy Blair in a Brooklyn dance hall. Hailed as a breakthrough in the way in which it focused on 'real' people, it looks rather tame today.

Mean Streets (Martin Scorsese: 1973). Scorsese's breakthrough film breathlessly follows small-time hood Harvey Keitel and his volatile, harum-scarum buddy Robert De Niro around Little Italy (actually Belmont in The Bronx) before reaching the inevitably violent climax.

Midnight Cowboy (John Schlesinger: 1969). The love story between Jon Voight's naive hustler Joe Buck and Dustin Hoffman's touching city creep Ratso Rizzo is the core of this ground-breaking Oscar winner. The pair are superlative. Much of the rest of the picture is empty, flashy aggression.

Miracle on 34th Street (George Seaton: 1947). Macy's Santa Claus Edmund Gwenn tries to prove he's real to young Natalie Wood and the courtroom.

Mixed Blood (Paul Morrisey: 1984). Blithely amoral comedy about flamboyant drug-pushing 'Godmother' Marilia Pera and her Alphabet City brood. Bloody cartoon action peppered with a hot salsa soundtrack.

Moscow on the Hudson (Paul Mazursky: 1984). Robin Williams as a Russian circus saxophonist who defects in this witty, sentimental comedy on the East/West divide. More schmaltzy propaganda for the US.

My Dinner With André (Louis Malle: 1981). Chamber version of the ultimate New York movie. It's all talk, analysis, philosophy, as playwright-actor Wallace Shawn and former *avant-garde* theatre director André Gregory play scripted (by Shawn) versions of themselves. Unique.

New York, New York (Martin Scorsese: 1977). Intense performances from Robert De Niro and Liza Minnelli in moody, impressive attempt to sour and splinter 1940s movie-musical conventions. The tone is dark, the narrative unbalanced, but occasionally it all really works, NY imaginatively recreated on studio soundstages.

Next Stop, Greenwich Village (Paul Mazursky: 1974). Brooklyn boy heads to the Village in 1953, hoping to become actor in endearing autobiographical comedy. Shelley Winters is outstandingly funny as his smothering, over-the-top mother.

On the Town (Gene Kelly, Stanley Donen: 1949). Exhilarating, landmark musical, ballet-inspired, about three sailors' romantic adventures on 24-hour leave in NYC. With Gene Kelly, Frank Sinatra, and Ann Miller flashing her gams in the Museum of Natural History. Partly shot on location (from Brooklyn Navy Yard to the top of the Empire State), it's as much New York travelogue as musical.

On the Waterfront (Elia Kazan: 1954). Oscar winner contains what is arguably Marlon Brando's greatest performance as anti-hero Terry Malloy, an inarticulate longshoreman reluctantly caught up in union racketeering. Superb location shooting. With Eva Marie Saint, Karl Malden and Rod Steiger.

Once Upon a Time In America (Sergio Leone: 1984). Sprawling, self-indulgent, but often brilliantly atmospheric saga starring Robert De Niro. Spanning decades, it comes close to capturing some of the pulp pleasures of 1930s and 1940s movies.

Panic in Needle Park (Jerry Schatzberg: 1971). Al Pacino and Kitty Winn give dedicated performances as pair of druggies in authentic-seeming downer.

The Pope of Greenwich Village (Stuart Rosenberg: 1984). Thin, shaky-footed retread of *Mean Streets* with Mickey Rourke and Eric Roberts as small-time thieves falling foul of the Mafia.

Radio Days (Woody Allen: 1987). Mia Farrow rises from cigarette girl to Manhattan personality in Allen's slender collection of vignettes from the days of 1930s radio. Some location shooting in Brooklyn and Times Square, but not a film to compare with his best work.

Ragtime (Milos Forman: 1981). Miscalculated adaptation of E. L. Doctorow's novel nevertheless has a fresh performance from Elizabeth McGovern as Evelyn Nesbit and an amusing one from James Cagney as the wily old police commissioner. See *Books*.

Rear Window (Alfred Hitchcock: 1954). Broken-legged photographer James Stewart plays Peeping Tom and discovers one of his neighbours is a killer. Peerless Hitchcock comedy-thriller, notable for its backlot recreation of a NYC courtyard, and the sexual chemistry between Stewart and Grace Kelly.

The Roaring 20s (Raoul Walsh: 1939). W.W.I. veteran gets involved with NY bootleggers. James Cagney supported by Humphrey Bogart. Definitive Warner's gangster formula, and crackling entertainment.

Rosemary's Baby (Roman Polanski: 1968). Seminal urban Gothic from Ira Levin's best-seller, about pregnant young married Mia Farrow plagued by satanic cult. The building she lives in is the famed Dakota, 72nd Street and Central Park West.

Saturday Night Fever (John Badham: 1977). Crudely-scripted, shrewdly-marketed flick that was a massive youth cult hit, with John Travolta as a sensitive stud using disco as his escape route over the Brooklyn Bridge to Manhattan. Not totally bad, unlike the 1983 sequel Staying Alive.

The Secret of My Success (Herbert Ross: 1987). Michael J. Fox plays the hick come to New York to make it whatever the costs, and becomes the bemused target of his boss's wife's advances. Scatty, funny and with some great shots of NYC.

Serpico (Sidney Lumet: 1973). Al Pacino is on target as real-life NYC cop, atypically cultured and incorruptible, in fast-paced tribute to loner righteousness that teems with atmosphere.

The Seven-Year Itch (Billy Wilder: 1955). When his wife and kid vacate humid Manhattan, Mitty-like pulp editor Tom Ewell is left guiltily leching over the innocent TV-toothpaste temptress upstairs – Marilyn Monroe, at her most wistfully comic. The sight of her pushing down her billowing skirt as she stands on a subway grating is one of the era's most resonant movie images.

Sid and Nancy (Alex Cox: 1986). The Chelsea Hotel is setting for the final scenes in the lives of punk's *enfants terribles*, Sid Vicious and Nancy Spungen. Their sad, shabby and often sick story is handled with warmth and humour.

Smithereens (Susan Seidelman: 1982). Cheaply and roughly made story of city's punks and dispossessed that has its moments. Very obviously a springboard for the same director's *Desperately Seeking Susan.*

Sophie's Choice (Alan J. Pakula: 1982). Meryl Streep sports a Polish accent as Jewish biologist Kevin Kline's mistress in this glum but honourable adaptation of William Styron's novel set in 1947 Flatbush Brooklyn. Guilt and retribution stirred with romantic melodrama.

Something Wild (Jonathan Demme: 1986). About the best of the Yuppie-in-peril nouvelle vogue with Melanie Griffith hijacking mild Manhattan businessman Jeff Daniels for a ride into New Jersey and her colourful past. The skill of the film is its ability to change gear several times – from screwball comedy to high-school nostalgia to something very wild and very nasty indeed.

The Sweet Smell of Success (Alexander Mackendrick: 1957). Broadway gossip columnist Burt Lancaster and sleazy press agent Tony Curtis are a great team in this biting study of showbiz corruption. British director Mackendrick handles the juicy on-location, night-time milieu with real flair.

Superman (Richard Donner: 1978). Chris Reeve struggles for Truth, Justice and the American Way in contemporary Manhattan by way of the Planet Krypton and a lovingly filmed Mid-West. Alter ego Clark Kent's offices are the *Daily News* Building on 42nd Street. The sequel

Superman 2 has stunning nightime vistas from atop the Verrazano Narrows Bridge.

Taxi Driver (Martin Scorsese: 1976). Superbly unsettling study of obsessive outsider Robert De Niro, with Jodie Foster as the pubescent hooker he tries to 'save' in horrifying gory climax. Scorsese's NYC is hallucinatorily seductive yet absolutely repellent.

Tootsie (Sydney Pollack: 1982). Dustin Hoffman's performance as an intense, out-of-work New York actor who dons female drag and becomes a soap opera celebrity is a work of comic genius.

A Tree Grows in Brooklyn (Elia Kazan: 1945). This touching working-class family saga, from a best-seller set in the earlier years of this century, was Kazan's directorial debut. See *Books.*

Up the Down Staircase (Robert Mulligan: 1967). Harren High School is the setting for screen version of Bel Kaufman's best-seller about beleaguered teacher Sandy Dennis. *Blackboard Jungle* with a sex-change.

West Side Story (Robert Wise, Jerome Robbins: 1961). Sex, Shakespeare and singing in an overlauded, hypercinematic Oscar-winning musical (via Broadway) about rival street gangs. Certainly it's excitingly assembled and impressively packaged.

Willie and Phil (Paul Mazursky: 1980) Under-nourished skim of 70s social fads and fashions as experienced by freeform ménage-à-trois Ray Sharkey, Michael Ontkean and Margot Kidder. An insult to its original, *Jules et Jim.*

Yankee Doodle Dandy (Michael Curtiz: 1942). James Cagney's Oscar winning performance as showbiz Rennaissance man George M. Cohan is a big, spirited bio-pic with music. Of its kind, probably the best ever.

Year of the Dragon (Michael Cimino: 1985). Mickey Rourke is a racist Vietnam veteran cop out to clean up Chinatown from newly appointed smack baron John Lone. Ostensibly anti-racist, but in fact falling into standard traps with glamoured violence and the condoning of its hero.

A GLOSSARY OF NEW YORK TERMS AND PEOPLE

New York has a jargon all its own – often unintelligible to non-natives. A guide to New York language appears on p.376. What follows here is a selection of words basic to an understanding of the city, a scattering of art/architecture terms used in the guide and, lastly, a roll-call of New York names, past and present.

New York terms and acronyms

ART DECO Style of decoration popular in the 1930s and characterised by geometrical shape and pattern.

ART NOUVEAU Art, architecture and design of the 1890s typified by stylised vegetable and plant forms.

ATRIUM Enclosed, covered pedestrian space usually forming the lobby of a corporate building.

AVENUE OF THE AMERICAS Recent and little-used name for Sixth Avenue.

BAG LADY Homeless woman who carries her possessions around in a bag.

BATHROOM / RESTROOM / WASHROOM / COMFORT STATION Euphemisms for a toilet.

BEAUX ARTS Style of Neo-Classical architecture taught at the Ecole des Beaux Arts in Paris at the end of the last century and widely adopted in New York City.

BIG APPLE New York City. Possibly from the slang of jazz musicians who referred to anything large as a 'big apple' – and, for them, New York was the biggest apple of all.

BROWNSTONE Originally a 19C terraced house with a facade of brownstone (a kind of sandstone): now any kind of row or townhouse.

CLAPBOARD House covered with overlapping timber boards.

COLONIAL Style of Neo-Classical architecture popular in the 17th and 18C.

COLONIAL DAMES OF AMERICA Patriotic organisation of women descended from worthy ancestors who became American residents before 1750.

CONDO Short for condominium, an individually owned apartment within a building.

CO-OP The most popular form of apartment ownership in the city. A co-op differs from a condo in that you buy shares in the building in which the apartment is sited, rather than the apartment itself.

FEDERAL Hybrid of French and Roman domestic architecture common in the last 18C and early 19C.

GREEK REVIVAL Style of architecture that mimicked that of Classical Greece. Highly popular for banks and larger houses in the early 19C.

GRIDLOCK Traffic freeze – when cars get trapped in street and avenue intersections, preventing traffic on the cross streets passing through.

HISTORICAL DISTRICT Official label for an area considered of historic interest or importance.

IRA Not what you might think but an abbreviation for *Individual Retirement Account* – portable pensions offered by most banks.

LEX Conversational shorthand for *Lexington Avenue*.

LOFT Large open space at the top of an apartment block, popular with artists because of the direct lighting.

MTA *(Metropolitan Transport Authority)*. Runs the city's buses and subway lines: the *IND* (Independent), *BMT* (Brooklyn-Manhattan Transport) and *IRT* (Interborough Rapid Transport).

PATH *(Port Authority Trans Hudson)*. The agency that operates the commuter train, also known as the PATH, between Manhattan and New Jersey.

PLAZA Wide open space that acts as a pedestrian forecourt to a skyscraper – and which gets it a prestigious address (One So-and-So Plaza) that can lead to much confusion when you try and work out just where the building actually *is*. See also **ZONING ORDINANCE**.

PORT AUTHORITY Conversational shorthand for the Port Authority bus terminal on 8th Avenue and 41st St.

ROBBER BARONS 19C magnates who made their fortunes at the expense and to the detriment of ordinary Americans.

SKYSCRAPER The word comes from the highest sail on a sailing ship, and hence refers to any high building.

SRO Single room occupancy hotel – most often lived in long-term by those on welfare (state benefit).

STOOP Open platform, with steps leading up to it, at the entrance to a house.

SUNY State University of New York.

TENEMENT Large, nowadays often slummy, building divided into apartments.

TRI-STATE AREA All-encompassing term for New York, New Jersey and Connecticut States.

VEST POCKET PARK Tiny park or open space.

WPA *(Works Project Administration)*. Agency begun by Roosevelt in 1935 to create employment. As well as much construction work the WPA art projects produced many murals in public buildings and a renowned set of guidebooks to the country.

ZONING ORDINANCES Series of building regulations. The first, passed in 1915, stated that the floor space of a building could not be more than 12 times the area of its site, discouraging giant monoliths and leading to the setback or wedding cake style of skyscraper. A later ordinance allowed developers to build higher provided they supplied a public space at the foot of the building. Hence the **PLAZA**.

New York names

Page numbers here detail (often expanded) references elsewhere.

ALLEN Woody Writer, director, comedian. Many people's cliché idea of the neurotic Jewish Upper East Side Manhattanite, his clever, crafted films *Annie Hall, Manhattan, Broadway Danny Rose* and *Hannah and Her Sisters* comment on and have become part of the New York myth. pp.131, 255, 264

ASTOR John Jacob (1822-1890) Robber baron, slum landlord and, when he died, the richest man in the world. Astor made his packet from exacting swingeing rents from those living in abject squalor in his many tenement blocks. By all accounts, a right bastard. p.89

BEECHER Henry Ward (1813-1887) Revivalist preacher famed for his support of women's suffrage, the abolition of slavery – and as the victim of a scandalous accusation of adultery that rocked 19C New York. His sister, **Harriet Beecher Stowe**, wrote the best-selling novel *Uncle Tom's Cabin*, which contributed greatly to the anti-slavery cause. p.159

BRADY James ('Diamond Jim') (1856-1917) Financier, wide boy and *bon vivant* of the Gay 90s. Famed for bespattering himself with diamonds – hence the nickname. One of the good guys of the era, he gave much money to philanthropic causes. p.313

BRESLIN Jimmy Bitter, Brit-hating but often brilliant columnist for the *Daily News*.

BRILL Diane Doyenne of the nightclub hangers-out and hangers-on.

BRYANT William Cullen (1794-1878) Poet, newspaper editor and main mover for Central Park and the Metropolitan Museum. The small park that bears his name at 42nd St and 5th Ave is a semi-seedy and ill-fitting memorial to a 19C *Wunderkind*. pp.115, 128

BURR Aaron (1756-1836) Fascinating politician whose action-packed career included a stint as Vice-President, a trial and acquittal for treason, and, most famously, the murder of Alexander Hamilton (qv) in a duel. His house, the Morris-Jumel Mansion, still stands. p.151

CARNEGIE Andrew (1835-1919) Emigré Scottish industrialist who spent most of his life amassing a vast fortune and his final years giving it all away. Unlike most of his wealthy contemporaries he was not an ostentatious man – as his house, now the Cooper-Hewitt Museum, shows. p.206

COHAN George M. (1878-1942) If you've seen the illustrious bio-pic *Yankee Doodle Dandy* you probably think this actor, dancer, composer, playwright and Broadway producer was a wonderful chap; in reality Cohan was a dislikeable and disreputable wheeler-dealer who ruined others for his success.

CRISP Quentin Writer (*The Naked Civil Servant*) and celebrated apologist for NYC, living in self-imposed exile from his native England. Frequently to be found giving readings. p.359

CUOMO Mario Governor of New York State and ongoing contender for the Democratic Party Presidential nomination. A liberalish politician whose main problem in achieving greater things will probably be his Italian ancestry.

FIELD Storm Only in New York could you find a TV weatherman with a name like this.

FRICK Henry Clay (1849-1919) John Jacob Astor minus the likeable side. Frick's single contribution to civilisation was to use his inestimable wealth to plunder some of the finest art treasures of Europe, now on show at his erstwhile home on 5th Avenue. p.193

FULTON Robert (1765-1815) Engineer, inventor and painter who got surburban commuting going with his ferry service to Brooklyn. The point where it landed now marks the beginning of Fulton St. He did not, as you'll read everywhere else, invent the steamboat. p.67

GARVEY Marcus (1887-1940) Activist who did much to raise the consciousness of blacks in the early part of the century (and is now a Rasta myth). When he started to become a credible political threat to the white-controlled government he was thrown in prison for fraud; pardoned but deported, he spent the last years of his life in London. p.145

GILBERT Cass (1859-1934) Architect of two of the city's most beguiling landmarks – the Woolworth Building and the Customs House. pp.71, 100

GOULD Jay (1836-1892) Robber baron extraordinaire. Using the telegraph network to be the first person in the know, Gould made his fortune during the Civil War, and went on to manipulate the stock market and make millions more. His most spectacular swindle cornered the gold market, netted him $11 million in a fortnight and provoked the 'Black Friday' crash of 1869. p.167

GREELEY Horace (1811-1872) Campaigning founder-editor of the *New Yorker* magazine and *Tribune* newspaper who said but never did 'Go West, young man!'. An advocate of women's rights, union rights, the abolition of slavery and other worthy, liberal matters. p.111

HAMILTON Alexander (1755-1804) Brilliant Revolutionary propagandist, fighter (battlefield aide to Washington), political thinker (drafted sections of the Constitution) and statesman (first Secretary to the Treasury). Shot and killed in a duel by Aaron Burr (qv). His house, Hamilton Grange, is preserved at the edge of Harlem. p.148

HARING Keith Big-name artist who uses crude animal forms for decoration/patterning. Designed bits of Palladium nightclub, sleeve to Malcolm McLaren's *Buffalo Girls*, etc. etc.

HELMSLEY Harry Property-owning tycoon who, like Donald Trump (qv), has a penchant for slapping his name on all that falls into his grasp. Hence many old hotels are now Helmsley Hotels, and, more offendingly, the New York Central Building on Park Avenue has become

the Helmsley Building. p.121

IRVING Washington (1783-1859) Satirist, biographer, short story writer (*The Legend of Sleepy Hollow, Rip Van Winkle*) and diplomat. His house, just outside the city at Tarrytown, is worth a visit. p.300

JOHNSON Philip Architect. As henchman to Ludwig Mies Van der Rohe, high priest of the International Style glass box skyscraper, he designed the Seagram Building on Park Avenue. In later years he has moved from Modernism to Post-Modernism, with the AT&T Building on 3rd Avenue (passable), the Federal Reserve Plaza on Liberty Street (puerile) and the thing at 53rd Street and 3rd (unspeakable). Other claims to fame: a brief stint as token intellectual for quasi-fascist senator Huey Long in the 1930s, and his personal founding of the thoroughly fascist *Youth and The Nation* organisation. pp.121, 191

KOCH Ed The most popular mayor of New York since Fiorello LaGuardia (qv). Elected by a slender majority in 1977, Koch won New Yorkers by his straight talking, no bullshit approach – and by appeasing the loudest liberal/ethnic groups when, and only when, politically necessary. His greatest fear for the city? 'My successor'. p.347

LAGUARDIA Fiorello (1882-1947) NYC mayor who replaced Jimmy Walker (qv) and who gained great popularity with his honest and down-to-earth administration.

MAILER Norman The old sexist slugger still breezes in from Brooklyn between novels.

MONTAUG Haoui Doorman at the now-defunct Danceteria, important nightperson and discoverer cf Madonna. To be on first-name terms with Haoui is the cool person's waking wish.

MORGAN J. Pierpoint (1837-1913) Top-of-the-pile industrialist and financier who bailed the country out of impending doom in 1907 and used a little of his spare cash to build the Morgan Library on 3rd Avenue. Morgan created a financial empire that was bigger even than the Gettys' and that enabled him to buy out Andrew Carnegie and Henry Frick. p.103

MOSES Robert (1889-1981) Moses is perhaps more than anyone responsible for the way the city looks today. Holding all key planning and building posts from the 30s to the 60s, his philosophy of urban development was to tear down whatever was old and in the way, and slap concrete over the green bits in between. p.286

OLMSTED Fredrick (1822-1903) Landscape designer and writer. Central Park and many others were the fruits of his partnership with architect Calvert Vaux. pp.128, 161

O'NEILL Eugene (1888-1953) NYC's (and America's) most influential playwright. Many of the characters from plays like *Mourning Becomes Electra*, *The Iceman Cometh* and *Long Day's Journey into Night* are based on his drinking companions in The Golden Swan bar. p.83

PARKER Dorothy (1893-1967) Playwright, essayist and acid wit. A founder member of the Round Table group. p.117

RIIS Jacob (1849-1914) Photo-journalist. His compassionate account of the poor and the horrors of slum dwelling, *How the Other Half Lives*, was instrumental in hastening the destruction of the worst tenements. p.91

ROCKEFELLER John D. (1839-1937) Multi-millionaire oil magnate and father of the dynasty.

ROCKEFELLER John D. Jr (1874-1960) Unlike his tight-fisted dad, Rockefeller Junior gave away tidy sums for philanthropic ventures in New York. The Cloisters Museum, The Museum of Modern Art, Lincoln Center, Riverside Church and most famously the Rockefeller Center were all (or mainly all) his doing. p.118

ROCKEFELLER Nelson (1908-1979) Politician son of John D. Jr. Elected governor of New York State in 1958 he held on to the post until 1974, when he turned to greater things and sought the Republican Party Presidential nomination. He didn't get it, but before his death served briefly as Vice-President under Gerald Ford. p.306

RUBELL Steve Entrepreneur. Founder and former owner of Studio 54, his latest venture (with business partner Ian Shrager) is Morgan's Hotel, the last word in with-it luxury. pp.104, 266

SABAN Steven Nightperson and writer. Chronicler of the after-hours in-crowd, Saban's column in *Details* magazine should be read by those who have to be in bed by midnight.

SIMON Neil Playwright. With a record of Broadway/film hits as big as his bank balance (*Brighton Beach Memoirs* the latest). Simon can lay claim to being the most popular MOR playwright today.

TRUMP Donald When you shell out $25 for your shoebox room, reflect that Donald sits on top of a real estate empire worth at least $1,300,000,000. Recent creations are the glammed-out Trump Tower on 5th Avenue, Trump Plaza near Bloomingdale's and Trump's Casino in Atlantic City, NJ. His latest loony scheme is to build a 2000 foot-plus skyscraper in what he's called 'TV City' on the Upper West Side. Watch that space. . . p.119

TWEED William Marcy 'Boss' (1823-78) Top banana of the NY Democratic Party who fiddled city funds to the tune of $200 million and gave Democratic Party headquarters Tammanny Hall its bad name. p.72

VANDERBILT Cornelius 'Commodore' (1794-1877) Builder and owner of much of the nation's railroads. At his death he was the wealthiest-ever American.

VANDERBILT Cornelius (1843-1899) Commodore's son and another hardnosed capitalist. He doubled the family wealth between his father's death and his own – a fortune that kept (and keeps) successive generations of Vanderbilts in spare change.

WALKER Jimmy (1881-1946) Professional songwriter who turned politician and was elected NYC mayor at the height of the jazz age. As a dapperdressed man-about-town he reflected much of its fizz but with the depression he lost popularity and office. p.84

WARHOL Andy (?-1987) Artist and media manoeuvrist. Instigator of Pop Art, The Factory, *Interview* magazine and *Empire* – a 24-hour movie of the Empire State Building (no commentary, no gorillas, nothing but the building). Died, oddly enough, after a routine gallstone operation.

WHITE Stanford (1853-1906) Partner of the architectural firm McKim, Mead and White, which designed such Neo-Classical piles as the General Post Office, Washington Square Arch, the Municipal Building and bits of Columbia University. Something of a *roué*, White's days ended with a bullet through the head from the gun of a cuckolded husband. p.100

NEW YORK SLANG: A GLOSSARY

New York City slang is essentially a kind of quickspeak, a shorthand which reflects the pace of the place, spat out brusquely (though never rudely) and without affectation. It's a language with its own variations – the corporate-based jargon of Madison Avenue is far from the street slang of the Lower East Side – but its roots, like so much else here, lie with New York's development as a city of immigrants. Yiddish words, in particular, now have currency as regular city slang; so too, though with narrower effect, do Italian. More recently, the Spanish spoken by New York's rapidly swelling Puerto Rican community has come close to making English the city's second language: adverts on the subway are in Spanish (significantly only those obviously directed at low-income brackets); there are specifically Spanish schools and TV stations; and there are parts of the city where you will not hear English spoken at all. What follows are a few of the most widely used New York phrases. Most of them were originally specific to the city, though several have spread through the US, and a few, over recent years, across the Atlantic.

Airhead	A stupid, ignorant person
Attitude adjustment	What you do during Happy Hour
AWOL	Mentally unbalanced
B'n'Ts	Bridge and Tunnel people, ie those unfortunate enough to live off Manhattan
BBQ	Acronym for the Outer Boroughs: Brooklyn, the Bronx and Queens
Catch the rays	Sunbathe
Cheap	Tacky
Chill out	Cool off, relax
Chutzpah	Playful arrogance
Cute	When used to describe a person: attractive, engaging. For things: nice, dinky – more like the British meaning
Funky	With no pretensions, Bohemian
Gross	Revolting
Grungy	Grotty, tatty, dirty
Jappie	Pertaining to a Jewish American Princess, ie young beautiful and rich
Kvetch	Complain
Maven	Buff, expert. As in *movie maven*
MIA	Missing In Action, ie not all there mentally. Similar to *AWOL*
Off the wall	Odd, out of the ordinary
Party pooper	One who sneaks off home early
Pig out	To stuff one's face
Pissed	Pissed off, fed up
Preppie	The predecessor of the yuppie, ie someone who went to an Ivy League University, buys clothes from Brooks Bros, etc.
Ritzy/glitzy	Swish, ostentatious
Schlep	To move around or carry out a task lazily or with difficulty
Schlmiel	Person, for example, who spills soup on someone
Schmozel	The person he or she spills the soup on
Schmuck	Person who laughs at both of them
Scuzzy	Grotty – like *Grungy*
Smart	Clever
Space cadet	A stupid, sometimes scatty person.
Stressed out	Suffering from extreme anxiety.
SOL	Shit Out of Luck
Veg out	Switch off your brain, perhaps in front of 'Dallas' or 'Lifestyles of the Rich and Famous'
WASP	White Anglo-Saxon Protestant

'What can I tell you? Not really a question, more of an intensifier of what's just been said, eg: 'this guy is a real asshole, what can I tell you?'

Yuppie Young Urban Professional. A person of either sex who lives in a major city, is between the ages of 25 and 45 and lives for personal prestige, money and power. Also known as 'Baby Boomers' and 'Fast Trackers'

Zoned/phased/
paced out Blitzed, worn out, knackered

INDEX

Abigail Adams Smith Museum 134
Abyssinian Baptist Church 147
THE ADIRONDACKS 317
Adirondack Museum 319
Albany 309
Algonquin Hotel 55, 117
Alphabet City 95
Alternative Museum 199
Amagansett 295
American International Building 66
American Museum of Natural History 208
Amityville 286
Antiques 231
Apollo Theater 145
Church of the Ascension 86
Asia Society gallery 198
Astor Place 89
ASTORIA 170
AT&T Building 121
Atlantic Avenue 160
Auburn 328
Audubon Terrace 150
Aunt Len's Doll and Toy Museum 206
Ausable Chasm 318

Babylon 286
Barnard College 141
Bars 234
Battery Park 65
Battery Park City 70
Bedford Street 84
Beekman Place 123
BELMONT 166
Black Fashion Museum 205
Bleecker Street 83
Bloomingdale's 134, 210
BOERUM HILL 160
Bowery 94
Bowling Green 65
Bowne House 171
Bridgehampton 295
BRIGHTON BEACH 163
THE BRONX 164
Bronx Museum of the Arts 199
Bronx Zoo 166
BROOKLYN 156
Brooklyn Academy of Music 161, 272
Brooklyn Botanical Garden 161
Brooklyn Bridge 68
Brooklyn Children's Museum 206

BROOKLYN HEIGHTS 157
Brooklyn Museum 199
Brunch 244
Bryant Park 115
Budget eats 241
Buffalo 336
Bully Hill 326

Cabaret 275
Canandaigua 325
Carl Schurz Park 133
Carnegie Hall 114
CARROLL GARDENS 160
Cast-iron architecture 78
Cathedral Church of St John the Divine 140
Catskill 304
THE CATSKILLS 304
Cazenovia 330
Center for African Arts 203
CENTRAL LEATHERSTOCKING 330
CENTRAL PARK 128
Chanin Building 106
Chase Manhattan Plaza 69
CHAUTAUQUA-ALLEGHENY 340
CHELSEA 108
Chelsea Hotel 55, 109
Children's Museum of Manhattan 206
CHINATOWN 74
Chinatown Museum 204
Christopher Street 85
Chrysler Building 106
Church of St Mary 93
Church of the Transfiguration 76
Citicorp Center 122
City Gallery 199
City Hall 72
City Island 168
CIVIC CENTER 71
Claremont 308
Classical Music 274
Climate 4
The Cloisters 197
Clothes 220
COBBLE HILL 160
Cold Spring Harbour 290
Columbia University 141
Columbus Avenue 138
Columbus Circle 137
Comedy 275

CONEY ISLAND 162
Cooper-Hewitt Museum 206
Cooper Square 88
Cooper Union Building 88
Cooperstown 331
Corning 326
CORONA 171
CROWN HEIGHTS 161
Cunard Building 65
Cutchogue 292

Dakota Building 138
Dance 272
Department stores 210
Diamond Row 115
Dykman House 151

East Hampton 295
EAST VILLAGE 87
EL BARRIO 148
Eldorado Building 140
Electrical equipment 232
Ellis Island 61
Elmira 327
Empire State Building 102
Episcopal Church of the Transfiguration 102
Erie Canal 329
The Esplanade 159
Essex Street Market 93
Ethnic crafts 231

Fashion Moda 200
Federal Hall National Memorial 64
Fifth Avenue 117
57th Street 116
Film 276
FINANCIAL DISTRICT 62
Finding a place to stay 53
FINGER LAKES 325
Fire Department Museum 207
Fire Island 287
First Avenue 123
First Presbyterian Chuch 86
Flatiron Building 100
Flower District 109
FLUSHING 171
Food and drink 20
Forbes Gallery 200
Ford Foundation Building 107
FOREST HILLS 172
Fort Ticonderoga 318
Fort Tryon Park 151

42nd Street 104
Fraunces Tavern 66
Free food 244
Frick Collection 193
Fulton Fish Market 67

Galleries (commercial) 228
Garden City 285
GARMENT DISTRICT 111
Gay New York 29, 238
General Electric Building 122
General Post Office 112
General Theological Seminary 109
George Washington Bridge 151
Getting there 4
Glens Falls 316
Gourmet shops 213
Governor's Island 62
Grace Church 89
Gracie Mansion 133
Gramercy Park 97
Grand Army Plaza 131
Grand Army Plaza (Brooklyn) 161
Grand Central Station 105
Grand Concourse 165
Grant's Tomb 142
Greeley Square 111
Greenport 292
GREENWICH VILLAGE 80
Greenwood Cemetery 162
Grey Art Gallery 200
Guggenheim Museum 192

HAMILTON HEIGHTS 148
Hamilton Grange 148
Hammondsport 326
The Hamptons 293
Hampton Bays 294
Happy hours 244
HARLEM 143
Haughwout Building 78
Hayden Planetarium 208
Health 10
HELL'S KITCHEN (CLINTON) 112
Herald Square 112
Hispanic Museum 204
Holography Museum 207
Horn & Hardart Automat 107
Hotel des Artistes 138
Howe Caverns 332
HUDSON VALLEY 298
The Hyde Collection 316
Hyde Park 307

IBM Building 121
IBM Gallery of Science and Art 200
Information 10
International Center of Photography 200
Intrepid Sea, Air Space Museum 207
Introduction 3
INWOOD 151
Ithaca 328

JACKSON HEIGHTS 171
Jacques Marchais Center of Tibetan Art 174
Jamaica Bay 172
Jamestown 341
Jazz and folk 262
Jefferson Market Courthouse 85
John Lennon 139
Jones Beach 286
Judson Memorial Church 82
KEW GARDENS 172
Kingsland House 172
Kingston 303

La Marqueta 148
Lake George 317
Lake Placid 319
Lesbian New York 29, 238
Lever House 122
Lexington Avenue 123
Lincoln Center for the Performing Arts 138, 274
Liquor stores 217
LITTLE INDIA 100
LITTLE ITALY 76
Locust Valley 289
Long Beach 286
LONG ISLAND 284
LONG ISLAND CITY 170
LOWER EAST SIDE 91
LOWER MANHATTAN 57

Macy's 111, 211
Madison Avenue 120
Madison Square 100
Madison Square Garden
Majestic Building 138
Manhattan Bridge 76
Manhattan Plaza 113
Marcus Garvey Park 145
Marie's Crisis Café 84
Markets 218
Massena 322

Media 16
Metropolitan Life Building 100
Metropolitan Museum of Art 178
MIDTOWN MANHATTAN 96
Mobil Building 106
Money 13
Montague Street 159
Montauk 296
MORNINGSIDE HEIGHTS 142
Morningside Park 142
Morris-Jumel Mansion 150
Mott Street 74
Mount Morris Park Historical District 145
Mulberry Street 76
MURRAY HILL 103
Museum Mile 132
Museum of Modern Art 188
Museum of American Crafts 205
Museum of American Folk Art 205
Museum of the American Indian 203
Museum of Broadcasting 207
Museum of Bronx History 202
Museum of the City of New York 202
Museo del Barrio 204

National Academy of Design 201
New Museum of Contemporary Art 201
New Paltz 302
New York Central Building 121
New York Conventions & Visitors Bureau 137
New York Experience 116
New York Life Building 100
New York Historical Society 202
New York Public Library 104
New York State Introduction 283
New York Stock Exchange 63
Niagara Falls 337
Nightclubs 265
NORTH BRONX 167
Northport 290

Oak Beach 286
Ogdensburg 321
Olana 308
Old Bethpage Village 286
Old Westbury Gardens 289
One UN Plaza 123
Opera 274
Orchard Beach 168
Orchard Street 94
Orient Point 292

Orientation 46
Oswego 321
Other things 38

Paley Park 121
Pan-Am Building 121
Parades and festivals 30
Park Avenue 121
PARK SLOPE 162
St Paul's Chapel 70
Penn Railroad Yards 139
Pennsylvania Station 111
Peter Cooper Village 97
Pharmacies 211
Pierpoint Morgan Library 201
Plattsburgh 318
Plaza Hotel 131
Plymouth Church of the Pilgrims 159
Poe Cottage 166
Points of arrival 45
Police Academy Museum 208
Police Headquarters 77
Police and trouble 18
PROSPECT PARK 161
Port Authority Terminal 112
Port Jefferson 292
Post 15
Prints, posters and cards 230

QUEENS 168
Queens Museum 203
Queensboro Bridge 134

Radio City Music Hall 118
Restaurants (Manhattan) 245
Restaurants (Outer Boroughs) 257
Richmondstown Restoration 174
RIVERDALE 168
Riverside Church 142
Riverside Park 140
Riverview Terrace 124
Rochester 334
Rock Music 261
The Rockaways 172
Rockefeller Center 118
Rockefeller Center Extension 116
ROOSEVELT ISLAND 134
Roslyn Heights 289

Sag Harbour 295
Sagamore Hill 289
St Bartholomew's Church 122

ST GEORGES 175
St Mark's Place 88
St Mark's-in-the-Bowery 89
St Patrick's Cathedral 119
Salamanca 341
Sands Point 288
Saranac Lake 319
Saratoga Springs 313
Schapiro's Winery 94
Schomberg Center 147
Seagram Building 122
Second Avenue 123
Seneca Falls 328
Setauket 291
Seventh Regiment Armory 133
79th Street Boat Basin 140
Shelter Island 296
Sheridan Square 85
Shoreham 292
Shrine of Elizabeth Ann Seton 66
Sixth Avenue 115
Skaneatles 329
Sleeping 19
Sleepy Hollow Restorations 300
Small's Paradise 147, 264
Snug Harbour Cultural Center 175
Society of Illustrators Museum 202
SOHO 77
South Street Seaport 67
Southampton 294
Southold 292
Speciality foodstores 214
Sport 33
STATEN ISLAND 172
Staten Island Ferry 173
Statue of Liberty 60
Staying on 36
STEINWAY 170
Stonewall Bar 85
Stony Brook 291
Strawberry Fields 139
Strivers' Row 147
Studio Museum of Harlem 205
Stuyvestant Square 100
Stuyvestant Town 97
Sunken Meadow 291
Supermarkets 213
Sutton Place 123
Syracuse 329

Tarrytown 300
Taughannock Falls 328

Telephones 14
Temple Emanual 132
Tenth Street Turkish Baths 90
Theatre 268
Theodore Roosevelt's Birthplace 97
THE THOUSAND ISLANDS 321
Times Square 113
Tompkins Square 90
Tours 11
Toys and games 233
Transport 47
Travel onwards 6
TRIBECA 80
Trinity Church 64
Trivia and oddities 233
Trump Tower 119
Tudor City 107
Tweed Courthouse 72
24 Hour Eating 256

Ukrainian Museum 205
Union Square 97
United Nations Building 107
UPPER EAST SIDE 131
UPPER MANHATTAN 125
UPPER WEST SIDE 135
Utica 330

Van Cortlandt Mansion 167
Vanderbilt Mansion 308
Vanderbilt Museum 290
Verdi Square 139
Verrazanno Narrows Bridge 174

Waldorf Astoria Hotel
Wall Street 63
WASHINGTON HEIGHTS 150
Washington Square 81
Watkins Glen 327
Wave Hill 168
West End Café 141, 243, 264
West Point 301
Westhampton 293
Whitney Museum of American Art 194
Williamsburg Bridge 93
Women's New York 27
Woodlawn Cemetery 167
Woodstock 305
Woolworth Building 71
World Trade Center 70

Yankee Stadium 165
YORKVILLE 133

Zabar's 140, 214

HELP US UPDATE

We've gone to a lot of trouble to ensure that this, the first edition of the **Rough Guide to New York**, is thoroughly up-to-date and accurate. However, things do change (in New York more rapidly than anywhere), and if you think we've got something wrong, missed something out, or that more should be said about a particular place, do get in touch. It won't be long before we do a second edition of the guide and we hope to make it better and even more comprehensive. We'll acknowledge any letters we use, and send a free copy of the next edition (or any other Rough Guide if you prefer) for the best ones. Write to us at: The Rough Guides, 149 Kennington Lane, London SE11 4EZ.